Martin Luther's
Basic Exegetical Writings

Edited by Carl L. Beckwith

Concordia Publishing House • Saint Louis

3558 S. Jefferson Ave., St. Louis, Missouri 63118-3968
1-800-325-3040 • www.cph.org

Manufactured in the United States of America

1 2 3 4 5 6 7 8 9 10 26 25 24 23 22 21 20 19 18 17

Contents

ABBREVIATIONS

LW	*Luther's Works: American Edition.* Volumes 1–30: Edited by Jaroslav Pelikan. St. Louis: Concordia, 1955–76. Volumes 31–55: Edited by Helmut Lehmann. Philadelphia/Minneapolis: Muhlenberg/Fortress, 1957–86. Volumes 56–82: Edited by Christopher Boyd Brown and Benjamin T. G. Mayes. St. Louis: Concordia: 2009–.
$NPNF^1$	*A Select Library of the Christian Church: Nicene and Post-Nicene Fathers: First Series.* Edited by Philip Schaff. 14 volumes. New York, 1886–89. Reprint, Peabody, MA: Hendrickson, 1994.
$NPNF^2$	*A Select Library of the Christian Church: Nicene and Post-Nicene Fathers: Second Series.* Edited by Philip Schaff and Henry Wace. 14 vols. New York, 1890–1900. Reprint, Peabody, MA: Hendrickson, 1994.
PL	*Patrologiae cursus completus: Series Latina.* Edited by J.-P. Migne. 221 volumes in 223. Paris: Garnier Fratres, 1844–64.
WA	*D. Martin Luthers Werke: Kritische Gesamtausgabe.* 73 volumes in 85. Weimar: H. Böhlau, 1883–.
WA Br	*D. Martin Luthers Werke: Briefwechsel.* 18 volumes. Weimar: H. Böhlau, 1930–.
WA TR	*D. Martin Luthers Werke: Tischreden.* 6 volumes. Weimar: H. Böhlau, 1912–21.
WSA	Edmund Hill and John E. Rotelle, eds. *The Works of St. Augustine: A Translation for the Twenty-First Century.* In three series. Hyde Park, NY: New City Press, 1990–.

Introduction

Martin Luther's Reformation is often seen through the lens of his formal theological writings such as the *Ninety-Five Theses, The Freedom of a Christian, The Babylonian Captivity of the Church*, and *Bondage of the Will.*[1] These important and significant works belong to any study of the Reformation. Often overlooked, however, are Luther's many lectures, sermons, and commentaries on the Bible. In Luther's day, the ordinary pastors and laypeople of Germany came to know and embrace the Reformation because of Luther's lectures at the University of Wittenberg and his sermons at St. Mary's, the city church of Wittenberg. Although many excellent anthologies of Luther's theological writings exist, until now there has not been a comparable volume of Luther's commentaries on the Bible. *Martin Luther's Basic Exegetical Writings* fills this gap by providing significant excerpts from the reformer's career as an interpreter of Scripture.

Twelve excerpts, spanning Luther's career, are presented in this volume. Each excerpt begins with an introduction that places the work, or the chief concern of the work, in its historical context. These introductions also provide an overarching historical narrative of Luther's academic, pastoral, and personal life from 1515 to 1546. The chronological arrangement of the excerpts allows the reader to appreciate Luther's development as a theologian and to observe the remarkable consistency of his theological concerns. Luther's interest in any biblical text always involves its grammar and historical context, its place in the history of God's people as a word of command or promise, and its abiding significance for believers today. These broad questions frequently entail digressions on church history, the history of interpretation, dogmatics, ethics, pastoral care, and spiritual warfare. Luther uses these digressions to illustrate the full significance of the text and to provide a responsible exposition for his students and parishioners. That responsibility also entails for Luther a careful critique of his opponents and their false interpretations of Scripture.

1 See LW 31:17–23, 327–77; 36:3–126; 33:1–295.

Luther's exposition of Scripture returns over and over again to the doctrines of sin, grace, and righteousness. These insights are almost always contrasted with the medieval schoolmen. Sometimes Luther will offer a lengthy rebuttal of these scholastic views on sin, grace, faith, and righteousness. More often than not, Luther simply makes a passing reference to a scholastic teaching and assumes the hearer understands. To make sense of these references by Luther a brief overview of what the schoolmen taught is provided below. This summary will also help the reader appreciate why so many people were drawn to Luther's teaching and preaching.

Related to Luther's critique of the schoolmen is his view of the Bible. Luther could not reconcile the opinions of the schoolmen with his reading of Scripture. Here, too, a brief word needs to be said about how Luther reads the Bible and particularly what he finds necessary for a proper understanding of it. These two issues, which inform all of the excerpts below, shed considerable light on Luther's exegetical and theological concerns.

Salvation according to the schoolmen

Most accounts of the Reformation begin with the posting of Luther's *Ninety-Five Theses* on October 31, 1517. These theses addressed the power and efficacy of indulgences. In Luther's day, people purchased indulgences because they guaranteed a full remission of the penalties accrued by their sins. The pope assured everyone that the Church possessed a treasury of merit from the good works of Christ and the saints. These extra merits could be used to remit the penalties for one's own sins or for those of a departed loved one in purgatory. Luther disagreed and argued that the true treasure of the Church is the most holy Gospel.

The world of late medieval piety struggled with uncertainty. All people inherited original sin because of Adam's fall, and God's justice required that sin be punished. Further, Adam's loss of original righteousness introduced a deformity or corrupt habit in the soul, and this deformity inclined all to sin. How could a person who had inherited Adam's sin and a soul inclined to sin avoid God's eternal punishment? The schoolmen distinguished between the guilt and punishment of original sin and actual sins. Christ's meritorious work upon the cross paid the price for original sin, and this was received by all in the Sacrament of Holy Baptism. Although freed from the inherited guilt and eternal punishment of original sin, people still struggled with the desire and inclination to sin, which the schoolmen referred to as concupiscence. When actual sins were committed, the faithful turned to the sacrament of penance and received Christ's forgiveness through an act of contrition, confession, and works of satisfaction. Salvation, however, required not just turning away from sin but also meritorious acts of love.

All of the schoolmen agreed that only grace led to salvation. They distinguished between a first grace (*gratia gratis data*) that prepared or disposed the soul to receive the sanctifying grace necessary for salvation (*gratia gratum faciens*). Most thought that these graces were qualities infused within the soul which enabled believers to do meritorious works. These works would earn an increase of grace, a greater infusion of God's love, and eventually merit eternal life. Significant debates arose among the schoolmen on whether this first grace (*gratia gratis data*) could also be merited or whether it must be bestowed as a gift by God. The question was asked whether fallen man apart from grace and by his own natural powers could love God above all things and keep the Commandments. Thomas Aquinas (ca. 1225–74) said no; John Duns Scotus (ca. 1265–1308) and Gabriel Biel (ca. 1410–95) said yes. For Scotus and Biel this meant that if people did their best, God would grant them grace (*facere quod in se est*). Although the schoolmen disagreed on whether first grace could be merited by our natural powers, they all agreed that eternal life must be merited by acts of love.

How can my works inherit eternal life? Once again the schoolmen offered a distinction. There is a difference between meritorious acts done by a person's own effort and those acts done by the Holy Spirit in the life of the believer. The merit of congruity (*meritum de congruo*), as they called it, is the reward received according to a person's own abilities. It is a merit proportionate to the value of the act. The merit of condignity (*meritum de condigno*), on the other hand, merits eternal life because it is worked by the Holy Spirit in cooperation with the believer. Although congruent merit earns further grace, it is not sufficient for eternal life. Condign merit alone earns eternal life.

The schoolmen could also use the Pauline language of justification and sanctification to describe the process of salvation. For example, Thomas Aquinas can say with Luther that we are justified by grace through faith. They do not, however, mean the same thing by justification, grace, or faith. For Thomas, God's grace moves the ungodly to faith, and this faith justifies when it is quickened by love. The schoolmen followed Aristotle (384–322 BC) in asserting that a thing works through its form. Paul said that faith works through love (Gal. 5:6). Therefore, for the schoolmen, love is the form of faith. This means that faith, which pertains to the intellect, does not save apart from love, which pertains to the will. Faith formed by love (*fides caritate formata*) produces acts of justice or righteousness, and these acts merit eternal life. By cooperating with God's grace, faith works through love, making a person less a sinner and more righteous. The righteousness that saves comes from the believer and increases with grace and meritorious acts of love.

The elaborate system of merit devised by the schoolmen explained how our works could satisfy God's justice and merit eternal life. They were certain that this was the case. And yet uncertainty lurked everywhere. Believers could never know if they had done enough to merit eternal life. Even worse, believers could not know if they were worthy of God's love and possessed the sanctifying grace which alone leads to salvation (*gratia gratum faciens*). The schoolmen were certain that eternal life must be earned and also certain that no person could know if he or she were in a state of sanctifying grace. For the believer in Luther's day, the only certainty available was the papal indulgence. Coin accomplished what faith could not.

Whether this description of late medieval piety is fair or not, it was Luther's view of it, and it was this teaching that led him to denounce the pope's indulgence and the false piety of his day. In the years leading up to the posting of the *Ninety-Five Theses*, Luther turned to the Scriptures and discovered a different teaching on sin, grace, faith, works, and righteousness than that taught by his university professors and the late medieval schoolmen. According to Paul, the righteousness of God, which alone avails for salvation, is received by grace through faith and not by our best efforts or works. Faith is not formed by love but by Christ, who is the form of faith. For Luther, the schoolmen failed to distinguish between active and passive righteousness, between the imperfect righteousness we have in ourselves, which is never sufficient for salvation, and the perfect righteousness of Christ, which is outside of us and is ours by faith alone. Certainty rests never in ourselves but always in Christ and His perfect and complete saving work for us. This was the good news proclaimed by Paul. When Luther came to this understanding, he felt that the gates of paradise had been opened. He immediately returned to the Scriptures and began to see everything in an entirely different light.[2]

Same old song

Luther's early lectures address sin, grace, and righteousness so often that he is accused of always singing the same old song and discussing nothing else. For Luther, this criticism is misguided. Rightly understanding these theological topics drives us to Christ and away from ourselves. Luther never stopped singing this song throughout his life. Twenty years later he insisted that one doctrine alone—faith in Christ—rules in his

2 *Preface to the Latin Writings* (1545), LW 34:336–38. Cf. *Commentary on Psalm 51* (1532), LW 12:313–14 (see below, p. 269).

heart: "From it, through it, and to it all my theological thought flows and returns, day and night."[3]

During the summer of 1530, the Evangelical princes and a number of Luther's colleagues gathered in Augsburg to present their faith to Emperor Charles V (r. 1519–56). After lengthy discussions and attempts at negotiation, the emperor ruled against the princes and their Augsburg Confession. The emperor issued an edict demanding that the Evangelical princes and their citizens return to the Roman Church by April 15, 1531. The emperor's edict and treatment of the princes infuriated Luther. He wrote to his "dear German people," warning them about the emperor's edict and reminding them of the true Gospel they had received. He writes: "Now—praise be to God—it has come to pass that man and woman, young and old, know the catechism; they know how to believe, to live, to pray, to suffer, and to die."[4] These things are understood because the Gospel has been rightly preached and taught to the people. If the emperor's edict succeeds, everyone will be forced to return to the old ways and be deprived of their trust and comfort in Christ.

The emperor's assault upon the Gospel led Luther to lecture on Paul's Epistle to the Galatians. Luther's lectures were published in 1535 and remain one of his greatest works. In these lectures, Luther succinctly states his position. The Gospel frees us from ourselves and from the monster of uncertainty—indeed, from the greatest of all monsters, the doubts of conscience. Luther explains:

> The chief point of all Scripture is that we should not doubt but hope, trust, and believe for a certainty that God is merciful, kind, and patient, that He does not lie and deceive but is faithful and true. He keeps His promises and has now accomplished what He had promised, handing over His only Son into death for our sins, so that everyone who believes in the Son should not perish but have eternal life (John 3:16).[5]

For Luther, God has been reconciled and is favorably disposed toward us because of Christ's victory over our sins. Christ's work of salvation is all sufficient and complete. He has paid the debt of our original sin and actual sins. His work is ours by grace through faith. This grace is not something infused into our souls but is God's unmerited benevolence and favor for us. The Holy Spirit works faith in our hearts through Word and Sacrament, and this faith receives Christ's perfect righteousness. Luther continues:

3 Preface to *Lectures on Galatians* (1531), LW 27:145.

4 *Warning to His Dear German People* (1531), LW 47:52.

5 *Lectures on Galatians* (1531), LW 26:386.

> And this is the reason why our theology is certain: it snatches us away from ourselves and places us outside ourselves, so that we do not depend on our own strength, conscience, experience, person, or works but depend on that which is outside ourselves, that is, on the promise and truth of God, which cannot deceive.[6]

The same old song, perhaps, but one that Luther never tired of singing from the pulpit and in the classroom.

Luther and the Bible

Luther took his oath as *Doctor in Biblia* on October 18, 1512. According to Johannes Mathesius (1504–65), Luther's student and biographer, Luther promised "to study the Holy Scriptures his entire life, to preach it and to defend the Christian faith in formal university disputations and in his writings against all heretics."[7] Luther loved the Bible. It was a source of great comfort and delight for him throughout his life. He said at table in 1532 that for some time he had been reading through the Bible twice a year and still could not exhaust its depths.[8] Not everyone shared Luther's fascination. He regretted that people either neglected the Bible entirely or thought it something easy to master. Luther writes: "There has never been an art or a book on earth that everyone has so quickly mastered as the Holy Scriptures."[9] Luther could understand none of this.

Luther spent his life preaching and lecturing on the Bible. This book and none other contained true wisdom. Everything else was foolishness compared to it.[10] Luther daily prayed the psalms and meditated upon the Ten Commandments and the Lord's Prayer. He read and reread. He pressed hard upon these words and prayed earnestly that the Holy Spirit would open his eyes and ears to better grasp their meaning. For Luther, however, prayer (*oratio*) and meditation (*meditatio*) alone would not bring you to understanding. Only by living and experiencing life itself could the person of faith come to understand and therefore to trust and repose in the comfort and consolation of God's promises. This understanding arises not when we are overcome with blessing and joy but when we find ourselves in the depths and contraries of life, amid suffering and anguish, disappointment and trial. Luther referred

6 *Lectures on Galatians* (1531), LW 26:387.

7 Quoted in Robert Kolb, *Martin Luther and the Enduring Word of God* (Grand Rapids, MI: Baker Academic, 2016), 31.

8 *Table Talk* no. 1877 (1532), LW 54:165.

9 *Commentary on Psalm 118* (1530), LW 14:46; cf. Luther's preface to Spangenberg, *German Postil* (1543), LW 60:283–85; and *Table Talk* no. 115 (1531), LW 54:13.

10 Cf. *Table Talk* no. 4691 (1539), LW 54:361.

to this third element as *tentatio* ("agonizing struggle") or *Anfechtung* in German. This final element, explains Luther, "teaches you not only to know and understand, but also to experience how right, how true, how sweet, how lovely, how mighty, how comforting God's Word is, wisdom beyond all wisdom."[11]

At the very end of his life, in the last recorded words from him, Luther continued to emphasize the importance of experience, of faithful living in the world, for right understanding.[12] No one, he tells us, can understand Virgil's poems on farming without first being a farmer for several years. Likewise, no one can understand Cicero's letters unless he has spent half his life engaged in public affairs. The ordinary and practical wisdom of life comes only with living that life, experiencing the highs and lows, the successes and failures. How much more must this be true of the Bible and the wisdom it bestows? For Luther, no one should think he has even tasted the Scriptures unless he has cared for the churches with the prophets for a hundred years. Although we daily pray and meditate upon the Scriptures, we cannot exhaust the depth of their wisdom. As long as we have life to live within us, we remain students of God's faithfulness and promises. As Luther's final words declare: "We are beggars. This is true."[13]

Christ, the key to Scripture

Luther and his colleagues studied Hebrew and Greek in order to better understand the grammar and sense of Scripture. Luther frequently offers grammatical insights in his lectures and sermons based on these ancient languages. At the same time, Luther insists that a proper interpretation requires more than grammar and languages alone. As early as 1517, he declared, "I see that not everyone is a truly wise Christian just because he knows Greek and Hebrew."[14] Luther had in mind Desiderius Erasmus (ca. 1467–1536). His problem, notes Luther, is that he fails to see Christ. Similarly, in 1540, toward the end of his life, Luther again declared that grammar was not enough. The wise interpreter of Scripture must observe the sense of Scripture.[15] Luther appeals to Virgil (70–19 BC) and his *Eclogues*. The reader will not understand Virgil's poems unless he recognizes their subject matter. Only when he understands that Virgil points

---

11 *Preface to the German Writings* (1539), LW 34:287.

12 *Luther's Last Observation Left in a Note* (*Table Talk* no. 5677), February 16, 1546, LW 54:476.

13 *Table Talk* no. 5677 (1546), WA TR 5:318.2–3: "Wir sein pettler. Hoc est verum."

14 Luther's letter to John Lang, March 1, 1517, LW 48:40.

15 *Table Talk* no. 5002 (1540), LW 54:375–76.

to the Roman emperor Augustus (r. 27 BC–AD 14) do the words, the grammar, make sense.[16]

In his early *Lectures on Romans*, Luther declares that the whole of Scripture points to Christ and finds its "meaning" in Him.[17] Everything must be understood in relation to Christ. The door of Scripture is thrown wide open when the interpreter sees Christ. Likewise, toward the end of his life, Luther declares that all of Scripture is pure Christ. All points to Him. Luther concludes: "To him who has the Son Scripture is an open book; and the stronger his faith in Christ becomes, the more brightly will the light of Scripture shine for him."[18]

In his debate with Erasmus over the bondage of the will, Luther acknowledges that there are many obscure and abstruse passages in Scripture. The obscurity, however, lies not in the subject matter of Scripture but in our ignorance of its vocabulary and grammar. The subject matter is known to all: "that Christ the Son of God has been made man, that God is three and one, that Christ has suffered for us and is to reign eternally." Luther ends with a question that summarizes his entire approach to Scripture: "Take Christ out of the Scriptures, and what will you find left in them?"[19] The purpose of Scripture is to drive us to Christ.[20]

A note to the reader

Luther often complained about how long it took the publisher to release his works. Luther's published commentaries can be dated either according to when they were given as lectures or sermons or when they were published. For example, Luther lectured on Galatians in 1531, but the lectures were not published until 1535. In this volume, the dates for Luther's lectures and sermons correspond to when they were delivered. There are three exceptions to this. Luther published and did not deliver his commentary on the Magnificat and on the last words of David. For these two works, I follow the date of publication. Finally, Luther lectured in Latin on the Book of Jonah in 1525. He revised these lectures and published them in German in 1526. The excerpt from Jonah in this volume uses Luther's German text of 1526.

---

16 Luther likely has in mind Virgil's *Fourth Eclogue* and its messianic prophecy. In the early church, Emperor Constantine (ca. 272–337) and many others argued that Virgil's prophecy pointed to Christ. Constantine, *Speech to the Assembly of Saints* 18. Cf. Augustine, *City of God* 10.27 and 18.23.

17 *Lectures on Romans* (1515–16), LW 25:405.

18 *Treatise on the Last Words of David* (1543), LW 15:339 (see below, p. 463).

19 *Bondage of the Will* (1525), LW 33:25–26.

20 *Preface to James and Jude* (1522, 1546), LW 35:396.

Each excerpt is divided according to the chapter and verse of the book being discussed by Luther. These divisions allow the reader to locate the excerpt easily in the appropriate volume of Luther's Works. Luther's commentaries are quite long, and therefore ellipses have been used to condense the material. On occasion, a hard break (indicated by an embellishment ⥱) has been inserted into the excerpt to indicate a significant jump in Luther's commentary.

Martin Luther's Basic Exegetical Writings

Lectures on Romans

1515–16

From spring 1515 to fall 1516, Martin Luther lectured every Monday and Friday at six in the morning on St. Paul's Epistle to the Romans. Luther requested from the local printer a specially formatted edition of the Latin Vulgate for his students. Each page contained sixteen lines of text with ample space for marginal and interlinear notes. In these early lectures, Luther followed the traditional pattern of providing both glosses and scholia. Luther's glosses gave brief summaries of the text and made slight corrections to the Latin translation based on Greek editions available to Luther. The scholia offered Luther's extended commentary on the text.

*Luther's commentary on Romans is lengthy. The excerpts below give a sense of Luther's early theological concerns and points of disagreement with his scholastic predecessors. Luther establishes in the opening glosses his Christological hermeneutic, which will guide his reading of Scripture throughout his career. Luther's extended commentary raises a number of critical issues concerning sin, grace, and righteousness. He insists that righteousness must precede works. As Luther puts it, God does not accept the person because of works but accepts the works because of the person. Luther's chief disagreement with his scholastic predecessors rests here. The value of our works derives from God and not from ourselves. The reason has to do with sin. Luther describes sin as curving us in upon ourselves. In this life we are never free of sin. It remains in the thoughts, words, and deeds of all believers. This means that even the good works of believers are tainted by sin and therefore may never be a source of merit for us. Luther famously declares at this point that we are at the same time both righteous and a sinner (*simul iustus et peccator*). For Luther, we cannot, as argued by some of the medieval schoolmen, do good works and love God above all things according to our natural powers. To say this is to misunderstand sin and to render grace useful but not necessary.*

Luther appeals to Augustine throughout his lectures on Romans to support his views on sin, grace, and righteousness. Luther's discovery of Augustine's anti-Pelagian writings contributed significantly to his Reformation breakthrough and to the reforming work of the faculty at the University of

Wittenberg.[1] *We glimpse the significance of these issues for Luther in a letter written in December 1516 to Erasmus by Georg Spalatin (1484–1545), who was charged with buying books for the university library and was asking about Erasmus's recent publications. In the letter, however, Spalatin turns to a question of theology. Spalatin says he has a friend, a certain Augustinian priest, who thinks Erasmus misunderstands St. Paul's teaching on justification and original sin. Spalatin's friend suggests Erasmus read Augustine's* On the Spirit and the Letter *and his other anti-Pelagian writings. Spalatin's Augustinian friend, of course, is young Martin Luther. Spalatin continues: "His [Luther's] view is that we do not become just by performing just actions, as Aristotle supposed, except in a manner of speaking, but that we become just first and then act justly. For the person must first be changed, and then his works; for Abel was pleasing to God, and afterwards his gifts."*[2]

The lectures on Romans and Spalatin's letter show that by 1515 a decisive turn has occurred in Luther's thinking on sin, grace, and righteousness.

Lectures on Romans[3]

Glosses

Romans 1:1

Paul, a servant of Jesus Christ.

The whole purpose and intention of the apostle in this Epistle is to break down all righteousness and wisdom of our own, to point out again those sins and foolish practices which did not exist (that is, those whose

1 Augustine of Hippo (345–430) is one of the most significant theologians in the history of Christianity. His works on grace, particularly *On the Spirit and the Letter*, exercised considerable influence on Luther and his university colleagues. In 1517, Luther declared to a friend: "Our theology and St. Augustine are progressing well, and with God's help rule at our University" (letter to John Lang, May 18, 1517, LW 48:42). Cf. Luther's preface to Augustine, *On the Spirit and the Letter* (1533?), LW 60:35–44.

2 Spalatin to Erasmus, December 11, 1516 (Ep. 501), in *The Correspondence of Erasmus*, trans. R. A. B. Mynors and D. F. S. Thompson, vol. 4 of *Collected Works of Erasmus* (Toronto: University of Toronto Press, 1977), 167–68. Luther had written to Spalatin in October about these issues and asked him to write to Erasmus. See LW 48:23–26.

3 The following excerpts are adapted from *Lectures on Romans*, volume 25 of *Luther's Works: American Edition*, ed. Hilton C. Oswald, trans. Walter G. Tillmanns and J. A. O. Preus (St. Louis: Concordia, 1971). Minor alterations have been made to the text for consistency in style, abbreviations, and capitalization. The annotations and subheadings are the work of the editor of this book.

existence we did not recognize on account of that kind of righteousness), to blow them up and to magnify them (that is, to cause them to be recognized as still in existence and as numerous and serious), and thus to show that for breaking them down Christ and His righteousness are needed for us. This he does up to chapter 12. From there to the end he teaches in what kind of works we should be involved, once that righteousness of Christ has been received. For in the presence of God this is not the way, that a person becomes righteous by doing works of righteousness (as the foolish Jews, Gentiles, and all other self-righteous people proudly think), but he who has been made righteous does works of righteousness, as it is written: "And the Lord had regard for Abel and for his offering" (Gen. 4:4), not in the first place "for his offering."[4]

Romans 1:3
Concerning His Son.

Here the door is thrown open wide for the understanding of Holy Scriptures, that is, that everything must be understood in relation to Christ, especially in the case of prophecy. But Scripture is completely prophetical, although not according to the superficial sense of the letter.

Romans 1:16
For I am not ashamed of the Gospel for it is the power of God for salvation.

That is, it is a power unto salvation for all who believe, or it is the Word that has power to save all who believe in it. And this is given through God and from God. It is as if you should say: "This jewel has this power from God, that he who wears it cannot be wounded." Thus the Gospel has this ingredient from God, that he who believes in it is saved. In this way, therefore, the person who has the Gospel is powerful and wise before, and from, God, even though in the eyes of men he may be considered foolish and weak.

Romans 3:21
But now, apart from the Law, the righteousness of God has been manifested.

Blessed Augustine in chapter 9 of *On the Spirit and the Letter* says: " 'The righteousness of God'; he did not say 'the righteousness of man' or

---

4 Cf. *Disputation against Scholastic Theology* (1517), Thesis 40: "We do not become righteous by doing righteous deeds but, having been made righteous, we do righteous deeds" (LW 31:12).

'the righteousness of one's own will,' but 'the righteousness of God,' not that righteousness by which God is righteous but that righteousness with which He covers man when He justifies the ungodly. As the term 'the faith of Christ' is used to describe not the faith by which Christ believes but the faith 'by which we believe in Christ,' so likewise this righteousness is not the righteousness by which God is righteous. For both are ours. But it is called God's righteousness and Christ's righteousness because He gives it to us out of His bounty."[5] The same things are said in chapter 11. Augustine continues in the same place: "How can it be witnessed in the Law if it is manifested without the Law? But it is a righteousness without the Law, which God through the Spirit of grace bestows on the believer without the aid of the Law, that is, unaided by the Law. For through the Law He has shown man his weakness, so that through faith he may flee to His mercy for cleansing. And concerning His wisdom it is said that it carries law and mercy on its tongue, namely, the Law by which He declares the proud guilty and mercy by which He justifies those who have been humbled."[6]

Lectures on Romans
Scholia

Romans 1:1

Paul, a servant of Jesus Christ.

The chief purpose of this letter is to break down, to pluck up, and to destroy all wisdom and righteousness of the flesh. This includes all the works which in the eyes of people or even in our own eyes may be great works. No matter whether these works are done with a sincere heart and mind, this letter is to affirm and state and magnify sin, no matter how much someone insists that it does not exist, or that it was believed not to exist. Therefore blessed Augustine, *On the Spirit and the Letter*, ch. 7, says: The apostle Paul "fights hard against the proud and the conceited and against those who are arrogant on the basis of their works, etc. . . . In the Letter to the Romans this question is treated so persistently and almost to the exclusion of all others that it may really weary the attention of the reader. But it is a profitable and salutary wearying."[7]

---

5 Augustine, *The Spirit and the Letter* 9.15 (WSA 1/23:158).

6 Augustine, *The Spirit and the Letter* 9.15 (WSA 1/23:158).

7 Augustine, *The Spirit and the Letter* 7.12 (WSA 1/23:156).

Romans 1:3–4

Concerning His Son, who was made for Him of the seed of David according to the flesh and predestined the Son of God in power.

This passage has, as far as I know, never been explained correctly or sufficiently by anyone. The exegetes of the ancient church were hindered by an inadequate explanation, and the more recent exegetes were lacking in Spirit. And yet, aided by the efforts of others, we venture to try our minds at it without doing violence to the piety of our faith. I think the meaning of the apostle is the following: The contents, or object, of the Gospel, or—as others say—its subject, is Jesus Christ, the Son of God, born of the seed of David according to the flesh and now appointed King and Lord over all things in power, and this according to the Holy Spirit, who has raised Him from the dead. Here the Greek text is very helpful, which reads as follows: "Concerning His Son, made of the seed of David, who was chosen, or designated, declared, ordained, etc., to be the Son of God in power according to the Spirit of sanctification by the resurrection from the dead, Jesus Christ, our Lord." Now let us look at the individual expressions.

Concerning His Son.

This is the Gospel, which deals not merely with the Son of God in general but with Him who has become incarnate and is of the seed of David. In effect he says: "He has emptied Himself and has become weak. He who was before all and created everything now has a beginning Himself and has been made." But the Gospel speaks not only of the humiliation of the Son of God, by which He emptied Himself, but also of His glory and the power which after His humiliation He received from God in His humanity. In other words, just as the Son of God became the Son of David by humbling and emptying Himself in the weakness of the flesh, so on the other hand the Son of David, though weak according to the flesh, has now in turn been established and designated the Son of God in all power and glory. And as according to His divine form He emptied Himself (Phil. 2:7) to the point of the nothingness of the flesh by being born into the world, so in the form of a servant He has brought Himself to completion to the point of fullness of divine essence by ascending into heaven. Observe the fitting expression of the apostle. He does not say: "He who was made the Son of God in power," in the same way as he says: "He who was made according to the flesh." For from the very beginning of Christ's conception, on account of the union of the two natures, it has been correct to say: "This God is the Son of David, and this man is the Son of God." The first is correct because His Godhead was emptied and hidden in the flesh. The second is correct because His humanity has been completed and translated to divine being. But even though it is true that He was not made the Son of God, but only the Son of Man, nevertheless one and the same person has always been the Son and is the Son of God even then.

Romans 1:17

The righteousness of God is revealed.

In human teachings the righteousness of man is revealed and taught, that is, who is and becomes righteous before himself and before other people and how this takes place. Only in the Gospel is the righteousness of God revealed (that is, who is and becomes righteous before God and how this takes place) by faith alone, by which the Word of God is believed, as it is written in the last chapter of Mark (16:16): "He who believes and is baptized will be saved; but he who does not believe will be condemned." For the righteousness of God is the cause of salvation. And here again, by the righteousness of God we must not understand the righteousness by which He is righteous in Himself but the righteousness by which we are made righteous by God. This happens through faith in the Gospel. Therefore blessed Augustine writes in chapter 11 of *On the Spirit and the Letter*: "It is called the righteousness of God because by imparting it He makes righteous people, just as 'Deliverance belongs to the Lord' refers to that by which He delivers."[8] Augustine says the same thing in chapter 9 of the same book. The righteousness of God is so named to distinguish it from the righteousness of man, which comes from works, as Aristotle describes it very clearly in Book 3 of his *Ethics*.[9] According to him, righteousness follows upon actions and originates in them. But according to God, righteousness precedes works, and thus works are the result of righteousness, just as no person can do the works of a bishop or priest unless he is first consecrated and has been set apart for this.[10] Righteous works of people who are not yet righteous are like the works of a person who performs the functions of a priest and bishop without being a priest; in other words, such works are foolish and tricky and are to be compared with the antics of hucksters in the marketplace.

8 Augustine, *The Spirit and the Letter* 11.18 (WSA 1/23:161). The Bible passage quoted here is Ps. 3:8.

9 Cf. Aristotle, *Nicomachean Ethics* 1113b7–14. Luther more often cites Aristotle, *Nicomachean Ethics* 1103a33–1103b1: "We become just by doing just acts."

10 Cf. *Freedom of a Christian* (1520), LW 31:360–61.

Romans 3:4

That Thou mayest be justified in Thy words.

. . . Thus God is justified in His words, that is, when we believe Him in the Gospel concerning the fulfillment of the promise, so that He is regarded as truthful and righteous. For these words of His in which He is justified are the word of the Gospel, when people believe Him, that He speaks the truth in them and that what is prophesied in this Word will come to pass. Not only will He be justified by those who believe, but He will also overcome when He is judged, that is, when He is reproved by those who deny that Christ has been sent and that the promises have been fulfilled. For they judge these words and condemn them and never consider them as righteous, that is, they never believe that these words are righteous and true; indeed, they even judge and condemn God in these words, while others justify Him. But these people shall not prevail. For He prevails and obtains the victory, because no matter how much they resist, this faithfulness of God, this "justification of God in His words" (that is, this trust in His Word) continues. The justification of God and trust in God are the same thing. For He prevails and remains—indeed, He always goes forward and increases, while they who do not believe will fail and perish.

That "God is justified in His words" (Ps. 51:4) means that He is made just and true in His words or that His words are made just and true. And this takes place in believing them, accepting them, and holding them as true and just. The only thing that can resist this justification is the pride of the human heart through unbelief. For this pride does not justify but condemns and judges. Therefore it does not believe His words, since it does not regard them as true. And it does not regard them as true because it regards its own understanding, which is contrary to them, as true. Hence for God to be judged in His words is the same as that He Himself or His words are condemned and thus become lying and unjust. This takes place through arrogant unbelief and rebellion. For thus it is obvious that this justification and judgment of God are outside of God and His Word, that is, in men. For intrinsically both God and His words are righteous and true. But they have not as yet become such in us until our wisdom yields to them and in faith gives them a place and accepts them. Thus it says in Ps. 51:4: "Against Thee have I sinned," that is, "I yield my righteousness and my understanding, which resists and condemns Thy words, and I confess that I am a sinner, unrighteous, and lying, in order that Thy words may have a place in me, be justified, be true, and become true," that they may become in us what they are in themselves, because in themselves they are justified oracles.

God is justified

Through the fact that "God is justified" we are justified. And this passive justification of God by which He is justified by us is our active justification by God. For He regards that faith which justifies His words as righteousness, as it says in chapter 4:5 and in chapter 1:17, "The just shall live by faith." And on the contrary, the passive justification of God, by which He is judged by unbelievers, is their own condemnation. For He rejects as unrighteousness and damnation that unbelief by which they judge and condemn His words. Thus it agrees with the Hebrew, which puts it this way: "Against Thee have I sinned, because Thou wilt justify," that is, Thou wilt bring justification, "in Thy Word and wilt cleanse when Thou art judged." For He justifies, overcomes, in His Word when He makes us to be like His Word, that is, righteous, true, wise, etc. And He thus changes us into His Word, but not His Word into us. And He makes us such when we believe His Word is such, that is, righteous and true. For then there is a similar form of the Word and the believer, that is, truth and righteousness. Therefore when He is justified, He justifies, and when He justifies, He is justified. . . .

Likewise, just as it is said that God or His words are justified, when in faith we believe them to be just and truthful (which they are in themselves even without our faith), so also we must understand that we have to become sinners and liars and fools and that all our righteousness, truthfulness, wisdom, and strength have to perish. And this takes place when we believe that we are sinners and liars, etc., and that our virtue and righteousness are absolutely nothing before God. Thus we become inwardly, inside ourselves, what we are outwardly (that is, before God), even though inside ourselves we are not this way, that is, even though we do not believe that we are such. For as God alone is truthful and righteous and powerful in Himself, so also He wishes to be such outside Himself, that is, in us, so that He may thus be glorified (for it is the glory of any good thing which is in anyone, that it be poured out of itself upon other people), so He wills that just as every man by himself is a liar, unrighteous, and weak outwardly (that is, before God), so he may become such inwardly, that is, he may confess and acknowledge himself to be such as he actually is. And thus God through His own coming forth causes us to enter into ourselves, and through this understanding of Him He gives to us also an understanding of ourselves. For unless God had first come forth and sought to be truthful in us, we could not have entered into ourselves and be made liars and unrighteous men. For man of himself could not know that he is such a person before God, unless God Himself had revealed it to him. "For who has known the mind of the Lord, or who has been His counselor?" (Rom. 11:34). Otherwise man would always believe that he is truthful, righteous, and wise, especially because in his own eyes and before his fellow men he is such. But now God has revealed what He thinks about us and what He judges us to be, namely, that all are in sin. Therefore we have to yield to this His revelation, His words, and believe and thus declare them righteous and true and thereby also confess that we ourselves are sinners according to them (a fact we did not know before).

Romans 3:27–28

Justified by faith apart from works of the Law.

. . . Hence we must note, as we have said above in quoting blessed Augustine, that "the principle of works says: 'Do what I command,' but the principle of faith says: 'Give what You command.' "[11] And thus the people of the Law say to the Law and to God, who speaks in the Law: "I have done what Thou hast commanded, it is done as Thou hast ordered." But the people of faith say: "I cannot do, I have not done, but give me what Thou commandest; I have not done it, but I desire to do it. And because I cannot, I beg and beseech of Thee the power whereby I may do it." And thus the former is made proud and boastful, and the latter humble and vile in his own eyes. And thus there is a very real difference between these classes of people, because the one says: "I have done it," and the other says, "I beg that I might be empowered to do it"; the one says: "Command what Thou dost wish, and I will do it," the other says: "Give what Thou hast commanded in order that I may do it"; the one is confident in the righteousness which he already possesses, the other prays for the righteousness which he hopes to acquire.

For this reason the whole life of the new people, the faithful people, the spiritual people, is nothing else but prayer, seeking, and begging by the sighing of the heart, the voice of their works, and the labor of their bodies, always seeking and striving to be made righteous, even to the hour of death, never standing still, never possessing, never in any work putting an end to the achievement of righteousness, but always awaiting it as something which still dwells beyond them, and always as people who still live and exist in their sins. Thus when the apostle says that a man is justified *apart from works of the Law* (v. 28), he is not speaking about the works which are performed in order that we may seek justification.

11 Augustine, *The Spirit and the Letter* 13.22 (WSA 1/23:164).

Because these are no longer the works of the Law but of grace and faith, since he who performs them does not trust in them for his justification, but he wants to be justified and he does not think that through these works he has fulfilled the Law, but he seeks its fulfillment.

Romans 4:6

So also David pronounces man righteous apart from works.

This passage must be understood in this way: *His faith is reckoned as righteousness. So David also pronounces* (that is, asserts) *a blessing upon the man* (that is, that that man is blessed, or that blessedness is of that man alone) *to whom God reckons righteousness apart from works.* And the expression "apart from works" must be understood, as we have pointed out above, of those works by the doing of which a person thinks he has received righteousness and now possesses it, as if he thereby is made righteous because he has performed those works, or as if God now regards him as a righteous man because he is doing them, although this is not true, because God does not accept a person because of his works but the works because of the person, therefore the person before the works. As it is written: "And the Lord had regard for Abel (first) and (afterward) for his offering" (Gen. 4:4). Hence it becomes obvious that it is not so much the works of that kind as the foolish opinion or estimation of these works which is disapproved. For the righteous do the same works as the unrighteous, but not from the same heart. That is, the righteous perform the works that they may seek and obtain righteousness through them, but the wicked do them that they may make a display of righteousness through them and boast of it as already found. The former are not content with the works they have performed and seek to have their heart justified and cleansed from sinful desires, but the latter care nothing for their inner life and are content with works performed externally. Therefore they are merely pretenders and are hypocrites, that is, they are like the righteous outwardly, but they are not really righteous inwardly.

Romans 4:7

Blessed are they whose iniquities are forgiven.

Sinners inwardly, justified outwardly

The saints are always sinners in their own sight, and therefore always justified outwardly.

But the hypocrites are always righteous in their own sight, and thus always sinners outwardly.

I use the term "inwardly" (*intrinsice*) to show how we are in ourselves, in our own eyes, in our own estimation; and the term "outwardly" (*extrinsice*) to indicate how we are before God and in His reckoning. Therefore we are righteous outwardly when we are righteous solely by the imputation of God and not of ourselves or of our own works. For His imputation is not ours by reason of anything in us or in our own power. Thus our righteousness is not something in us or in our power. As Hosea 13:9 says, "Destruction is your own, O Israel; your help is only in Me," that is, within yourself there is nothing but destruction, and your deliverance is from outside of you. And Ps. 121:2: "My help comes from the Lord," which is to say, it is not from myself. But inwardly we are sinners according to the law of mutual relationship. For if we are righteous only because God reckons us to be such, then it is not because of our mode of living or our deeds. Thus inwardly and of ourselves we are always unrighteous. Thus we read in Ps. 51:3–4: "My sin is ever before me," that is, I always have it in my mind that I am a sinner. "Against Thee have I sinned" (that is, I am a sinner), "so that Thou art justified in Thy Word, etc." And on the contrary, the hypocrites, because they are righteous in their own sight, by force and necessity of this relationship are outwardly unrighteous (that is, in the reckoning of God), as Ps. 95:10 says, "And I said, 'They are a people who err in heart.'" They pervert every word of Scripture, as, for example, this statement: "My sin is ever before me" (Ps. 51:3), for they say: "My righteousness is always before me" (that is, always in view), and "Blessed are they who work righteousness, etc." "Before Thee," they say (not, "I have sinned," but), "I do righteous works." Indeed, before themselves they perform such works.

Every saint a sinner

"God is wonderful in His saints" (Ps. 68:35). To Him they are at the same time both righteous and unrighteous.

And God is wonderful in the hypocrites. To Him they are at the same time both unrighteous and righteous.

For inasmuch as the saints are always aware of their sin and seek righteousness from God in accord with His mercy, for this very reason they are always also regarded as righteous by God. Thus in their own sight and in truth they are unrighteous, but before God they are righteous because He reckons them so because of their confession of sin. They are actually sinners, but they are righteous by the imputation of a merciful God. They are unknowingly righteous and knowingly unrighteous; they are sinners in fact but righteous in hope. And this is what he is saying here: "Blessed are they whose iniquities are forgiven, and whose sins are covered" (Ps. 32:1). Hence, these words follow (v. 5), "I said, I will confess my transgressions to the Lord" (that is, I am always conscious of my sin, because I confess it to Thee). Therefore, "Then Thou didst forgive the guilt of my sin," not to me only but to all. Hence these words follow (v. 6): "Therefore let everyone who is godly offer prayer to Thee." Note that every saint is a sinner and prays for his sins. Thus the righteous man is in the first place his own accuser. And again (Ecclus. 39:5), the righteous man "will make supplication for his sins." And again, Ps. 38:18: "I confess my iniquity, I am sorry for my sin." Therefore, wonderful and sweet is the mercy of God, who at the same time considers us both as sinners and nonsinners. Sin remains and at the same time it does not remain. Therefore, this psalm must be understood according to its title. On the other hand, His wrath is also wonderful and severe, for at the same time He regards the ungodly as both righteous and unrighteous. And at the same time He both takes away their sin and does not take it away.

Simul iustus et peccator

He is speaking not only of sins in deed, word, and thought but also of the tinder,[12] as later in Rom. 7:20: "It is no longer I that do it, but sin which dwells within me." And in the same chapter he speaks of "our sinful passions" (Rom. 7:5), that is, the desires, feelings, and inclinations toward sin which he says produce fruit for death. Therefore, act of sin (as it is called by the theologians) is more correctly sin in the sense of the work and fruit of sin, but sin itself is the passion, the tinder, and the concupiscence, or the inclination, toward evil and the difficulty of doing good, as he says below (Rom. 7:7): "I should not have known concupiscence to be sin." For if these passions "work," then they are not the works themselves, but they work to bring forth fruit, and thus they are not the fruit. Conversely, just as our righteousness from God is the very turning toward the good and the avoiding of evil which is given to us inwardly through grace, but our works are the fruits of righteousness, so also sin is the actual turning away from good and the inclination toward evil. And the works of sin are the fruits of this sin, as will be seen very clearly later on in chapters 7 and 8. And all the passages previously cited must be understood in the light of this kind of sin. Thus (Rom. 4:7; Ps. 32:1): "Blessed are those whose iniquities are forgiven," and again (Ps. 32:5–6): "I said, I will confess my transgressions to the Lord . . . Therefore let everyone who is godly offer prayer to Thee," and again (Ps. 51:3): "For I know my transgression, and

12 The schoolmen referred to the inclination toward sin as the *fomes peccati* ("tinder of sin"). They further distinguished between the inclination to sin, which they also called concupiscence, and actual sin. The schoolmen did not regard this inclination or concupiscence to be sin until it was acted upon. Cf. Aristotle, *Nicomachean Ethics* 1105b30–1106a10.

my sin is ever before me," and likewise (Ps. 51:4): "Against Thee only have I sinned, etc." For this is the evil, since it is truly sin, which God forgives through His nonimputation out of His mercy toward all who acknowledge and confess and hate their sin and plead to be cleansed from it. This is the basis for the statement (1 John 1:8): "If we say we have no sin, we are liars." And the mistake lies in thinking that this evil can be cured through works, since experience bears witness that in whatever good work we perform, this concupiscence toward evil remains, and no one is ever cleansed of it, not even the one-day-old infant. But the mercy of God is that this does remain and yet is not imputed as sin to those who call upon Him and cry out for His deliverance. For such people easily avoid also the error of works, because they so zealously seek to be justified. Thus in ourselves we are sinners, and yet through faith we are righteous by God's imputation. For we believe Him who promises to free us, and in the meantime we strive that sin may not rule over us but that we may withstand it until He takes it from us.

It is similar to the case of a sick man who believes the doctor who promises him a sure recovery and in the meantime obeys the doctor's order in the hope of the promised recovery and abstains from those things which have been forbidden him, so that he may in no way hinder the promised return to health or increase his sickness until the doctor can fulfill his promise to him. Now is this sick man well? The fact is that he is both sick and well at the same time. He is sick in fact, but he is well because of the sure promise of the doctor, whom he trusts and who has reckoned him as already cured, because he is sure that he will cure him; for he has already begun to cure him and no longer reckons to him a sickness unto death. In the same way Christ, our Samaritan, has brought His half dead man into the inn to be cared for, and He has begun to heal him, having promised him the most complete cure unto eternal life, and He does not impute his sins, that is, his wicked desires, unto death, but in the meantime in the hope of the promised recovery He prohibits him from doing or omitting things by which his cure might be impeded and his sin, that is, his concupiscence, might be increased. Now, is he perfectly righteous? No, for he is at the same time both a sinner and a righteous man [*simul peccator et iustus*]; a sinner in fact, but a righteous man by the sure imputation and promise of God that He will continue to deliver him from sin until He has completely cured him. And thus he is entirely healthy in hope, but in fact he is still a sinner; but he has the beginning of righteousness, so that he continues more and more always to seek it, yet he realizes that he is always unrighteous. But now if this sick man should like his sickness and refuse every cure for his disease, will he not die?

Certainly, for thus it is with those who follow their lusts in this world. Or if a certain sick man does not see that he is sick but thinks he is well and thus rejects the doctor, this is the kind of operation that wants to be justified and made well by its own works.

Luther versus the schoolmen

Since this is the case, either I have never understood, or else the scholastic theologians have not spoken sufficiently clearly about sin and grace, for they have been under the delusion that original sin, like actual sin, is entirely removed,[13] as if these were items that can be entirely removed in the twinkling of an eye, as shadows before a light, although the ancient fathers Augustine and Ambrose spoke entirely differently and in the way Scripture does. But those men speak in the manner of Aristotle in his *Ethics*, when he bases sin and righteousness on works, both their performance or omission.[14] But blessed Augustine says very clearly that "sin, or concupiscence, is forgiven in Baptism, not in the sense that it no longer exists, but in the sense that it is not imputed."[15] And blessed Ambrose says, "I always sin, therefore I always go to Communion."[16] And on the basis of this in my foolishness I could not understand in which way I should regard myself a sinner like other men and thus prefer myself to no one, even though I was contrite and made confession; for I then felt that all my sins had been taken away and entirely removed, even inwardly. For if because of sins that were past, which they say must always be remembered (and here they speak the truth, but not strongly enough), I still had to consider myself a sinner, then I felt that these past sins had not been forgiven. Yet God has promised that they are forgiven to those who confess them. Thus I was at war with myself, not knowing that it was a true forgiveness indeed, but that this is nevertheless not a taking away of sin except in hope, that is, that the taking away is to be done, and that by the gift of grace, which begins to take sin away, so that it is not imputed as sin. For this reason it is plain insanity to say that man of his own powers can love God above all things[17] and can perform the works

---

13 Whether original sin remains after Baptism or not will become a principal point of disagreement between Luther and his Roman opponents. Cf. *Against Latomus* (1521), LW 32:220–21. See also Philip Melanchthon's (1497–1560) lengthy discussion of this question in Apology of the Augsburg Confession II.

14 Aristotle, *Nicomachean Ethics* 1103a32–1103b26.

15 Augustine, *Marriage and Desire* 1.25 (WSA 1/24:46).

16 Ambrose (ca. 339–397), *De sacramentis* 4.6.28 (PL 26:464).

17 Thomas Aquinas had argued that man could love God above all things in the state of perfect nature, but after the fall, in the state of corrupt nature, grace was needed (*Summa Theologiae*, I–II, q. 109, a. 3). John Duns Scotus, the most significant medieval theologian after Thomas Aquinas, argued that man could love God

of the Law according to the substance of the act, even if not according to the intentions of Him who gave the commandment,[18] because he is not in a state of grace.

O fools, O pig-theologians (*Sawtheologen*)! By your line of reasoning grace was not necessary except because of some new demand above and beyond the Law. For if the Law can be fulfilled by our powers, as they say, then grace is not necessary for the fulfilling of the Law, but only for the fulfilling of some new exaction imposed by God above the Law. Who can endure these sacrilegious notions? When the apostle says that "the Law works wrath" (4:15) and that the Law "was weakened by the flesh" (Rom. 8:3), it certainly cannot be fulfilled without grace. They could have been made aware of their own foolishness and brought to shame and repentance even by their own experience. For willy-nilly they recognize the evil lusts in themselves. For this reason I say: "Hah! Get busy now, I beg you. Be men! Work with all your might, so that these lusts may no longer be in you. Prove that it is possible by nature to love God, as you say, 'with all your strength' (Luke 10:27) and without any grace. If you are without concupiscence, we will believe you. But if you live with and in these lusts, then you are no longer fulfilling the Law." Does not the Law say, "You shall not covet" (Exod. 20:17), but rather, "You shall love God" (Deut. 6:5)? But when a person desires and loves something else, can he really love God? But this concupiscence is always in us, and therefore the love of God is never in us, unless it is begun by grace, and until the concupiscence which still remains and which keeps us from "loving God with all our heart" (Luke 10:27) is healed and by mercy not imputed to us as sin, and until it is completely removed and the perfect love for God is given to the believers and those who persistently agitate for it to the end.

All of these monstrosities have come from the fact that they did not know what sin is nor forgiveness. For they reduced sin to some very minute activity of the soul, and the same was true of righteousness. For

---

above all things by his own natural abilities even after the fall (*Sententiarum*, III, d. 27, q. 1; *Ordinatio*, III, suppl. d. 27). Cf. Luther, *Disputation against Scholastic Theology* (1517), Thesis 13, LW 31:10; *Lectures on Galatians* (1531), LW 26:128 (see below, p. 232); *Commentary on Psalm 51* (1532), LW 12:308, 345 (see below, p. 291); *Lectures on Genesis* (1535–45), LW 2:124 (see below, p. 325).

18 Luther, who studied Gabriel Biel in detail at the University of Erfurt, paraphrases Biel's distinction between the substance of the act (*quoad substantiam actus*) and the intention of the lawgiver (*quoad intentionem praecipientis*). Biel, *Collectorium circa quattuor libros Sententiarum*, II, d. 28, q. 1, a. 2, concl. 3; and *Collectorium*, III, d. 27, q. 1., a. 3, dub. 2, prop. 2. See also Luther, *Lectures on Galatians* (1531), LW 26:128 (see below, p. 233); and *Commentary on Psalm 51* (1532), LW 12:308 (see below, pp. 264–65).

they said that since the will has this synteresis,[19] "it is inclined," albeit weakly, "toward the good." And this minute motion toward God (which man can perform by nature) they imagine to be an act of loving God above all things! But take a good look at man, entirely filled with evil lusts (notwithstanding that minute motion). The Law commands him to be empty, so that he may be taken completely into God. Thus Isaiah in 41:23 laughs at them and says, "Do good or evil if you can!" This life, then, is a life of being healed from sin, it is not a life of sinlessness, with the cure completed and perfect health attained. The church is the inn and the infirmary for those who are sick and in need of being made well. But heaven is the palace of the healthy and the righteous. As blessed Peter says in his Second Epistle 3:13 that the Lord will build "new heavens and a new earth in which righteousness dwells." Righteousness does not yet dwell here, but it is preparing a dwelling place for itself here in the meantime by healing sin. All the saints have had this understanding of sin, as David prophesied in Ps. 32:5ff. And thus they all have confessed that they were sinners, as is clear in the books of St. Augustine. Our theologians, however, have deflected the discussion of sin to the matter of good works only and have undertaken to teach only those things by which works might be safeguarded but not how through much agony men should humbly seek healing grace and confess themselves to be sinners. Thus of necessity they make men proud and cause them to think that they are already entirely righteous when they have performed certain outward works. And thus they are not at all concerned about declaring war on their evil lusts through unceasing prayer to the Lord. And the result is that there is now in the church a great deal of falling away after confession. For the people do not realize that they need to be justified but are confident that they have been justified, and thus they are ruined through their own sense of security without any effort on the part of the devil. This is certainly a case of basing righteousness upon works. And although they implore the grace of God, they do not do so rightly, but only for the sake of forgiveness for an act of sin. But those who truly belong to Christ have the spirit of Christ and act rightly, even though they do not understand what we have just stated; for they act before they understand, indeed, they understand more from life than from what they have been taught.

There is still one more point which is raised in objection to what we have just said, namely, that the righteousness of God even without works

19 *Synteresis* refers to the major premise of a scholastic syllogism that asserted the natural inclination of the soul toward the good. Luther conveys this meaning with the quoted words.

is imputed to those who believe. We read in the stories of many of the saints that certain of their works or prayers were well regarded by God and commended to others for an example. And thus they were justified by works of this kind. I reply: A great argument, for it both sets forth a glaring error and makes clearer a useful understanding of what we have been saying up to this point. The error is committed by those who immediately want to imitate with their presumed powers all of those things which have been well regarded by God and thus want to be so regarded themselves, because they are doing the same things as the saints to whom works have been reckoned as righteous. This is merely seeking a righteousness of works and in no way an imitation of the saints but rather a perversion of their example. For those saints to whom these works were reckoned for righteousness and commended as an example surely did not do them in order that they might be so reckoned; indeed, they were entirely ignorant that they were reckoned righteous by God, but did what they could in their humble faith, always praying that their works might be pleasing to God according to His mercy. Thus after they had first been reckoned as righteous because of the humble prayer of faith, then also their works were so reckoned and approved. But you stupid perverter, you first begin with the works which have been reckoned, ignoring the inner groaning by which you were already reckoned as righteous, just as these saints were. You want to be reckoned as righteous only by your works, that is, you want first "regard for the offering" and then "for Abel," which cannot be. And this insanity now rages everywhere in the pulpits of those who should be preaching the Word of God.

Excursus on Psalm 51

This verse speaks most explicitly of original sin, according to the Hebrew text: "Behold, I was conceived in iniquities," that is, in unrighteousness (*iniustitia*), "and in sin did my mother bear me" (Ps. 51:5). For the meaning is that this unrighteousness and sin do not refer to the mother who conceives and bears but to the child who is conceived and brought forth. It is as if he were saying: "Behold when I was conceived, I was in a state of unrighteousness before Thee; I was not righteous because through Adam I had lost this righteousness and thus was conceived without it. For Thou imputest unrighteousness to all those who are conceived because of the sin which is poured out by their parents, even when they do not sin." And "in sin," that is, with the tinder of sin, with sinful lust, "did my mother bear me." Now a mother does not sin by the act of bearing a child, but the son who is born sins, that is, he is a sinner. Surely the psalmist is confessing not someone else's sins but his own, not only in this verse but also in the preceding verses, where he always uses such terms as "my" and "mine." But the reason why in this verse he does not speak of "my" or "mine" is that the sin in which he says that he has been conceived is the common possession of all. And the sin which belongs to all, he asserts, has now become his too. Therefore he introduces the statement by saying, "Wash me thoroughly from my iniquity, etc." (v. 2). And another reason is that this sin is his own and not his own. Therefore he did not say "in my iniquities" but "in iniquities," as if to say that this iniquity exists whether I perform it or even know about it. I am conceived in it, but I did not do it. It began to rule in me before I began to live. It is simultaneous with me. For if this were only the sin of my parents who conceived me, then surely I would not have been conceived in it, for they would have sinned even before I was conceived. Therefore this iniquity and sin existed and they were not mine; I was conceived in them without my consent. But now they have become mine. For now I understand that I do evil and disobey the Law. The Law commands, "You shall not covet" (Exod. 20:17). And if I do not observe the Law, I am now sinning, and behold, I covet. Therefore the sin is now my own, that is, by my will it has been approved and accepted by my consent, because without grace I have been unable to overcome it in myself; therefore it has overcome me, and I am, because of that same tinder and evil lust, through my work also an actual sinner and not merely under original sin. Therefore I have said, "For I know my transgression, etc." (Ps. 51:3).

We sin even when we do good

Scripture uses the terms "righteousness" and "unrighteousness" very differently from the philosophers and lawyers. This is obvious, because they consider these things as a quality of the soul. But the "righteousness" of Scripture depends upon the imputation of God more than on the essence of a thing itself. For he does not have righteousness who only has a quality, indeed, he is altogether a sinner and an unrighteous man; but he alone has righteousness whom God mercifully regards as righteous because of his confession of his own unrighteousness and because of his prayer for the righteousness of God and whom God wills to be considered righteous before Him. Therefore we are all born in iniquity, that is, in unrighteousness, and we die in it, and we are righteous only by the imputation of a merciful God through faith in His Word. . . .

From all of this it is obvious that there is no sin which is venial according to its substance and its nature,[20] but also no merit. For even the good

20 Augustine distinguished between sins that merit damnation and those that do not. The medieval schoolmen continued to use this distinction and named these sins "mortal" and "venial." Mortal sins destroy the relationship with God, deprive a person of grace and love, and lead to eternal damnation. Venial sins do not destroy

works which are done while the tinder of sin and sensuality are fighting against them are not of such intensity and purity as the Law requires, since they are not done with all of our strength, but only with the spiritual powers which struggle against the powers of the flesh. Thus we sin even when we do good, unless God through Christ covers this imperfection and does not impute it to us. Thus it becomes a venial sin through the mercy of God, who does not impute it for the sake of faith and the plea in behalf of this imperfection for the sake of Christ. Therefore, he who thinks that he ought to be regarded as righteous because of his works is very foolish, since if they were offered as a sacrifice to the judgment of God, they still would be found to be sins. As Ps. 36:2 says, "For he has acted deceitfully in His sight, so that his iniquity is found to be for wrath," that is, before God and within his own spirit there was deceit and not the truth of righteousness, even though before men he makes a display of righteousness in his works. For he could not be righteous within himself without the mercy of God, since he is corrupt because of the tinder of sin. Therefore iniquity will be found in his righteousness, that is, even his good works will be unrighteous and sinful. This iniquity will not be found in believers and those who cry to Him, because Christ has brought them aid from the fullness of His purity and has hidden this imperfection of theirs. For they seek also this and hope for it from Him, but the others do not seek it but presumptuously think they have it.

Romans 5:4
Suffering produces endurance, and endurance trial.

Why do believers suffer?

If God should not test us by tribulation, it would be impossible for any man to be saved.

The reason is that our nature has been so deeply curved in upon itself because of the viciousness of original sin that it not only turns the finest gifts of God in upon itself and enjoys them (as is evident in the case of legalists and hypocrites), indeed, it even uses God Himself to achieve these aims, but it also seems to be ignorant of this very fact, that in acting so iniquitously, so perversely, and in such a depraved way, it is even seeking God for its own sake. Thus the prophet Jeremiah says in Jer. 17:9: "The heart is perverse above all things, and desperately corrupt; who can understand it?" that is, it is so curved in on itself that no man, no matter

---

the relationship with God, nor do they deprive a person of grace and love. These sins dull a person's affections for God and hamper acts of love. For the schoolmen, believers have the ability to avoid all mortal sins but not all venial sins. See also below, p. 37 n. 5.

how holy (if a testing is kept from him) can understand it. Thus Ps. 19:12 reads: "Who can discern his errors? Clear Thou me from hidden faults, etc.," and Ps. 32:6: "Therefore let everyone who is godly offer prayer to Thee at a proper time." And the Scripture calls this viciousness by a name most proper to it, that is, iniquity, depravity, or crookedness. . . . Therefore our good God, after He has justified us and given us His spiritual gifts, quickly brings tribulation upon us, exercises us, and tests us so that this godless nature of ours does not rush in upon these enjoyable sins, lest in his ignorance man should die the eternal death. For they are very lovely and vigorously excite enjoyment. Thus man learns to love and worship God purely for Himself, and not just because of His grace and His gifts; but he worships God for His own sake alone. Thus "He chastises every son whom He receives" (Heb. 12:6). And unless He did this, the son would quickly be drawn away by the sweetness of his new inheritance, he would luxuriate in his enjoyment of the grace which he had received and would offend his Father more deeply than before. Therefore in very good order the apostle says, "Suffering produces endurance, and endurance trial," that is, a proving or a testing.

Romans 6:6

Our old man.

The term "old man" describes what kind of person is born of Adam, not according to his nature but according to the defect of his nature. For his nature is good, but the defect is evil. However, the term "old man" is used not only because he performs the works of the flesh but more especially when he acts righteously and practices wisdom and exercises himself in all spiritual good works, even to the point of loving and worshiping God Himself. The reason for this is that in all these things he "enjoys" the gifts of God and "uses" God.[21] Nor can he be freed of his perversity (which in the Scriptures is called curvedness, iniquity, and crookedness) except by the grace of God. Eccl. 1:15: "The perverse are hard to be corrected." This is said not only because of the stubbornness of perverse people but particularly because of the extremely deep infection of this inherited weakness and original poison, by which a man seeks his own advantage even in God Himself because of his love of concupiscence. Ps. 72:14: "From usuries and iniquities He redeems their life." Furthermore, this iniquity is so bottomless that no one can ever understand its depth, and

21 Luther refers to Augustine's distinction in *On Christian Doctrine* 1.3–4, 22. For Augustine, we are "to use" (*uti*) the things of this world but not "to enjoy" (*frui*) them. The true objects of enjoyment are Father, Son, and Holy Spirit.

in Scripture, by the grace of God, not the iniquity itself but only the love of it is rebuked. Ps. 11:5: "His soul hates him that loves iniquity." And Ps. 32:6: "Therefore," that is, because of iniquity, "let everyone who is godly offer prayer to Thee," because He hates iniquity. This is symbolized in the curvedness of that woman in the Gospel whom Satan had held captive for eighteen years, as the Savior said (Luke 13:11).

Romans 8:3
For what the Law could not do.

Where now is free will? Where are those people who are trying to affirm that we of our own natural powers can produce the act of loving God above all things?[22] If I said that impossible demands are made of us, I would be roundly cursed. But now the apostle is saying that it was impossible for the Law to condemn sin, indeed, that it was itself infirmity because of the flesh. This is what I have previously said very often, namely, that it is simply impossible for us of ourselves to fulfill the Law, and that it is of no value to say that we can fulfill the Law according to the substance of the deed but not according to the intention of the Lawgiver, as if it were in our power to will and to be able, but not in the way God wills it, namely, in grace. And because of such reasoning grace is useful but not necessary, and we do not incur the wickedness of our nature through the sin of Adam, but we are complete in our natural powers. For this reason philosophy stinks in our nostrils, as if our reason always spoke for the best things,[23] and we make up many stories about the law of nature.

It is certainly true that the law of nature is known to all men and that our reason does speak for the best things, but what best things? It speaks for the best not according to God but according to us, that is, for things that are good in an evil way. For it seeks itself and its own in all things, but not God. This only faith does in love.

Hence knowledge and virtue and whatever good things are desired, sought, and found by natural capacity are good in an evil way. For they are not brought into relation to God but to the creature, that is, to oneself. For how would one relate things to God, if one does not love Him above all things? How would one love Him whom one has not known? How would a man know, when he is under the wickedness of the first sin and in shadows and chains as far as his intellect and feeling is concerned? Therefore, unless faith gives the light and love makes us free, no man can

22 See above, pp. 16–17 and n. 17.

23 Aristotle, *Nicomachean Ethics* 1102b15–16.

either have or do anything good, but only evil, even when he performs the good.

Incurvatus in se

The common saying that human nature in a general and universal way knows and wills the good but errs and does not will it in particular cases would be better stated if we were to say that in particular cases human nature knows and wills what is good but in general neither knows nor wills it. The reason is that it knows nothing but its own good, or what is good and honorable and useful for itself, but not what is good for God and other people. Therefore it knows and wills more what is particular, yes, only what is an individual good. And this is in agreement with Scripture, which describes man as so turned in on himself that he uses not only physical but even spiritual goods for his own purposes and in all things seeks only himself.

This curvedness is now natural for us, a natural wickedness and a natural sinfulness. Thus man has no help from his natural powers, but he needs the aid of some power outside of himself. This is love, without which he always sins against the Law "You shall not covet," that is, turn nothing in on yourself and seek nothing for yourself, but live, do, and think all things for God alone. For then a man will know the good in every way along with all particular good things, and he will judge all things. Thus the Law is impossible for us.

For this reason blessed Augustine in *On Grace and Free Will*, ch. 16, says: "He commands something which we cannot do in order that we may know what we must ask of Him. For this is faith which demands in prayer what the Law demands."[24]

Nature versus grace

In vain do some people magnify the light of nature and compare it with the light of grace, since it is actually more a shadow and something contrary to grace. Thus it is cursed by Job and Jeremiah [Job 3:1ff.; Jer. 20:14], because it is an evil day and a foul sight, because this light came into being right after sin did, as the Scripture says, "Their eyes were opened" (Gen. 3:7). For grace has set before itself no other object than God toward which it is carried and toward which it is moving; it sees only Him, it seeks only Him, and it always moves toward Him, and all other things which it sees between itself and God it passes by as if it had not seen them and directs itself only toward God. This is the "upright heart" (Ps. 7:10) and the "right spirit" (Ps. 51:10).

24 Augustine, *Grace and Free Choice* 16 (WSA 1/26:92).

But nature set for itself no object but itself toward which it is borne and toward which it is directed; it sees, seeks, and works only toward itself in all matters, and it passes by all other things and even God Himself in the midst, as if it did not see them, and is directed only toward itself. This is the "perverse heart" (Ps. 101:4) and the "wicked heart" (Prov. 27:21). Just as grace has placed God in the place of all things it sees, even its own interests, and prefers Him to itself and seeks only those things which belong to God and not its own things, so nature on the other hand sets itself in the place of all other things, even in the place of God, and seeks only those things which are its own and not the things of God. Therefore it is its own first and greatest idol. Second, it makes God into an idol and the truth of God into a lie, and finally it makes idols of all created things and of all gifts of God. But grace is never content in the things which it sees except as it sees God in and above them, and it wills, hopes, and rejoices in the fact that all things exist, are seen, and are accomplished for the glory of God. Nature, on the contrary, thinks that all the things it sees are nothing unless they serve to its advantage, exist for it and are done for it. And then it esteems them, if it can appropriate them for its own benefit, use, and good.

This is spiritual fornication, iniquity, and a terrible curving in on itself. Therefore, this wisdom is not a light, but it can much better be called darkness, unless someone would call it light because it sees and understands these things by its own reason and sense, but otherwise insofar as it turns all knowledge in upon itself, it is the most complete darkness. Nor can it by its nature do anything else than turn in upon itself. For it cannot love God and His Law, as the apostle here says.

Romans 14:1–2

As for the man who is weak in faith, welcome him, but not for disputes over opinions. One person believes he may eat anything, while the weak person eats only vegetables.

The word "weak" must not be understood in this passage in the sense of "impotent," as in the following chapter, where he speaks of the "failings of the weak" (Rom. 15:1), that is, of people who are impotent, but rather in the sense of "debility," which is contrasted with strength or good health. For example, a boy to be sure is impotent in comparison with a man, but he is not weak. Therefore the first term must be understood in a relative and transitive sense, but the second in an absolute sense. For thus the apostle in his letters speaks of some people as weak and others as sound in faith, understanding the term "weak" as referring to people who are overly careful or still superstitious in some respect, who think they ought to do what they really do not need to do. But not that he compliments those who are superstitious and of their own will remain such but rather those who of necessity are still weak in faith, who because of this are not yet in a state of salvation yet are on the way and thus should be cherished and cultivated, so that they might reach the goal. . . .

Christian freedom and indifferent things

Thus the meaning of the apostle is that in the new law all things are free and nothing is necessary for those who believe in Christ, but love is sufficient for them . . . .

Thus it does not belong to the new law to set aside certain days for fasting and others not, as the Law of Moses did. Nor does it belong that we make an exception of and a distinction between certain kinds of food, such as meat, eggs, etc., as again is done in the Law of Moses, for example, in Leviticus 11 and Deuteronomy 14. Nor does it belong to designate some days as feast days and others not. Nor does it belong to the new law that we build this or that church or that we ornament them in such and such a way, or that the singing be of a certain kind or the organ or the altar decorations, the chalices, the statues, and all of the other paraphernalia which are contained in our temples. Finally, it is not necessary that the priest and other religious[25] wear the tonsure or go about in distinctive garb, as they did under the old law. For all of these things are shadows and signs of the real thing and thus are childish. For every day is a feast, all food is permitted, every place is sacred, every time is a time of fasting, every kind of apparel is allowed, all things are free, only that we observe moderation in their use and that love and the other things which the apostle teaches us be practiced. Many false apostles have preached against this liberty which has been asserted by the apostle, so that they might lead the people to consider these matters as being necessary for salvation. These things the apostle resists with magnificent zeal. To what end? Are we now going to confirm the heresy of the Picards?[26] For they brought themselves to this rule. And thus are we going to say that all churches, all their ornamentation, all offices in them, all sacred places, all fast days, all feast days; finally all the distinctions between priests, bishops, and religious in rank, garb, and ceremonies observed for so many centuries right up to this day; and so many monasteries, foundations, benefices,

25 "Religious" are those who have taken vows and live in community under a monastic rule.

26 The name Picards is a corruption of Beghards, a mystical religious movement that flourished in Germany during the thirteenth and fourteenth centuries. They were condemned by the Council of Vienne (1311–12).

and prebends[27]—are we going to say that all of these should be abolished? For that is what the Picards are doing, and this is what the liberty of the new law requires. God forbid! . . .

Hence although all of these things are now matters of the greatest liberty, yet out of love for God each is permitted to bind himself by oath to this or that goal. But he is thereby no longer bound to these matters by the new law but by his own oath, which he has taken upon himself by reason of his love for God. For who is so foolish as to deny that a person can give up his liberty out of deference to another person and make himself a servant and bind himself to a certain place on such and such a day with such and such a work? But this must be done out of love and the faith that does not believe that he is doing these things as necessary for salvation but only of his own free will and out of a sense of freedom.

And thus all things are free, but because of our oath and out of love they can be offered up. And when this has been done, then these works are necessary, not because of their own nature but because of the oath freely given. And thus we must take care that our oaths are fulfilled with the same love with which they were promised, for without this they cannot be fulfilled. And if they are fulfilled without it, that is, in an unwilling spirit, it would be better not to have made the vow. For he who makes a vow and does not keep it is like this: he keeps it with his body, but he has reservations in his heart, and thus he is sacrilegious, since he does not perform it willingly. Thus there are many apostates, but they do not appear as such. However, he who omits love and directs his attention to various commandments which he considers necessary for salvation, as now is the case everywhere among the priests and the religious, indeed, even among the seculars who are preoccupied with their own laws and the doctrines of men—then we surely have returned to superstitions of the Jews and have reestablished the Mosaic servitude. For we do these things not only unwillingly but in the belief that without them there is no salvation and that with them there is salvation without everything else. But then what about the general commandments of the church, about fasts and feasts? The answer is: Whatever has been imposed on us by the ancient consensus of the whole church and by the love of God and righteous causes must surely be kept, not because they are themselves necessary or immutable, but because we owe God obedience out of our love for Him and the church. However, the higher clergy ought to carry on their work in such a way that they make as few commandments as possible and be on their guard as to when, how much, and how these

27 Benefices and prebends were endowments used by churches to support clergy and their pastoral work.

commandments either promote or hinder love, and change them accordingly. For example, when they fill the churches with a loud noise, make the organs resound, and perform the Mass with all pomp, they think they have done such a good work that they can consider help given to the poor as worth nothing. For perjury, lying, slander are committed even on feast days, and nobody cares. But if a person eats meats or eggs on the sixth day of the week, the people are stunned. So stupid is everybody today. The result is that today we should abolish the fast days and many of the feast days. For the common people observe them with such conscience that they believe there is no salvation without them. And yet nearly all of them are acting against their conscience. The people have come to this foolish idea because of the neglect of the preaching of the true Word, so that again the people are in need of the apostles so that they might learn true piety.

For this reason it would be useful to revise and reform nearly the entire book of decretals[28] and to curtail displays, and especially the ceremonies of prayer services and vestments. For every day these increase, and they increase to such an extent that under the load of them faith and love decrease, but avarice, pride, vainglory are fostered, and what is still worse, that men hope in these things for salvation and are not at all concerned about the inner man.

Becoming a monk

The question therefore is whether it is good to become a religious in our day. The answer is: If you think you cannot have salvation in any other way except by becoming a religious, do not even begin. For the proverb is so true: "Despair makes a monk," actually not a monk but a devil.[29] For there will never be a good monk who is one out of despair of this kind, but only when he becomes a monk out of love, namely, when he sees that his sins are very serious and he wishes to do something great for God because of his love, when he willingly gives up his liberty and dons the habit as a fool and subjects himself to degrading duties.

For this reason I believe that it is better to become a monk today than it was at any time in the last two hundred years, because up to this time the monks drew away from the cross and there was a glory in being a religious. But now again it has become displeasing to men, even to those who are good, because of the foolish garb. But this is what it means to be a religious, that one be hated by the world and regarded as a fool. And he who out of love submits himself to this situation does a very good work.

28 The collection of medieval canon law, gathered from papal bulls, decrees, letters, and conciliar decisions.

29 Cf. *Sermon on the Mount* (1531), LW 21:27 (see below, p. 166).

For I am not afraid when the bishops and the priests persecute us. For this has to happen. But this alone displeases me, that we give them such a poor reason for their dislike. Moreover, those who have no reason and yet dislike the monks, not knowing why they dislike them, are the best friends that the religious have in the whole world. For the monks should rejoice as able to fulfill their vows by being despised and shamed for the sake of a vow taken to God, for they wear their foolish habit to induce all men to hold them in contempt. But in our day they do something entirely different, having only the appearance of the religious. But I know that they would be the happiest of men if they had love, and they would be more blessed than the hermits in the desert because of the fact that they are exposed to the cross and the shame every day. But now there is no more arrogant class of people than they are, sad to say!

And now let us return to the text. The apostle desires above all that those who are weak be tolerated and helped by those who are stronger, and, secondly, that the weak should not make hasty judgment. And thus he is encouraging them to peace and unity.

The Seven Penitential Psalms

1516

Martin Luther's first course of lectures as professor of Bible was on the Psalms (1513–15). After completing his lectures on Romans in 1516, Luther prepared for publication a revision of his comments on the seven penitential psalms (6, 32, 38, 51, 102, 130, and 143). This commentary constitutes the first publication by Luther of his own work. Of even greater significance, however, is how Luther revised the psalms. He shifted the audience for the commentary from the classroom to the church. He translated the psalms and his comments into German. As Luther put it, the commentary was not meant for the cultured but for his coarse Saxons.[1] *This work also marks Luther's first published translation of Scripture into German—a task that would occupy him for the rest of his life.*

Luther's theology of humility, which can be seen in all the selections from his early years, stands at the heart of our relationship to God. By despairing of our own righteousness and rejecting any claim to merit, we are brought low and into the depths. For Luther, this humility, which proceeds from God's gift of faith, knows that sin continues to cling closely in the believer and remains even in our best works. For this reason, the whole of a person's life is that of repentance—a point Luther will famously make at the beginning of the Ninety-Five Theses *in October 1517. At this stage in his theological development, Luther emphasizes that the humble who acknowledge they are sinners and confess their sins have forgiveness from God. Although sin remains in our thoughts, words, and deeds, God does not impute this sin to the believer who looks to Christ and His suffering for forgiveness.*

Luther's commentaries and theological works from his early years relentlessly address sin, grace, and righteousness. Luther returns to these themes so often that he is accused of discussing nothing else, of always singing the same old song. Luther defends himself in the conclusion to this work. He argues that only by focusing on these issues are we driven to Christ and away from ourselves.

The brief excerpt below focuses on the beginning of Psalm 51 and Luther's conclusion to the whole commentary on the pentiential psalms. Luther lightly revised and republished his commentary in 1525. The translation in the American edition

1 Luther's letter to Christoph Scheurl, May 6, 1517, WA Br 1:93.6–8. Cf. Luther's letter to Georg Spalatin, May 6, 1517, WA Br 1:96.13–16.

of Luther's Works was based on the 1525 edition. Luther did not add material to the following selection from Psalm 51 in 1525 but rather deleted a few repetitive phrases and sentences. Luther's conclusion was unchanged in the 1525 edition. The excerpt below reflects only material from 1516.

The Seven Penitential Psalms[2]
Psalm 51

1. *Have mercy on me, O God, according to Thy steadfast love.*

A true and penitent heart sees nothing but its sin and misery of conscience. He who still finds any counsel and help in himself cannot in all earnestness speak these words; for he is not yet altogether miserable but feels some comfort in himself, apart from God's mercy. The sense, then, is this: "O God, no man or creature can help or comfort me, so great is my misery; for my affliction is not bodily or temporal. Thou alone, therefore, who art God and eternal, canst help me. Have mercy on me, for without Thy mercy all things are terrible and bitter to me."

According to Thy abundant mercy blot out my transgressions.

These are all words of a true repentance which magnifies and multiplies the grace of God by magnifying and multiplying sin. The apostle says (Rom. 5:20): "Where sin increased, grace abounded all the more." Therefore the proud have no taste for grace, because their sins do not yet taste bitter to them.

2. *Wash me thoroughly from my iniquity, and cleanse me from my sin!*

Before this he began, after the manner of men, to pray for grace, for remission of sins which had been committed, and for the beginning of a new life. Now he prays almost until the end of the psalm in increasing measure that he be washed and cleansed more and more. For first grace is a beginning of washing and cleansing. Anyone who looks upon sin as something outward only cannot remain in this grace but must slide backward and thus remain without grace and become worse than before, although he does not see or realize it. Now with us the situation is that Adam must get out and Christ come in, Adam become as nothing, and Christ alone remain and rule. For this reason there is no end of washing

2 The following excerpt is adapted from *Seven Penitential Psalms*, in volume 14 of *Luther's Works: American Edition*, ed. Jaroslav Pelikan and Daniel E. Poellot, trans. Arnold Guebert (St. Louis: Concordia, 1958). Minor alterations have been made to the text for consistency in style, abbreviations, and capitalization. The annotations and subheadings are the work of the editor of this book.

and cleansing in this life. For the old Adam, with which we are born, makes sinful and nullifies also the good works, in which we make a start and some progress, if God did not look upon the grace and cleansing which has begun.

3. *For I know my transgressions, and my sin is ever before me.*

The difference between the true saints and the sham saints is this: the former see their transgressions and realize that they are not what they should be and want to be. Therefore they judge themselves and are not concerned about others. The others, however, do not perceive their own wickedness; they imagine they are as they should be. They always forget about themselves and sit in judgment on the wickedness of others. They pervert this psalm and say: "I perceive the sins of others, and the sins of others are always before me." This is because they have their own sins on their back and a log in their eyes (Matt. 7:3–5).

4. *Against Thee, Thee only, have I sinned, and done that which is evil in Thy sight.*

This is the verse from which we learn thoroughly to disregard our outward good works and to put no faith in the praise and honor of them by others. They are done in uncleanness and weakness, and are not counted good in God's sight unless we confess them as such. Hence the interpretation which takes this verse to mean outward sins is far from right. For without question we sin and do evil also by outward sins, not only before God but before men as well.

So that Thou art justified in Thy sentence and blameless in Thy judgment.

What is this? Can God not be justified unless we are sinners? Or who will judge God? It is obvious that God in Himself and in His nature is not judged or justified by anyone. He is the eternal, constant, essential, and never-changing Justice itself and the supreme Judge of all things. But in His words and works He is constantly resisted, opposed, judged, and condemned by self-righteous and self-satisfied men. There is a constant legal war between Him and them over His words and works. To say that you are justified in your words is, therefore, the same as saying that your words are justified and found and acknowledged to be true. Now here we cannot enumerate all the words that are subject to the contradiction of the proud. We shall put them all in one heap and say: All Scripture and the Word of God point to the suffering of Christ, as He Himself declares in the last chapter of Luke (24:46–47), that Scripture contains nothing else than the promised grace and forgiveness of sin through the suffering of Christ, that whoever believes in Him, and none other, shall be saved.

This truth and Christ's suffering and faith are resisted by all those who refuse to be sinners, especially those who have just begun to live. They do not want to admit that they are sinners, and they do not sigh for Christ, although God has promised in all His words that Christ should die because of sin.

Therefore anyone who will not consider himself, or be considered, a sinner tries to make God a liar and himself the truth. This is the most grievous sin and idolatry of all idolatries. Therefore the apostle John says (1 John 1:8): "If we say we have no sin, we deceive ourselves, and the truth is not in us." And again (1 John 1:10): "If we say we have not sinned, we make Him a liar, and His Word is not in us." Hence the prophet says here: "In order that this terrible sin of pride may not infect me, I confess that I am a sinner before Thee and do no good, so that Thou mightest remain in truth and prevail, and also overcome all who contend with Thee, justify themselves, and judge Thee in Thy words." For in the end God will prevail and gain the victory, either here by His goodness or hereafter by His severity. It will do no good to be justified before men or in our own eyes, for we must ignore this and wait with fear to learn what God thinks about it.

5. *Behold, I was brought forth in iniquity, and in sin did my mother conceive me.*

Behold, it is so true that before Thee I am a sinner that even my nature, my very beginning, my conception, is sin, to say nothing of the words, works, thoughts, and life which follow. How could I be without sin if I was made in sin and sin is my nature and manner? I am an evil tree and by nature a child of wrath and sin. Therefore as long as this same nature and essence remains with us, we will be sinners and must say; "Forgive us our trespasses" until the body dies and is destroyed. Adam must die and decay before Christ can arise completely, and this begins with a penitent life and is completed through death. Hence death is a wholesome thing to all who believe in Christ; for it does nothing else than destroy and reduce to powder everything born of Adam, so that Christ alone may be in us.

6. *Behold, Thou desirest truth.*

That is, the outward righteousness and apparent piety is pure deception, without foundation and without truth, because it covers the sin within and is only a type of the real and true righteousness. This type is hateful to Thee, but man loves it. Therefore Thou lovest the inner truth, but they the outer falsehood; Thou the real, they the apparent. Hence they do not say: "I am a sinner before Thee."

Thou teachest me the wisdom which is hidden away.

The wisdom of God is revealed to the proud only in its outward appearance, but it is revealed to the humble in its inner truth and hidden foundation. Now the outward appearance of this wisdom consists in this, that man believes he serves God with many words, thoughts, and works, and measures up to God's standard. It is all an outward show, which is apparent and possible to anyone, as there are many ways and means of doing this. In all this, men seek God, but entirely in reverse and outwardly. Inwardly they know Him less than all others, because they seek themselves, and under the pretext of studying and learning about God!

The inner and hidden part of this wisdom is nothing else than knowing oneself thoroughly, and therefore hating oneself. It is seeking all righteousness not in self but in God, always dissatisfied with oneself and yearning for God, that is, humbly loving God and looking away from self. This inner, unknown righteousness is revealed in all kinds of outward behavior, manner, words, and works, in which the proud remain and harden themselves. Therefore God, who loves reality and truth, hates them, because they love the outward appearance and hypocrisy.

7. *Purge me with hyssop, and I shall be clean.*

Here he supports, as it were with an example, what he has said before. It is as if he were saying: "When Moses and the priest of the Law sprinkled themselves and the people with hyssop dipped in the blood of a goat (Num. 19:18ff.) and considered themselves clean, this was only an outward sign and type of the real thing which Thou hast in mind and which Thou considerest highly. Nor was it the inner truth which Thou hast revealed to me. Sprinkle me, therefore, with the true goat's blood of Jesus Christ. Then I will be truly and thoroughly cleansed, without all my works and efforts."

Wash me, and I shall be whiter than snow.

That is, the outward washing of hands and feet according to the Law does not make me white; but with its outward appearance it misleads those who do not recognize the inner value, the true and real wisdom which it only signifies. Now as the outward sprinkling with hyssop and the washing with water in no way aids the inner washing and sprinkling but is only a figure and an empty sign, so all other outward means and gestures have no other purpose than that God should thus inwardly sprinkle, wash, work, speak, serve, etc., with the grace of the Holy Spirit. Thus the old beloved fathers looked upon the type in the Old Testament, and in it they understood the inward and hidden things of the true meaning and wisdom of God.

8. *Let me hear joy and gladness.*

That is, all outward righteousness, behavior, and actions cannot bring comfort to my conscience and take away sin. Despite all efforts and good works the timid, frightened, and terrified conscience remains until Thou sprinklest and washest me with grace and thus createst in me a good conscience, so that I hear that mysterious prompting: "Your sins are forgiven" (Matt. 9:2). No one notices, sees, or understands this except him who hears it. It can be heard, and the hearing produces a calm and joyful conscience, and confidence in God.

Let the bones which Thou hast broken rejoice.

The bones which are weary and crushed, as it were, because of the sinful conscience rejoice and are revived when the conscience hears the joy of absolution. Sin is a heavy, grievous, and terrifying burden; yet it cannot be taken away through the outward works of man, but only through the inner work of God.

9. *Hide Thy face from my sins.*

That is: "Do not take strict notice of my works, for they are all sin if Thou shouldst set them before Thy face and judgment." Therefore he does not say: "Turn my sin from Thy face," as though there were some works pleasing in God's sight, so that He would turn away only the sin and let the good remain. He must turn His face away, so that the works and we ourselves can exist and remain; that is, by grace He does not impute what in reality is sin, as we read in Ps. 32:1: "Blessed is he whose transgression is forgiven."

And blot out all my iniquities.

That is: "Whatever is lacking of righteousness, forgive, just as I have prayed Thee to turn Thy face from the evil that is still present." For, as already said, before God all our works have what they should not have; that is, they are done in sin, in which we are born. They do not have what they should have, namely, complete purity; for of this we have been deprived by the sin of Adam. . . .

17. *The sacrifice acceptable to God is a broken spirit; a broken and contrite heart, O God, Thou wilt not despise.*

It is as if he said: Everything else He despises except a heart that is humble and broken, for it ascribes honor to God and sin to itself. Such a heart gives God nothing but only takes from Him. This is also what God wants so that He may be truly God. For it behooves God to give, not to take.

Conclusion

Now someone might say to me: "Can't you ever do anything but speak only about the righteousness, wisdom, and strength of God rather than of man, always expounding Scripture from the standpoint of God's righteousness and grace, always harping on the same string and singing the same old song?" To this I answer: Let each one look to himself. As for me, I confess: Whenever I found less in the Scriptures than Christ, I was never satisfied; but whenever I found more than Christ, I never became poorer. Therefore it seems to me to be true that God the Holy Spirit does not know and does not want to know anything besides Jesus Christ, as He says of Him (John 16:13–14): "He will glorify Me; He will not speak of Himself, but He will take of Mine and declare it to you."

Christ is God's grace, mercy, righteousness, truth, wisdom, power, comfort, and salvation, given to us by God without any merit on our part. Christ, I say, not as some express it in blind words, "causally," that He grants righteousness and remains absent Himself, for that would be dead.[3] Yes, it is not given at all unless Christ Himself is present, just as the radiance of the sun and the heat of fire are not present if there is no sun and no fire.

Now there are some who think lightly of these words of grace and arrogantly say: "Who does not know that without grace there is no good in us?" They insist they know all this very well. In fact, if you ask them whether they think little of their own righteousness, they are quick to say: "Of course, I am certain of that!"

It is indeed grave and wretched blindness that they consider themselves to have attained the highest degree of perfection when they have not even understood or tasted the lowest grade. For who can be prouder than the person who has the presumption to claim that he is free of all pride and evil inclination? Spiritual pride is the last and deepest vice, since they are not yet free from carnal and human inclinations.

No saint has ever been so bold as to claim that his righteousness and wisdom meant nothing to him. They are steeped in strife and are always at war among themselves about these things.

Now these come with the deceptive argument: "Yes, but the inclination is not a mortal sin."[4] They insist that they are not blind but know very well which are daily sins and which are deadly sins, and in this blindness

3 There were many theories on the process of justification among the medieval schoolmen. Luther rejects here any position that separates the bestowal of Christ's righteousness from the giving of Christ Himself to the believer.

4 On mortal and venial (here called "daily") sins, see above, pp. 20–21 n. 20.

they practically sit in the judgment seat of Christ. It is true that daily sins do not damn.

But they are not "daily" sins by their nature; it is only because by grace God looks upon them as "daily."[5] However, He does this only in the case of those who do not underrate them.

For this reason it is dangerous to speak about "daily" sins if one does so to gain a feeling of security and false comfort. This leads to striving against the fear of God and to secret contempt for the judgment of God. For if man must give account on the Last Day of every idle word (Matt. 12:36), who will be so bold as not to shun daily sins with fear, to weep over them, and then with humble awe to long earnestly for grace and mercy?

---

5 The medieval schoolmen argued that venial sins or daily sins were either by nature or by imperfection not mortal. For example, by nature, stealing a dollar from your friend is not so grievous as to destroy the relationship with your friend. Although these sorts of sin deserve temporal punishment and offend God, they do not destroy the relationship with God. For sins that do destroy your relationship with God, they are venial and not mortal by imperfection when consent and act are withheld. The schoolmen argued that mortal sin involves temptation, taking pleasure in the temptation, consenting to the temptation, and acting upon your consent. If a person consents and acts upon the temptation, he commits a mortal sin; if a person takes some amount of pleasure in the temptation but withholds consent and action, he is said to commit a venial sin. The schoolmen further argued that penance was needed only for mortal sins. Venial sins were forgiven by corporate confession and absolution, receiving the Lord's Supper, praying the Lord's Prayer, or extreme unction, among a number of other ways.

The Magnificat
1521

The Roman Church officially excommunicated Martin Luther on January 3, 1521. Luther's excommunication affected all who provided safe haven for him or who supported his teachings. Guilt by association meant that any church, city, or territory protecting Luther would also be declared outside the Church and its sacramental ministry. Cities complied with Luther's excommunication by publicly burning his books. In some cities, confessors interrogated penitents in the confessional about Luther. If they admitted to owning any of his books, absolution was withheld, and they were ordered to surrender the books for burning. To resist such an order was to risk not only one's own standing in the Church but also one's family and town.[1]

Frederick the Wise (1463–1525), the elector of Saxony and Luther's political protector, understood the seriousness of Luther's excommunication and the risk involved for himself and the people of Electoral Saxony. Despite the pope's verdict, Frederick petitioned Emperor Charles V to hear Luther's case at the imperial diet at Worms. The emperor assented and summoned Luther to Worms in March 1521. There would be, however, no debate. Luther was summoned to recant. He appeared before the emperor on April 17. His books were laid before him. The titles were read. He was told to recant. Luther requested time to think matters over and was given a day to do so. He returned on April 18 and declared: "I cannot and I will not retract anything . . . . [H]ere I stand, may God help me, Amen."[2]

Luther's excommunication would remain in force, and soon an imperial ban was placed upon him. In the meantime, Frederick secretly arranged for Luther to be taken to the Wartburg fortress near Eisenach. Luther used his time in exile—his "Patmos," as he called it—to defend and clarify his scriptural understanding of justification by faith alone and his insistence that we are at one and the same time both saint and sinner. He also completed projects he had begun before leaving for Worms. He finished a collection of sermons for Advent and Christmas, which had been requested by Frederick, and wrote a commentary

1 In February 1521, Luther addressed this matter in *An Instruction to Penitents concerning the Forbidden Books of Dr. M. Luther*. See LW 44:219–42.

2 LW 32:112–13.

on the Magnificat, which he dedicated to Prince John Frederick (1503–54), the young duke of Saxony and future elector.

Luther began his commentary on Mary's Magnificat (Luke 1:46–55) in November 1520 and completed it at the Wartburg in June 1521. Luther's work on the commentary coincided with his excommunication from the Roman Church, his summons to Worms, as well as the emperor's verdict against him. Remarkably, the commentary bears little evidence of these personal trials. Luther's commentary focuses at length on the undeserved grace and mercy of God. The Virgin Mary is a model of Christian piety. She teaches us all with her words and by her example how to know, love, and praise God.

Luther describes our sin and pride as residing always in the heights, in the exalted things of the world, in power, riches, and pious appearances. God resides, however, in the depths, among the poor, despised, and lowly. He dwells in the darkness of faith where there is no light, no seeing, and no feeling. In this place we come to know that we are made pious, righteous, and blessed by no work of our own but solely by faith. It is this faith that sings forth the great works and deeds of God. It is this faith, Mary's faith, that all believers seek to imitate in word and deed.

Luther's commentary shows his understanding of God's activity in our history. It reveals his high regard for the blessed Virgin Mary, the mother of God,[3] *which never diminishes in his lifetime. But his commentary chiefly sketches his evangelical piety in terms borrowed from medieval mystical and monastic traditions. Here we see a life peacefully reposing in the grace and mercy of God, flourishing in the depths.*

The Magnificat[4]

In order properly to understand this sacred hymn of praise, we need to bear in mind that the Blessed Virgin Mary is speaking on the basis of her own experience, in which she was enlightened and instructed by the Holy Spirit. No one can correctly understand God or His Word unless he

3 On this title for Mary, which Luther uses throughout the commentary on the Magnificat, see below, p. 397 n. 16.

4 The following excerpt is adapted from *The Magnificat*, in volume 21 of *Luther's Works: American Edition*, ed. Jaroslav Pelikan, trans. A. T. W. Steinhaeuser (St. Louis: Concordia, 1956). Minor alterations have been made to the text for consistency in style, abbreviations, and capitalization. The annotations and subheadings are the work of the editor of this book.

has received such understanding immediately from the Holy Spirit.[5] But no one can receive it from the Holy Spirit without experiencing, proving, and feeling it. In such experience the Holy Spirit instructs us as in His own school, outside of which nothing is learned but empty words and prattle. When the holy virgin experienced what great things God was working in her despite her insignificance, lowliness, poverty, and inferiority, the Holy Spirit taught her this deep insight and wisdom, that God is the kind of Lord who does nothing but exalt those of low degree and put down the mighty from their thrones, in short, break what is whole and make whole what is broken.

Just as God in the beginning of creation made the world out of nothing, whence He is called the Creator and the Almighty, so His manner of working continues unchanged. Even now and to the end of the world, all His works are such that out of that which is nothing, worthless, despised, wretched, and dead, He makes that which is something, precious, honorable, blessed, and living. On the other hand, whatever is something, precious, honorable, blessed, and living, He makes to be nothing, worthless, despised, wretched, and dying. In this manner no creature can work; no creature can produce anything out of nothing. Therefore His eyes look only into the depths, not to the heights; as it is said in Dan. 3:55 (Vulgate): "Thou sittest upon the cherubim and beholdest the depths"; in Ps. 138:6: "Though the Lord is high, He regards the lowly; but the haughty He knows from afar." Ps. 113:5–6: "Who is like the Lord, our God, who is seated on high, who looks far down upon the heavens and the earth?" For since He is the Most High, and there is nothing above Him, He cannot look above Him, nor yet to either side, for there is none like Him. He must needs, therefore, look within Him and beneath Him; and the farther one is beneath Him, the better does He see him.

The eyes of the world and of men, on the contrary, look only above them and are lifted up with pride, as it is said in Prov. 30:13: "There is a people whose eyes are lofty, and their eyelids lifted up on high." This we experience every day. Everyone strives after that which is above him, after honor, power, wealth, knowledge, a life of ease, and whatever is lofty and great. And where such people are, there are many hangers-on; all the world gathers round them, gladly yields them service, and would be at their side and share in their exaltation. Therefore it is not without reason that the Scriptures describe so few kings and rulers who were godly men. On the other hand, no one is willing to look into the depths with their

5 Following his encounter with the Zwickau prophets and enthusiasts in the early and mid-1520s, Luther will emphasize that the Holy Spirit works through the external Word and never apart from it.

poverty, disgrace, squalor, misery, and anguish. From these all turn away their eyes. Where there are such people, everyone takes to his heels, forsakes and shuns and leaves them to themselves; no one dreams of helping them or of making something out of them. And so they must remain in the depths and in their low and despised condition. There is among men no creator who would make something out of nothing, although that is what St. Paul teaches in Rom. 12:16 when he says, "Dear brethren, set not your mind on high things, but go along with the lowly."

Therefore to God alone belongs that sort of seeing that looks into the depths with their need and misery, and is near to all that are in the depths; as St. Peter says (1 Pet. 5:5): "God opposes the proud but gives grace to the humble." And this is the source of men's love and praise of God. For no one can praise God without first loving Him. No one can love Him unless He makes Himself known to him in the most lovable and intimate fashion. And He can make Himself known only through those works of His which He reveals in us, and which we feel and experience within ourselves. But where there is this experience, namely, that He is a God who looks into the depths and helps only the poor, despised, afflicted, miserable, forsaken, and those who are nothing, there a hearty love for Him is born. The heart overflows with gladness and goes leaping and dancing for the great pleasure it has found in God. There the Holy Spirit is present and has taught us in a moment such exceeding great knowledge and gladness through this experience.

For this reason God has also imposed death on us all and laid the cross of Christ together with countless sufferings and afflictions on His beloved children and Christians. In fact, sometimes He even lets us fall into sin, in order that He may look into the depths even more, bring help to many, perform manifold works, show Himself a true Creator, and thereby make Himself known and worthy of love and praise. Alas, the world with its proud eyes constantly thwarts Him in this, hinders His seeing, working, and helping, and our knowledge, love, and praise of Him, depriving Him of all His glory and itself of its pleasure, joy, and salvation. He also cast His only and well-beloved Son, Christ, into the depths of all woe and showed in Him most plainly to what end His seeing, work, help, method, counsel, and will are directed. Therefore, having most fully experienced all these things, Christ abounds through all eternity in the knowledge, love, and praise of God; as it is said in Ps. 21:6: "Thou dost make Him glad with the joy of Thy presence," namely, in that He sees Thee and knows Thee. Here, too, belongs Ps. 44:7–8, where it is said that all the saints will do nothing in heaven but praise God, because He looked upon them when they were in the depths and there made Himself known to them and loved and praised by them.

The tender mother of Christ does the same here and teaches us, with her words and by the example of her experience, how to know, love, and praise God. For since she boasts, with heart leaping for joy and praising God, that He regarded her despite her low estate and nothingness, we must believe that she came of poor, despised, and lowly parents. Let us make it very plain for the sake of the simple. Doubtless there were in Jerusalem daughters of the chief priests and counselors who were rich, comely, youthful, cultured, and held in high renown by all the people, even as it is today with the daughters of kings, princes, and men of wealth. The same was also true of many another city. Even in her own town of Nazareth she was not the daughter of one of the chief rulers, but a poor and plain citizen's daughter, whom none looked up to or esteemed. To her neighbors and their daughters she was but a simple maiden, tending the cattle and doing the housework, and doubtless esteemed no more than any poor maidservant today, who does as she is told around the house.

For thus Isaiah announced (Isa. 11:1–2): "There shall come forth a rod out of the stem of Jesse, and a flower shall rise up out of his root, and the Holy Spirit shall rest upon Him." The stem and root is the generation of Jesse or David, in particular the Virgin Mary; the rod and flower is Christ. Now, as unlikely—indeed, incredible—a thing it is that a fair branch and flower should spring from a dry and withered stem and root, just so unlikely was it that Mary the Virgin should become the mother of such a Child. For I take it that she is called a stem and root not only because she became a mother in a miraculous manner without violation of her virginity—just as it is miraculous to make a branch grow out of a dead tree stump—but also for the following reason. In the days of David and Solomon the royal stem and line of David had been green and flourishing, fortunate in its great glory, might, and riches, and famous in the eyes of the world. But in the latter days, when Christ was to come, the priests had usurped this honor and were the sole rulers, while the royal line of David had become so impoverished and despised that it was like a dead stump, so that there was no hope or likelihood that a king descended from it would ever attain to any great glory. But when all seemed most unlikely—comes Christ, and is born of the despised stump, of the poor and lowly maiden! The rod and flower springs from her whom Sir Annas's or Caiaphas's daughter would not have deigned to have for her humblest lady's maid. Thus God's work and His eyes are in the depths, but man's only in the height.

So much for the occasion of Mary's canticle, which we shall now consider in detail.

Luke 1:46

My soul magnifies God, the Lord.

These words express the strong ardor and exuberant joy with which all her mind and life are inwardly exalted in the Spirit. Therefore she does not say, "I exalt the Lord," but, "My soul doth exalt Him." It is as if she said: "My life and all my senses float in the love and praise of God and in lofty pleasures, so that I am no longer mistress of myself; I am exalted, more than I exalt myself, to praise the Lord." This is the experience of all those who are saturated with the divine sweetness and Spirit: they cannot find words to utter what they feel. For to praise the Lord with gladness is not a work of man; it is rather a joyful suffering and the work of God alone. It cannot be taught in words but must be learned in one's own experience. Even as David says in Ps. 34:8: "Oh, taste and see that the Lord is sweet; blessed is the man that trusts in Him." He puts tasting before seeing, because this sweetness cannot be known unless one has experienced and felt it for himself; and no one can attain to such experience unless he trusts in God with his whole heart when he is in the depths and in sore straits. Therefore David makes haste to add, "Blessed is the man that trusteth in God." Such a person will experience the work of God within himself and will thus attain to His sensible sweetness and through it to all knowledge and understanding.

Let us take up the words in their order. The first is "my soul." Scripture divides man into three parts, as St. Paul says in 1 Thess. 5:23: "May the God of peace Himself sanctify you wholly; and may your spirit and soul and body be kept sound and blameless at the coming of our Lord Jesus Christ." There is yet another division of each of these three, and the whole of man, into two parts, which are called "spirit" and "flesh." This is a division not of the nature of man, but of his qualities. The nature of man consists of the three parts—spirit, soul and body; and all of these may be good or evil, that is, they may be spirit or flesh. But we are not now dealing with this division. The first part, the spirit, is the highest, deepest, and noblest part of man. By it he is enabled to lay hold on things incomprehensible, invisible, and eternal. It is, in brief, the dwelling place of faith and the Word of God. Of it David speaks in Ps. 51:10: "Lord, create in my inward parts a right spirit," that is, a straight and upright faith. But of the unbelieving he says in Ps. 78:37: "Their heart was not right with God, nor was their spirit faithful to Him."

The second part, the soul, is this same spirit, so far as its nature is concerned, but viewed as performing a different function, namely, giving life to the body and working through the body. In the Scriptures it is frequently put for the life; for the spirit may live without the body, but the body has no life apart from the spirit. Even in sleep the soul lives and works without ceasing. It is its nature to comprehend not incomprehensible things but such things as the reason can know and understand. Indeed, reason is the light in this dwelling; and unless the spirit, which is lighted with the brighter light of faith, controls this light of reason, it cannot but be in error. For it is too feeble to deal with things divine. To these two parts of man the Scriptures ascribe many things, such as wisdom and knowledge—wisdom to the spirit, knowledge to the soul; likewise hatred, love, delight, horror, and the like.

The third part is the body with its members. Its work is only to carry out and apply that which the soul knows and the spirit believes. Let us take an illustration of this from Scripture. In the tabernacle fashioned by Moses there were three separate compartments. The first was called the Holy of Holies: here was God's dwelling place, and in it there was no light. The second was called the holy place; here stood a candlestick with seven arms and seven lamps. The third was called the outer court; this lay under the open sky and in the full light of the sun. In this tabernacle we have a figure of the Christian man. His spirit is the Holy of Holies, where God dwells in the darkness of faith, where no light is; for he believes that which he neither sees nor feels nor comprehends. His soul is the holy place, with its seven lamps, that is, all manner of reason, discrimination, knowledge, and understanding of visible and bodily things. His body is the forecourt, open to all, so that men may see his works and manner of life.

Now Paul prays God, who is a God of peace, to sanctify us not in one part only, but wholly, through and through, so that spirit, soul, body, and all may be holy. We might mention many reasons why he prays in this manner, but let the following suffice. When the spirit is no longer holy, then nothing is holy. This holiness of the spirit is the scene of the sorest conflict and the source of the greatest danger. It consists in nothing else than in faith pure and simple, since the spirit has nothing to do with things comprehensible, as we have seen. But now there come false teachers and lure the spirit out of doors; one puts forth this work, another that mode of attaining to godliness. And unless the spirit is preserved and is wise, it will come forth and follow these men. It will fall upon the external works and rules and imagine it can attain to godliness by means of them. And before we know it, faith is lost, and the spirit is dead in the sight of God.

Then commence the manifold sects and orders. This one becomes a Carthusian, that one a Franciscan; this one seeks salvation by fasting, that one by praying; one by one work, another by another.[6] Yet these are all self-chosen works and orders, never commanded by God, but invented by men. Engrossed in them, they have no eye for faith but only go on teaching men to put their trust in works, until they are so sunk in works that they fall out among themselves. Everyone claims to be the greatest and despises the others, as our bragging and blustering Observantines do today. Over against such work-saints and teachers of pious appearance Paul prays, calling God a God of peace and unity. Such a God these divided, unpeaceable saints cannot have or keep unless they give up "their own things," agree together in the same spirit and faith, and learn that works breed nothing but discrimination, sin, and discord, while faith alone makes men pious, united, and peaceable. As it is said in Ps. 68:6: "God makes us dwell in unity in the house"; and in Ps. 133:1: "Behold how good and pleasant it is when brothers dwell in unity."

There is no peace except where men teach that we are made pious, righteous, and blessed by no work nor outward thing but solely by faith, that is, a firm confidence in the unseen grace of God that is promised us, as I showed at greater length in the *Treatise on Good Works*.[7] But where there is no faith, there must necessarily be many works; and where these are, peace and unity depart, and God cannot remain. . . .

Let this suffice in explanation of these two words, soul and spirit; they occur very frequently in the Scriptures. We come to the "magnifies," which means to make great, to exalt, to esteem one highly, as having the power, the knowledge, and the desire to perform many great and good things, such as those that follow in this canticle. Just as a book title indicates what is the contents of the book, so this word "magnifies" is used by Mary to indicate what her hymn of praise is to be about, namely, the great works and deeds of God, for the strengthening of our faith, for the comforting of all those of low degree, and for the terrifying of all the mighty ones of earth. We are to let the hymn serve this threefold purpose; for she sang it not for herself alone but for us all, to sing it after her. Now, these great works of God will neither terrify nor comfort anyone unless he believes that God has not only the power and the knowledge but also the willingness and hearty desire to do such great things. In fact, it is not

6 The Carthusian order, founded in 1084, was known for its austerity, prayer, and silent contemplation. The Franciscan order, founded by Francis of Assisi (ca. 1181–1226) in 1209, emphasized total poverty for its members and community. The ideal of poverty proved too difficult for some, and the order eventually split between the Observants (here "Observantines"), who adhered to Francis's ideal, and the Conventuals, who adopted a more moderate position.

7 See LW 44:15–114; *Treatise on Good Works, 1520*, ed. Timothy J. Wengert (Minneapolis, MN: Fortress, 2016).

even enough to believe that He is willing to do them for others but not for you. This would be to put yourself beyond the pale of these works of God, as is done by those who, because of their strength, do not fear Him, and by those of little faith who, because of their tribulations, fall into despair.

That sort of faith is nothing; it is dead; it is like an idea learned from a fairy tale. You must rather, without any wavering or doubt, realize His will toward you and firmly believe that He will do great things also to you, and is willing to do so. Such a faith has life and being; it pervades and changes the whole man; it constrains you to fear if you are mighty and to take comfort if you are of low degree. And the mightier you are, the more must you fear; the lowlier you are, the more must you take comfort. This no other kind of faith is able to effect. How will it be with you in the hour of death? There you must believe that He has not only the power and the knowledge but also the desire to help you. For it requires indeed an unspeakably great work to deliver you from eternal death, to save you and make you God's heir. To this faith all things are possible, as Christ says (Mark 9:23); it alone abides; it also comes to experience the works of God and thus attains to the love of God and thence to songs and praise of God, so that man esteems Him highly and truly magnifies Him.

For God is not magnified by us so far as His nature is concerned—He is unchangeable—but He is magnified in our knowledge and experience when we greatly esteem Him and highly regard Him, especially as to His grace and goodness. Therefore the holy mother does not say: "My voice or my mouth, my hand or my thoughts, my reason or my will, magnifies the Lord." For there are many who praise God with a loud voice, preach about Him with high-sounding words, speak much of Him, dispute and write about Him, and paint His image; whose thoughts dwell often upon Him and who reach out after Him and speculate about Him with their reason; there are also many who exalt Him with false devotion and a false will. But Mary says, "My soul magnifies Him"—that is, my whole life and being, mind and strength, esteem Him highly. She is caught up, as it were, into Him and feels herself lifted up into His good and gracious will, as the following verse shows. It is the same when anyone shows us a signal favor; our whole life seems to incline to him, and we say: "Ah, I esteem him highly"; that is to say, "My soul magnifies him." How much more will such a lively inclination be awakened in us when we experience the favor of God, which is exceeding great in His works. All words and thoughts fail us, and our whole life and soul must be set in motion, as though all that lived within us wanted to break forth into praise and singing.

But here we find two kinds of false spirits that cannot sing the Magnificat aright. First, there are those who will not praise Him unless

He does well to them; as David says (Ps. 49:18): "He will praise Thee when Thou shalt do well to him." These seem indeed to be greatly praising God; but because they are unwilling to suffer oppression and to be in the depths, they can never experience the proper works of God, and therefore can never truly love or praise Him. The whole world nowadays is filled with praise and service to God, with singing and preaching, with organs and trumpets, and the Magnificat is magnificently sung; but it is regrettable that this precious canticle should be rendered by us so utterly without salt or savor. For we sing only when it fares well with us; as soon as it fares ill, we stop our singing and no longer esteem God highly, but suppose He can or will do nothing for us. Then the Magnificat also must languish.

The other sort are more dangerous still. They err on the opposite side. They magnify themselves by reason of the good gifts of God and do not ascribe them to His goodness alone. They themselves desire to bear a part in them; they want to be honored and set above other men on account of them. When they behold the good things that God has done for them, they fall upon them and appropriate them as their own; they regard themselves as better than others who have no such things. This is really a smooth and slippery position. The good gifts of God will naturally produce proud and self-complacent hearts. Therefore we must here give heed to Mary's last word, which is "God." She does not say, "My soul magnifies itself" or "exalts me." She does not desire herself to be esteemed; she magnifies God alone and gives all glory to Him. She leaves herself out and ascribes everything to God alone, from whom she received it. For though she experienced such an exceeding great work of God within herself, yet she was ever minded not to exalt herself above the humblest mortal living. Had she done so, she would have fallen, like Lucifer, into the abyss of hell (Isa. 14:12).

She had no thought but this: if any other maiden had got such good things from God, she would be just as glad and would not grudge them to her; indeed, she regarded herself alone as unworthy of such honor and all others as worthy of it. She would have been well content had God withdrawn these blessings from her and bestowed them upon another before her very eyes. So little did she lay claim to anything, but left all of God's gifts freely in His hands, being herself no more than a cheerful guest chamber and willing hostess to so great a Guest. Therefore she also kept all these things forever. That is to magnify God alone, to count only Him great and lay claim to nothing. We see here how strong an incentive she had to fall into sin, so that it is no less a miracle that she refrained from pride and arrogance than that she received the gifts she did. Tell me, was not hers a wondrous soul? She finds herself the mother of God, exalted above all mortals, and still remains so simple and so calm that she does not think of any poor serving maid as beneath her. Oh, we poor mortals! If we come into a little wealth or might or honor, or even if we are a little prettier than other men, we cannot abide being made equal to anyone beneath us, but are puffed up beyond all measure. What should we do if we possessed such great and lofty blessings?

Therefore God lets us remain poor and hapless, because we cannot leave His tender gifts undefiled or keep an even mind, but let our spirits rise or fall according to how He gives or takes away His gifts. But Mary's heart remains the same at all times; she lets God have His will with her and draws from it all only a good comfort, joy, and trust in God. Thus we, too, should do; that would be to sing a right Magnificat.

Luke 1:47
And my spirit rejoices in God, my Savior.

We have seen what is meant by "spirit"; it is that which lays hold by faith on things incomprehensible. Mary, therefore, calls God her Savior, or her Salvation, even though she neither saw nor felt that this was so, but trusted in sure confidence that He was her Savior and her Salvation. This faith came to her through the work God had done within her. And, truly, she sets things in their proper order when she calls God her Lord before calling Him her Savior, and when she calls Him her Savior before recounting His works. Thereby she teaches us to love and praise God for Himself alone, and in the right order, and not selfishly to seek anything at His hands. This is done when one praises God because He is good, regards only His bare goodness, and finds his joy and pleasure in that alone. That is a lofty, pure, and tender mode of loving and praising God and well becomes this Virgin's high and tender spirit.

But the impure and perverted lovers, who are nothing else than parasites and who seek their own advantage in God, neither love nor praise His bare goodness, but have an eye to themselves and consider only how good God is to them, that is, how deeply He makes them feel His goodness and how many good things He does to them. They esteem Him highly, are filled with joy and sing His praises, so long as this feeling continues. But just as soon as He hides His face and withdraws the rays of His goodness, leaving them bare and in misery, their love and praise are at an end. They are unable to love and praise the bare, unfelt goodness that is hidden in God. By this they prove that their spirit did not rejoice in God, their Savior, and that they had no true love and praise for His bare goodness. They delighted in their salvation much more than in their Savior, in the gift more than in the Giver, in the creature rather than in the Creator. For they are unable to preserve an even mind in plenty and in want, in wealth and in poverty; as St. Paul says (Phil. 4:12): "I know how to abound and how to suffer want."

Here apply the words in Ps. 49:18: "They will praise Thee when Thou shalt do well with them." That is to say: "They love not Thee but themselves; if they have but Thy good and pleasant things, they care nothing for Thee." As Christ also said to those who sought Him (John 6:26): "Truly, truly, I say to you, you seek Me, not because you saw signs, but because you ate your fill of the loaves."

Such impure and false spirits defile all of God's gifts and prevent His giving them many gifts, especially the gift of salvation. The following is a good illustration of this: Once a certain godly woman saw in a vision three virgins seated near an altar. During the Mass, a beautiful boy leaped from the altar and, approaching the first virgin in a most friendly manner, lavished caresses upon her and smiled lovingly in her face. Then he approached the second virgin, but was not so friendly with her; he did not give her a caress, though he did lift her veil and give her a pleasant smile. But for the third virgin he had not a friendly sign, struck her in the face and tore her hair, thrust her from him and dealt most ungallantly with her. Then he ran swiftly back upon the altar and disappeared.

Afterward the vision was interpreted for the woman as follows: The first of the three virgins was a figure of the impure and self-seeking spirits, on whom God must lavish many good things and whose will He must do rather than they His; they are unwilling to suffer want but must always find joy and comfort in God and are not content with His goodness. The second virgin was a figure of the spirits that make a beginning of serving God and are willing to do without some things, but not without all or to be free from all self-seeking and enjoyment. God must now and then smile upon them and let them feel His good things, in order that they may learn from this to love and praise His bare goodness. But the third virgin, that poor Cinderella—for her there is nothing but want and misery; she seeks to enjoy nothing and is content to know that God is good, even though she should never once experience it, though that is impossible. She keeps an even mind in both situations, and she loves and praises God's goodness just as much when she does not feel it as when she does. She neither falls upon the good things when they are given nor falls away when they are removed. That is the true bride of Christ, who says to Him: "I seek not Thine, but Thee; Thou art to me no dearer when it goes well with me, nor any less dear when it goes ill."

Such spirits fulfill what is written (Isa. 30:21): "You shall not stray from the even and right way of God, neither to the left hand nor to the right."

That is to say, they are to love and praise God evenly and rightly and not seek their own advantage or enjoyment. Such a spirit was David's; when he was driven from Jerusalem by his son Absalom and was likely to be cast out forever and to lose his kingdom and the favor of God, he said (2 Sam. 15:25–26): "If I find favor in the eyes of the Lord, He will bring me back; but if He says, 'I have no pleasure in you,' behold, here I am." Oh, how pure a spirit that was, not to stop loving, praising, and following the goodness of God even in the direst distress! Such a spirit is manifested here by Mary, the mother of God. Standing in the midst of such exceedingly great good things, she does not fall upon them or seek her own enjoyment in them, but keeps her spirit pure in loving and praising the bare goodness of God, ready and willing to have God withdraw them from her and leave her spirit poor and naked and needy.

Now, it is much more difficult to practice moderation amid riches, honor, and power than amid poverty, dishonor, and weakness, since the former are mighty incentives to evildoing. So the wondrous pure spirit of Mary is worthy of even greater praise, because, having such overwhelming honors heaped upon her head, she does not let them tempt her, but acts as though she did not see it, remains "even and right in the way," clings only to God's goodness, which she neither sees nor feels, overlooks the good things she does feel, and neither takes pleasure nor seeks her own enjoyment in it. Thus she can truly sing, "My spirit rejoices in God, my Savior." It is indeed a spirit that exults only in faith and rejoices not in the good things of God that she felt, but only in God, whom she did not feel and who is her Salvation, known by her in faith alone. Such are the truly lowly, naked, hungry, and God-fearing spirits, as we shall see below.

From all this we may know and judge how full the world is nowadays of false preachers and false saints, who fill the ears of the people with preaching good works. There are indeed a few who teach them how to do good works, but the greater part preach human doctrines and works that they themselves have devised and set up. Even the best of them, unfortunately, are so far from this "even and straight road" that they constantly drive the people to "the right hand" by teaching good works and a godly life, not for the sake of the bare goodness of God, but for the sake of one's own enjoyment. For if there were no heaven or hell and if they could not enjoy the good gifts of God, they would let His good things go unloved and unpraised. These men are mere parasites and hirelings; slaves, not sons; aliens, not heirs. They turn themselves into idols, whom God is to love and praise and for whom He is to do the very things they ought to do for Him. They have no spirit, nor is God their Savior. His good gifts are their Savior, and with them God must serve them as their lackey. They are the children of Israel, who were not content in the desert with eating bread from heaven, but wanted meat, onions, and garlic too (Num. 11:4–6).

Alas, all the world, all the monasteries, and all the churches are now filled with such people. They all walk in their false, perverted, and uneven spirit, and urge and drive others to do the same. They exalt good works to such a height that they imagine they can merit heaven through them. But the bare goodness of God is what ought rather to be preached and known above all else, and we ought to learn that, just as God saves us out of pure goodness, without any merit of works, so we in our turn should do the works without reward or self-seeking, for the sake of the bare goodness of God. We should desire nothing in them but His good-pleasure, and not be anxious about a reward. That will come of itself, without our seeking. For though it is impossible that the reward should not follow, if we do well in a pure and right spirit, without thought of reward or enjoyment; nevertheless God will not have such a self-seeking and impure spirit, nor will it ever obtain a reward. A son serves his father willingly and without reward, as his heir, solely for the father's sake. But a son who served his father merely for the sake of the inheritance would indeed be a wicked child and deserve to be cast off by his father.

Luke 1:48

For He has regarded the low estate of His handmaiden. For behold, henceforth all generations will call me blessed.

The word "low estate" has been translated "humility" by some, as though the Virgin Mary referred to her humility and boasted of it; hence certain prelates also call themselves *humiles*. But that is very wide of the mark, for no one can boast of any good thing in the sight of God without sin and perdition. In His sight we ought to boast only of His pure grace and goodness, which He bestows upon us unworthy ones; so that not our love and praise but His alone may dwell in us and may preserve us. Thus Solomon teaches us to do (Prov. 25:6–7): "Do not put yourself forward in the king's presence or stand (that is, pretend to be something) in the place of the great; for it is better to be told, 'Come up here,' than to be put lower in the presence of the prince." How should such pride and vainglory be attributed to this pure and righteous Virgin, as though she boasted of her humility in the presence of God? For humility is the highest of all the virtues, and no one could boast of possessing it except the very proudest of mortals. It is God alone who knows humility; He alone judges it and brings it to light, so that no one knows less about humility than he who is truly humble.

In scriptural usage, "to humble" means "to bring down" or "to bring to naught." Hence, in the Scriptures, Christians are frequently called poor, afflicted, despised. Thus in Ps. 116:10: "I am greatly afflicted"—that is, humbled. Humility, therefore, is nothing else than a disregarded, despised, and lowly estate, such as that of men who are poor, sick, hungry, thirsty, in prison, suffering, and dying. Such was Job in his afflictions, David when he was thrust out of his kingdom, and Christ as well as all Christians in their distresses. Those are the depths of which we said above that God's eyes look only into them, but men's only to the heights, namely, to that which is splendid and glorious and makes a brave show. Therefore in the Scriptures (Zech. 12:4) Jerusalem is called a city upon which God's eyes are open—that is to say, Christendom lies in the depths and is despised by the world; therefore God regards her, and His eyes are always fixed upon her, as He says in Ps. 32:8: "I will fix My eyes upon you."

St. Paul also says in 1 Cor. 1:27–28: "God chose what is foolish in the world to shame the wise. God chose what is weak in the world to shame the strong. God chose what is low and despised in the world, even things that are not, to bring to nothing things that are." In this way He turns the world with all its wisdom and power into foolishness and gives us another wisdom and power. Since, then, it is His manner to regard things that are in the depths and disregarded, I have rendered the word "humility" with "nothingness" or "low estate." This, therefore, is what Mary means: "God has regarded me, a poor, despised, and lowly maiden, though He might have found a rich, renowned, noble, and mighty queen, the daughter of princes and great lords. He might have found the daughter of Annas or of Caiaphas, who held the highest position in the land. But He let His pure and gracious eyes light on me and used so poor and despised a maiden, in order that no one might glory in His presence, as though he were worthy of this, and that I must acknowledge it all to be pure grace and goodness and not at all my merit or worthiness."

Now, we described above at length how lowly was the estate of this tender Virgin and how unexpectedly this honor came to her, that God should regard her in such abundant grace. Hence she does not glory in her worthiness nor yet in her unworthiness, but solely in the divine regard, which is so exceedingly good and gracious that He deigned to look upon such a lowly maiden, and to look upon her in so glorious and honorable a fashion. They, therefore, do her an injustice who hold that she gloried not indeed in her virginity, but in her humility. She gloried neither in the one nor in the other, but only in the gracious regard of God. Hence the stress lies not on the word "low estate," but on the word "regarded." For not her humility but God's regard is to be praised. When a prince takes a poor beggar by the hand, it is not the beggar's lowliness but the prince's grace and goodness that is to be commended. . . .

True humility, therefore, never knows that it is humble, as I have said; for if it knew this, it would turn proud from contemplation of so fine a virtue. But it clings with all its heart and mind and senses to lowly things, sets them continually before its eyes, and ponders them in its thoughts. And because it sets them before its eyes, it cannot see itself nor become aware of itself, much less of lofty things. And therefore, when honor and elevation come, they must take it unawares and find it immersed in thoughts of other things. Thus Luke tells us (Luke 1:29) that Mary was troubled at the angel's saying and considered in her mind what sort of greeting this might be, since she had never expected anything like it. Had it come to Caiaphas's daughter, she would not have considered in her mind what sort of greeting it was, but would have accepted it immediately, thinking: "Oh, how wonderful! This is just as it should be."

False humility, on the other hand, never knows that it is proud; for if it knew this, it would soon grow humble from contemplation of that ugly vice. But it clings with heart and mind and senses to lofty things, sets them continually before its eyes, and ponders them in its thoughts. And because it does this, it cannot see itself nor become aware of itself. Hence honors come to it not unawares or unexpectedly, but find it immersed in thoughts of them. But dishonor and humiliation take it unawares and when it is thinking of something far different. . . .

But this holy virgin points to nothing except her low estate. In it she was content to spend the remainder of her days, never seeking to be honored or exalted or ever becoming aware of her own humility. For humility is so tender and precious a thing that it cannot abide beholding its own face; that belongs to God's eyes alone, as it is said in Ps. 113:6: "He looks far down upon the lowly in the heavens and the earth." For if anyone could see his own humility, he could judge himself worthy of salvation and thus anticipate God's judgment; for we know that God certainly saves the humble. Therefore God must reserve to Himself the right to know and look at humility, and must hide it from us by setting before our eyes things of low degree and exercising us in them so that we may forget to look at ourselves. That is the purpose of the many sufferings, of death, and all manner of afflictions we have to bear on earth; by means of the trouble and pain they cause us we are to pluck out the evil eye.

Thus the word "low estate" shows us plainly that the Virgin Mary was a poor, despised, and lowly maiden, who served God in her low estate nor knew it was so highly esteemed by Him. This should comfort us and teach us that though we should willingly be humbled and despised, we ought not to despair as though God were angry at us. Rather, we should set our hope on His grace, concerned only lest we be not cheerful and contented enough in our low estate and lest our evil eye be opened too wide and deceive us by secretly lusting after lofty things and satisfaction with self, which is the death of humility. What profit is it to the damned that they are humbled to the lowest degree, since they are not willing and content to be where they are? Again, what harm is it to all angels that they are exalted to the highest degree, so long as they do not cling to their station with false desire? In short, this verse teaches us to know God aright, because it shows us that He regards the lowly and despised. For he knows God aright who knows that He regards the lowly, as we have said above. From such knowledge flows love and trust in God, by which we yield ourselves to Him and gladly obey Him.

As Jeremiah says (Jer. 9:23–24): "Let no one glory in his might, riches, or wisdom; but if anyone wants to glory, let him glory in this, that he understands and knows Me." And St. Paul teaches (2 Cor. 10:17): "Let him who boasts, boast in the Lord." Now, after lauding her God and Savior with pure and single spirit, and after truly singing the praises of His goodness by not boasting of His gifts, the mother of God addresses herself in the next place to the praise also of His works and gifts. For, as we have seen, we must not fall upon the good gifts of God or boast of them, but make our way through them and ascend to Him, cling to Him alone, and highly esteem His goodness. Thereupon we should praise Him also in His works, in which He showed forth that goodness of His for our love, trust, and praise. Thus His works are simply that many incentives to love and praise His bare goodness that rules over us.

Mary begins with herself and sings what He has done for her. Thus she teaches us a twofold lesson. First, every one of us should pay attention to what God does for him rather than to all the works He does for others. For no one will be saved by what God does to another, but only by what He does to you. When St. Peter asked about John (John 21:21): "What about this man?" Christ answered him by saying (John 21:22): "What is that to you? Follow Me." It is as though He were to say: "John's works will not help you. You yourself must take hold and await what I will do for you." But now the world is captive to a dreadful abuse—the sale and distribution of good works—by which certain audacious spirits would assist others, especially such as live or die without good works of their own, just as if these spirits had a surplus of good works. But St. Paul plainly says in 1 Cor. 3:8: "Each man shall receive his wages according to his labor"—certainly not according to that of anyone else. . . .

In the second place, she teaches us that everyone should strive to be foremost in praising God by showing forth the works He has done to him, and then by praising Him for the works He has done to others. Thus we read (Acts 15:12) that Paul and Barnabas declared to the apostles the works God had done by them, and that the apostles in turn rehearsed those He had done by them. The same was done by the apostles, in Luke 24:34–35, with respect to the appearances of Christ after His resurrection. Thus there arose a common rejoicing and praising of God, each one praising the grace bestowed on another, yet most of all that bestowed on himself, however much more modest it was than that of the other. So simplehearted were they that all desired to be foremost, not in possessing the gifts but in praising and loving God; for God Himself and His bare goodness were sufficient for them, however small His gifts. But the hirelings and mercenaries grow green with envy when they observe that they are not first and foremost in possessing the good things of God; instead of praising, they murmur because they are made equal to, or lower than, others, like the laborers in the Gospel (Matt. 20:11–12) who murmured against the householder, not because he did them any wrong, but because he made them equal to the other laborers by giving to all the same pfennig. . . .[8]

Mary confesses that the foremost work God did for her was that He regarded her, which is indeed the greatest of His works, on which all the rest depend and from which they all derive. For where it comes to pass that God turns His face toward one to regard him, there is nothing but grace and salvation, and all gifts and works must follow. Thus we read in Gen. 4:4–5 that He had regard for Abel and his offering, but for Cain and his offering He had no regard. Here is the origin of the many prayers in the Psalter—that God would lift up His countenance upon us, that He would not hide His countenance from us, that He would make His face shine upon us, and the like. And that Mary herself regards this as the chief thing she indicates by saying: "Behold, since He has regarded me, all generations will call me blessed."

Note that she does not say men will speak all manner of good of her, praise her virtues, exalt her virginity or her humility, or sing of what she has done. But for this one thing alone, that God regarded her, men will call her blessed. That is to give all the glory to God as completely as it can be done. Therefore she points to God's regard and says: "For, behold, henceforth all generations will call me blessed. That is, beginning with the time when God regarded my low estate, I shall be called blessed." Not *she* is praised thereby, but God's *grace* toward her. In fact, she is despised, and she despises herself in that she says her low estate was regarded by

8 On "pfennig," see below, p. 170 n. 13.

God. Therefore she also mentions her blessedness before enumerating the works that God did to her, and ascribes it all to the fact that God regarded her low estate.

From this we may learn how to show her the honor and devotion that are her due. How ought one to address her? Keep these words in mind, and they will teach you to say: "O Blessed Virgin, mother of God, you were nothing and all despised; yet God in His grace regarded you and worked such great things in you. You were worthy of none of them, but the rich and abundant grace of God was upon you, far above any merit of yours. Hail to you! Blessed are you, from thenceforth and forever, in finding such a God." Nor need you fear that she will take it amiss if we call her unworthy of such grace. For, of a truth, she did not lie when she herself acknowledged her unworthiness and nothingness, which God regarded, not because of any merit in her, but solely by reason of His grace.

But she does take it amiss that the vain chatterers preach and write so many things about her merits. They are set on proving their own skill and fail to see how they spoil the Magnificat, make the mother of God a liar, and diminish the grace of God. For in proportion as we ascribe merit and worthiness to her, we lower the grace of God and diminish the truth of the Magnificat. The angel salutes her only as highly favored of God and because the Lord is with her (Luke 1:28), which is why she is blessed among women. Hence all those who heap such great praise and honor upon her head are not far from making an idol of her, as though she were concerned that men should honor her and look to her for good things, when in truth she thrusts this from her and would have us honor God in her and come through her to a good confidence in His grace.

Whoever, therefore, would show her the proper honor must not regard her alone and by herself, but set her in the presence of God and far beneath Him, must there strip her of all honor, and regard her low estate, as she says; he should then marvel at the exceedingly abundant grace of God, who regards, embraces, and blesses so poor and despised a mortal. Thus regarding her, you will be moved to love and praise God for His grace, and drawn to look for all good things to Him, who does not reject but graciously regards poor and despised and lowly mortals. Thus your heart will be strengthened in faith and love and hope. What do you suppose would please her more than to have you come through her to God this way, and learn from her to put your hope and trust in Him, notwithstanding your despised and lowly estate, in life as well as in death? She does not want you to come to her, but through her to God.

Again, nothing would please her better than to have you turn in fear from all lofty things on which men set their hearts, seeing that even in

His mother God neither found nor desired anything of high degree. But the masters who so depict and portray the Blessed Virgin that there is found in her nothing to be despised, but only great and lofty things—what are they doing but contrasting us with her instead of her with God? Thus they make us timid and afraid and hide the Virgin's comfortable picture, as the images are covered over in Lent. For they deprive us of her example, from which we might take comfort; they make an exception of her and set her above all examples. But she should be, and herself gladly would be, the foremost example of the grace of God, to incite all the world to trust in this grace and to love and praise it, so that through her the hearts of all men should be filled with such knowledge of God that they might confidently say: "O Blessed Virgin, mother of God, what great comfort God has shown us in you, by so graciously regarding your unworthiness and low estate. This encourages us to believe that henceforth He will not despise us poor and lowly ones, but graciously regard us also, according to your example."

What do you think? David, St. Peter, St. Paul, St. Mary Magdalene, and the like are examples to strengthen our trust in God and our faith, by reason of the great grace bestowed on them without their worthiness, for the comforting of all men. Will not the blessed mother of God also gladly be such an example to all the world? But now she cannot be this because of the fulsome eulogists and empty chatterers, who do not show the people from this verse how the exceeding riches of God joined in her with her utter poverty, the divine honor with her low estate, the divine glory with her shame, the divine greatness with her smallness, the divine goodness with her lack of merit, the divine grace with her unworthiness. On this basis our love and affection toward God would grow and increase with all confidence, which is why her life and works, as well as the lives and works of all the saints, have been recorded. But now we find those who come to her for help and comfort, as though she were a divine being, so that I fear there is now more idolatry in the world than ever before. But enough of this for the present.

Luke 1:49

For He who is mighty has done great things for me, and holy is His name.

Here she sings in one breath of all the works that God has done to her and observes the proper order. In the preceding verse she sang of God's regard and gracious goodwill toward her, which is indeed the greatest and chief work of grace, as we have said. Now she comes to the works and gifts. For God indeed gives to some many good things and richly adorns them, as He did Lucifer in heaven. He scatters His gifts broadcast among the multitude; but He does not therefore regard them. His good things are merely gifts, which last for a season; but His grace and regard are the inheritance, which lasts forever, as St. Paul says in Rom. 6:23: "The grace of God is eternal life." In giving us the gifts He gives only what is His, but in His grace and His regard of us He gives His very self. In the gifts we touch His hand; but in His gracious regard we receive His heart, spirit, mind, and will. Hence the Blessed Virgin puts His regard in the first and highest place and does not begin by saying: "All generations will call me blessed, because He has done great things for me," as this verse says; but she begins: "He has regarded my low estate," as the preceding verse shows. Where God's gracious will is, there are also His gifts; but, on the other hand, where His gifts are, there is not also His gracious will. This verse therefore logically follows the preceding verse. We read in Gen. 25:5–6 that Abraham gave gifts to the sons of his concubines; but to Isaac, his natural son by his true helpmate Sarah, he gave the whole inheritance. Thus God would not have His true children put their trust in His goods and gifts, spiritual or temporal, however great they be, but in His grace and in Himself, yet without despising the gifts.

Nor does Mary enumerate any good things in particular, but gathers them all together in one word and says, "He has done great things for me." That is: "Everything He has done for me is great." She teaches us here that the greater devotion there is in the heart, the fewer words are uttered. For she feels that however she may strive and try, she cannot express it in words. Therefore these few words of the Spirit are so great and profound that no one can comprehend them without having, at least in part, the same Spirit. But for the unspiritual, who deal in many words and much loud noise, such words seem utterly inadequate and wholly without salt or savor. Christ also teaches us in Matt. 6:7 not to speak much when we pray, as the unbelievers do, for they think that they will be heard for their many words. Even so there is today in the churches a great ringing of bells, blowing of trumpets, singing, shouting, and intoning, yet I fear precious little worship of God, who wants to be worshiped in spirit and truth, as He says in John 4:24. . . .

The "great things" are nothing less than that she became the mother of God, in which work so many and such great good things are bestowed on her as pass man's understanding. For on this there follows all honor, all blessedness, and her unique place in the whole of mankind, among which she has no equal, namely, that she had a Child by the Father in heaven, and such a Child. She herself is unable to find a name for this work, it is too exceedingly great; all she can do is break out in the fervent cry: "They are great things," impossible to describe or define. Hence men have crowded all her glory into a single word, calling her the mother of God. No one can say anything greater of her or to her, though he had as many tongues as there are leaves on the trees or grass in the fields or stars in the sky or sand by the sea. It needs to be pondered in the heart what it means to be the mother of God.

Mary also freely ascribes all to God's grace, not to her merit. For though she was without sin, yet that grace was far too great for her to deserve it in any way.[9] How should a creature deserve to become the mother of God? Although certain scribblers make much ado about her worthiness for such motherhood, I prefer to believe her rather than them. She says her low estate was regarded by God, not thereby rewarding her for anything she had done, but "He has done great things for me," He has done this of His own accord without any doing of mine. For never in all her life did she think to become the mother of God, still less did she prepare or make herself meet for it. The tidings took her all unawares, as Luke reports (Luke 1:29). Merit, however, is not unprepared for its reward, but deliberately seeks and awaits it.

It is no valid argument against this to cite the words of the hymn "Regina coeli laetare":[10] "Whom thou didst merit to bear" and, again, "Whom thou wast worthy to bear." For the same things are sung about the holy cross, which was a thing of wood and incapable of merit. The words are to be understood in this sense: In order to become the mother of God, she had to be a woman, a virgin, of the tribe of Judah, and had to believe the angelic message in order to become worthy, as the Scriptures foretold. As the wood had no other merit or worthiness than that it was suited to be made into a cross and was appointed by God for that purpose, so her sole worthiness to become the mother of God lay in her being fit and

9 The church fathers and medieval schoolmen affirmed the bodily assumption of Mary into heaven following her death. They argued further that if she was assumed into heaven she must have been without actual sin. Although Scripture mentions none of this, which they acknowledged, they concluded that Mary must have been sanctified before her birth in the womb. Thomas Aquinas understood this sanctification to mean that she was freed from the stain of original sin but not the guilt of original sin. She required, like all people, the redeeming work of Christ. To say otherwise would be unfitting and would imply that Christ is not the Savior of all. Thomas's position echoes the arguments of the church fathers, Bernard of Clairvaux (1090–1153), and Bonaventure (1221–74), among others. John Duns Scotus, however, went further and argued that Mary was also preserved from original sin. Scotus's teaching on the immaculate conception of Mary was formally dogmatized by the Roman Catholic Church in 1854.

10 An Eastertide hymn to the Virgin Mary, which begins "Queen of Heaven, rejoice." Luther continues by quoting two lines from the hymn.

appointed for it; so that it might be pure grace and not a reward, that we might not take away from God's grace, worship, and honor by ascribing too great things to her. For it is better to take away too much from her than from the grace of God. Indeed, we cannot take away too much from her, since she was created out of nothing, like all other creatures. But we can easily take away too much from God's grace, which is a perilous thing to do and not well-pleasing to her. It is necessary also to keep within bounds and not make too much of calling her "Queen of Heaven," which is a true-enough name and yet does not make her a goddess who could grant gifts or render aid, as some suppose when they pray and flee to her rather than to God. She gives nothing, God gives all, as we see in the words that follow.

"He who is mighty." Truly, in these words she takes away all might and power from every creature and bestows them on God alone. What great boldness and robbery on the part of so young and tender a maiden! She dares, by this one word, to make all the strong feeble, all the mighty weak, all the wise foolish, all the famous despised, and God alone the possessor of all strength, wisdom, and glory. For this is the meaning of the phrase: "He who is mighty." There is none that does anything, but as St. Paul says in Ephesians 1: "God accomplishes all in all," and all creatures' works are God's works. Even as we confess in the Creed: "I believe in God the Father, the Almighty." He is almighty because it is His power alone that works in all and through all and over all. Thus St. Anna, the mother of Samuel, sings in 1 Sam. 2:9: "Not by might shall a man prevail." St. Paul says in 2 Cor. 3:5: "Not that we are sufficient of ourselves to claim anything as coming from us; our sufficiency is from God." This is a most important article of faith, including many things; it completely puts down all pride, arrogance, blasphemy, fame, and false trust, and exalts God alone. It points out the reason why God alone is to be exalted—because He does all things. That is easily said but hard to believe and to translate into life. For those who carry it out in their lives are most peaceable, composed, and simplehearted folk, who lay no claim to anything, well knowing it is not theirs but God's.

This, then, is the meaning of these words of the mother of God: "In all those great and good things there is nothing of mine, but He who alone does all things, and whose power works in all, has done such great things for me." For the word "mighty" does not denote a quiescent power, as one says of a temporal king that he is mighty, even though he may be sitting still and doing nothing. But it denotes an energetic power, a continuous activity, that works and operates without ceasing. For God does not rest, but works without ceasing, as Christ says in John 5:17: "My Father is working still, and I am working." In the same sense St. Paul says in

Eph. 3:20: "He is able to do more than all that we ask"; that is, He always does more than we ask; that is His way, and thus His power works. That is why I said Mary does not desire to be an idol; she does nothing, God does all. We ought to call upon her, that for her sake God may grant and do what we request. Thus also all other saints are to be invoked, so that the work may be every way God's alone.[11]

Therefore she adds, "And holy is His name." That is to say: "As I lay no claim to the work, neither do I to the name and fame. For the name and fame belong to Him alone who does the work. It is not proper that one should do the work and another have the fame and take the glory. I am but the workshop in which He performs His work; I had nothing to do with the work itself. No one should praise me or give me the glory for becoming the mother of God, but God alone and His work are to be honored and praised in me. It is enough to congratulate me and call me blessed, because God used me and did His works in me." Behold, how completely she traces all to God, lays claim to no works, no honor, no fame. She conducts herself as before, when she still had nothing of all this; she demands no higher honors than before. She is not puffed up, does not vaunt herself or proclaim with a loud voice that she is become the mother of God. She seeks not any glory, but goes about her usual household duties, milking the cows, cooking the meals, washing pots and kettles, sweeping out the rooms, and performing the work of maidservant or housemother in lowly and despised tasks, as though she cared nothing for such great gifts and graces. She was esteemed among other women and her neighbors no more highly than before, nor desired to be, but remained a poor townswoman, one of the great multitude. Oh, how simple and pure a heart was hers, how strange a soul was this! What great things are hidden here under this lowly exterior! How many came in contact with her, talked, and ate and drank with her, who perhaps despised her and counted her but a common, poor, and simple village maiden, and who, had they known, would have fled from her in terror.

---

11 Luther's early works encourage believers to call upon the saints and Mary. See *Sermon on Preparing to Die* (1519), LW 42:113. By 1530, Luther had thoroughly repudiated the practice. In *On Translating*, Luther writes: "Since in the matter of divine worship, however, it is not proper for us to undertake anything without God's command—whoever does so is tempting God—it is therefore neither to be advised nor tolerated that one should call upon the departed saints to intercede for him or teach others to call upon them. Rather this is to be condemned, and men should be taught to avoid it. . . . Moreover this is in itself a dangerous and offensive way of worship, because people are easily accustomed to turning from Christ; they quickly learn to put more confidence in the saints than in Christ himself" (LW 35:199).

That is the meaning of the clause: "Holy is His name." For "holy" means "separated," "dedicated to God," that none should touch or defile it but all should hold it in honor. And "name" means a good report, fame, praise, and honor. Thus everyone should let God's name alone, not lay hands on it or appropriate it to himself. It is a symbol of this when we read in Exod. 30:25–32 that Moses made an oil of holy ointment, at God's command, and strictly forbade that it be poured on any man's flesh. That is, no man should ascribe to himself the name of God. For we desecrate God's name when we let ourselves be praised or honored, or when we take pleasure in ourselves and boast of our works or our possessions, as is the way of the world, which constantly dishonors and desecrates the name of God. But as the works are God's alone, so, too, the name should be His. And all that thus hallow His name and deny themselves all honor and glory, rightly honor His name, and therefore are hallowed by it. Thus we read in Exod. 30:29 that the precious ointment was so holy that it hallowed whatever it touched. That is, when God's name is hallowed by us, so that we lay claim to no work, fame, or self-satisfaction in it, it is rightly honored, and in turn touches and hallows us.

Therefore we must be on our guard, because we cannot do without God's good things while we live on earth, and therefore we cannot be without name and honor. When men accord us praise and honor, we ought to profit by the example of the mother of God and at all times arm ourselves with this verse to make the proper reply and to use such honor and praise correctly. We should openly say, or at least think in our heart: "O Lord God, Thine is this work that is being praised and celebrated. Thine be also the name. Not I have done it but Thou, who art able to do all things, and holy is Thy name." We ought neither to reject this praise and honor as though they were wrong nor to despise them as though they were nothing, but refuse to accept them as too precious or noble, and ascribe them to Him in heaven, to whom they belong. This is one lesson from this precious verse. It also furnishes us an answer to the question that some may ask, whether no man ought to honor another. St. Paul says in Rom. 12:10 that we should "outdo one another in showing honor." But no one should accept the honor as accorded to him, nor take it to himself, but should hallow it and ascribe it to God, to whom it belongs, by performing all manner of good works, from which honor comes. For no one should lead a dishonorable life. But if he is to live honorably, honor will have to be shown him. Yet as an honorable life is the gift and work of God, so, too, the name should be His alone, holy and undefiled by self-complacency. For this we pray in the Lord's Prayer: "Hallowed be Thy name."

Luke 1:50

And His mercy is on those who fear Him, from generation to generation.

. . . Having finished singing about herself and the good things she had from God, and having sung His praises, Mary now rehearses all the works of God that He works in general in all men, and sings His praises also for them, teaching us to understand the work, method, nature, and will of God. Many philosophers and men of great acumen have also engaged in the endeavor to find out the nature of God; they have written much about Him, one in this way, another in that, yet all have gone blind over their task and failed of the proper insight. And, indeed, it is the greatest thing in heaven and on earth, to know God correctly if that may be granted to one. This the mother of God teaches us here in a masterly fashion, if we would only listen, just as she taught the same above, in and by her own experience. How can one know God better than in the works in which He is most Himself? Whoever understands His works correctly cannot fail to know His nature and will, His heart and mind. Hence to understand His works is an art. And in order that we may learn it, Mary enumerates, in the following four verses, six divine works among as many classes of persons. She divides all the world into two parts and assigns to each side three works and three classes of men, so that either side has its exact counterpart in the other. She describes the works of God in each of these two parts, portraying Him so well that it could not be done better. . . .

Let us now consider these six works in order.

The first work of God, mercy

Of this our verse treats: "His mercy is on those who fear Him from generation to generation." She begins with the highest and greatest things, with the spiritual and inward goods, which produce the most vain, proud, and stiff-necked people on earth. No rich or mighty man is so puffed up and bold as one such smart aleck who feels and knows that he is in the right, understands all about a matter, and is wiser than other people. Especially when he finds he ought to give way or confess himself in the wrong, he becomes so insolent and is so utterly devoid of the fear of God that he dares to boast of being infallible, declares God is on his side and the others on the devil's side, and has the effrontery to appeal to the judgment of God. If such a man possesses the necessary power, he rushes on headlong, persecuting, condemning, slandering, slaying, banishing, and destroying all who differ with him, saying afterward he did it all to the honor and glory of God. He is as certain and sure as hardly an angel in heaven of earning much thanks and merit before God. Oh, how big a bubble we have here! How much Scripture has to say about such men, and how many grievous things it threatens them with! But they feel them less than the anvil feels the smith's hammer. This is a great and widespread evil.

Christ says of such men in John 16:2: "The hour is coming when whoever kills you will think that he is offering service to God." And Ps. 10:5–6 says about the same crowd: "As for all his foes, he puffs at them and says, I shall not meet adversity"; as if he were to say: "I am in the right, I do well, God will richly reward me." Such were the people of Moab, of whom we read in Isa. 16:6 and Jer. 48:29–30: "We have heard of the pride of Moab—he is very proud—of his loftiness, his pride, and his arrogance; his reputation and his wrath are greater than his power." Thus we see that such men would gladly do more in their great arrogance than they are able. Such were the people of the Jews in their dealings with Christ and the apostles. Such were the friends of St. Job, who argued against him with extraordinary wisdom and praised and preached God in the loftiest terms. Such people will not give you a hearing; it is impossible that they should be in the wrong or give way. They must have their way though all the world perish. . . . Such, above all others, are the pope and his herd today and these many days. They do all of these things, and worse than were ever done; there is no hearing nor giving way, it profits nothing to speak, to counsel, beg, or threaten. It is simply, "We are in the right," and there is an end of it, in spite of everyone else, though it be the whole world.

But someone might say: "How is that? Are we not bound to defend the right? Should we let the truth go? Are we not commanded to die for the sake of the right and the truth? Did not the holy martyrs suffer for the sake of the Gospel? And Christ Himself, did not He desire to be in the right? It happens indeed that such men are now and then in the right publicly (and as they prate, before God) and that they do wisely and well." I reply: Here it is high time and most necessary that we open our eyes, for here lies the crux of the whole matter. Everything depends on our proper understanding of "being in the right." It is true, we are to suffer all things for the sake of the truth and the right, and not to deny it, however unimportant the matter be. It may also be that those men are now and then in the right; but they spoil all by not rightly asserting their right, by not going about it in fear or setting God before their eye. They suppose it is sufficient that it is right, and then they desire to continue and carry it out by their own power. Thus they turn their right into a wrong, even if it was in itself right. But it is much more dangerous when they only think they are in the right, yet are not certain, as they do in the important matters that pertain to God and His right. Let us, however, deal first with the more tangible human right and use a simple illustration that all may grasp.

Is it not true that money, property, body, wife, child, friends, and the like are good things created and given by God Himself? Since, then, they are God's gifts and not your own, suppose He were to try you, to learn whether you were willing to let them go for His sake and to cleave to Him rather than to such gifts of His. Suppose He raised up an enemy, who deprived you of them in whole or in part, or you lost them by death or some other mischance. Do you think you would have just cause to rage and storm and to take them again by force or to sulk impatiently until they were restored to you? And if you said that they were good things and God's creatures, made with His own hands, and that, since all the Scriptures called such things good, you were resolved to fulfill God's Word and defend or get back such good at cost of life and limb, not suffering their loss voluntarily or surrendering them patiently—what a farce that would be! To do right in this case, you should not rush in headlong, but fear God and say: "Dear Lord, they are good things and gifts of Thine, as Thine own Word and Scripture; nevertheless I do not know whether Thou wilt permit me to keep them. If I knew that I was not to have them, I would not move a finger to get them back. If I knew that Thou wouldst rather have them remain in my possession than in that of others, I would serve Thy will by taking them back at risk of life and property. But now, since I know neither and see that for the present Thou permittest them to be taken from me, I commit the case to Thee. I will await what I am to do, and be ready to have them or to do without them."

That, mark you, is a right soul, and one that fears God. There is God's mercy, as the mother of God sings. . . .

In the same manner we must treat the right and the manifold good things of reason or wisdom. Who can doubt that right is a good thing and a gift of God? God's Word itself says right is good, and no one should admit that his good and righteous cause is unrighteous or evil, but should sooner die for it and let go everything that is not God. To do otherwise would be to deny God and His Word, for He says right is good and not evil. But if such right is snatched from you or suppressed, would you cry out, storm and rage, and slay the whole world? Some do this; they cry to heaven, work all manner of mischief, ruin land and people, and fill the world with war and bloodshed. How do you know whether or not it is God's will that you keep such a gift and right? It belongs to Him, and He can take it from you today or tomorrow, outwardly or inwardly, by friend or foe, just as He wills. He tries you to see whether you will dispense with your right for His will's sake, be in the wrong and suffer wrong, endure shame for Him, and cleave to Him alone. If you fear God and think: "Lord, it is Thine; I will not keep it unless I know Thou willest me to have it. Let go what will: only be Thou my God"—then this verse is fulfilled: "His mercy is on those who fear Him," who refuse to do anything apart from His will. Then both sides of God's Word are observed. In the first place, you confess that the right, your reason, knowledge, wisdom, and all your thoughts are right and good, as God's Word teaches. In the second place, you are willing to dispense with such good things for God's sake, to be wrongfully despoiled and put to shame before the world, as God's Word also teaches. To confess the right and good is one thing; to obtain it is another. It is enough for you to confess that you are in the right; if you cannot obtain it, commit that to God. To you is committed the confession; the obtaining God has reserved to Himself. If He desires you also to obtain, He will perform it Himself or put it in your way, without any thought of yours, so that you must come into possession of it and win the victory, above all that you asked or thought (Eph. 3:20). If He does not desire you to obtain it, let His mercy be sufficient for you (2 Cor. 12:9). Although they deprive you of the victory of the right, they cannot deprive you of the confession. Thus we must refrain, not from the good things of God but from wickedly and falsely cleaving to them, so that we may use them or suffer the lack of them with equanimity, and cling, whatever befalls, to God alone. Oh, this is a thing that ought to be known to all princes and rulers who, not content with confessing the right, immediately want to obtain it and win the victory, without the fear of God; they fill the world with bloodshed and misery, and think what they do is right and well done because they have, or think they have, a just cause. What else is that but proud and haughty Moab, which calls and makes itself worthy to possess the right, that fine and noble good and gift of God; while if it regards itself right in the sight of God, it is not worthy to live on earth or eat a crust of bread, because of its sins. Oh, blindness, blindness! Who is worthy of the least creature of God? Yet we desire not only to possess the highest creatures, right, wisdom, and honor, but to keep them or regain possession of them with furious shedding of blood and every disaster. Thereupon we go and pray, fast, hear Mass, and found churches, with such bloody, furious, raving hearts, it is a wonder the stones do not burst asunder in our face.

Here a question arises. If a ruler did not defend his land and subjects against injustice, but followed my advice, made no resistance, and let all be taken from him, what would the world come to? I will briefly set down my view of the matter. Temporal power is in duty bound to defend its subjects, as I have frequently said; for it bears the sword in order to keep in fear those who do not heed such divine teaching, and to compel them to leave others in peace. And in this the temporal power seeks not its own but its neighbor's profit and God's honor; it would gladly remain quiet and let its sword rust, if God had not ordained it to be a hindrance to evildoers. Yet this defense of its subjects should not be accompanied by still greater harm; that would be but to leap from the frying pan into the fire. It is a poor defense to expose a whole city to danger for the sake of one person, or to risk the entire country for a single village or castle, unless God enjoined this by a special command, as He did in former times. If a robber knight robs a citizen of his property and you, my lord, lead your army against him to punish this injustice, and in so doing lay waste the whole land, who will have wrought the greater harm, the knight or the lord? David overlooked many things when he was unable to punish without bringing harm upon others. All rulers must do the same. On the other hand, a citizen must endure a certain measure of suffering for the sake of the community, and not demand that all other men undergo the greater injury for his sake. Christ did not want the weeds to be gathered up, lest the wheat also be rooted up with them (Matt. 13:29). If men went to war on every provocation and passed by no insult, we should never be at peace and have nothing but destruction. Therefore, right or wrong is never a sufficient cause indiscriminately to punish or to make war. It is a sufficient cause to punish within bounds and without destroying another. The lord or ruler must always look to what will profit the whole mass of his subjects rather than any one portion. That householder will never grow rich who, because someone has plucked a feather from his goose, flings the whole goose after him. There is no time now to go into the subject of war.

We must do the same in things divine, such as faith and the Gospel, which are the highest goods and which no one should let go. But the right, favor, honor, and acceptance of them we must cast in the balance and commit them to God. We should be concerned not to obtain but to confess, and willingly endure being reviled before all the world, being persecuted, banished, burned at the stake, or otherwise slain, as unrighteous, deceivers, heretics, apostates, blasphemers, and what not; for then God's mercy is upon us. They cannot take the faith and the truth from us, even though they take our life. There are not very many, however, who rage and fret to obtain and to win the victory in this matter, as men do in temporal goods and rights. There are also few who confess it aright and on principle. But we should grieve and lament for the others who through the defeat of the Gospel are hindered in their soul's salvation. In fact, we should lament and labor (yet as in the sight of God) because of the injury to souls inflicted by the Moabites for the sake of their own temporal goods and rights, as we said above. For it is a lamentable thing when God's Word does not win the victory, lamentable not so far as the confessor is concerned, but so far as those are concerned who should have been saved by it. Hence we find in the prophets, in Christ, and in the apostles such sorrow and lamentation for the suppression of the Word of God, though they were glad to bear any injustice and injury. For far more depends on the obtaining of this good than of any other. Yet no one should employ force or keep or regain such right of the Gospel by rage and unreason; he should rather humble himself before God as one who may not be worthy that such a great and good thing be done through him, and commit all to His mercy with prayer and lamentation.

This, then, is the first work of God—that He is merciful to all who are ready to do without their own opinion, right, wisdom, and all spiritual goods, and willing to be poor in spirit. These are the ones who truly fear God, who count themselves not worthy of anything, be it ever so small, and are glad to be naked and bare before God and man; who ascribe whatever they have to His pure grace, bestowed on the unworthy; who use it with praise and fear and thanksgiving, as though it belonged to another; and who seek not their own will, desire, or honor, but His alone to whom it belongs. Mary also indicates how much more gladly God shows such mercy, which is His noblest work, than its counterpart, His strength; for she says this work of God endures without ceasing from generation to generation of those that fear Him, while His strength endures only to the third and fourth generation, though in the verse that follows it has no time or limit set to it.

The second work of God, breaking spiritual pride

Luke 1:51

He has shown strength with His arm, He has scattered the proud in the imagination of their hearts.

I trust no one will be confused by my translation. Above I rendered this verse, "He shows strength," and here, "He has shown strength." I have done this in order that we may the better understand these words, which are not bound to any one time, but are intended to set forth in general the works of God that He always has done, always does, and always will do. Hence the following would be a fair translation: "God is a Lord whose works are of such a nature that He mightily scatters the proud and is merciful to those who fear Him." In the Scriptures, the "arm" of God means God's own power, by which He works without the medium of any creature. This work is done quietly and in secret, and no one becomes aware of it until all is accomplished, so that this power, or arm, can be known and understood only by faith. Therefore Isaiah complains (Isa. 53:1) that so few have faith in this arm, saying: "Who has believed what we have heard, and to whom has the arm of the Lord been revealed?" These things are so because, as he goes on to say (Isa. 53:2ff.), all is done in secret and without the semblance of power. We also read in Hab. 3:4 that there are horns coming out of God's hands, to indicate His mighty power; and yet it is said: "There He veiled His power." What is the meaning of this?

It means that when God works by means of His creatures, it is plainly seen where the strength is and where the weakness. Hence the proverb, "God helps those who help themselves." For example, whichever prince wins a battle, it is seen that God defeated the other by him. When a man is devoured by a wolf or otherwise injured, it is evident that it took place by means of the creature. Thus God makes or breaks one creature by means of another. Whoever falls, falls; whoever stands, stands. But it is different when God Himself works, with His own arm. Then a thing is destroyed or raised up before one knows it, and no one sees it done. Such works as these He does only among the two divisions of mankind, the godly and the wicked. He lets the godly become powerless and to be brought low, until everyone supposes their end is near, whereas in these very things He is present to them with all His power, yet so hidden and in secret that even those who suffer the oppression do not feel it but only believe. There is the fullness of God's power and His outstretched arm. For where man's strength ends, God's strength begins, provided faith is present and waits on Him. And when the oppression comes to an end, it becomes manifest what great strength was hidden underneath the weakness. Even so, Christ was powerless on the cross; and yet there He performed His mightiest work and conquered sin, death, world, hell, devil, and all evil. Thus all the martyrs were strong and overcame. Thus, too, all who suffer and are oppressed overcome. Therefore it is said in Joel 3:10: "Let the weak say, 'I am strong' "—yet in faith, and without feeling it until it is accomplished.

On the other hand, God lets the other half of mankind become great and mightily to exalt themselves. He withdraws His power from them and lets them puff themselves up in their own power alone. For where man's strength begins, God's strength ends. When their bubble is full-blown, and everyone supposes them to have won and overcome, and they themselves feel smug in their achievement, then God pricks the bubble, and it is all over. The poor dupes do not know that even while they are puffing themselves up and growing strong they are forsaken by God, and God's arm is not with them. Therefore their prosperity has its day, disappears like a bubble, and is as if it had never been. To this the psalmist refers in Ps. 73:16–20. It bothered him when he saw the riches, pride, and prosperity of the wicked in the world. At last he said: "When I thought how to understand this, it seemed to me a wearisome task, until I looked into the secrets of God; then I perceived their end. I saw that they were exalted only in their self-deception, and were brought to ruin in their exaltation. How they are destroyed in a moment, how quickly it is all over for them! It is as though they had never existed, like a dream when one awakes." And Ps. 37:35–36: "I have seen a wicked man overbearing and towering like a cedar of Lebanon. Again I passed by, and, lo, he was no more; though I sought him, he could not be found."

It is because of our lack of faith that we cannot wait a little, until the time comes when we, too, shall see how the mercy of God together with all His might is with those who fear Him, and the arm of God with all severity and power against the proud. O faithless! We grope with our hands for the mercy and the arm of God, and, unable to feel them, suppose our cause lost and that of our enemies won, as though God's grace and mercy had forsaken us and His arm turned against us. This we do because we do not know His proper works and therefore do not know Him, neither His mercy nor His arm. For He must and will be known by faith; hence our sense and our reason must close their eyes. This is the eye that offends us; therefore it must be plucked out and cast from us. These, then, are the two contrary works of God, from which we learn that He is minded to be far from the wise and prudent and near to the foolish and those compelled to be in the wrong. This makes God worthy of love and praise and comforts soul and body and all our powers.

We come to the words: "He scatters the proud in the imagination of their hearts." This scattering takes place, as we have said, when their prudence is at its height and when they are filled with their own wisdom; then, truly, God's wisdom is no longer with them. And in what better way could He scatter them than by depriving them of His eternal wisdom and permitting them to be filled with their own temporal, short-lived, and perishing wisdom? For Mary says "the proud in the imagination of their hearts," that is, those who delight in their own opinions, thoughts, and reason, which not God but their heart inspires, and who suppose that these are right and good and wise above all others. Therefore they exalt themselves above those who fear God, put down and pour shame upon the opinion and right of others, and persecute them to the utmost, so that their own cause may by all means be right and be maintained. When they have accomplished this, they boast and loudly brag, as the Jews did with Christ. Yet the Jews did not see that by this their cause was destroyed and brought down, while Christ was exalted to glory. We observe, then, that our verse treats of spiritual goods and how one can know God's twofold work in them. It shows us that we ought gladly to be poor in spirit and in the wrong and let our adversaries be in the right. They will not long continue; the promise is too strong for them. They cannot escape God's arm but must succumb and be brought as low as they once were high, if we will only believe it. But where there is no faith, God does not perform such works; He withdraws His arm and works openly by means of the creatures, as we said above. But these are not His proper works, by which He may be known; for in them the creatures' strength is mingled with His own. They are not God's own pure works, as they must be when no one works with Him and He alone does the work, which He does when we become powerless and oppressed in our right or our opinion and let God's power work in us. What precious works these are!

With what mastery Mary here hits the perverse hypocrites! She looks not at their hands or in their eyes, but in their hearts when she says "the proud in the imagination of their hearts." She refers in particular to the enemies of divine truth, such as the Jews in their opposition to Christ and the men of today. For these scholars and saints are not proud of their dress or conduct; they pray much, fast much, preach and study much; they also say Mass, go meekly with bowed head, and shun costly clothes. They think there are no greater foes to pride, error, and hypocrisy, nor any better friends of truth and of God than they themselves. How else could they bring such great harm upon the truth if they were not such holy, pious, and learned men? Their doings make a brave outward show and impress the common people. Oh, they have good hearts and mean well; they call upon the good God and pity the poor Jesus, who was so unrighteous and proud, and not so pious as they. He says of them in Matt. 11:19: "Divine wisdom is justified by her children," that is: "They are more righteous and wise than I, who am divine wisdom itself; whatever I do is wrong, and I am mastered by them."

These are the most venomous and pernicious men on earth, their hearts abysses of satanic pride. There is no helping them; they will not heed our counsel. It does not concern them; they leave that to poor sinners, for whom such teaching is necessary, but not for them. John calls them "a brood of vipers" in Luke 3:7, and so does Christ (Matt. 12:34). These are the right guilty ones, who do not fear God and are fit only that God should scatter them with their pride, because no one persecutes the right and wisdom more than they—yet for the sake of God and of righteousness, as we have said. Hence they must be first and foremost among the three enemies of God on this side. For the rich are the least His enemies; the mighty are much more hostile; but these smart alecks are the worst of all because of their influence on others. The rich destroy the truth among themselves; the mighty drive it away from others; but these wise ones utterly extinguish the truth itself and replace it with other things, the imagination of their own heart, so that the truth cannot come into its own again. As much as the truth itself is better than the men among whom it dwells, so much worse are the wise than the mighty and the rich. Oh, God is their special enemy, as they well deserve.

The third work, putting down the mighty

Luke 1:52

He has put down the mighty from their seats.

This work and those that follow are easily understood from the two foregoing works. God scatters the wise and prudent in their own thoughts and imaginations, on which they depend, venting their pride on those who fear God, who must needs be in the wrong and see their right and their opinion rejected; which happens chiefly for the sake of God's Word. Just so He destroys and puts down the mighty and the great with their strength and authority, on which they depend, venting their pride on their inferiors, the godly and weak, who must suffer injury, pain, death, and all manner of evil at their hands. And just as He comforts those who must suffer wrong and shame for the right, truth, and Word, so He comforts those who must suffer injury and evil. And as much as He comforts the latter, so much He terrifies the former. But this, too, must all be known and waited for in faith. For He does not destroy the mighty as suddenly as they deserve, but lets them go for a season, until their might has reached its highest point. When it has done this, God does not support it, neither can it support itself; it breaks down of its own weight without any crash or sound, and the oppressed are raised up, also without any sound, for God's strength is in them, and it alone remains when the strength of the mighty has fallen.

Observe, however, that Mary does not say He breaks the seats, but He casts the mighty from their seats. Nor does she say He leaves those of low degree in their low degree, but He exalts them. For while the world stands, authority, rule, power, and seats must remain. But God will not long permit men to abuse them and turn them against Him, inflict injustice and violence on the godly, and enjoy it, boast of them, and fail to use them in the fear of God, to His praise and in defense of righteousness. We see in all histories and in experience that He puts down one kingdom and exalts another, lifts up one principality and casts down another, increases one people and destroys another, as He did with Assyria, Babylon, Persia, Greece, and Rome, though they thought they would sit in their seats forever. Nor does He destroy reason, wisdom, and right; for if the world is to go on, these things must remain. But He does destroy pride and the proud, who use these things for selfish ends, enjoy them, do not fear God, but persecute the godly and the divine right by means of them, and thus abuse the fair gifts of God and turn them against Him.

Now, in things divine, the smart alecks and proud sages usually make common cause with the mighty and persuade them to take sides against the truth, as it is written in Ps. 2:2: "The kings of the earth set themselves, and the rulers take counsel together, against the Lord and His Anointed." For truth and right must always be assailed by the wise, the mighty, and the rich, that is, by the world with its greatest and best ability. Hence the Holy Spirit comforts truth and right by the mouth of this mother and bids them not to be deceived or afraid. Let them be wise, mighty, rich: it will not be for long. For if the saints and scholars, together with the mighty lords and the rich, were not against but for the right and the truth, what would become of the wrong? Who would there be to suffer evil? But this must never come to pass. The learned, saintly, mighty, great and rich, and the best that the world has must fight against God and the right, and be the devil's own. As it is said in Hab. 1:16: "His food is rich and choice"; that is to say, the evil spirit has a most delicate palate and is fond of feasting on the very best, daintiest, and choicest morsels, as a bear on honey. Hence the learned and saintly hypocrites, the great lords and the rich, are the devil's own tidbits. On the other hand, as St. Paul says in 1 Cor. 1:28, those whom the world rejects, the poor, lowly, simplehearted, and despised, God has chosen, causing the best part of mankind to bring suffering upon the lowest part, in order that men may know that our salvation consists not in man's power and works but in God's alone, as St. Paul also says (1 Cor. 3:7). Hence there is much truth in these sayings, "The more men know, the worse they grow"; "A prince, a rare bird in heaven"; "Rich here, poor yonder." For the learned will not surrender the pride of their hearts, nor the mighty their oppression, nor the rich their pleasures. And so it goes.

The fourth work, exalting the lowly

Luke 1:52

And exalted those of low degree.

Those of low degree are here not the humble, but all those who are contemptible and altogether nothing in the eyes of the world. It is the same expression that Mary applied to herself above: "He has regarded the low estate of His handmaiden." Nevertheless, those who are willing to be nothing and lowly of heart, and do not strive to be great, are truly humble. Now, when He exalts them, it does not mean that He will put them in the seats of those He has cast out any more than that when He shows mercy to those who fear Him, He puts them in the place of the learned, that is, the proud. Rather, He lets them be exalted spiritually and in God, and be judges over seats and power and all might, here and hereafter; for they have more knowledge than all the learned and the mighty. How this is done was said above under the first work and need not be repeated. All this is said for the comfort of the suffering and for the terror of the tyrants, if we only had faith enough to believe that it is true.

The fifth and sixth works

Luke 1:53
He has filled the hungry with good things, and the rich He has sent empty away.

We said above that by those of low degree are meant not those who are despised and nothing in appearance, but those who are willing to be in such a state, especially if they have been forced into it for the sake of God's Word or the right. Even so, by the hungry are not meant those who have little or nothing to eat, but those who gladly suffer want, especially if they are forcibly compelled by others to do so for the sake of God or the truth. Who is lowlier, more despised, and needier than the devil and the damned, or than men who are tortured, starved, or slain on account of their evil deeds, or all who are lowly and in want against their will? Yet that does not help them but only adds to their misery. Of them the mother of God does not speak, but of those who are one with God and God with them, and who believe and trust in Him. . . .

But our wretched unbelief always hinders God from working such works in us, and ourselves from experiencing and knowing them. We desire to be filled and have plenty of everything before hunger and want arrive. We lay up provision against future hunger and need, so that we no longer have need of God and His works. What sort of faith is that which trusts in God when all the while you feel and know that you have goods laid up to help yourself? It is because of our unbelief that we see God's Word, the truth, and the right defeated and wrong triumph and yet remain silent, do not rebuke, speak out, or prevent it, but let things go as they will. Why? We are afraid that we, too, might be attacked and made poor and might then perish of hunger and be forever laid low. That is to esteem temporal goods more than God and to put them in God's place as an idol. If we do this, we do not deserve to hear or to understand this comfortable promise of God: that He exalts the lowly, puts down the mighty, fills the poor, and empties the rich. We do not deserve ever to come to the knowledge of His works, without which there is no salvation. We must therefore be damned forever, as Ps. 28:5 says: "Because they do not regard the works of the Lord or the work of His hand, He will break them down and build them up no more."

And this is only fair, because they do not believe His promises but count Him a fickle, lying God. They dare not venture or begin anything on the strength of His words, so little do they esteem His truth. It is indeed necessary that we make a trial and venture out on His words; for Mary does not say that He has filled the full and exalted those of high degree, but: "He has filled the hungry and exalted those of low degree." You must feel the pinch of poverty in the midst of your hunger and learn by experience what hunger and poverty are, with no provision on hand and no help in yourself or any other man, but in God only, so that the work may be God's alone and impossible to be done by any other. You must not only think and speak of a low estate but actually come to be in a low estate and caught in it, without any human aid, so that God alone may do the work. Or if it should not come to such a pass, you must at least desire it and not shrink from it. We are Christians and have the Gospel, which neither the devil nor men can abide, in order that we may come into poverty and lowliness and God may thereby have His work in us.

Luke 1:54

He has helped His servant Israel in remembrance of His mercy.

After enumerating the works of God in her and in all men, Mary returns to the beginning and to the chief thing. She concludes the Magnificat by mentioning the very greatest of all God's works—the incarnation of the Son of God. She freely acknowledges herself as the handmaiden and servant of all the world, confessing that this work which was performed in her was not done for her sake alone, but for the sake of all Israel. But she divides Israel into two parts and refers only to that part that is God's servant. Now, no one is God's servant unless he lets Him be his God and perform His works in him, of which we spoke above. Alas, the word "service of God" has nowadays taken on so strange a meaning and usage that whoever hears it thinks not of these works of God, but rather of the ringing of bells, the wood and stone of churches, the incense pot, the flicker of candles, the mumbling in the churches, the gold, silver, and precious stones in the vestments of choirboys and celebrants, of chalices and monstrances, of organs and images, processions and churchgoing, and, most of all, the babbling of lips and the rattling of rosaries. This, alas, is what the service of God means now. Of such service God knows nothing at all, while we know nothing but this. We chant the Magnificat daily, to a special tone and with gorgeous pomp; and yet the more often we sing it, the more we silence its true music and meaning. Yet the text stands firm. Unless we learn and experience these works of God, there will be no service of God, no Israel, no grace, no mercy, no God, though we kill ourselves with singing and ringing in the churches and drag into them all the goods in all the world. God has not commanded any of these things; undoubtedly, therefore, He takes no pleasure in them.

Now, the Israel that is God's servant is the one whom the incarnation of Christ benefits. That is His own beloved people, for whose sake He also became man, to redeem them from the power of the devil, of sin, death, and hell, and to lead them to righteousness, eternal life, and salvation. That is the help of which Mary sings. As Paul says in Titus 2:14: "Christ gave Himself for us, to purify for Himself a people of His own"; and St. Peter in 1 Pet. 2:9: "You are a holy nation, a chosen people, a royal priesthood." These are the riches of the boundless mercy of God, which we have received by no merit but by pure grace. Therefore she sings: "He has remembered His mercy." She does not say: "He has remembered our merit and worthiness." We were in need, to be sure, but completely unworthy. That is the basis of His praise and glory, while our boasting and presumption must keep quiet. There was nothing for Him to regard that could move Him except His mercy, and this name He desired to make known. But why does she say "He remembered" rather than "He regarded"? Because He had promised this mercy, as the following verse shows. Now, He had waited a long time before showing it, until it seemed as though He had forgotten—even as all His works seem as though He were forgetting us—but when He came, it was seen that He had not forgotten but had continually had in mind to fulfill His promise.

Luke 1:55

As He spoke to our fathers, to Abraham, and to his seed forever.

Here all merit and presumption are brought low, and God's grace and mercy alone are exalted. For God has not helped Israel on account of their merits, but on account of His own promise. In pure grace He made the promise; in pure grace He also fulfilled it. Wherefore St. Paul says in Gal. 3:17 that God gave the promise to Abraham four hundred years before He gave the Law to Moses, that no one might glory, saying he had merited and obtained such grace and promise through the Law or the works of the Law. This same promise the mother of God here lauds and exalts above all else, ascribing this work of the incarnation of God solely to the undeserved promise of divine grace made to Abraham.

The promise of God to Abraham is recorded especially in Gen. 12:3 and Gen. 22:18, and is referred to in many other places besides. It runs thus: "By Myself I have sworn: in your Seed shall all families or nations of the earth be blessed." These words are highly esteemed by St. Paul (Gal. 3:16) and by all the prophets, and well might they be. For in these words Abraham and all his descendants were preserved and saved, and in them we, too, must all be saved; for here Christ is contained and promised as the Savior of the whole world. This is Abraham's bosom (Luke 16:22), in which were kept all who were saved before Christ's birth; without these words no one was saved, even though he had performed all good works. Let us examine them more fully.

In the first place, it follows from these words of God that without Christ all the world is in sin and under condemnation and is accursed with all its doing and knowing. For if He says that not some but all nations shall be blessed in Abraham's Seed, then without Abraham's Seed no nation shall be blessed. What need was there for God to promise so solemnly and with so mighty an oath, that He would bless them, if they were already blessed and not rather cursed? From this saying the prophets drew many inferences, namely, that all men are evil, liars all, false and blind, in short, without God, so that in the scriptural usage to be called a man is no great honor, since in God's sight the name "man" is no better than the name "liar" or "faithless" in the eyes of the world. So completely is man corrupted through Adam's fall that the curse is innate with him and become, as it were, his nature and being.

It follows, in the second place, that this Seed of Abraham could not be born in the common course of nature, of a man and a woman; for such a birth is cursed and results in nothing but accursed seed, as we have just said. Now, if all the world was to be redeemed from the curse by this Seed of Abraham and thereby blessed, as the word and oath of God declare, the Seed itself had to be blessed first, neither touched nor tainted by that curse, but pure blessing, full of grace and truth (John 1:14). Again, if God, who cannot lie, declared with an oath that it should be Abraham's natural seed, that is, a natural and genuine child, born of his flesh and blood, then this Seed had to be a true, natural man, of the flesh and blood of Abraham. Here, then, we have a contradiction—the natural flesh and blood of Abraham, and yet not born in the course of nature, of man and wife. Therefore He uses the word "your seed," not "your child," to make it very clear and certain that it should be his natural flesh and blood, such as seed is. For a child need not be one's natural child, as everyone knows. Now, who will find the means to establish God's Word and oath, where such contradictory things lie side by side?

God Himself has done this thing. He is able to keep what He has promised, even though no one may understand it before it comes to pass; for His Word and work do not demand the proof of reason, but a free and pure faith. Behold, how He combined the two. He raises up seed for Abraham, the natural Son of one of his daughters, a pure virgin, Mary, through the Holy Spirit, and without her knowing a man. Here there was no natural conception with its curse, nor could it touch this Seed; and yet it is the natural seed of Abraham, as truly as any of the other children of Abraham. That is the blessed Seed of Abraham, in whom all the world is set free from its curse. For whoever believes in this Seed, calls upon Him, confesses Him, and abides in Him, to him all his curse is forgiven and all blessing given, as the Word and oath of God declare—"In your Seed shall all the nations of the earth be blessed." That is to say: "Whatever is to be blessed must and shall be blessed through this Seed, and in no other way." This is Abraham's Seed, begotten by none of his sons, as the Jews always confidently expected, but born of this one daughter of his, Mary, alone.

That is what the tender mother of this Seed means here by saying: "He has helped His servant Israel, as He promised to Abraham and to all his seed." She found the promise fulfilled in herself; hence she says: "It is now fulfilled; He has brought help and kept His word, solely in remembrance of His mercy." Here we have the foundation of the Gospel and see why all its teaching and preaching drive men to faith in Christ and into Abraham's bosom. For where there is not this faith, no other way can be devised and no help given to lay hold of this blessed Seed. And indeed, the whole Bible depends on this oath of God, for in the Bible everything has to do with Christ. Furthermore, we see that all the fathers in the Old Testament, together with all the holy prophets, had the same faith and Gospel as we have, as St. Paul says in 1 Cor. 10:1–4; for they all remained with a strong faith in this oath of God and in Abraham's bosom and were preserved in it. The sole difference is, they believed in the coming and promised Seed; we believe in the Seed that has come and has been given. But it is all the one truth of the promise, and hence also one faith, one Spirit, one Christ, one Lord (Eph. 4:5), now as then, and forever, as Paul says in Heb. 13:8.

But the subsequent giving of the Law to the Jews is not on a par with this promise. The Law was given in order that by its light they might the better come to know their cursed state and the more fervently and heartily desire the promised Seed; in this they had an advantage over all the heathen world. But they turned this advantage into a disadvantage; they undertook to keep the Law by their own strength, and failed to learn from it their needy and cursed state. Thus they shut the door upon themselves, so that the Seed was compelled to pass them by. They still continue in this state, but God grant not for long. Amen. This was the cause of the quarrel all the prophets had with them. For the prophets well understood the purpose of the Law, namely, that men should thereby know their accursed nature and learn to call upon Christ. Hence they condemned all the good works and everything in the life of the Jews that did not agree with this purpose. Therefore the Jews became angry with them and put them to death as men who condemned the service of God, good works, and godly living; even as the hypocrites and graceless saints ever do, of which we might say a great deal.

When Mary says, "His seed forever," we are to understand "forever" to mean that such grace is to continue to Abraham's seed (that is, the Jews) from that time forth, throughout all time, down to the Last Day. Although the vast majority of them are hardened, yet there are always some, however few, that are converted to Christ and believe in Him. For this promise of God does not lie: the promise was made to Abraham and to his seed, not for one year or for a thousand years, but "for the ages," that is, from one generation to another, without end. We ought, therefore, not to treat the Jews in so unkindly a spirit, for there are future Christians among them, and they are turning every day. Moreover, they alone, and not we Gentiles, have this promise, that there shall always be Christians among Abraham's seed, who acknowledge the blessed Seed, who knows how or when? As for our cause, it rests upon pure grace, without a promise of God. If we lived Christian lives, and led them with kindness to Christ, there would be the proper response. Who would desire to become a Christian when he sees Christians dealing with men in so unchristian a spirit? Not so, my dear Christians. Tell them the truth in all kindness; if they will not receive it, let them go. How many Christians are there who despise Christ, do not hear His Word, and are worse than Jews or heathen! Yet we leave them in peace and even fall down at their feet and well-nigh adore them as gods. Let this suffice for the present. We pray God to give us a right understanding of this Magnificat, an understanding that consists not merely in brilliant words but in glowing life in body and soul. May Christ grant us this through the intercession and for the sake of His dear mother, Mary! Amen.

Sermons on the First Epistle of St. Peter 1522

While at the Wartburg, news of unrest in Wittenberg came to Martin Luther. Dressed as a knight and traveling under the name of Junker Jörg, Luther secretly visited Wittenberg in early December and met with Philip Melanchthon and others. By mid-December he was back at the Wartburg and hard at work on translating the New Testament into German—a task he completed in less than eleven weeks. As unrest in Wittenberg escalated, Luther determined—against the wishes of Elector Frederick the Wise—to return to Wittenberg for good. The imperial ban placed upon Luther after the Diet of Worms meant he was an outlaw. To appear in public at Wittenberg threatened his own safety and created significant political difficulties for the elector.

The circumstances of Luther's return prevented him from resuming his classroom lectures. His chief activity at this time was preaching. It is through his sermons that Luther introduced the people of Wittenberg to the Reformation and to an evangelical life of faith. On Sunday morning Luther preached the appointed Gospel lesson, and in the afternoon he preached through individual books of the Bible. The first book Luther chose was the First Epistle of Peter. His choice was not accidental. Luther had been engaged in a protracted debate with Jerome Emser (1478–1527)—the "goat of Leipzig," as Luther was fond of calling him—concerning church and ministry and particularly the priesthood of all believers (1 Pet. 2:9).[1] *Luther's sermons on First Peter allowed him to address these disputed issues of the day from the pulpit for the people at Wittenberg.*

Luther emphasizes two themes throughout his sermons. First, he shows at length and with great clarity the relationship between faith and good works. If we are justified by faith apart from works, do works matter? Are they necessary? For Luther, faith works, and it does so automatically and unbidden. Moreover, for Luther, faith works in the places God calls us. We do not manufacture works for God; rather, we serve our neighbors in our divinely appointed vocations.

1 For a detailed account of this debate and for Luther's writings against Emser, see LW 39:105–238.

Luther's second theme focuses on biblical interpretation. In his introduction to the Epistle, he distinguishes the Gospel as a theological term, as proclamation of the saving work of Christ for us, from the four Gospels of Matthew, Mark, Luke, and John. Luther further explains the unity and diversity of the Scriptures. Although each apostle retains his own distinctive literary style, they all preach one and the same Gospel. Luther's opening reflection shows the reader how to distinguish between the good news of what God has done for us from what God commands us to do. Further, the reader of Scripture should not be misled by the differing literary styles of Peter and Paul. Their evangelical substance remains the same.

Luther traces out these two themes throughout his sermons on First Peter. In the excerpts below, Luther discusses at length the relationship between the Old and New Testament and between faith and works. Here we find Luther's well-known discussion of the priesthood of all believers. He explains what it means for believers to be royal priests who offer spiritual sacrifices and proclaim the wonderful deeds of God.

Finally, the life of faith is a life of service to our neighbors, and this involves suffering. Luther shows how Christ is both our gift and example. We lay hold of Christ as gift by faith and receive the free forgiveness of our sins. This, explains Luther, is the chief article and best part of the Gospel. We also receive Christ as an example and pattern to follow. We imitate Him in our life and in our suffering.

Sermons on the First Epistle of St. Peter[2]

Before we take up St. Peter's Epistle, it is necessary for us to say a few words by way of instruction. One must know how this Epistle is to be regarded, and one must get a proper understanding of it.

First of all, we must realize that all the apostles teach one and the same doctrine, and that it is incorrect to speak of four evangelists and four gospels; for everything the apostles wrote is one Gospel. And the word "Gospel" signifies nothing else than a sermon or report concerning the grace and mercy of God merited and acquired through the Lord Jesus Christ with His death. Actually, the Gospel is not what one finds in books and what is written in letters of the alphabet; it is, rather, an oral sermon and a living Word, a voice that resounds throughout the world and is

2 The following excerpt is adapted from *Sermons on the First Epistle of St. Peter*, in volume 29 of *Luther's Works: American Edition*, ed. Jaroslav Pelikan and Walter A. Hansen, trans. Martin H. Bertram (St. Louis: Concordia, 1967). Minor alterations have been made to the text for consistency in style, abbreviations, and capitalization. The annotations and subheadings are the work of the editor of this book.

proclaimed publicly, so that one hears it everywhere. Therefore it is not a book of laws that contains many good teachings, as it has been regarded in the past. It does not tell us to do good works to make us pious, but it announces to us the grace of God bestowed gratis and without our merit, and tells us how Christ took our place, rendered satisfaction for our sins, and destroyed them, and that He makes us pious and saves us through His work.

Now he who preaches these facts and writes about them teaches the true Gospel, just as all the apostles, particularly St. Paul and St. Peter, do in their Epistles. Therefore what is preached about Christ is all one Gospel, although every writer has his own distinctive literary style. The discussion may be short or long and may be presented briefly or at some length. But whenever it deals with Christ as our Savior and states that we are justified and saved through faith in Him without our works, then there is one Word and one Gospel, just as there is but one faith and one Baptism (Eph. 4:5) in all Christendom.

Thus one apostle has recorded the same things that are found in the writings of the other. But those who stress most frequently and above all how nothing but faith in Christ justifies are the best evangelists. Therefore St. Paul's Epistles are Gospel to a greater degree than the writings of Matthew, Mark, and Luke. For the latter do little more than relate the history of the deeds and miracles of Christ. But no one stresses the grace we have through Christ so valiantly as St. Paul does, especially in his Epistle to the Romans. Now since greater value attaches to the words of Christ than to His works and deeds—and if we had to dispense with one or the other, it would be better for us to do without the deeds and the history than to be without the words and the doctrine—those books that treat mainly of Christ's teaching and words should in all conscience be esteemed most highly. For even if Christ's miracles were nonexistent, and if we knew nothing about them, His words would be enough for us. Without them we could not have life.

Accordingly, this Epistle of St. Peter is also one of the noblest books in the New Testament; it is the genuine and pure Gospel. For St. Peter does the same thing that St. Paul and all the evangelists do; he teaches the true faith and tells us that Christ was given to us to take away our sin and to save us, as we shall hear.

On this basis you can now determine concerning all books and doctrines what is and what is not Gospel. For with regard to what is not preached or written in this way you may freely judge that it is false, no matter how good it seems to be. All Christians have this power to judge, not the pope or the councils, who boast that they alone have the power to judge doctrine. Let this suffice as introduction and foreword. Now we want to hear the Epistle.

1 Peter 1:1–2

Peter, an apostle of Jesus Christ.

This is the superscription and the signature. Here you see at once that this is the Gospel. St. Peter states that he is an apostle, that is, a messenger. . . . Thus St. Peter wants to say: I am an apostle of Jesus Christ; that is, Jesus Christ has commanded me to preach about Christ. Take note that all who preach human doctrines are immediately excluded. For he who carries out what Christ has commanded is a messenger of Jesus Christ. If he preaches anything else, he is not a messenger of Christ. Therefore we should not listen to him. But if he preaches what Christ has commanded, this is no different from hearing Christ Himself in person.

To the exiles.

. . . The exiles are people whom we call foreigners. St. Peter calls them exiles because they were heathen. It is surprising that while St. Peter was an apostle to the Jews, he is nevertheless writing here to the heathen. The Jews called them proselytes, that is, converts to Judaism and its Law but not of the Jewish house and blood of Abraham. Accordingly, he is writing to those who had formerly been heathen but had now been converted to the faith and had joined the believing Jews. He calls them chosen foreigners who surely are Christians. He writes only to these. This is an important point, as we shall hear.

Chosen and destined by God the Father.

St. Peter declares that they are chosen. How? Not by themselves but according to God's arrangement. For we shall not be able to bring ourselves to heaven or to create faith in ourselves. God will not admit all men to heaven; He will count His own very exactly. Now the human doctrine of free will and of our own powers no longer amounts to anything. Our will is unimportant; God's will and choosing are decisive.

And sanctified by the Spirit.

God has predestined us to be holy, and in such a way that we become spiritually holy. The belly-preachers have also perverted the precious words "holy" and "spiritual" for us; they have called their priestly and monastic estate holy and spiritual. So shamefully have they abused this dear and noble name. They have done the same thing with the name "church" by asserting that the pope and the bishops are the church. When they willfully do what they please, they say that the church has commanded it. Holiness does not consist in being a monk, priest, or nun, in wearing tonsures and cowls. It is a spiritual word which states that inwardly we are sincerely holy in the spirit before God. And his real reason for making this statement was to point out that nothing is holy but the holiness that God works in us. For at that time the Jews had much external holiness, but this was not a true holiness. Therefore St. Peter means: God has chosen you to be truly holy. Thus in Eph. 4:24 St. Paul also speaks of being "in true righteousness and holiness," that is, in a genuine and completely good holiness; for the external holiness of the Jews has no validity before God.

Thus Scripture calls us holy while we are still living here on earth, if we believe. The Papists have taken this name away from us and say: "We should not be holy; only the saints in heaven are holy." Therefore we must get the noble name back. You must be holy. But you must be prepared not to think that you are holy of yourself or on the strength of your merit. No, you must be holy because you have the Word of God, because heaven is yours, and because you have become truly pious and holy through Christ. This you must avow if you want to be a Christian. For it would be the greatest slander and blasphemy of the name of Christ if we refused to honor Christ's blood for washing away our sin or refused to believe that this blood makes us holy. Hence you must believe and confess that you are holy, but by this blood and not by reason of your own piety. Therefore you must be willing to surrender life and all possessions for this and to face whatever may be your lot on this account.

For obedience to Jesus Christ and for sprinkling with His blood.

With these words St. Peter says that we become holy if we obey and believe the Word of Christ and are sprinkled with His blood. He expresses himself differently from St. Paul. But the purport is identical with Paul's declaration that we are saved through faith in Christ. For faith makes us obedient and subject to Christ and His Word. Therefore to be submissive to the Word of God and Christ and to be sprinkled with His blood is the same as believing. For it is difficult for nature to submit completely to Christ and to desist from all its doings, despise them, and regard them as sin; it struggles against this and tortures itself in the process. Yet it must surrender itself.

The psalm *Miserere* also speaks of this sprinkling. "Purge me with hyssop," it says, "and I shall be clean" (Ps. 51:7). This alludes to the Law of Moses, from which St. Peter took this expression. He wants to uncover Moses for us (2 Cor. 3:14) and lead us into Scripture. When Moses built the tabernacle, he took the blood of goats and sprinkled the tabernacle and all the people, as Exod. 24:6, 8 says (cf. Heb. 9:19). But the sprinkling does not sanctify in the spirit; this is only an external sanctification. Consequently, there must be a spiritual purification (Heb. 9:13–14). The former was a fleshly and external holiness that does not avail before God. Therefore with this sprinkling God typified the spiritual sprinkling. Accordingly, Peter says: The Jews are outwardly holy; in the eyes of the people they are pious and lead a respectable life, while you are regarded as wicked. But you have a better sprinkling; you are sprinkled in the spirit, in order that you may be pure inwardly. The Jews sprinkled themselves externally with the blood of goats. We, however, are sprinkled inwardly in our conscience, so that the heart becomes clean and glad.

Thus the heathen are no longer heathen. The pious Jews, with their sprinkling, are no longer pious. Now the situation is reversed. There must be a sprinkling which converts us and makes us spiritual. But to sprinkle means to preach that Christ shed His blood, intercedes for us before His Father, and says: "Dear Father, here Thou seest My blood, which I shed for this sinner." If you believe this, you are sprinkled. Then you know the right way to preach. If all the popes, monks, and priests were to melt what they do and say into one big pile, they could not teach and accomplish as much as St. Peter does here with a few words.

This is the signature St. Peter appends to this chapter, in which he tells what his office is and what he preaches, as we have heard. Therefore only this is the Gospel. Everything not in agreement with this must be trodden underfoot, and you must forswear all other books where you find beautiful titles dealing with works, prayers, and indulgences—books that do not teach the Gospel and are not obviously founded on it. All the papistic books do not contain one letter about this obedience, about this blood and sprinkling. Now comes the greeting to those to whom Peter is writing.

May grace and peace be multiplied to you.

Here St. Peter's greeting is almost like the one used by the apostle Paul. He means: You now have peace and grace, but not yet in perfect measure. Therefore you must grow constantly until the old Adam dies completely. Grace is God's goodwill. It begins in us now, but it must continue to be active and grow until we die. And he who realizes and believes that he has a gracious God, he has Him. Then his heart gains peace, and he fears neither the world nor the devil. For he knows that God, who is omnipotent, is his friend and will rescue him from death, hell, and all adversity. Therefore his conscience has peace and joy. This is what St. Peter wishes for the believers, and this is a true Christian greeting. All Christians should greet one another in this way. Thus we have the superscription and the greeting.

1 Peter 1:3–9

Blessed be the God and Father of our Lord Jesus Christ! By His great mercy we have been born anew.

In this foreword you see a truly apostolic speech and an introduction to the theme. It bears out what I said earlier, namely, that this Epistle is a paragon of excellence. For here St. Peter begins without further ado to tell us what Christ is and what we have acquired through Him. He says that by God's mercy "we have been born anew to a living hope through the resurrection of Jesus Christ from the dead." He also says that everything has been given to us by the Father out of pure mercy and without any merit on our part. These are genuinely evangelical words. They must be proclaimed. God help us, how little preaching of this kind one finds in all the books, even in those that are said to be the best, as, for example, the writings of St. Jerome and St. Augustine![3] How little they have in common with these words! Therefore one must preach about Jesus Christ that He died and rose from the dead, and why He died and rose again, in order that people may come to faith through such preaching and be saved through faith. This is what it means to preach the genuine Gospel. Preaching of another kind is not the Gospel, no matter who does it.

These words can be summarized by saying that through His resurrection Christ has led us to the Father. Here St. Peter wants to lead us to the Father through the Lord Christ and sets Him up as the Mediator between God and us. Up to now preachers have told us to call upon the saints in order that they may be our intercessors before God. Then we hied ourselves to Our Dear Lady, made her our mediatrix, and let Christ remain an angry judge. Scripture does not do this; it insists on going to the truth of the matter and praises the Lord Christ as our Mediator through whom we must come to the Father. Oh, what an inestimable blessing has been given to us through Christ! It enables us to step before the Father and to demand the inheritance of which St. Peter speaks here.

These words point out what the apostle had in mind by beginning to praise the Father with such great devotion and asking us to laud and bless Him because of the inestimable riches He conferred on us by bringing about our rebirth, and by doing so before we thought of or expected such a thing. Here there is nothing to praise but sheer mercy. Therefore we can boast of no works, but we must confess that everything we have

3 Jerome (ca. 345–420) was a gifted translator, biblical scholar, and historian. He translated many books of the Bible into Latin from Hebrew and Greek, produced numerous biblical commentaries, and compiled a widely used bibliography of the apostles and early Christian and Jewish writers. See also below, p. 420 n. 5. On Augustine, see above, p. 4 n. 1.

is ours because of pure mercy. No longer does the Law or God's wrath frighten us as the Jews were terrified when they had to flee and did not dare approach the mountain (Exod. 19:16; 20:19). No longer does God drive and smite us. No, He deals with us in the friendliest manner possible and renews us. He does not give us the ability to do one work or two but brings about a completely new birth and a new existence in us, so that we become something different from what we were before, when we were the children of Adam. This means that He has transplanted us from the inheritance of Adam into the inheritance of God, so that God is our Father and we are His children and thus also heirs of all His blessings. Note how thoroughly Scripture deals with this. Everything is alive. We are not dealing with unnecessary words here. Since we are now born anew and are God's children and heirs, we become equal in honor and glory with St. Paul, St. Peter, Our Dear Lady, and all the saints; for we possess the treasure and all the blessings from God as richly as they do. For they had to be born anew, just as we did. Therefore they have no more than all Christians have.

To a living hope through the resurrection of Jesus Christ from the dead.

We have no other reason for living on earth than to be of help to others. If this were not the case, it would be best for God to kill us and let us die as soon as we are baptized and have begun to believe. But He permits us to live here in order that we may bring others to faith, just as He brought us. But as long as we are on earth, we must live in hope. For although we are sure that we have all the blessings of God through faith—for faith is surely accompanied for you by the new birth, the filial relationship, and the inheritance—we do not yet see this. It is still something to be hoped for and still somewhat remote. We cannot see it with our eyes. St. Peter calls this the hope of life. This is a Hebrew way of speaking, as if one said in Latin *homo peccati*, "a man of sin." We speak of a living hope, that is, a hope in which we may hope with certainty and be sure of eternal life. But this is still concealed. It is still covered with a cloth. One does not see it. At present it can be grasped only with the heart and through faith, as St. John says in 1 John 3:2: "Beloved, we are God's children; it does not yet appear what we shall be, but we know that when He appears, we shall be like Him; for we shall see Him as He is." For this life and the life to come are mutually exclusive and cannot exist together in such a way that we eat, drink, sleep, wake, and do other natural things of this life and are in heaven at the same time. We cannot enter into eternal life unless we have died and this life passes away. Therefore we must be in hope while we are here and until God wants us to see the blessings we have.

But how do we attain the living hope? Peter says that we do so "through the resurrection of Jesus Christ from the dead." I have often said that no one should believe in God without employing means. Therefore we cannot deal with God on our own initiative, for we are all children of wrath (Eph. 2:3). We must have someone else through whom we can come before God—someone to represent us and to reconcile us with God. And there is no other Mediator than the Lord Christ, who is the Son of God. Therefore the faith of the Jews and the Turks is false. They say: "I believe that God created heaven and earth." The devil believes the same thing (cf. James 2:19), but it does not help him. For the Jews and the Turks have the audacity to come before God without Christ the Mediator.

St. Paul states in Rom. 5:2: "We have obtained access to God in faith"—not through ourselves but "through Christ." Therefore we must bring Christ, come with Him, pay God with Him, and carry out all our dealings with God through Him and with Him. This is what St. Peter means here. He wants to say: We are looking forward with certainty to life, even though we are still on earth. But we owe all this to Christ's resurrection from the dead, to His ascension into heaven, and to the fact that He sits at the right hand of God. For He ascended into heaven to bestow His Spirit on us, to give us a new birth, and to give us the courage to come to the Father and say: "Behold, I come before You and pray, not in reliance on my petition, but my Lord Christ represents me and is my Intercessor." These are all words of fire where there is a heart that believes. Otherwise everything is cold and does not go to the heart.

But from this one can judge what true Christian doctrine or preaching is. For when one wants to preach the Gospel, one must treat only of the resurrection of Christ. He who does not preach this is no apostle. For this is the chief article of our faith. And those books that teach and stress this most are indeed the noblest books, as has been stated above. This enables one to observe that the Epistle of James is no truly apostolic Epistle, for it does not contain a single word about these things.[4] The greatest power of faith is bound up in this article of faith. For if there were no resurrection, we would have no consolation or hope, and everything else Christ did and suffered would be futile (1 Cor. 15:17).

4 *Preface to the New Testament* (1522, 1546), LW 35:362–63: "In a word St. John's Gospel and his First Epistle, St. Paul's Epistles, especially Romans, Galatians, and Ephesians, and St. Peter's First Epistle are the books that show you Christ and teach you all that is necessary and salvatory for you to know, even if you were never to see or hear any other book or doctrine. Therefore St. James' Epistle is really an epistle of straw, compared to these others, for it has nothing of the nature of the Gospel about it." Cf. *Preface to James and Jude* (1522, 1546), LW 35:395–98.

Therefore one must teach as follows: "Behold, Christ died for you! He took sin, death, and hell upon Himself and submitted Himself. But nothing could subdue Him, for He was too strong; He rose from the dead, was completely victorious, and subjected everything to Himself. And He did all this in order that you might be free from it and lord over it. If you believe this, you have it. For we are not able to do all this with our own power. Consequently, Christ had to do it. Otherwise there would have been no need for Him to come down from heaven." When we preach about our works, it is impossible for this message to be accepted and understood. Oh, how well we Christians should be aware of this! How clear this Epistle should be to us!

And to an inheritance which is imperishable, undefiled, and unfading.

That is, we do not hope for a blessing or inheritance that does not exist. On the contrary, we live in the hope of an inheritance that does exist and is imperishable and also undefiled and unfading. This blessing is ours forever and ever, even though we do not see it now. These are powerful and extraordinary words. He who knows what they mean will, I think, not be greatly concerned about a temporal blessing and pleasure. How can anyone cling to a perishable blessing and to pleasure if he really believes this?

For if one compares the worldly blessing with this, one sees that the former passes away completely and lasts only for a time. Only the latter remains forever and is not consumed. Furthermore, the former is totally unclean and defiles us; for no one is so pious that the temporal blessing does not make him unclean. But this inheritance alone is pure. He who has it is forever undefiled. Nor does it fade, wither, and rot. Everything on earth is changeable, even if it is as hard as iron and stone; it lacks permanency. A human being is ugly as soon as he becomes old. But this inheritance does not change; it remains fresh and green forever. On earth no pleasure is so great that it does not become unpleasant as time goes on. We see that one becomes weary of everything. But this blessing is different. All this is ours in Christ, by God's mercy, if we believe. It is given to us gratis. For how could we poor people merit such a great blessing with our works? No human reason and intelligence can grasp it.

Kept in heaven for you.

This imperishable, undefiled, and unfading inheritance is surely ours. Only now it is hidden for a short time until we close our eyes and are buried. Then we shall certainly find and see it, if we believe.

Who by God's power are guarded through faith for a salvation.

St. Peter declares that we await the precious inheritance in the hope into which we have entered through faith. For this is the sequence: Faith follows from the Word, the new birth follows from faith, and from this birth we enter into the hope of looking forward to the blessing with certainty. Therefore Peter has stated here in a truly Christian manner that this must come to pass through faith and not through one's own works.

But in reality St. Peter says here: "You are guarded for salvation by the power of God." For there are many people who—when they hear the Gospel that faith alone, without any works, makes pious—plump in and say: "Yes, I, too, believe." They regard their own self-invented notions as faith. Now we have taught on the basis of Scripture that we are unable to perform even the slightest works without the Spirit of God. How, then, could we by our own strength perform the greatest work, namely, to believe? Therefore such notions are nothing else than a dream and fiction. God's power must be present and work faith in us, as Paul says in Eph. 1:17–19: "That God . . . may give you a spirit of wisdom . . . that you may know . . . what is the immeasurable greatness of His power in us who believe, according to the working of His great might." It is not only God's will but also His power to spend a great deal. For when God creates faith in man, this is as great a work as if He were to create heaven and earth again.

Therefore those fools do not know what they are saying when they declare: "Ah, how can faith alone do it? After all, many a person who does not perform a single good work believes." For they suppose that their own dream is faith and that faith can exist without good works. We, however, declare with Peter that faith is a power of God. Where God works faith, man must be born again and become a new creature. Then good works must follow from faith as a matter of course. Therefore one should not say to a believing Christian: "Do this or that work!" For he does good works automatically and unbidden. But he must be told not to be deluded by a false and imaginary faith. Therefore pay no attention to the windbags who can speak volubly about this yet talk nothing but nonsense and balderdash. Of these Paul says in 1 Cor. 4:19–20: "But I will come to you . . . and I will find out not the talk of these arrogant people but their power. For the kingdom of God does not consist in talk but in power." Now where this power of God is lacking, there can be no true faith and no good works. Therefore those people who boast of the Christian name and faith and yet lead an evil life are liars. If this were the power of God, they would be different.

But what does St. Peter mean when he says that you are guarded for salvation by the power of God? This is his meaning: The faith which works in us the power of God—which dwells in us and with which we are filled—is such a tender and precious thing that it gives us a true and clear understanding of everything that pertains to salvation, so that we are able to judge everything on earth and say: "This doctrine is right. That one is false. This life is right. That one is not. This work is good and well done. That one is evil." What such a person concludes is right and true; for he cannot be misled but is preserved and protected, and he remains a judge of all doctrine.

On the other hand, where faith and this power of God are lacking, there one finds nothing but error and blindness. There reason lets itself be led hither and thither from one work to another; for it would like to go to heaven by means of its works and always thinks: "Ah, this work will bring you to heaven! Do it, and you will be saved." This is why so many foundations, cloisters, altars, priests, monks, and nuns have arisen in the world. God lets unbelievers come into such blindness. But He keeps us believers in a proper understanding in order to save us and preserve us from damnation.

For a salvation ready to be revealed in the last time.

That is, the inheritance for which you are destined was acquired and prepared a long time ago, ever since the beginning of the world. But it is still hidden, is still covered, locked and sealed up. Yet in a short time it will be revealed and exposed to our view.

In this you rejoice, though now for a little while you may have to suffer various trials.

If you are a Christian and look forward to the inheritance or salvation, you must cling only to this goal, despise everything on earth, and acknowledge that all worldly reason, wisdom, and holiness are nothing. The world will not be able to tolerate this. Therefore you must be prepared to be condemned and persecuted. In this way St. Peter sums up faith, hope, and the holy cross; for one follows from the other.

And he also gives us consolation when we suffer and are persecuted. Your mourning will last for a short time. Then you will rejoice, for salvation is already prepared for you. Therefore be patient in your suffering. This is true Christian consolation. It does not comfort as the teachings of men do. They seek no more than how to find help for external misfortune. St. Peter says: I am not speaking of physical comfort. The fact that you must have outward misfortune does no harm. Go ahead boldly, and stand firm. Do not think that you will be rid of misfortune, but think as follows: "My inheritance is already prepared and at hand. My suffering will last but a short while. Then it will cease." Thus one must lay the temporal consolation aside and oppose to it the eternal comfort which we have in God.

Furthermore, one must note that the apostle says: "You may have to suffer." Later, in the third chapter, he will say: "If that should be God's will" (v. 17). Many want to take heaven by storm and would like to enter at once. Therefore they impose a cross on themselves at their own discretion. After all, reason always wants to extol only its own works. God does not want this. We should not choose our own works, but we should wait to see what God imposes on us and sends for us, in order that we may go and follow as He leads us. Therefore you need not run after it yourself. If it is to be, that is, if God disposes that you must suffer, accept it, and console yourself with bliss that is eternal, not temporal.

So that the genuineness of your faith, more precious than gold which though perishable is tested by fire, may redound to praise and glory and honor at the revelation of Jesus Christ. Without having seen Him, you love Him; though you do not now see Him, you believe in Him.

It is the purpose of the cross and adversities of all kinds to enable one to differentiate between the false and the true faith. God afflicts us in this way in order that our faith may be proved and made manifest before the world, with the result that others are attracted to the faith and we are praised and extolled. For God will praise, extol, and honor us as we praise Him. Then the false hypocrites, who do not approach the cross and adversities in the proper way, will necessarily be put to shame.

All Scripture compares temptation to fire. Thus here St. Peter also likens the gold that is tested by fire to the testing of faith by temptation and suffering. Fire does not impair the quality of gold, but it purifies it, so that all alloy is removed. Thus God has imposed the cross on all Christians to cleanse and to purge them well, in order that faith may remain pure, just as the Word is, so that one adheres to the Word alone and relies on nothing else. For we really need such purging and affliction every day because of the coarse old Adam.

It is characteristic of a Christian life to improve constantly and to become purer. When we come to faith through the preaching of the Gospel, we become pious and begin to be pure. But as long as we are still in the flesh, we can never become completely pure. For this reason God throws us right into the fire, that is, into suffering, disgrace, and misfortune. In this way we are purged more and more until we die. No works can do this for us. For how can an external work cleanse the heart inwardly? But when faith is tested in this way, all alloy and everything false must disappear. Then, when Christ is revealed, splendid honor, praise, and glory will follow. Therefore Peter continues:

You believe in Him and rejoice with unutterable and exalted joy. As the outcome of your faith you obtain the salvation of your souls.

St. Peter says that unutterable and exalted joy will redound to honor and glory. The world has the kind of joy which results in nothing but dishonor and of which one must be ashamed. Here St. Peter has spoken clearly of the joy that is to come, and in Scripture there is hardly another verse like this one about the future joy. Yet St. Peter cannot express it.

This is a part of the foreword, in which the apostle has pointed out what faith in Christ is and how this faith must be proved and become pure through the adversities and the sufferings which God sends us. And now we hear how this faith is recorded and promised in Scripture.

1 Peter 1:10–12

Here St. Peter refers us to Holy Scripture in order that we may see there how God keeps His promise not because of any merit on our part but out of pure grace. For it is the purpose of all Scripture to tear us away from our works and to bring us to faith. And it is necessary for us to study Scripture well in order to become certain of faith. Thus St. Paul also leads us into Scripture when he says in Rom. 1:2 that God promised the Gospel "beforehand through His prophets in the Holy Scriptures." And in Rom. 3:21 he says that the Law and the prophets bear witness to the faith through which one is justified.

In Acts 17:2ff. we read that Paul preached the faith to the Thessalonians, led them into Scripture, and expounded it to them, and that they returned to Scripture every day and searched to see whether his teachings were in agreement with it (v. 11). Therefore we must do the same thing. We must go back to the Old Testament and learn to prove the New Testament from the Old. There we shall see the promise concerning Christ, as Christ Himself declares in John 5:39: "You search the Scriptures . . . and it is they that bear witness to Me." Likewise (v. 46): "If you believed Moses, you would believe Me; for he wrote of Me."

Therefore we must ignore the good-for-nothing babblers who despise the Old Testament and say that it is no longer necessary; for we must derive from it alone the basis of our faith. For God sent the prophets to the Jews to bear witness to the Christ who was to come. Consequently, the apostles also convicted the Jews everywhere from their own Scriptures and proved that this was the Christ.

Thus the books of Moses and the prophets are also Gospel, since they proclaimed and described in advance what the apostles preached or wrote later about Christ. But there is a difference. For although both have been put on paper word for word, the Gospel, or the New Testament, should really not be written but should be expressed with the living voice which resounds and is heard throughout the world. The fact that it is also written is superfluous. But the Old Testament is only put in writing. Therefore it is called "a letter." Thus the apostles call it Scripture; for it only pointed to the Christ who was to come. But the Gospel is a living sermon on the Christ who has come.

Furthermore, there is also a difference among the books of the Old Testament. First, the five Books of Moses are the chief part of Scripture. They are actually what is meant by the Old Testament. Then come histories and historical books. They contain all kinds of examples of those who either kept or did not keep the Law of Moses. In the third place, we have the prophets. They are based on Moses and have enlarged on and explained the writings of Moses more clearly. But Moses and all the prophets have one purpose.

The statement that the Old Testament has been abolished and cast aside must be understood in the following way: In the first place, the difference between the Old and the New Testament, as we have just stated, is this, that the former pointed to Christ, while the New Testament now gives us what was promised and prefigured in the Old Testament. Therefore the figures are now done away with, for they have served their purpose and have accomplished and fulfilled all that they promised. Henceforth no distinction is to be made of food, clothing, place, and time. Everything is the same in Christ, to whom all was directed. The Jews were not saved through the Old Testament, for it was not given to them to make them pious; it was given to foreshadow for them the Christ who was to come.

Furthermore, in the Old Testament God carried on a twofold government: external and internal. He determined to rule the people Himself, both inwardly and outwardly—inwardly in their hearts and outwardly in their bodies and their property. This explains why He gave them so many kinds of laws mingled together. Thus it was an instance of physical government when a husband could give his wife a bill of divorce and send her out of his house if he did not want her (Deut. 24:1). But the commandment which says: "You shall love your neighbor as yourself" (Lev. 19:18) is part of the spiritual government. Now, however, God reigns only spiritually in us through Christ. He executes the physical and external rule through the civil government. Therefore the external rule was abrogated when Christ came. Now God no longer assigns external persons, times, and places; but He governs us spiritually by means of the Word, so that we are lords over everything external and are not bound to anything physical. What belongs to the spiritual government, however, has not been repealed but always continues to be in force, as, for instance, the laws in Moses concerning the love for God and one's neighbor. God still wants these laws observed, and with this Law He will condemn all unbelievers.

In addition, the figures remained spiritual; that is, the spiritual meaning set forth by means of the external figures remained, although it was externally abolished. Thus the fact that a husband divorces his wife because of adultery is a figure and has a meaning which has now also been fulfilled spiritually. For in this way God also cast off the Jews and chose the heathen, because the Jews refused to believe in Christ. God does the same thing today. If a person refuses to walk in faith, He has him put out of the Christian congregation in order that he may change for the better.

The same thing is true of the law that after her husband's death a wife must take her husband's brother and bear him children, and that he must succeed to the name of his brother and come into his property (Deut. 25:5–6). Although this is no longer in force, or has really become a matter of choice, so that one may do or not do it without sinning, yet it is a figure that points to Christ. For Christ is our Brother. He died for us, ascended into heaven, and commanded us to make souls pregnant and fruitful through the Gospel. In this way we retain His name, succeed to His name, and also come into His property. Therefore I dare not boast of converting people, but I must ascribe all this to the Lord Christ. This is true of all other figures of the Old Testament. It would take too long to enumerate them.

Thus all that is not external in the Old Testament still stands. I mean everything the prophets say about faith and love. Therefore Christ also confirms this in Matt. 7:12: "Whatever you wish that men would do to you, do so to them; for this is the law and the prophets." In addition, Moses and the prophets bear witness to the Christ who is to come. If I, for instance, want to preach about Christ that He is the only Savior and that everyone must be saved through Him, I can choose the statement in Gen. 22:18: "In your Seed shall all the nations of the earth be blessed." I transform this into a living voice and say: "Through Christ, who is Abraham's Seed, all men must be blessed." From this it follows that we are all cursed and condemned in Adam. Therefore we must believe in the Seed if we want to escape condemnation. On such statements we must base our faith. We must let them stand in order that we may see in them how they testify of Christ for the strengthening of faith. This is what St. Peter means when he says:

The prophets who prophesied of the grace that was to be yours searched and inquired about this salvation.

This is the way Paul also speaks in Rom. 16:25–26. "According to the revelation of the mystery which was kept secret for long ages," he says, "but is now disclosed and through the prophetic writings is made known." Thus in the New Testament you find many statements taken from the prophets with which the apostles show that everything has happened as the prophets foretold. Thus Christ Himself shows this from the prophet Isaiah when He says in Matt. 11:5: "The blind receive their sight, and the lame walk, etc." It is as if He were saying: "Just as it is written there (cf. Isa. 35:5–6), so it is happening." We also read in Acts 9:22 about Paul and in Acts 18:28 about Apollos how they drove the Jews into a corner and proved from Scripture that this was the Christ. For what the prophets had proclaimed, all this now took place in the case of Christ. And in Acts 15:14ff. the apostles show how the Gospel had to be preached to the heathen in order that they might believe. All this proceeded and was accomplished in such a way that the Jews were convinced and had to admit that it was happening as Scripture had predicted.

They inquired what person or time was indicated by the Spirit of Christ within them.

St. Peter wants to say: Although the prophets had no knowledge of a fixed and definite time, they nevertheless indicated in general all the circumstances of time and place, as, for example, how Christ would suffer, how He would die, and how the heathen would believe in Him. Thus one could know for certain from the signs when the time had come. The prophet Daniel came close, yet he spoke vaguely about when Christ would suffer and die, when this or that would take place (Dan. 9:25–27). The Jews also had a definite prophecy that their kingdom would cease before the coming of Christ. But the day and the definite time when this would occur were not specified. For it was sufficient for them to have the certain knowledge that when this time came, Christ was not far away. Thus the prophet Joel also prophesied concerning the time of the coming of the Holy Spirit when he said: "And it shall come to pass afterward, that I will pour out My Spirit on all flesh" (2:28). St. Peter quotes this verse in Acts 2:17 and shows that Joel was speaking about that time and about definite persons.

From all this you see how painstakingly the apostles always pointed out the basis and the proof of their preaching and teaching. Today the councils and the pope come along and want to deal with us only without Scripture. They command us to believe them because we owe obedience to the church, and they threaten us with excommunication if we refuse to believe. The apostles were filled with the Holy Spirit and were certain that they had been sent by Christ and that they preached the true Gospel. Yet they humbled themselves and did not want to be believed unless they proved completely from Scripture that what they said was true. It was also their purpose to stop the mouths of the unbelievers, to prevent them from being able to bring up anything against what they preached. And we are expected to believe the stupid, uneducated persons who never preach one word of God and can do nothing else than cry out incessantly: "Indeed, the fathers could not err. This was settled long ago. Therefore one need not account for it." To be sure, we can prove from Scripture that no one is saved unless he believes in Christ. They cannot say anything against this. But they will not be able to adduce Scripture passages to prove their nonsense that he who does not fast on this or that day will be damned. Therefore we will not believe them, and we are not obligated to do so. Now St. Peter continues:

The Spirit of Christ within them when predicting the sufferings of Christ and the subsequent glory.

This can be taken to mean both Christ's and our sufferings. St. Paul also calls the sufferings of all Christians the sufferings of Christ (Col. 1:24). For just as faith, the name, the Word, and the work of Christ are mine by reason of my belief in Him, so His sufferings are also mine; for I suffer for His sake. Thus Christ's sufferings are fulfilled in the Christians every day until the end of the world.

In all our sufferings we take comfort in the knowledge that we have all these sufferings in common with Christ and that He regards all our sufferings as His own, as well as in the certainty that glory will immediately follow the suffering. But we must also know that just as Christ did not enter into His glory before His suffering, so we must also first bear the cross with Him. Then we shall also have joy with Him.

St. Peter declares that everything we preach today was clearly proclaimed and foretold in times past by the prophets because the Holy Spirit revealed it to them. The fact that we have so little understanding of the prophets today is the result of our inability to understand the language. In any case, they spoke clearly enough. Therefore those who are familiar with the language and have the Spirit of God, as all believers do, understand without any difficulty, since they know the purport of all Scripture. But if one does not understand their language and does not have the Spirit or Christian discernment, the prophets seem to be drunk and full of wine. Yet if one of these is lacking, the Spirit without the language is better than the language without Spirit. The prophets have a special way of speaking, but they mean exactly what the apostles preach; for both have said much about the suffering and the glory of Christ and of those who believe in Him. Thus David says of Christ in Ps. 22:6: "I am a worm, and no man." With these words he shows the depth of His abject humiliation in His suffering. David also writes of the afflictions of his people and the Christians in Ps. 44:22: "We are accounted as sheep for the slaughter."

It was revealed to them that they were serving not themselves but you, in the things which have now been announced to you by those who preached the good news to you through the Holy Spirit sent from heaven.

That is, it was sufficient for the prophets to know this. But for our sakes they handed it down to us, became our servants, and served us with it, in order that we might go to their school and learn it from them. Now we have a foundation, so that our faith becomes all the stronger and we can arm and defend ourselves against all false doctrine.

Things into which angels long to look.

Through the Holy Spirit, who descended on them from heaven, the apostles proclaimed to us great things of the kind the angels like to see. St. Peter orders us to close our eyes and see what the Gospel is. This will give us joy and delight. As yet we cannot see this with our physical eyes; but we must believe that we partake of and share in the righteousness, truth, blessedness, and all the good things God has. For since He gave us Christ, His only Son, the highest Good, He, through Him, also gives us all His good things, riches, and treasures, from which the angels in heaven derive all pleasure and joy. All this is offered to us in the Gospel; and if we believe, we necessarily take such joy in it. But while we are living on earth, our joy cannot be perfect like that of the angels. Through faith we are now beginning to feel some of it. In heaven, however, it is so great that no human heart can grasp it. But when we get there, we, too, shall feel it.

Thus you see how St. Peter teaches us to outfit and equip ourselves with Scripture. Up to this point he has been describing what it means to preach the Gospel, and how the prophets proclaimed beforehand that it was to happen and was to be preached this way. Now in this chapter he proceeds to admonish us to cling to this proclamation of the Gospel by faith and to follow up on it with our love.

1 Peter 1:13–16

This is an exhortation to faith. It means: Since things in which even the angels rejoice and which they are delighted to see have been proclaimed and given to you through the Gospel, cling to them and place full confidence in them, so that it is a genuine faith and not a colored or fictitious delusion and dream.

Gird up your minds.

Here Peter is speaking about a spiritual girding of the mind, just as one girds a sword physically to one's loins. Christ also touched on girding when He said: "Let your loins be girded" (Luke 12:35). In several places in Scripture the loins denote physical unchastity. But here St. Peter is speaking of spiritual loins. In a physical sense Scripture calls the loins the source of the natural descent from the father. Thus we read in Gen. 49:10 that Christ is to come from the loins of Judah. Thus the physical girding of the loins is nothing else than chastity, as Isa. 11:5 states: "Righteousness shall be the girdle of His waist, and faithfulness the girdle of His loins." That is, one suppresses and overcomes evil lust only through faith.

But the spiritual girding—of which the apostle is speaking here—takes place as follows: Just as a virgin is physically pure and blameless, so the soul is spiritually blameless because of faith, through which it becomes the bride of Christ. But if it falls from faith into false doctrine, it must go to ruin. For this reason Scripture consistently calls idolatry and unbelief adultery and whoring, that is, if the soul clings to the teachings of men and thus surrenders faith and Christ. St. Peter forbids this here when he tells us to gird the loins of the mind. It is as if he were saying: You have now heard the Gospel and have come to faith. Therefore see to it that you remain in faith and not be moved by false doctrine, that you do not waver and run hither and thither with works.

Here St. Peter adopts a peculiar expression—different from that of St. Paul—when he speaks of "the loins of your mind." He uses the word "mind" for what we mean when we speak of being minded, as if I said: "I regard this as right," or, as St. Paul expresses himself (Rom. 3:28), "We hold that"; that is, "So we are minded." With this he actually means faith and wants to say: "You have come to the proper understanding, namely, that one is justified by faith alone. Now cling to this understanding. Gird it well. Hold fast to it, and do not let anyone wrest it from you. Then all is well with you. For many false teachers will appear and will set up human doctrines, to take away your understanding and loosen the girdle of faith. Therefore be warned, and give careful thought to this." The hypocrites, who rely on their works and lead a fine moral life, think that God must take them to heaven because of their works. They become puffed up and arrogant. Like the Pharisee in Luke 18:11–12, they insist on their understanding and opinion. Mary speaks about them in the *Magnificat*, where she uses the same little word Peter employs here. She says: "He has scattered the proud in the imagination of their hearts" (Luke 1:51), that is, in their understanding.

Be sober.

Sobriety serves the body externally and is the chief work of faith. For even though man has become righteous, he is not yet completely rid of evil lusts. To be sure, faith has begun to subdue the flesh; but the flesh continues to bestir itself and rages nevertheless in all sorts of lusts that would like to assert themselves again and do what they want. Therefore the spirit must busy itself daily to tame the flesh and to bring it into subjection, must wrestle with it incessantly, and must take care that it does not repel faith. Therefore those who say that they have faith, think that this is enough, and, in addition, live as they please are deceiving themselves. Where faith is genuine, it must attack the body and hold it in check, lest the body do what it pleases. For this reason, St. Peter says that we must be sober.

But he does not want the body to be destroyed or to be weakened too much. Thus one finds many who have fasted themselves mad and have tortured themselves to death. Even though St. Bernard was a saintly man, he, too, was afflicted for a time with such folly. He denied his body so much that his breath stank and he could not associate with people.[5] Later,

5 Luther praises Bernard of Clairvaux throughout his writings. See, e.g., *Sermons on John 1–2* (1537–38), LW 22:52: "We read that when St. Bernard was at the point of death, he remarked: 'I have misspent and wasted my life disgracefully; but I take comfort in the knowledge that Jesus Christ, my Lord, has a twofold claim on heaven. In the first place, He can lay claim to it for Himself, because He is the true and natural Son of God, governing with the Father from eternity. Hence He is entitled to heaven as an heir from eternity. But this is not the source of my comfort. In the second place, however, He has gained heaven through His holy suffering and death and then presented this to me. In this manner I, too, fall heir to heaven.' Had St. Bernard not died in this faith, he would have gone to the devil and into the abyss of hell with his monkery and monastic life. It is the same with all the monks in the papacy. No matter how holy and ascetic their life may have been, if they were saved, they must have come to this same realization and confessed: 'I have conducted my life shamefully. I cannot put my trust in my cowl, in rules, or in my order. But I do believe in Jesus Christ, who died for my sins and for the sins of the whole world. To Him I cling, and I depart this life with implicit confidence in His consoling promise: Come to Me, all who labor and are heavy laden, and I will give you rest (Matt. 11:28).' I hope that Francis and Dominic also embraced this faith; if not, I would not want to go to the heaven they entered!" See also *Sermon on the Mount* (1532), LW 21:283.

however, he came to his senses and also told his brothers not to hurt the body too much. For he realized that he had made himself unable to serve his brothers. Therefore St. Peter demands no more than that we be sober, that is, that we stint the body as long as we feel that it is still too lascivious. He does not prescribe any definite length of time for fasting, as the pope has done; but he leaves it to everyone's discretion to fast in such a way that he always remains sober and does not burden the body with gluttony. He must remain reasonable and sensible, and he must see to what extent it is necessary for him to mortify the body. It does no good at all to impose a command about this on a whole crowd or community, since we are so different from one another. One has a strong body; another has a body that is weak. Therefore one person must deny it much, and another person must deny it little, in such a way that when this is done, the body remains healthy and able to do good.

But it is also wrong for the other crowd to come along and say that they are getting on well by not fasting and by feeling free to eat meat. For these people, like the others, do not understand the Gospel either and are of no importance. They do no more than disdain the pope's command. Yet they do not want to gird the mind and the understanding, as Peter says. They let the body have its way, with the result that it remains indolent and lascivious. It is good to fast. But one fasts in the right way by not giving the body more food than is needed to keep it healthy, and by letting it work and wake, in order that the old ass may not become too reckless, go dancing on the ice, and break a leg but may be bridled and follow the spirit. It should not imitate those who, when they fast, fill themselves so full of fish and the best wine at one time that their bellies are bloated.

This is what St. Peter means by being sober. Now he continues:

Set your hope fully upon the grace that is coming to you.

Christian faith is ready to rest completely on God's Word with all confidence and courage, and then to go joyfully on its way. Therefore Peter says: Then the loins of your mind are girded, and your faith is genuine, if you have such courage, no matter whether property, honor, body, or life are involved. With these words he has surely given an excellent description of a genuine and true faith. It must not be an indolent and sleepy faith and only a dream. No, it must be a living and active thing, so that one devotes oneself to it with all confidence and clings to the Word, no matter what happens, in order that we may press forward through fortune and misfortune. Thus when I must die, I must rely boldly on Christ, readily put forth my neck, and trust in the Word of God, which cannot lie to me. Then faith must go straight ahead, let nothing lead it astray, and ignore everything it sees, hears, and feels. This is the kind of faith St. Peter demands—a faith that consists in such power, not in thoughts or words.

In the second place, St. Peter says: Set your hope upon the grace that is offered you. This means that you did not earn this great grace, but that it is offered to you completely without cost. For the Gospel, which proclaims this grace, is not our invention or fabrication. No, the Holy Spirit let it come down into the world from heaven. But what is being offered to us? That which we heard above, namely, that he who believes in Christ and clings to the Word has Him with all His blessings, so that he becomes lord over sin, death, devil, and hell, and is sure of eternal life. This treasure is brought to our door and laid into our laps without our cooperation or merit, yes, unexpectedly and without our knowledge or thoughts. Therefore the apostle wants us to set our hope cheerfully on this grace, for the God who offers it to us will surely not lie to us.

At the revelation of Jesus Christ.

God does not let His grace be offered to anyone in any other way than through Christ. Hence no man should presume to approach Him without this Mediator, as we have heard sufficiently above. For God will listen to no one who does not bring Christ, His dear Son, with him. God has regard for Him alone, and for His sake He also has regard for those who cling to Him. He wants us to acknowledge that we are reconciled to the Father through the blood of the Son and for this reason need not be afraid to come before Him. For the Lord Christ came, assumed flesh and blood, and attached Himself to us for the purpose of acquiring such grace for us before the Father. Thus all the patriarchs and prophets were preserved and saved through such faith in Christ; for they all had to believe in the words which God spoke to Abraham: "In your Seed shall all the nations of the earth be blessed" (Gen. 22:18). Therefore, as we have said, the faith of the Jews, the Turks, and of those who rely on their own works and want to go to heaven because of them is invalid. Peter says: "Grace is offered to you," but at the revelation of Jesus Christ, or, to translate it more clearly, because Jesus Christ is revealed to you.

Through the Gospel we are told who Christ is, in order that we may learn to know that He is our Savior, that He delivers us from sin and death, helps us out of all misfortune, reconciles us to the Father, and makes us pious and saves us without our works. He who does not learn to know Christ in this way must go wrong. For even though you know that He is God's Son, that He died and rose again, and that He sits at the right hand of the Father, you have not yet learned to know Christ aright, and this knowledge still does not help you. You must also know and believe that He did all this for your sake, in order to help you. Consequently, all that has hitherto been preached and taught at the schools of higher learning is sheer rubbish. They had no understanding of this, and they never went beyond the thought that Christ suffered intensely and that He is now sitting in heaven above with nothing to do and is enjoying Himself. Thus their hearts remain barren, and faith cannot come to life in them. The Lord Christ should not be isolated as existing for Himself but should be preached as belonging to us. Otherwise why would it have been necessary for Him to come down to earth and shed His blood? But since, as He says in John 3:17, He was sent into the world that the world might be saved through Him, He must have accomplished what the Father sent Him to do. The fact that He was sent by and came from the Father should not be understood as having taken place only according to the divine nature. No, this must also be understood of the human nature and of His office. As soon as He was baptized, He began to carry out what He had been sent and had come into the world to accomplish, namely, to proclaim the truth and to announce to us that all who believe in Him should be saved. Thus He revealed and manifested Himself, and He offered us grace. . . .

So far the apostle has described the grace that is offered to us through the Gospel and the preaching about Jesus Christ, and he has taught us what our attitude toward this should be, namely, that we should hold to a pure and unchanged meaning of faith, in such a way that we know that no work we are able to do or devise can be of any help to us. Now when this is preached, reason comes along and says: "Ah, if this is true, then I need not do a single good work!" Thus stupid minds seize upon this and change Christian life into carnal liberty. They think they should do what they please. St. Peter confronts these people here, anticipates them, and teaches them that Christian liberty must be exercised solely over against God. For here nothing else is necessary than faith, that I give God His due honor and regard Him as my God, who is just, truthful, and merciful. Such faith liberates us from sin and all evil. Now when I have given God this honor, then whatever life I live, I live for my neighbor, to serve and help him. The greatest work that comes from faith is this, that I confess Christ with my mouth and, if it has to be, bear testimony with my blood and risk my life. Yet God does not need the work; but I should do it to prove and confess my faith, in order that others, too, may be brought to faith. Then other works will follow. They must all tend to serve my neighbor. All this God must bring about in us. Therefore we should not make up our minds to begin to lead a carnal life and to do what we please. For this reason St. Peter now says:

1 Peter 1:17–21

And if you invoke as Father Him who judges each one impartially according to his deeds, conduct yourselves with fear throughout the time of your exile.

Thus St. Peter says: By faith you are now children of God, and He is your Father. You have acquired an imperishable inheritance in heaven [as he stated above]. Therefore nothing remains now but that the veil be taken away and that what is now hidden be revealed. You must still wait until you see this. It is now possible for you to address God confidently as Father; but though He is your Father, He is so just that He gives to everyone according to his deeds and does not respect the person. Therefore even though you have the great distinction to be called a Christian and a child of God, you dare not think that God will spare you on this account if you live without fear and imagine that it is now sufficient for you to boast of such a distinction. To be sure, the world judges according to the person. It does not punish all in the same way. It spares those who are friends, rich, beautiful, learned, wise, and powerful. But God has no regard for this. No matter how great the person is, all this is immaterial to Him. Thus in Egypt He slew the son of King Pharaoh just as readily as He slew the son of a common miller.

The apostle wants us to expect such judgment of God and to be in fear, lest we boast of being called Christians and depend on it, as if God would be more indulgent with us on this account than He would be with others. In times past the Jews, too, were deluded by this assumption; they boasted of being Abraham's seed and the people of God. Scripture does not differentiate according to the flesh; it differentiates according to the spirit. It is true that God had promised that Christ should be born from Abraham and that a holy people should come from him; but it does not follow from this that all who are born from Abraham are God's children. God also promised that the heathen shall be saved. But He did not say that He would save all the heathen.

But a question now arises here. Since we say that God saves us solely through faith and without regard to works, why, pray, does St. Peter say that God does not judge according to the person, but that He judges according to the works? Answer: What we have taught, that faith alone justifies before God, is undoubtedly true, since it is so clear from Scripture that it cannot be denied. Now what the apostle says here, that God judges according to the works, is also true. But one should maintain with certainty that where there is no faith, there can be no good works either, and, on the other hand, that there is no faith where there are no good works. Therefore link faith and good works together in such a way that both make up the sum total of the Christian life. As you live, so you will fare. God will judge you according to this. Therefore even though God judges us according to our works, it nevertheless remains true that the works are only the fruits of faith. They are the evidence of our belief or unbelief. Therefore God will judge and convict you on the basis of your works. They show whether you have believed or have not believed, just as one cannot condemn and judge a liar better than from his words. Yet it is evident that the words have not made him a liar, but that he has become a liar before he tells a lie; for the lie must come into the mouth from the heart. Therefore the only way to understand this is the simplest way, namely, that the works are fruits and signs of faith and that God judges people according to these fruits, which certainly have to follow, in order that one may see publicly where belief or unbelief is in the heart. God will not judge according to whether you are called a Christian or have been baptized. No, He will ask you: "If you are a Christian, then tell Me: Where are the fruits with which you can show your faith?" . . .

As we have heard, a sincere Christian believer has all the possessions of God and is a child of God. The time of his life, however, is but a pilgrimage. For through faith the spirit is already in heaven, and this makes him lord over all things. But God permits him to remain alive in the flesh and lets his body walk the earth in order that he may help others and bring them to heaven too. Therefore we must use everything on earth in no other way than as a guest who travels across country, comes to an inn where he must spend the night, and takes nothing but food and lodging from the innkeeper.[6] He does not say that the innkeeper's property belongs to him. Thus we must also deal with temporal goods as if they did not belong to us. We must limit our enjoyment of them to what is necessary for the preservation of the body. With the rest we must help our neighbor. Thus the Christian life is only a night's lodging; "for here we have no lasting city" (Heb. 13:14), but we must go where the Father is, namely, to heaven. Therefore we should not indulge in riotous revelry here; but, as St. Peter says, we must conduct ourselves with fear. . . .

So far we have heard St. Peter exhort us to gird our minds, in order that we may remain pure and live in faith; then, since it has cost so much, to "conduct ourselves with fear" and not to rely on the fact that we are called Christians, since God is a judge who does not care about anybody but judges one as He judges the other, without respect of persons. Now Peter continues and concludes the first chapter.

---

6 Many years later Luther will make this same point. Cf. *Sermons on the Gospel of St. John* (1537–39), LW 22:291 (see below, p. 395).

1 Peter 1:22–25

In Gal. 5:22–23 Paul enumerates the fruits that follow from faith. "The fruit of the Spirit," he says, "is love, joy, peace, patience, kindness, goodness, faithfulness, gentleness, self-control." Thus here St. Peter also speaks of the fruits of faith, namely, that we should purify our souls by obedience to the truth through the Spirit. For where faith is genuine, it subdues the body and constrains the lust of the flesh. Even though it does not slay the body, it nonetheless makes it subject and obedient to the Spirit and holds it in check. This is what St. Paul also means when he speaks of fruits of the Spirit. It is a great work that the Spirit is lord over the flesh and curbs the evil lust that is innate in us from our father and mother. For without grace it is impossible for us to live properly in wedlock, let alone out of wedlock.

But why does the apostle say that we should purify our souls? He is well aware of the fact that after Baptism the lust of the flesh abides in us until death. Therefore it is not enough for one to abstain from the deed, to remain chaste outwardly, and to let evil lust stay in the heart. No, one must strive to purify the soul, so that evil lust and desire depart from our heart and the soul is hostile to them and constantly fights against them until it is rid of them.

And now St. Peter makes a beautiful addition, namely, that one should purify the soul by obedience to the truth in the Spirit. Many sermons have been preached and many books have been written about chastity. There they have said that one should fast for a certain length of time, not eat meat, not drink wine, etc., in order to get rid of the affliction. Although this has helped to some extent, it has not been enough; it has not subjugated lust. Thus St. Jerome writes about himself that he abused his body until it resembled that of an Ethiopian, but that this did not help and that he still dreamed he was singing and dancing among harlots in Rome.[7] Thus St. Bernard also hurt and ruined his body until it stank. . . . These men were sorely tried, and they undertook to subdue this by external means. But since this is external, the poultice has been applied only on the outside, not on the inside. Therefore it does not suffice to quell lust.

But here St. Peter has given a real remedy for this, namely, obedience to the truth in the Spirit. Scripture gives the same remedy in other passages, as, for example, in Isa. 11:5: "Faithfulness shall be the girdle of his loins." This is the right poultice; it girds the loins. The evil must come out, not go in; for it has grown inside in the flesh and blood, in the marrow

7 Jerome, *Letter to Eustochium* 22.7.1–2 (PL 22:398–99; NPNF[2] 6:24–25).

and the veins, not outside in the cloth or in the garment. Therefore it is useless to attempt to curb lust with external means. To be sure, one can weaken and mortify the body with fasting and work; but one does not expel evil lust in this way. Faith, however, can subdue and restrain it, so that it gives room to the Spirit.

Thus the prophet Zechariah speaks in chapter 9:17 about a wine which Christ has. He gives it to maidens to drink, and they flourish. Other wine tends to incite to evil lust; but this wine, that is, the Gospel, subdues lust and makes chaste hearts. This is what St. Peter says: When one takes hold of the truth with the heart and is obedient to it in the Spirit, this is the right help and the most powerful remedy. Otherwise you will find no remedy that could quell all evil thoughts in this way. For when it enters the heart, the evil inclination soon departs. Let him who wants to, try this. He will find that this is true, and those who have tried it are well aware of this. But the devil does not easily let anyone come to the point of taking hold of and enjoying the Word of God; for he knows well what power it has to subdue evil lust and thoughts.

Thus St. Peter now wants to say: If you want to remain chaste, you must take hold of obedience to the truth in the Spirit; that is, one must not only hear and read the Word of God, but one must take it to heart. Consequently, it is not enough to preach or hear the Gospel once. No, one must constantly move forward and progress. For the Word has such grace that the more one deals with it, the sweeter it becomes. Although the doctrine of faith is always one and the same, one cannot hear it too often, unless there are impertinent and coarse hearts.

Now the apostle adds:

For a sincere love of the brethren.

To what end should we now lead a chaste life? To be saved by doing so? No, but for the purpose of serving our neighbor. What should I do to check my sin? I must take hold of the obedience to the truth in the Spirit, that is, faith in God's Word. Why do I check sin? To enable me to be of service to others. For first I must hold body and flesh in subjection through the Spirit. Then I can also be of service to others.

We read on:

Love one another earnestly from the heart.

The apostles Peter and Paul differentiate between brotherly love and love in general. Brotherhood means that Christians should all be like brothers and make no distinction among them; for since we all have one Christ in common, one Baptism, one faith, one treasure, I am no better than you are. For what you have I also have, and I am just as rich as you are. The treasure is the same except that I may have understood it better than you, so that I have it lying in gold, while you have it in a plain bit of cloth. Therefore just as we have the grace of Christ and all spiritual blessings in common, so we should also have body and life, property and honor in common, so that one serves the other with all things. . . .

You have been born anew.

In the third place, this should be done because you are no longer what you formerly were, he says, but are new persons. Works have not brought this about, but for it a birth has been required. For you cannot make the new man. No, he must grow or be born. Just as a carpenter cannot make a tree, but the tree itself must grow out of the earth, and just as we all were not made children of Adam but were born as such and have inherited sin from our father and mother, so we cannot become children of God by means of works but must be born again. This is what the apostle wants to say: Since you are now new creatures, you must also conduct yourselves differently now and lead a new life. Just as you formerly lived in hatred, so you must now walk in love, contradictory in every respect. But how did the new birth come about? In the following way:

Not of perishable seed but of imperishable, through the living and abiding Word of God.

We have been born anew through a seed. For, as we see, the only way anything grows is through a seed. Now if the old birth originated from a seed, the new birth must also be from a seed. But what is the seed? Not flesh and blood. What then? It is not perishable, but it is an eternal Word. This is everything from which we live put together, food and nourishment. But it is chiefly the seed from which we are born anew, as the apostle says here.

How does this take place? In the following way: God lets the Word, the Gospel, go forth. He causes the seed to fall into the hearts of men. Now where it takes root in the heart, the Holy Spirit is present and creates a new man. There an entirely new man comes into being, other thoughts, other words and works. Thus you are completely changed. Now you seek everything from which you formerly fled; and what you formerly sought, that you flee. Physical birth takes place in the following way: When man has received the seed, the seed is changed, so that it is no longer seed. But this is a seed that cannot be changed; it remains eternally. But it changes me in such a way that I am changed into it and what evil there is in me because of my nature disappears completely. Therefore this is an extraordinary birth—a birth from an unusual seed. Now St. Peter continues:

All flesh is like grass and all its glory like the flower of the grass. The grass withers, and the flower falls, but the Word of the Lord abides forever.

This verse is taken from Isa. 40:6–8, where the prophet says: "A voice says: 'Cry!' And I said: 'What shall I cry?' All flesh is grass, and all its beauty is like the flower of the field. The grass withers, the flower fades, but the Word of our God will stand forever." These are the words quoted here by St. Peter. For, as I have said, this is a rich Epistle, and one that is well interlarded with Scripture passages. Thus Scripture now says that God's Word abides forever. That which is flesh and blood is as perishable as grass, even though it is young and therefore flourishing. When it is rich, powerful, clever, pious, and therefore flourishing—all this pertains to the flower—the flower nonetheless begins to wither. What is young and beautiful becomes old and ugly. What is rich becomes poor, etc. Everything has to perish through the Word of God. But this seed cannot pass away.

Now St. Peter finishes:

That Word is the good news which was preached to you.

It is as though the apostle were saying: You need not open your eyes wide when you come to the Word of God. You have it before your eyes. It is the Word which we are preaching. With it you can subdue all evil lusts. You need not search far. Do no more than take hold of it when it is preached. For it is so near that one can hear it, as Moses also says in Deut. 30:11–14: "For this commandment which I command you this day is not too hard for you, neither is it far off. It is not in heaven; neither is it beyond the sea. But the Word is very near to you; it is in your mouth and in your heart." To be sure, it is quickly spoken and heard; but when it enters the heart, it cannot die or pass away. Nor does it let you die. It holds you as long as you cling to it. Thus when I hear that Jesus Christ died, took away my sin, gained heaven for me, and gave me all that He has, I am hearing the Gospel. The Word is soon gone when it is preached; but when it falls into the heart and is grasped by faith, it can never slip away. No creature can invalidate this truth. The depths of hell can do nothing against it; and even if I am already in the jaws of the devil, I must come out and remain where the Word remains, if I can take hold of it. Therefore St. Peter says with good reason that you need not look for anything else than what we have preached.

St. Paul also says in Rom. 1:16: "I am not ashamed of the Gospel; it is the power of God for salvation to everyone who has faith." The Word is a divine and eternal power; for although the voice or speech soon fades away, yet the core remains, that is, the meaning, the truth expressed with the voice. Thus when I put a cup of wine to my lips, I drink the wine even though I do not force the cup down my throat along with the wine. Thus the Word which the voice speaks enters the heart and comes to life even though the voice remains outside and passes away. Therefore it is surely a divine power. Indeed, it is God Himself. For thus God says to Moses in Exod. 4:12: "I will be with your mouth." And in Ps. 81:10 He says: "Open your mouth wide"; that is, "Preach boldly. Speak out, be hungry; I will fill you. I will be present there and say enough." Thus Christ says in John 14:6: "I am the Way and the Truth and the Life." He who clings to this is born of God (cf. 1 John 5:1). Thus the seed is our Lord God Himself. All this points out that we cannot be helped with works. Although the Word is unimposing and seems to be nothing while it proceeds from the mouth, yet there is such boundless power in it that it makes all who cleave to it children of God, as John 1:12 says. It is on such a precious blessing that our salvation rests.

This is the first chapter of this Epistle. In it you see how masterfully St. Peter preaches faith and treats of it. Hence one sees clearly that this Epistle is the true Gospel. Now the second chapter follows. It will teach us how we should conduct ourselves toward our neighbor so far as deeds are concerned.

1 Peter 2:1–5

Here the apostle begins to teach us what the works and fruits of a Christian life should be, For we have said often enough that a Christian life is composed of two parts: faith in God and love toward one's neighbor. Likewise, that the Christian faith is given in such a way that many evil lusts still remain in the flesh as long as we live, since there is no saint who is not in the flesh. But that which is in the flesh cannot be completely pure. Therefore St. Peter says: Be armed in such a way that you guard against sins which still cling to you, and that you constantly fight against them. For our worst foes are in our bosom and in our flesh and blood. They wake, sleep, and live with us like an evil guest whom we have invited to our house and cannot get rid of. Therefore since the Lord Christ is now completely yours through faith, and you have received salvation and all His blessings, you must henceforth let it be your concern to cast off all wickedness, or all that is evil, and all guile. This means that no one should deal unfaithfully and falsely with the other person. The world has a proverb which says: "The world is full of perfidy." This is true. But we Christians must deal uprightly and with purity of heart, not perfidiously, with people as well as with God, fair and square, so that no one overreaches the other person in selling, buying, or promising, and the like.

Thus St. Paul also says in Eph. 4:25: "Therefore putting away falsehood, let everyone speak the truth with his neighbor." It is the truth when yes means yes and no means no. But it is hypocrisy when the outward bearing belies one's thoughts. For it is important to behave according to what is in the heart. A Christian must act in such a way that he can let everybody see and know what he thinks in his heart. In all his behavior and in everything he does he must think only of praising God and serving his neighbor. He should fear no one. And at heart everyone should be what he appears to be. He should not resort to dissimulation and in this way cause people to gape.

Furthermore, St. Peter says that we must put away envy and slander. Here he strikes a telling blow at the common vices that are prevalent among people in their dealings with one another. Slander is very common and reckless. Since people are quick to engage in slander, no one becomes aware of it. Therefore guard against it, says St. Peter, even though you are spiritual and know what the fruits of the Spirit are.

Like newborn babes, long for the pure spiritual milk.

Here the apostle employs an analogy. He wants to say: Through the Word of God you are now born anew. Therefore conduct yourselves like newborn babes, who seek nothing else than milk. Just as they long for the breasts and milk, so you, too, should yearn for the Word, strive for it, and have a liking for it, in order that you may imbibe the pure spiritual milk.

These, too, are figurative words. For the apostle has neither physical milk nor physical longing in mind, just as he is also not speaking of a physical birth. No, he is speaking of another milk, that is, a spiritual milk which is taken with the soul and which the heart must imbibe. This milk must be unadulterated. It must not be like the false commodity that is usually sold. It is truly very important and decidedly necessary to give the newborn young Christians milk that is pure and unadulterated. But the milk is nothing but the Gospel, which is also the very seed by which we were conceived and born, as we heard above. This is also the food that nourishes us when we grow up; it is the armor which we put on and with which we equip ourselves. Yes, it is everything put together. But the admixture is the human doctrines with which the Word of God is adulterated. Consequently, the Holy Spirit wants every Christian to see what kind of milk he drinks; he himself must learn what to think of all teachings.

But the breasts which give this milk and which the babes suck are the preachers in Christendom, as the groom says to the bride in Song of Sol. 4:5: "Your two breasts are like two fawns." They should have a bag of myrrh hanging around them, as the bride says in Song of Sol. 1:13: "My beloved is to me a bag of myrrh that lies between my breasts." This means that one must always preach Christ. The groom must constantly be between the breasts. Otherwise things are not as they should be. The milk is adulterated if anything but Christ is preached.

This is what happens: When one preaches that Christ died for us and rescued us from sin, death, and hell, this is pleasing and sweet like milk. But then one must also preach the cross, so that one suffers as Christ did. This is a strong potion and strong wine. Therefore one must give Christians the softest food first, that is, the milk. For one cannot preach better to them than one can do by first preaching Christ alone. He is not bitter. No, He is nothing but sweet, fat grace. Here you need not yet suffer any pains at all. This is the true, pure, and unadulterated milk. . . .

That by it you may grow up to salvation; for you have tasted the kindness of the Lord.

It is not enough to hear the Gospel once; one must study it constantly, in order that we may grow up. Then, when faith is strong, one must provide for and feed everyone. But this is not said to those who have never heard the Gospel; they know neither what is milk nor what is wine. Therefore St. Peter adds: "For you have tasted the kindness of the Lord." It is as if he were saying: It does not touch the heart of him who has not tasted it; to him it is not sweet. But those who have tried it—they always eat this food and busy themselves with the Word. To them it tastes right; to them it is sweet.

But to have tasted means when I believe in my heart that Christ gave Himself to me and became my own, that my sin and my misery are His, and that His life is now mine. If this goes to the heart, then one relishes it. For how could I not derive joy and delight from it? Surely I rejoice heartily if a good friend gives me 100 guldens.[8] But he whose heart is not touched by this cannot rejoice over it. But those who are lying in the throes of death or are oppressed by an evil conscience relish it most. Then hunger is a good cook, as the saying goes. It makes the food taste good, for the heart and the conscience can hear nothing more delightful. When they feel their misery, they long for this food; they smell the roast from afar and cannot be satisfied. Thus Mary says in the *Magnificat:* "He has filled the hungry with good things" (Luke 1:53). But those hardened people who live in their own holiness, rely on their works, and do not feel their sin and misery—they do not relish it. Everything tastes good to him who sits at table and is hungry. But he who is sated beforehand relishes nothing; to him the very best food gives gray hair. Therefore the apostle

8 A gulden was the most valuable gold coin in common circulation.

says: "For you have tasted the kindness of the Lord." It is as if he were saying: "If you have not tasted it, I am preaching in vain."

He continues:

Come to Him, to that Living Stone.

Here he again reaches back into Scripture and quotes from the prophet Isaiah, who says in chapter 28:14–16: "Therefore hear the Word of the Lord, you scoffers . . . you have said: 'We have made a covenant with death, and with Sheol we have an agreement. . . . We have made lies our refuge. . . .' Therefore thus says the Lord God: 'Behold, I am laying in Zion for a foundation a Stone . . . a precious Cornerstone, of a sure foundation, etc.'" St. Paul cites this verse too (Rom. 9:33). It is also an exceedingly important Scripture passage. For Christ is the precious cornerstone on which we must be built.

And look how St. Peter takes these words and applies them to Christ. Then what Isaiah says about putting one's trust in Him means, as St. Peter states, to build on Him. This is the proper interpretation of Scripture. The builders place the cornerstone where it lies firmly and securely, so that it can support the entire structure. Thus the Living Stone, which is Christ, supports the whole building. To build, therefore, means that we all intertwine our trust and confidence and put them in Him. . . .

And like living stones be yourselves built into a spiritual house.

How can we build ourselves? Through the Gospel and preaching. The preachers are the builders. The Christians, who hear the Gospel, are those who are built and the stones one must join to this Cornerstone, so that we place our confidence in Him and our hearts rest and repose on Him. Then I must also be prepared to retain the form of this Stone; for if I am placed on Him through faith, I and everyone with me must do the kind of works He did and lead the kind of life He led. It is now a fruit of faith and a work of love that we all should accommodate ourselves to one another and become one building. Thus St. Paul also speaks of this, although in another way, when he says in 1 Cor. 3:16: "Do you not know that you are God's temple?" The house of stone or wood is not His house. He wants to have a spiritual building, that is, the Christian congregation, in which we are all equal in one faith, one like the other, and are all placed and fitted on one another and joined together through love without malice, guile, hypocrisy, hatred, and slander, as the apostle has said.

To be a holy priesthood.

Here He has abolished both the external, physical priesthood and the external church which existed previously in the Old Testament. All this He takes away and wants to say: All the externals of the priesthood have now come to an end. Therefore another priesthood begins and offers other sacrifices. This means that everything is spiritual. We have argued extensively that those who are called priests today are not priests in the sight of God. And we have substantiated this with what Peter says here. Therefore understand it well, and if someone comes along and wants to explain it—as some have done—by saying that Peter is speaking about a twofold priesthood, namely, about external and spiritual priests, then ask him to put spectacles on to be able to see and take hellebore to sweep out his brain.[9] St. Peter says: Be yourselves built to be a spiritual or holy priesthood. Now ask those priests whether they, too, are holy. Their life shows, as one sees, that the wretched people are up to the ears in greed, whoring, and vices of all kinds. He who has the priesthood must, of course, be holy; but he who is not holy does not have it. Therefore St. Peter is speaking here of only one priesthood. . . .

Thus only those are the holy and spiritual priesthood who are true Christians and are built on the Stone. For since Christ is the groom and we are the bride, the bride has everything that the groom has, even His own body. When He gives Himself to the bride, He gives Himself entirely as what He is; and the bride, in turn, also gives herself to Him. Now Christ is the High and Chief Priest anointed by God Himself. He also sacrificed His own body for us, which is the highest function of the priestly office. Then He prayed for us on the cross. In the third place, He also proclaimed the Gospel and taught all men to know God and Him Himself. These three offices He also gave to all of us. Consequently, since He is the Priest and we are His brothers, all Christians have the authority, the command, and the obligation to preach, to come before God, to pray for one another, and to offer themselves as a sacrifice to God. Nevertheless, no one should undertake to preach or to declare the Word of God unless he is a priest.

To offer spiritual sacrifices acceptable to God through Jesus Christ.

A spiritual sacrifice is not money contributed as a sacrifice to the pope. Nor is it, as in the Old Testament, the obligatory sacrificing of the tenth part of everything. Such physical sacrifices and such a priesthood have all ceased now. Today everything is new and spiritual. Christ is the Priest, and we are all priests. Just as He sacrificed His body, so we, too, must sacrifice ourselves. Here everything foreshadowed by the external sacrifices

9 Hellebore, a flowering plant, was used by the ancients to purge the body of various ailments. According to Pliny (23–79), some philosophers took it to sharpen the mind. Isidore of Seville (ca. 560–636) says the Romans used it to return a disturbed mind to health, which seems to be Luther's meaning here. See Pliny, *Natural History* 25.21–25; Isidore of Seville, *Etymologies* 27.9.24.

as they took place in the Old Testament is now fulfilled. Briefly stated, all this means that the Gospel is preached. He who preaches the Gospel practices and does all this. He slaughters the calf, namely, the carnal mind; he strangles the old Adam. For one must slay with the Gospel what is irrational in the flesh and blood. Then we let ourselves be sacrificed and put to death on the cross. The true priestly office is practiced when we sacrifice that villainous rogue, the lazy old ass, to God. If the world does not do this, we must do it ourselves; for in the end we must put aside every vestige of the old Adam, as we heard above in the first chapter. This is the only sacrifice that is acceptable and pleasing to God. From this you can now see where our fools and blind leaders have taken us and how this text has been neglected.

Now you might say: "What kind of situation will arise if it is true that we are all priests and should all preach? Should no distinction be made among the people, and should the women, too, be priests?" Answer: In the New Testament no priest has to be tonsured. Not that this is evil in itself, for one surely has the right to have the head shaved clean. But one should not make a distinction between those who do so and the common Christian. Faith cannot tolerate this. Thus those who are now called priests would all be laymen like the others, and only a few officiants would be elected by the congregation to do the preaching. Thus there is only an external difference because of the office to which one is called by the congregation. Before God, however there is no distinction, and only a few are selected from the whole group to administer the office in the stead of the congregation. They all have this office, but nobody has any more authority than the other person has. Therefore nobody should come forward of his own accord and preach in the congregation. No, one person must be chosen from the whole group and appointed. If desired, he may be deposed.

Now those people have created a special estate and say that it was established by God. They have acquired such freedom that almost in the midst of Christendom there is a greater distinction than there is between us and Turks. As St. Paul says in Gal. 3:28, you must pay no attention to distinctions when you want to look at Christians. You must not say: "This is a man or a woman; this is a servant or a master; this person is old or young." They are all alike and only a spiritual people. Therefore they are all priests. All may proclaim God's Word, except that, as St. Paul teaches in 1 Cor. 14:34, women should not speak in the congregation. They should let the men preach, because God commands them to be obedient to their husbands. God does not interfere with the arrangement. But He makes no distinction in the matter of authority. If, however, only women were present and no men, as in nunneries, then one of the women might be authorized to preach.

This is the true priesthood. As we have heard, it embraces these three things: to offer spiritual sacrifices, to pray for the congregation, and to preach. He who can do this is a priest. They are all obliged to preach the Word, to pray for the congregation, and to sacrifice themselves before God. Let those fools go their way who call the spiritual estate "priests," who, after all, exercise no other office than being tonsured and anointed. If shaving the head and anointing made one a priest, I could even oil and anoint the hooves of an ass and make him a priest too.

Finally, St. Peter says that we must offer up spiritual sacrifices that are acceptable to God through Jesus Christ. Since Christ is the cornerstone on whom we are built, all our dealings with God must be carried on through Him, as we have heard exhaustively above. Otherwise God would not regard my cross, even if I tortured myself to death. But He does regard Christ. Through Him my works have validity before God. Otherwise they would not be worth a blade of straw. Therefore Scripture fittingly calls Christ a precious cornerstone who imparts His virtues to all who are built on Him through faith. Thus in the verse which speaks of Christ as the Living Stone, St. Peter teaches us what Christ is. This is a fine figure of speech from which one can readily understand how one should believe in Christ.

1 Peter 2:9–10

But you are a chosen race, a royal priesthood, a holy nation, God's own people.

Here the apostle gives the Christians a proper title. He took this statement from Moses, who tells the Jews in Deut. 7:6: "You are a people holy to the Lord your God; the Lord your God has chosen you to be a people for His own possession, out of all the peoples that are on the face of the earth." And in Exod. 19:5–6 we read: "You shall be My own possession among all peoples . . . and you shall be to Me a kingdom of priests and a holy nation." Here you see what Peter is speaking about. I repeat what I said earlier, namely, that one must become accustomed to the way Scripture is wont to speak about priests. Let no one be concerned about those whom people call priests. Let everyone call them what they choose. You must remain with the pure Word of God. What it calls priests, you, too, must call priests. We will permit those whom the bishops and the pope consecrate to call themselves priests. They may call themselves what they choose, provided that they do not call themselves "priests of God"; for they cannot adduce a single word from Scripture in defense of this.

But if they come along with this verse and say that it is speaking to them, answer them as I taught above, and ask them to whom Peter is speaking here. Then they will have to confess the truth to their shame. For it is certainly clear and manifest enough that the apostle is addressing the whole multitude, all Christians, when he says: "You are a chosen race . . . a holy nation." Up to this point, of course, he has spoken about no one except those who are built on the Stone and believe. Therefore it must follow that he who does not believe is no priest. Then they say: "Ah, one must explain the words as the saintly fathers interpreted them!" Then you must say: "Let the fathers and teachers, whoever they may be, explain as they choose. This is what St. Peter tells me. He has greater testimony from God than they have. Besides, he is older. Therefore I will agree with him." Thus this verse requires no commentary; for it speaks explicitly of those who believe. Now not only those who are anointed and tonsured are believers. Therefore we are willing to let them call themselves priests, for we do not care how they want to be dubbed. No, the question at issue is whether they are called priests in Scripture and whether God calls them priests. Some can be selected from the congregation who are office-holders and servants and are appointed to preach in the congregation and to administer the Sacraments. But we are all priests before God if we are Christians. For since we have been laid on the Stone who is the Chief Priest before God, we also have everything He has.

It would please me very much if this word "priest" were used as commonly as the term "Christians" is applied to us. For priests, the baptized, and Christians are all one and the same. For just as I should not put up with it when those who have been anointed and tonsured want to have exclusive right to the terms "Christians" and "baptized," so I should also not put up with it when they alone want to be called priests. Yet they have monopolized this title. Thus they have called "the church" what the pope, together with his pointed hats, decrees. But Scripture turns this around. Therefore note this well, in order that you may know how to differentiate between those whom God calls priests and those who call themselves priests. For it must be our aim to restore the little word "priests" to the common use which the little word "Christians" enjoys. For to be a priest does not belong in the category of an external office; it is exclusively the kind of office that has dealings before God.

The same thing is true with regard to the fact that we are all kings. "Priests" and "kings" are all spiritual names just as "Christians," "saints," and "church" are. And just as you are not called a Christian because you have a great deal of money and property but because you have been built on the Stone and believe in Christ, so you are not called a priest because you are tonsured or wear a long coat but because you may approach God. In like manner, you are not a king because you wear a golden crown and have many lands and people under you, but because you are a lord over all things, death, sin, and hell. If you believe in Christ, you are a king just as He is a King. Now He is not a King after the manner of earthly monarchs. He does not wear a golden crown. Nor does He ride along with great pomp and many horses. No, He is a King over all kings—a King who has power over all things and at whose feet everything must lie. Just as He is a Lord, so I, too, am a lord. For what He has, that I, too, have.

Now someone may say: "St. Peter declares here, too, that the Christians also are kings. On the other hand, it is evident that we are not all kings. Therefore this verse cannot be understood to mean that he is speaking about all in general. For he who is a Christian is not a king in France or a priest in Rome." So I also ask now whether the king of France is also a king before God. This he concedes, for God will not judge according to the crown. To be sure, he is a king on earth and before the world; but when death comes, his rule has ended. Then he will have to lie at the feet of those who believe. We are speaking of an eternal kingdom and priesthood. Here every believer is truly a king before God. But who does not know that we are not all tonsured and anointed priests? The fact that those men are anointed does not make them priests before God. Thus they are not kings before God either because they have been crowned. Crowned kings and anointed priests belong in the world and have been made kings and priests by men. The pope may make as many priests of that kind as he pleases, provided that he does not make priests before God; for God wants to make these Himself.

Therefore when St. Peter says here: "You are a royal priesthood," this is tantamount to saying: "You are Christians." If you want to know what kind of title and what kind of power and praise Christians have, you see here that they are kings and priests and a chosen race. But what is the priestly office? The answer follows:

That you may declare the wonderful deeds of Him who called you out of darkness into His marvelous light.

A priest must be God's messenger and must have a command from God to proclaim His Word. You must, says Peter, exercise the chief function of a priest, that is, to proclaim the wonderful deed God has performed for you to bring you out of darkness into the light. And your preaching should be done in such a way that one brother proclaims the mighty deed of God to the other, how you have been delivered through Him from sin, hell, death, and all misfortune, and have been called to eternal life. Thus you should also teach other people how they, too, come into such light. For you must bend every effort to realize what God has done for you. Then let it be your chief work to proclaim this publicly and to call everyone into the light into which you have been called. Where you find people who do not know this, you should instruct and also teach them as you have learned, namely, how one must be saved through the power and strength of God and come out of darkness into the light.

And here you see that Peter states clearly that there is only one light and concludes that all our reason, no matter how clever, is utter darkness. For although reason can count one, two, three, can also see what is black or white, large and small, and can judge about outward things, yet it cannot see what faith is. Here it is stone-blind. And even if all men were to put all their wisdom together, they could not understand one letter of the divine wisdom. Therefore St. Peter is speaking here of another light, a light that is marvelous; and he tells us bluntly that we are all in darkness and in blindness if God does not call us into His true light.

Experience also teaches us this. For when one preaches that we cannot come before God with works, but that we must have a Mediator who could come before God and reconcile us to Him, then reason must admit that it could have absolutely no knowledge of this. Therefore it must have a different light and knowledge if it is to understand this. Consequently everything that is not God's Word and faith is darkness. For there reason gropes about like a blind man, always falls from one thing upon another, and does not know what it is doing. If we tell this to the learned and wise in the world, they do not want to hear it and begin to cry out and rage against it. Therefore St. Peter is truly a bold apostle. What everybody calls light he designates as darkness.

Thus we see that the first and foremost duty we Christians should perform is to proclaim the wonderful deeds of God. Now what are the wonderful deeds and the noble works God has done? They are the deeds and works we have often mentioned, namely, that by the power of God Christ has swallowed up death, devoured hell, drunk sin to the dregs, and placed us into eternal life. These are such great deeds that man cannot understand them, let alone perform them. Therefore it is completely useless to preach human doctrines to us Christians. No, one should preach to us about the kind of power that overcomes the devil, sin, and death. And here St. Peter has again referred to many Scripture passages, just as throughout his writings he nearly always quotes one verse after the other. For all the prophets say that God's name and honor, and His arm or power, should be honored and praised, and that He would perform a deed of which the whole world would sing and speak. The prophets are full of this everywhere. Here St. Peter points to all these places. Moreover, the prophets also said much about light and darkness. They said that we must be illumined with the light of God. In this way they also show that all human reason is darkness. St. Peter continues:

Once you were no people, but now you are God's people; once you had not received mercy, but now you have received mercy.

This verse is found in Hosea 2:23. St. Paul also quoted it in Rom. 9:25, where he says: "Those who were not My people I will call My people." All this points to the fact that almighty God chose the people of Israel in particular, conferred great honor on them, gave them many prophets, and also performed many miraculous deeds with them because He wanted Christ to become man from this nation. All this took place for the sake of the Child. For this reason they are called God's people in Scripture. But the prophets amplify this and said that this promise should become known and should also concern the Gentiles.

Therefore St. Peter says here: "Once you were no people, but now you are God's people." From this it is clear that he wrote the Epistle to the Gentiles, not to the Jews. With these words he now wants to point out that the statement of the prophet has now been fulfilled, that they are now a holy nation, God's own people, the priesthood and kingdom, and that they have everything Christ has—provided that they believe.

1 Peter 4:1

Since therefore Christ suffered in the flesh, arm yourselves with the same thought; for whoever has suffered in the flesh has ceased from sin.

St. Peter continues on the same path. Just as so far he has exhorted us all to suffer if it is God's will and has presented Christ to us as an example, so he now confirms this further and repeats it. He wants to say: Since Christ, who is our Leader and Head, suffered in the flesh and gave us all an example—besides, He redeemed us through His suffering—we should imitate Him, equip ourselves in this way, and put on armor of this kind. For in Scripture the life of the Lord Christ, and particularly His suffering, is presented to us in a twofold manner. In the first place, as a gift, as St. Peter has already done in the third chapter. First, he stressed faith and taught that we are redeemed by the blood of Christ, that our sins have been taken away, and how He has been given to us as a gift. This cannot be grasped in any other way than through faith. The apostle spoke about this when he said: "Christ also died for sins once for all" (3:18). This is the chief article and the best part of the Gospel.

In the second place, Christ is held up and given to us as an example and a pattern for us to follow, for if we now have Christ as a gift through faith, we should go forward and do as He does for us. We should imitate Him in our whole life and in all our suffering. That is the way St. Peter presents this here. But here St. Peter is not speaking primarily of the works of love with which we serve and benefit our neighbor, which are really good works—for he has said enough about this above—but he is speaking about works that relate to our bodies and serve us ourselves—works through which faith is strengthened, so that we mortify sin in the flesh and thus are able to serve our neighbor better. For if I subdue my body, so that it does not become lascivious, I can also let my neighbor's wife and child alone. Thus if I suppress hatred and envy, I become all the more willing to be kind and friendly to my neighbor.

Now we have stated often enough that although we are righteous through faith and have the Lord Christ as our own, we are nonetheless also obliged to perform good works and to serve our neighbor. For we never become perfectly pure while we are living on earth, and everyone still finds evil lust in his body. To be sure, faith begins to slay sin and to bestow heaven; but it has not yet become perfect and really strong, as Christ says about the Samaritan (Luke 10:33ff.), whose wounds were not yet healed. But he was bandaged and looked after, in order that his wounds might be healed. This is also how it is here. If we believe, our sin, that is, the wound we have brought from Adam, is bandaged and begins to heal. But in one person this healing is less, and in another person it is more, the more each one chastises and subdues the flesh, and the more firmly he believes. Therefore if we have these two things, faith and love, we should henceforth devote ourselves to sweeping out sin entirely until we die completely.

For this reason St. Peter says: "Arm yourselves with the same thought"; that is, make a firm resolution, and strengthen your hearts with the thought you receive from Christ. For if we are Christians, we have to say: "My Lord suffered for me and shed His blood. He died for my sake. Should I, then, be so worthless as not to be willing to suffer?" For since the Lord steps to the front in the fray, how much more should His servants rejoice to step forward! In this way we gain courage to prevail and to arm ourselves in our thoughts, in order that we may go through with joy.

In Scripture the little word "flesh" means not only the body externally, where there is flesh and blood, bone and skin, but everything that comes from Adam. Thus God says in Gen. 6:3: "My Spirit shall not abide in man forever, for he is flesh." And in Isa. 40:5 we read that all flesh shall see the glory of the Lord; that is, this glory will be revealed to all mankind. Thus we also confess in the Creed: "I believe in the resurrection of the flesh";

that is, that mankind will rise again. Accordingly, flesh means the whole man through and through, as he lives here in this life.

Now the works of the flesh are enumerated by Paul one by one in Gal. 5:19–21, not only the coarse, carnal works, such as unchastity, but also the costliest and most sublime vices, such as idolatry and heresy, which are not only in the flesh but also in reason. Therefore one must understand this to mean that man, together with his reason and will, internally and externally, together with body and soul, is called flesh because with all his powers, externally and internally, he sees only that which is carnal and which benefits the flesh. Accordingly, St. Peter now adds here that "Christ suffered in the flesh." Now it is certain that His suffering extended farther than into the flesh alone; for, as the prophet Isaiah says (53:11), His soul suffered the great travail.

In this way you must also understand what follows here: "Whoever has suffered in the flesh has ceased from sin." For this, too, refers not only to cutting off someone's head and to dismembering the body but to everything that can hurt man, to whatever misery and distress he suffers. For many people have sound bodies, and yet inwardly they feel much heartache and wretchedness. If this happens for Christ's sake, it is profitable and good. For, as St. Peter says, "whoever has suffered in the flesh has ceased from sin." The holy cross is a good means with which to subdue sin. When it attacks you in this way, your tickling, envy, and hatred, and your other rascality, vanish. God has laid the holy cross on us in order that it may drive and compel us, so that we have to believe and to extend a helping hand to one another.

1 Peter 4:9–10

Practice hospitality ungrudgingly to one another. As each has received a gift, employ it for one another.

The person who is glad to provide lodging is called hospitable. Thus when the apostles went jointly in the country to preach, and when they sent their disciples to and fro, then one person had to provide lodging for the other person. This is how it should still be. One should travel from one place to another to preach, from city to city, from house to house; and one should not tarry too long at one place. One should be able to see: if a person is weak, he should get help; if a person has fallen, he should be encouraged; and the like. This, says St. Peter, should be done ungrudgingly, and no one should let this be too much. Now this is also a work of love, as is also the injunction that follows, namely, that we should serve one another. With what? With the gifts of God which everyone has received. The Gospel wants everyone to be the other person's servant and, in addition, to see that he remains in the gift which he has received, which God has given him, that is, in the position to which he has been called. God does not want a master to serve his servant, the maid to be a lady, a prince to serve the beggar. For He does not want to destroy the government. But the apostle means that one person should serve the other person spiritually from the heart. Even if you are in a high position and a great lord, yet you should employ your power for the purpose of serving your neighbor with it. Thus everyone should regard himself as a servant. Then the master can surely remain a master and yet not consider himself better than the servant. Thus he would also be glad to be a servant if this were God's will. The same thing applies to other stations in life.

Lectures on Jonah

1526

By the mid-1520s theological controversy and political turmoil surrounded Martin Luther. Disagreement over infant Baptism, the presence of Christ in the Lord's Supper, and the use of images in worship divided the Protestant reformers. Many rejected God's objective work through Word and Sacrament and directed people to the internal working of the Spirit. Some were convinced that the Spirit spoke through them as through the prophets of old. The divine call to preach, they thought, would come not from a city council or church but from the direct working of the Holy Spirit. The spirit of revolution was also in the air. Some thought they were the elect of God and had been set apart to cleanse Germany of corrupt Christianity by use of the sword. It was also at this time that grievances by the peasants of Germany arose. Their economic and social concerns led to rioting and plundering. Violence erupted throughout Germany, resulting in the bloody Peasants' War of 1524–25.

During this upheaval, Luther lectured on the minor prophets. In his preface to the lectures on Jonah, he laments that the devil has divided the various reforming groups in Germany, embroiled them in controversy, and used rebellion to draw the reformers away from the Gospel and the study of the Scriptures. Luther's lectures returned him to the classroom and to the task of interpreting the Bible. The lectures on Jonah were first published in Latin in 1525. Luther produced an expanded version in German in 1526. The German version is used below.

In the excerpts that follow, Luther offers reflections on biblical interpretation and the importance of history for understanding the prophets. The beginning of Jonah also provides warrant for St. Paul's teaching on natural knowledge of God. When God raised a mighty tempest on the sea, the mariners in the ship with Jonah called out to their own gods. Luther reflects at length on natural knowledge and the defects of natural reason. Luther turns next to the nature of Jonah's sin and why God's mercy for the Ninevites displeased him. Finally, Luther ends with an allegorical reading of the wild plant provided for Jonah and the worm sent to destroy it.

Lectures on Jonah[1]

Since the prince of this world has sowed his tares everywhere and Germany has become glutted with factions and spirits through whom he not only seduces many but also turns those who remain faithful to many unprofitable and vain pursuits and thereby detracts them from Scripture and entices them into his disputes and thus, in the end, cunningly catches them off the base of Scripture and works their ruin, it is imperative that we recognize this sly and malicious attack and not become too engrossed in his altercations, lest he lure us far away from our defenses and our fortress and surreptitiously defeat us. "For," as St. Paul declares, "we are not ignorant of his designs" (2 Cor. 2:11). And St. Peter informs us that the devil does not take a holiday but "prowls around like a roaring lion, seeking someone to devour" (1 Pet. 5:8). For some time I have entered the lists and fought against these spirits and factions. Now that others have joined the fray, I have decided to take Scripture in hand again to feast our hearts, to strengthen, to comfort, and to arm them, lest fatigue and lassitude subdue us in our daily struggle. May God grant me grace that we, by His Word and the comfort of Scripture, may be refreshed and invigorated to fight with ever greater courage. . . .

I have therefore chosen to expound the holy prophet Jonah, for he is indeed well suited for this situation and represents an excellent, outstanding, and comforting example of faith and a mighty and wonderful sign of God's goodness to all the world. For who would not trust God with all his heart, proudly defy all the devils, the world, and all the fulminating tyrants, and exult over God's kindness, when he contemplates this story and beholds how easily God's power and grace are able to preserve Jonah in the midst of the deep sea, even in the belly of the whale, thus saving him not only from one death but also from various deaths, deserted and forgotten as he is by all men and all creatures? Apparently without effort God sustains Jonah and brings him back merely by uttering a word. It is as if God were saying: "Behold, this is what I can do with one word. In view of this, what do you suppose I could do with My Spirit and power?" The human mind cannot conceive of a greater work than this. For that reason Christ Himself prizes this story so highly, citing this Jonah above all other prophets as an illustration of His own death and resurrection.

1 The following excerpt is adapted from *Lectures on Jonah: The German Text*, in volume 19 of *Luther's Works: American Edition*, ed. Hilton C. Oswald, trans. Martin H. Bertram (St. Louis: Concordia, 1974). Minor alterations have been made to the text for consistency in style, abbreviations, and capitalization. The annotations and subheadings are the work of the editor of this book.

In Matt. 12:39 He says: "No sign shall be given this generation except the sign of the prophet Jonah, etc."

Furthermore, Jonah is also an object of comfort for all who administer the Word. It teaches them not to despair of the fruit of the Gospel, no matter how badly it appears to be devoid of fruit and profit. For here a single man, Jonah, is dispatched to the mightiest king and the greatest kingdom of that day. When we compare the two, Jonah and this king, it impresses us as ridiculous and completely impossible that such a mighty king and such a powerful kingdom should be moved, converted, and frightened by the words of one weak individual, a stranger to boot, and by a message which the king himself did not even hear—he heard it only as a report. In view of this, I am tempted to say that no apostle or prophet, not even Christ Himself, performed and accomplished with a single sermon the great things Jonah did. His conversion of the city of Nineveh with one sermon is surely as great a miracle as his rescue from the belly of the whale, if not an even greater one. For just as the whale had to spew Jonah forth in obedience to the words of God, so Jonah by the Word of God also tore the city of Nineveh from the belly and the jaws of the devil, that is, from sin and death. Would it not be reasonable to assume that such a king would rely on his great might and regard this one man a liar, a man whom even his own fellow Hebrews disobeyed? Thus the apostles and, as we hear in Ps. 2:2, even Christ Himself were shamefully despised by kings and princes on earth. And there are princes, bishops, and lords today who are veritable beggars compared with the king of Nineveh but who rely so vaingloriously on their tawdry beggary that they do not only despise the Word of God but also persecute it.

That is why Christ in Matt. 12:41 cites the men of Nineveh against all unbelievers and scorners of His Word, saying: "The men of Nineveh will arise at the judgment with this generation and condemn it; for they repented at the preaching of Jonah, and behold, something greater than Jonah is here." And that is not at all unfair, for it will forever stand as a great miracle that the people of Nineveh were converted so quickly by a foreign preacher and by means of such simple words, without any attendant miraculous signs. And these Jews were not converted by their own Savior, who preached to them so often and lavished miracles on them. What a shame to hear that now! And what a shame it will be also to see this! But it is of no avail; they are and remain hardened. Therefore we let them go their way, and we take comfort from the prophet and learn our lesson from him as God grants us grace. Amen.

Jonah 1:1
Now the word of the Lord came to Jonah the son of Amittai.

Some people concur in Jerome's[2] opinion that this prophet Jonah was the son of the widow of Zarephath at Sidon, who fed the prophet Elijah in a time of famine, according to 1 Kings 17 and Luke 4:26. These people base their assumption on the fact that Jonah here calls himself son of Amittai (v. 1), that is, "son of the truthful one." This they relate to the widow's words to Elijah after he had raised her son from the dead: "Now I know that the word of the Lord in your mouth is true" (1 Kings 17:24). Whoever wants to may believe this; I do not. No, his father's name was Amittai; in Latin it would be *Verax*, in German, *Wahrlich*. And he came from Gath-hepher, a town within the borders of the tribe of Zebulun, according to Josh. 19:13. For in 2 Kings 14:25 we find recorded: "[King Jeroboam] restored the border of Israel from the entrance of Hamath as far as the Sea of the Arabah, according to the word of the Lord, the God of Israel, which He spoke by His servant Jonah the son of Amittai, the prophet, who was from Gath-hepher." Moreover, the widow of Zarephath was a Gentile, as Christ also tells us in Luke 4:26; but Jonah confesses here in chapter 1:9 that he is a Hebrew.

I am enlarging on this because I regard it advantageous to know the time of a prophet's life and the country in which he lived. Wherever available, these facts should be mentioned. It contributes to a proper understanding of a man's book if one knows his time, his place of residence, his person, and his background. Of Jonah we know that he lived in the days of King Jeroboam, whose grandfather was King Jehu, a contemporary of King Uzziah in Judah. The prophets Hosea, Amos, and Joel lived in the kingdom of Israel at the same time, although in different places and towns. From this I suppose we can infer that Jonah was an excellent and estimable man in the kingdom of Israel and that God worked great things through him, for by means of his preaching King Jeroboam was fortunate enough to recover all the land that Hazael, the king of Syria, had taken from the kingdom of Israel. He had inflicted such great injury that also the prophet Elisha had wept over it when he foresaw it, according to 2 Kings 8:11. God bestowed these favors on Israel despite the fact that the kingdom was still idolatrous, worshiping the golden calves in Samaria beside the true God. So great is the mercy when God grants a country one man with His Word and for his sake not only endures the whole country's misdeeds and disobedience but even comes to the aid of that country and showers untold benefits on it. What would God not be

2 On Jerome, see above, p. 86 n. 3.

willing to do or abstain from doing for a country that contains more than one godly person?

Scripture does not indicate whether these events in Nineveh and in the whale happened to Jonah before he proved so helpful to Jeroboam or later, after his return from Nineveh. It seems credible, however, that he first served and aided Jeroboam in his country until he had reestablished the kingdom of Israel and that thereupon he was sent farther afield, out of his country to Nineveh. In his own country he observed with his own eyes what kindness and mercy God was showing to the idolatrous kingdom of Israel. And from this he very likely gathered that God would be just as kind and gracious to Nineveh, so that his preaching would be useless and unnecessary, as he himself angrily confesses in chapter 4:1–2.

Jonah 1:2–3

"Arise, go to Nineveh, that great city, and cry against it . . . ." But Jonah rose to flee to the sea, away from the presence of the Lord.

. . . Now the question suggests itself whether or not Jonah committed a sin by fleeing from the Lord. The ancient holy fathers were all inclined to make excuses for the prophets, apostles, and great saints. They carried this silly deference to them to such extremes that they even preferred to violate Holy Scripture, to force it and stretch it, before they would admit that the saints were sinners. Although we can bear with their humility, which grew from their hatred of sin and their respect for righteousness, it is nevertheless dangerous to bend Scripture thus and to follow their interpretation. Christ speaks a different language; in Matt. 5:18 He declares that heaven and earth would have to pass away before an iota or a dot of Holy Scripture would vanish. It is better to concede the saints too little than too much; it is better to detract from them than to disparage God Himself and His Word. We can be saved without the saints but not without God's Word.

Thus we shall stick rigidly and inflexibly to the Word of God and agree that Jonah here committed a grave and serious sin, which would have damned him eternally, had his name not been recorded in the Book of Life amid the number of the elect. It is obvious, and no one can deny it, that God here issues an order to Jonah, bidding him to go to Nineveh and preach there. Moreover, it is certain that God did not view this matter lightly but that He was in earnest about this, even as He was in the Garden of Eden at the time when He gave orders to Adam. He says: "The wickedness of the city of Nineveh has come up before Me." This means that He purposed to punish the entire kingdom. In short, God is very angry. Thus it is also evident that Jonah is disobedient to this earnest command of God by fleeing and refusing to execute God's command. Thereby he sinned as gravely as Adam did in Paradise. Jonah should not merely have accepted the divine will, but he should also have been most happy to carry it out. He should rather have suffered a hundred deaths than to become disobedient to God's Word. For what can be more flagrant and heinous than disobedience to God's will? Behold, what a price Adam, Saul, and the people of Israel paid for this sin! Yes, witness what happened to Jonah here because of his disobedience! It seems to me that the enormous and terrible punishment meted out to his disobedience is an index of the gravity of this sin. How miserably he evades obedience to God on the sea! I am sure that he wished he could have died three times on land instead. Since he refuses to go to Nineveh, he must sail into the jaws of the whale far out at sea. . . .

Sinning against grace

It is also a source of great comfort to us to see that even the greatest and best saints sin grievously against God and that we are not the only poor, miserable sinners. We observe that they, too, were human, that they had flesh and blood as we do, and now we, too, must not despair, even though we fall into sin. If only we do not defect from the kingdom of grace through false doctrine and superstition! For just as there is no sin so great as to be unforgivable in that kingdom, so there is no work so good, no life so holy, as not to be damnable without this grace. However, I declare that to remain in the kingdom of grace implies that we do not sin against grace. Sinning against grace is done in a twofold manner: first, by sinning against God's commandment and then aggravating this by adding the devilish sin to despond and despair, believing and disturbing my conscience with the thought that God will not forgive my sin and that there is no longer any mercy for me. Under those circumstances there is, in fact, no longer any mercy, but God with all His mercy is denied and thwarted. This is no longer a human but a devilish sin, a sin against the Holy Spirit, which is unforgivable so long as it remains, for it directly counteracts the mercy by which sin is to be remitted. . . .

The second manner in which I sin against grace is if I perform good works with the simultaneous devilish thought that I comfort myself with these or rely on them, that I tell my conscience that I can stand before God with these, as if there were no sin here. Thereby I neutralize grace for myself, acting as though grace were neither necessary nor beneficial, since works could do this. That, too, is denying God with all His mercy, and that is no longer human but devilish righteousness, which cannot be forgiven so long as it remains and is not recognized. If a person becomes so pious in his works and his being that he does not require forgiveness or grace but regards his works in themselves good and pure enough to render grace and forgiveness superfluous, he remains outside the kingdom of grace and sins against grace.

Jonah 1:4–5

But the Lord hurled a great wind upon the sea, and there was a mighty tempest on the sea . . . . Then the mariners were afraid, and each cried to his god.

Here you find St. Paul's statement in Rom. 1:19 concerning the universal knowledge of God among all the heathen, that is, that the whole world talks about the Godhead and natural reason is aware that this Godhead is something superior to all other things. This is here shown by the fact that the people in our text called upon a god, heathen though they were. For if they had been ignorant of the existence of God or of a Godhead, how could they have called upon him and cried to him? Although they do not have true faith in God, they at least hold that God is a being able to help on the sea and in every need. Such a light and such a perception is innate in the hearts of all men; and this light cannot be subdued or extinguished. There are, to be sure, some people, for instance, the Epicureans, Pliny, and the like, who deny this with their lips.[3] But they do it by force and want to quench this light in their hearts. They are like people who purposely stop their ears or pinch their eyes shut to close out sound and sight. However, they do not succeed in this; their conscience tells them otherwise. For Paul is not lying when he asserts that they know something about God, "because God has shown it to them" (Rom. 1:19).

Defects of natural reason

Let us here also learn from nature and from reason what can be known of God. These people regard God as a being who is able to deliver from every evil. It follows from this that natural reason must concede that all that is good comes from God; for He who can save from every need and misfortune is also able to grant all that is good and that makes for happiness. That is as far as the natural light of reason sheds its rays—it regards God as kind, gracious, merciful, and benevolent. And that is indeed a bright light. However, it manifests two big defects: first, reason does admittedly believe that God is able and competent to help and to bestow; but reason does not know whether He is willing to do this also

3 The ancient Greek philosopher Epicurus (341–270 BC) and his followers denied divine providence and were often accused of atheism (see below, p. 343 n. 32). Pliny the Elder wrote a monumental work on the natural world that was widely used throughout the history of the church. See above, p. 114 n. 9.

for us. That renders the position of reason unstable. Reason believes in God's might and is aware of it, but it is uncertain whether God is willing to employ this in our behalf, because in adversity it so often experiences the opposite to be true. That is very obvious here. These people indeed call upon God and thereby acknowledge that He can help if He is thus inclined; they even believe that He may help others. But that is as far as they can go; they cannot transcend that. They exhaust every means at their command; they try their utmost. Free will cannot go beyond that. But they do not believe that God is disposed to help them. For if they did, they would not "throw the wares that were in the ship into the sea," nor would they turn to Jonah and urge him to call upon his God. No, they would calmly await the help of God. Moreover, the sea would also have become tranquil as a result of their faith. But this situation calls for a faith that does not doubt but is convinced that God wants to be gracious not only to others but also to me. That is a genuine and a live faith; it is a great and rich and rare gift of the Holy Spirit, and so we shall see it in Jonah.

The second defect is this: Reason is unable to identify God properly; it cannot ascribe the Godhead to the one who is entitled to it exclusively. It knows that there is a God, but it does not know who or which is the true God. It shares the experience of the Jews during Christ's sojourn on earth. When John the Baptist bore witness of His presence in their midst, they were aware that Christ was among them and that He was moving about among them; but they did not know which person it was. It was incredible to them that Jesus of Nazareth was the Christ. Thus reason also plays blindman's buff with God; it consistently gropes in the dark and misses the mark. It calls that God which is not God and fails to call Him God who really is God. Reason would do neither the one nor the other if it were not conscious of the existence of God or if it really knew who and what God is. Therefore it rushes in clumsily and assigns the name God and ascribes divine honor to its own idea of God. Thus reason never finds the true God, but it finds the devil or its own concept of God, ruled by the devil. So there is a vast difference between knowing that there is a God and knowing who or what God is. Nature knows the former—it is inscribed in everybody's heart; the latter is taught only by the Holy Spirit.

Reason makes idols

We shall illustrate this with a few examples. Let us first consider the Papists and the religious.[4] These are laboring under the delusion that God is a being who is moved and satisfied by good works. That explains their many vocations, sects, and modes of life, in all of which they presume to serve and please God. Now tell me, what are these people worshiping

4 On the "religious," see above, p. 26 n. 25.

as God if there is no God whose mind and will conforms to theirs? Is it not true that they are honoring their own delusion and their own fancy as God? For in truth there is no God who is of one mind with them. Therefore they go awry with their illusion. They miss the true God, and nothing remains but their own false notion. That is their god. To him they assign the name and honor of God. Of course, no one but the devil can be behind this delusion, for he inspires and governs these thoughts. Thus their delusion is their idol; it is the image of the devil they hold in their hearts. For the real and the true God is He who is properly served not with works but with the true faith and with sincerity of heart, who gives and bestows mercy and benefactions entirely gratis and without our works and merits. That they do not believe, and therefore they do not know God but are bound to blunder and to miss the mark.

Here you see where all idolatry comes from and why it is rightly called idol (*Abgott*) and superstition (*Abglaube*) and idolatry (*Abgötterei*), undoubtedly because such delusion draws us away from God (*Ab-Gott*) and alienates us from the true worship of God. Indeed, this is an idol and a superstition that directs us away from God and directs us to the devil in hell. For since everybody proposes to do something which he regards and believes to be pleasing to God and imagines that God is minded as he supposes He is—but in reality God is not pleased by this, and in reality God is not minded as each one supposes—it follows that as many idolatries must arise as there are illusions of that kind. Every idea of pleasing God comes into being except that of faith; this the Holy Spirit must inspire. Thus the idol Baal came to the mind of King Ahab. Since he knew that there was a God, he imagined that it was God who was pleased with his type of worship. Thus he called God Baal, and Baal God, as is evident from Hosea 2:16.

Furthermore, King Jeroboam supposed that it was God who was pleased with the worship of the golden calves. And therefore calves had to be called the God of Israel, and, again, God had to be called a calf (1 Kings 12:28). That is like calling Christ our Lord a lover of cowls or of tonsures today because people assume that He is a God who is in love with cowls and tonsures and is well-pleased with such service. I am sure that monks and priests have that conception of Him in their hearts and also call Him that. But this is an idol and superstition and delusion which falls wide of the mark; it is genuine archidolatry. There are innumerable types of idolatry; in fact, there are as many varieties as there are illusions and self-chosen concepts of pleasing God. All but faith in Christ come into this category. And since there is nowhere a God who is pleased with this service, it follows that they are all serving the devil and not God.

Thus you also note that the people in the ship all know of God, but they have no definite God. For Jonah relates that each one calls on his own god, that is, his concept of God, whatever he conceives of God in his mind. And in that way they all fail to encounter the one true God and have nothing but idols whom they call God and honor as God. Therefore their faith, too, was false; it was superstition and idolatry and of no avail. For their god lets them down in the hour of need; he lets them call in vain, so that they despair and find themselves at a loss to know where to find a god who might help them. They run down to Jonah, arouse him, and command him to call on his God. They are curious to see whether there might be another god besides their own to aid them. There you can see that a false faith will not stand the test of adversity, but that both god and faith, idol and superstition, become engulfed and vanish, and that nothing but despair remains. Therefore only the one living God is entitled to the name and reputation of being a helper in every trouble, Ps. 9:10; Ps. 46:1; for He can rescue from death, Ps. 68:20.

You also perceive how humble these people are now as they turn to Jonah in their distress, whom they had ignored so long as all was safe and tranquil. And if they had known that he was a Jew, they would have despised him still more, since the Gentiles were hostile to the Jews. But now that they are beset by perils and their idol is letting them down, how happy their proud contempt is to call on poor Jonah, expecting more good from him than from all their idols and all their power. That is always the experience of a false and fictitious faith. So long as all goes well, it retains its conceit; it is arrogant even toward God and all that is God; it is obdurate and harder than any anvil ever was. But when such a faith begins to give way and despond, then there is nothing more timid and discouraged in heaven and on earth, and it would then like to crawl into a mousehole. The wide world becomes too confining for it, and it gladly seeks and accepts help and counsel from friend and foe, from those it respects and those it despises.

Jonah's sin

Meanwhile, Jonah is sleeping down below in the ship, completely insensible to the tempest. That may indeed be termed a sleep of death, which has come over him shortly before he is doomed to die. That is always the way with sinners. God deals with them as He does here with Jonah. Jonah had sinned grievously against God. But because God remains silent, tarries with His punishment, does not restrain the sin, or does not immediately strike the offender, it is the nature and way of sin to blind and to harden man. He becomes secure and loses his fear, lies down, goes to sleep, and fails to see the disaster and the great storm gathering over him which will arouse him horribly. Meanwhile God appears to have forgotten the sins, since He delays the punishment. Thus He tests the children of men and waits to see whether they will repent, as Ps. 11:4 says: "His eyelids test the children of men." But nothing comes of this; they do not repent, they do not weigh the consequences. Jonah would probably continue to sleep to the end of his days; if God would forget his sins, he would surely never give them a thought himself. This is indicated by Jonah's deep sleep in the midst of the storm, and far down below in the ship besides. It is like saying that he is blinded, obdurate, and submerged in sin, yes, dead, lying in the pit of his unrepentant heart. He would remain there eternally and perish too; for sin would not permit any power for good to bestir itself, free will or no free will, reason or no reason. There he lies and snores in his sin, hears nothing and sees nothing, nor does he feel what God's wrath contemplates doing with him.

But when the captain wakes Jonah and bids him call upon his God, matters change. He becomes aware that God with His punishment is pursuing him and that God has not forgotten his sin. Now conscience raises its voice; now the consciousness of sin is revived; now "sin is the sting of death" (1 Cor. 15:56) and manifests the anger of God. Now not only the ship but the whole world becomes too small for Jonah. The irony of it—he should now call upon God! He is more fear-stricken than all the others on the ship taken together; for he feels and senses, and his conscience also tells him, that this tempest is aimed at him and that God's wrath has overtaken him. Oh, how humble he is now. He absolves all other people on the ship from sin; he does not regard them as sinners. He sees no sin but his own. That is the way of remorse. When that comes to a person and stings and terrifies the conscience, the entire world looks pious to him, and only he himself is a sinner. Then God appears gracious to all the world but to him; then God's anger strikes none but him alone. He also assumes that there is no other wrath than that felt by him, and he regards himself as the most wretched person. That was also the experience of Adam and Eve after their fall into sin. If God had not come to them in the cool of the day, they would never have paid any attention to their sin. But when He appeared to them, they hid from Him. Peter, too, went his way after he had denied Christ. He felt no sin; he also slept, as it were, down below in the ship; he was dead until Christ looked at him. Then he again came to and wept bitterly. Thus we behold here how obstinate, callous, and virtually dead sin makes man; he is sensitive neither to himself nor to God and walks along securely and unafraid until God comes and arouses him. Thus the glory of free will is laid low.

Jonah shrinks from calling on his God; he sits there, trembles before God's wrath, and struggles with death, which threatens to devour him any moment. At the same time the other people cry to their gods in vain, doing all they can for their rescue. Jonah surely sees and senses that all this is happening because of him. However, he is not pious enough to come out into the open and confess his sin, but he lets these poor people endure such terror and danger and distress for his sake until he is betrayed by the casting of lots and God wrests a confession of his sin from him. That is also one of the tender virtues of sin: it renders people mute. It conceals itself; it is ashamed; it would like to remain beautiful, like Adam and Eve when they covered their nakedness with an apron and refused to come to confession. Oh, it hurts to uncover your own shame and to turn your glory into disgrace. But in the end this will have to be done, or man will find no rest and peace of mind. As Ps. 32:3 says: "When I declared not my sin, my body wasted away through my groaning all day long." Thus God ordered the children of Israel to strip themselves of their ornaments before Mount Sinai (Exod. 33:5). This is really a time for donning sackcloth and sitting in ashes, for crushing oneself before God and also, if God wants this, before man. Since these people have incurred loss and danger because of Jonah's sin, it is necessary that he, in turn, suffer loss, forfeit his honor, and speak his own shame. He must restore the honor of these people and establish their innocence. He must pronounce his own death sentence, obliging them to drown him. Thus he pays his debt and, with life and limb, with honor and goods, and with all he is and has, atones for the sin with which he has so deeply injured his fellow men. He has jeopardized their life against their will, and now they must take his life, also against their will, but by reason of his own verdict and wish. That, I think, is stern and righteous judgment.

Jonah 1:9

I am a Hebrew; and I fear the Lord, the God of heaven, who made the sea and the dry land.

Now Jonah's confession is forthcoming; now the sin is brought to the light of day. Now the real struggle between Jonah and death ensues, although the most difficult phase of the conflict is over. For although death and the wrath of God advance on Jonah and furiously attack him, the heavy burden of sin has already been rolled from his heart, his conscience has become lighter through his confession of sin, and his faith begins to catch fire, though only dimly. For Jonah confesses the true God, Creator of heaven and earth, and this is no insignificant beginning of faith and of bliss. A despondent and despairing conscience will not open its lips that far; it grows mute or blasphemes God, and it cannot think, regard, and mention God otherwise than as a horrible tyrant or as a devil. It would only like to flee from Him and put as much distance as possible between itself and God. Indeed, it would prefer it if He were not God, so that it would not have to experience this at His hands. Such a conscience also is unmindful of confession and does not admit its sin. It is so lost in fear and so hardened that it sees and feels nothing but fear and thinks only about ridding itself of this fear, which is impossible, since it keeps on charging itself with sin. And thus it remains engulfed in sin and in death eternally.

From this let us learn the real art and skill of extricating ourselves from all distress and fear. To do this, we must first of all take note of our sin, forthwith make a clean breast of it, and confess it. That disposes of the most urgent danger and need. For help must first be brought to the heart; this must be lightened and given air to breathe. Then it is easier to aid the whole person. Thus the conscience must first of all be disencumbered and given room to breathe, and then aid can be found for all trouble. Two things are involved when God's anger strikes, sin and fear. Imprudent hearts cope with this situation incorrectly. They let the sin remain and are intent only on ridding themselves of the fear. That will not profit them, and they must despair. That is the way reason, if not accompanied by grace and spirit, always attacks the problem. But sensible hearts turn their minds away from fear and concentrate mainly on sin, confess this, and free themselves of it; and no matter if they should be haunted by fear forever, they reconcile themselves to this, as Jonah does here. But it is the way of all the ungodly that they fear and heed the punishment but pay no heed to the sin. They would like to continue to sin with impunity; but that is impossible, since punishment regularly follows in the wake of sin. On the other hand, it is in the nature of the godly to fear and to heed sin and to have less regard for the punishment. They would rather suffer punishment and be delivered of sin than to remain in sin and be free of punishment.

Jonah 1:12, 17

Throw me into the sea; then the sea will quiet down for you; for I know it is because of me that this great tempest has come upon you. . . . And Jonah was in the belly of the fish three days and three nights.

Jonah must have thought these the longest days and nights ever lived under the sun. It must have seemed an interminably long time that he sat there in the dark. Yes, I suppose, that he occasionally lay down and stood up. He saw neither sun nor moon and was unable to compute the passage of time. Nor did he know where in the sea he was traveling about with the fish. How often lung and liver must have pained him! How strange his abode must have been among the intestines and the huge ribs! However, death was crowding in upon him, and he paid scant attention to the fish. His one thought was: When, when, when will this come to an end? O God, what a great miracle this is! Who can really comprehend how a man can survive three days and three nights within a fish, in the middle of the sea, all alone, without light and without food, and in the end return to dry land again? That must have been a strange voyage. Who would believe this story and not regard it a lie and a fairy tale if it were not recorded in Scripture?

God proves here that He holds death and everything in His almighty hand and that it is an easy matter for Him to help us even in indescribable and desperate situations. This seems incredible to us. He is present everywhere, in death, in hell, in the midst of our foes, yes, also in their hearts. For He has created all things, and He also governs them, and they must all do as He wills. This story is recorded for our sakes, and God's omnipotence is here displayed so forcefully to induce us to trust and to believe Him, whether we find ourselves in the grasp of death or in the hands of our enemies. It was not necessary for God to have this story recorded for His own sake, nor for Jonah's own good. The world can talk glibly about divine omnipotence, and it seems easy for everyone to believe that God is almighty whenever this is asserted, but experience demonstrates how many really and genuinely believe this when it is a question of staking life and limb on God's omnipotence and when it is a matter of experiencing the truth of these words for oneself in death and in sin. To come by this truth is hard even for the greatest saints. And yet to know this and to be familiar with examples illustrating it is comforting. Thus the prophet glories in Ps. 119:52: "When I think of Thy ordinances from of old, I take comfort, O Lord."

The people in the ship are convinced that Jonah must drown and die. This is evident from the fact that they pray God not to let them perish because of Jonah's soul nor to hold them responsible for innocent blood. Thereby they imply that they consider him dead; in fact, they themselves had to be instrumental in killing him, although reluctantly and only in compliance with God's will. However, now that Jonah has disappeared from sight, now that he has died to himself and to the world and that all hope for his life is abandoned, his life and the fruit of his death first begin; for in death he is mightily kept alive. And in that way the people in the ship are also delivered from death, also from unbelief and from sin, and they are brought to a knowledge of God so that they now become pious and true servants of God, such humble and timid servants that they even fear and stand in awe of sinning where they are in reality doing nothing but obeying God. They would like to preserve Jonah's life. They are apprehensive of murdering him by drowning him, although they see that God wants it that way. What pure, God-fearing, and Christian consciences these people now have! The same people who prior to this did not hesitate to commit murder and who were entirely indifferent to obeying God now proceed to make sacrifices to God and to make vows. The various gods on whom they had called earlier are all forgotten. And this was all effected by Jonah and his dying. A servant of God must prove himself so useful that there is nothing about him that does not accrue to the benefit and the welfare of others. We stated earlier that the fear of God is just another term for the service of God; for true service of God is to fear and to honor God. Thus these people, too, feared God, that is, they became God's servants and God-fearing men.

Jonah 2:1–2

Then Jonah prayed to the Lord his God from the belly of the fish, saying, I called to the Lord out of my distress, and He answered me; out of the belly of Sheol I cried, and Thou didst hear my voice.

Jonah begins by praising God's mercy and help and by thanking Him for His deliverance from distress. Thus he first of all holds God's goodness up before our view and then his own need from which he was helped. This first verse of Jonah's prayer teaches us two important and necessary lessons: first, that we must above all else pray and cry to God in time of adversity and place our wants before Him. For God cannot resist helping him who cries to Him and implores Him. His divine goodness cannot hold aloof; it must help and lend an ear. All depends on our calling and crying to Him. We dare not keep silent. Turn your gaze upward, raise your folded hands aloft, and pray forthwith: "Come to my aid, God my Lord! etc.," and you will immediately find relief. If you can cry and supplicate, then there is no longer any reason for worry to abide. Even hell would not be hell or would not remain hell if its occupants could cry and pray to God. It is vain to lament and to bemoan your condition and to fret and to worry about your sad estate and to cast about for a helper. That will not extricate you from your woes; it will only drag you in deeper. Listen and hear what Jonah does. He, too, consumed himself a long time with his distress before he resorted to prayer, as he himself will tell us later. If he had not delayed, he would presumably have been delivered sooner. He also bids and teaches you not to emulate his example in this respect, but he immediately states that he prayed and thus was granted deliverance. . . .

The second lesson that we derive from this is that we must feel that our crying to God is of a nature that God will answer, that we may glory with Jonah in the knowledge that God answers us when we cry to Him in our necessity. That means nothing else but to cry to God with the heart's true voice of faith; for the head cannot be comforted, nor can we raise our hands in prayer, until the heart is consoled. And as I have already said, the heart finds solace when it hastens to the angry God with the aid of the Holy Spirit and seeks mercy amid the wrath, lets God punish and at the same time dares to find comfort in His goodness. Take note what sharp eyes the heart must have, for it is surrounded by nothing but tokens of God's anger and punishment and yet beholds and feels no punishment and anger but only kindness and grace; that is, the heart must be so disposed that it does not want to see and feel punishment and anger, though in reality it does see and feel them, and it must be determined to see and feel grace and goodness, even though these are completely hidden from view. Oh, what a difficult task it is to come to God. Penetrating to Him through His wrath, His punishment, and His displeasure is like making your way through a wall of thorns, yes, through nothing but spears and swords. The crying of faith must feel in its heart that it is making contact with God, just as Christ felt that "a power had gone forth from Him" when He had stopped a woman's flow of blood (Mark 5:30). One perceives that the Spirit's words and works hit their mark and do not miss. But if we cry and pray indifferently, hit or miss, we accomplish nothing. That is rather mockery and hypocrisy in the sight of God.

Jonah 2:10

And the Lord spoke to the fish, and it vomited out Jonah upon the dry land.

To say that God does and effects all things by means of speaking or through the agency of words is fully in accord with Scripture. In John 1:3 we read: "All things were made through the Word, and without the Word was not anything made that was made"; and in Ps. 33:9: "For He spoke, and it came to be; He commanded, and it stood forth." Thus the fish was kept from digesting Jonah. Not only was the digestive process of nature in the fish suspended, but the fish also had to vomit the food out again; it had to disgorge Jonah and return him to land unharmed. Thus God worked great miracles in Jonah. Now the former order of things is reversed: What a moment ago served the purpose of death must now serve to further life. The fish who was but recently the tool of death must now be life's implement; it must be a gateway to life, though just a short time before it held Jonah captive and consigned him to death. The ocean, too, must make way for Jonah and give its guest free access to the land. The roots of the mountains no longer hold him; earth's bars are pushed aside; the weeds cover him no more; etc. All of this is a source of comfort and confidence for us. It teaches us to rely on God, with whom life and death are alike. They are both trivial to Him, playthings as it were, as He bestows the one and takes the other, or exchanges one for the other. But for us these are momentous and impossible things, which God employs to display His power and skill to us, as Psalm 104 declares.

Jonah 3:1–2

Then the Word of the Lord came to Jonah the second time, saying: Arise, go to Nineveh, that great city.

This is written that we may guard against undertaking anything without God's word and command. The first command of God had been nullified by Jonah's disobedience. Thus if God had not repeated His order, Jonah would not have known whether or not he was still to execute it. He might have shared the experience of the children of Israel (Num. 14:1ff.; Deut. 1:41ff.), who at first refused to comply with God's command to fight and later presumed to do this on their own responsibility and then suffered defeat because of their presumption. It is utterly futile and wrong for man to undertake a project of his own choosing and will without God's command and word. Moreover, this second commission contains the added command to preach what God tells him. Thus both the office and the Word employed in the office must be comprehended in the divine command. If that is done, the work will prosper and bear fruit. But when men run without God's command or proclaim other messages than God's Word, they work nothing but harm. Jeremiah, too, drives both these facts home, saying (Jer. 23:21): "I did not send the prophets, yet they ran; I did not speak to them, yet they prophesied." You who are to preach, impress these two points on your minds! Note them well! They are directed to you and the people; they enable you to instruct souls. Peter also emphasized these two facts (1 Pet. 4:11): "Whoever speaks, as one who utters oracles of God; whoever renders service, as one who renders it by the strength which God supplies," so that he may be sure that both the Word and the office are divine and commanded by God. For it is decreed that whenever God speaks, it comes to be (Ps. 33:9), that all things are to come to pass by His Word (John 1:3). Therefore "every plant which My heavenly Father has not planted will be rooted up" (Matt. 15:13). Even if they are planted and begin to sprout, they will not reach the state of fruition. Thus man's petty baubles may have their day, but they work havoc and do not effect their purpose; after they have run their course and wrought enough harm, they perish.

Jonah 3:4

And he cried: Yet forty days, and Nineveh shall be overthrown!

Jonah goes into the city "a day's journey" and preaches. It is not known, however, how many days he spent before he covered that area with his message. His sermon is briefly summarized in the words: "In forty days Nineveh shall be overthrown." Undoubtedly he did not confine himself to these words, but he must have enlarged on the themes why such wrath of God would overtake them, what sorts of wickedness were rampant in the city, how one should be a godly person, and all that is involved in this. We are still in the habit of summarizing a sermon today, saying, for example: "He preached on sin" or "He preached on the Mass."

Jonah 3:5

And the people of Nineveh believed God; they proclaimed a fast and put on sackcloth, from the greatest of them to the least of them.

I hold that none but saints inhabited the city and that Jonah rightly called it "a city of God." Show me another city in the wide world comparable to Nineveh, even if it were the holy city Jerusalem. Just look at this city! Jonah preached only a day's journey, and not every citizen heard him; yet they were all converted. Neither Christ nor all the apostles and prophets were ever able to bring Jerusalem to that point by means of their words and their miracles, though they ministered to it for a long time and preached from one end of the city to the other. God might exclaim here, too, as Christ did in Matt. 8:10 about the centurion: "Not even in Israel have I found such faith." Yes, in the days of Jonah, Israel and Jerusalem were very wicked as Nineveh turned to God. If Jerusalem had done this, as it did in the days of David, Solomon, Ezekiel, and Josiah, it would not have been so miraculous, since it had the Law, many prophets, many God-fearing kings, princes, priests, and other excellent people who daily preached and admonished. However, at the time of Jonah, Nineveh was the best and greatest city on earth, a city without equal.

Jonah 4:1–2
But it displeased Jonah exceedingly, and he was angry. And he prayed to the Lord, etc.

This is, I think, a queer and odd saint who is angry because of God's mercy for sinners, begrudging them all benefits and wishing them every evil. This militates against the nature of love, which does everything good and wishes everything good even to enemies. It is still more amazing to find this attitude in Jonah after he had experienced the great sternness of the divine will in the ocean and in the whale. He does not even change when God punishes him for this unreasonable anger. And yet he has enough faith at the same time to ask God to let him die; he does not care to live any longer. He could not have prayed thus if he had not trusted God implicitly. What comment are we to add here? How can such faith and such evil exist side by side? Here questions are pertinent. Here you might benefit by them. We cannot deny that Jonah is angry without cause and that he is indeed doing wrong. This is evidenced by the fact that God punishes him for this with words and with deed, and that He chides him with the token of the wild plant. But at the same time we must concede that he remained in the faith and was acceptable to God, since He conversed so affably with Jonah and granted him a token, acting like a man who chats and deals in a friendly way with his fellow man. . . .

We must note first of all how wondrous God is in His saints, lest we be tempted to judge and condemn them thoughtlessly because of any of their actions. This work here may be evil—as indeed it is. But for all of that, I must not despise and reject the person. For if we regard Jonah in this act, we must agree that his actions are surely wrong; for God Himself punishes him. And yet he is God's dear child. He chats so uninhibitedly with God as though he were not in the least afraid of Him—as indeed he is not; he confides in Him as in a father. Second, we learn that God permits His children to blunder and err greatly and grossly. We see in the Gospels that Christ does likewise with His apostles. This redounds to the consolation of all believers who sin and stray occasionally. Third, we observe how very kindly, paternally, and amiably God deals with those who place their trust in Him in times of need. The Epistle to the Hebrews (Heb. 12:11) tells us how gracious God is to us after first whipping and flogging us, which punishment "yields the peaceful fruit of righteousness to those who have been trained by it." For here we perceive that this cannot harm us nor be imputed to us as sin, though, in fact, it is sin and culpable. But it is the daily sin of a child that the heavenly Father willingly bears in His mercy. However, God does not treat the ungodly in that manner. Nor would such treatment befit their character; for they grow inordinately insolent and ungovernable when they sense that God is gracious and inclined to spare them. They demean themselves as though God should be expected to endure and tolerate their ungodly conduct.

God desires all to be saved

However, it is not at all surprising that Jonah is loath to see God's grace extended also to the heathen. For judge for yourself and consider that the Jews always believed that Israel alone was God's people, as I have said before, and that all the Gentiles were under God's wrath. Thus Ps. 79:6 exclaims: "Pour out Thy anger on the nations that do not know Thee and on the kingdoms that do not call on Thy name." Consequently, they insisted that no man would partake of God's grace before he adopted the laws of Moses and became a Jew. The apostles and the other early Christians conceived of this matter in the same way. Luke writes in Acts 8 that they went about preaching the Word to none but the Jews, and he writes in Acts 10 and 11 that the Jews were displeased with Peter because he had preached to the Gentiles. And it is nothing short of a miracle that Jonah was not persecuted and killed by the Jews because he had preached in Nineveh and had called it a city of God. The mere thought that Jonah should praise the people of Nineveh as being people of God, without having and without observing the laws of Moses, was intolerable to the Jews. And I ask you, what judgment can all they expect today who teach that there are Christians and that there may well be Christians who do not have and do not observe the ordinances of the pope and the customs and precepts of the Roman Church? They must, of course, be accounted heretics—yes, heretics—and are fit to be burned at the stake.

It seems plausible to assume that this was the true reason why Jonah was so unwilling to go to Nineveh, why he grumbled because the city was not destroyed, and why he preferred death to the spectacle of seeing people in receipt of God's grace and of being regarded as people of God without adoption of the laws of Moses and the customs of the Jews. What else was that than infamy for the people of Israel, implying that their laws were useless and unnecessary, since a man could well be saved without them? Would it not be reasonable for them to say, as the men do in the Gospel (Matt. 20:12): "Why are we slaving and drudging if these last arrivals work but an hour and receive the same compensation as we who have borne the heat and toil of the day?" Should that not cause eyes to go green with jealousy? Should they not be regarded as better than the others? Should they not receive more? Thus it also happens here that the people of Nineveh obtain mercy without the Law and the prophets, and the Jews, despite their great labors, receive no more than they; yes, in the end the Jews forfeit grace completely. Their grumbling and their jealousy demand something better than the Gospel. They begrudge the Gentiles the privilege of becoming Christians. It is the expectation that he should convey these benefits to the people of Nineveh that irks Jonah so. To think that he should be the first to make Judaism contemptible and superfluous! How could he, under those circumstances, remain in his country? It was not without cause that he fled and refused to preach. For to be a Jew and yet to proclaim that Judaism was unnecessary and that God's grace was available without it is the same as to depreciate and disparage his fellow countrymen and to exalt the Gentiles. That was the experience of Paul, as we find recorded by Luke in the Book of Acts (13:45ff.).

In order to dispel Jonah's scruples and also to supply him with an answer to give to his angry fellow Jews, God toys with him and gives him a sign, just as He did to Peter in Acts 10:11ff., when Peter labored under a similar illusion as Jonah here. God showed him a vision from heaven, a linen cloth containing all kinds of animals, and told him that everything was pure, although he saw nothing but heathen without the laws of Moses, etc. Thus God also gives Jonah a sign here. He causes a wild plant to grow that provides Jonah with a delightful arbor. And now while he is enjoying this shelter, the Lord creates a worm early in the morning before Jonah is aware of it. This worm "attacked the plant, so that it withered," and that deprived Jonah of his great joy. Furthermore, God let the sun burn down on his uncovered head. This vexed Jonah again and added indignation to indignation. Everything goes contrary to his wishes. And in order to forestall further disappointment, Jonah again asks God to let him die. And now God appears and silences him. Like the householder in the Gospel, He announces that He can do as He wants (Matt. 20:15). He also shows that Jonah is annoyed without cause. "Behold," He says, "you are angry because an insignificant plant withered and did not continue to flourish. Of how much less value is such a shrub than a person, to say nothing of such a city? Should you who wish to see the wild plant preserved not also wish and rejoice to see the city saved?" What could Jonah say to refute this? He had to remain mute, vanquished in his own judgment, to which he had nicely been misled on the spot concerning the plant. So human ingenuity is a lost cause before God. . . .

From all of this we learn that God is a helper of all men, not only of the Jews. Thus St. Paul says in 1 Tim. 2:4: "God desires all men to be saved and to come to the knowledge of the truth." We learn that we are heathen who have come into God's grace in the last hour without having toiled and with no promise of God's grace such as was given the Jews. God grant that we might show our gratitude and avail ourselves of this as these people of Nineveh did, lest we also finally perish more miserably by reason of our ingratitude, as the people of Nineveh did later on. The story of Jonah has been transmitted to us because God wants to show us His miracles, namely, that God's Word bears fruit mainly where this is least expected and, conversely, produces least where most is expected. Here we find the heathen of Nineveh coming to faith, though they had not heard the Word of God before; and we find that the Jews, who heard the Word of God daily, abandon their faith. From this we must learn, on the one hand, not to despair of anyone and, on the other, not to place undue confidence in anyone. . . .

Let that suffice on this subject. Now we must also consider the spiritual meanings of this book . . . .

Allegory of plant and worm

Finally, we have the plant and the worm which attacked the former at the dawn of day. This phase of the story pertains not only to Jonah, to his anger and his thoughts described in the text, but it is applicable also to Judaism, which was a real wild plant. The plant, in the first place, has large leaves. That is its best part, as these leaves afforded Jonah welcome shade. It formed a sheltering hut against the sun's heat over his head. Nothing is said about fruit. In fact, the plant bore no fruit. The leaves represent the words and laws of God. St. Paul says in Rom. 3:2: "The Jews are entrusted with the oracles of God." Jonah is seated under these leaves, that is, the prophets and holy fathers dwelt in the midst of Judaism as under a temporal hut and given to external divine worship until the days of Christ. It was an arbor for the summer season or a tabernacle which served but for a time and then ceased to exist. But it bore no fruit, for the Law, devoid of the Spirit, could profit no one of itself, although many holy people dwelt under it in the Spirit. Therefore Christ cursed the fig tree, which had leaves but no fruit, and it withered (Matt. 21:19). The same fate befell the wild plant in our story. However, Jonah takes delight in the arbor as he there awaits the devastation of the city of Nineveh. For the Jews gloried in and also boasted of the exclusive possession of God's Word and divine service. They regarded the Gentiles as altogether doomed, just as Jonah does the people of Nineveh here.

And now while the Jews complacently rely on being God's people to the exclusion of all others, and just as Jonah is basking in the enjoyment of this wild plant, God appoints a worm to smite the plant. This signifies that Christ appeared with His Gospel at a time when the Jews vaunted most vaingloriously that they alone were God's people. He attacked the wild plant, that is, He preached against it and abolished the Law through His Holy Spirit and liberated us all from the Law and its power. Therefore Judaism withered and decayed in all the world, and thus we see it today.

Its verdure is gone, it flourishes no longer, nor is there a saint or a prophet sitting in its shade today. Its day is spent. Christ is a worm, as He says in Ps. 22:6: "I am a worm, and no man." He is this by reason of His shameful crucifixion and the shame heaped upon Him. And yet this poor crucified Worm stings such a fine shrub that it withers. With this slight sting, that is, with the despised Gospel, He dashes such a mighty kingdom and people to pieces.

The fact that the worm works this harm not in the evening but early in the morning, at the break of day, signifies that this fall of Judaism occurred at the dawn of the day of grace, of the New Testament, at the time when the era of grace broke upon the world through the Gospel. For He who caused the plant to grow so marvelously also permitted the worm to attack it and make it wither. Similarly, Judaism sprang into being overnight and prospered through many marvelous miracles of God's might; it did not grow by its own power and strength. The history of Moses, of all the kings, etc., demonstrates that adequately. In like manner it also withered and perished by God's will and command when the hour of the Gospel had struck. Jonah is vexed here for two weighty reasons: first, because the plant withered and deprived him of the enjoyment of its shade; second, because Nineveh is not to perish. It seems unfair to him, as it also did to several great saints, that the Jews should be so forsaken and wither and come to an end and that the people of Nineveh, the Gentiles, should accept the Gospel and become God's children. Then the sun beats upon Jonah's head, and a sultry east wind appears, and he becomes faint. The thought of the perdition of the Jews also caused St. Paul much anguish of heart in Rom. 9:3, and he was ready to wish that he himself "were accursed and cut off from Christ" for their sake. But Jonah is informed that it would be better for him to display this anger over the prospect of Nineveh's destruction than over the withering of this plant, that it would be better that Nineveh be preserved than this plant. This reflects what St. Paul says in Rom. 11:11: "Through their" (the Jews') "trespass salvation has come to the Gentiles," that is, it is better and fairer that Judaism should die (which, after all, was unprofitable and without spirit, all leaves and no fruit) than that it be preserved and the whole world be brought to ruin. That is the judgment which was pleasing to God. And therefore it is fitting that we Gentiles thank Him for His mercy. For the Jews sustained no loss if they were willing to believe and abandon their Judaism; and for us, all of salvation depends on this. May God help us to attain this. Amen.

Sermon on the Mount

1531

In 1521, from the Wartburg, Martin Luther wrote to Philip Melanchthon and complained that his very capable colleagues thought only of proclaiming the Gospel to the people of Wittenberg. "For goodness' sake, do you want the kingdom of God to be proclaimed only in your town? Don't others also need the Gospel? Will your Antioch not release a Silas or a Paul or a Barnabas for some other work of the Spirit?"[1] *We must not live for ourselves, continued Luther. The harvest is plentiful, and we are the harvesters. Let us be ready to go where God sends us. Over the course of the 1520s, amid great theological and political difficulties, Luther's colleagues heeded his words and began the hard work of spreading the Gospel throughout Germany and beyond.*

In 1523, Johann Bugenhagen (1485–1558) was called by the city council to be pastor of St. Mary's Church, the city church of Wittenberg. Bugenhagen became Luther's pastor, confessor, and dear friend. He was an exceptional administrator and was regularly asked to introduce the Reformation to various cities throughout Germany and countries beyond. In 1528, Bugenhagen left Wittenberg for the city of Braunschweig. Luther expected Bugenhagen to be away for several days, but days turned into months. Bugenhagen completed his work in October only to be summoned to Hamburg. He would not return to Wittenberg until June 1529. During Bugenhagen's absence, Luther assumed the preaching and administrative duties at St. Mary's in addition to his already full schedule of teaching and writing.

When a similar request for help arrived from Lübeck in the summer of 1530, Bugenhagen again departed. He was in Lübeck from October 1530 to April 1532. The preaching and administrative duties for St. Mary's once again fell to Luther, who complained in a letter that he had to be Luther, Bugenhagen, Moses, and Jethro.[2] *Luther's preaching increased significantly. He preached from the lectionary Sunday mornings and afternoons, preached a series on the Gospel of Matthew on Wednesdays, and preached another series on the Gospel*

1 Luther's letter to Philip Melanchthon, July 13, 1521, LW 48:262.

2 Luther's letter to Wenzeslaus Link, December 1, 1530, WA Br 5:692.13–14.

of John on Saturdays.[3] *The sermons on Matthew below were given during 1531 and published in 1532.*

The following excerpt focuses on the Beatitudes (Matt. 5:1–12) and includes Luther's final postscript on grace and merit. Luther's sermons address the relationship between the goods of this world and Christian faith. The religion of the world wrongly ties prosperity to piety. People falsely think the rich are blessed by God and the poor are rejected by God. On the other hand, the Anabaptists reject all money and property in the name of the Gospel.[4] *For Luther, both of these views produce counterfeit saints who recreate the order of God's creation by misunderstanding His blessings and by manufacturing good and holy works. Luther counters both views by appealing to a proper understanding of vocation. God calls us to different offices, and we serve Him by providing for our neighbors in these places. This means we neither despise riches nor praise poverty.*

When God says that our works will be rewarded and that our labor is not in vain, what reward does He promise? Luther's postscript on grace and merit advances a number of subtle distinctions to answer this question. He admits that his discussion belongs more properly to the classroom than to the pulpit. Nevertheless, because Scripture says these things and many twist their proper meaning, he offers an explanation. The reward promised pertains not to eternal life but to the glory of eternal life. Greater suffering in our vocations will bring greater glory in heaven. As Luther puts it, St. Paul's star will be more brilliant and brighter than others.

Luther's sermons on the Beatitudes address the practical concerns of living faithfully in the world for others. His discussion of wealth and poverty and of vocation and good works lies at the heart of his mature thoughts on the Christian way of life according to the Gospel.

3 Luther had suggested that these two Gospels be especially preached during the week. See *German Mass and Order of Service* (1526), LW 53:68.

4 The Anabaptists (from the Greek for "rebaptizers") rejected infant Baptism and practiced believers' baptism. Beyond this shared commitment, a great deal of diversity prevailed among the Anabaptist groups in the sixteenth century. Some embraced pacifism and expressed reservations with the orthodox doctrines of the Trinity and Christ. Some questioned the use of all externals in worship, including water for Baptism or bread and wine for the celebration of the Lord's Supper. Some favored violence in bringing about their reformation, practiced polygamy, and required the communal sharing of all goods. Still others enthusiastically predicted the exact date and place of Christ's return.

Sermon on the Mount[5]

Preface

I am very happy to see the publication of these sermons of mine on the three chapters of St. Matthew which St. Augustine calls "the Lord's Sermon on the Mount."[6] May God grant His grace so that they may help to preserve and keep the true, sure, and Christian understanding of this teaching of Christ, because these are such common sayings and texts that are used so often throughout Christendom. I do not doubt that here I have presented their true, pure, and Christian meaning to my friends and to anyone else that is interested. It is beyond understanding how through his apostles the wicked devil has managed so cleverly to twist and pervert especially the fifth chapter, making it teach the exact opposite of what it means. Christ here deliberately wanted to oppose all false teaching and to open up the true meaning of God's commandments, as He emphasizes when He says (Matt. 5:17): "I have not come to abolish the Law." He takes it up piece by piece and tries to make it completely dear. Still the infernal Satan has not found a single text in the Scriptures that he has more shamefully distorted and into which he has imported more error and false teaching than this very one, which Christ Himself ordered and appointed in order to head off false doctrine. This is really the devil's masterpiece!

... So long as the devil lives and the world stands, he will not stop attacking this chapter. His aim is in this way to suppress good works altogether, as happened under the papacy; or to institute false good works and fictitious holiness, as he has now begun to do through the new monks or schismatic spirits. Even if both the papistic and the schismatic jurists and monks were to perish, he would still find or raise up others; for he has to have such a following. From the beginning of the world, his kingdom has been ruled by monks. Although they may not have been called "monk," yet their teaching and life have been monkish, that is, different and special and better than what God has commanded. ... From this fifth chapter have come the pope's monks, who on the basis of this chapter have laid claim to a more perfect station in life than other Christians, and have maintained this claim until they are full of greed, pride, and finally every kind of devil. May Christ, our dear Lord and Master, who

5 The following excerpt is adapted from *The Sermon on the Mount*, in volume 21 of *Luther's Works: American Edition*, ed. and trans. Jaroslav Pelikan (St. Louis: Concordia, 1956). Minor alterations have been made to the text for consistency in style, abbreviations, and capitalization. The annotations and subheadings are the work of the editor of this book.

6 On Augustine, see above, p. 4 n. 1.

has opened up the true meaning for us, increase and strengthen it for us, and may He help us to live and act according to it. To Him be praise and thanks, with the Father and the Holy Spirit forever. Amen.

Matthew 5:1–2

Seeing the crowds, He went up on the mountain; and when He sat down, His disciples came to Him. And He opened His mouth and taught them and spoke.

Here the evangelist opens with a preface stating how Christ prepared Himself for the sermon He wanted to deliver: He went up on a mountain, sat down, and opened His mouth, to make it evident that He was in earnest. These are the three things, so to speak, which every good preacher should do: First, he takes his place; second, he opens his mouth and says something; third, he knows when to stop. "Takes his place" means that he presents himself as a master, a preacher with both the ability and the responsibility, one who comes with a call and not on his own, one to whom it is a matter of duty and obedience. Then he can say: "I am not coming because my own purpose and preference impel me, but I must do so because it is my office." This is said against those who have been causing us so much toil and trouble and still are, the schismatic rascals and fanatics who roam all over the country. They poison the people before the clergy and the government can discover it; and so they defile one household after another, until they have poisoned an entire city, and from the city an entire country.

To guard against such sneaks and cheats, one ought not to let anyone preach unless he has been appointed and commissioned for it. Nor should anyone take it upon himself, even though he is a preacher, to preach against a lying preacher whom he hears misleading the people in a papal or other church. Nor should anyone sneak around into the houses and set up private preaching meetings. He should stay at home and mind his own official business and pulpit. If he neither will nor can enter the pulpit publicly, he should keep quiet. God does not want people running all over the place with His Word as though they were driven by the Holy Spirit and had to preach, or were seeking nooks or corners or pulpits to preach where they have no official call. Even though St. Paul was called as an apostle by God, he did not want to preach in places where other apostles had preached before (Rom. 15:20). Therefore it says here that Christ went up the mountain openly and publicly when He began His preaching ministry. A little later He said to His disciples (Matt. 5:14–15): "You are the light of the world. Men do not light a lamp and put it under a bushel, but on a stand, to give light to all in the house." The Office of the Ministry and the Word of God are supposed to shine forth like the sun. We should not go around sneaking and plotting in the dark, as when we play blindman's buff, but deal openly in broad daylight, to make it perfectly plain that both preacher and hearer are sure about the propriety of the teaching and the legitimacy of the office, so that concealment is unnecessary. Act the same way if you are in the ministry and have the commission to preach. Take your place openly, and fear no one; then you can boast with Christ (John 18:20): "I have spoken openly and freely before the world, and I have said nothing in the corner."

But you say: "What? Does this mean that no one should teach anything except in public? Should not the head of a household teach his servants in his house or keep a pupil or someone there who recites to him?" Answer: Of course that is all right and in its proper place here. The head of every family has the duty of training and teaching his children and servants, or of having them taught. In his house he is like a minister or bishop over his household, and he has the command to supervise what they learn and to be responsible for them. But you have no right to do this outside your own household and to force yourself upon other households or upon your neighbors. Nor should you put up with it if some such sneak comes to you and sets up a special preaching meeting in your household for which he has no authorization. If someone comes into a house or city, let him be required to furnish proof that he is known, or let him show by letter and seal that he has proper authorization. Not every vagabond is to be believed who boasts that he has the Holy Spirit and who uses this to insinuate himself into this or that household. In short, this means that the Gospel or proclamation should not be listened to in a corner, but high up on a mountain and openly in the free daylight. That is the first thing that Matthew wants to show here.

The second thing is that He opens His mouth. As I have said, this is also part of a preacher's duty. He should not keep his mouth shut, nor perform his office publicly merely so that everyone must keep quiet and let him take his place as one who has a divine right and command. But he should also open his mouth vigorously and confidently, to preach the truth that has been entrusted to him. He should not be silent or mumble, but testify without being frightened or bashful. He should speak out candidly without regarding or sparing anyone, let it strike whomever or whatever it will. It is a great hindrance to a preacher if he looks around and worries about what people like or do not like to hear, or what might make him unpopular or bring harm or danger upon him. As he stands high on a mountain in a public place and looks around freely, so he should also speak freely and fear no one, though he sees many kinds of people and faces. He should not hold a leaf in front of his mouth. He should look at neither the pleasure nor the anger of lords and squires, neither money nor riches, neither popularity nor power, neither disgrace nor poverty nor harm. He should think of nothing except that he is speaking what his office demands—his very reason for standing there.

For Christ did not establish and institute the ministry of proclamation to provide us with money, property, popularity, honor, or friendship, nor to let us seek our own advantage through it; but to have us publish the truth freely and openly, rebuke evil, and announce what pertains to the advantage, health, and salvation of souls. The Word of God is not here to teach a maid or a servant how to work in the household and to earn his bread, nor a burgomaster how to rule, nor a farmer how to plow or make hay. In brief, it neither gives nor shows temporal goods for the preservation of this life, for reason has already taught all this to everyone. But it is intended to teach how we are to come to that other life. It tells you to make use of this life and to feed your belly here as long as it lasts, knowing all the while where you will remain and live when this has ended. When the preacher begins to preach concerning another life about which we should be concerned and for the sake of which we should not behave as though we wanted to stay here forever, then arguments and battles begin. The world cannot stand it. Then if a preacher loves his belly and this temporal life more, he is not doing his job. He may stand up and jabber in the pulpit, but he is not preaching the truth, he is not really opening his mouth. If trouble threatens, he keeps quiet and does not bite the fox.

Now you see why Matthew wrote the introductory statement that Christ as a true preacher goes up on the mountain and vigorously opens His mouth, teaching the truth and condemning both false teaching and false life, as we shall hear.

Matthew 5:3

Blessed are the spiritually poor, for theirs is the kingdom of heaven.

This is a fine, sweet, and friendly beginning for His instruction and preaching. He does not come like Moses or a teacher of the Law, with demands, threats, and terrors, but in a very friendly way, with enticements, allurements, and pleasant promises. In fact, if it were not for this report which has preserved for us all the first dear words that the Lord Christ preached, curiosity would drive and impel everyone to run all the way to Jerusalem, or even to the end of the world, just to hear one word of it. You would find plenty of money to build such a road well! And everyone would proudly boast that he had heard or read the very word that the Lord Christ had preached. How wonderfully happy the man would seem who succeeded in this! That is exactly how it would really be if we had none of this in written form, even though there might be a great deal written by others. Everyone would say: "Yes, I hear what St. Paul and His other apostles have taught, but I would much rather hear what He Himself spoke and preached."

But now since it is so common that everyone has it written in a book and can read it every day, no one thinks of it as anything special or precious. Yes, we grow sated and neglect it, as if it had been spoken by some shoemaker rather than the high Majesty of heaven. Therefore it is in punishment for our ingratitude and neglect that we get so little out of it and never feel nor taste what a treasure, power, and might there is in the words of Christ. But whoever has the grace to recognize it as the Word of God rather than the word of man will also think of it more highly and dearly, and will never grow sick and tired of it.

Friendly and sweet as this sermon is for Christians, who are His disciples, just so irksome and unbearable it is for the Jews and their great saints. From the very beginning He hits them hard with these words, rejecting and condemning their teaching, preaching the exact opposite, yes, pronouncing woe upon their life and teaching, as Luke 6:24–26 shows. The essence of their teaching was this: "If a man is successful here on earth, he is blessed and well-off." That was all they aimed for, that if they were pious and served God, He should give them plenty upon earth and deprive them of nothing. Thus David says of them in Ps. 144:13–15: "This is their teaching, that all their corners and garners should be full of grain and their fields full of sheep that bear often and much, and of cattle that labor much, with no harm or failure or mischance or distress coming upon them. Happy are such people!"

In opposition to this, Christ opens His mouth here and says that something is necessary other than the possession of enough on earth; as if He were to say: "My dear disciples, when you come to preach among the people, you will find out that this is their teaching and belief: 'Whoever is rich or powerful is completely blessed; on the other hand, whoever is poor and miserable is rejected and condemned before God.'" The Jews were firmly persuaded that if a man was successful, this was a sign that he had a gracious God, and vice versa. The reason for this was the fact that they had many great promises from God regarding the temporal, physical goods that He would grant to the pious. They counted upon these, in the opinion that if they had this, they were right with Him. The Book of Job is addressed to this theory. His friends argue and dispute with him about this and insist that he is being punished this way because of some great sin he must have knowingly committed against God. Therefore he ought to admit it, be converted, and become pious, that God might lift the punishment from him.

At the outset, therefore, it was necessary for His sermon to overthrow this delusion and to tear it out of their hearts as one of the greatest obstacles to faith and a great support for the idol Mammon in their heart. Such a doctrine could have no other consequence than to make people greedy, so that everyone would be interested only in amassing plenty and in having a good time, without need or trouble. And everyone would have to conclude: "If that man is blessed who succeeds and has plenty, I must see to it that I do not fall behind."

This is still what the whole world believes today, especially the Turks, who draw their reliance and strength from it, coming to the conclusion that they could not have had so much success and victory if they had not been the people of God to whom He was gracious in preference to all others. Among us, too, the whole papacy believes this. Their doctrine and life are founded only upon their having enough; and therefore they have assembled all the goods of the world, as everyone can see. In short, this is the greatest and most universal belief or religion on earth. On it all men depend according to their flesh and blood, and they cannot regard anything else as blessedness. That is why He preaches a totally new sermon here for the Christians: If they are a failure, if they have to suffer poverty and do without riches, power, honor, and good days, they will still be blessed and have not a temporal reward, but a different, eternal one; they will have enough in the kingdom of heaven.

But you say: "What? Must all Christians, then, be poor? Dare none of them have money, property, popularity, power, and the like? What are the rich to do, people like princes, lords, and kings? Must they surrender all their property and honor, or buy the kingdom of heaven from the poor, as some have taught?" Answer: No. It does not say that whoever wants to have the kingdom of heaven must buy it from the poor, but that he must be poor himself and be found among the poor. It is put clearly and candidly, "Blessed are the poor." Yet the little word "spiritually" is added, so that nothing is accomplished when someone is physically poor and has no money or goods. Having money, property, land, and retinue outwardly is not wrong in itself. It is God's gift and ordinance. No one is blessed, therefore, because he is a beggar and owns nothing of his own. The command is to be "spiritually poor." I said at the very beginning that Christ is not dealing here at all with the secular realm and order, but that He wants to discuss only the spiritual—how to live before God, above and beyond the external.

Having money, property, honor, power, land, and servants belongs to the secular realm; without these it could not endure. Therefore a lord or prince should not and cannot be poor, because for his office and station he must have all sorts of goods like these. This does not mean, therefore, that one must be poor in the sense of having nothing at all of his own. The world could not endure if we were all to be beggars and to have nothing. The head of a household could not support his household and servants if he himself had nothing at all. In short, physical poverty is not the answer. There is many a beggar getting bread at our door more arrogant and wicked than any rich man, and many a miserly, stingy peasant who is harder to get along with than any lord or prince.

So be poor or rich physically and externally, as it is granted to you—God does not ask about this—and know that before God, in his heart, everyone must be spiritually poor. That is, he must not set his confidence, comfort, and trust on temporal goods, nor hang his heart upon them and make Mammon his idol. David was an outstanding king, and he really had his wallet and treasury full of money, his barns full of grain, his land full of all kinds of goods and provisions. Despite all this he had to be a poor beggar spiritually, as he sings of himself (Ps. 39:12): "I am poor, and a guest in the land, like all my fathers." Look at the king, sitting amid such possessions, a lord over land and people; yet he does not dare to call himself anything but a guest or a pilgrim, one who walks around on the street because he has no place to stay. This is truly a heart that does not tie itself to property and riches; but though it has, it behaves as if it had nothing, as St. Paul boasts of the Christians (2 Cor. 6:10): "As poor, yet making many rich; as having nothing, and yet possessing everything."

All this is intended to say that while we live here, we should use all temporal goods and physical necessities, the way a guest does in a strange place, where he stays overnight and leaves in the morning. He needs no more than bed and board and dare not say: "This is mine, here I will stay." Nor dare he take possession of the property as though it belonged to him by right; otherwise he would soon hear the host say to him: "My friend, don't you know that you are a guest here? Go back where you belong." That is the way it is here too. The temporal goods you have, God has given to you for this life. He does permit you to use them and with them to fill the bag of worms[7] that you wear around your neck. But you should not fasten or hang your heart on them as though you were going to live forever. You should always go on and consider another, higher, and better treasure, which is your own and which will last forever.

7 This along with "maggot sack" and "stinking sack of worms" were Luther's favorite colorful expressions for human mortality.

This is said coarsely for the common man. Thus he will learn to understand what it means in scriptural language to be "spiritually poor" or poor before God. We should not evaluate things externally, on the basis of money and property or of deficits and surpluses. For, as we have said above, we see that the poorest and most miserable beggars are the worst and most desperate rascals and dare to commit every kind of mischief and evil tricks, which fine, upstanding people, rich citizens or lords and princes, do not do. On the other hand, many saintly people who had plenty of money and property, honor, land, and retinue, still were poor amid all this property. We should evaluate things on the basis of the heart. We must not be overconcerned whether we have something or nothing, much or little. And whatever we do have in the way of possessions, we should always treat it as though we did not have it, being ready at any time to lose it and always keeping our hearts set on the kingdom of heaven (Col. 3:2).

Then, too, a man is called "rich" in Scripture, even though he does not have any money or property, if he scrambles and scratches for them and can never get enough of them. These are the very ones whom the Gospel calls "rich bellies," who in the midst of great wealth have the very least and are never satisfied with what God grants them. That is so because the Gospel looks into the heart, which is crammed full of money and property, and evaluates on the basis of this, though there may be nothing in the wallet or the treasury. On the other hand, it also calls a man "poor" according to the condition of his heart, though he may have his treasury, house, and hearth full. Thus the Christian faith goes straight ahead. It looks at neither poverty nor riches, but only at the condition of the heart. If there is a greedy belly there, the man is called "spiritually rich"; on the other hand, he is called "spiritually poor" if he does not depend upon these things and can empty his heart of them. As Christ says elsewhere (Matt. 19:29): "He who forsakes houses, land, children, or wife will receive a hundredfold, and besides he will inherit eternal life." By this He seeks to rescue their hearts from regarding property as their treasure, and to comfort His own who must forsake it; even in this life they will receive more than they leave behind.

We are not to run away from property, house, home, wife, and children, wandering around the countryside as a burden to other people. This is what the Anabaptist sect does, and they accuse us of not preaching the Gospel rightly because we keep house and home and stay with wife and children. No, He does not want such crazy saints! This is what it means: In our heart we should be able to leave house and home, wife and children. Even though we continue to live among them, eating with them and serving them out of love, as God has commanded, still we should be able, if necessary, to give them up at any time for God's sake. If you are able to do this, you have forsaken everything, in the sense that your heart is not taken captive but remains pure of greed and of dependence, trust, and confidence in anything. A rich man may properly be called "spiritually poor" without discarding his possessions. But when the necessity arises, then let him do so in God's name, not because he would like to get away from wife and children, house and home, but because, as long as God wills it, he would rather keep them and serve Him thereby, yet is also willing to let Him take them back.

So you see what it means to be "poor" spiritually and before God, to have nothing spiritually and to forsake everything. Now look at the promise which Christ appends when He says, "For of such is the kingdom of heaven." This is certainly a great, wonderful, and glorious promise. Because we are willing to be poor here and pay no attention to temporal goods, we are to have a beautiful, glorious, great, and eternal possession in heaven. And because you have given up a crumb, which you still may use as long and as much as you can have it, you are to receive a crown, to be a citizen and a lord in heaven. This would stir us if we really wanted to be Christians and if we believed that His words are true. But no one cares who is saying this, much less what He is saying. They let it go in one ear and out the other, so that no one troubles himself about it or takes it to heart.

With these words He shows that no one can understand this unless he is already a real Christian. This point and all the rest that follow are purely fruits of faith, which the Holy Spirit Himself must create in the heart. Where there is no faith, there the kingdom of heaven also will remain outside; nor will spiritual poverty, meekness, and the like follow, but there will remain only scratching and scraping, quarrels and riots over temporal goods. Therefore it is all over for such worldly hearts, so that they never learn or experience what spiritual poverty is, and neither believe nor care what He says and promises about the kingdom of heaven.

Yet for their sakes He so arranges and orders things that whoever is not willing to be spiritually poor in God's name and for the sake of the kingdom of heaven must still be poor in the devil's name and not have any thanks for it. God has so hung the greedy to their bellies that they are never satisfied or happy with their greedily gained goods. Sir Greed is such a jolly guest that he does not let anyone rest. He seeks, pushes, and hunts without stopping, so that he cannot enjoy his precious property for a single hour. Thus Solomon the preacher wonders and says (Eccl. 6:2): "Is it not a sore affliction that God gives a man wealth and possessions, land and retinue, and yet he is not capable of enjoying them?" He must always be afraid, troubled, and concerned about how he is going to keep it and expand it, lest it disappear or diminish. He is so completely its prisoner that he cannot enjoy spending a heller of it.[8] But if there were a heart that could be content and satisfied, it would have rest and the kingdom of heaven besides. Otherwise, amid great possessions and with its greed, it must have purgatory here and hellfire hereafter. As they say: "Here you travel in a wheelbarrow, but there on one wheel"; that is, you have trouble and anxiety here, but bitter grief hereafter.

Look, this is the way God always works, so that His Word remains true and no one is saved or satisfied except the Christian. Although the others have everything, their lot is never any better; indeed, it is never as good, and they must still remain poor beggars as far as their heart is concerned. The difference is that the former are glad to be poor and depend upon an imperishable, eternal possession, that is, upon the kingdom of heaven, and are the blessed children of God; but the latter are greedy for temporal goods, and yet they never get what they want, but must eternally be the victims of the devil's tortures besides. In short, there is no difference between a beggar before the door and such a miserable belly, except that the one has nothing and lets himself be put off with a crust of bread, while the other, the more he has, the less satisfied he is, even though he were to get all the goods and money in the world in one pile.

As I have said, therefore, this sermon does the world no good and accomplishes nothing for it. The world stubbornly insists upon being right. It refuses to believe a thing, but must have it before its very eyes and hold it in its hand, saying, "A bird in the hand is worth two in the bush." Therefore Christ also lets them go. He does not want to force anyone or drag him in by the hair. But He gives His faithful advice to all who will let Him advise them, and He holds before us the dearest promises. If you want it, you have peace and quiet in your heart here, and hereafter whatever your heart desires forever. If you do not want it, have your own way, and rather have sorrow and misfortune both here and hereafter. For we see and experience that everything depends upon being content and not clinging to temporal goods. There are many people whose heart God can fill so that they may have only a morsel of bread and yet are cheerful and more content than any prince or king. In brief, such a person is a rich lord and emperor, and he need have no worry, trouble, or sorrow. This is the first point of this sermon: Whoever wants to have enough here and hereafter, let him see to it that he is not greedy or grasping. Let him accept and use what God gives him, and live by his labor in faith. Then he will

8 The heller was the smallest coin in circulation.

have paradise and even the kingdom of heaven here, as St. Paul also says (1 Tim. 4:8): "Godliness is of value in every way, as it holds promise for the present life and also for the life to come."

Matthew 5:4

Blessed are those who mourn, for they shalt be comforted.

He began this sermon against the doctrine and belief of the Jews—in fact, not only of the Jews but of the whole world as well, even at its best, which sticks to the delusion that it is well-off if it just has property, popularity, and its Mammon here, and which serves God only for this purpose. In the same way He now continues, overturning even what they thought was the best and most blessed life on earth, one in which a person would attain to good and quiet days and would not have to endure discomfort, as Ps. 73:5 describes it: "They are not in trouble as other men are; they are not stricken like other men."

For that is the highest thing that men want, to have joy and happiness and to be without trouble. Now Christ turns the page and says exactly the opposite; He calls "blessed" those who sorrow and mourn. Thus throughout, all these statements are aimed and directed against the world's way of thinking, the way it would like to have things. It does not want to endure hunger, trouble, dishonor, unpopularity, injustice, and violence; and it calls "blessed" those who can avoid all these things.

So He wants to say here that there must be another life than the life of their quests and thoughts, and that a Christian must count on sorrow and mourning in the world. Whoever does not want to do this may have a good time here and live to his heart's desire, but hereafter he will have to mourn forever. As He says (Luke 6:25): "Woe unto you that laugh and have a good time now! For you shall have to mourn and weep." This is how it went with the rich man in Luke 16. He lived luxuriously and joyfully all his life, decked out in expensive silk and purple. He thought he was a great saint and well-off in the sight of God because He had given him so much property. Meanwhile he let poor Lazarus lie before his door daily, full of sores, in hunger and trouble and great misery. But what kind of judgment did he finally hear when he was lying in hell? "Remember that in your lifetime you received good things, but Lazarus evil things. Therefore you are now in anguish, but he is comforted" (Luke 16:25).

See, this is the same text as: "Blessed are those who mourn, for they shall be comforted," which is as much as saying, "Those who seek and have nothing but joy and fun here shall weep and howl forever."

You may ask again: "What are we to do, then? Is everyone to be damned who laughs, sings, dances, dresses well, eats, and drinks? After all, we read about kings and saints who were cheerful and lived well. Paul is an especially wonderful saint; he wants us to be cheerful all the time (Phil. 4:4), and he says (Rom. 12:15): 'Rejoice with those who rejoice,' and again: 'Weep with those who weep.' That sounds contradictory, to be joyful all the time and yet to weep and mourn with others."

Answer: I said before that having riches is not sinful, nor is it forbidden. So also being joyful, eating and drinking well, is not sinful or damnable; nor is having honor and a good name. Still I am supposed to be "blessed" if I do not have these things or can do without them, and instead suffer poverty, misery, shame, and persecution. So both of these things are here and must be—being sad and being happy, eating and going hungry, as Paul boasts about himself (Phil. 4:11–12): "I have learned the art, wherever I am, to be content. I know how to be abased, and I know how to abound; in any and all circumstances I have learned the secret of facing plenty and hunger, abundance and want." And in 2 Cor. 6:8–10: "In honor and dishonor, in ill repute and good repute; as dying, and, behold, we live; as sorrowful, yet always rejoicing."

So this is what it means: A man is called "spiritually poor," not because he has no money or anything of his own, but because he does not covet it or set his comfort and trust upon it as though it were his kingdom of heaven. So also a man is said to "mourn and be sorrowful"—not if his head is always drooping and his face is always sour and never smiling; but if he does not depend upon having a good time and living it up, the way the world does, which yearns for nothing but having sheer joy and fun here, revels in it, and neither thinks nor cares about the state of God or men.

In this way many great and outstanding people, kings and others, who were Christians, have had to mourn and be sorrowful, though in the eyes of the world they lived a glorious life. Thus throughout the Psalter David complains about his weeping and sorrow. Now, too, I could easily cite examples of great men, lords and princes, who have experienced and learned this about the gracious Gospel, at the recent Diet of Augsburg and elsewhere.[9] Externally they lived well, dressed in princely fashion in silk and gold, and looked like people for whom life was a bed of roses. But daily they had to be right in the midst of poisonous snakes; and in their heart they had to experience such unheard-of arrogance, insolence, and shame, so many evil tricks and words from the vile Papists, who delighted in embittering their hearts and, as far as possible, in denying them a single happy hour. Thus they had to stew within themselves and do nothing but lament before God with sighs and tears. Such people know something of

9 See the introduction to *Lectures on Galatians* (1531), below, p. 198.

what the statement means: "Blessed are those who mourn and are sorrowful," though they do not always show it. They eat and drink with other people and sometimes laugh and joke with them, to forget their sorrow. You must not suppose that "to mourn" means only to weep and cry and scream, like women and children. It is not the real and most profound mourning when it has come over the heart and breaks forth through the eyes, but when really great shocks come, which strike and shake the heart so that one cannot cry and dare not complain to anyone.

Therefore mourning and sorrow are not a rare plant among Christians, despite outward appearances. They would like to be joyful in Christ, outwardly, too, as much as they can. Daily, whenever they look at the world, they must see and feel in their heart so much wickedness, arrogance, contempt, and blasphemy of God and His Word, so much sorrow and sadness, which the devil causes in both the spiritual and the secular realm. Therefore they cannot have many joyful thoughts, and their spiritual joy is very weak. If they were to look at this continually and did not turn their eyes away from time to time, they could not be happy for a moment. It is bad enough that this really happens more often than they would like, so that they do not have to go out looking for it.

Therefore simply begin to be a Christian, and you will soon find out what it means to mourn and be sorrowful. If you can do nothing else, then get married, settle down, and make a living in faith. Love the Word of God, and do what is required of you in your station. Then you will experience, both from your neighbors and in your own household, that things will not go as you might wish. You will be hindered and hemmed in on every side, so that you will suffer enough and see enough to make your heart sad. But especially the dear preachers must learn this well and be disciplined daily with all sorts of envy, hatred, scorn, ridicule, ingratitude, contempt, and blasphemy. In addition, they have to stew inside, so that their heart and soul is pierced through and continually tormented.

Because the world does not want to have such mourning and sorrow, it seeks out those stations and ways of life where it can have fun and does not have to suffer anything from anyone, as the monks' and priests' station used to be. It cannot stand the idea that in a divine station it should serve other people with nothing but care, toil, and trouble, and get nothing as a reward for this but ingratitude, contempt, and other malicious treatment. Therefore, when things do not go with it as it wishes and one person looks at another with a sour face, all they can do is to batter things with cursing and swearing, and with their fists, too, and be ready to put up property and reputation, land and servants. But God arranges things so that they still cannot get off too easily, without seeing or suffering any trouble at all. What He gives them as a reward for not wanting to suffer is this: they still have to suffer, but by their anger and impatience they make it twice as great and difficult, and without finding any comfort or a good conscience. The Christians have the advantage that though they mourn, too, they shall be comforted and be blessed both here and hereafter. . . .

Those who mourn this way are entitled to have fun and to take it wherever they can so that they do not completely collapse for sorrow. Christ also adds these words and promises this consolation so that they do not despair in their sorrow nor let the joy of their heart be taken away and extinguished altogether, but mix this mourning with comfort and refreshment. Otherwise, if they never had any comfort or joy, they would have to languish and wither away. No man can stand continual mourning. It sucks out the very strength and savor of the body, as the wise man says (Ecclus. 30:25): "Sadness has killed many people"; and again (Prov. 17:22): "A downcast spirit dries up the marrow in the bones." Therefore we should not neglect this but should command and urge such people to have a good time once in a while if possible, or at least to temper their sorrow and forget it for a while.

Thus Christ does not want to urge continual mourning and sorrow. He wants to warn against those who seek to escape all mourning and to have nothing but fun and all their comfort here. And He wants to teach His Christians, when things go badly for them and they have to mourn, to know that it is God's good-pleasure and to make it theirs as well, not to curse or rage or despair as though their God did not want to be gracious. . . .

Matthew 5:5

Blessed are the meek, for they shall inherit the earth.

This statement fits the first one well, when He said: "Blessed are the spiritually poor." For as He promises the kingdom of heaven and an eternal possession there, so here He also adds a promise about this temporal life and about possessions here on earth. But how does being poor harmonize with inheriting the land? It might seem that the preacher has forgotten how He began. Whoever is to inherit land and possessions cannot be poor. By "inheriting the land" here and having all sorts of possessions here on earth, He does not mean that everyone is to inherit a whole country; otherwise God would have to create more worlds. But God confers possessions upon everyone in such a way that He gives a man wife, children, cattle, house, and home, and whatever pertains to these, so that he can stay on the land where he lives and have dominion over his possessions. This is the way Scripture customarily speaks, as Psalm 37 says several times (Ps. 37:34): "Those who wait for the Lord will inherit the land"; and again (Ps. 37:22): "His blessed ones inherit the land." Therefore He adds His own gloss here: to be "spiritually poor," as He used the expression before, does not mean to be a beggar or to discard money and possessions. For here He tells them to live and remain in the land and to manage earthly possessions, as we shall hear later.

What does it mean, then, to be meek? From the outset here you must realize that Christ is not speaking at all about the government and its work, whose property it is not to be meek, as we use the word in German, but to bear the sword (Rom. 13:4) for the punishment of those who do wrong (1 Pet. 2:14), and to wreak a vengeance and a wrath that are called the vengeance and wrath of God. He is only talking about how individuals are to live in relation to others, apart from official position and authority—how father and mother are to live, not in relation to their children nor in their official capacity as father and mother, but in relation to those for whom they are not father and mother, like neighbors and other people. I have often said that we must sharply distinguish between these two, the office and the person. The man who is called Hans or Martin is a man quite different from the one who is called elector or doctor or preacher. Here we have two different persons in one man. The one is that in which we are created and born, according to which we are all alike—man or woman or child, young or old. But once we are born, God adorns and dresses you up as another person. He makes you a child and me a father, one a master and another a servant, one a prince and another a citizen. Then this one is called a divine person, one who holds a divine office and goes about clothed in its dignity—not simply Hans or Nick, but the prince of Saxony, father, or master. He is not talking about this person here, letting it alone in its own office and rule, as He has ordained it. He is talking merely about how each individual, natural person is to behave in relation to others.

Therefore if we have an office or a governmental position, we must be sharp and strict, we must get angry and punish; for here we must do what God puts into our hand and commands us to do for His sake. In other relations, in what is unofficial, let everyone learn for himself to be meek toward everyone else, that is, not to deal with his neighbor unreasonably, hatefully, or vengefully, like the people whom they call "Headlong Hans." They refuse to put up with anything or to yield an inch, but they tear up the world and the hills and want to uproot the trees. They never listen to anyone nor excuse him for anything. They immediately buckle on their armor, thinking of nothing but how to take vengeance and hit back. This does not forbid the government to punish and to wreak vengeance in the name of God. But neither does it grant license to a wicked judge, burgomaster, lord, or prince to confuse these two persons and to reach beyond his official authority through personal malice or envy or hate or hostility, as commonly happens, under the cloak and cover of his office and legal right. This would be as though, in the name of the government, our neighbors wanted to take some action against us which they could not get away with otherwise. . . .

You see, then, that here Christ is rebuking those crazy saints who think that everyone is master of the whole world and is entitled to be delivered from all suffering, to roar and bluster and violently to defend his property. And He teaches us that whoever wants to rule and possess his property, his possessions, house, and home in peace, must be meek, so that he may overlook things and act reasonably, putting up with just as much as he possibly can. It is inevitable that your neighbor will sometimes do you injury or harm, either accidentally or maliciously. If he did it accidentally, you do not improve the situation by refusing or being unable to endure anything. If he did it maliciously, you only irritate him by your violent scratching and pounding; meanwhile he is laughing at you and enjoying the fact that he is baiting and troubling you, so that you still cannot have any peace or quietly enjoy what is yours.

So select one of the two, whichever you prefer: either to live in human society with meekness and patience and to hold on to what you have with peace and a good conscience; or boisterously and blusterously to lose what is yours, and to have no peace besides. There stands the decree: "The meek shall inherit the earth." Just take a look for yourself at the queer characters who are always arguing and squabbling about property and other things. They refuse to give in to anybody, but insist on rushing everything through headlong, regardless of whether their quarreling and squabbling costs them more than they could ever gain. Ultimately they lose their land and servants, house and home, and get unrest and a bad conscience thrown in. And God adds His blessing to it, saying: "Do not be meek, then, so that you may not keep your precious land, nor enjoy your morsel in peace."

But if you want to do right and have rest, let your neighbor's malice and viciousness smother and burn itself out. Otherwise you can do nothing more pleasing to the devil or more harmful to yourself than to lose your temper and make a racket. Do you have a government? Then register a complaint, and let it see to it. The government has the charge not to permit the harsh oppression of the innocent. God will also overrule so that His Word and ordinance may abide and you may inherit the land according to this promise. Thus you will have rest and God's blessing, but your neighbor will have unrest together with God's displeasure and curse. This sermon is intended only for those who are Christians, who believe and know that they have their treasure in heaven, where it is secure for them and cannot be taken away: Hence they must have enough here, too, even though they do not have treasuries and pockets full of yellow guldens.[10] Since you know this, why let your joy be disturbed and taken away? Why cause yourself disquiet and rob yourself of this magnificent promise?

Matthew 5:6

Blessed are those who hunger and thirst for righteousness, for they shall be satisfied.

"Righteousness" in this passage must not be taken in the sense of that principal Christian righteousness by which a person becomes pious and acceptable to God. I have said before that these eight items are nothing but instruction about the fruits and good works of a Christian. Before these must come faith, as the tree and chief part or summary of a man's righteousness and blessedness, without any work or merit of his; out of which faith these items all must grow and follow. Therefore take this in the sense of the outward righteousness before the world, which we maintain in our relations with each other. Thus the short and simple meaning of these words is this: "That man is righteous and blessed who continually works and strives with all his might to promote the general welfare and the proper behavior of everyone and who helps to maintain and support this by word and deed, by precept and example."

Now, this is also a precious point, embracing very many good works, but by no means a common thing. Let me illustrate with an example. If a preacher wants to qualify under this point, he must be ready to instruct and help everyone to perform his assigned task properly and to do what it requires. And when he sees that something is missing and things are not going right, he should be on hand to warn, rebuke, and correct by whatever method or means he can. Thus as a preacher I dare not neglect my office. Nor dare the others neglect theirs, which is, to follow my teaching and preaching. In this way the right thing is done on both sides. Now, where there are people who earnestly take it upon themselves to do right gladly and to be found engaged in the right works and ways—such people "hunger and thirst for righteousness." If this were the situation, there would be no rascality or injustice, but sheer righteousness and blessedness on earth. What is the righteousness of the world except that in his

10 On "gulden," see above, p. 112 n. 8.

station everyone should do his duty? That means that the rights of every station should be respected—those of the man, the woman, the child, the manservant, and the maid in the household, the citizen of the city in the land. And it is all contained in this, that those who are charged with overseeing and ruling other people should execute this office diligently, carefully, and faithfully, and that the others should also render their due service and obedience to them faithfully and willingly.

It is not by accident that He uses the term "hunger and thirst for righteousness." By it He intends to point out that this requires great earnestness, longing, eagerness, and unceasing diligence and that where this hunger and thirst is lacking, everything will fail. The reason is that there are too many great hindrances. They come from the devil, who is blocking and barricading the way everywhere. They also come from the world—that is, his children—which is so wicked that it cannot stand a pious man who wants to do right himself or to help other people do so, but plagues him in every way, that he finally becomes tired and perplexed over the whole business. It is painful to see how shamefully people behave, and to get no reward for pure kindness except ingratitude, contempt, hate, and persecution. For this reason, many people who could not stand the sight of such evil conduct finally despaired over it, ran away from human society into the desert, and became monks, so that the saying has repeatedly been verified: "Despair makes a man a monk."[11] A person may not trust himself to make his own living and run into the monastery for his belly's sake, as the great crowd has done; otherwise a person may despair of the world and not trust himself in it, either to remain pious or to help people.

But this is not hungering and thirsting for righteousness. Anyone who tries to preach or rule in such a way that he lets himself become tired and impatient and be chased into a corner will not be of much help to other people. The command to you is not to crawl into a corner or into the desert, but to run out, if that is where you have been, and to offer your hands and your feet and your whole body, and to wager everything you have and can do. You should be the kind of man who is firm in the face of firmness, who will not let himself be frightened off or dumbfounded or overcome by the world's ingratitude or malice, who will always hold on and push with all the might he can summon. In short, the ministry requires a hunger and thirst for righteousness that can never be curbed or stopped or sated, one that looks for nothing and cares for nothing except the accomplishment and maintenance of the right, despising everything that hinders this end. If you cannot make

11 Cf. *Lectures on Romans* (1515–16), LW 25:491–92 (see above, pp. 28–29).

the world completely pious, then do what you can. It is enough that you have done your duty and have helped a few, even if there be only one or two. If others will not follow, then in God's name let them go. You must not run away on account of the wicked, but rather conclude: "I did not undertake this for their sakes, and I shall not drop it for their sakes. Eventually some of them might come around; at least there might be fewer of them, and they may improve a little."

Here you have a comforting and certain promise, with which Christ allures and attracts His Christians: "Those who hunger and thirst for righteousness shall be filled." That is, they will be recompensed for their hunger and thirst by seeing that their work was not in vain and that at last a little flock has been brought around who have been helped. Although things are not going now as they would like and they have almost despaired over it, all this will become manifest, not only here on earth, but even more in the life hereafter, when everyone will see what sort of fruit such people have brought by their diligence and perseverance. For example, a pious preacher has snatched many souls out of the jaws of the devil and brought them to heaven; or a pious, faithful ruler has helped many lands and people, who testify that he has done so and who praise him before the whole world.

The counterfeit saints are exactly the opposite. Because of their great sanctity they forsake the world and run into the desert, or they sneak away into a corner somewhere, to escape the trouble and worry that they would otherwise have to bear. They do not want to pay attention to what is going on in the world. Never once do they think of the fact that they should help or advise other people with teaching, instruction, warning, reproof, correction, or at least with prayers and sighs to God. Yes, it even disgusts and grieves them when other people become pious; for they want to be thought of as the only ones who are holy so that anyone who wants to get to heaven has to buy their good works and merits from them. In brief, they are so full of righteousness that they look down their noses at other poor sinners. Just so in Luke 18:11 the great St. Pharisee in his intoxication looks down at the poor publican and spits on him. He is so much in love with himself that he pays court to God and thanks Him that he alone is pious and other people are bad.

Note that these are the people against whom Christ is speaking here, the shameful, proud, and self-sufficient spirits, who are tickled, pleased, and overjoyed over the fact that other people are not pious, whereas they ought to pity them, sympathize with them, and help them. All they can do is to despise, slander, judge, and condemn everyone else; everything must be stench and filth except what they themselves do. But going out to admonish and help a poor, frail sinner—this they avoid as they would avoid the devil. Hence they will have to hear again what Christ cries out against them in Luke 6:25: "Woe to you that are full, for you shall hunger." As those who now hunger and thirst shall be filled, so these others must hunger forever; though they are full and sated now, no one has ever got any benefit from them or been able to praise them for ever helping anyone or setting him aright. There you have a summary of the meaning of this passage, which, as I have said, embraces many good works, indeed, all the good works by which a man may live right by himself in human society and help to give success to all sorts of offices and stations, as I have often said in more detail elsewhere.

Matthew 5:7

Blessed are the merciful, for they shall obtain mercy.

This is also an outstanding fruit of faith, and it follows well upon what went before. Anyone who is supposed to help other people and to contribute to the common weal and success should also be kind and merciful. He should not immediately raise a rumpus and start a riot if something is missing or if things do not go as they should, as long as there is still some hope for improvement. One of the virtues of counterfeit sanctity is that it cannot have pity or mercy for the frail and weak, but insists on the strictest enforcement and the purest selection; as soon as there is even a minor flaw, all mercy is gone, and there is nothing but fuming and fury. St. Gregory also teaches us how to recognize this when he says: "True justice shows mercy, but false justice shows indignation." True holiness is merciful and sympathetic, but all that false holiness can do is to rage and fume. Yet it does so, as they boast, "out of zeal for justice"; that is, it is done through love and zeal for righteousness.[12]

The whole world is being forced to the conclusion that they have been carrying on their mischief and violence under the lovely and excellent pretext and cover of doing it for the sake of righteousness. In the same way, both in the past and in the present, they have been exercising their enmity and treachery against the Gospel under the guise of defending the truth and exterminating heresy. For this they want God to crown them and to elevate them to heaven, as a reward for those who out of great thirst and hunger for righteousness persecute, strangle, and burn His saints.

12 Pope Gregory the Great (ca. 540–604), *Homily 34 on the Gospels*. Gregory's statement is quoted by Gratian (fl. 1140), *Decretum*, d. 45, c. 15.

They want to make the claim and to give the impression, even more than the true saints, that they hunger and thirst for righteousness. They put up such a good front and use such beautiful words that they think even God Himself will not know any better. But the noble tree is known by its fruits. When they should demand justice, that is, the proper administration of both the spiritual and the temporal realm, they do not do so. It never enters their mind to instruct and improve anyone. They themselves live in continual vice; and if anyone denounces their behavior or does not praise it and do as they want, he must be a heretic and let himself be damned to hell. You see, that is how it is with every counterfeit saint. His self-made holiness makes him so proud that he despises everyone else and cannot have a kind and merciful heart.

Therefore this is a necessary warning against such abominable saints. If a man deals with his neighbor in an effort to help and correct him in his station and way of life, he should still take care to be merciful and to forgive. In this way people will see that your aim really is righteousness and not the gratification of your own malice and anger; for you are righteous enough to deal in a friendly and gentle manner with the man who is willing to forsake his unrighteousness and improve himself, and you tolerate and endure his fault or weakness until he comes around. But if you try all this and find no hope for improvement, then you may give him up and turn him over to those whose duty it is to punish.

Now, this is the one aspect of mercy, that one gladly forgives the sinful and the frail. The other is to do good also to those who are outwardly poor or in need of help; on the basis of Matt. 25:35ff. we call these "works of mercy." The arrogant Jewish saints knew nothing about this aspect either. There was nothing in them but ice and frost—yes, a heart as hard as a block of stone—and not a single loving drop of blood that took pleasure in doing good for a neighbor, nor any mercy that forgave sin. All they were concerned about and thought about was their own belly, even though another man might have been starving to death. Thus there is much more mercy among public sinners than there is in such a saint. This is how it has to be; for they praise only themselves and regard only themselves as holy, despising everyone else as worthless and supposing that the whole world must serve them and give them plenty, while they are under no obligation to give anyone anything or any service.

Hence this sermon and exhortation seems contemptible and useless to such saints. The only pupils it finds are those who already cling to Christ and believe in Him. They know of no holiness of their own. On the basis of the preceding items they are poor, miserable, meek, really hungry and thirsty; they are inclined not to despise anyone, but to assume and to sympathize with the need of everyone else. To them applies the comforting promise: "It is well with you who are merciful. For you will find pure mercy in turn, both here and hereafter, and a mercy which inexpressibly surpasses all human kindness and mercy." There is no comparison between our mercy and God's, nor between our possessions and the eternal possessions in the kingdom of heaven. So pleased is He with our kindness to our neighbor that for one pfennig[13] He promises us a hundred thousand guldens if we have need of them, and for a drink of water, the kingdom of heaven (Matt. 10:42).

Now, if anyone will not let himself be moved by this wonderful and comforting promise, let him turn the page and hear another judgment: "Woe and curses upon the unmerciful, for no mercy shall be shown to them." At the present time the world is full of people, among the nobles and city people and peasants, who sin very grievously against the dear Gospel. Not only do they refuse to give support or help to poor ministers and preachers; but besides they commit theft and torment against it wherever they can, and act as if they meant to starve it out and chase it out of the world. Meanwhile they go along quite smugly, supposing that God must keep quiet about it and approve of everything they do. But it will hit them someday. I am afraid that someone will come along who will make a prophet out of me—for I have given ample warning—and treat them mercilessly, taking away their reputation and their property, their body and their life, so that the Word of God might remain true and so that he who refuses to show or to have mercy might experience endless wrath and eternal displeasure. As St. James also says (James 2:13): "Judgment without mercy will be spoken over the one who has shown no mercy." At the Last Day, therefore, Christ will also cite this lack of mercy as the worst injury done to Him, whatever we have done out of a lack of mercy. He Himself will utter the curse (Matt. 25:41–42): "I was hungry and thirsty, and you gave Me no food, you gave Me no drink. Depart from Me, therefore, you cursed, into eternal hellfire." He warns and exhorts us faithfully, out of sheer grace and mercy. Whoever does not want to accept this, let him choose the curse and eternal damnation. Think of the rich man in Luke 16; daily he saw poor Lazarus lying before his door full of sores, yet he did not have enough mercy to give him a bundle of straw or to grant him the crumbs under his table. But look how terribly he was requited; in hell he would gladly have given a hundred thousand guldens for the privilege of boasting that he had given him even a thread.

13 A coin worth approximately two hellers (see above, p. 158 n. 8). The etymology is similar to the English "penny."

Matthew 5:8

Blessed are those of a pure heart, for they shall see God.

This item is rather obscure, and not very intelligible to us who have such coarse and carnal hearts and minds. It is also hidden from all the sophists,[14] who have the reputation of being most learned; none of them can say what it means to have a "pure heart," much less what it means to "see God." With mere dreams and random thoughts they walk around things of which they have no experience. Therefore we must look at these words according to the Scriptures and learn to understand them correctly.

They have imagined that having a pure heart means for a man to run away from human society into a corner, a monastery, or a desert, neither thinking about the world nor concerning himself with worldly affairs and business, but amusing himself only with heavenly thoughts. By this delusive doctrine they have not only beguiled and dangerously deceived themselves and other people, but have even committed the murderous crime of calling "profane" the act and stations which the world requires and which, as a matter of fact, God Himself has ordained. But Scripture speaks of this pure heart and mind in a manner that is completely consistent with being a husband, loving wife and children, thinking about them and caring for them, and paying attention to other matters involved in such a relationship. For God has commanded all of this. Whatever God has commanded cannot be profane (Acts 10:15); indeed it must be the very purity with which we see God. For example, when a judge performs his official duty in sentencing a criminal to death, that is not *his* office and work but God's. If he is a Christian, therefore, this is a good, pure, and holy work, one he could not do if he did not already have a pure heart. In the same way it must be regarded as a pure work and a pure heart when a servant in the household does a dirty and repulsive job, like hauling manure or washing and cleaning children. Hence it is a shameful perversion to disparage the relationships covered by the Ten Commandments this way and to gape at other special and showy works. As though God did not have as pure a mouth or eyes as we, or as pure a heart and hand when He creates both man and woman! Then how can such works and thoughts make a heart impure? This is the blindness and foolishness that comes upon men who despise the Word of God and who determine purity only by the outward mask and the show of works. Meanwhile they are causing trouble with their own wandering thoughts

14 Those who use subtle reasoning or argumentation designed to deceive. Luther refers to his scholastic opponents as sophists.

and gaping as though they wanted to climb up to heaven and grope for God, until they break their own necks in the process.

Let us understand correctly, then, what Christ calls a "pure heart." Note again that the target and object of this sermon were principally the Jews. They did not want to suffer, but sought a life of ease, pleasure, and joy; they did not want to hunger nor to be merciful, but to be smug in their exclusive piety while they judged and despised other people. In the same way, their holiness also consisted in outward cleanliness of body, skin, hair, clothes, and food, so that they did not dare to have even a speck on their clothing; if anyone touched a dead body, or had a scab or a rash on his body, he did not dare to approach other people. This is what they called "purity." "But that does not do it," says He; "the ones I praise are those who take pains to have a pure heart." So He says in Matt. 23:25: "You cleanse the outside of the cup and of the plate, but inside you are full of extortion and rapacity." Again (Matt. 23:27): "You are like whitewashed tombs, which outwardly appear beautiful, but within they are full of dead men's bones and all uncleanness." This is the way it is with our clergy today. Outwardly they lead a decent life, and in the churches everything is conducted with such excellent taste and formality that it is beautiful to behold. But He does not ask for such purity. He wants to have the heart pure, though outwardly the person may be a drudge in the kitchen, black, sooty, and grimy, doing all sorts of dirty work.

Then what is a pure heart? In what does it consist? The answer can be given quickly, and you do not have to climb up to heaven or run to a monastery for it and establish it with your own ideas. You should be on your guard against any ideas that you call your own, as if they were just so much mud and filth. And you should realize that when a monk in the monastery is sitting in deepest contemplation, excluding the world from his heart altogether, and thinking about the Lord God the way he himself paints and imagines Him, he is actually sitting—if you will pardon the expression—in the dung, not up to his knees but up to his ears. For he is proceeding on his own ideas without the Word of God; and that is sheer deception and delusion, as Scripture testifies everywhere.

What is meant by a "pure heart" is this: one that is watching and pondering what God says and replacing its own ideas with the Word of God. This alone is pure before God, yes, purity itself, which purifies everything that it includes and touches. Therefore, though a common laborer, a shoemaker, or a blacksmith may be dirty and sooty or may smell because he is covered with dirt and pitch, still he may sit at home and think: "My God has made me a man. He has given me my house, wife, and child and has commanded me to love them and to support them with my work."

Note that he is pondering the Word of God in his heart; and though he stinks outwardly, inwardly he is pure incense before God. But if he attains the highest purity so that he also takes hold of the Gospel and believes in Christ—without this, that purity is impossible—then he is pure completely, inwardly in his heart toward God and outwardly toward everything under him on earth. Then everything he is and does, his walking, standing, eating, and drinking, is pure for him; and nothing can make him impure. So it is when he looks at his own wife or fondles her, as the patriarch Isaac did (Gen. 26:8), which a monk regards as disgusting and defiling. For here he has the Word of God, and he knows that God has given her to him. But if he were to desert his wife and take up another, or neglect his job or duty to harm or bother other people, he would no longer be pure; for that would be contrary to God's commandment.

But so long as he sticks to these two—namely, the Word of faith toward God, which purifies the heart, and the Word of understanding, which teaches him what he is to do toward his neighbor in his station—everything is pure for him, even if with his hands and the rest of his body he handles nothing but dirt. If a poor housemaid does her duty and is a Christian in addition, then before God in heaven she is a lovely and pure beauty, one that all the angels admire and love to look at. On the other hand, if the most austere Carthusian fasts and whips himself to death, if he does nothing but weep out of sheer devotion, if he never gives the world a thought, and yet lacks faith in Christ and love for his neighbor, he is nothing but a stench and a pollution, inwardly and outwardly, so that both God and the angels find him abhorrent and disgusting.[15]

So you see that everything depends on the Word of God. Whatever is included in that and goes in accordance with it must be called clean, pure, and white as snow before both God and man. Therefore Paul says (Titus 1:15): "To the pure all things are pure", and again: "To the corrupt and unbelieving nothing is pure." Why is this so? Because both their minds and their consciences are impure. How does this happen? Because "they profess to know God, but with their deeds they deny it" (Titus 1:16). These are the people who are abominable in the sight of God. Look how horribly the apostle paints and denounces these great Jewish saints. Take, for example, a Carthusian monk. He thinks that if he lives according to his strict rule of obedience, poverty, and celibacy, if he is isolated from the world, he is pure in every way. What is this but their own way of thinking, growing up in their own heart without the Word of God and faith? In this way they think that they alone are pure and that other people are impure. St. Paul calls this an "impure mind,"

15 On the Carthusians, see above, p. 45 n. 6.

that is, everything they think and imagine. Since this delusion and idea is impure, everything they do on the basis of it must also be impure for them. As their mind is, so is their conscience too. Although they should and could be of help to other people, they have a conscience that functions on the basis of their ideas and is bound to their cowls, cloisters, and rules. They think that if they neglected this routine even for a moment to serve their neighbor and had relations with other people, they would be committing a most grievous sin and defiling themselves altogether. The cause of all this is that they do not acknowledge God's Word and creatures, although, as St. Paul says (Titus 1:16): "With their mouths they profess that they do." If they knew the means and the purpose of their creation by God, they would not despise these other stations nor exalt their own so highly; they would recognize the purity of these as the works and creatures of God, and would honor them, willingly remain in them, and be of service to their neighbor. That would be the true recognition of God, both in His Word and in His creatures, and the true purity of both heart and conscience, which comes to this faith and conclusion: Whatever God does and ordains must be pure and good. For He makes nothing impure, and He consecrates everything through the Word which He has attached to every station and creature.

Therefore be on guard against all your own ideas if you want to be pure before God. See to it that your heart is founded and fastened on the Word of God. Then you will be purer than all the Carthusians and saints in the world. When I was young, people used to take pride in this proverb: "Enjoy being alone, and your heart will stay pure." In support of it they would cite a quotation from St. Bernard, who said that whenever he was among people, he defiled himself.[16] In the lives of the fathers we read about a hermit who would not let anyone come near him or talk to him, because, he said: "The angels cannot come to anyone who moves around in human society." We also read about two others, who would not let their mother see them. She kept watch, and once she caught them. Immediately they closed the door and let her stand outside for a long time, crying; finally, they persuaded her to go away and to wait until they would see each other in the life hereafter.

Look, this is what they call a noble deed, the highest kind of sanctity and the most perfect kind of purity. But what was it really? Here is the Word of God (Exod. 20:12): "Honor your father and your mother." If they had regarded this as holy and pure, they would have shown their mother and their neighbor all honor, love, and friendship. On the contrary, they followed their own ideas and a holiness they chose for themselves; hence

16 For Luther's high esteem for Bernard of Clairvaux, see above, p. 100 n. 5.

they isolated themselves from them, and by their very effort to be most pure they most shamefully profaned themselves before God. As though even the most desperate scoundrels could not have such thoughts and put on such a show that people would have to say: "These are living saints! They can despise the world and have to do only with angels." With angels all right—from the abyss of hell! The angels like nothing more than to watch us deal with the Word of God; with such people they enjoy dwelling. Therefore leave the angels up there in heaven undisturbed. Look for them here on earth below, in your neighbor, father and mother, children, and others. Do for these what God has commanded, and the angels will never be far away from you.

I have said this to help people evaluate this matter correctly and not go so far away to look for it as the monks do. They have thrown it out of the world altogether and stuck it into a corner or a cowl. All this is stench and filth and the devil's real dwelling. Let it be where God has put it, in a heart that clings to God's Word and that regards its tasks and every creature on the basis of it. Then the chief purity, that of faith toward God, will also manifest itself outwardly in this life; and everything will proceed from obedience to the Word and command of God, regardless of whether it is physically clean or unclean. I spoke earlier of a judge who has to condemn a man to death, who thus sheds blood and defiles himself with it. A monk would regard this as an abominably impure act, but Scripture says it is the service of God. In Rom. 13:4 Paul calls the government, which bears the sword, "God's servant." This is not its work and command, but His, which He imposes on it and demands from it.

Now you have the meaning of "pure heart": it is one that functions completely on the basis of the pure Word of God. What is their reward, what does He promise to them? It is this: "They shall see God." A wonderful title and an excellent treasure! But what does it mean to "see God"? Here again the monks have their own dreams. To them it means sitting in a cell and elevating your thoughts heavenward, leading a "contemplative life," as they call it in the many books they have written about it. That is still a far cry from seeing God, when you come marching along on your own ideas and scramble up to heaven, the way the sophists and our schismatic spirits and crazy saints insist on using their own brains to measure and master God together with His Word and works. But this is what it is: if you have a true faith that Christ is your Savior, then you see immediately that you have a gracious God. For faith leads you up and opens up the heart and will of God for you. There you see sheer, superabundant grace and love. That is exactly what it means "to see God," not with physical eyes, with which no one can see Him in this life, but with faith, which sees His fatherly, friendly heart, where there is no anger or displeasure. Anyone who regards Him as angry is not seeing Him correctly, but has pulled down a curtain and cover, more, a dark cloud over His face. But in scriptural language "to see His face" means to recognize Him correctly as a gracious and faithful Father, on whom you can depend for every good thing. This happens only through faith in Christ.

Therefore, if according to God's Word and command you live in your station with your husband, wife, child, neighbor, or friend, you can see God's intention in these things; and you can come to the conclusion that they please Him, since this is not your own dream, but His Word and command, which never deludes or deceives us. It is a wonderful thing, a treasure beyond every thought or wish, to know that you are standing and living in the right relation to God. In this way not only can your heart take comfort and pride in the assurance of His grace, but you can know that your outward conduct and behavior is pleasing to Him. From this it follows that cheerfully and heartily you can do and suffer anything, without letting it make you fearful or despondent. None of this is possible for those who lack this faith and pure heart, guided only by God's Word. Thus all the monks have publicly taught that no one can know whether or not he is in a state of grace. It serves them right that because they despise faith and true godly works and seek their own purity, they must never see God or know how they stand in relation to Him.

Ask one who has most diligently observed his canonical hours of prayer,[17] celebrated Mass and fasted daily, whether he is also sure that this is pleasing to God. He must say he does not know, that he is doing it all as a risk: "If it succeeds, let it succeed." It is impossible for anyone to say anything else. None of them can make a boast and say: "God gave me this cowl, He commanded me to wear it, He ordered me to celebrate this Mass." Until now we have all been groping in such blindness as this. We performed many works, contributed, fasted, prayed our rosaries; and yet we never dared to say: "This work is pleasing to God; of this I am sure, and I would be willing to die for it." Hence no one can boast that in all his life and activity he has ever seen God. Or if in his pride someone glorifies such works and thinks that God must be well disposed to them and reward him for them, he is not seeing God but the devil in place of God. There is no word of God to support him; it is all the invention of men, grown up in their own hearts. That is why it can never assure or pacify any heart, but remains hidden by pride until it comes to its final

17 The canonical hours of prayer divided the day and night for monks. These offices (Matins, Prime, Terce, Sext, None, Vespers, Compline) consisted mostly of Scripture reading, especially the Psalms, hymns, and prayer.

gasps, when it all disappears and brings on despair, so that one never gets around to seeing the face of God. But anyone who takes hold of the Word of God and who remains in faith can take his stand before God and look at Him as his gracious Father. He does not have to be afraid that He is standing behind him with a club, and he is sure that He is looking at him and smiling graciously, together with all the angels and saints in heaven.

You see, that is what Christ means by this statement, that only those who have such a pure heart see God. By this He cuts off and puts aside every other kind of purity. Where this kind is absent, everything else in a man may be pure; but it is worth nothing before God, and he can never see God. Where the heart is pure, on the other hand, everything is pure; and it does not matter if outwardly everything is impure, yes, if the body is full of sores, scabs, and leprosy.

Matthew 5:9

Blessed are the peacemakers, for they shall be called the children of God.

With an excellent title and wonderful praise the Lord here honors those who do their best to try to make peace, not only in their own lives but also among other people, who try to settle ugly and involved issues, who endure squabbling and try to avoid and prevent war and bloodshed. This is a great virtue, too, but one that is very rare in the world and among the counterfeit saints. Those who are not Christians are both liars and murderers, as is their father, the devil (John 8:44). Therefore they have no other goal than to stir up unrest, quarrels, and war. Thus among the priests, bishops, and princes nowadays practically all we find are bloodhounds. They have given many evidences that there is nothing they would rather see than all of us swimming in blood. If a prince loses his temper, he immediately thinks he has to start a war. Then he inflames and incites everyone, until there has been so much war and bloodshed that he regrets it and gives a few thousand guldens for the souls that were killed. These are bloodhounds, and that is what they remain. They cannot rest until they have taken revenge and spent their anger, until they have dragged their land and people into misery and sorrow. Yet they claim to bear the title "Christian princes" and to have a just cause.

You need more to start a war than having a just cause. As we have said, this does not prohibit the waging of war; for Christ has no intention here of taking anything away from the government and its official authority, but is only teaching individuals who want to lead a Christian life. Still it is not right for a prince to make up his mind to go to war against his neighbor, even though, I say, he has a just cause and his neighbor is in the wrong. The command is: "Blessed are the peacemakers." Therefore anyone who claims to be a Christian and a child of God not only does not start war or unrest, but he also gives help and counsel on the side of peace wherever he can, even though there may have been a just and adequate cause for going to war. It is sad enough if one has tried everything and nothing helps, and then he has to defend himself, to protect his land and people. Therefore not "Christians" but "children of the devil" is the name for those quarrelsome young noblemen who immediately draw and unsheathe their sword on account of one word. Even worse are the ones that are now persecuting the Gospel and ordering the burning and murder of innocent preachers of the Gospel, who have done them no harm but only good and have served them with body and soul. We are not talking about these right now, but only about those who claim that they are in the right and have a just cause and think that as high and princely personages they ought not to suffer, even though other people do.

This also means that if you are the victim of injustice and violence, you have no right to take the advice of your own foolish head and immediately start getting even and hitting back; but you are to think it over, try to bear it and have peace. If that is impossible and you cannot stand it, you have law and government in the country, from which you can seek legitimate redress. It is ordained to guard against such things and to punish them. Therefore anyone who does violence to you sins not only against you but also against the government itself; for the order and command to maintain peace was given to the government and not to you. Therefore leave the vengeance and punishment to your judge, who has the command; it is against him that your enemy has done wrong. If you take it upon yourself to wreak vengeance, you do an even greater wrong. You become guilty of the same sin as he who sins against the government and interferes with its duties, and by doing so you invalidate the justice of your own righteous cause. For the proverb says: "The one who strikes back is in the wrong, and striking back makes a quarrel."

Note that this is one demand that Christ makes here in opposition to those who are vengeful and violent. He gives the name "peacemakers," in the first place, to those who help make peace among lands and people, like pious princes, counselors, or jurists, to people in government who hold their rule and reign for the sake of peace; and in the second place, to pious citizens and neighbors, who with their salutary and good tongues adjust, reconcile, and settle quarrels and tensions between husband and wife or between neighbors, brought on by evil and poisonous tongues. Thus St. Augustine boasts that when his mother, Monica, saw two people at odds, she would always speak the best to both sides. Whatever good she heard about the one, she brought to the other; but whatever evil she heard, that she kept to herself or mitigated as much as possible. In this way she often brought on a reconciliation.[18] It is especially among womenfolk that the shameful vice of slander is prevalent, so that great misfortune is often caused by an evil tongue. This is the work of those bitter and poisonous brides of the devil, who when they hear a word about another, viciously make it sharper, more pointed, and more bitter against the others, so that sometimes misery and murder are the result.

All this comes from the shameful, demonic filth which naturally clings to us, that everyone enjoys hearing and telling the worst about his neighbor and it tickles him to see a fault in someone else. If a woman were as beautiful as the sun but had one little spot or blemish on her body, you would be expected to forget everything else and to look only for that spot and to talk about it. If a lady were famous for her honor and virtue, still some poisonous tongue would come along and say that she had once been seen laughing with some man and defame her in such a way as to eclipse all her praise and honor. These are really poisonous spiders that can suck out nothing but poison from a beautiful, lovely rose, ruining both the flower and the nectar, while a little bee sucks out nothing but honey, leaving the roses unharmed. That is the way some people act. All they can notice about other people are the faults or impurities which they can denounce, but what is good about them they do not see. People have many virtues which the devil cannot destroy, yet he hides or disfigures them to make them invisible. For example, even though a woman may be full of faults and have no other virtue, she is still a creature of God. At least she can carry water and wash clothes. There is no person on earth so bad that he does not have something about him that is praiseworthy. Why is it, then, that we leave the good things out of sight and feast our eyes on the unclean things? It is as though we enjoyed only looking at—if you will pardon the expression—a man's behind, while God Himself has covered the unpresentable parts of the body and, as Paul says (1 Cor. 12:24), has given them "greater honor." We are so filthy that we only look for what is dirty and stinking, and wallow in it like pigs. . . .

So be on your guard against such people, and neither listen nor pay attention to them. Learn to put the best interpretation on what you hear about your neighbor, or even to conceal it, so that you may establish and preserve peace and harmony. Then you can honorably bear the title "child of God" before the whole world and before the angels in heaven. You should let this honor draw and attract you; in fact, you should chase it to the end of the world, if need be, and gladly surrender everything you have for it. Now you have it offered to you here and spread out in front

18 Augustine, *Confessions* 9.9.

of you for nothing. There is nothing that you have to do or give for it, except that if you want to be a child of God, you must also show yourself to be one and do your Father's works toward your neighbor. This is what Christ, our Lord, has done for us by reconciling us to the Father, bringing us into His favor, daily representing us, and interceding on our behalf.

You do the same. Be a reconciler and a mediator between your neighbors. Carry the best to both sides; but keep quiet about the bad, which the devil has inspired, or explain it the best way you can. If you come to Margaret, do what is said of Monica, Augustine's mother, and say: "My dear Margaret, why are you so bitter? Surely she does not intend it so badly. All I notice about her is that she would like to be your dear sister." In the same way, if you meet Catherine, do the same thing. Then, as a true child of God, you will have made peace on both sides as far as possible.

But if you will or must talk about an evil deed, do as Christ has taught you. Do not carry it to others, but go to the one who has done it, and admonish him to improve. Do not act ostentatiously when you come and expose the person involved, speaking when you ought to be quiet and being quiet when you ought to speak. This is the first method: You should discuss it between yourself and your neighbor alone (Matt. 18:15). If you must tell it to others, however, when the first method does not work, then tell it to those who have the job of punishing, father and mother, master and mistress, burgomaster and judge. That is the right and proper procedure for removing and punishing a wrong. Otherwise, if you spread it among other people, the person remains unimproved; and the wrong remains unpunished, besides being broadcast by you and by others, so that everyone washes out his mouth with it. Look what a faithful physician does with a sick child. He does not run around among the people and broadcast it; but he goes to the child and examines his pulse or anything else that is necessary, not to gratify his pleasure at the cost of the child, nor to make fun of him, but with the good, honest intention of helping him. So we read about the holy patriarch Joseph in Genesis 37. He was tending the cattle with his brothers; and when he heard an evil report about them, he went and brought it to their father as their superior, whose task it was to investigate and to punish them because they would not listen to him.

But you may say: "Then why do you yourself publicly attack the pope and others, instead of keeping the peace?" Answer: A person must advise and support peace while he can and keep quiet as long as possible. But when the sin is evident and becomes too widespread or does public damage, as the pope's teaching has, then there is no longer time to be quiet but only to defend and attack, especially for me and others in public office whose task it is to teach and to warn everyone. I have the commission and charge, as a preacher and a doctor, to see to it that no one is misled, so that I may give account of it at the last judgment (Heb. 13:17). So St. Paul (Acts 20:28) commands the preachers to watch and guard their whole flock against the wolves that were to appear among them. Thus it is my duty to chastise public sinners so that they may improve, just as a judge must publicly condemn and punish evildoers in the performance of his office. As we have said often enough, Christ is not talking here about public office, but in general about all Christians insofar as we are all alike before God.

Matthew 5:10

Blessed are those who are persecuted for righteousness' sake, for theirs is the kingdom of heaven.

I have said earlier that all these items and promises must be understood by faith in reference to things that are neither seen nor heard and that they are not talking about outward appearances. How can the poor and the mourners be said to look outwardly successful and blessed when, in addition, they have to suffer all sorts of persecution—all things that the whole world and our reason calls trouble and that they say should be avoided? Therefore whoever wants to have the blessedness and the possessions that Christ is talking about here must lift up his heart far above all senses and reason. He must not evaluate himself on the basis of his feelings, but he must argue this way: "If I am poor, then I am not poor. I am poor outwardly, according to the flesh; but before God, in faith, I am rich." Thus when he feels sad, troubled, and worried, he must not use this standard and say that he is not a blessed man. But he must turn himself over and say: "I feel sorrow, misery, and sadness of heart; but still I am blessed, happy, and settled on the basis of the Word of God." The situation in the world is the exact counterpart of this, for those who are called rich and happy are not. Christ calls out His "Woe!" against them and calls them unhappy (Luke 6:24–25), although it appears that they are well-off and having the greatest possible success. Therefore they should lift up their thoughts above the riches and fun which they are having and say: "Yes, I am rich and living in the midst of pure fun. But too bad for me if I have nothing else; for there must certainly be plenty of trouble, misery, and sorrow in all this that will come over me before I feel it or know it." This applies to all these items; every one of them looks different before the world from the way it looks according to these words.

So far we have been treating almost all the elements of a Christian's way of life and the spiritual fruits under these two headings: first, that in his own person he is poor, troubled, miserable, needy, and hungry; second, that in relation to others he is a useful, kind, merciful, and peaceable man, who does nothing but good works. Now He adds the last: how he fares in all this. Although he is full of good works, even toward his enemies and rascals, for all this he must get this reward from the world: he is persecuted and runs the risk of losing his body, his life, and everything.

If you want to be a Christian, therefore, consider this well, lest you be frightened, lose heart, and become impatient. But be cheerful and content, knowing that you are not badly off when this happens to you. He and all the saints had the same experience, as He says a little later. For this reason He issues a warning beforehand to those who want to be Christians, that they should and must suffer persecution. Therefore you may take your choice. You have two ways before you—either to heaven and eternal life or to hell, either with Christ or with the world. But this you must know: if you live in order to have a good time here without persecution, then you will not get to heaven with Christ, and vice versa. In short, you must either surrender Christ and heaven or make up your mind that you are willing to suffer every kind of persecution and torture in the world. Briefly, anyone who wants to have Christ must put in jeopardy his body, life, goods, reputation, and popularity in the world. He dare not let himself be scared off by contempt, ingratitude, or persecution.

The reason is this: the devil is a wicked and angry spirit. He will not and cannot stand seeing a man enter the kingdom of God. And if the man undertakes to do so, he blocks the way himself, arousing and attempting every kind of opposition he can summon. If you want to be God's child, therefore, prepare yourself for persecution, as the wise man says. Paul says in 2 Tim. 3:12: "All who desire to live a godly life in Christ Jesus will be persecuted." And Christ Himself says (John 15:20): "The disciple should not be better off than his master. If they persecuted Me, they will also persecute you." There is no other way out, and therefore the statement is: "Blessed are those who are persecuted for the sake of the kingdom of heaven," to let us know how to console ourselves. Otherwise this would look outwardly like a troubling and unhappy situation, and it wears us down to be sitting constantly amid danger to life and property. But when faith takes over, we can lift ourselves up above this and think: "Nevertheless Christ has said that I am blessed and well-off. Because He has said so, I let it be my comfort and pleasure. The Word will make my heart great, yes, greater than heaven and earth. What are all my persecutors in comparison with this Man or His Word? If there are one or two persecuting us, there are many more (2 Kings 6:16) defending us, cheering us up, consoling us, and blessing us—yes, 10,000 angels over against one of them, together with all the saints, who act in concert with Christ and with God Himself." Hence we must not be so coarse and cold, letting this Word lie around, but blow it up and magnify it, pitting it against every persecution. Then we shall see and learn that we should despise all our suffering as nothing at all when compared with this great consolation and eternal blessing.

But it is significant that He should add the phrase "for righteousness' sake," to show that where this condition is absent, persecution alone will not accomplish this. The devil and wicked people also have to suffer persecution. Rascals often get into each other's hair, and there is no love lost between them. So one murderer persecutes another, and the Turk battles against the Tartar;[19] but this does not make them blessed. This statement applies only to those who are persecuted for righteousness' sake. So also 1 Pet. 4:15 says: "Let none of you suffer as a murderer or a thief or a wrongdoer." Therefore bragging and yelling about great suffering is worthless without this condition. So the godless monks have deceived the poor people whom they have led away to be punished, consoling them with the statement that with their death they were paying for their sins. Beware of any death that is supposed to pay for your sin, for it belongs in the abyss of hell. First there must come righteousness and the death of Christ, the Lord.

See to it, therefore, that you have a genuine divine cause for whose sake you suffer persecution, and that you are really convinced of it so that your conscience can take a stand and stick by it, even though the whole world should stand up against you. The primary thing is that you grasp the Word of God firmly and surely so that there can be no doubt or hesitation there. Suppose that the emperor, the bishops, or the princes were to forbid marriage, freedom in the choice of food, the use of both kinds in the Sacrament,[20] and the like, and were to persecute you for these things. Then you would have to see to it that your heart is convinced and persuaded that the Word of God has made these things free and unprohibited, that it even commands us to take them seriously and to stake our lives upon them. Then you can have the confidence to say: "This cause does not belong to me but to Christ, my Lord. For I have not concocted it out of my own head. I have not assumed or begun it on my own or at the advice or suggestion of any man. But it has been brought and announced

19 The Tartars were a Central Asian people, associated in the medieval European mind with the thirteenth-century Mongol conquests.

20 During the thirteenth century, churches began withholding the chalice from the laity. Many feared that the people were not careful enough in their reception of the chalice and risked spilling it. Therefore, only the priest should commune under both kinds. See Thomas Aquinas, *Summa Theologiae*, III, q. 80, a. 12.

to me from heaven through the mouth of Christ, who never deludes or deceives me but is Himself sheer Truth and Righteousness. At this man's Word I will take the risk of suffering, of doing and forsaking whatever I should. All by itself, His Word will accomplish more to comfort and strengthen my heart than the raging and threatening of all the devils and of the world can accomplish to frighten me."

Who cares if a crazy prince or foolish emperor fumes in his rage and threatens me with sword, fire, or the gallows! Just as long as my Christ is talking dearly to my heart, comforting me with the promises that I am blessed, that I am right with God in heaven, and that all the heavenly host and creation call me blessed. Just let my heart and mind be ready to suffer for the sake of His Word and work. Then why should I let myself be scared by these miserable people, who rage and foam in their hostility to God but suddenly disappear like a puff of smoke or a bubble, as the prophet Isaiah says (Isa. 51:12–13): "I, I am He that comforts you; who are you that you are afraid of man who dies, of the son of man who is made like grass, and have forgotten the Lord, who made you, who stretched out the heavens and laid the foundations of the earth?" That is to say: "He who comforts you and takes pleasure in you is almighty and eternal. When it is all over with them, He will still be sitting up there, and so will you. Why, then, let the threatening and fuming of a miserable, stinking bag of worms concern you more than this divine comfort and approval? Be grateful to God and happy in your heart that you are worthy of suffering this, as the apostles went forth (Acts 5:41) leaping for joy over the fact that they were disgraced and beaten down."

You see, these words are a great blessing to us if only we receive them with love and thanks, since we have no shortage of persecution. But our great advantage is that our enemies themselves cannot condemn our cause and must acknowledge—no thanks to them!—that it is right and true. What is wrong is the fact that we are teaching it, for they refuse to learn or accept it from us. Such a thing is unprecedented and unheard of. What we suffer on this account, therefore, is a holy and blessed suffering, as they themselves must testify. This is no longer a human persecution, but a truly demonic one, when they say that we must not and dare not call it the Word of God but must keep our mouth shut and not preach unless first we go and fall at the pope's feet, asking for approval from him and from his masks.

So let us be all the more willing and happy to suffer everything they can do against us, since we have the strong and certain comfort and the great and glorious satisfaction that their own mouth confirms our teaching and our cause. In addition, we hear the wonderful and delightful promise here that we shall be well rewarded in heaven and that we should be happy and rejoice over this, as people who do not have to yearn for heaven but already have it. All they do by their persecution is to further this, actually driving and chasing us to heaven. Now tell me whether these simple, short words do not encourage you as much as the whole world can, and provide more comfort and joy than all the suffering and torture our enemies can inflict on us. We should not listen to them with only *half* an ear, but take them to heart and ponder them.

This applies to persecution with deeds and fists, involving person or property, when Christians are seized and tortured, burned, hanged, and massacred, as happens nowadays and has happened before. There is, in addition, another kind of persecution. It is called defamation, slander, or disgrace, involving our reputation and good name. In this way Christians have to suffer more than others. Now Christ discusses this.

Matthew 5:11
Blessed are you when men revile you and persecute you and utter all kinds of evil against you falsely on My account.

This, too, is a great and severe persecution and, as I have said, the real suffering of Christians, that they endure bitter slander and poisonous defamation. Although other people must also suffer persecution, violent and unjust treatment, still men are willing to let them keep their reputation and good name. So this is not yet really Christian suffering, which requires not merely all sorts of tortures and troubles, but more; their good name must be spit upon and slandered, and the world must boast loudly that in murdering the Christians it has executed the worst kind of criminal, whom the earth could no longer carry, and that it has done God the greatest and most acceptable service, as Christ says (John 16:2). Thus no name has ever appeared on earth so slanderous and disreputable as the name "Christian." No nation has ever experienced so much bitter opposition and attack by wicked and poisonous tongues as have the Christians.

Right now they are proving this in the slander, defamation, lies, deceit, vicious tricks, and wicked misinterpretations they have perpetrated against the dear Gospel and its preachers, such that one would die many times rather than endure these poisonous, malicious darts (Eph. 6:16). Along comes the pope with his thunderbolts, damning us to the ninth hell as the children of the devil. In the same way his retinue, the bishops and princes, rage and roar with such terrible blasphemies and slanders that our whole body trembles and we would soon tire and give up if we did not have a comfort stronger and more powerful than all their malice and rage. Thus we let them rage and blaspheme. They will only plague themselves, and their poisonous hatred and insatiable envy will give them a burning pain. But we are content and courageous. If they want to rage and storm, we can still laugh and be joyful.

Therefore I say it again: Anyone who wants to be a Christian should learn to expect such persecution from poisonous, evil, slanderous tongues, especially when they cannot do anything with their fists. He should let the whole world sharpen its tongue on him, aim at him, sting and bite. Meanwhile he should regard all this with defiant contempt and laughter in God's name, letting them rage in the name of their god, the devil, and being firmly persuaded, as we have said above, that our cause is the right cause and is God's own cause. This they themselves have to confirm; even though they condemn us, they have to say it is the truth. Besides, before God our heart and conscience are sure that our teaching is right. We are not teaching on the basis of our own brains, reason, or wisdom, or using this to gain advantage, property, or reputation for ourselves before the world. We are preaching only God's Word and praising only His deeds. Our enemies, on the other hand, brag about nothing but their own deeds, merits, and holiness. They persecute us for refusing to join them in this.

They do not persecute us for being adulterers, robbers, or thieves. In fact, they can tolerate the most desperate scoundrels and criminals in their midst. But they are raising such a hue and cry because we refuse to approve their teaching and life; because we praise nothing but the Gospel, Christ, faith, and truly good works; and because we do not suffer for ourselves but suffer everything for the sake of Christ, the Lord. Therefore we will sing it to the end with them. No matter how hard their head, ours is still harder. In short, they must let that Man alone, whether they like it or not.

Matthew 5:12

Rejoice and be glad, for your reward is great in heaven.

These are really sweet and comforting words. They should gladden and encourage our hearts against all kinds of persecution. Should not the dear Lord's Word and comfort be dearer and more important to us than that which comes from a helpless bag of worms, or the rage, threats, excommunication, curses, and lightning of the miserable pope, even though he deluged us with the very dregs and the whole hell of his wrath and cursing? For I hear my Lord Christ telling me that He is truly delighted, and commanding me to be happy about it. In addition, He promises me such a wonderful reward: the kingdom of heaven shall be mine and everything that Christ has, together with all the saints and all

Christendom—in short, such a treasure and comfort that I should not trade it for all the possessions, joy, and music in the whole world, even though all the leaves and all the blades of grass were tongues singing my praises. This is not a Christian calling me "blessed," nor even an angel, but the Lord of all the angels, before whom they and all the creatures must kneel and adore. With all the other creatures, therefore, with the leaves and the grass, they must cheerfully sing and dance in my honor and praise.

And those who slander and curse me, what are they by comparison but nits and lousy paunches—if you will pardon the expression—so shameful that there is no name for them. If every creature, the leaves and the blades of grass in the forest and the sand on the shore, were all tongues to accuse and destroy them, what would all that be in comparison with a single word of this Man? His voice sounds clear enough to fill heaven and earth and to echo through them, silencing the slobbering coughs and the hoarse scratching of His enemies.

You see, that is how we should learn something about using these words for our benefit. They are not put here for nothing, but were spoken and written for our strengthening and comfort. By them our dear Master and faithful Shepherd, or Bishop, arms us. Then we shall be unafraid and ready to suffer if for His sake they lay all kinds of torment and trouble upon us in both words and deeds, and we shall despise whatever is offensive to us, even though contrary to our own reason and heart.

For if we cling to our own thoughts and feelings, we are dismayed and hurt to learn that for our service, help, counsel, and kindness to the world and to everyone we should get no thanks except the deepest and bitterest hatred and cursed, poisonous tongues. If flesh and blood were in charge here, it would soon say: "If I am to get nothing else out of this, then let anyone who wants to, stick with the Gospel and be a Christian! The world can go to the devil for help if that is what it wants!" This is the reason for the general complaint and cry that the Gospel is causing so much conflict, strife, and disturbance in the world and that everything is worse since it came than it was before, when things moved along smoothly, when there was no persecution, and when the people lived together like good friends and neighbors.

But here is what it says: "If you do not want to have the Gospel or be a Christian, then go out and take the world's side. Then you will be its friend, and no one will persecute you. But if you want to have the Gospel and Christ, then you must count on having trouble, conflict, and persecution wherever you go." Reason: because the devil cannot bear it otherwise, nor will he stop egging people on against the Gospel, so that all the world is incensed against it. Thus at the present time peasants, city people, nobles, princes, and lords oppose the Gospel from sheer cussedness, and they themselves do not know why. . . .

For so men persecuted the prophets who were before you.

"When this happens," He wants to say, "you are not alone. Look around, count back to all the holy fathers who ever lived before you, and you will find that their lot was the same. Why should you expect any special treatment? Should He forsake His method for your sake? He had to put up with it when His dear fathers and prophets were persecuted and killed, slandered, and ridiculed by everyone, and made the mockery of the world." As we see from the Scriptures, it had become a common and proverbial expression that if someone wanted to refer to a prophet, he called him a "fool." So in the history of Jehu (2 Kings 9:11), they said of a prophet: "Why did this mad fellow come to you?" And Isaiah shows (Isa. 57:4) that they opened their mouths and put out their tongues against him. But all they accomplished by this was to become a terrible stench and a curse, while the dear prophets and saints have honor, praise, and acclaim throughout the world and are ruling forever with Christ, the Lord. "This is what you should expect for yourselves too," Christ says, "that you will receive the same reward that they did, a reward more abundant and glorious than you can believe or dare to wish. For you are members of the same company and congregation."

What a dear and wonderful Preacher and faithful Master! He leaves out nothing that will help to strengthen and console, whether it be His Word and promise or the example and testimony of all the saints and of Himself. And all the angels in heaven and all the creatures support this. What more would you want and need? With such comfort, should we not put up with the anger and spite of the world and the devil for His sake? What would we do if we did not have a righteous and divine cause, if we had no splendid sayings and assurances like these and still had to suffer, as other people do who have no comfort? In the world it is impossible to avoid all suffering. And for the sake of the Gospel, as we have said, there must be some suffering; it reinforces the faithful and advances them to their promised comfort, joy, and bliss, and it punishes and damns the wicked despisers and enemies of the Gospel.

So far Christ has been equipping and preparing His Christians to live and suffer in the world, especially those who are to hold public office in Christendom. Even apart from this, however, every Christian should be ready at all times to take a stand, by himself if necessary, to confess his Lord and to represent his faith, always being armed against the world, the devil, the sects, and whatever else may be lined up against him. Now He goes on. He commits the office to them and teaches them how to carry it out; later on He will also put into their mouths what and how they are to preach. These are the elements that go in to make a Christian perfect: that in his person he lives properly and suffers in all sorts of ways on this account and that he properly administers and carries out his office, in which he is to serve and help other people.

Postscript: Grace and merit

Here at the end one more question remains to be discussed. In this sermon we have heard Christ emphasizing works very vigorously. He says (Matt. 5:3): "The poor shall have the kingdom of heaven"; (Matt. 5:7): "The merciful shall obtain mercy." He says again (Matt. 5:11–12) that those who suffer persecution for His sake will be rewarded in heaven. What is more, He says at the end of the fifth chapter (Matt. 5:46): "If you love those who love you, what reward have you?" In the sixth chapter He says about almsgiving, fasting, and praying (Matt. 6:4, 6, 18): "Your Father who sees in secret will reward you openly." From these statements those silly false preachers have drawn the conclusion that we enter the kingdom of heaven and are saved by our own works and actions. On this they build their endowments, monasteries, pilgrimages, Masses, and the like.

This question is a little subtle and would be more appropriate in a school before the learned people than in a pulpit before simple, common people. But since it occurs so often in the text, we must not bypass it completely but have to say something about it. It is necessary that everyone should know at least a little about the distinction between grace and merit, for the two are mutually exclusive. When grace is being preached, certainly merit cannot be preached; and what is grace cannot be merit, for "otherwise grace would no longer be grace," says St. Paul (Rom. 11:6). Since that is beyond every doubt, anyone who confuses these two causes the people to go astray and misleads both himself and those who listen to him.

For the present, we shall ignore the subtle answer and discuss the question in the most obvious possible terms. First of all, it must be maintained that faith or being a Christian is quite distinct from its fruit, as I have often said. So far as being a Christian and bearing the Christian name is concerned, one is no different from the other; everyone has an identical treasure and the identical possessions. The Baptism of St. Peter is no different or better than that of St. Paul, and the Baptism of a child born yesterday is no less a Baptism than that of St. John the Baptist or

St. Peter and all the apostles. Nor do they have any different or better Christ than the most insignificant Christian.

Now, from this perspective, no merit or distinction means a thing. The most insignificant Christian receives the same body and blood of Christ in the Sacrament; and when he listens to the Gospel, he is listening to the same Word of God that Peter and Paul listened to and preached. Similarly, no saint can pray a different Our Father or a better one, or confess a different Creed, or recite a different Decalogue from what is my daily prayer and every child's. This is so obvious that anyone can understand and comprehend it. In that which entitles us to the name "Christian" there is no inequality or discrimination among persons, but one is like the next—man or woman, young or old, learned or unlearned, noble or ignoble, prince or peasant, master or servant, major or minor saint. There is only one kind of Christ and one kind of faith. The sun in the heavens is the same toward everyone. It shines on a peasant as well as on a king, on a blind man as well as on a man with sharp vision, on a sow in the street as well as on the loveliest woman on earth. It shines on a thorn no less than on a rose, on a clod no less than on a purple robe. The same sun shines on the poorest beggar and on the greatest king or emperor.

But it is in the outward sphere and in our activity that the inequalities and the various distinctions among Christians appear—not as Christians nor as to what makes them Christians, but as to the fruit. I am a baptized Christian, but over and above this I am also a preacher, though I could be a Christian without that. As a preacher I am the kind of Christian that is supposed to present the Word to the people, to console the sorrowful, and to instruct the erring and ignorant. Another person is the head of a household or a manual laborer, who is supposed to govern his household, take care of his work, and support his wife and children. Such a man is quite different from you and me, and yet I have to say: "He is just as much of a Christian, and he has as much of Baptism, the grace of God, and eternal life as I and everyone else. In Christ he is no less significant than I, and here there is no distinction between women and men." A woman's task is different from a man's, a servant's from a master's, a preacher's from an ordinary citizen's, a child's from a father's, a pupil's or disciple's from a teacher's. Every one of them has his own task or fruit. So throughout the outward sphere there are differences, while in the inward sphere they are all Christians and identical. There is only one Christian estate and only one natural condition of all men.

We see the same thing in the heavens, St. Paul says (1 Cor. 15:41). There are so many varieties of stars, and they are all dissimilar—one great and the other small, one bright and the other dim. Yet there is only one sun and only one heaven. They are all alike in that they all stand in one heaven and have one kind of sun, and still they are unlike in their size and brightness. It is the same on earth, too, St. Paul continues (1 Cor. 15:39): "Not all flesh is alike, but there is one kind for men, another for animals, another for birds." They are all alike in being flesh; each has its limbs, head, heart, stomach, etc., as well as the others. Still there is a distinction of natures between men, animals, birds, and fish.

Now if you want to describe or portray a Christian, you must paint him in such a way that there is no distinction among the different ones; each one must be like each other one in every way. You must not portray him on the basis of the fact that he is a man or a woman, a preacher or a layman, a prince or a pauper, a manual laborer or a Carthusian monk. None of these distinctions makes him what he is; and compared in this respect with Peter and Paul, he is as good and as holy as they. In fact, no one amounts to more or is any better than he. If St. Peter were better than I in what makes a Christian a Christian, he would have to have a better Christ, Gospel, and Baptism. But since the possession we have is identical in all respects, we must all be alike so far as this is concerned, with no one elevated above the other. It is possible that one does more and greater deeds than another, as St. Peter raised the dead (Acts 9:40). Performing miracles that I do not perform makes him a greater and a brighter star than me in heaven, but not a different kind of star; and he does not have a different heaven either. St. Paul did more and worked harder than all the apostles (1 Cor. 15:10); but this does not mean that he had a better apostolic office or preached a different and better Christ.

Regarding merit, then, we say this. If the subject is what makes a Christian a Christian, how to become pious before God and obtain forgiveness of sins and eternal life, here we are all alike; here all our merit is completely excluded, and we must not hear or know anything about it. You have not merited the Gospel or Christ or Baptism, but it is purely a gift, freely given. Our sins are forgiven free, and we become God's children and are put into heaven without any contribution on our part. Our quarrel here is with the abomination of the sophists, who exalt our works to the point that by them we get a gracious God and merit heaven. In fact, they are so brazen that they dare to say that even in mortal sin a man is capable of doing so much on his own, of performing such acts of devotion, and of achieving such good works that by this he may still and propitiate the wrath of God. That amounts to throwing the roof to the ground, upsetting the foundation, building salvation on mere water, hurling Christ from His throne completely, and putting up our works in

His place. From this it must follow that we do not need Baptism or Christ or the Gospel or faith; for even in mortal sin I find enough goodness and power in myself to pull myself up by my own works and to merit forgiveness of sins and eternal life. From this you can see that all their drivel about merit is a slander and a blasphemy of God, when it comes to the subject we are now discussing, namely, how and by what means we come to the grace of God and eternal life. As if it were not bad enough that they teach this abominable blasphemy, they are actually defending it and condemning us as heretics on account of it.

It is easy to figure out and understand that one of these two must be false: Either we do merit grace by our actions, or Christ with His Baptism must be useless and worthless. Then Christ acted like a fool, to let Himself be tortured and to shed His blood so dearly and to expend so much, in gaining and granting to us something that was unnecessary and that we already have by ourselves. Although they denounce us as heretics for refusing to agree with them regarding this merit of works, we will bide our time, letting them call us heretics and turning it over to God, our Judge. And we shall withstand them all the more firmly, telling them that they are not heretics, but the worst blasphemers under the sun. They shamefully deny and curse Christ, as Peter prophesied about them (2 Pet. 2:1); and as the Epistle to the Hebrews says (Heb. 10:29), they punch Christ in the teeth and trample Him underfoot, along with His Baptism, the Sacrament, and the whole Gospel, and whatever God has given us through Him.

I would really like to hear how these miserable people could reply to this. They assert that by our works we can move toward receiving grace; when this is done and we have merited so much, we merit the kingdom of heaven and eternal salvation over and above what they call "first grace." What, then, is merited by the other works that follow? Let us assume that a Papist has performed his Mass or other work in grace and that by this precious work, which is worthy of eternal life, he has merited the kingdom of heaven. They call this the merit of condignity.[21] What, then, will he merit by the works and Masses that he does tomorrow and thereafter in the same grace? Since they do not know what to say, they begin to distinguish between "essential and accidental reward," saying: "These subsequent works make it possible to merit something extra, a sort of little gift or bonus, which God gives us over and above eternal life." If this is true, then it seems to me that the first works are the best but that the others are not so good; for otherwise they would have to merit the same. Usually, the subsequent works tend to be better, since they are practiced

21 See the volume introduction above, p. ix; and below, p. 229 n. 10.

and cultivated more carefully. Now since the last works do not merit the kingdom of heaven, the first must not merit it either. Or, if they are all equal and if every work can merit it, then God would have to build as many heavens as there are good works performed. And where would our Lord God find all those heavens to pay for every good work? Those are really smart people, being able to measure everything so smoothly and accurately! What shall we say then? Everything they present is sheer lying and deception. None of these things is true: first, that any man can merit grace by his own works, much less that a man in mortal sin can do so; secondly, even if, as their lie says, a man were in grace through his works, that such works done in grace should be precious enough to be worthy of the kingdom of heaven. There stands Christ, stating the exact opposite in frank and plain words (Luke 17:10): "When you have done all that is commanded you, say, 'We are unworthy servants.'"

Here we should steadfastly maintain our teaching so that we never let any work take credit for gaining the favor and grace of God, for liberating us from sin, and for bringing us to heaven. My merit is worthless for this. And if someone should want to use it for this, I must trample it underfoot and damn it to the devil himself in hell, as a thing that denies Christ and seeks to hinder my faith. All that avails here is the fact that God has given all this free, out of pure grace, by sending Christ, His Son, and letting Him die for me, announcing and granting this to me, and commanding me simply to believe it and to be baptized in it. None of my works has anything to do with this, but it is purely a gift, bestowed from heaven and brought to me by Christ. Let all merit be simply discarded here in favor of the conclusion that it is impossible to obtain grace and the forgiveness of sins in any other way, manner, or measure than by hearing the Word of God about Christ and by receiving it through faith. And why should we brag about our merit in order to make God applaud us? They themselves and all the saints have to pray in the Lord's Prayer every day as long as we live: "Forgive us our debts." And yet these desperate saints have the audacity to say that a man in mortal sin can prepare himself for grace, and then can merit eternal life!

How do you deal with the fact that there are so many passages about reward and merit? For the benefit of the simple people, we give the answer now that these are simply intended to comfort Christians. Once you have become a Christian and have a gracious God and the forgiveness of sins, both of past sins and of those that cling to you every day, a certain result will be that you will have to do much and suffer much on account of your faith and your Baptism. As these three chapters have shown in detail (Matthew 5–7), the devil himself, together with the world and the flesh, will attach himself to you and torment you from every side, making the world seem too narrow for you. If we were left to be stuck in this, without Word or consolation, we would despair and say: "Who wants to be a Christian or preach or do good works? You see what happens to them. The world tramples them underfoot, defames and slanders them, and tries every kind of villainy and evil trick on them, finally robbing them of their honor, their property, and their life. All Christ can call me is poor, troubled, hungry, meek, peaceable, afflicted, and persecuted! Is this supposed to last forever and never change?"

Then He has to speak out, strengthening and comforting us and saying: "Now you are in grace, and you are the children of God. Although you have to suffer for that in the world now, do not let it frighten you. Hold on tight, and do not let what you see tire you out or wear you down. Let everyone do his duty. If this causes him trouble, it will not do him any damage. He should know that the kingdom of heaven is his and that he will be richly repaid." Repaid, but how? We already have it through Christ, apart from, and prior to, any action of ours. As St. Paul says (1 Cor. 15:41), God will make you a big, bright star and give you a special gift, even in this life. Even here on earth, a Christian can obtain so much from God through his prayer and good works: He can save a whole country, prevent war, famine, and pestilence. This is not because the work is so precious in its own right, but because He has promised this to strengthen and comfort us and to keep us from thinking that our works, troubles, and sorrows have been lost and forgotten.

Now, none of this implies any merit on our part for earning grace or Baptism or Christ and heaven, which is what they mean when they talk about merit; but it all refers to the fruit of Christianity. As we have seen, Christ is saying nothing in this sermon about how we become Christians, but only about the works and fruit that no one can do unless he already is a Christian and in a state of grace. This is evident from the words that they have to endure poverty, suffering, and persecution simply because they are Christians and have the kingdom of heaven. Now, if we are discussing the fruit that follows grace and the forgiveness of sins, we will let the terms "merit" and "reward" be used. What we oppose is the idea that works of ours like these are the highest good, which must precede them and without which they do not take place or please God. If the insistence on grace alone without any merit is preserved, then we have no objection to giving the name "merits" to the fruit that follows. Only such statements should not be distorted and applied in an antiscriptural way to our meriting grace, but interpreted correctly, the way they were intended, as a consolation to Christians—especially when they have to suffer opposition, when they get the feeling and the impression that our life, suffering, and activity are pointless and useless. This is the consolation that Scripture uses everywhere in urging perseverance in good works. So in Jer. 31:16 it says: "Your works shall be rewarded"; and St. Paul says in 1 Cor. 15:58: "In the Lord your labor is not in vain." If we did not have this consolation, we could not stand the misery, persecution, and trouble we get in exchange for doing so much good, nor let our teaching and preaching be rewarded with nothing but ingratitude and abuse. Finally, we would have to stop working and suffering, though it is our obvious duty to do so.

God wants to wake us up and to strengthen us with this beautiful promise. Then we will not pay attention to the ingratitude, hate, envy, and contempt of the world, but pay attention to Him who says: "I am your God. If the world refuses to thank you and deprives you of your reputation and property, even of your body and life, just cling to Me, and find your consolation in the fact that I still have a heaven with so much in it that I can easily recompense you and give you ten times as much as they can take away from you now." And we can defy the world this way: "If it refuses to be kind to us, then it can leave, and take its kindness and everything else along. I did not start anything for its sake, and I will not do anything or stop anything for its sake. But I will do everything and suffer everything for the sake of Him whose promises are so generous and who says: 'Through Christ you already have all the treasure in heaven, and more than enough. Yet I will give you even more, as a bonus. You will have the kingdom of heaven revealed to you, and the Christ whom you now have in faith you will have in sight as well, in eternal glory and joy, the more you suffer and labor now.' "

Here we should also put wonderful statements and admonitions like Heb. 10:35: "Do not throw away your confidence, which has a great reward." And in Matt. 19:29 Christ says: "Everyone who has left houses or brothers or sisters or father or mother or children or lands, for My name's sake, will receive a hundredfold in this life, and in the world to come eternal life." Here He says (Matt. 5:12): "Your reward is great in heaven." Thus He shows that they already have the kingdom of heaven, and yet that they will have it even more gloriously when it is revealed.

You see, these passages are correctly interpreted when they are applied not to any confidence in our own works contrary to faith, but to the consolation of Christians and believers. If the sophists had directed their discussion of merit to this, it would have been fine. But they built their own works-holiness and monkery on this, expecting God to regard them as special saints and to be a peddler selling heaven to them and giving them the highest seats, because they are people with whom ordinary Christians should not even be compared. This was not an unwise thing to do, since it brought them not poverty, misery, sorrow, and persecution, but money, property, and honor. No order was ever established to let its members exercise themselves in the Word of Christ, the Sacrament, faith, love, and patience, but only to gain a reputation before God and His extra favor with their cowls and special ascetic life, as people who needed neither Christ nor faith.

In this sense we concede that Christians have merit and a reward with God, but not in order to make them children of God and heirs of eternal life. Rather, it is intended to console believers who already have this, to let them know that He will not leave unrewarded what they suffer here for Christ's sake, but that if they suffer much and labor much, He will adorn them specially on the Last Day, more and more gloriously than the others, as special stars that are greater than others. So St. Paul will be more brilliant, more bright and clear than others. This does not refer to the forgiveness of sins nor to meriting heaven, but to a recompense of greater glory for greater suffering. We refuse to tolerate the way they treat this issue; for it is a slander and a blasphemy to Christ, God, and the Holy Spirit, and to everything that God has given us through Him. We would rather be denounced as heretics and scoundrels and be burned at the stake than surrender or deny this treasure. We will also hold to this consolation, though we may have to suffer trouble, shame, and persecution on account of it, since this is inevitable. The devil will not make any concessions to us here, nor come to any agreement with us. He intends to uphold the pope's teaching and to make us believe the way he believes. Because he sees that we refuse, he attacks us with all his might. He knows very well that once this doctrine is granted—that Christ and the forgiveness of sins are purely a gift—then anyone can count on his fingers and come to the conclusion that the papacy with its Masses, monkery, purgatory, and worship of saints must amount to nothing; and it will all collapse by itself.

Learn to give this answer regarding the passages that refer to merit and reward: "Of course I hear Christ saying (Matt. 5:3): 'Blessed are the poor, for they shall have the kingdom of heaven'; and (Matt. 5:11–12): 'Blessed are you when you suffer persecution for My sake, for your reward is great in heaven.' But by these statements He is not teaching me where to build the foundation of my salvation, but giving me a promise that is to console me in my sufferings and in my Christian life. You must not confuse this and throw the two into the same pot, nor make my merit out of what God gives me in Christ through Baptism and the Gospel. It does not say that I can merit this and that I do not need Christ and Baptism for it. Rather, those who are Christ's pupils, those to whom He has been preaching here and who have to suffer many things for His sake, should know how to console themselves. Because people refuse to tolerate them on earth, they will have everything that much more abundantly in heaven; and he who does the most work and endures the most suffering will also get the most glorious recompense."

In Christ, as I have said, they are all alike. Grace is granted equally to all and brings full salvation to each individual, as the highest and most common possession; thus whoever has Christ has everything. And yet there will be a distinction in the glory with which we shall be adorned, and in the brightness with which we shall shine. In this life there is a distinction among gifts, and one labors and suffers more than another. But in that life it will all be revealed for the whole world to see what each one has done from the degree of glory he has; and the whole heavenly host will rejoice. Let this be sufficient on the matter.

Lectures on Galatians
1531

While Martin Luther preached at St. Mary's, the Wittenberg city church, on the Sermon on the Mount, he lectured at the university on St. Paul's Epistle to the Galatians. Luther's early lectures on Romans (1515–16) and Galatians (1516–17) were instrumental in clarifying his understanding of sin, grace, and righteousness. And yet Luther never lectured again on Romans and only returned to Galatians in the summer of 1531. A great deal had happened to Luther and his world since those early lectures.

Although Luther had been excommunicated by the Roman Church and had been declared an outlaw by the emperor in 1521, he was permitted to remain in Electoral Saxony under the protection of Frederick and his successors. Political maneuverings and the westward advance of the Ottoman Turks worried the emperor more than the troublesome monk in Wittenberg. By 1530 this was no longer the case. The political winds had shifted, and the emperor determined to resolve the Luther affair. He summoned a diet to be held in Augsburg. In March 1530, Elector John (1468–1532), Frederick's brother and successor, headed for Augsburg with Luther and a number of his colleagues. The situation was still too precarious for Luther to appear at the diet. He also could not risk leaving Electoral Saxony. He went as far south as he could and remained in the fortress at Coburg, about 150 miles north of Augsburg.

On June 25, 1530, the German Lutheran princes presented their confession of faith, the Augsburg Confession, to the emperor. After three months of further negotiations and a Roman refutation of the Confession, the emperor ruled against the Lutheran princes. They had until April 15, 1531, to return to the Roman Church or face the consequences. Luther thought war likely. The Lutheran princes and the other Protestant leaders of Germany who did not sign the Augsburg Confession feared the same, and in February 1531 they formed the Smalcald League. This Protestant alliance aimed to protect the religious and political interests of the Evangelical territories against the Holy Roman emperor. The political winds once again shifted, and April 15 came and passed. The Turks were again threatening the borders, and the emperor could not risk losing the military assistance of the Protestants. Negotiations resumed between the emperor and the Protestants, and a temporary peace was signed at Nürnberg in 1532.

Amid the political turmoil of 1531, Luther lectured on Galatians and produced one of his finest theological works. Once again Luther's choice of biblical material was not accidental. St. Paul's Epistle to the Galatians mirrored for Luther the struggle of his day. Paul stood for the purity of the Gospel and the believer's freedom in Christ from all laws and ceremonies. This was the very issue now facing the German people following the emperor's edict at Augsburg and any subsequent negotiations with Rome. Would they enslave themselves once more to works and human traditions by returning to Rome as the emperor demanded, or would they stand with the outlawed Luther for the purity of the Gospel? The following excerpt from Luther's lectures on Galatians demonstrates his mature understanding of Law and Gospel, Christ's universal atoning work, the relationship between faith and works, the freedom of the Christian, and true Christian holiness.

Lectures on Galatians[1]

We have taken it upon ourselves in the Lord's name to lecture on this Epistle of Paul to the Galatians once more. This is not because we want to teach something new or unknown, for by the grace of God Paul is now very well-known to you. But it is because, as I often warn you, there is a clear and present danger that the devil may take away from us the pure doctrine of faith and may substitute for it the doctrines of works and of human traditions. It is very necessary, therefore, that this doctrine of faith be continually read and heard in public. No matter how well-known it may be or how carefully learned, the devil, our adversary, who prowls around and seeks to devour us (1 Pet. 5:8), is not dead. Our flesh also goes on living. Besides, temptations of every sort attack and oppress us on every side. Therefore this doctrine can never be discussed and taught enough. If it is lost and perishes, the whole knowledge of truth, life, and salvation is lost and perishes at the same time. But if it flourishes, everything good flourishes—religion, true worship, the glory of God, and the right knowledge of all things and of all social conditions. To keep from doing nothing, we shall begin again where we broke off, according to the saying (Ecclus. 18:7): "When a man has finished, he is just beginning."

1 The following excerpt is adapted from *Lectures on Galatians (1531)*, volumes 26–27 of *Luther's Works: American Edition*, ed. Jaroslav Pelikan and Walter A. Hansen, trans. Jaroslav Pelikan (St. Louis: Concordia, 1963–64). Minor alterations have been made to the text for consistency in style, abbreviations, and capitalization. The annotations and subheadings are the work of the editor of this book.

The Argument of St. Paul's Epistle to the Galatians

Active and passive righteousness

First of all, we must speak of the argument, that is, of the issue with which Paul deals in this Epistle. The argument is this: Paul wants to establish the doctrine of faith, grace, the forgiveness of sins or Christian righteousness, so that we may have a perfect knowledge and know the difference between Christian righteousness and all other kinds of righteousness. For righteousness is of many kinds. There is a political righteousness, which the emperor, the princes of the world, philosophers, and lawyers consider. There is also a ceremonial righteousness, which human traditions teach, as, for example, the traditions of the pope and other traditions. Parents and teachers may teach this righteousness without danger, because they do not attribute to it any power to make satisfaction for sin, to placate God, and to earn grace; but they teach that these ceremonies are necessary only for moral discipline and for certain observances. There is, in addition to these, yet another righteousness, the righteousness of the Law or of the Decalogue, which Moses teaches. We, too, teach this, but after the doctrine of faith.

Over and above all these there is the righteousness of faith or Christian righteousness, which is to be distinguished most carefully from all the others. For they are all contrary to this righteousness, both because they proceed from the laws of emperors, the traditions of the pope, and the commandments of God, and because they consist in our works and can be achieved by us with "purely natural endowments," as the scholastics teach, or from a gift of God. For these kinds of the righteousness of works, too, are gifts of God, as are all the things we have. But this most excellent righteousness, the righteousness of faith, which God imputes to us through Christ without works, is neither political nor ceremonial nor legal nor works-righteousness but is quite the opposite; it is a merely passive righteousness, while all the others, listed above, are active. For here we work nothing, render nothing to God; we only receive and permit someone else to work in us, namely, God. Therefore it is appropriate to call the righteousness of faith or Christian righteousness "passive." This is a righteousness hidden in a mystery, which the world does not understand. In fact, Christians themselves do not adequately understand it or grasp it in the midst of their temptations. Therefore it must always be taught and continually exercised. And anyone who does not grasp or take hold of it in afflictions and terrors of conscience cannot stand. For there is no comfort of conscience so solid and certain as is this passive righteousness.

But such is human weakness and misery that in the terrors of conscience and in the danger of death we look at nothing except our own works, our worthiness, and the Law. When the Law shows us our sin, our past life immediately comes to our mind. Then the sinner, in his great anguish of mind, groans and says to himself: "Oh, how damnably I have lived! If only I could live longer! Then I would amend my life." Thus human reason cannot refrain from looking at active righteousness, that is, its own righteousness; nor can it shift its gaze to passive, that is, Christian righteousness, but it simply rests in the active righteousness. So deeply is this evil rooted in us, and so completely have we acquired this unhappy habit! Taking advantage of the weakness of our nature, Satan increases and aggravates these thoughts in us. Then it is impossible for the conscience to avoid being more seriously troubled, confounded, and frightened. For it is impossible for the human mind to conceive any comfort of itself, or to look only at grace amid its consciousness and terror of sin, or consistently to reject all discussion of works. To do this is beyond human power and thought. Indeed, it is even beyond the Law of God. For although the Law is the best of all things in the world, it still cannot bring peace to a terrified conscience but makes it even sadder and drives it to despair. For by the Law sin becomes exceedingly sinful (Rom. 7:13).

Therefore the afflicted conscience has no remedy against despair and eternal death except to take hold of the promise of grace offered in Christ, that is, this righteousness of faith, this passive or Christian righteousness, which says with confidence: "I do not seek active righteousness. I ought to have and perform it; but I declare that even if I did have it and perform it, I cannot trust in it or stand up before the judgment of God on the basis of it. Thus I put myself beyond all active righteousness, all righteousness of my own or of the divine Law, and I embrace only that passive righteousness which is the righteousness of grace, mercy, and the forgiveness of sins." In other words, this is the righteousness of Christ and of the Holy Spirit, which we do not perform but receive, which we do not have but accept, when God the Father grants it to us through Jesus Christ.

As the earth itself does not produce rain and is unable to acquire it by its own strength, worship, and power but receives it only by a heavenly gift from above, so this heavenly righteousness is given to us by God without our work or merit. As much as the dry earth of itself is able to accomplish in obtaining the right and blessed rain, that much can we men accomplish by our own strength and works to obtain that divine, heavenly, and eternal righteousness. Thus we can obtain it only through the free imputation and indescribable gift of God. Therefore the highest art and wisdom of Christians is not to know the Law, to ignore works and all active righteousness, just as outside the people of God the highest wisdom is to know and study the Law, works, and active righteousness.

Law and Gospel

It is a marvelous thing and unknown to the world to teach Christians to ignore the Law and to live before God as though there were no Law whatever. For if you do not ignore the Law and thus direct your thoughts to grace as though there were no Law but as though there were nothing but grace, you cannot be saved. "For through the Law comes knowledge of sin" (Rom. 3:20). On the other hand, works and the performance of the Law must be demanded in the world as though there were no promise or grace. This is because of the stubborn, proud, and hard-hearted, before whose eyes nothing must be set except the Law, in order that they may be terrified and humbled. For the Law was given to terrify and kill the stubborn and to exercise the old man. Both words must be correctly divided, according to the apostle (2 Tim. 2:25ff.).

This calls for a wise and faithful father who can moderate the Law in such a way that it stays within its limits. For if I were to teach men the Law in such a way that they suppose themselves to be justified by it before God, I would be going beyond the limit of the Law, confusing these two righteousnesses, the active and the passive, and would be a bad dialectician who does not properly distinguish. But when I go beyond the old man, I also go beyond the Law. For the flesh or the old man, the Law and works, are all joined together. In the same way the spirit or the new man is joined to the promise and to grace. Therefore when I see that a man is sufficiently contrite, oppressed by the Law, terrified by sin, and thirsting for comfort, then it is time for me to take the Law and active righteousness from his sight and to set forth before him, through the Gospel, the passive righteousness which excludes Moses and the Law and shows the promise of Christ, who came for the afflicted and for sinners. Here a man is raised up again and gains hope. Nor is he any longer under the Law; he is under grace, as the apostle says (Rom. 6:14): "You are not under Law but under grace." How not under Law? According to the new man, to whom the Law does not apply. For the Law had its limits until Christ, as Paul says below (Gal. 3:24): "The Law, until Christ." When He came, Moses and the Law stopped. So did circumcision, sacrifices, and the Sabbath. So did all the prophets.

This is our theology, by which we teach a precise distinction between these two kinds of righteousness, the active and the passive, so that morality and faith, works and grace, secular society and religion may not be confused. Both are necessary, but both must be kept within their limits. Christian righteousness applies to the new man, and the righteousness of the Law applies to the old man, who is born of flesh and blood. Upon this latter, as upon an ass, a burden must be put that will oppress him. He must not enjoy the freedom of the spirit or of grace unless he has first put on the new man by faith in Christ, but this does not happen fully in this life. Then he may enjoy the kingdom and the ineffable gift of grace. I am saying this in order that no one may suppose that we reject or prohibit good works, as the Papists falsely accuse us because they understand neither what they themselves are saying nor what we are teaching. They know nothing except the righteousness of the Law; and yet they claim the right to judge a doctrine that is far above and beyond the Law, a doctrine on which the carnal man is unable to pass judgment. Therefore it is inevitable that they be offended, for they cannot see any higher than the Law. Therefore whatever is above the Law is the greatest possible offense to them.

We set forth two worlds, as it were, one of them heavenly and the other earthly. Into these we place these two kinds of righteousness, which are distinct and separated from each other. The righteousness of the Law is earthly and deals with earthly things; by it we perform good works. But as the earth does not bring forth fruit unless it has first been watered and made fruitful from above—for the earth cannot judge, renew, and rule the heavens, but the heavens judge, renew, rule, and fructify the earth, so that it may do what the Lord has commanded—so also by the righteousness of the Law we do nothing even when we do much; we do not fulfill the Law even when we fulfill it. Without any merit or work of our own, we must first be justified by Christian righteousness, which has nothing to do with the righteousness of the Law or with earthly and active righteousness. But this righteousness is heavenly and passive. We do not have it of ourselves; we receive it from heaven. We do not perform it; we accept it by faith, through which we ascend beyond all laws and works. "As, therefore, we have borne the image of the earthly Adam," as Paul says, "let us bear the image of the heavenly one" (1 Cor. 15:49), who is a new man in a new world, where there is no Law, no sin, no conscience, no death, but perfect joy, righteousness, grace, peace, life, salvation, and glory.

Then do we do nothing and work nothing in order to obtain this righteousness? I reply: Nothing at all. For this righteousness means to do nothing, to hear nothing, and to know nothing about the Law or about works but to know and believe only this: that Christ has gone to the Father and is now invisible; that He sits in heaven at the right hand of the Father, not as a judge but as one who has been made for us wisdom, righteousness, sanctification, and redemption from God (1 Cor. 1:30); in short, that He is our High Priest, interceding for us and reigning over us and in us through grace. Here one notices no sin and feels no terror or remorse of conscience. Sin cannot happen in this Christian righteousness; for where there is no Law, there cannot be any transgression (Rom. 4:15). If, therefore, sin does not have a place here, there is no conscience, no terror, no sadness. Therefore John says: "No one born of God commits sin" (1 John 3:9). But if there is any conscience or fear present, this is a sign that this righteousness has been withdrawn, that grace has been lost sight of, and that Christ is hidden and out of sight. But where Christ is truly seen, there there must be full and perfect joy in the Lord and peace of heart, where the heart declares: "Although I am a sinner according to the Law, judged by the righteousness of the Law, nevertheless I do not despair. I do not die, because Christ lives who is my righteousness and my eternal and heavenly life. In that righteousness and life I have no sin, conscience, and death. I am indeed a sinner according to the present life and its righteousness, as a son of Adam where the Law accuses me, death reigns and devours me. But above this life I have another righteousness, another life, which is Christ, the Son of God, who does not know sin and death but is righteousness and eternal life. For His sake this body of mine will be raised from the dead and delivered from the slavery of the Law and sin, and will be sanctified together with the spirit."

Thus as long as we live here, both remain. The flesh is accused, exercised, saddened, and crushed by the active righteousness of the Law. But the spirit rules, rejoices, and is saved by passive righteousness, because it knows that it has a Lord sitting in heaven at the right hand of the Father, who has abolished the Law, sin, and death, and has trodden all evils underfoot, has led them captive and triumphed over them in Himself (Col. 2:15). In this Epistle, therefore, Paul is concerned to instruct, comfort, and sustain us diligently in a perfect knowledge of this most excellent and Christian righteousness. For if the doctrine of justification is lost, the whole of Christian doctrine is lost. And those in the world who do not teach it are either Jews or Turks or Papists or sectarians. For between these two kinds of righteousness, the active righteousness of the Law and the passive righteousness of Christ, there is no middle ground. Therefore he who has strayed away from this Christian righteousness will necessarily relapse into the active righteousness; that is, when he has lost Christ, he must fall into a trust in his own works.

Faith and works

We see this today in the fanatical spirits and sectarians, who neither teach nor can teach anything correctly about this righteousness of grace. They have taken the words out of our mouth and out of our writings, and these only they speak and write. But the substance itself they cannot discuss, deal with, and urge, because they neither understand it nor can understand it. They cling only to the righteousness of the Law. Therefore they are and remain disciplinarians of works; nor can they rise beyond the active righteousness. Thus they remain exactly what they were under the pope. To be sure, they invent new names and new works; but the content remains the same. So it is that the Turks perform different works from the Papists, and the Papists perform different works from the Jews, and so forth. But though some do works that are more splendid, great, and difficult than others, the content remains the same, and only the quality is different. That is, the works vary only in appearance and in name. For they are still works. And those who do them are not Christians; they are hirelings, whether they are called Jews, Mohammedans, Papists, or sectarians.

Therefore we always repeat, urge, and inculcate this doctrine of faith or Christian righteousness, so that it may be observed by continuous use and may be precisely distinguished from the active righteousness of the Law. (For by this doctrine alone and through it alone is the church built, and in this it consists.) Otherwise we shall not be able to observe true theology but shall immediately become lawyers, ceremonialists, legalists, and Papists. Christ will be so darkened that no one in the church will be correctly taught or comforted. Therefore if we want to be preachers and teachers of others, we must take great care in these issues and hold to this distinction between the righteousness of the Law and that of Christ. This distinction is easy to speak of; but in experience and practice it is the most difficult of all, even if you exercise and practice it diligently. For in the hour of death or in other conflicts of conscience these two kinds of righteousness come together more closely than you would wish or ask.

Therefore I admonish you, especially those of you who are to become instructors of consciences, as well as each of you individually, that you exercise yourselves by study, by reading, by meditation, and by prayer, so that in temptation you will be able to instruct consciences, both your own and others, console them, and take them from the Law to grace, from active righteousness to passive righteousness, in short, from Moses to Christ. In affliction and in the conflict of conscience it is the devil's habit to frighten us with the Law and to set against us the consciousness of sin, our wicked past, the wrath and judgment of God, hell and eternal death, so that thus he may drive us into despair, subject us to himself, and pluck us from Christ. It is also his habit to set against us those passages in the Gospel in which Christ Himself requires works from us and with plain words threatens damnation to those who do not perform them. If here we cannot distinguish between these two kinds of righteousness; if here by faith we do not take hold of Christ, who is sitting at the right hand of God, who is our life and our righteousness, and who makes intercession for us miserable sinners before the Father (Heb. 7:25), then we are under the Law and not under grace, and Christ is no longer a Savior. Then He is a lawgiver. Then there can be no salvation left, but sure despair and eternal death will follow.

Therefore let us learn diligently this art of distinguishing between these two kinds of righteousness, in order that we may know how far we should obey the Law. We have said above that in a Christian the Law must not exceed its limits but should have its dominion only over the flesh, which is subjected to it and remains under it. When this is the case, the Law remains within its limits. But if it wants to ascend into the conscience and exert its rule there, see to it that you are a good dialectician and that you make the correct distinction. Give no more to the Law than it has coming, and say to it: "Law, you want to ascend into the realm of conscience and rule there. You want to denounce its sin and take away the joy of my heart, which I have through faith in Christ. You want to plunge me into despair, in order that I may perish. You are exceeding your jurisdiction. Stay within your limits, and exercise your dominion over the flesh. You shall not touch my conscience. For I am baptized; and through the Gospel I have been called to a fellowship of righteousness and eternal life, to the kingdom of Christ, in which my conscience is at peace, where there is no Law but only the forgiveness of sins, peace, quiet, happiness, salvation, and eternal life. Do not disturb me in these matters. In my conscience not the Law will reign, that hard tyrant and cruel disciplinarian, but Christ, the Son of God, the King of peace and righteousness, the sweet Savior and Mediator. He will preserve my conscience happy and peaceful in the sound and pure doctrine of the Gospel and in the knowledge of this passive righteousness."

When I have this righteousness within me, I descend from heaven like the rain that makes the earth fertile. That is, I come forth into another kingdom, and I perform good works whenever the opportunity arises. If I am a minister of the Word, I preach, I comfort the saddened, I administer the Sacraments. If I am a father, I rule my household and family, I train my children in piety and honesty. If I am a magistrate, I perform the office which I have received by divine command. If I am a servant, I faithfully tend to my master's affairs. In short, whoever knows for sure that Christ is his righteousness not only cheerfully and gladly works in his calling but also submits himself for the sake of love to magistrates, also to their wicked laws, and to everything else in this present life—even, if need be, to burden and danger. For he knows that God wants this and that this obedience pleases Him.

So far the argument of the Epistle, which Paul sets forth because of the false teachers who had obscured this righteousness of faith among the Galatians. Against them he asserts his authority and office.

Galatians 1:1
Paul an apostle—not from men nor through man.

Now that we have set forth the argument and have shown the summary of this Epistle to the Galatians, it seems appropriate, before we come to the content itself, to indicate the occasion for Paul's composition of this Epistle. He had planted the pure doctrine of the Gospel and the righteousness of faith among the Galatians. But immediately after his departure false teachers crept in; they subverted everything that he had planted and taught so well. For the devil cannot do otherwise than attack this doctrine vehemently, with might and with craft; nor does he rest as long as he sees even a spark of it remaining. We, too, merely because we preach the Gospel purely, suffer all sorts of evils both on the right hand and on the left from the world, the devil, and his apostles.

For the Gospel is a doctrine that teaches something far more sublime than the wisdom, righteousness, and religion of the world. It leaves these things at their proper level and commends them as good creatures of God. But the world prefers these creatures to the Creator. Finally, through them it wants to abolish sin, to be delivered from death, and to merit eternal life. This the Gospel condemns. But the world cannot bear the condemnation of that which it regards as best. Therefore it charges the Gospel with being a seditious and erroneous doctrine that subverts commonwealths, principalities, kingdoms, empires, and religions; it accuses the Gospel of sinning against God and Caesar, of abrogating the laws, of subverting morality, and of granting men the license to do with impunity whatever they please. With righteous zeal, therefore, and with the appearance of high service to God (John 16:2), the world persecutes this doctrine and despises its teachers and followers as the greatest plague there can be on earth. . . .

The divine call

At the very outset Paul deals with those false teachers. They claimed to be the pupils of the apostles, sent by them; and they despised Paul as one who was neither the pupil of the apostles nor sent by them to preach the Gospel but had entered in some other way and had intruded himself upon the ministry on his own initiative. Against them Paul defends his calling and says: "Your preachers look down on my calling. But whoever it is that has come to you, he is sent either from men or through man; that is, he has either entered on his own, without a call, or has been called by someone else. But my calling is not from men or through man; it is superior to any calling that can come after the apostles. For it is 'through Jesus Christ and God the Father.'"

When Paul says "from men," I take this to refer to those who call and intrude themselves, when neither God nor man calls or sends them, but who run and speak on their own. Today the sectarians do this. Either they lurk in corners, look for some place to spew forth their venom, and do not come into public churches; or they go where the Gospel has already been planted. These I call "from men." But when he says "through man," I take this to refer to those who have a divine calling, but one that has come through man.

God calls in two ways, either by means or without means. Today He calls all of us into the ministry of the Word by a mediated call, that is, one that comes through means, namely, through man. But the apostles were called immediately by Christ Himself, as the prophets in the Old Testament had been called by God Himself. Afterward the apostles called their disciples, as Paul called Timothy, Titus, etc. These men called bishops, as in Titus 1:5ff.; and the bishops called their successors down to our own time, and so on to the end of the world. This is a mediated calling, since it is done by man. Nevertheless, it is divine.

Thus when someone is called by a prince or a magistrate or me, he has his calling through man. Since the time of the apostles this has been the usual method of calling in the world. It should not be changed; it should be exalted, on account of the sectarians, who despise it and lay claim to another calling, by which they say that the Spirit drives them to teach. But they are liars and impostors, for they are being driven by a spirit who is not good but evil. It is not lawful for me to forsake my assigned station as a preacher, to go to another city where I have no call, and to preach there. (As a doctor of divinity, of course, I could preach throughout the papacy, provided that they let me.) I have no right to do this even if I hear that false doctrine is being taught and that souls are being seduced and condemned which I could rescue from error and condemnation by my sound doctrine. But I should commit the matter to God, who in His own time will find the opportunity to call ministers lawfully and to give the Word. For He is the Lord of the harvest who will send laborers into His harvest; our task is to pray (Matt. 9:38).

Therefore we should not intrude into someone else's harvest, as the devil does through his sectarians. With ardent zeal they claim to be saddened that men are being so miserably led astray, and to want to teach them the truth and rescue them from the devil's clutches. Therefore even when a man seeks, with pious zeal and good intentions, to rescue with his sound doctrine those who have been led astray into error, this is still a bad example, which gives ungodly teachers an excuse to intrude themselves, after which Satan himself occupies the see. This example does a great deal of damage.

But when the prince or some other magistrate calls me, then, with firm confidence, I can boast against the devil and the enemies of the Gospel that I have been called by the command of God through the voice of a man; for the command of God comes through the mouth of the prince, and this is a genuine call. Therefore we, too, have been called by divine authority—not by Christ immediately, as the apostles were, but "through man."

Certainty of the call

Now this doctrine of the certainty of the call is extremely necessary on account of the pernicious and demonic spirits. Every minister of the Word may boast with John the Baptist (Luke 3:2): "The Word of the Lord has come upon me." Therefore when I preach, baptize, or administer the Sacraments, I do so as one who has a command and a call. For the voice of the Lord has come to me, not in some corner, as the sectarians boast, but through the mouth of a man who is carrying out his lawful right. But if one or two citizens were to ask me to preach, I should not follow such a private call; for this would open the window to the ministers of Satan, who would follow this example and work harm, as we have said above. But when those who are in public office ask me, then I should obey.

Therefore when Paul says "not from men nor through man," he is knocking down the false apostles. It is as though he were saying: "No matter how much these vipers may brag, of what more can they brag than that they have come either 'from men,' that is, on their own, without any call, or 'through man,' that is, being sent by someone else? I am not concerned about any of this; nor should you be. But as for me, I have been called and sent neither from men nor through man but immediately, that is, by Jesus Christ Himself. In every way my call is like that of the apostles, and I am indeed an apostle." Therefore Paul deals thoroughly with this doctrine of the call of the apostles. Elsewhere he distinguishes between apostleship and other ministries, as in 1 Cor. 12:28ff. and in Eph. 4:11, where he says: "And God has ordained some in the church as apostles, prophets, etc." He puts apostles into first place, so that those may properly be called apostles who have been sent immediately by God Himself without any other person as the means. Thus Matthias was called by God alone; for when the other apostles had chosen two men, they did not dare decide between them but cast lots and prayed God to indicate whom He preferred (Acts 1:23–26). Since he was to be an apostle, it was necessary that he be called by God. Thus Paul was called to be the apostle to the Gentiles (Rom. 11:13). This is why the apostles are called saints; for they are sure of their calling and doctrine and have remained faithful in their ministry, and no one of them has become an apostate except Judas, because their call is a holy one.

This is the first attack Paul makes against the false apostles, who ran when no one sent them. The call, therefore, is not to be despised. For it is not sufficient if a man has the Word and the pure doctrine. He must also have the assurance of his call, and whoever enters without this assurance enters only in order to kill and destroy (John 10:10). For God never prospers the work of those who are not called. Even if they teach something good and useful, it does not edify. Thus in our time the sectarians have the vocabulary of faith in their mouths, but they do not produce any fruit. Their chief aim is to attract men to their false opinions. To remain in their saving task, those who have a sure and holy call must often bear many severe conflicts, as must those whose teaching is pure and sound, against the devil with his constant and endless wiles and against the world with its attacks. In these conflicts what is one to do whose call is unsure and whose doctrine is corrupt?

Therefore we who are in the ministry of the Word have this comfort, that we have a heavenly and holy office; being legitimately called to this, we prevail over all the gates of hell (Matt. 16:18). On the other hand, it is dreadful when the conscience says: "You have done this without a call!" Here a man without a call is shaken by such terror that he wishes he had never heard the Word he preaches. For by his disobedience he sullies all his works, regardless of how good they are, so that even his greatest works and deeds become his greatest sins.

Thus you see how necessary it is to boast and glory in our ministry this way. In the past, when I was only a young theologian and doctor, I thought it was imprudent of Paul in his Epistle to boast of his call so often. But I did not understand his purpose, for I did not know that the ministry of the Word of God was so weighty a matter. I did not know anything about the doctrine of faith and a true conscience. In the schools and churches no certainty was being taught, but everything was filled with the sophistic trifles and nursery rhymes of the canonists and commentators on the *Sentences*.[2] Therefore no one could understand how forceful

---

2 Aspiring masters of theology were required to lecture upon the *Sentences* of Peter Lombard (ca. 1095–1160). No other Christian work outside of Scripture has been

and powerful is this holy and spiritual boasting about a call, which serves first to the glory of God, secondly to the advancement of our own ministry, and also to our own benefit and to that of the people. When we boast this way, we are not looking for prestige in the world or praise from men or money, or for pleasure or the goodwill of the world. The reason for our proud boasting is that we are in a divine calling and in God's own work, and that the people need to be assured of our calling, in order that they may know that our word is in fact the Word of God. This, then, is not a vain pride; it is a most holy pride against the devil and the world. And it is a true humility in the sight of God.

Galatians 1:2
To the churches of Galatia.

The Church of Rome is holy

. . . Jerome[3] raises an important question here: Why does Paul call "churches" those that were not churches? For Paul, he says, is writing to the Galatians, who had been led astray and turned away from Christ and from grace to Moses and the Law. I reply: When Paul calls them the "churches of Galatia," he is employing synecdoche, a very common practice in the Scriptures.[4] Writing in a similar vein to the Corinthians, he congratulates them that the grace of God was given them in Christ, that is, that they were enriched in Him with all speech and all knowledge (1 Cor. 1:4–5). And yet many of them had been perverted by false apostles and did not believe in the resurrection of the dead, etc. So today we still call the Church of Rome holy and all its sees holy, even though they have been undermined and their ministers are ungodly. For God "rules in the midst of His foes" (Ps. 110:2), Antichrist "takes his seat in the temple of God" (2 Thess. 2:4), and Satan is present among the sons of God (Job 1:6). Even if the church is "in the midst of a crooked and perverse generation," as Paul says to the Philippians (2:15), and even if it is surrounded by wolves and robbers, that is, spiritual tyrants, it is still the church. Although the city of Rome is worse than Sodom and Gomorrah, nevertheless there remain in it Baptism, the Sacrament, the voice and text of the Gospel, the Sacred Scriptures, the ministries, the name of Christ, and the name of God. Whoever has these, has them;

---

commented upon more. Theologians as diverse as Bonaventure, Thomas Aquinas, John Duns Scotus, William of Ockham (ca. 1285–ca. 1348), Gabriel Biel, and Martin Luther—to name only a few—commented upon the *Sentences*.

3 On Jerome, see above, p. 86 n. 3.

4 A figure of speech that refers to a part by naming the whole or vice versa.

whoever does not have them, has no excuse, for the treasure is still there. Therefore the Church of Rome is holy, because it has the holy name of God, the Gospel, Baptism, etc. If these are present among a people, that people is called holy. Thus this Wittenberg of ours is a holy village, and we are truly holy, because we have been baptized, communed, taught, and called by God; we have the works of God among us, that is, the Word and the Sacraments, and these make us holy.

I say this in order that we may distinguish sharply between Christian holiness and other kinds of holiness. The monks called their orders holy, although they did not dare call themselves holy; but they are not holy, because, as we said above, Christian holiness is not active but passive. Therefore let no one call himself holy on the basis of his way of life or of his works—fasting, prayer, flagellation, almsgiving, or the consolation of the sad and afflicted. Otherwise the Pharisee in Luke (18:11ff.) would be holy too. Such works, of course, are holy, and God strictly demands them of us; but they do not make us holy. You and I are holy; the church, the city, and the people are holy—not on the basis of their own holiness but on the basis of a holiness not their own, not by an active holiness, but by a passive holiness. They are holy because they possess something that is divine and holy, namely, the calling of the ministry, the Gospel, Baptism, etc., on the basis of which they are holy.

The church is universal

Therefore even though the Galatians had been led astray, Baptism, the Word, and the name of Christ still continued among them. Besides, there were still some good men who had not defected from Paul's doctrine and who had a proper understanding of the Word and the Sacraments, which could not be defiled by those who did rebel. For Baptism, the Gospel, etc., do not become unholy because I am defiled and unholy and have a false understanding of them. On the contrary, they remain holy and exactly what they were, regardless of whether they are among the godly or the ungodly; men can neither defile them nor hallow them. By our good or evil behavior, by our good or evil life and morals, they are defiled or hallowed in the sight of the Gentiles (Rom. 2:24) but not in the sight of God. Therefore the church is holy even where the fanatics are dominant, so long as they do not deny the Word and the Sacraments; if they deny these, they are no longer the church. Wherever the substance of the Word and the Sacraments abides, therefore, there the holy church is present, even though Antichrist may reign there; for he takes his seat not in a stable of fiends or in a pigpen or in a congregation of unbelievers but in the highest and holiest place possible, namely, in the temple of God

(2 Thess. 2:4).[5] Thus our brief answer to this question is this: The church is universal throughout the world, wherever the Gospel of God and the Sacraments are present. The Jews, the Turks, and the fanatics are not the church, because they oppose and deny these things. Now there follows the salutation.

Galatians 1:3

Grace to you and peace from God the Father and our Lord Jesus Christ.

I hope that you are not ignorant of the meaning of "grace" and "peace," since these terms occur frequently in Paul and are easy to understand. But since we are taking it upon ourselves to expound this Epistle—something we are doing not because it is necessary or because the Epistle is very difficult, but in order to confirm our consciences against future heresies—it should not bore you if we repeat here what we teach, preach, sing, and write at other times and places. For if we lose the doctrine of justification, we lose simply everything. Hence the most necessary and important thing is that we teach and repeat this doctrine daily, as Moses says about his Law (Deut. 6:7). For it cannot be grasped or held enough or too much. In fact, though we may urge and inculcate it vigorously, no one grasps it perfectly or believes it with all his heart. So frail is our flesh and so disobedient to the Spirit!

The apostle's greeting is new to the world and had never been heard before the proclamation of the Gospel. Grace and peace—these two words embrace the whole of Christianity. Grace forgives sin, and peace stills the conscience. The two devils who plague us are sin and conscience, the power of the Law and the sting of sin (1 Cor. 15:56). But Christ has conquered these two monsters and trodden them underfoot, both in this age and in the age to come. The world does not know this; therefore it cannot teach anything sure about how to overcome sin, conscience, and death. Only Christians have this kind of teaching and are equipped and armed with it, so that they can overcome sin, despair, and eternal death. It is a teaching that is given only by God; it does not proceed from free will, nor was it invented by human reason or wisdom.

These two words, "grace" and "peace," contain a summary of all of Christianity. Grace contains the forgiveness of sins, a joyful peace, and a quiet conscience. But peace is impossible unless sin has first been forgiven, for the Law accuses and terrifies the conscience on account of sin. And the sin that the conscience feels cannot be removed by pilgrimages,

5 For Luther's identification of the papacy as the Antichrist, see *On the Papacy in Rome* (1520), LW 39:49–104.

vigils, labors, efforts, vows, or any other works; in fact, sin is increased by works. The more we work and sweat to extricate ourselves from sin, the worse off we are. For there is no way to remove sin except by grace. This deserves careful notice. For the words are easy; but in temptation it is the hardest thing possible to be surely persuaded in our hearts that we have the forgiveness of sins and peace with God by grace alone, entirely apart from any other means in heaven or on earth.

Because the world does not understand this doctrine, it neither can nor will tolerate it. It brags about free will, about our powers, about our works—all these as means by which to earn and attain grace and peace, that is, the forgiveness of sins and a joyful conscience. But the conscience cannot be quiet and joyful unless it has peace through this grace, that is, through the forgiveness of sins promised in Christ. Many have worked hard, inventing various religious orders and disciplines, to find peace and a quiet conscience; but instead they have plunged even more deeply into even greater misery, for such tactics are merely ways of multiplying doubt and despair. Therefore your bones and mine will know no rest until we hear the Word of grace and cling to it firmly and faithfully.

The apostle clearly distinguishes this grace and peace from any other kind of grace and peace. He wishes the Galatians grace and peace—not from Caesar or from kings and princes, for these usually persecute the pious and rise up against the Lord and against His Christ (Ps. 2:1); nor from the world, for "in the world," Christ said, "you have tribulation" (John 16:33); but from God our Father. In other words, he wishes them a heavenly peace. So Christ says: "Peace I leave with you; My peace I give to you; not as the world gives do I give to you" (John 14:27).

The world's peace grants nothing except the peace of our property and of our bodies, so that we can live happily and peacefully in the flesh; and the world's grace permits us to enjoy our property and does not deprive us of our possessions. But in trouble and in the hour of death the grace and peace of the world cannot help us or deliver us from trouble, despair, and death. But when the grace and peace of God are present, a man is so strong that he can bear both the cross and peace, both joy and sorrow. He is heartened by the victory that comes from the death of Christ. In his conscience the assurance of this victory begins to prevail over sin and death, for he has the guarantee of the forgiveness of sins. Once he has received this forgiveness, his conscience is gladdened and consoled. Thus when a man is consoled and encouraged by the grace of God—that is, by the forgiveness of sins and the peace of conscience—he can bravely endure and overcome all troubles, including even death itself. This peace of God is given only to those who believe and not to the world, for the world neither desires it nor understands it. And the only way it comes is by the grace of God alone.

Speculation about God

But why does the apostle add "and from our Lord Jesus Christ"? Did it not suffice to say "from God the Father"? Why does he link Jesus Christ with the Father? You have often heard from us that it is a rule and principle in the Scriptures, and one that must be scrupulously observed, to refrain from speculation about the majesty of God, which is too much for the human body, and especially for the human mind, to bear. "Man shall not see Me and live," says Scripture (Exod. 33:20). The pope, the Turks, the Jews, and all the sectarians pay no attention to this rule. They put Christ the Mediator out of their sight, speak only of God, pray only to Him, and act only in relation to Him. The monk, for example, imagines this to himself: "The works I am doing are pleasing to God. God will look upon my vows, and on their account He will grant me salvation." The Turk says: "If I live this way and bathe this way, God will accept me and give me eternal life." The Jew thinks to himself: "If I obey the Law of Moses, I shall find God gracious to me, and so I shall be saved." Thus the fanatics of our time boast about the Spirit, visions, and I do not know what other monstrous things; they go around in miracles beyond their comprehension. These new monks invent a new cross and new works, and they imagine that by performing these they will please God. In short, whoever does not know the doctrine of justification takes away Christ the Propitiator.

But true Christian theology, as I often warn you, does not present God to us in His majesty, as Moses and other teachings do, but Christ born of the Virgin as our Mediator and High Priest. Therefore when we are embattled against the Law, sin, and death in the presence of God, nothing is more dangerous than to stray into heaven with our idle speculations, there to investigate God in His incomprehensible power, wisdom, and majesty, to ask how He created the world and how He governs it. If you attempt to comprehend God this way and want to make atonement to Him apart from Christ the Mediator, making your works, fasts, cowl, and tonsure the mediation between Him and yourself, you will inevitably fall, as Lucifer did (Isa. 14:12), and in horrible despair lose God and everything. For as in His own nature God is immense, incomprehensible, and infinite, so to man's nature He is intolerable. Therefore if you want to be safe and out of danger to your conscience and your salvation, put a check on this speculative spirit. Take hold of God as Scripture instructs you (1 Cor. 1:21, 24): "Since, in wisdom, the world did not know God through wisdom, it pleased God through the folly of what we preach to save those who believe. We preach Christ crucified, a stumbling block to Jews and folly to Gentiles, but to those who are called, both Jews and Greeks, Christ the power of God and the wisdom of God." Therefore begin where Christ began—in the Virgin's womb, in the manger, and at His mother's breasts. For this purpose He came down, was born, lived among men, suffered, was crucified, and died, so that in every possible way He might present Himself to our sight. He wanted us to fix the gaze of our hearts upon Himself and thus to prevent us from clambering into heaven and speculating about the divine Majesty.

Therefore whenever you consider the doctrine of justification and wonder how or where or in what condition to find a God who justifies or accepts sinners, then you must know that there is no other God than this man Jesus Christ. Take hold of Him; cling to Him with all your heart, and spurn all speculation about the divine Majesty; for whoever investigates the majesty of God will be consumed by His glory. I know from experience what I am talking about. But these fanatics, who deal with God apart from this man, will not believe me. Christ Himself says: "I am the Way and the Truth and the Life; no one comes to the Father but by Me" (John 14:6). Outside Christ, the Way, therefore, you will find no other way to the Father; you will find only wandering; not truth, but hypocrisy and lies; not life, but eternal death. Take note, therefore, in the doctrine of justification or grace that when we all must struggle with the Law, sin, death, and the devil, we must look at no other God than this incarnate and human God.

But when you leave the doctrine of justification and have to engage in controversy with Jews, Turks, or sectarians, etc., about the power, wisdom, etc., of God, then you must use all your cleverness and effort and be as profound and subtle a controversialist as possible; for then you are in another area. But when it comes to the conscience, to righteousness and life (which I want to be noted carefully here) against the Law, sin, death, and the devil; or when it comes to satisfaction for sin, the forgiveness of sins, reconciliation, and eternal salvation, then you must disabuse your mind completely of all speculation and investigation into the majesty of God, and you must pay attention only to this man, who presents Himself to us as the Mediator and says: "Come to Me, all who labor, etc." (Matt. 11:28). When you do this, you will see the love, the goodness, and the sweetness of God. You will see His wisdom, His power, and His majesty sweetened and mitigated to your ability to stand it. And in this lovely picture you will find everything, as Paul says to the Colossians: "In Christ are hid all the treasures of wisdom and knowledge" (2:3); and "In

Him the whole fullness of Deity dwells bodily" (2:9). The world does not see this, because it looks at Him only as a man in His weakness.

This is why Paul makes such a frequent practice of linking Jesus Christ with God the Father, to teach us what is the true Christian religion. It does not begin at the top, as all other religions do; it begins at the bottom. It bids us climb up by Jacob's ladder; God Himself leans on it, and its feet touch the earth, right by Jacob's head (Gen. 28:12). Therefore whenever you are concerned to think and act about your salvation, you must put away all speculations about the Majesty, all thoughts of works, traditions, and philosophy—indeed, of the Law of God itself. And you must run directly to the manger and the mother's womb, embrace this Infant and Virgin's Child in your arms, and look at Him—born, being nursed, growing up, going about in human society, teaching, dying, rising again, ascending above all the heavens, and having authority over all things. In this way you can shake off all terrors and errors, as the sun dispels the clouds. This vision will keep you on the proper way, so that you may follow where Christ has gone. When Paul wishes grace and peace not only from God the Father but also from Jesus Christ, therefore, this is what should be noted first.

Christ is true God

The second thing that Paul teaches us here is a substantiation of our faith that Christ is true God. Statements like this about the divinity of Christ should be assembled and carefully noted, not only against the Arians and other sectarians past or future but also for the substantiation of our own faith.[6] For until our death Satan will never stop attacking all the doctrines of the Creed in us. He is the implacable enemy of faith, for he knows that it is the victory that overcomes the world (1 John 5:4). Therefore it is our obligation to hold constantly to our faith and to establish it, in order that we may be able to stand up to Satan.

The true deity of Christ is proved by this conclusion: Paul attributes to Him the ability to grant the very same things that the Father does—grace, peace of conscience, the forgiveness of sins, life, and victory over sin, death, the devil, and hell. This would be illegitimate, in fact, sacrilegious, if Christ were not true God. For no one grants peace unless he himself has it in his hands. But since Christ grants it, He must have it in His hands.

---

6 Arius (ca. 280–336), a presbyter from Alexandria, taught that the Son was created and therefore there was a time when the Son was not. Although called "God" by Scripture, He was not true God by nature and therefore not coeternal and coequal with the Father. Arius's teaching was condemned at the Council of Nicaea in 325.

Christ gives grace and peace, not as the apostles did, by preaching the Gospel, but as its Author and Creator. The Father creates and gives life, grace, peace, etc.; the Son creates and gives the very same things. To give grace, peace, eternal life, the forgiveness of sins, justification, life, and deliverance from death and the devil—these are the works not of any creature, but only of the divine Majesty. The angels can neither create these things nor grant them. Therefore these works belong only to the glory of the sovereign Majesty, the Maker of all things. And since Paul attributes the very same power to create and give all this to Christ just as much as to the Father, it follows necessarily that Christ is truly God by nature.

Many such arguments appear in John, where it is proved and concluded from the works ascribed to the Son as well as to the Father that the deity of the Father and of the Son is one. Therefore the gifts we receive from the Father are no other than those we receive from the Son; the same things come both from the Father and the Son. Otherwise Paul would have spoken otherwise and would have said: "Grace from God the Father, and peace from our Lord Jesus Christ." But by knitting them together he attributes them equally to Christ and to the Father.

I am warning you about this matter so earnestly on account of the danger that, amid the many errors and various sects today, some Arians, Eunomians, Macedonians, and other such heretics might arise and damage the churches with their subtlety.[7] The Arians were truly sharp. They conceded that Christ has a double nature and that He is called "God of true God"—but only in name. Christ, they said, is a most noble and perfect creature, higher than the angels; through Him God then created heaven and earth and everything else. Thus Mohammed also speaks of Christ in a laudatory way. But all this is nothing but fallacious reasoning and words that are pleasant and reasonable, by which the fanatics deceive men unless they are careful. But Paul speaks of Christ differently. You, he says, are rooted and grounded in this knowledge, that Christ is not only a perfect creature but true God, who performs the very same works that God the Father performs. He performs divine works, not those of a creature but of the Creator. For He grants grace and peace; and to give these is to condemn sin, to conquer death, and to trample the devil underfoot. No angel can grant any of this; but since it is ascribed to Christ, it necessarily follows that He is God by nature.

7 Eunomius of Cyzicus (ca. 335–ca. 394) argued that the Son was unlike the Father in essence or substance. The Macedonians or Pneumatomachi, as they were more commonly called, rejected the divinity of the Holy Spirit. Both groups were vigorously opposed by the Cappadocian fathers: Basil of Caesarea (ca. 329–379), Gregory of Nazianzus (ca. 330–ca. 390), and Gregory of Nyssa (ca. 331–ca. 396).

Galatians 1:4

Who gave Himself for our sins.

In a sense Paul treats the argument of this Epistle in every word. He has nothing in his mouth but Christ. Therefore in every word there is a fervor of spirit and life. Note how precisely he speaks. He does not say: "Who has received our works from us" or "Who has received the sacrifices required by the Law of Moses—acts of worship, monastic orders, Masses, vows, and pilgrimages." Instead, he says: "Who has given." Has given what? Neither gold nor silver nor cattle nor Passover lambs nor an angel, but "Himself." For what? Neither for a crown nor for a kingdom nor for our holiness or righteousness, but "for our sins." These words are a veritable thunderbolt from heaven against every kind of righteousness, as is the statement (John 1:29): "Behold, the Lamb of God, who takes away the sin of the world!" Therefore we must pay careful attention to every word and not look at it casually or pass over it lightly; for these words are filled with comfort, and they give great encouragement to timid consciences.

But the question is: What are we to do with sins—not only other people's but our own? Paul answers that the man who is called Jesus Christ, the Son of God, has given Himself for them. These are wonderful words of consolation and promises of the old Law: that our sins are not removed by any other means than by the Son of God given into death. Such bullets and such artillery must be used to destroy the papacy, all the religions of the heathen, all ceremonies, all works, all merits. For if our sins can be removed by our own satisfactions, why did the Son of God have to be given for them? But since He *was* given for them, it follows that we cannot remove them by works of our own.

In addition, it follows that our sins are so great, so infinite and invincible, that the whole world could not make satisfaction for even one of them. Certainly the greatness of the ransom—namely, the blood of the Son of God—makes it sufficiently clear that we can neither make satisfaction for our sin nor prevail over it. The force and power of sin is amplified by these words: "Who gave Himself for our sins." We are indifferent, and we regard sin as something trivial, a mere nothing. Although it brings with it the sting and remorse of conscience, still we suppose that it has so little weight and force that some little work or merit of ours will remove it. But we should note here the infinite greatness of the price paid for it. Then it will be evident that its power is so great that it could not be removed by any means except that the Son of God be given for it. Anyone who considers this carefully will understand that this one word "sin" includes the eternal wrath of God and the entire kingdom of Satan, and that sin is no trifle.

Therefore this text concludes that all men are the captives and slaves of sin and, as Paul says, are "sold under sin" (Rom. 7:14); and that sin is a very cruel and powerful tyrant over all men throughout the world, a tyrant who cannot be overthrown and expelled by the power of any creatures, whether angels or men, but only by the infinite and sovereign power of Jesus Christ, the Son of God, who was given for it. . . .

For our sins

Pay careful attention to Paul's every word, and note particularly this pronoun "our." For we find very often in the Scriptures that their significance consists in the proper application of pronouns, which also convey vigor and force. It is easy for you to say and believe that Christ, the Son of God, was given for the sins of Peter, Paul, and other saints, who seem to us to have been worthy of this grace. But it is very hard for you, who regard yourself as unworthy of this grace, to say and believe from your heart that Christ was given for *your* many great sins. In general, therefore, and without the pronoun, it is easy to praise and exalt the blessing of Christ extravagantly, namely, that Christ was given for sins, but for the sins of other men, who are worthy. But when it comes to applying this pronoun "our," there our weak nature and reason is thrown back; it does not dare approach God or promise itself that it is to receive such a great treasure freely. Therefore it refuses to have anything to do with God unless it is pure and sinless first. Accordingly, even though it reads or hears this sentence, "who gave Himself for our sins," or something similar, it does not apply this pronoun "our" to itself; it applies it to others, who are worthy and holy, and decides to wait until it has been made worthy by its own works. . . .

The main knowledge and true wisdom of Christians, then, is this: to regard as very serious and true these words of Paul, that Christ was given over to death, not for our righteousness or holiness but for our sins, which are real sins—great, many, in fact, infinite and invincible. Therefore you must not think of them as minor or suppose that your own works can remove them. Nor must you despair on account of their gravity if you feel them oppressing you either in life or in death. But you must learn from Paul here to believe that Christ was given, not for sham or counterfeit sins, nor yet for small sins, but for great and huge sins; not for one or two sins but for all sins; not for sins that have been overcome—for neither man nor angel is able to overcome even the tiniest sin—but for invincible sins. And unless you are part of the company of those who say "our sins," that is, who have this doctrine of faith and who teach, hear, learn, love, and believe it, there is no salvation for you.

Therefore you must make thorough preparations not only for the time of temptation but also for the time and struggle of death. Then your conscience will be terrified by the recollection of your past sins. The devil will attack you vigorously and will try to swamp you with piles, floods, and whole oceans of sins, in order to frighten you, draw you away from Christ, and plunge you into despair. Then you must be able to say with confident assurance: "Christ, the Son of God, was given, not for righteousness and for saints but for unrighteousness and for sinners. If I were righteous and without sin, I would have no need of Christ as my Propitiator. Satan, you cantankerous saint, why do you try to make me feel holy and look for righteousness in myself, when in fact there is nothing in me but sins, and real and serious sins at that? These are not counterfeit or trivial sins; they are sins against the First Table, namely, infidelity, doubt, despair, contempt for God, hatred, ignorance, blasphemy, ingratitude, the abuse of the name of God, neglect, loathing, and contempt for the Word of God, and the like. In addition, there are sins of the flesh against the Second Table: failure to honor my parents, disobedience to rulers, coveting another man's property, wife, etc., although these vices are less grave than those against the First Table.[8] Of course, I have not been guilty of murder, adultery, theft, and other sins like those against the Second Table. Nevertheless, I have committed them in my heart; therefore I have broken every one of God's Commandments, and the number of my sins is so great that an ox's hide would not hold them; they are innumerable. "For the sins I have committed are more in number than the sands of the sea" (Prayer of Manasseh 9). The devil is such a clever trickster that he can make great sins out of my righteousness and good works. Because my sins are so grave, so real, so great, so infinite, so horrible, and so invincible that my righteousness does me no good but rather puts me at a disadvantage before God, therefore Christ, the Son of God, was given into death for my sins, to abolish them and thus to save all men who believe.

The meaning of eternal salvation, then, consists in taking these words to be serious and true. I am not speaking empty words. I have often experienced, and still do every day, how difficult it is to believe, especially amid struggles of conscience, that Christ was given not for the holy, righteous, and deserving, or for those who were His friends, but for the godless, sinful, and undeserving, for those who were His enemies, who deserved the wrath of God and eternal death. . . .

---

8 See Exod. 20:3–8 for the commandments of the First Table and Exod. 20:12–17 for those of the Second Table.

For the sins of the whole world

Against this temptation we must use these words of Paul in which he gives this very good and true definition of Christ: "Christ is the Son of God and of the Virgin; He was delivered and put to death for our sins." If the devil cites any other definition of Christ, you must say: "The definition and the subject are false; therefore I refuse to accept the definition." I am not speaking vainly here, for I know why I define Christ so strictly from the words of Paul. For Christ is not a cruel master; He is the Propitiator for the sins of the whole world. If you are a sinner therefore—as indeed we all are—do not put Christ on a rainbow as the judge; for then you will be terrified and will despair of His mercy. No, grasp the true definition of Him, namely, that Christ, the Son of God and of the Virgin, is not one who terrifies, troubles, condemns us sinners or calls us to account for our evil past, but one who has taken away the sins of the whole world, nailing them to the cross (Col. 2:14) and driving them all the way out by Himself.

Learn this definition carefully. Especially practice this pronoun "our" in such a way that this syllable, once believed, may swallow up and absorb all your sins, that is, that you may be certain that Christ has taken away not only the sins of some men but your sins and those of the whole world. The offering was for the sins of the whole world, even though the whole world does not believe. So do not permit your sins to be merely sins; let them be your very own sins. That is, believe that Christ was given not only for the sins of others but also for yours. Hold to this firmly, and do not let anything deprive you of this sweet definition of Christ, which brings joy even to the angels in heaven: that Christ is, in the strictest of terms, not a Moses, a tormentor, or an executioner but the Mediator for sins and the Donor of grace, who gave Himself, not for our merits, holiness, glory, and holy life but for our sins. Christ also interprets the Law, to be sure; but this is not His proper and chief work. . . .

This is why I am so earnest in my plea to you to learn the true and correct definition of Christ on the basis of these words of Paul: "who gave Himself for our sins." If He gave Himself into death for our sins, then undoubtedly He is not a tormentor. He is not one who will cast down the troubled, but one who will raise up the fallen and bring propitiation and consolation to the terrified. Otherwise Paul would be lying when he says "who gave Himself for our sins." If I define Christ this way, I define Him correctly, grasp the authentic Christ, and truly make Him my own. I avoid all speculations about the divine Majesty and take my stand in the humanity of Christ. There is no fear here; there is sheer sweetness, joy, and the like. This kindles a light that shows me the true knowledge of

God, of myself, of all creatures, and of all the wickedness of the kingdom of the devil.

We are not teaching anything novel; we are repeating and confirming old doctrines. Would that we could teach and confirm them in such a way that we would have them not only in our mouth but in the meditations at the very core of our heart and especially that we might be able to use them in the struggle of death!

Galatians 2:4–5

But because of false brethren secretly brought in, who slipped in to spy out our freedom which we have in Christ Jesus, that they might bring us into bondage—to them we did not yield submission even for a moment, that the truth of the Gospel might be preserved for you.

Here Paul states why he went up to Jerusalem and conferred with the other apostles about his Gospel; he also states why he did not circumcise Titus. It was not to be confirmed by the apostles or to become more certain of his Gospel, for he had no doubts about this. It was rather that the truth of the Gospel might abide among the Galatians and in all the churches of the Gentiles. Thus you see that what was at stake for Paul was no joke and no trifle.

Two uses of the Gospel

Now when Paul speaks of "the truth of the Gospel," he shows that there are two uses of the Gospel, a true one and a false one, or a true and a false gospel. It is as though he were saying: "The false apostles proclaim a faith and a gospel too, but their gospel is a false gospel. Hence my stubbornness and refusal to yield. I did this in order that the truth of the Gospel might be preserved among you." Thus in our day the pope and the sectarians brag that they proclaim the Gospel and faith in Christ. Yes, they do, but with the same results that the false apostles once had, those whom Paul (Gal. 1:7) calls troublers of the churches and perverters of the Gospel of Christ. By contrast he says that he is teaching "the truth of the Gospel," the pure and true Gospel, as though he were saying: "Everything else is a lie masquerading as the Gospel." For all the heretics lay claim to the names of God, of Christ, of the church, etc.; and they pretend that they want to teach not errors, but the most certain truth and the purest Gospel.

The truth of the Gospel is this, that our righteousness comes by faith alone, without the works of the Law. The falsification or corruption of the Gospel is this, that we are justified by faith but not without the works of the Law. The false apostles preached the Gospel, but they did so with this condition attached to it. The scholastics do the same thing in our day. They say that we must believe in Christ and that faith is the foundation of salvation, but they say that this faith does not justify unless it is "formed by love."[9] This is not the truth of the Gospel; it is falsehood and pretense. The true Gospel, however, is this: Works or love are not the ornament or perfection of faith; but faith itself is a gift of God, a work of God in our hearts, which justifies us because it takes hold of Christ as the Savior. Human reason has the Law as its object. It says to itself: "This I have done; this I have not done." But faith in its proper function has no other object than Jesus Christ, the Son of God, who was put to death for the sins of the world. It does not look at its love and say: "What have I done? Where have I sinned? What have I deserved?" But it says: "What has Christ done? What has He deserved?" And here the truth of the Gospel gives you the answer: "He has redeemed you from sin, from the devil, and from eternal death." Therefore faith acknowledges that in this one person, Jesus Christ, it has the forgiveness of sins and eternal life. Whoever diverts his gaze from this object does not have true faith; he has a phantasy and a vain opinion. He looks away from the promise and at the Law, which terrifies him and drives him to despair.

Therefore what the scholastics have taught about justifying faith "formed by love" is an empty dream. For the faith that takes hold of Christ, the Son of God, and is adorned by Him is the faith that justifies, not a faith that includes love. For if faith is to be sure and firm, it must take hold of nothing but Christ alone; and in the agony and terror of conscience it has nothing else to lean on than this pearl of great value (Matt. 13:45–46). Therefore whoever takes hold of Christ by faith, no matter how terrified by the Law and oppressed by the burden of his sins he may be, has the right to boast that he is righteous. How has he this right? By that jewel, Christ, whom he possesses by faith. Our opponents fail to understand this. Therefore they reject Christ, this jewel; and in His place they put their love, which they say is a jewel. But if they do not know what faith is, it is impossible for them to have faith, much less to teach it to others. And as for what they claim to have, this is nothing but a dream, an opinion, and natural reason, but not faith.

I am saying all this in order that you may recognize that when Paul speaks emphatically of "the truth of the Gospel," he is vehemently attacking the opposite. He wanted to show that they were abusing the Gospel. By these words he is condemning the false apostles for teaching a false gospel when they required that circumcision be observed. In addition, they used subtle tricks and devices to trap Paul. They watched

9 Cf. below, p. 231 n. 13.

him closely to see whether he would circumcise Titus and whether he would dare oppose them in the presence of the apostles. On this account he severely condemns them. "They slipped in," he says, "to spy out our freedom which we have in Christ Jesus, that they might bring us into bondage." The false apostles equipped and trained themselves in every possible way to attack and convict Paul in the presence of the church. They also tried to abuse the authority of the apostles, saying: "Paul has brought this uncircumcised Titus into the sight of the whole church. He is denying and condemning the Law in the very presence of you who are apostles. If he has the audacity to try this here in your presence, what would he be willing to try among the Gentiles in your absence?"

When Paul saw that he was being attacked with such tricks, he resisted the false apostles vigorously and said: "We did not permit the liberty we have in Christ Jesus to be imperiled, even though the false brethren tried in every way to trap us and caused us a great deal of trouble. But we overcame them by the very judgment of the apostles themselves, and we did not yield submission to them even for a moment. (For undoubtedly they said: 'Paul, surrender this liberty at least for a while!') For we saw that they wanted to require the observance of the Law as necessary for salvation." If all they had urged was charitable patience with the brethren, Paul would have yielded to them. But they were after something quite different, namely, to bring Paul and all the adherents of his doctrine into bondage. And this was why he refused to yield submission to them even for a moment.

Negotiations with Rome

In the same way we are willing to concede everything possible to the Papists, in fact, more than we should; but we will not give up the freedom of conscience that we have in Christ Jesus. We will not be forced, or let our conscience be forced, into any work, as though we could be righteous by doing this or that, or as though we could be damned for failing to do it. We are willing to eat the same foods that they eat and to keep the same feasts and fasts, provided that they permit us to do so with a free will and refrain from the threats by which they have terrified and subjugated the whole world, as when they say: "We command, we require, we require once more, we excommunicate, etc." But we cannot obtain the concession of this freedom any more than Paul could. Therefore we do what he did. When he could not obtain this freedom, he refused to yield submission to the false apostles even for a moment.

Just as our opponents refuse to concede to us the freedom that faith in Christ alone justifies, so we refuse to concede to them, in turn, that faith formed by love justifies. Here we intend and are obliged to be rebellious and stubborn with them, for otherwise we would lose the truth of the Gospel. We would lose that freedom which we have, not in the emperor or in kings and princes or in the pope or in the world or in the flesh, but in Christ Jesus. We would lose faith in Christ, which, as I have said, takes hold of nothing but Christ, the jewel. If our opponents will let us keep intact this faith by which we are born again, justified, and incorporated into Christ, we are willing to do anything for them that is not contrary to this faith. But because we cannot obtain this concession from them, we for our part will not budge the least little bit. For the issue before us is grave and vital; it involves the death of the Son of God, who, by the will and commandment of the Father, became flesh, was crucified, and died for the sins of the world. If faith yields on this point, the death of the Son of God will be in vain. Then it is only a fable that Christ is the Savior of the world. Then God is a liar, for He has not lived up to His promises. Therefore our stubbornness on this issue is pious and holy; for by it we are striving to preserve the freedom we have in Christ Jesus and to keep the truth of the Gospel. If we lose this, we lose God, Christ, all the promises, faith, righteousness, and eternal life.

Galatians 2:12

For before certain men came from James, he [Peter] ate with the Gentiles. But when they came, he drew back and separated himself, fearing the circumcision party.

Peter's sin

Here you see Peter's sin. Paul describes it carefully. He accuses Peter of weakness, not of malice or ignorance. Peter was afraid of the Jews who had come from James, and he fell on account of his fear of them; for he did not want to scandalize them in this way. Thus he was more concerned about the Jews than about the Gentiles and was responsible for endangering Christian freedom and the truth of the Gospel. By drawing back, separating himself, and avoiding foods prohibited by the Law—foods which he had previously eaten—he injected a scruple into the consciences of the faithful, who could draw this conclusion from his actions: "Peter abstains from foods prohibited by the Law. Therefore whoever eats foods prohibited by the Law sins and transgresses the Law, but whoever abstains is righteous and keeps the Law. Otherwise Peter would not have drawn back. But because he does so and deliberately avoids the food he ate before, this is a most certain sign that those who eat contrary to the Law sin, but that those who abstain from the foods prohibited in the Law are justified." . . .

It is astonishing that Peter, such an outstanding apostle, should do this. Previously, at the council of Jerusalem, he had stood almost alone in obtaining the adoption of his position that righteousness comes to believers by faith, without the Law (Acts 15:7–11). He who had so steadfastly defended the truth and freedom of the Gospel now avoids foods prohibited by the Law, and thus he falls; not only is he the cause of great offense, but he offends against his own decree. "Therefore let anyone who thinks that he stands take heed, lest he fall" (1 Cor. 10:12). No one believes how dangerous traditions and ceremonies are, and yet we cannot do without them. What is more necessary in the world than the Law and its works? Yet there is always the danger that from these will come a denial of Christ. For the Law often produces trust in works; and where this is present, there cannot be trust in Christ. Thus Christ is soon denied and lost, as we can see in the case of Peter. He knew the doctrine of justification better than we do. And yet how easily he could have been responsible for such a terrible ruin by his deed and example if Paul had not opposed him! All the Gentiles would have fallen away from the preaching of Paul and would thus have lost the Gospel and Christ Himself. And this would all have happened with the appearance of holiness. For they could have said: "Paul, until now you have been teaching us that we must be justified by grace alone, without the Law. Now you see Peter doing the very opposite, for he abstains from foods prohibited by the Law. Thus he teaches us that we cannot be saved unless we undergo circumcision and observe the Law."

Galatians 2:14

But when I saw that they were not straightforward about the truth of the Gospel.

This is a wonderful story to tell about very great men and pillars of the churches. Paul is the only one who has his eyes open and sees the sin of Peter, Barnabas, and the other Jews, who were acting insincerely along with Peter. . . . It was a serious matter for Peter to be accused by Paul of falling and of swerving from the truth of the Gospel; there could be no graver reproach. Yet he bears it patiently and undoubtedly accepted it with real gratitude. . . . For although they were preaching the Gospel, still by their pretense, which could not stand with the truth of the Gospel, they were establishing the Law. But the establishment of the Law is the abrogation and overthrow of the Gospel.

Distinguishing Law and Gospel

Therefore whoever knows well how to distinguish the Gospel from the Law should give thanks to God and know that he is a real theologian.

I admit that in the time of temptation I myself do not know how to do this as I should. The way to distinguish the one from the other is to locate the Gospel in heaven and the Law on earth, to call the righteousness of the Gospel heavenly and divine and the righteousness of the Law earthly and human, and to distinguish as sharply between the righteousness of the Gospel and that of the Law as God distinguishes between heaven and earth or between light and darkness or between day and night. Let the one be like the light and the day, and the other like the darkness and the night. If we could only put an even greater distance between them! Therefore if the issue is faith, heavenly righteousness, or conscience, let us leave the Law out of consideration altogether and let it remain on the earth. But if the issue is works, then let us light the lamp of works and of the righteousness of the Law in the night. So let the sun and the immense light of the Gospel and of grace shine in the day, and let the lamp of the Law shine in the night. . . .

Galatians 2:16

Yet who know that a man is not justified by works of the Law but through faith in Jesus Christ.

Works of the Law

These words, "works of the Law," are to be taken in the broadest possible sense and are very emphatic. I am saying this because of the smug and idle scholastics and monks, who obscure such words in Paul—in fact, everything in Paul—with their foolish and wicked glosses, which even they themselves do not understand. Therefore take "works of the Law" generally, to mean whatever is opposed to grace: Whatever is not grace is Law, whether it be the civil law, the ceremonial law, or the Decalogue. Therefore even if you were to do the work of the Law, according to the commandment "You shall love the Lord your God with all your heart, etc." (Matt. 22:37), you still would not be justified in the sight of God; for a man is not justified by works of the Law. But more detail on this later on.

Thus for Paul "works of the Law" means the works of the entire Law. Therefore one should not make a distinction between the Decalogue and ceremonial laws. Now if the work of the Decalogue does not justify, much less will circumcision, which is a work of the ceremonial law. When Paul says, as he often does, that a man is not justified by the Law or by the works of the Law, which means the same thing in Paul, he is speaking in general about the entire Law; he is contrasting the righteousness of faith with the righteousness of the entire Law, with everything that can be done on the basis of the Law, whether by divine power or by human. For by the righteousness of the Law, he says, a man is not pronounced righteous in the sight of God; but God imputes the righteousness of faith freely through His mercy, for the sake of Christ. It is, therefore, with a certain emphasis and vehemence that he said "by works of the Law." For there is no doubt that the Law is holy, righteous, and good; therefore the works of the Law are holy, righteous, and good. Nevertheless, a man is not justified in the sight of God through them. . . .

Therefore the dangerous and wicked opinion of the Papists is to be condemned. They attribute the merit of grace and the forgiveness of sins to the mere performance of the work. For they say that a good work performed before grace can earn a "merit of congruity"; but once grace has been obtained, the work that follows deserves eternal life by the "merit of condignity."[10] If a man outside a state of grace and in mortal sin performs a good work by his own natural inclination—such as reading or hearing Mass, giving alms, etc.—this man deserves grace "by congruity." Once he has obtained grace this way, he goes on to perform a work that merits eternal life "by condignity." Now in the first case God is not indebted to anyone. But because He is good and righteous, it is proper for Him to approve such a good work, even though it is performed in mortal sin, and to grant grace for such a deed. But once grace has been obtained, God has become a debtor and is obliged by right to grant eternal life. For now this is not only a work of the free will, carried out externally, but it is performed in the grace that makes a man pleasing before God, that is, in love.

. . . By this wicked and blasphemous teaching they have not only obscured the Gospel but have removed it altogether and have buried Christ completely. For if in a state of mortal sin I can do any tiny work that is not only pleasing before God externally and of itself but can even deserve grace "by congruity"; and if, once I have received grace, I am able to perform works according to grace, that is, according to love, and receive eternal life by a right—then what need do I have of the grace of God, the forgiveness of sins, the promise, and the death and victory of Christ? Then Christ has become altogether useless to me; for I have free will and the power to perform good works, and through this I merit grace "by congruity" and eventually eternal life "by condignity." . . .

10 For the medieval schoolmen, a distinction existed between meritorious acts done by a person's own effort and those acts done by the Holy Spirit in the life of the believer. The merit of congruity is the reward received according to a person's own abilities. It is a merit proportionate to the value of the act. The merit of condignity, on the other hand, merits eternal life because it is worked by the Holy Spirit in the individual. Late medieval theology argued further that an initial act of good done by the unimpaired natural powers (*ex puris naturalibus*) would merit an initial gift of grace. This is the position of John Duns Scotus and Gabriel Biel that Luther describes and rejects throughout this section.

With Paul, therefore, we totally deny the "merit of congruity" and the "merit of condignity"; and with complete confidence we declare that these speculations are merely the tricks of Satan, which have never been performed or demonstrated by any examples. For God has never given anyone grace and eternal life for the merit of congruity or the merit of condignity. Therefore these disputations of the scholastics about merit of congruity and of condignity are nothing but empty fictions, the dreams of idle men; and yet the entire papacy is founded on these nonexistent things and depends on them to this day. For every monk imagines as follows to himself: "By the observance of my holy rule I am able to merit grace 'by congruity.' And by the works I perform after receiving this grace I am able to accumulate such a treasure of merit that it will not only be enough for me to obtain eternal life but can also be given or sold to others."[11] This is how all the monks have taught and lived. In defense of this horrible blasphemy against Christ there is nothing that the Papists will not attempt against us today. Among them all, the more holy and self-righteous a hypocrite is, the more vicious an enemy he is of the Gospel of Christ.

True meaning of Christianity

Now the true meaning of Christianity is this: that a man first acknowledge, through the Law, that he is a sinner, for whom it is impossible to perform any good work. For the Law says: "You are an evil tree. Therefore everything you think, speak, or do is opposed to God. Hence you cannot deserve grace by your works. But if you try to do so, you make the bad even worse; for since you are an evil tree, you cannot produce anything except evil fruits, that is, sins. 'For whatever does not proceed from faith is sin' (Rom. 14:23)." Trying to merit grace by preceding works, therefore, is trying to placate God with sins, which is nothing but heaping sins upon sins, making fun of God, and provoking His wrath. When a man is taught this way by the Law, he is frightened and humbled. Then he really sees the greatness of his sin and finds in himself not one spark of the love of God; thus he justifies God in His Word and confesses that he deserves death and eternal damnation. Thus the first step in Christianity is the preaching of repentance and the knowledge of oneself.

The second step is this: If you want to be saved, your salvation does not come by works; but God has sent His only Son into the world that we might live through Him. He was crucified and died for you and bore your sins in His own body (1 Pet. 2:24). Here there is no "congruity"

11 Thomas Aquinas argues that a man may not merit condignly for another because he cannot merit salvation for another. A man may merit congruently first grace for another. See Thomas Aquinas, *Summa Theologiae*, I–II, q. 114, a. 6.

or work performed before grace, but only wrath, sin, terror, and death. Therefore the Law only shows sin, terrifies, and humbles; thus it prepares us for justification and drives us to Christ. For by His Word God has revealed to us that He wants to be a merciful Father to us. Without our merit—since, after all, we cannot merit anything—He wants to give us forgiveness of sins, righteousness, and eternal life for the sake of Christ. For God is He who dispenses His gifts freely to all, and this is the praise of His deity. But He cannot defend this deity of His against the self-righteous people who are unwilling to accept grace and eternal life from Him freely but want to earn it by their own works. They simply want to rob Him of the glory of His deity. In order to retain it, He is compelled to send forth His Law, to terrify and crush those very hard rocks as though it were thunder and lightning.

Scholastic errors

This, in summary, is our theology about Christian righteousness, in opposition to the abominations and monstrosities of the sophists about "merit of congruity and of condignity" or about works before grace and after grace.[12] Smug people, who have never struggled with any temptations or true terrors of sin and death, were the ones who made up these empty dreams out of their own heads; therefore they do not understand what they are saying or what they are talking about, for they cannot supply any examples of such works done either before grace or after grace. Therefore these are useless fables, with which the Papists delude both themselves and others.

The reason is that Paul expressly states here that a man is not justified by the deeds of the Law, whether they are those that precede (of which he is speaking here) or those that follow justification. Thus you see that Christian righteousness is not an "inherent form," as they call it.[13] For they say: When a man does a good work, God accepts it; and for this work He infuses charity into him. This infused charity, they say, is a

---

12 On "sophists," see above, p. 171 n. 14.

13 Generally speaking, the medieval schoolmen believed that people are saved by created grace or love. Faith (intellect) does not save apart from love (will) because faith is formed by love (*fides caritate formata*). This love and the works that follow from it are brought about by God's infused grace, which, for some schoolmen, becomes a quality of the soul. This infused grace creates a proper disposition or *habitus* in us which cultivates the works that produce our own righteousness and merit eternal life. Luther rejects the very premise of faith formed by love and argues that faith is formed by Christ—indeed, that Christ is the form of faith. The righteousness that avails for our salvation is not the righteousness worked by us in faith (or love) but the righteousness of Christ that faith receives. On the distinction between righteousness as a possession or property, see *Disputation concerning Justification* (1536), LW 34:177–78.

quality that is attached to the heart; they call it "formal righteousness." (It is a good idea for you to know this manner of speaking.) Nothing is more intolerable to them than to be told that this quality, which informs the heart as whiteness does a wall, is not righteousness. They cannot climb any higher than this cogitation of human reason: Man is righteous by means of his formal righteousness, which is grace making him pleasing before God, that is, love. Thus they attribute formal righteousness to an attitude and "form" inherent in the soul, namely, to love, which is a work and gift according to the Law; for the Law says: "You shall love the Lord" (Matt. 22:37). And they say that this righteousness is worthy of eternal life; that he who has it is "formally righteous"; and, finally, that he is righteous in fact, because he is now performing good works, for which eternal life is due him. This is the opinion of the sophists—and of the best among them at that.

Others are not even that good, such as Scotus and Occam.[14] They said that this love which is given by God is not necessary to obtain the grace of God, but that even by his own natural powers a man is able to produce a love for God above all things. Scotus disputes this way: "If a man can love a creature, a young man love a girl, or a covetous man love money—all of which are a lesser good—he can also love God, who is a greater good. If by his natural powers he has a love for the creature, much more does he have a love for the Creator."[15] This argument left all the sophists confounded, and none of them could refute it. Nevertheless, this is what they said:

"Scripture requires us to say that in addition to our natural love, with which He is not satisfied, God also demands a love that He Himself grants." Thus they accuse God of being a severe tyrant and a cruel taskmaster, who is not content that I observe and fulfill His Law but demands also that beyond the Law, which I can easily fulfill, I dress up my obedience with additional qualities and adornments. It is as though the lady of the house were not content that her cook had prepared the food very well but scolded her for not wearing precious garments and adorning herself with a golden crown while she prepared the food. What sort of housewife

14 On John Duns Scotus, see above, pp. 16–17 n. 17. William of Ockham, a rigorous and independent thinker, ushered in a new way of thinking (*via moderna*) that departed from the old way (*via antiqua*) represented by Aquinas and Scotus. Both Scotus and Ockham influenced the late medieval theologian Gabriel Biel.

15 John Duns Scotus, *Sententiarum*, III, d. 27, q. 1. Cf. Gabriel Biel, *Collectorium circa quattuor libros Sententiarum*, III, d. 27, q. 1, a. 3, dub. 2, prop 1. See Luther, *Lectures on Romans* (1515–16), LW 25:261 (see above, p. 16 and n. 17); *Commentary on Psalm 51* (1532), LW 12:345 (see below, p. 291); and *Lectures on Genesis* (1535–45), LW 2:124 (see below, p. 325).

would that be who, after her cook has done everything she is required to do and has done it superbly, would demand that she should also wear a golden crown, which it is impossible for her to have? Likewise, what sort of God would that be who would demand that we fulfill His Law, which we otherwise observe by our natural powers, with an ornamentation that we cannot possess?

To avoid the impression of contradicting themselves, they make a distinction at this point and say that the Law can be fulfilled in two ways: first, according to the content of the act; secondly, according to the intention of Him who gave the commandment.[16] According to the content of the act, that is, so far as the deed itself is concerned, we can simply fulfill everything that the Law commands. But we cannot do so according to the intention of Him who gave the commandment; for this means that God is not content that you have performed and fulfilled everything commanded in the Law (although He has no more than this to demand of you), but He requires in addition that you keep the Law in love—not the natural love that you have but a supernatural and divine love that He Himself confers. What is this but to make God a tyrant and a tormentor who demands of us what we cannot produce? In a sense it is as though they were saying that if we are damned, the fault is not so much in us as in God, who requires us to keep His Law in this fashion.

I am reciting all this to make you see how far they have strayed from the meaning of Scripture with their declaration that by our own natural powers we are able to love God above all things, or at least that by the mere performance of the deed we are able to merit grace and eternal life. And because God is not content if we fulfill the Law according to the content of the act but also wants us to fulfill it according to the intention of Him who gave the commandment, therefore Sacred Scripture requires us to have a supernatural quality infused into us from heaven, namely, love, which they call the formal righteousness that informs and adorns faith and makes it justify us. Thus faith is the body, the shell, or the color; but love is the life, the kernel, or the form.

Such are the dreams of the scholastics. But where they speak of love, we speak of faith. And while they say that faith is the mere outline but love is its living colors and completion, we say in opposition that faith takes hold of Christ and that He is the form that adorns and informs faith as color does the wall. Therefore Christian faith is not an idle quality or an empty husk in the heart, which may exist in a state of mortal sin until

16 Luther refers to Gabriel Biel's distinction between the substance of the act (*quoad substantiam actus*) and the intention of the lawgiver (*quoad intentionem praecipientis*). See *Lectures on Romans* (1515–16), LW 25:261 (see above, p. 17 and n. 18).

love comes along to make it alive. But if it is true faith, it is a sure trust and firm acceptance in the heart. It takes hold of Christ in such a way that Christ is the object of faith, or rather not the object but, so to speak, the one who is present in the faith itself. Thus faith is a sort of knowledge or darkness that nothing can see. Yet the Christ of whom faith takes hold is sitting in this darkness as God sat in the midst of darkness on Sinai and in the temple. Therefore our "formal righteousness" is not a love that informs faith; but it is faith itself, a cloud in our hearts, that is, trust in a thing we do not see, in Christ, who is present especially when He cannot be seen.

Therefore faith justifies because it takes hold of and possesses this treasure, the present Christ. But how He is present—this is beyond our thought; for there is darkness, as I have said. Where the confidence of the heart is present, therefore, there Christ is present, in that very cloud and faith. This is the formal righteousness on account of which a man is justified; it is not on account of love, as the sophists say. In short, just as the sophists say that love forms and trains faith, so we say that it is Christ who forms and trains faith or who is the form of faith. Therefore the Christ who is grasped by faith and who lives in the heart is the true Christian righteousness, on account of which God counts us righteous and grants us eternal life. Here there is no work of the Law, no love; but there is an entirely different kind of righteousness, a new world above and beyond the Law. For Christ or faith is neither the Law nor the work of the Law. But we intend later on to go into more detail on this issue, which the sophists have neither understood nor written about. For the present let it be enough for us to have shown that Paul is speaking here not only about the ceremonial law but about the entire Law.

I have warned in passing of the dangerous error of the scholastic theologians, who taught that a man obtains forgiveness of sins and justification in the following manner: By his works that precede grace, which they call a "merit of congruity," he merits grace, which, according to them, is a quality that inheres in the will, granted by God over and above the love we have by our natural powers. They say that when a man has this quality, he is formally righteous and a true Christian. I say that this is a wicked and dangerous notion, which does not make a man a Christian but makes him a Turk, a Jew, an Anabaptist,[17] or a fanatic. For who cannot perform a good work by his own powers without grace and thus merit grace? In this way these dreamers have made faith an empty quality in the soul, which is of no use alone, without love, but becomes effective and justifies when love is added to it.

17 On Anabaptists, see above, p. 148 n. 4.

They go on to say that the works that follow have the power to merit eternal life "by condignity," because God accepts the work that follows and applies it to eternal life, on account of the love that He has infused into man's will. Thus they say that God "accepts" a good work for eternal life but "disaccepts" an evil work for damnation and eternal punishment. They have heard something in a dream about "acceptance" and have ascribed this relation to works. All this is false and blasphemous against Christ. Nevertheless, they do not all speak even this well; but some, as we have said, have taught that by our purely natural powers we are able to love God above all things. These things are useful to know, to make Paul's argument clearer. . . .

Proper understanding of Christ

But by the true definition Christ is not a lawgiver; He is a Propitiator and a Savior. Faith takes hold of this and believes without doubting that He has performed a superabundance of works and merits of congruity and condignity. He might have made satisfaction for all the sins of the world with only one drop of His blood, but now He has made abundant satisfaction. Heb. 9:12: "With His own blood He entered once for all into the Holy Place." And Rom. 3:24–25: "Justified by His grace as a gift, through the redemption which is in Christ Jesus, whom God put forward as an expiation by His blood." Therefore it is something great to take hold, by faith, of Christ, who bears the sins of the world (John 1:29). And this faith alone is counted for righteousness (Romans 3–4).

Here it is to be noted that these three things are joined together: faith, Christ, and acceptance or imputation. Faith takes hold of Christ and has Him present, enclosing Him as the ring encloses the gem. And whoever is found having this faith in the Christ who is grasped in the heart, him God accounts as righteous. This is the means and the merit by which we obtain the forgiveness of sins and righteousness. "Because you believe in Me," God says, "and your faith takes hold of Christ, whom I have freely given to you as your Justifier and Savior, therefore be righteous." Thus God accepts you or accounts you righteous only on account of Christ, in whom you believe.

Now acceptance or imputation is extremely necessary, first, because we are not yet purely righteous, but sin is still clinging to our flesh during this life. God cleanses this remnant of sin in our flesh. In addition, we are sometimes forsaken by the Holy Spirit, and we fall into sins, as did Peter, David, and other saints. Nevertheless, we always have recourse to this doctrine, that our sins are covered and that God does not want to hold us accountable for them (Romans 4). This does not mean that there is no sin in us, as the sophists have taught when they said that we must go on doing good until we are no longer conscious of any sin; but sin is always present, and the godly feel it. But it is ignored and hidden in the sight of God, because Christ the Mediator stands between; because we take hold of Him by faith, all our sins are sins no longer. But where Christ and faith are not present, here there is no forgiveness of sins or hiding of sins. On the contrary, here there is the sheer imputation and condemnation of sins. Thus God wants to glorify His Son, and He Himself wants to be glorified in us through Him.

When we have taught faith in Christ this way, then we also teach about good works. Because you have taken hold of Christ by faith, through whom you are righteous, you should now go and love God and your neighbor. Call upon God, give thanks to Him, preach Him, praise Him, confess Him. Do good to your neighbor, and serve him; do your duty. These are truly good works, which flow from this faith and joy conceived in the heart because we have the forgiveness of sins freely through Christ.

Then whatever there is of cross or suffering to be borne later on is easily sustained. For the yoke that Christ lays upon us is sweet, and His burden is light (Matt. 11:30). When sin has been forgiven and the conscience has been liberated from the burden and the sting of sin, then a Christian can bear everything easily. Because everything within is sweet and pleasant, he willingly does and suffers everything. But when a man goes along in his own righteousness, then whatever he does and suffers is painful and tedious for him, because he is doing it unwillingly.

Definition of a Christian

Therefore we define a Christian as follows: A Christian is not someone who has no sin or feels no sin; he is someone to whom, because of his faith in Christ, God does not impute his sin. This doctrine brings firm consolation to troubled consciences amid genuine terrors. It is not in vain, therefore, that so often and so diligently we inculcate the doctrine of the forgiveness of sins and of the imputation of righteousness for the sake of Christ, as well as the doctrine that a Christian does not have anything to do with the Law and sin, especially in a time of temptation. For to the extent that he is a Christian, he is above the Law and sin, because in his heart he has Christ, the Lord of the Law, as a ring has a gem. Therefore when the Law accuses and sin troubles, he looks to Christ; and when he has taken hold of Him by faith, he has present with him the Victor over the Law, sin, death, and the devil—the Victor whose rule over all these prevents them from harming him.

Therefore a Christian, properly defined, is free of all laws and is subject to nothing, internally or externally. But I purposely said, "to the extent that he is a Christian" (not "to the extent that he is a man or a woman"); that is, to the extent that he has his conscience trained, adorned, and enriched by this faith, this great and inestimable treasure, or, as Paul calls it, "this inexpressible gift" (2 Cor. 9:15), which cannot be exalted and praised enough, since it makes men sons and heirs of God. Thus a Christian is greater than the entire world. For in his heart he has this seemingly small gift; yet the smallness of this gift and treasure, which he holds in faith, is greater than heaven and earth, because Christ, who is this gift, is greater.

Galatians 3:6

Thus Abraham believed God, and it was reckoned to him as righteousness.

Up to this point Paul has been arguing on the basis of experience. And he vigorously urges this argument that is based on experience. "You have believed," he says, "and having believed, you have done miracles and have performed many outstanding and powerful deeds. You have also suffered evils. All this is the effect and operation not of the Law, but of the Holy Spirit." This the Galatians were obliged to admit, for they could not deny the things that were going on before their eyes and were available to their senses. Hence this argument, based on experience or on its effects in the Galatians themselves, is very strong and clear.

Now Paul adds the example of Abraham and recites testimonies from Scripture. The first is from Gen. 15:6: "Abraham believed, etc." He urges this passage strongly here, just as he does especially in Rom. 4:2. "If Abraham was justified by works," he says, "he has righteousness and something to boast about, but not before God," only before men; for before God he has sin and wrath. But he was justified before God, not because he worked but because he believed. For Scripture says: "Abraham believed, and it was reckoned to him as righteousness." Paul expounds and develops this passage there as magnificently as it deserves (Rom. 4:19–24): "Abraham," he says, "did not weaken in faith when he considered his own body, which was as good as dead, because he was about a hundred years old, or when he considered the barrenness of Sarah's womb. No distrust made him waver concerning the promise of God; but he grew strong in his faith as he gave glory to God, fully convinced that God was able to do what He had promised. That is why his faith was 'reckoned to him as righteousness.' But the words 'it was reckoned to him' were written not only for his sake but also for our sakes."

Faith and reason

With these words Paul makes faith in God the supreme worship, the supreme allegiance, the supreme obedience, and the supreme sacrifice. Whoever is an orator, let him develop this topic. He will see that faith is something omnipotent, and that its power is inestimable and infinite; for it attributes glory to God, which is the highest thing that can be attributed to Him. To attribute glory to God is to believe in Him, to regard Him as truthful, wise, righteous, merciful, and almighty, in short, to acknowledge Him as the Author and Donor of every good. Reason does not do this, but faith does. It consummates the Deity; and, if I may put it this way, it is the creator of the Deity, not in the substance of God but in us. For without faith God loses His glory, wisdom, righteousness, truthfulness, mercy, etc., in us; in short, God has none of His majesty or divinity where faith is absent. Nor does God require anything greater of man than that he attribute to Him His glory and His divinity; that is, that he regard Him not as an idol but as God, who has regard for him, listens to him, shows mercy to him, helps him, etc. When He has obtained this, God retains His divinity sound and unblemished; that is, He has whatever a believing heart is able to attribute to Him. To be able to attribute such glory to God is wisdom beyond wisdom, righteousness beyond righteousness, religion beyond religion, and sacrifice beyond sacrifice. From this it can be understood what great righteousness faith is and, by antithesis, what a great sin unbelief is.

Therefore faith justifies because it renders to God what is due Him; whoever does this is righteous. The laws also define what it means to be righteous in this way: to render to each what is his. For faith speaks as follows: "I believe Thee, God, when Thou dost speak." What does God say? Things that are impossible, untrue, foolish, weak, absurd, abominable, heretical, and diabolical—if you consult reason. For what is more ridiculous, foolish, and impossible than when God says to Abraham that he is to get a son from the body of Sarah, which is barren and already dead?

Thus when God proposes the doctrines of faith, He always proposes things that are simply impossible and absurd—if, that is, you want to follow the judgment of reason. It does indeed seem ridiculous and absurd to reason that in the Lord's Supper the body and the blood of Christ are presented; that Baptism is "the washing of regeneration and renewal in the Holy Spirit" (Titus 3:5); that Christ, the Son of God, was conceived and carried in the womb of the Virgin, that He was born, that He suffered the most ignominious of deaths on the cross, that He was raised again, that He is now sitting at the right hand of the Father, and that He now has "authority in heaven and on earth" (Matt. 28:18). Paul calls the Gospel of Christ the crucified "the Word of the cross" (1 Cor. 1:18) and "the folly of preaching" (1 Cor. 1:21), which the Jews regarded as offensive and the Greeks as a foolish doctrine. Reason judges this way about all the doctrines of the faith; for it does not understand that the supreme form of worship is to hear the voice of God and to believe, but it supposes that what it chooses on its own and what it does with a so-called good intention and from its own devotion is pleasing to God. When God speaks, reason, therefore, regards His Word as heresy and as the word of the devil; for it seems so absurd. Such is the theology of all the sophists and of the sectarians, who measure the Word of God by reason. . . .

Righteousness of faith

Therefore faith alone attributes glory to God. Paul testifies to this in the case of Abraham in Rom. 4:20, when he says: "Abraham grew strong in faith as he gave glory to God." And he adds from Gen. 15:6 that this was imputed to him as righteousness. This is not without cause. For Christian righteousness consists in two things, namely, faith in the heart and the imputation of God. Faith is indeed a formal righteousness; but this does not suffice, for after faith there still remain remnants of sin in the flesh. The sacrifice of faith began in Abraham, but it was finally consummated only in death. Therefore the second part of righteousness has to be added, which perfects it in us, namely, divine imputation. Faith does not give enough to God formally, because it is imperfect; in fact, it is barely a little spark of faith, which only begins to attribute divinity to God. We have received the firstfruits of the Spirit, but not the tithes. Nor is reason completely killed in this life. Hence lust, wrath, impatience, and other fruits of the flesh and of unbelief still remain in us. Not even the more perfect saints have a full and constant joy in God. But, as Scripture testifies concerning the prophets and the apostles, their feelings change; sometimes they are sad, sometimes joyful. But because of their faith in Christ such faults are not laid to their charge; for otherwise no one could be saved. From these words, "It was imputed to him as righteousness," we conclude, therefore, that righteousness does indeed begin through faith and that through it we have the firstfruits of the Spirit. But because faith is weak, it is not perfected without the imputation of God. Hence faith begins righteousness, but imputation perfects it until the day of Christ. . . .

I have said this in interpretation of the sentence "And it was reckoned to him as righteousness," in order that the students of the Sacred Scriptures may understand how Christian righteousness is to be defined properly and accurately, namely, that it is a trust in the Son of God or a trust of the heart in God through Christ. Here this clause is to be added to provide the differentia for the definition: "which faith is imputed as righteousness for the sake of Christ." For, as I have said, these two things make Christian righteousness perfect: The first is faith in the heart, which is a divinely granted gift and which formally believes in Christ; the second is that God reckons this imperfect faith as perfect righteousness for the sake of Christ, His Son, who suffered for the sins of the world and in whom I begin to believe. On account of this faith in Christ God does not see the sin that still remains in me. For so long as I go on living in the flesh, there is certainly sin in me. But meanwhile Christ protects me under the shadow of His wings and spreads over me the wide heaven of the forgiveness of sins, under which I live in safety. This prevents God from seeing the sins that still cling to my flesh. My flesh distrusts God, is angry with Him, does not rejoice in Him, etc. But God overlooks these sins, and in His sight they are as though they were not sins. This is accomplished by imputation on account of the faith by which I begin to take hold of Christ; and on His account God reckons imperfect righteousness as perfect righteousness and sin as not sin, even though it really is sin.

Thus we live under the curtain of the flesh of Christ (Heb. 10:20). He is our "pillar of cloud by day and pillar of fire by night" (Exod. 13:21), to keep God from seeing our sin. And although we see it and feel remorse of conscience, still we keep running back to Christ, our Mediator and Propitiator, through whom we reach completion and are saved. In Him is everything; in Him we have everything; and He supplies everything in us. On His account God overlooks all sins and wants them to be covered as though they were not sins. He says: "Because you believe in My Son, even though you have sins, they shall be forgiven, until you are completely absolved from them by death."

Let Christians strive to learn completely and perfectly this doctrine of Christian righteousness, which the sophists neither understand nor are able to understand. But let them not suppose that they can learn it thoroughly all at once. Therefore let them make the effort to read Paul often and with the greatest diligence. Let them compare the first with the last; in fact, let them compare Paul as a whole with himself. Then they will find that this is the situation, that Christian righteousness consists in two things: first, in faith, which attributes glory to God; secondly, in God's imputation. For because faith is weak, as I have said, therefore God's imputation has to be added. That is, God does not want to impute the remnant of sin and does not want to punish it or damn us for it. But He wants to cover it and to forgive it, as though it were nothing, not for our sakes or for the sake of our worthiness or works but for the sake of Christ Himself, in whom we believe.

Simul iustus et peccator

Thus a Christian man is righteous and a sinner at the same time, holy and profane, an enemy of God and a child of God. None of the sophists will admit this paradox, because they do not understand the true meaning of justification. This was why they forced men to go on doing good works until they would not feel any sin at all. By this means they drove to the point of insanity many men who tried with all their might to become completely righteous in a formal sense but could not accomplish it. And innumerable persons even among the authors of this wicked dogma were driven into despair at the hour of death, which is what would have happened to me if Christ had not looked at me in mercy and liberated me from this error.

We, on the other hand, teach and comfort an afflicted sinner this way: "Brother, it is impossible for you to become so righteous in this life that your body is as clear and spotless as the sun. You still have spots and wrinkles (Eph. 5:27), and yet you are holy." But you say: "How can I be holy when I have sin and am aware of it?" "That you feel and acknowledge sin—this is good. Thank God, and do not despair. It is one step toward health when a sick man admits and confesses his disease." "But how will I be liberated from sin?" "Run to Christ, the Physician, who heals the contrite of heart and saves sinners. Believe in Him. If you believe, you are righteous, because you attribute to God the glory of being almighty, merciful, truthful, etc. You justify and praise God. In short, you attribute divinity and everything to Him. And the sin that still remains in you is not imputed but is forgiven for the sake of Christ, in whom you believe and who is perfectly righteous in a formal sense. His righteousness is yours; your sin is His." . . .

Therefore this is a marvelous definition of Christian righteousness: it is a divine imputation or reckoning as righteousness or to righteousness, for the sake of our faith in Christ or for the sake of Christ. When the sophists hear this definition, they laugh; for they suppose that righteousness is a certain quality that is first infused into the soul and then distributed through all the members. They cannot strip off the thoughts of reason, which declares that righteousness is a right judgment and a right will. Therefore this inestimable gift excels all reason, that without any works God reckons and acknowledges as righteous the man who takes hold by faith of His Son, who was sent into the world, who was born, who suffered, and who was crucified for us.

Galatians 3:11–12

Now it is evident that no man is justified before God by the Law; for the righteous shall live by faith. But the Law does not rest on faith.

The sophists say: "The righteous shall live if his faith is formed." Paul, on the other hand, says: "The Law does not rest on faith." But what is the Law? Is it not also a commandment of love? In fact, the Law commands nothing else but love, as the text says (Matt. 22:37): "You shall love the Lord your God with all your heart, etc." Again (Deut. 5:10): "Showing steadfast love to thousands of those who love Me." And again (Matt. 22:40): "On these two commandments depend all the Law and the prophets." Thus if the Law commanding love conflicts with faith, then love is not of faith. In this way Paul clearly refutes the gloss made up by the sophists about a "formed faith," and, putting the Law aside, he speaks only about faith. Once the Law has been put aside, love is also put aside, as well as everything that belongs to the Law; all that is kept is faith, which justifies and makes alive.

Paul is arguing on the basis of a very clear testimony of the prophet that there is simply no one who attains to justification and life in the sight of God except the believer, who attains to righteousness and life on the basis of faith, without the Law or love. The reason: The Law does not rest on faith, that is, the Law is not faith or anything about faith; it does not believe. Nor are the works of the Law faith. Therefore faith is something different from the Law, just as the promise is something different from the Law. But the promise is not grasped by doing; it is grasped only by believing.

As in philosophy, at the first division, substance and accident are distinct, so in theology the promise and the Law are as distinct as heaven and earth. But if the promise and the Law are distinct, then faith and works are distinct also. Hence it is impossible for faith to rest on the Law, because faith rests only on the promise. Therefore it only accepts and knows God, and it consists only in receiving good things from God. But the Law and works consist in doing and in giving to God. Thus Abel the sacrificer gives to God, but Abel the believer receives from God. Therefore from this passage in the prophet Paul draws the very forceful conclusion that the righteous shall live by faith, that is, by faith alone, because the Law does not belong to faith at all. The Law is not the promise, but faith clings to and rests on the promise. Accordingly, just as the Law and the promise are distinct, so are works and faith. Hence the gloss of the sophists, which joins the Law to faith, is false and wicked; in fact, it extinguishes faith and puts the Law in place of faith.

Paul is speaking continually about those who want to keep the Law morally, not theologically. But whatever is said about theological good works is simply attributed to faith alone.

For he who does them shall live by them.

I understand this part of the statement as irony, although it can be expounded in a moral sense, namely, that those who keep the Law morally, that is, without faith, shall live by it; that is, they will not be punished but will have physical rewards from it. But I take this passage as a general statement, like that saying of Christ (Luke 10:28): "Do this, and you will live," so that it is a kind of irony or ridicule. "Yes, just go ahead and do it!" Paul wants to show here what the righteousness of the Law and of the Gospel is, exactly and accurately. The righteousness of the Law is to keep the Law, according to the statement: "He who does them, etc." The righteousness of faith is to believe, according to the statement, "The righteous shall live by faith." Therefore the Law requires that we perform something for God. Faith does not require our doing; it requires that we believe the promise of God and accept something from Him. Therefore the function of the Law, at its highest level, is to work, just as that of faith is to assent. Thus the Law provides doing, and faith provides believing; for faith is faith in the promise, and the work is the work of the Law. This is why Paul lingers over the term "doing." To show clearly what the righteousness of the Law and what that of faith is, he contrasts the one with the other, the promise with the Law and faith with works. He says that nothing follows from the Law except doing; but faith is something altogether different, namely, that which clings to the promise.

Therefore these four things must be distinguished perfectly. For just as the Law has its proper task, so the promise has its proper task. Refer doing to the Law, believing to the promise. As widely as the Law and the promise are distinct, so far apart are faith and works—even if you understand "doing works" in a theological sense. For Paul is discussing something else here. He is urging the distinction between doing and believing, so that he may separate love from faith and show that faith alone justifies, because the Law, whether it is done morally or theologically or not at all, contributes nothing whatever to justification. The Law pertains to doing. But faith is not of this sort; it is something completely different—something that is required before the Law is kept, so that when faith is preexistent, a beautiful incarnation can take place.

Believing and doing

Therefore faith always justifies and makes alive; and yet it does not remain alone, that is, idle. Not that it does not remain alone on its own level and in its own function, for it always justifies alone. But it is incarnate and becomes man; that is, it neither is nor remains idle or without love. Thus Christ, according to His divinity, is a divine and eternal essence or nature, without a beginning; but His humanity is a nature created in time. These two natures in Christ are not confused or mixed, and the properties of each must be clearly understood. It is characteristic of the humanity to have a beginning in time, but it is characteristic of the divinity to be eternal and without a beginning. Nevertheless, these two are combined, and the divinity without a beginning is incorporated into the humanity with a beginning. Just as I am obliged to distinguish between the humanity and the divinity, and to say: "The humanity is not the divinity, and yet the man is God," so I make a distinction here and say: "The Law is not faith, and yet faith does works. Faith and works are in agreement concretely or compositely, and yet each has and preserves its own nature and proper function."

Thus you have the reason why Paul puts such stress on this passage, namely, in order to distinguish faith plainly from love. Therefore let the sophists go to the devil with their accursed gloss, and let that expression "faith formed" be damned! You should constantly say that these terms, "faith formed," "unformed," "acquired," etc., are monstrosities of the devil, produced to destroy Christian doctrine and faith, to blaspheme Christ and tread Him underfoot, and to establish the righteousness of works. You should say this, I mean, in order to keep the one true and correct faith—the faith without works. Although works follow faith, yet faith should not be works, and works should not be faith, lest they be confused; but the boundaries and the realms of the Law or works and of faith should be correctly distinguished from one another.

When we believe, therefore, then we live simply on account of Christ, who is without sin, who is also our mercy seat and forgiveness of sins. On the other hand, when we keep the Law, we do indeed perform works; but we do not have righteousness and life. For it belongs to the Law not to justify and give life but to disclose sin and to kill. Of course, the Law says: "He who does them shall live by them." But where is the one who does them? Where is the one who loves God with all his heart, etc., and his neighbor as himself? Therefore there is no one who keeps the Law. And even though he tries his best to keep it, yet in keeping it he does not keep it; therefore he remains under the curse. Faith, however, does not perform works; it believes in Christ, the Justifier. And so a man does not live because of his doing; he lives because of his believing. Yet a believer does keep the Law; but what he does not keep is forgiven him through the forgiveness of sins for Christ's sake, and what sin there is left is not imputed to him.

Galatians 3:13

Christ redeemed us from the curse of the Law, having become a curse for us—for it is written: Cursed be everyone who hangs on a tree.

Here again Jerome and the sophists who followed him are distressed. They most miserably lacerate this passage, which is filled to overflowing with comfort; and they strive anxiously with what they think is godly zeal not to permit the insult of being called a curse or an execration to come to Christ. Therefore they evade this statement this way: "Paul was not speaking in earnest here." Thus they said, in a way that was as reprehensible as it was wicked, that Scripture, whose passages do not contradict themselves, does contradict itself in Paul. They show this as follows: "The statement from Moses that Paul cites here does not speak about Christ. In addition, the universal expression 'everyone' that Paul has is not added in Moses. Furthermore, Paul omits the phrase 'by God,' which occurs in Moses. In short, it is obvious enough that Moses is speaking about a criminal or a thief who has deserved the cross by his wicked deeds, as Scripture testifies clearly in Deut. 21:22–23." Therefore they ask how this sentence can be applied to Christ, that He is accursed by God and hanged on a tree, since He is not a criminal or a thief but righteous and holy. Perhaps this may impress the inexperienced; for they suppose that the sophists are speaking in a way that is not only subtle but also very pious, and that they are defending the honor of Christ and are religiously admonishing all Christians not to suppose wickedly that Christ was a curse. Therefore it must be determined what Paul's intent and meaning are.

Christ became a curse for us

Paul guarded his words carefully and spoke precisely. And here again a distinction must be made; Paul's words clearly show this. For he does not say that Christ became a curse on His own account, but that He became a curse "for us." Thus the whole emphasis is on the phrase "for us." For Christ is innocent so far as His own person is concerned; therefore He should not have been hanged from the tree. But because, according to the Law, every thief should have been hanged, therefore, according to the Law of Moses, Christ Himself should have been hanged; for He bore the person of a sinner and a thief—and not of one but of all sinners and thieves. For we are sinners and thieves, and therefore we are worthy of death and eternal damnation. But Christ took all our sins upon Himself, and for them He died on the cross. Therefore it was appropriate for Him to become a thief and, as Isaiah says (53:12), to be "numbered among the thieves."

And all the prophets saw this, that Christ was to become the greatest thief, murderer, adulterer, robber, desecrator, blasphemer, etc., there has ever been anywhere in the world. He is not acting in His own person now. Now He is not the Son of God, born of the Virgin. But He is a sinner, who has and bears the sin of Paul, the former blasphemer, persecutor, and assaulter; of Peter, who denied Christ; of David, who was an adulterer and a murderer, and who caused the Gentiles to blaspheme the name of the Lord (Rom. 2:24). In short, He has and bears all the sins of all men in His body—not in the sense that He has committed them but in the sense that He took these sins, committed by us, upon His own body, in order to make satisfaction for them with His own blood. Therefore this general Law of Moses included Him, although He was innocent so far as His own person was concerned; for it found Him among sinners and thieves. Thus a magistrate regards someone as a criminal and punishes him if he catches him among thieves, even though the man has never committed anything evil or worthy of death. Christ was not only found among sinners, but of His own free will and by the will of the Father He wanted to be an associate of sinners, having assumed the flesh and blood of those who were sinners and thieves and who were immersed in all sorts of sin. Therefore when the Law found Him among thieves, it condemned and executed Him as a thief.

This knowledge of Christ and most delightful comfort, that Christ became a curse for us to set us free from the curse of the Law—of this the sophists deprive us when they segregate Christ from sins and from sinners and set Him forth to us only as an example to be imitated. In this way they make Christ not only useless to us but also a judge and a tyrant who is angry because of our sins and who damns sinners. But just as Christ is wrapped up in our flesh and blood, so we must wrap Him and know Him to be wrapped up in our sins, our curse, our death, and everything evil.

"But it is highly absurd and insulting to call the Son of God a sinner and a curse!" If you want to deny that He is a sinner and a curse, then deny also that He suffered, was crucified, and died. For it is no less absurd to say, as our Creed confesses and prays, that the Son of God was crucified and underwent the torments of sin and death than it is to say that He is a sinner or a curse. But if it is not absurd to confess and believe that Christ was crucified among thieves, then it is not absurd to say as well that He was a curse and a sinner of sinners. Surely these words of Paul are not without purpose: "Christ became a curse for us" and "For our sake God made Christ to be sin, who knew no sin, so that in Him we might become the righteousness of God" (2 Cor. 5:21).

In the same way John the Baptist called Christ "the Lamb of God" (John 1:29). He is, of course, innocent, because He is the Lamb of God without spot or blemish. But because He bears the sins of the world, His innocence is pressed down with the sins and the guilt of the entire world. Whatever sins I, you, and all of us have committed or may commit in the future, they are as much Christ's own as if He Himself had committed them. In short, our sin must be Christ's own sin, or we shall perish eternally. The wicked sophists have obscured this true knowledge of Christ which Paul and the prophets have handed down to us.

Isaiah 53:6 speaks the same way about Christ. It says: "God has laid on Him the iniquity of us all." These words must not be diluted but must be left in their precise and serious sense. For God is not joking in the words of the prophet; He is speaking seriously and out of great love, namely, that this Lamb of God, Christ, should bear the iniquity of us all. But what does it mean to "bear"? The sophists reply: "To be punished." Good. But why is Christ punished? Is it not because He has sin and bears sin? That Christ has sin is the testimony of the Holy Spirit in the Psalms. Thus in Ps. 40:12 we read: "My iniquities have overtaken Me"; in Ps. 41:4: "I said: 'O Lord, be gracious to Me; heal Me, for I have sinned against Thee!' "; and in Ps. 69:5: "O God, Thou knowest My folly; the wrongs I have done are not hidden from Thee." In these psalms the Holy Spirit is speaking in the person of Christ and testifying in clear words that He has sinned or has sins. These testimonies of the psalms are not the words of an innocent one; they are the words of the suffering Christ, who undertook to bear the person of all sinners and therefore was made guilty of the sins of the entire world.

Therefore Christ not only was crucified and died, but by divine love sin was laid upon Him. When sin was laid upon Him, the Law came and said: "Let every sinner die! And therefore, Christ, if You want to reply that You are guilty and that You bear the punishment, You must bear the sin and the curse as well." Therefore Paul correctly applies to Christ this general law from Moses: "Cursed be everyone who hangs on a tree." Christ hung on a tree; therefore Christ is a curse of God.

He bore the sins of the entire world

And this is our highest comfort, to clothe and wrap Christ this way in my sins, your sins, and the sins of the entire world, and in this way to behold Him bearing all our sins. When He is beheld this way, He easily removes all the fanatical opinions of our opponents about justification by works. For the Papists dream about a kind of faith "formed by love." Through this they want to remove sins and be justified. This is clearly to unwrap Christ and to unclothe Him from our sins, to make Him innocent, to burden and overwhelm ourselves with our own sins, and to behold them, not in Christ but in ourselves. This is to abolish Christ and make Him useless. For if it is true that we abolish sins by the works of the Law and by love, then Christ does not take them away, but we do. But if He is truly the Lamb of God who takes away the sins of the world, who became a curse for us, and who was wrapped in our sins, it necessarily follows that we cannot be justified and take away sins through love. For God has laid our sins not upon us but upon Christ, His Son. If they are taken away by Him, then they cannot be taken away by us. All Scripture says this, and we confess and pray the same thing in the Creed when we say: "I believe in Jesus Christ, the Son of God, who suffered, was crucified, and died for us."

This is the most joyous of all doctrines and the one that contains the most comfort. It teaches that we have the indescribable and inestimable mercy and love of God. When the merciful Father saw that we were being oppressed through the Law, that we were being held under a curse, and that we could not be liberated from it by anything, He sent His Son into the world, heaped all the sins of all men upon Him, and said to Him: "Be Peter the denier; Paul the persecutor, blasphemer, and assaulter; David the adulterer; the sinner who ate the apple in Paradise; the thief on the cross. In short, be the person of all men, the one who has committed the sins of all men. And see to it that You pay and make satisfaction for them." Now the Law comes and says: "I find Him a sinner, who takes upon Himself the sins of all men. I do not see any other sins than those in Him. Therefore let Him die on the cross!" And so it attacks Him and kills Him. By this deed the whole world is purged and expiated from all sins, and thus it is set free from death and from every evil. But when sin and death have been abolished by this one man, God does not want to see anything else in the whole world, especially if it were to believe, except sheer cleansing and righteousness. And if any remnants of sin were to remain, still for the sake of Christ, the shining Sun, God would not notice them.

This is how we must magnify the doctrine of Christian righteousness in opposition to the righteousness of the Law and of works, even though there is no voice or eloquence that can properly understand, much less express, its greatness. Therefore the argument that Paul presents here is the most powerful and the highest of all against all the righteousness of the flesh; for it contains this invincible and irrefutable antithesis: If the sins of the entire world are on that one man, Jesus Christ, then they are not on the world. But if they are not on Him, then they are still on the world. Again, if Christ Himself is made guilty of all the sins that we have all committed, then we are absolved from all sins, not through ourselves or through our own works or merits but through Him. But if He is innocent and does not carry our sins, then we carry them and shall die and be damned in them. "But thanks be to God, who gives us the victory through our Lord Jesus Christ! Amen" (1 Cor. 15:57).

Now let us see how two such extremely contrary things come together in this person. Not only my sins and yours, but the sins of the entire world, past, present, and future, attack Him, try to damn Him, and do in fact damn Him. But because in the same person, who is the highest, the greatest, and the only sinner, there is also eternal and invincible righteousness, therefore these two converge: the highest, the greatest, and the only sin; and the highest, the greatest, and the only righteousness. Here one of them must yield and be conquered, since they come together and collide with such a powerful impact. Thus the sin of the entire world attacks righteousness with the greatest possible impact and fury. What happens? Righteousness is eternal, immortal, and invincible. Sin, too, is a very powerful and cruel tyrant, dominating and ruling over the whole world, capturing and enslaving all men. In short, sin is a great and powerful god who devours the whole human race, all the learned, holy, powerful, wise, and unlearned men. He, I say, attacks Christ and wants to devour Him as he has devoured all the rest. But he does not see that He is a person of invincible and eternal righteousness. In this duel, therefore, it is necessary for sin to be conquered and killed, and for righteousness to prevail and live. Thus in Christ all sin is conquered, killed, and buried; and righteousness remains the victor and the ruler eternally. . . .

In Himself

This circumstance, "in Himself," makes the duel more amazing and outstanding; for it shows that such great things were to be achieved in the one and only person of Christ—namely, that the curse, sin, and death were to be destroyed, and that the blessing, righteousness, and life were to replace them—and that through Him the whole creation was to be renewed. If you look at this person, therefore, you see sin, death, the wrath of God, hell, the devil, and all evils conquered and put to death. To the extent that Christ rules by His grace in the hearts of the faithful, there is no sin or death or curse. But where Christ is not known, there these things remain. And so all who do not believe lack this blessing and this victory. "For this," as John says, "is our victory, faith" (1 John 5:4).

This is the chief doctrine of the Christian faith. The sophists have completely obliterated it, and today the fanatics are obscuring it once more. Here you see how necessary it is to believe and confess the doctrine of the divinity of Christ. When Arius denied this, it was necessary also for him to deny the doctrine of redemption. For to conquer the sin of the world, death, the curse, and the wrath of God in Himself—this is the work not of any creature, but of the divine power. Therefore it was necessary that He who was to conquer these in Himself should be true God by nature. For in opposition to this mighty power—sin, death, and the curse—which of itself reigns in the whole world and in the entire creation, it is necessary to set an even higher power, which cannot be found and does not exist apart from the divine power. Therefore to abolish sin, to destroy death, to remove the curse in Himself, to grant righteousness, to bring life to light (2 Tim. 1:10), and to bring the blessing in Himself, that is, to annihilate these things and to create those—all these are works solely of the divine power. Since Scripture attributes all these to Christ, therefore He Himself is Life, Righteousness, and Blessing, that is, God by nature and in essence. Hence those who deny the divinity of Christ lose all Christianity and become Gentiles and Turks through and through.

As I often warn, therefore, the doctrine of justification must be learned diligently. For in it are included all the other doctrines of our faith; and if it is sound, all the others are sound as well. Therefore when we teach that men are justified through Christ and that Christ is the Victor over sin, death, and the eternal curse, we are testifying at the same time that He is God by nature. . . .

With gratitude and with a sure confidence, therefore, let us accept this doctrine, so sweet and so filled with comfort, which teaches that Christ became a curse for us, that is, a sinner worthy of the wrath of God; that He clothed Himself in our person, laid our sins upon His own shoulders, and said: "I have committed the sins that all men have committed." Therefore He truly became accursed according to the Law, not for Himself but, as Paul says, ὑπὲρ ἡμῶν. For unless He had taken upon Himself my sins, your sins, and the sins of the entire world, the Law would have had no right over Him, since it condemns only sinners and holds only them under a curse. Therefore He could neither have become a curse nor have died, since the cause of the curse and of death is sin, of which He was innocent. But because He took upon Himself our sins, not by compulsion but of His own free will, it was right for Him to bear the punishment and the wrath of God—not for His own person, which was righteous and invincible and therefore could not become guilty, but for our person.

Fortunate exchange

By this fortunate exchange with us He took upon Himself our sinful person and granted us His innocent and victorious person. Clothed and dressed in this, we are freed from the curse of the Law, because Christ Himself voluntarily became a curse for us, saying: "For My own person of humanity and divinity I am blessed, and I am in need of nothing whatever. But I shall empty Myself (Phil. 2:7); I shall assume your clothing and mask; and in this I shall walk about and suffer death, in order to set you free from death." Therefore when, inside our mask, He was carrying the sin of the whole world, He was captured, He suffered, He was crucified, He died; and for us He became a curse. But because He was a divine and eternal person, it was impossible for death to hold Him. Therefore He arose from death on the third day, and now He lives eternally; nor can sin, death, and our mask be found in Him any longer; but there is sheer righteousness, life, and eternal blessing.

We must look at this image and take hold of it with a firm faith. He who does this has the innocence and the victory of Christ, no matter how great a sinner he is. But this cannot be grasped by loving will; it can be grasped only by reason illumined by faith. Therefore we are justified by faith alone, because faith alone grasps this victory of Christ. To the extent that you believe this, to that extent you have it. If you believe that sin, death, and the curse have been abolished, they have been abolished, because Christ conquered and overcame them in Himself; and He wants us to believe that just as in His person there is no longer the mask of the sinner or any vestige of death, so this is no longer in our person, since He has done everything for us.

Therefore if sin makes you anxious, and if death terrifies you, just think that this is an empty specter and an illusion of the devil—which is what it surely is. For in fact there is no sin any longer, no curse, no death, and no devil, because Christ has conquered and abolished all these. Accordingly, the victory of Christ is utterly certain; the defects lie not in the fact itself, which is completely true, but in our incredulity. It is difficult for reason to believe such inestimable blessings. In addition, the devil and the sectarians—the former with his flaming darts (Eph. 6:16), the latter with their perverse and wicked doctrine—are bent on this one thing: to obscure this doctrine and take it away from us. It is above all for this doctrine, on which we insist so diligently, that we bear the hate and persecution of Satan and of the world. For Satan feels the power and the results of this doctrine.

Now that Christ reigns, there is in fact no more sin, death, or curse—this we confess every day in the Apostles' Creed when we say: "I believe in the holy church." This is plainly nothing else than if we were to say: "I believe that there is no sin and no death in the church. For believers in Christ are not sinners and are not sentenced to death but are altogether holy and righteous, lords over sin and death who live eternally." But it is faith alone that discerns this, because we say: "I believe in the holy church." If you consult your reason and your eyes, you will judge differently. For in devout people you will see many things that offend you; you will see them fall now and again, see them sin, or be weak in faith, or be troubled by a bad temper, envy, or other evil emotions. "Therefore the church is not holy." I deny the conclusion that you draw. If I look at my own person or at that of my neighbor, the church will never be holy. But if I look at Christ, who is the Propitiator and Cleanser of the church, then it is completely holy; for He bore the sins of the entire world.

Therefore where sins are noticed and felt, there they really are not present. For, according to the theology of Paul, there is no more sin, no more death, and no more curse in the world, but only in Christ, who is the Lamb of God that takes away the sins of the world and who became a curse in order to set us free from the curse. On the other hand, according to philosophy and reason, sin, death, etc., are not present anywhere except in the world, in the flesh, and in sinners. For the theology of the sophists is unable to consider sin any other way except metaphysically, that is: "A quality clings to a substance or a subject. Therefore just as color clings to a wall, so sin clings to the world, to the flesh, or to the conscience. Therefore it must be washed away by some opposing motivations, namely, by love." But the true theology teaches that there is no more sin in the world, because Christ, on whom, according to Isa. 53:6, the Father has laid the sins of the entire world, has conquered, destroyed, and killed it in His own body. Having died to sin once, He has truly been raised from the dead and will not die any more (Rom. 6:9). Therefore wherever there is faith in Christ, there sin has in fact been abolished, put to death, and buried. But where there is no faith in Christ, there sin remains. And although there are still remnants of sin in the saints because they do not believe perfectly, nevertheless these remnants are dead; for on account of faith in Christ they are not imputed.

Galatians 3:18–19

For if the inheritance is by the Law, it is no longer by promise. Why, then, the Law?

When we teach that a man is justified without the Law and works, this question necessarily follows: "If the Law does not justify, why, then, was it given?" Again: "Why does God prod and burden us with the Law if it does not give life?" . . .

The grumbling, "If the Law does not justify, it is nothing," is a fallacious conclusion. For just as the conclusion is not valid if one says: "Money does not justify; therefore it is nothing. The eyes do not justify; therefore I shall pluck them out. The hands do not justify; therefore I shall cut them off"—so this conclusion is not valid: "The Law does not justify; therefore it is nothing." To each thing one must attribute its proper function and use. When we deny that the Law justifies, we are not destroying or condemning it. But to the question, "Why, then, the Law?" we give an answer that is different from the one given by our opponents, who, in their distorted thinking, imagine for the Law a function and use that does not lie in the nature of things.

We are debating against this abuse and this imaginary function of the Law, and we reply with Paul that the Law does not pertain to justification. But by this we are not asserting that the Law is nothing, as they immediately infer: "If the Law does not justify, it was given to no purpose." No. The Law has its proper function and use; but this is not the one that our opponents attribute to it, namely, that of justifying. It does not belong to the Law to be used for justification; therefore we teach that it must be separated from this as far as heaven is from earth. With Paul we say that "the Law is good, if anyone uses it lawfully" (1 Tim. 1:8), that is, if anyone uses the Law as Law. If I define the Law with a proper definition and keep it in its own function and use, it is a very good thing. But if I transfer it to another use and attribute to it what should not be attributed to it, I distort not only the Law but all theology. . . .

Double use of the Law

Here one must know that there is a double use of the Law. One is the civic use. God has ordained civic laws—indeed, all laws—to restrain transgressions. Therefore every law was given to hinder sins. Does this mean that when the Law restrains sins, it justifies? Not at all. When I refrain from killing or from committing adultery or from stealing, or when I abstain from other sins, I do not do this voluntarily or from the love of virtue but because I am afraid of the sword and of the executioner. This prevents me, as the ropes or the chains prevent a lion or a bear from ravaging something that comes along. Therefore restraint from sins is not righteousness but rather an indication of unrighteousness. Therefore just as a rope holds a furious and untamed beast and keeps it from attacking whatever it meets, so the Law constrains an insane and furious man, lest he commit further sins. This restraint makes it abundantly clear that those who have need of it—as does everyone who is outside Christ—are not righteous but unrighteous and insane, whom it is necessary to tame with the rope and with prison to keep them from sinning. Therefore the Law does not justify.

Thus the first understanding and use of the Law is to restrain the wicked. For the devil reigns in the whole world and drives men to all sorts of shameful deeds. This is why God has ordained magistrates, parents, teachers, laws, shackles, and all civic ordinances, so that, if they cannot do any more, they will at least bind the hands of the devil and keep him from raging at will. Therefore just as ropes and chains are bound upon men who are possessed and in whom the devil is ruling powerfully, to keep them from harming someone, so the whole world, which is possessed by the devil and is being led headlong into every crime, has the magistrate with his ropes and chains, that is, his laws, restraining its hands and feet, lest it rush headlong into all sorts of evil. If it does not permit itself to be restrained this way, it will pay with the price of its head. This civic restraint is extremely necessary and was instituted by God, both for the sake of public peace and for the sake of preserving everything, but especially to prevent the course of the Gospel from being hindered by the tumults and seditions of wild men. Paul is not discussing that civic use here; it is indeed very necessary, but it does not justify. For as a possessed person is not free and mentally balanced just because his hands and feet are bound, so when the world is most restrained from external acts of disgrace by the Law, it is not righteous on that account but remains unrighteous. In fact, this very restraint indicates that the world is wicked and insane and that it is driven by its prince, the devil; otherwise there would be no need for it to be kept from sinning by laws.

The other use of the Law is the theological or spiritual one, which serves to increase transgressions. This is the primary purpose of the Law of Moses, that through it sin might grow and be multiplied, especially in the conscience. Paul discusses this magnificently in Romans 7. Therefore the true function and the chief and proper use of the Law is to reveal to man his sin, blindness, misery, wickedness, ignorance, hate and contempt of God, death, hell, judgment, and the well-deserved wrath of God. Yet this use of the Law is completely unknown to the hypocrites, the sophists in the universities, and to all men who go along in the presumption of the righteousness of the Law or of their own righteousness. To curb and crush this monster and raging beast, that is, the presumption of religion, God is obliged, on Mount Sinai, to give a new Law with such pomp and with such an awesome spectacle that the entire people is crushed with fear. For since the reason becomes haughty with this human presumption of righteousness and imagines that on account of this it is pleasing to God, therefore God has to send some Hercules, namely, the Law, to attack, subdue, and destroy this monster with full force. Therefore the Law is intent only on this beast, not on any other.

Hence this use of the Law is extremely beneficial and very necessary. For if someone is not a murderer, adulterer, or thief, and abstains from external sins, as that Pharisee did (Luke 18:11), he would swear, being possessed by the devil, that he is a righteous man; therefore he develops the presumption of righteousness and relies on his good works. God cannot soften and humble this man or make him acknowledge his misery and damnation any other way than by the Law. Therefore the proper and absolute use of the Law is to terrify with lightning (as on Mount Sinai), thunder, and the blare of the trumpet, with a thunderbolt to burn and crush that brute which is called the presumption of righteousness. Hence God says through Jeremiah (23:29): “My Word is a hammer which breaks the rock in pieces.” For as long as the presumption of righteousness remains in a man, there remain immense pride, self-trust, smugness, hate of God, contempt of grace and mercy, ignorance of the promises and of Christ. The proclamation of free grace and the forgiveness of sins does not enter his heart and understanding, because that huge rock and solid wall, namely, the presumption of righteousness by which the heart itself is surrounded, prevents this from happening. . . .

Rightly distinguishing Law and Gospel

I urge you, who are to be the teachers of others, to learn this doctrine of the true and proper use of the Law carefully; for after our time it will be obscured again and will be completely wiped out. Today, while we are still alive and are insistently urging this doctrine, there are nevertheless very few, even among those who want to seem “evangelical” and who acknowledge the Gospel with us, who correctly understand the use of the Law. What do you think will happen when we have been taken away? Right now I am not even speaking about the Anabaptists, the neo-Arians, and the spirits who blaspheme the Sacrament of the body and blood of Christ; they are all as ignorant of this proper use and function of the Law as the Papists are. They have long since defected from the pure doctrine of the Gospel to laws. Therefore they do not teach Christ. They boast and swear that they are intent on nothing except the glory of God and the salvation of the brethren, and that they teach the Word of God purely; but in fact they distort the Word of God and twist it into an alien meaning, so that it is forced to tell them what they themselves imagine. Under the name of Christ, therefore, they teach their own dreams; and under the name of the Gospel, nothing but laws and ceremonies. And so they are and remain true to form, that is, monks, performers of works, legalists, and ritualists; all they do is to think up new names and new works.

Therefore it is a matter of no small moment to believe correctly about what the Law is and what its use and function are. Thus it is evident that we do not reject the Law and works, as our opponents falsely accuse us. But we do everything to establish the Law, and we require works. We say that the Law is good and useful, but in its proper use, namely, first, as we have said earlier, to restrain civic transgressions; and secondly, to reveal spiritual transgressions. Therefore the Law is a light that illumines and shows not the grace of God or righteousness and life, but the wrath of God, sin, death, our damnation in the sight of God, and hell. For just as on Mount Sinai the lightning, the thunder, the dark cloud, the smoking and burning mountain, and the whole horrendous sight did not make the children of Israel happy or alive but terrified them, made them almost helpless, and disclosed a presence of God speaking from the cloud that they could not bear for all their sanctity and purity, so when the Law is being used correctly, it does nothing but reveal sin, work wrath, accuse, terrify, and reduce the minds of men to the point of despair. And that is as far as the Law goes.

On the other hand, the Gospel is a light that illumines hearts and makes them alive. It discloses what grace and the mercy of God are; what the forgiveness of sins, blessing, righteousness, life, and eternal salvation are; and how we are to attain to these. When we distinguish the Law from the Gospel this way, we attribute to each its proper use and function. You will not find anything about this distinction between the Law and the Gospel in the books of the monks, the canonists, and the recent and ancient theologians. Augustine taught and expressed it to some extent.[18] Jerome and others like him knew nothing at all about it. In other words, for many centuries there has been a remarkable silence about this in all the schools and churches. This situation has produced a very dangerous condition for consciences; for unless the Gospel is clearly distinguished from the Law, Christian doctrine cannot be kept sound. But when this distinction is recognized, the true meaning of justification is recognized. Then it is easy to distinguish faith from works, and Christ from Moses, as well as from the magistrate and all civil laws. For everything apart from Christ is a ministry of death for the punishment of the wicked.

Galatians 5:18–19

But if you are led by the Spirit, you are not under the Law. Now the works of the flesh are plain.

. . . When I was a monk, I often had a heartfelt wish to see the life and conduct of at least one saintly man. But meanwhile I was imagining the sort of saint who lived in the desert and abstained from food and drink, subsisting on nothing but roots and cold water. I had derived this notion about unnatural saints from the books not only of the sophists but even of the fathers. For Jerome writes somewhere as follows: "I am not saying anything about food and drink, since it is a luxury even for those who are

18 Cf. Augustine, *The Spirit and the Letter* 9.15 and 13.34.

feeble to take a little cold water and to eat some cooked food."[19] But now that the light of truth is shining, we see with utter clarity that Christ and the apostles designate as saints not those who lead a celibate life, who are abstemious, or who perform other works that give the appearance of brilliance or grandeur, but those who, being called by the Gospel and baptized, believe that they have been sanctified and cleansed by the blood and death of Christ. Thus whenever Paul writes to Christians, he calls them saints, sons and heirs of God, etc. Therefore saints are all those who believe in Christ, whether men or women, whether slaves or free. And they are saints on the basis not of their own works, but of the works of God, which they accept by faith, such as the Word, the Sacraments, the suffering, death, resurrection, and victory of Christ, the sending of the Holy Spirit, etc. In other words, they are saints not by active holiness, but by passive holiness.

Such genuine saints include ministers of the Word, political magistrates, parents, children, masters, servants, etc., if they, first of all, declare that Christ is their wisdom, righteousness, sanctification, and redemption (1 Cor. 1:30), and if, in the second place, they all do their duty in their callings on the basis of the command of the Word of God, abstaining from the desires and vices of the flesh for the sake of Christ. They are not all of equal firmness of character, and many weaknesses and offenses are discernible in every one of them; it is also true that many of them fall into sin. But this does not hinder their holiness at all, so long as they sin out of weakness, not out of deliberate wickedness. For, as I have already said several times, the godly are conscious of the desires of the flesh; but they resist them and do not gratify them. When they fall into sin unexpectedly, they obtain forgiveness, if by faith they return to Christ, who does not want us to chase away the lost sheep but to look for it. On no account, therefore, am I to jump to the conclusion that those who are weak in faith or morals are unholy, when I see that they love and revere the Word, receive the Lord's Supper, etc.; for God has received them and regards them as righteous through the forgiveness of sins. It is before Him that they stand or fall (Rom. 14:4).

This is how Paul speaks about the saints everywhere. And I am happy to give thanks to God for His superabundant gift, which I sought when I used to be a monk; for I have seen not one saint, but many, in fact, innumerable genuine saints, not the kind that the sophists portrayed but the kind that Christ and the apostles portray and describe, the kind to which, by the grace of God, even I belong. For I have been baptized; and I believe that Christ, my Lord, has redeemed me from sin by His death

19 Cf. Jerome, *Against Jovinian* 2.5–17.

and has granted me eternal righteousness and holiness. And let anyone be accursed who does not give Christ the honor of believing that he has been justified and sanctified by His death, the Word, the Sacraments, etc.

Galatians 6:18

The grace of our Lord Jesus Christ be with your spirit, brethren. Amen.

This is Paul's final farewell. He ends the Epistle with the same words with which he began it, as though he were saying: "I have proclaimed Christ to you purely. I have begged you and scolded you. I have not omitted anything that I thought you needed. There is nothing further that I can do for you except to pray from my heart that our Lord Jesus Christ may add His blessing and His increase to my labor, and may rule you by His Spirit forever. Amen."

So far the exposition of the Epistle of St. Paul to the Galatians. May the Lord Jesus Christ, our Justifier and Savior, who has granted me the grace and ability to expound this Epistle and has granted you the grace and ability to hear it, preserve and confirm both you and me. From the heart I pray that we may grow more and more in the knowledge of grace and of faith in Him, so that we may be blameless and beyond reproach until the day of our redemption. To Him, with the Father and the Holy Spirit, be praise and glory forever and ever. Amen. Amen.

Commentary on Psalm 51

1532

Martin Luther prayed the Psalms *daily as a monk and could summon them from memory with little effort. When Luther became professor of Bible, he turned naturally to the Psalms for his first lectures (1513–15). Three years later he offered a second course of lectures on the Psalms. The first publication of his own work was on the penitential psalms (see above, p. 30). Luther often turned to the Psalms throughout his career in his sermons, lectures, and writings. This was especially the case during difficult times.*

During the imperial diet at Augsburg, while Luther's colleagues were revising their confession and preparing to present it to the emperor, Luther was stewing at the fortress in Coburg. Frustrated with the lack of information coming to him and feeling helpless, Luther offered, as he put it, the only thing of value he possessed—his comments on Scripture.[1] *Luther worried that too many concessions were being made at Augsburg to secure a temporal peace. From June 13 to June 26, he wrote a commentary on Psalm 118, his favorite psalm and beloved treasure, and gave his opinion on these negotiations.*[2] *Psalm 118, titled* Confitemini Domino *in Latin, confesses the steadfast love of the Lord, in whom we take refuge, trusting not in man or princes.*

Luther's concerns at Coburg guided his lectures of the early 1530s. When Luther returned to Wittenberg, he preached on the Sermon on the Mount and he lectured on Galatians. After a brief break, he lectured next on selected psalms. The psalms he chose addressed the matters now facing the German people and the purpose of the Reformation. Luther began with Psalm 2 and Psalm 51. His lectures on Psalm 2 confidently set forth Christ, the Son of God, as our true King.[3] *Although the world and its powers rage against Christ, He will be victorious in the end. This Luther knew with certainty. Luther's lectures on Psalm 51 return him to the familiar themes of sin and grace, the true subject of theology. Luther's exposition of these two psalms stands alongside his great*

1 See Luther's prefatory letter for *Commentary on Psalm 118* (1530), LW 14:45–46.

2 See LW 14:41–106.

3 See LW 12:1–93.

accomplishment with Galatians. They are, in their own right, exceptional works of Luther's mature theology.

The Reformation is often dated to the posting of Luther's Ninety-Five Theses. *Luther's first thesis declared that when Jesus said "repent" (Matt. 4:17) He meant for the entire life of the believer to be one of repentance.*[4] *Luther said this against his scholastic predecessors and their notions of penance. Psalm 51, a penitential psalm, was used in the church's liturgy and daily prayers. Luther often commented on it throughout his career. The lectures from 1532 are his most thorough exposition of Psalm 51. Luther divides the psalm into two parts. Part one (vv. 1–9) addresses the principal doctrines of the Christian faith: repentance, sin, grace, and justification. Part two (vv. 10–19) explains the gifts of the Spirit that follow forgiveness and the worship offered to God. The excerpt below is from part one.*

Luther's disagreement with his scholastic predecessors begins with their understanding of sin. For Luther, they minimize sin and do not consider it deeply enough. They think only in terms of actual sins rather than the origin of sin. They regard people as sinners because they commit sins, but the Scriptures declare that we sin because we are sinners. For Luther, the scholastic failure to understand sin necessarily leads to a misunderstanding of grace. Sin and grace mutually inform each other. The false appraisal of sin also leads to a false assessment of human nature and our natural powers after the fall. All of this results in a false teaching on penance that emphasizes our acts of contrition and satisfaction. For Luther, the failure to understand sin and grace properly ends in devising a false doctrine of God.

Psalm 51[5]

Last year, we expounded the Second Psalm, on Christ the King and His spiritual and heavenly kingdom, how He is received in this world, vexed and wounded by kings and people, yet how He conquers and triumphs. Now I have begun the exposition of the Psalm *Miserere*, which teaches about repentance. I cannot promise that I shall lecture satisfactorily, for I admit that I have not fully grasped the Spirit who speaks there. Still it gives us an opportunity and a basis for thought and study, so that I can

4 See LW 31:25.

5 The following excerpt is adapted from *Commentary on Psalm 51*, in volume 12 of *Luther's Works: American Edition*, ed. and trans. Jaroslav Pelikan (St. Louis: Concordia, 1955). Minor alterations have been made to the text for consistency in style, abbreviations, and capitalization. The annotations and subheadings are the work of the editor of this book.

become a student with you and await the Spirit. Whatever He gives, we shall receive with thanks.

A knowledge of this psalm is necessary and useful in many ways. It contains instruction about the chief parts of our religion, about repentance, sin, grace, and justification, as well as about the worship we ought to render to God. These are divine and heavenly doctrines. Unless they are taught by the great Spirit, they cannot enter the heart of man. We see that our opponents have expended great effort and discussed this doctrine in many huge volumes. Yet none of them really understands the nature of repentance, sin, or grace. These words are like a dream to them, which leaves some traces in the mind but itself has utterly disappeared from the mind and the eyes. The reason for this blindness and ignorance is that true knowledge of these doctrines does not depend upon the intelligence and wisdom of human reason, nor is it born, so to speak, in our home or our hearts. But it is revealed and given from heaven. Where is there a man who could speak about repentance and the forgiveness of sins the way the Holy Spirit speaks in this psalm?

This psalm is commonly called a "penitential psalm," and among them all it is the most widely used in church and daily prayers. Whoever first gave it this name knew what he was doing. But the rest of the crowd, who either chant or pray it daily in order to perform the works required by the bishops, have understood nothing of it at all. They have applied this psalm to the penance of works, to actual sin, which they define as "anything said, done, or thought against the Law of God." This definition is far too narrow to portray the greatness or power of sin. We must look at sin more deeply and show more clearly the root of wickedness or sin, not simply remain with the "elicited acts," as they call them. From this error, their failure to understand sin properly, there comes, of course, the other error, their failure to understand the nature of grace properly either. This accounts for their ineptitude in comforting timid consciences and consoling hearts against death and divine judgment. How can anyone give consolation if he does not understand what grace is? Hence they fell into the foolishness of persuading men troubled with sorrows of conscience to put on cowls, accept monastic rules, and the like, by which they believed they would please God. This clearly shows that they did not properly understand either sin or grace and that they were simply teaching a theology of reason without the Word of God.

They taught the same way about repentance: People were to collect all the transgressions of the past year, sorrow over them, and expiate them by satisfaction. I ask you, does not a judge hang a thief if he confesses his theft and is sorry for it? Yet these people think God is satisfied if they pretend to be sorry by dressing differently, walking differently, and eating differently. The reading of this psalm will be especially useful in teaching us to understand these points of our doctrine properly and in providing us with a learned and serious refutation of our opponents, who argue so wrongly about such serious issues. I have experienced for myself how useless their profane arguments were when my conscience was in need. I have also urged the church very often to be grateful for this great gift of the Word and pure doctrine, that with the darkness driven away He has lighted the clear lamp of the Word.

Content and title of the psalm

Now let us come to the psalm. Here the doctrine of true repentance is set forth before us. There are two elements in true repentance: recognition of sin and recognition of grace; or, to use the more familiar terms, the fear of God and trust in mercy. These two parts David sets forth before us in this prayer as in a beautiful picture for us to look at. At the beginning of the psalm we see him troubled by the knowledge of his sin and the burden of his conscience. At the end he consoles himself with trust in the goodness of God and promises that he will also instruct others so that they might be converted. So it is apparent that in this psalm the prophet wanted to set down the true wisdom of divine religion in the right words with the right meaning, with the express purpose of teaching us the nature of sin, grace, and total repentance. There are also other psalms of this type, like Psalm 32, *Beati quorum*, and Psalm 130, *De profundis*. David is a master in teaching this doctrine, but in such a way that in using this doctrine he remains a pupil with us; for all men, be they ever so illumined by the Holy Spirit, still remain pupils of the Word. They remain under and near the Word, and they experience that they can hardly draw out a drop from the vast ocean of the Holy Spirit.

I have briefly summarized the content and arrangement of the psalm. Now something has to be said about the title. The story from 2 Samuel 12 is well-known. Therefore I have no doubt that this title gave the scholastics an excuse to interpret the psalm only in relation to the person of David and his actual sins, since David seems to be speaking in his own person about his own sins of adultery and murder. It is strange that they have not also taught that this psalm should be prayed only for this one sin, but have permitted it to serve as an example of prayer for all other sins. Thus when Paul says (1 Tim. 1:16), "In me the Lord Jesus displayed His patience for an example to those who were to believe in Him," even though not all believers were persecutors of the church, this means that in Paul Christ showed His patience, gentleness, and infinite mercy, lest others despair in their sins. In the same way they have set forth this psalm as an example of prayer for all sins, even though they interpret it only in relation to the actual sins of David referred to in the title.

We must not concentrate on those external sins, but go further and look at the whole nature, source, and origin of sin. The psalm talks about the whole of sin, about the root of sin, not merely about the outward work, which springs like fruit from the root and tree of sin. When he complains (v. 5) that he was conceived in sin, this clearly does not refer only to adultery but to his whole nature contaminated by sin, though I have no objection if David's deed is set forth as an example. In this deed there appear other sins than merely the one with Bathsheba. To his adultery he added a very wicked plan. He pronounced the man who had stolen his poor neighbor's ewe lamb worthy of death. Meanwhile he did not see his own sin when he murdered Uriah, who was undoubtedly a good man and faithful to his king, and took away his wife. He wanted to look like a holy man who loved right and justice. This doubled the sin. Not only did he cover up the vicious murder of Uriah, but other Israelites also perished, and the name of the Lord was blasphemed. Thus he went beyond the Fifth and Sixth Commandment to sin against the First, Second, and Third as well. Nor would he have left inviolate the Fourth, about duty toward parents, if it had stood in the way of the adultery he desired. Actually it is with blasphemy that God specially charges him (2 Sam. 12:14): "You have caused the Ammonites to blaspheme." The collapse of his people aroused the minds of the Gentiles against the people and the God of Israel, so that they cried out that the God of Israel was nothing but the god of the Ammonites was God and was victorious. Therefore David is an outstanding example. One by one he broke almost the whole Decalogue. Yet he would not have acknowledged these sins if Nathan had not come, but would still have wanted to be known as a righteous and holy king.

Explained this way, David's sin is a very moving example of grace and sin. Indeed, if the Holy Scriptures had not told this story, who would ever have believed that such a holy man could sink so low? Through the Holy Spirit he had instituted the worship of the tabernacle. He had adorned this worship with holy songs. He had waged wars with great success. God had declared him to be a chosen man. He had a most glorious promise about the future Seed, Christ, whom the prophets called the Son of David and the King of David. Why say more? There is no reason why he could not be rightly compared with Moses and Samuel. Yet such a man fell, not into some peccadillo, but at one time into a whole mass of sins. What is even worse, he fell into impenitence and deep smugness, so that if Nathan had not come, David might have sinned against the Holy Spirit.

The fact that such a great man—filled with the Holy Spirit, with the highest good works and divine wisdom, and famous above all for his outstanding gift of divine prophecy—should have fallen so miserably is an example for us, to comfort us when we are beset by sin and fall, or when our consciences are touched by a sense of the wrath and judgment of God. Here in a glorious example there shines the goodness and mercy of God, who is ready to forgive sins and to justify us, just as long as we do not add to our sin a denial that we have sinned. This is shown by the history of Saul. Although he had sinned against the voice of the Lord, this would have been forgiven him if he had not added a defense of his sin and said (1 Sam. 15:13), "I have performed the commandments of the Lord." When he was warned a second time, he stubbornly denied it and said (v. 20), "I have obeyed the voice of the Lord; I have gone on the mission on which the Lord sent me." For this he heard the sad sentence from Samuel (v. 23): "Because you have rejected the word of the Lord, He has also rejected you from being king." This is as if he would say: "The Lord is indeed ready to forgive sins, but only to those who acknowledge their sins and yet do not despair, but who believe that a door is open to the God who promises forgiveness of sins to the penitent." . . .

Human nature after the fall

The scholastic statement that "the natural powers are unimpaired" is a horrible blasphemy, though it is even more horrible when they say the same about demons.[6] If the natural powers are unimpaired, what need is there of Christ? If by nature man has good will, if he has true understanding to which, as they say, the will can naturally conform itself, what is it, then, that was lost in Paradise through sin and that had to be restored through the Son of God alone? Yet in our day, men who seem to be masters of theology defend the statement that the natural powers are unimpaired, that is, that the will is good. Even though through malice it occasionally wills and thinks something besides what is right and good, they attribute this to the malice of men, not to the will as it is in itself. The mind must be fortified against these dangerous opinions, lest the knowledge of grace be obscured; this cannot remain sound and right if we believe this way about the nature of man. Nor can this scholastic teaching be tolerated in the church: that man can keep the Law according to the substance of

6 Medieval theologians debated how Adam and Eve maintained their original righteousness before the fall. It was argued that they received—either as part of their creation or by meriting it after creation—a superadded gift of grace (*donum superadditum*). Following the fall, they lost this gift, and only their natural powers remained. Scholastic theologians generally agreed that our natural powers remained unimpaired. For an affirmation that this was true of demons, too, see Thomas Aquinas, *Summa Theologiae*, I, q. 64, a. 1.

the act, but not according to the intention of Him who commanded it,[7] since according to His intention not only the work is required, but also a disposition in the heart which is called grace. This would be just like saying that a man who is sound in hands and feet can properly do his job, except that he is hindered by not being dressed in black or white clothes. In exactly the same way they say that God requires something beyond the Decalogue and is not satisfied when someone keeps the Decalogue, but requires a right disposition as well. All these monstrosities have arisen from the fact that they do not rightly know the nature of sin. I have listed them to show the great difference between our sound doctrine and the monstrous and deceptive doctrine of the pope.

We say that the natural powers are corrupt in the extreme. When he was created, Adam had a right will and understanding. He could hear and see perfectly, and he took care of earthly things perfectly, with praise and faith in God. Through the fall his will, understanding, and all natural powers were so corrupted that man was no longer whole, but was diverted by sin, lost his correct judgment before God, and thought everything perversely against the will and Law of God. He no longer had an adequate knowledge or love of God, but fled from Him and hated Him, supposing that He was not God, that is, merciful and good, but a judge and a tyrant. From this loss of the knowledge of God proceed endless other sins, because men sin smugly when things are going well for them, like our enemies, who persecute the Word by trusting in their own power. They believe it is God's will that they earn something before Him by their diligence and devotion and thus reconcile Him to themselves. From this there have arisen monasteries, monastic rules, cowls, cords, Masses, pilgrimages, and similar foolish services, which nature has invented for itself against and beyond the Word, because it lacks the knowledge of God. Are these not sure signs that as far as God and the worship of God are concerned, natural powers are very corrupt? In the Old Testament this was proved by the various services to idols, by the contempt of the prophets and of the Word of God, and by similar sins which through the prophets God condemned in His thankless people.

We cannot say that the natural powers are perfect even in civil matters. We see what great contempt there is for laws that prescribe what is right, how great is the breakdown of the discipline on account of which God instituted laws and authority. A physician is often deceived in mixing

7 Luther refers here to Gabriel Biel's distinction between the substance of the act (*quoad substantiam actus*) and the intention of the lawgiver (*quoad intentionem praecipientis*). See *Lectures on Romans* (1515–16), LW 25:261 (see above, pp. 16–17); *Lectures on Galatians* (1531), LW 26:128 (see above, p. 233).

drugs, and sometimes by his inexperience he kills a sick man. Thus the very light of the eyes, the ears, and all the other organs acquired a fault through sin. They are not as sound and perfect as they were in Adam before sin. This corruption of the senses is obvious. Now what condition do you suppose exists in spiritual matters? Through sin we are completely turned away from God, so that we do not think correctly about God but think of Him simply as we do of an idol. . . .

The proper subject of theology

Therefore our sin is that we are born and conceived in sin. This David learned from his own experience. He defines sin as the corruption of all powers, inward and outward. No member performs its function now as it did in Paradise before sin. We have turned away from God, full of an evil conscience and subject to illness and death, as the words of the punishment show (Gen. 2:17): "In the day that you eat of it you shall die." We learn this only from the Word. The Gentiles who are without the Word do not properly understand these evils even though they lie right in the middle of them. They suppose that death is some sort of natural necessity, not a punishment for sin. Thus they cannot properly evaluate any of human nature, because they do not know the source from which these calamities have come upon mankind. The psalm teaches this knowledge of sin and of all human nature. It does not only present an example—though we are grateful to the scholastics for at least leaving us that much—but includes the whole teaching of spiritual religion about the knowledge of God, the knowledge of our own nature, sin, grace, and the like. Therefore we believe that this psalm is a general instruction for all the people of God from the time it was composed until the present day. In it David, or rather the Holy Spirit in David, instructs us in the knowledge of God and of ourselves. He does both of these gloriously. First he clearly shows sin, then the knowledge of God, without which there is despair.

This knowledge of sin, moreover, is not some sort of speculation or an idea which the mind thinks up for itself. It is a true feeling, a true experience, and a very serious struggle of the heart, as he testifies when he says (v. 3), "I know (that is, I feel or experience) my transgressions." This is what the Hebrew word really means. It does not mean, as the pope taught, to call to mind what one has done and what one has failed to do; but it means to feel and to experience the intolerable burden of the wrath of God. The knowledge of sin is itself the feeling of sin, and the sinful man is the one who is oppressed by his conscience and tossed to and fro, not knowing where to turn. Therefore we are not dealing here with the philosophical knowledge of man, which defines man as a rational animal and so forth. Such things are for science to discuss, not for theology. So a lawyer speaks of man as an owner and master of property, and a physician speaks of man as healthy or sick. But a theologian discusses man as a sinner. In theology, this is the essence of man. The theologian is concerned that man become aware of this nature of his, corrupted by sins. When this happens, despair follows, casting him into hell. In the face of the righteous God, what shall a man do who knows that his whole nature has been crushed by sin and that there is nothing left on which he can rely, but that his righteousness has been reduced to exactly nothing? When the mind has felt this much, the other part of this knowledge should follow. This is not a matter of speculation either, but completely of practice and feeling. A man hears and learns what grace and justification are, what God's plan is for the man who has fallen into hell, namely, that He has decided to restore man through Christ. Here the dejected mind cheers up, and on the basis of this teaching of grace it joyfully declares: "Although I am a sinner in myself, I am not a sinner in Christ, who has been made righteousness for us (1 Cor. 1:30). I am righteous and justified through Christ, the Righteous and the Justifier, who is and is called the Justifier because He belongs to sinners and was sent for sinners."

This is the twofold theological knowledge which David teaches in this psalm, so that the content of the psalm is the theological knowledge of man and also the theological knowledge of God. Let no one, therefore, ponder the divine Majesty, what God has done and how mighty He is; or think of man as the master of his property, the way the lawyer does; or of his health, the way the physician does. But let him think of man as sinner. The proper subject of theology is man guilty of sin and condemned, and God the Justifier and Savior of man the sinner. Whatever is asked or discussed in theology outside this subject is error and poison. All Scripture points to this, that God commends His kindness to us and in His Son restores to righteousness and life the nature that has fallen into sin and condemnation. The issue here is not this physical life—what we should eat, what work we should undertake, how we should rule our family, how we should till the soil. All these things were created before man in Paradise and were put into man's hands when God said (Gen. 1:28), "Have dominion over the fish of the sea and over the birds of the air." The issue here is the future and eternal life; the God who justifies, repairs, and makes alive; and man, who fell from righteousness and life into sin and eternal death. Whoever follows this aim in reading the Holy Scriptures will read holy things fruitfully.

Therefore this theological knowledge is necessary: A man should know himself, should know, feel, and experience that he is guilty of sin and subject to death; but he should also know the opposite, that God is the Justifier and Redeemer of a man who knows himself this way. The care of other men, who do not know their sins, let us leave to lawyers, physicians, and parents, who discuss man differently from the way a theologian does. Now I come to the psalm.

Psalm 51:1

Have mercy on me, O God, according to Thy steadfast love; according to Thy abundant mercy blot out my transgressions.

David mentions God and makes no reference to Christ. Here at the very beginning you should be reminded of something so that you do not think that David is talking about God like a Mohammedan or like some other Gentile. David is talking with the God of his fathers, with the God who promised. The people of Israel did not have a God who was viewed "absolutely," to use the expression, the way the inexperienced monks rise into heaven with their speculations and think about God as He is in Himself. From this absolute God everyone should flee who does not want to perish, because human nature and the absolute God—for the sake of teaching we use this familiar term—are the bitterest of enemies. Human weakness cannot help being crushed by such majesty, as Scripture reminds us over and over. Let no one, therefore, interpret David as speaking with the absolute God. He is speaking with God as He is dressed and clothed in His Word and promises, so that from the name "God" we cannot exclude Christ, whom God promised to Adam and the other patriarchs. We must take hold of this God, not naked but clothed and revealed in His Word; otherwise certain despair will crush us. This distinction must always be made between the prophets who speak with God and the Gentiles. The Gentiles speak with God outside His Word and promises, according to the thoughts of their own hearts; but the prophets speak with God as He is clothed and revealed in His promises and Word. This God, clothed in such a kind appearance and, so to speak, in such a pleasant mask, that is to say, dressed in His promises—this God we can grasp and look at with joy and trust. The absolute God, on the other hand, is like an iron wall, against which we cannot bump without destroying ourselves. Therefore Satan is busy day and night, making us run to the naked God so that we forget His promises and blessings shown in Christ and think about God and the judgment of God. When this happens, we perish utterly and fall into despair. . . .

Have mercy on me

I wanted to mention this first because of other passages in the prophets. Now we must consider whether it is appropriate for him to say, "Have mercy on me." If you look at the persons dealing with each other here, God and the sinner David, their great dissimilarity and an insoluble contradiction will appear. Is it not the feeling of all nature and a judgment of all men that God hates sin? As the blind man says (John 9:31), "We know that God does not listen to sinners, but if anyone is a worshiper of God and does His will, God listens to him." In the Decalogue it says (Exod. 20:5), "I, the Lord, your God, am a jealous God." Yes, throughout Moses there is almost nothing but sheer threats against the wicked and disobedient, and the feeling of nature agrees with the Law of Moses, a feeling we cannot eradicate in any way. All men judge this way: "You are a sinner, but God is righteous. Therefore He hates you, therefore He inflicts punishments upon you, therefore He does not hear you." Nothing in our nature can deny this conclusion. Hence almost all the holy fathers who wrote about the psalms expounded "the righteous God" to mean that He righteously avenges and punishes, not that He justifies. So it happened to me when I was a young man that I hated this name for God, and from this deep habit I still shudder today when I hear someone say, "the righteous God." So great is the power of wicked teaching if the mind is imbued with it from childhood. Yet almost all the early theologians expound it this way. But if God is righteous in such a way that He righteously punishes according to deserts, who can stand before this righteous God? For we are all sinners and bring before God a righteous reason for Him to inflict punishment. Out of here with such a righteousness and such a righteous God! He will devour us all like a consuming fire (Deut. 4:24). Because God sent Christ as Savior, He certainly does not want to be righteous in punishing according to deserts. He wants to be righteous and to be called righteous in justifying and having mercy on those who acknowledge their sins.

Therefore when David the sinner says, "Have mercy on me, O God," it sounds as though he were speaking against the whole Decalogue, in which God commands you not to be a sinner and threatens sinners with punishment. What harmony can there be between a sinner and God, who is righteous and truthful, the enemy and foe of sinners, who by His very nature cannot stand sins? Yet David, who later says (v. 3), "I know my transgressions, and my sin is ever before me," this David, I say, calls on God and says, "Have mercy on me." This is really what they call the conjunction of two things that are incompatible. So at the very beginning David shows an art and a wisdom that is above the wisdom of the

Decalogue, a truly heavenly wisdom, which is neither taught by the Law nor imagined or understood by reason without the Holy Spirit.

Nature always thinks this way, and it says to itself: "I dare not lift my eyes to heaven; I am afraid of the sight of God. I know both that I am a sinner and that God hates sins. So what shall I pray?" Here a very hard battle begins. Either the mind is confused within itself by the consciousness of sin and believes that it should delay praying until it finds some worthiness within itself, so to speak; or it looks around at human counsels and sophistic consolations so that it first thinks about satisfactions that will enable it to come before God with some confidence in its own worthiness and say, "Have mercy on me, O God." This is the constant belief of our nature, but it is highly dangerous. It encourages our minds to trust in our own righteousness and to think we can please God with our own works. This is a blasphemous presumption of our own merits against the merit of Christ. Since we are born in sins, it follows that we shall never pray unless we pray before we feel that we are pure of all sins.

Therefore we must drive away this blasphemous notion. In the very midst of our sins, or to put it more meaningfully, in the very sea of our sins, we must use the means David uses here, so that we do not put off praying. What does the word "have mercy" accomplish if those who pray are pure and do not need mercy? As I have said, this is a very bitter battle, that in the very feeling of sin a mind can be aroused to cry to God, "Have mercy on me." From my own example I have sometimes learned that prayer is the most difficult of almost all works, I who teach and command others! Therefore I do not profess to be a master of this work, but rather confess that in great danger I have often repeated the words very coldly, "Have mercy on me, O God," because I was offended by my unworthiness. Still the Holy Spirit won out by telling me: "Whatever you may be, surely you must pray! God wants you to pray and to be heard because of His mercy, not because of your worthiness."

Two types of sinners

For a proper understanding of the fact that God hates sinners and loves the righteous, we must distinguish between the sinner who feels his sins and the sinner who does not feel his sins. God does not want the prayer of a sinner who does not feel his sins, because he neither understands nor wants what he is praying for. Thus a monk living in superstition often sings and mumbles, "Have mercy on me, O God." But because he lives with trust in his own righteousness and does not feel the uncleanness of his own heart, he is merely reciting syllables and neither understands nor wants the thing itself. Besides, he adds things that contradict his prayer. He prays for forgiveness, he prays for mercy; meanwhile, by this means or that he is looking for expiation of his sin and for satisfaction. Is not this really an open mockery of God? It is just as though a beggar were constantly crying out for alms and when someone offered him some, he would begin to brag about his riches, that is, his poverty, and thus clearly show that he does not need the alms.

Thus the enemies of the Gospel count words. Not only do they fail to understand this, but they do things that contradict it, when they undertake various acts of worship, when they look for the forgiveness of sins by wicked Masses, pilgrimages, invocation of the saints, and the like. Such sinners, who are sinners but do not feel that they are sinners, who go along with stubborn brow and justify themselves, who persecute the Word of God—such people, I say, should be kept far away from all mercy. Before them you should set sayings of wrath, in which God does not offer mercy but eternal punishments, as in the First Commandment (Exod. 20:5): "I am a jealous God, visiting the iniquity of the fathers upon the children to the third and the fourth generation." To them you should set forth examples of divine wrath, the destruction of Sodom, the coming of the flood over all flesh, the scattering of the holy people, and whatever other fearful spectacles of the judgment and wrath of God there may be in the Scriptures. Thus the callous and impenitent sinners will be brought to a knowledge of themselves, and they will begin a serious plea for mercy. These are the ones of whom it is said, "God hates the sinners; God does not hear the sinners."

The other sinners are those who feel their sins and the wrath of God and who are afraid before the face of God. These people apply to themselves the threats set forth in the Word of God, and the fearful examples of divine wrath so depress them that they are afraid of the very same punishments because of their sins. When, amid these terrors, the mind has thus been crushed by the hammer of the Law and the judgment of God, this is really the place, time, and occasion to grasp this divine wisdom. Then the heart consoles itself and is sure that when God is wrathful against sinners, He is wrathful only against those who are hard and callous. About those who feel the burden of their sins, it is said (Ps. 147:11): "The Lord takes pleasure in those who fear Him." Then the Law has done enough, the lightning flashes of the wrathful God should stop, and in their place should shine the lights of mercy set forth in the Word of God: that the Lord takes pleasure in those who fear Him; that God does not despise a contrite and humble heart (Ps. 51:17); that His ears are open (Ps. 10:17) and His eyes attentive to the needy to lift him from the ash heap (Ps. 113:7); that He helps the bruised reed and restores the dimly burning wick (Isa. 42:3). Such people are "the most tender little worm"—as Jerome's translation says of David in 2 Sam. 23:8, though it is not in the Hebrew—and the tender flower, which is moved and shaken by even the slightest breeze of divine threatening. The others, the callous, meanwhile stand unmoved by any preaching of repentance, like iron mountains in a great storm. Amid these terrors of conscience, therefore, you must see to it that these terrified minds do not judge according to their nature and sense, since this would plunge them into despair. Just as sicknesses that are different in nature have different remedies, so those who are terrified should be strengthened with words of grace, while those who are hard should be smashed with a rod of iron. In such dangers of conscience the pope with his theologians cannot give sound advice, as I experienced for myself. They all judge according to nature, which says, "I am a sinner, but God is righteous; therefore the same punishment awaits me as awaits other sinners." Here nature shrinks back and cannot see the rays of mercy in the clouds of divine wrath.

Have mercy "on me"

But here comes our true theology and teaches that when minds are terrified this way, then one part of theology is finished, the part that uses the Law and its threats. Thus the sinner begins to know himself and casts out the smugness in which we all naturally live before this revelation of wrath. We must not stop here, but go on to the knowledge of the other part of theology, the part that fulfills the whole of theological knowledge: that God gives grace to the humble (1 Pet. 5:5). Those threats and horrible examples apply to the hardened and smug sinners; to them God is jealous and a devouring fire (Deut. 4:24). The contrite and fearful are the people of grace, whose wounds the Good Shepherd wants to bind up and heal, the Shepherd who gives His life for the sheep (John 10:11). Such people should not give in to the thoughts of their hearts, which persuade them that because of their sins they ought not to pray or hope for grace. With David they should cry out, "Have mercy on me, O God," for such people are well-pleasing to God. The theology of this psalm is unknown to the schools of the Papists. Look at David here. With his mouth open he breaks out in the words "Have mercy on me, O God." Thus he combines things that by nature are dissimilar, God and himself the sinner, the Righteous and the unrighteous. That gigantic mountain of divine wrath that so separates God and David, he crosses by trust in mercy and joins himself to God. This is really what our theology adds to the Law. To call on God and to say, "Have mercy," is not a great deal of work. But to add the particle "on me"—this is really what the Gospel inculcates so earnestly, and yet we experience how hard it is for us to do it. This "on me" hinders almost all our prayers, when it ought to be the only reason and highest occasion for praying.

Therefore we must first study David's example so that we may rightly look at the pronoun "on me" and be sure that it means a sinner, as he clearly points out later when he says (v. 5), "I was conceived in sin." There he confesses that this "me" is the greatest of sinners. Let us also learn this so that the crowd of thoughts that seek to hinder us might rather urge us on even more to cry out to God, as we read of the blind man in the Gospel that, when he was rebuked, "he cried out all the more" (Mark 10:48). In ourselves we experience this crowd of thoughts upbraiding us: "Why do you want to pray? Do you not know what you are and what God is?" This crowd of thoughts is very burdensome for the spirit, and it hinders very many. We must despise it and pray for the very reason that seems to call us away from prayer, so that somehow we break through that crowd to Christ and ask for mercy. Those who do this pray rightly, but a truly great struggle of spirit is necessary. I have learned from my own experience that these thoughts often drove prayer away from me. Nevertheless, by the grace of God I came to the knowledge that I must not surrender to Satan as he attacked me with his arrows, but tearing them from him by the power of the Spirit I turned the weapons against the enemy himself and said: "You frighten me away from prayer because I am a sinner. But I see that I must pray most of all because of this one reason, that I am a very great sinner and have need of mercy."

The same must be done in the very heat of temptation, when the mind is tempted with thoughts of lust or vengeance. If someone is urged to pray under these circumstances, the mind immediately protests that it is impure, as though among these dirty thoughts there could be no room for prayer. Here you should insist on the contrary that we must not expect temptation to end or thoughts of lust or other vice to disappear completely from the mind. In the very moment in which you feel that the temptation is strongest and that you are least prepared for prayer, go off into a solitary place (Matt. 6:6), and pray the Lord's Prayer or whatever you can say against Satan and his temptation. Then you will feel the temptation subsiding and Satan turning tail. If anyone thinks that prayer should be put off until the mind is clean of impure thoughts, he is doing nothing but using his wisdom and strength to help Satan, who is already more than strong enough. This is really heathen and sophistic religion, the very teaching of Satan. Against it we must maintain the example and teaching of this psalm, where we see that David, viewing his total impurity and his special sin of the flesh, does not flee from God, the way Peter foolishly said in the ship (Luke 5:8), "Depart from me, for I am a sinful man, O Lord." But with trust in mercy he breaks out in prayer and says, "Lord, if I am a sinner, just as I am, have mercy on me." Just because our hearts really feel sin, we ought to come to God through prayer all the more. Formerly we had to flee and be afraid of God, when there was danger that we might fall into sin. Since the fall we ought to hope for forgiveness and ask for it instead of remaining in thoughts of wrath and fear. Now Satan is trying to turn that order around, so that in committing sins we are smug and without the fear of God, and after they have been committed, we remain in fear, without hope or trust in mercy.

Look at David, as I said, clearly taking refuge in mercy and saying, "Have mercy on me, O God." It is as though he were saying: "I know that I am evil and a sinner, and that Thou art righteous. That I arise and dare to pray, all this I do with trust in Thy Word and promises. I know that Thou art not the god of the Mohammedans or the monks, but the God of our fathers, who hast promised that Thou wilt redeem sinners—not simply sinners but such sinners as know and feel that they are sinners." Therefore let us also dare to say: "Have mercy on me, O God. I am a sinner, tempted by flesh and blood, anger and hate. But my hope is in Thy mercy and goodness, which Thou hast promised to those who thirst for righteousness (Matt. 5:6)." This cannot be adequately expressed in words, but our own experience is necessary in addition. This teaches what hard work it is to climb over the mountain of our own unworthiness and sins standing between God and us as we are about to pray. Although it is here that we feel the weakness of faith most, still we ought to hold to the consolation that we are not alone in saying, "Have mercy on me, O God." The Spirit is saying and praying the same thing with us in our hearts, "with sighs too deep for words" (Rom. 8:26). As we do not see or fully understand these sighs, so God, who is also a spirit, sees them most clearly and understands them most fully. Struggling in the midst of conflict or of temptation, therefore, we ought to resist Satan with trust in this Intercessor and say: "If I am a sinner, so what? God is merciful. If I am unfit for prayer because of my sins, well and good. I do not want to become more fit. For, alas, to God I am more than fit for prayer, because I am an exceedingly great sinner."

It is the teaching of this passage that conscious sinners—I call them this for instruction's sake—should have courage, and that God the Righteous and man the sinner should be reconciled, so that in our sins we are not afraid of God but sing with David, "Have mercy." To keep the pronoun "on me" and the name "God" from hindering us, let us put between them the verb "have mercy," by which God and man the sinner are reconciled. Unless this happens, we shall not only be unable to sing this psalm properly, but we shall also be unable to pray the Lord's Prayer correctly, because in this life it will never happen that we are pure of all sins. Even though "actual sins," as they are called, may be absent—and this is very rare—still original sin will not be absent. Since we are continually in sin, we must also continually pray, as the reverent hearts of Christians pray every moment, because every moment they see their unworthiness and want it forgiven. These constant sighs of the Christian heart are disturbed and covered by thoughts, and sometimes by duties, so that we do not always see them. Therefore it is really a theological virtue to cover our sin with prayer this way, and when we feel our weakness, to take refuge in this song: "Have mercy on me, O God." . . .

God's abundant mercy

At the outset we reminded you that we should not only look at the example of David here, but should change the psalm into a general teaching that applies to all men without exception. Thus the Epistle to the Romans (3:4) quotes as a general statement the words (Ps. 116:11) that all men are liars, and also says (Rom. 11:32): "God has consigned all men to disobedience, that He may have mercy upon all." In the same way we said about David that he includes the death and life of the whole human race, not merely his own sin. Therefore God is the same sort of God to all men that He was to David, namely, one who forgives sins and has mercy upon all who ask for mercy and acknowledge their sins.

Also pertinent here is his use of repetition or, rather, amplification, when he adds: "According to Thy abundant mercy blot out my transgression." He asked previously that God in mercy should turn His eyes away from his sins; in this phrase he does the same, but with greater agitation and spirit. He takes hold of God the Promiser and turns the whole vision of his heart upon His mercy. He could not do this if he had not taken hold of God the Promiser with the help of the Spirit and known that in God there remained a hope of forgiveness for sinners, as he says in another psalm (Ps. 130:4): "There is forgiveness with Thee, that Thou mayest be feared." He is not looking for satisfaction, nor for a corner where he can prepare for grace, but by a direct course he steers for the countenance of God and His mercy. This he knows not from his own heart nor from the dictates of right reason—for in sin, reason flees from God, and the conscience cannot raise itself to the light by which it believes that God has mercy, grace, and favor left for sinners—but from the promises which he sees broadcast everywhere, even in the Law and the Decalogue. Even though God threatens sinners here, He still keeps the name "a God merciful" (Exod. 34:6). The promises to Adam, to Abraham, and to others testify to the same thing. In our temptations we must do likewise.

Whenever we are stung and vexed in our conscience because of sins, let us simply turn our attention from sin and wrap ourselves in the bosom of the God who is called Grace and Mercy, not doubting at all that He wants to show grace and mercy to miserable and afflicted sinners, just as He wants to show wrath and judgment to hardened sinners. This is true theology, which this verse of the psalm also manifests when it says, "According to Thy abundant mercy blot out my transgressions." . . .

Now look how beautifully David combines these two things: first, that God is merciful, that is, that He freely blesses us undeserving ones; second, that He gives us the forgiveness of sins, which we accept by faith through the Holy Spirit and His promises. If God did not freely forgive, we should have no satisfaction and no remedy left. Not by our fasting nor by other works, not by angels nor by any other creature, is there salvation. Our only salvation is if we flee to the mercy of God and seek blessing and forgiveness from God, asking Him not to look at our sins and transgressions, but to close His eyes and to deal with us according to His steadfast love and abundant mercy. Unless God does this, we are not worthy of being granted one hour of life or one morsel of bread.

Here, too, we experience that it is a great and difficult art to combine these two things and to fix our eyes only on the steadfast love of God and His abundant mercy. For these words are not born in our house, but are brought down from heaven by the Holy Spirit. On the other hand, these thorns are born in our hearts: "I am a sinner, and God is righteous and angry at me the sinner." The conscience cannot pluck out these thorns; it cannot put the sinner before a gracious and forgiving God. This is the gift of the Holy Spirit, not of our free will or strength. When men are without the Spirit of God, either their hearts are hardened in sins or they despair; but both are contrary to the will of God. Therefore by the Holy Spirit David navigates between this satanic Scylla and Charybdis and throws himself securely on the abundant and endless mercy of God, saying: "Many and great are Thy abundant mercies, O Lord. But I am a sinner. I have lived badly, I am living badly, and I shall live badly as long as I live. If I want to come before Thee, I must bring other thoughts than those which my heart grants me. Therefore I confess my sins before Thee, for they are many (as he says in Ps. 32:5). But I confess my sin in such a way that at the same time I confess Thy steadfast love and Thy abundant mercies, immensely greater than my sin; as well as Thy righteousness, by which Thou dost justify sinners, infinitely more abundant than that I should despair over it." Hence he says "abundant mercy." By saying that the mercies are abundant, he simply denies and rejects any holiness, whether his own or other people's. What connection could there be between abundant mercy and human holiness? If mercy is this abundant, then there is no holiness in us. Then it is a fictitious expression to speak of a "holy man," just as it is a fictitious expression to speak of God's falling into sin; for by the nature of things, this cannot be.

What is holiness?

For this reason we must reject those very ancient and deep-rooted errors by which in monastic fashion we speak of Jerome or Paul as "holy." In themselves they are sinners, and only God is holy, as the church sings. Those whom we call "holy" are made holy by an alien holiness, through Christ, by the holiness of free mercy. In this holiness the whole church of the faithful is the same, there is no difference. As Peter is holy, so I am holy. As I am holy, so the thief on Christ's right hand is holy. It does not matter that Peter and Paul did greater things than you or I. On both sides we are sinners by nature, and we have need of steadfast love and abundant mercy. Although the apostles had fewer outward sins, still in their hearts they often felt presumption, loathing, thoughts of despair, denial of God, and similar defects of human weakness. So you see nothing holy, nothing good in man, as the psalm says (Ps. 53:2–3): "God looks down from heaven upon the sons of men. . . . There is none that does good, no, not one." If there are not good people among the sons of men, where else could they be? Therefore let us keep quiet about holiness and holy people. We know that those have been made holy who have become conscious sinners instead of unconscious sinners. They do not presume to have any righteousness of their own—for it is nonexistent—but begin to have an enlightened heart. Thus they know themselves and God. They know that everything that is ours is evil before God and is forgiven by the free forgiveness of mercy. We and all "saints" must take refuge in this bosom, or we must be damned. God sent His Son to reveal these abundant mercies to the world and to make known this teaching, which the human heart and reason do not know. David presents it to us here when he confesses his sins and yet confesses that mercy is greater.

Let all men sing this verse with David and acknowledge that they are sinners but that God is righteous, that is, merciful. This confession is a sacrifice acceptable and pleasing to God, and David invites us to it. He wants this to be a teaching for the whole world. When the devil or our conscience accuses us because of our sins, we can freely confess that our sins are many and great, but not despair because of them. For though our sins are many and great, nevertheless we are taught here that the mercies of God are also many and great. With this argument all the saints have defended themselves against Satan, that though they were sinners, yet they are made holy by this knowledge, according to Isa. 53:11: "The knowledge of Christ will justify many."

When we have once heard this, we suppose that it is easy and can be learned quickly, but it takes effort and work to hold on to this in temptation. This is no quibble about trifles. The danger of eternal death is involved, and we are struggling over the salvation of our souls. We also experience not only our conscience crying out, but Satan inspiring thoughts of death because of the sins of which we are conscious. Therefore it is completely a divine power to be able to say that I am a sinner and yet not to despair. We do not come to it, as do our adversaries, by minimizing sin. Rather we should do it this way: As by its nature sin is very great and serious, so we believe that grace or mercy is immense and inexhaustible. Thus David confesses here with a loud voice, "According to Thy abundant mercy blot out my transgressions."

Psalm 51:2

Wash me more abundantly from my iniquity, and cleanse me from my sin.

So far he has been asking for grace and the remission of sins, or forgiveness, that God would be favorable to him and to us all, forgive sin, and blot it out according to His mercy. After the recognition of sin, this is the first part or the first stage, to accept grace, to have a God of favor and blessing, to be in the lap of God's mercy, and to have confidence in the sure promises that have been given us about the grace of God. Just as we have those promises in Baptism, they had them in the Christ who was promised. In this verse, where he asks to be washed from his sin, he sets forth a distinction of sin different from the one we discussed earlier. Earlier we divided sin into conscious sin, to use the word, and unconscious sin, just as we made two kinds of sinners, conscious and unconscious sinners, or true and holy sinners and hypocrites, who in their hardness and smugness do not feel their sin.

Here he shows that this "conscious sin" is also of two kinds, or can be looked at from two points of view. There is the sin forgiven through grace, and there is the sin left in the flesh. The sin forgiven through grace is that for Christ's sake God does not want to forsake us, great sinners though we may be, but wants mercifully to forgive us, who are condemned and corrupted by sins. It is not enough that this sin is forgiven through grace, for through our infirmity we fall right back into sin. Therefore we want sin not only to be forgiven, but to be completely removed. As Augustine says, "Sin remains in fact but passes away in guilt."[8] That is, the thing itself, which is truly sin and is remitted and forgiven by God, still remains in the flesh and is not completely dead. Although the head of the serpent has been crushed by Christ, as it is said in Gen. 3:15, still it is quivering with its tongue and threatening His heel with its tail. Because the grace and mercy of God reign over us, sin cannot condemn us nor make God wrathful against us. Nevertheless, in the justified there are still remnants of sin, like lust and other vices. These the prophet sees in himself as dung or seed plots; and as earlier he asked for the forgiveness of sins, so here he prays for the cleansing and uprooting of these remnants.

Thus this is the second part of the petition, which, as I have said, shows us the second distinction of sin: God wants to wipe out the sins as far as the forgiveness of their guilt and their power are concerned, but not as far as the thing itself or the nature of sin is concerned. The power of sin is to accuse, condemn, sting, sadden, disquiet the heart, show a wrathful God, hell, and the like. This power of sin is done away with through free mercy, and yet there remain true remnants of this poison. Therefore both statements are true: "No Christian has sin" and "Every Christian has sin." From this there arises the distinction that with Christians there are two kinds of sin, the sin that is forgiven and the sin that remains, which must still be destroyed and washed away. This latter kind of sin is forgiven; it has been crushed by trust in mercy so that it no longer condemns or accuses. Yet because of this flesh it still sprouts and struggles within our flesh to bring forth fruits like the old fruits, to make us smug, thankless, and ignorant of God, as we used to be. These are the efforts of the remnants of sin in us, which even the saints feel, but through the Holy Spirit they do not give in to them.

Alien righteousness

Once a Christian is righteous by faith and has accepted the forgiveness of sins, he should not be so smug, as though he were pure of all sins. For only then does he face the constant battle with the remnants of sin, from which the prophet here wants to be cleansed. He is righteous and holy by an alien or foreign holiness—I call it this for the sake of instruction—that is, he is righteous by the mercy and grace of God. This mercy and grace is not something human; it is not some sort of disposition or quality in the heart. It is a divine blessing, given us through the true knowledge of the Gospel, when we know or believe that our sin has been forgiven us through the grace and merit of Christ and when we hope for steadfast love and abundant mercy for Christ's sake, as the prophet says here. Is not this righteousness an alien righteousness? It consists completely in

8 Augustine, *Marriage and Desire* 1.26 (WSA 1/24:46).

the indulgence of another and is a pure gift of God, who shows mercy and favor for Christ's sake.

This becomes clear through an analogy. If someone has earned capital punishment in the court of some prince and if the prince remits this out of grace, would you not say that this guilt was forgiven him by the gracious blessing of the kind prince, not by his own merit? He merited nothing but execution. But for such a man it is not enough to forgive the guilt he has committed. His bonds must be loosed, he must be clothed, something must be put into his hands to live by. The same thing happens to us in the transaction of our justification. When by mercy we are free of guilt, then we still need the gift of the Holy Spirit to clean out the remnants of sin in us, or at least to help us, lest we succumb to sin and to the lusts of the flesh. As Paul says (Rom. 8:13) that by the Spirit we "put to death the deeds of the body." What happens to us is that most of us live in such smugness as though we were all spirit and nothing of the flesh were left at all. Therefore we must learn that the flesh still remains and that the task of the Spirit is to war against the flesh, lest the flesh accomplish that for which it lusts.

Therefore the Christian is not formally righteous, he is not righteous according to substance or quality—I use these words for instruction's sake.[9] He is righteous according to his relation to something: namely, only in respect to divine grace and the free forgiveness of sins, which comes to those who acknowledge their sin and believe that God is gracious and forgiving for Christ's sake, who was delivered for our sins (Rom. 4:25) and is believed in by us. After we have attained this righteousness by faith, then we need the bath or washing of which the psalm speaks. Sin does not condemn anymore, but it still remains to vex us. It keeps us from being caught up by love for God and believing with all our heart, the way we should like in spirit or the way God commands, and from being chaste, contented, and kindly. It is as though all our members were working against the Law of God with their vices. Unless we oppose and fight this with great effort, there is danger that these vices will grow stronger and drag us back into our old wickedness. Many examples of our own people teach us this; now that they have heard the Gospel, they are much worse than before, as the examples of the sects also testify. They are so smug as though their reason could not deceive them, as though they were without flesh. They admire the demonic thoughts that they add to the Word of God, and they broadcast them as though they were some sort of oracles. When this happens, there is no remedy left.

9 By these terms Luther means to say that a Christian is not righteous in himself but only in Christ.

To be washed daily

Against this smugness it is useful to consider David's prayer well. After he has asked for the forgiveness of sins as far as their guilt is concerned, and rejoices in God's mercy, he still asks for what remains: that he might be washed from his iniquities; that he might be granted the Holy Spirit, the power and gift that lives within the heart and cleanses the remnants of sin, which began to be buried through Baptism but have not been completely buried. This is the Christian life, as it is marvelously described in Col. 3:1–3, that we seek the things that are above, as men who are dead to the world and whose life is hid in Christ; and in 2 Cor. 7:1, that we "cleanse ourselves from every defilement of body and spirit." He means that in him and in all Christians there remain such defilements of the spirit, that is, evil opinions about God, and defilements of the flesh, that is, vicious lusts; and that it should be our labor and effort to clean these out with the help of the Spirit. Those who seem to themselves to be completely holy and without faults defile themselves in spirit, lose the faith, and develop opinions that resemble faith but actually come from the devil. These opinions make them smug and gradually lead them from the Word into ungodliness.

You can readily say, "I believe in Christ." But it takes the hardest kind of work to keep this faith fixed and sure and permanent in the heart. The defilement of the spirit remains, and neither our reason nor Satan stops working with all their powers to make us do without the Word and rule ourselves by our own opinions. From this there come sects and heresies, which hate us with bitter hatred and yet think of this hate of theirs not as sin, but as zeal. So they do not cleanse or wash away this sin, but increase it daily. Let us take care to be washed daily, to become purer day by day, so that daily the new man may arise and the old man may be crushed, not only for his death but also for our sanctification. It also belongs to this exercise of Christians not only that God lets the church be oppressed by various physical troubles, but also that He permits sects and heresies to arise so that the church might be exercised to keep the Word and faith and to clean out these remnants of sin. The Holy Spirit is given to believers in order to battle against the masks of wisdom in our hearts, which exalt themselves against the righteousness of God; and in order to arouse us to prayer and to the performance of the duties of humanity to all men, especially to the brethren, so that thus both mind and body might be exercised and we might become more holy day by day.

The confession is clear: "Christians are sinners." When washing is needed, this means that there is defilement and dirt. Because the scholastics understand only philosophical righteousness or a quality in the mind, they cannot harmonize this discord. They take righteousness to be a quality in the heart; when this is present, they suppose that the whole man is holy in spirit and flesh. When they hear that Paul was elected and yet was a sinner because of the remnants of sin clinging to his nature, they think they are hearing about some chimera that exists nowhere in all of nature. Hence they condemn us as heretics and threaten to burn us at the stake. Let them answer this noble and well-known psalm for us. What is the reason why, after steadfast love and mercy, that is, after justification, David still asks that he be cleansed? Having the forgiveness of sins and existing in grace, being neither accused nor condemned by any sin, David is nevertheless unclean and has a sin so unclean that all it lacks to make it a real sin is that it cannot condemn him. David the righteous and the justified still has sin, and is still partly unrighteous. He prays for the greatest gift of the Holy Spirit to clean out these dirty spots, and this gift surely proves that the washing is no game or joke.

We must avoid minimizing these remnants of sin. If you minimize them, you also minimize Him who cleanses them and the gift of cleansing—the Holy Spirit. The prophet expressly calls these remnants sin and iniquity, even though it is not the sin that it was previously, since its head has been cut off by the forgiveness of sins. The prophet does not simply say, "Wash me," but he adds: "more abundantly, or much, today, tomorrow, and so throughout life, from the defilements of body and spirit. Thus day by day I can become stronger and surer against the terrors of the Law, till I finally become master of the Law and of sin through full confidence in Thy mercy." This is the teaching of this psalm and our perpetual school, from which we never graduate as perfect masters, neither we nor the apostles nor the prophets. We all remain students here, and as long as we live, we all ask to be washed thoroughly.

These are the two parts of justification. The first is grace revealed through Christ, that through Christ we have a gracious God, so that sin can no longer accuse us, but our conscience has found peace through trust in the mercy of God. The second part is the conferring of the Holy Spirit with His gifts, who enlightens us against the defilements of spirit and flesh (2 Cor. 7:1). Thus we are defended against the opinions with which the devil seduces the whole world. Thus the true knowledge of God grows daily, together with other gifts, like chastity, obedience, and patience. Thus our body and its lusts are broken so that we do not obey them. Those who do not have this gift or do not use it this way, but fall into the uncleanness of either the flesh or the spirit, so that they approve of all doctrines without discrimination—they are dominated by the flesh, and they do not know the bath of the Holy Spirit for which David is asking here.

Psalm 51:3

For I know my iniquity, and my sin is ever before me.

We have heard two verses of the psalm, in which David asked first for grace and the forgiveness of sins, then for the gift that would purify and cleanse the dirt or remnants of sin. These two things perfectly absolve a righteous and holy man in the sight of God, without all our preparations and satisfactions and without the counterfeit repentance which we have taught the people until now and which the Papists still teach. There is only one cause for justification, namely, the merit of Christ, or the gracious mercy which hearts that are ignited by the Holy Spirit grasp by faith. If someone wants to, he may list the acknowledgment of sin as a second cause . . . . It is the sort of cause that the whole thing still depends on the mercy of God or on the promise, that God has promised He will have mercy on those who acknowledge their sins and thirst for righteousness (Matt. 5:6). Otherwise, if you are talking about the nature of sin, even about the "conscious sinner," as we called him above, on the basis of Law and nature, he deserves nothing but the deepest punishment and wrath. When such people escape punishment and wrath, it is all by the mercy of God, who has promised that by freely forgiving their sin He wants to give life to those who feel their sins and the horrors of divine judgment. There is nothing that could in any way be cited as merit, because even the acknowledgment of sin is nothing except what the divine promise makes it. When sin is denounced and revealed by the Holy Spirit—as David in his mind looks not only at his own adultery, but generally at all of nature, which is completely deformed through sin—then if there were no other recourse than our rendering satisfaction, David would be crushed by the fear of the judgment of God and by despair, as we have often been taught by our own experience.

In the monasteries we were told to render satisfactions and to give an accurate confession of our sins, but our conscience did not find peace that way. We were advised to take the cowl, but in the cowl the same sorrows of mind continued that we had suffered before, and it did not help to throw off the cowl again. But this we experienced, by the kindness of God, that the readiest and surest remedy was to know or believe that God wants to forgive those who are terrified by their sin, and that He commands them to hope for the forgiveness of sins. By his example David shows that this doctrine of the promise was the reason he asked for mercy and the gifts that would purify him. The causative particle "for" which he uses here does not mean that the recognition of sin is the primary cause that merits the forgiveness of sins. For sin is sin, and by its nature it merits punishment, whether you acknowledge it or not. The acknowledgment of sin is a sort of corequisite in that God wishes to forgive sins to those who acknowledge them and does not wish to forgive sins to those who do not acknowledge them. This promise is the sole cause, the first, middle, and last cause; that is, it is everything in justification. At this promise David looks when he says, "For I know my iniquity." It is as though he would say: "I am not citing as some sort of merit the fact that I acknowledge my sin. But because Thou hast promised grace to those who acknowledge their sin, therefore I come before Thee to acknowledge my sin."

I know my sin

The word "know" is far more meaningful in Hebrew than it is in other languages. It means "to feel and experience something as it is according to its very nature." Thus Scripture says of Adam (Gen. 4:1) that he "knew" his wife, that is, that he experienced and felt her. Thus "God does not know the proud" (Ps. 138:6); that is, He does not care for them or advance them. In the same sense it is said here, "I know my sin." It is as though he were to say: "I have come to this place at the time for mercy and help. I have been changed from an unconscious to a conscious sinner. Now I know, that is, I truly feel my sin and God's judgment." This feeling is, indeed, the very death of nature, unless the Holy Spirit grants us thoughts of peace and the knowledge of the mercy of God, that God does not want to destroy such sinners. Here we need statements like those which the holy fathers undoubtedly used to ponder a great deal. Although He is talking there about physical blessing, the Lord says in Deut. 9:5: "Not because of your righteousness or the uprightness of your heart are you going in to possess the land of the nations." Again (Isa. 43:25): "I am the Lord, who blots out your transgressions." Again (Ezek. 33:11): "I do not want the death of the sinner." Here we also need some examples. When the people of Nineveh do penance, that is, when they are humbled in the acknowledgment of their sin, God retracts His sentence and says (Jon. 3:10): "I shall not destroy them." In the same way He forgives Ahab, whom He had threatened with the destruction of his family, and says to the prophet (1 Kings 21:29): "Have you seen how Ahab has humbled himself before Me?" From these histories there arises this theological knowledge of God: that God is the God of the humble, the afflicted, and the poor who acknowledge that they are sinners and fear God in such a way that they hope still more in His mercy. The holy fathers in the Old Testament undoubtedly knew such statements and examples very well and held them very dear. . . .

"And my sin is ever before me." That is: "It lies on my neck, it presses me, I cannot get rid of it." Be careful not to suppose that he is talking about the actual sin. The prophet is looking at his whole life, with all its own holiest righteousness, and he feels that none of these things will help him at all unless mercy comes. Thus the story is told of Bernard, a man of admirable holiness, that as his last word he said, "I have lived shamefully."[10] This is really to be looking at sin, not this or that misdeed, but our whole nature and our universal sin, with all our powers, with all the righteousness and wisdom of our flesh—to say that all these are nothing in the judgment of God. Bernard says with David, and David with all the saints (Ps. 143:2): "Lord, enter not into judgment with Thy servant." Sadoletus takes this to refer to actual sin.[11] He could not have found a better way to show his total ignorance of real theology. This is not said in an elegant address, but in actual experience, which the examples of David and other saints in the Holy Scriptures so marvelously illuminate, but which Sadoletus does not understand at all. I stress this all the more diligently because I have experienced how hard it is to teach it to those who have been brought up in scholastic theology. Yet we need this knowledge not only for ourselves but also for others when they must be consoled in a similar feeling of their sin. When it is looking at its sin, the mind does not dare to lift itself up, but it keeps singing this song to itself: "You are a sinner, therefore God hates you."

Such a conclusion is true in nature, in civil courts and judgment, and in all human affairs. There this conclusion certainly remains true, that you say, "You are a sinner in this or that sin, therefore the emperor or judge hates you." You must avoid, as the poison of Satan or the most loathsome pestilence, the transfer of this conclusion from the law court to the tribunal of Christ. Here it does not follow: "You are a sinner, therefore God hates you." But it follows: "You are a sinner, therefore have confidence, because God wants sinners who feel their sins." Otherwise no man would have been saved, neither the apostles nor the prophets. God has consigned all things to sin (Rom. 11:32; Gal. 3:22), but in order to have mercy on all. If, therefore, you acknowledge that you have sin, if you tremble, if you are troubled by a feeling of God's wrath and by a horror of God's judgment and of hell, then have confidence. You are the one with whom God wants to speak, to whom God wants to show His mercy, and whom He wants to save. This is what His promises say, that He is the God of the poor, who does not want the death of the sinner. He is not a God of

10 See above, p. 100 n. 5.

11 Jacopo Sadoleto (d. 1547), a cardinal and theologian, wrote a commentary on Psalm 51, published in 1526, from which Luther quotes here and below.

fury but of grace and peace. Therefore He wants the sinner to "turn from his way and live" (Ezek. 33:11). These consolations are not light words, based on the decrees of the fathers or the rules of the order. They are based on divine promises and on the almighty Word of God, and therefore hearts are lifted up and feel a firm and certain consolation.

Psalm 51:4

Against Thee only have I sinned and done that which is evil in Thy sight, so that Thou art justified in Thy sentences and victorious in Thy judgment.

This verse has been treated in various ways by various interpreters, and it has always been thought that this one piece is the most difficult in this psalm. Because Paul quoted it in the Epistle to the Romans (3:4), it came to be listed among the more difficult passages in all of Scripture. Although I freely leave it to others to remain with their interpretation, still I have the good hope that we shall not wander away from the true and proper meaning. Above all I want to remind the reader of what we pointed out at the beginning of the psalm, that David is speaking in the name of all the saints, not merely in his own name, in the name of the adulterer. I would not deny the possibility that his fall brought him to a knowledge of himself and of all human nature; as though he were to think: "Look at me, such a holy king! I have been so earnestly engaged in the holy service of the Law and of the worship of God. Now I have been so crushed and conquered by the inborn evil of the flesh and by sin that I have murdered an innocent man and adulterously taken away his wife. Is not this an obvious proof that human nature is more seriously infected and corrupted by sin than I could ever have suspected? Yesterday I was chaste; today I am an adulterer. Yesterday my hands were innocent of blood; now I am a man of blood." In this way it could have happened that from his fall into adultery and murder he acquired this general feeling of all sin and concluded from this that neither the tree nor the fruit of human nature is good, but that everything has been so deformed and destroyed by sin that there is nothing sound left in all of human nature. I want to remind the reader of this first of all, if he wants a sound interpretation of this passage.

Secondly, we must explain the grammar, which is somewhat obscure. What the translator rendered in the past tense ought to be in the present tense: "Against Thee only do I sin." That is: "I acknowledge that in Thy sight I am nothing but a sinner." And again: "I always do that which is evil in Thy sight." That is: "My whole life is evil and corrupt because of sin. In Thy sight I cannot boast of my merit or righteousness, but I am completely evil. Before Thee this is my name, that I do evil, that I have sinned, that I am sinning, that I shall sin forever." In this way the change of past tense into present takes us from the actual sin to universal sin. As a thoroughly inexperienced theologian but a man of great eloquence, Sadoletus tortures himself in various ways and so changes the sense that you cannot guess what he means. He takes the word "only" to mean that no one sees the sin but God. But who cannot see how inept this interpretation is!

Our first grammatical correction, then, is that these verbs in the past tense should be rendered in the present. The second is that the word "only" should be taken adverbially. Thus the proper, accurate, and simple interpretation is: "Only and solely against Thee do I sin. In Thy sight I am nothing but a sinner. Before Thy judgment I boast of no merit or righteousness, but I acknowledge that I am a sinner, and I implore Thy mercy." Thus the sentence becomes universal, as in John 1:9: "That enlightens every man." There he says that all human nature has been blinded by sin. Paul also supports this interpretation of this passage in Rom. 3:4, where he seems to have quoted it purposely in order to show how it is to be understood. In the same verse he sets up this universal statement: "Every man is a liar, so that He alone is true." The word "that" is to be interpreted the same way here. He does not mean that God's righteousness is increased by our sins, as slanderous people charged Paul with saying (Rom. 3:8). He simply says, "I sin only in Thy sight, I do evil only in Thy sight, so that it stands as true that Thou alone art righteous and the Justifier of sinners, that Thou alone dost free from sin in that Thou dost not impute it to those who trust in Thy mercy." . . .

Thus the sure and proper meaning of this verse is that when David looks at all of human nature, he denies any self-made righteousness to himself and to all men; and in a general confession he ascribes nothing to himself but sin, so that God has sole and complete claim to the title that He alone is righteous. Therefore this sentence does not imply what the blasphemers infer from it: "If God is justified from our sin, we shall sin even more." But something else does follow. The whole world is guilty of sin. Because God alone is righteous, the world cannot be freed from sin by any efforts, strivings, or works of its own. This glory of righteousness must be left to God alone, who is righteous and who justifies the wicked through faith in Christ. Therefore all those who feel and see this unhappiness of their nature should look for no other form or way of righteousness than through Him who alone is righteous. These two principal teachings of all Scripture are set down here: first, that our whole nature is condemned and destroyed by sin and cannot emerge from this calamity and death by its own powers or efforts; second, that God alone is righteous. Those who want to be freed from sin should take refuge in the righteous God by the confession of their sin, and should beg for His mercy, after the example of David. It is clear that this psalm is a most beautiful reminder, which the Holy Spirit has established in the church to teach us about very great and serious matters, which the age before could neither understand nor properly teach, because they had turned away from the Word to human dreams. We must judge and teach others from the Word, which clearly declares that God alone is righteous. Political or domestic righteousness will not free us, nor will any ceremonies. Even a prince or a husband who is righteous in the external administration of his office must say in the sight of God, "Against Thee only have I sinned; Thou only art righteous." But we shall discuss this in greater detail later. . . .

Our sin divinely revealed

Now since it is also part of sin that sin remains hidden in our nature and cannot be fully recognized, it had to be divinely revealed. This revelation of sin takes place through the Law and through the Gospel, or promise. Both teachings denounce sins, which we would neither know nor feel nor believe to be sins unless we were admonished by the Word of God. Hence the prophet expressly adds the clause "so that Thou art justified in Thy sentences." It is as though he were to say: "We are all sinners, but Thou art righteous, as Thy Word proclaims. To Thee I ascribe righteousness. To myself and to all men I ascribe sin, so that there is no righteousness with me but only with Thee. I do this, however, being informed by Thy sentences and Thy Word. If I were without the Word, I could not have the knowledge to talk this way about myself and all men. Whoever does not believe the Word will not confess that God alone is righteous nor that he is only a sinner. Therefore I believe Thy Word and declare that Thou knowest my nature and that of all men better than we do. According to the Word, I proclaim that we are sinners and will remain sinners as far as our nature is concerned, so that Thou art righteous and dost justify and glorify through this confession, which declares that I am a sinner while Thou art righteous and holy."

The Holy Spirit speaks the same way in Ps. 32:5: "I said, I will confess my transgression to the Lord; then Thou didst forgive the guilt of my sin." For the forgiveness of sins, therefore, this confession or knowledge is necessary, that we believe and confess that we are sinners and that the whole world is under the wrath of God. Thus the First Commandment denounces sin by its very promise. God promises: "I am the Lord, your God; that is, I am He through whom salvation will come to you against death and sin." This itself argues that our whole nature is punishable by death and sin. Why else should He promise that He will be God to us? Thus the Word of God—that is, both the Law and the Gospel, or promise—proves with clear and certain arguments that we are sinners and are saved by grace alone. If God promises life, it follows that we are under death. If He promises forgiveness of sins, it follows that sins dominate and possess us. Now, the wages of sin is death (Rom. 6:23). Both the threats and the promises all show the same thing. They were not addressed to the beasts, which abide in death. The divine voice and the promise of salvation were addressed to us men, against death, sin, and hell.

I have said this at length to show that this sentence is not metaphysical but theological, denouncing sin through the Word. Thus Paul clearly says (Rom. 7:7): "If it had not been for the Law, I should not have known sin"; not that he would not have had sin or would not have been in the world, but he would not have known sin. The issue here is not the essence of sin or sin metaphysically considered, but the knowledge of sin, that it is recognized and felt when the voice and sentences of God come and say in our heart, "You are a sinner, you are under the wrath of God and death." When this happens, then at last there begins that battle in which David admits he succumbed and was defeated. In the battle human nature struggles with God over whether this Word is true which declares that all men are under sin but God alone is righteous. Human nature rejects this statement and will not agree to it, that all its works are evil and sinful in the judgment of God. Thus the scholastics bitterly defend the statement that man has the right light of reason and his natural powers intact. This means not only a denial of sin, which has been divinely revealed, but also a denial that God alone is righteous when He declares that we are sinners.

The whole papacy and all the schools of the scholastics live in this perpetual contradiction. They do not want to acknowledge that they are nothing but sinners. They argue that reason has its light intact and that if there is any fault in our nature, only its lower part has been corrupted and is dragged along by lust and evil desire, while the higher part has an inextinguishable and pure light. If someone were to maintain this about civil matters, it would be true to some extent, though not altogether. Even in these matters we feel how much has been taken away from our nature by sin. When the issue is the knowledge of God or of sin or of human nature, however, then nothing could be farther from the truth. What remains, therefore, is that only through divine revelation in the Word can we know that we are sinners and that God is righteous.

When sins are thus revealed by the Word, two different kinds of men manifest themselves. One kind justifies God and by a humble confession agrees to His denunciation of sin; the other kind condemns God and calls Him a liar when He denounces sin. The greater part of the world belongs to this latter group, condemning and persecuting the Word by which sins are denounced. By this I do not mean only the Turks and the Jews, who are inflamed against Christian teaching with an obvious hatred. The pope is doing the same with his church. When they say that by the dictates of right reason they can elicit and perform the good, what is this but to deny that our nature is corrupted by sin? Then, too, there is the familiar and common statement of the schools: "If a man does as much as is in him, God inevitably grants His grace."[12] Is not this calling God a liar, since He says in His Word (Rom. 3:9–12): "They have all sinned; no one does good, not even one; all have turned aside and become useless." He is not denouncing merely shameful lust, evil desire, and greed, but worse things: that men turn aside from God; that nature neither needs nor cares about God; that it is without faith in times of calamity and without fear in times of prosperity. This proves that human reason as well as the will has been blinded and turned away from the good and the true. Yet because we teach and defend this, we are condemned as heretics and seized for punishment. Still that is what the psalm says here, that the wicked do not call God just in His sentence, but denounce and condemn Him.

Let us therefore learn that it is a sin to dispute with God this way and to denounce Him in His Word. Rather, this is what we should do. Even though we do not fully understand, we should believe our Creator when He declares something about us. He knows what sort of frame or dust we are (Ps. 103:14); we do not. Just as the vase of a potter may have acquired a crack through a blow or some other way and does not know it has a crack, whereas the potter knows and sees it, so also we do not fully know our faults. Therefore let us confess our infirmity and reverently say: "O Lord, I am Thy clay, Thou art my former and potter (Isa. 64:8). Therefore because Thou dost declare that I am a sinner, I agree to Thy Word. I freely acknowledge and confess this wickedness hiding in my flesh and my whole nature. That Thou mightest be glorified, let me be confounded. That Thou mightest be righteous and the Life, let me and all men be sin and death. That Thou mightest be the highest good, let me and all men

12 This is Luther's paraphrase of an important late medieval axiom. Some medieval theologians thought a person could do a minimal act of good that would elicit God's grace. Hence the axiom: "God will not deny grace to those who do what is in them" (*facientibus quod in se est, Deus non denegat gratiam*). Luther often assails this teaching and assigns it to the whole of scholasticism. See *Disputation against Scholastic Theology* (1517), Theses 5–7 and 33, LW 31:9, 11. Cf. *Heidelberg Disputation* (1518), Thesis 16, LW 31:40; *Preface to Romans* (1522, 1546), LW 35:367–68.

be the lowest evil. I acknowledge and confess this, being instructed in this by Thy promises and Thy Law, not by my reason, which would like to cover up this wickedness or even decorate it. But I am more concerned that Thy glory increase." Whoever confesses his sin in this way, prays this verse with sound mind: "Against Thee only have I sinned and done that which is evil in Thy sight, so that Thou art justified in Thy sentences." . . .

So there are two kinds of men. One kind confesses with David that God alone is righteous, truthful, and holy. The others are wicked and are "God-fighters" like the giants, saying: "Thy Word is not true. We are not blind. There is still some light in us toward God. If I obey it, I shall be in grace." This is to make God a merchant and to tell Him, "If You give, I will give." Yet on this idea all the scholastic theologians agree. It is well-known that Scotus said: "If a man can love what is a lesser good, he can also love what is a greater good. But man loves the creature; therefore much more does he love the Creator above all things."[13] That is really a theological conclusion, one worthy of a teacher of darkness in the church! He does not see that when a man loves a creature most, he loves it least as a creature. Who has there ever been who loved a girl as girl, or gold as gold? This love is spotted by lust and greed, and in this flesh it can never be perfectly pure. There are innumerable other statements of this sort in recent theologians which show the battle that human reason wages against the sentences of God. Now we are saying nothing here about domestic and political righteousness. Even if this were to be most perfect, the statement would still stand: "Against Thee only do I sin and do that which is evil in Thy sight."

Psalm 51:5

Behold, I was conceived in iniquity, and in sin did my mother conceive me.

The prophet proceeds in a most beautiful sequence in the doctrine of repentance. He asks for mercy and then gives the reason: "because I am a sinner and acknowledge my sin so that Thou mightest be righteous and we all be confounded." Then he adds the cause of this knowledge, the sentence of God, because sin is revealed through the Word. What follows now is connected with the preceding in such a way as to illumine it. He shows the cause of sin and, as it were, opens up the basis of the whole transaction, explaining why he confesses his sin and begs for mercy:

13 Luther often cites this statement by Scotus. Cf. *Lectures on Romans* (1515–16), LW 25:261 (see above, p. 16); *Lectures on Galatians* (1531), LW 25:128 (see above, p. 232); and *Lectures on Genesis* (1535–45), LW 2:124 (see below, p. 325).

"because," he says, "I was conceived in iniquity." What could be said more clearly and meaningfully? He does not say, "I murdered Uriah." He does not say, "I committed adultery." But he wraps up all of human nature as in one bundle and says, "I was conceived in sin." He is not talking about certain actions but simply about the matter, and he says: "The human seed, this mass from which I was formed, is totally corrupt with faults and sins. The material itself is faulty. The clay, so to speak, out of which this vessel began to be formed is damnable. What more do you want? This is how I am; this is how all men are. Our very conception, the very growth of the fetus in the womb, is sin, even before we are born and begin to be human beings."

Furthermore, he is not talking about sin in marriage or about the sin of parents, as though he were accusing his parents of sin when he says, "I was conceived in sin." He is not saying, "My mother sinned when she conceived me"; nor is he saying, "I sinned when I was conceived." He is talking about the unformed seed itself and declaring that it is full of sin and a mass of perdition. Thus the true and proper meaning is this: "I am a sinner, not because I have committed adultery nor because I have had Uriah murdered. But I have committed adultery and murder because I was born, indeed conceived and formed in the womb, as a sinner." So we are not sinners because we commit this or that sin, but we commit them because we are sinners first. That is, a bad tree and bad seed also bring forth bad fruit, and from a bad root only a bad tree can grow.

But someone may ask: "Why, then, was marriage instituted? Why did God bless marriage? Why does He list posterity as a blessing since the mass from which the fetus comes is completely corrupt and faulty?" I reply: Although God is not bound to give us reasons, still this reason may be conveniently given, that God did not want His creature to be destroyed because it had been spotted by sin. Just because the flesh is leprous, is the whole body thrown away? Just because eyes now are less sharp than Adam's were in Paradise, shall He not give a man eyes at birth? There is no doubt that several members of the body had a much more excellent nature before sin than they have now, after they have become corrupted and faulty through sin. As He did not take the eyes away from human nature, nor other members that have now been weakened by sin, so He did not take away the powers of reproduction or procreation. . . .

Still God puts up with these faults so that at least some form of government exists, children are educated, the earth is tilled, and business can go on. To take all the faults out of public affairs and laws would be to do away with governments and laws themselves. All the more insane is it when some lawyers first come into court or public life and want to cut everything to the quick and bring about an arithmetic equality in everything. Those who do this disturb the peace. Why not also abolish this very lovely arrangement for the procreation of children, since it cannot be without sin? Wise government ought to work more on how to keep the peace than on how to correct the laws; for those who do the latter and neglect the former are neglecting the log and getting very excited about a speck (Matt. 7:3–5). How different God's activity looks. Although He sees that marriage is spotted with desire, He does not abolish marriage for this reason or do away with the procreation of children. He would rather put up with the fault than abolish His creation. Thus a wise lawyer ought to have his eyes above all on this in the commonwealth: how to promote peace and the public tranquility of the citizens so that education and other political and domestic duties might be preserved. And if certain faults should occur, he should ignore them rather than disturb the public peace on account of them. . . .

We are by nature sinful

This verse of the psalm teaches us about the cause of sin, why we are sinners. The prophet confesses publicly that he was wicked by his own fault, not only by that of his parents, while he was growing and being formed as an embryo in the womb. Thus before she gave him birth, his mother was nourishing a sinner with her blood in the womb. We should hold the same thing about everyone who is born, ever was born, or ever will be born into this world, except Christ. The fact that John the Baptist and others were sanctified in the womb (Luke 1:15) does not abolish the fact that they were conceived in sin, just as the flesh still remains wicked in adults who have been sanctified by the Spirit and faith.

This doctrine of original sin is one of those outstanding doctrines which reason does not know, but which, like others, is learned from the Law and the promises of God. Paul is the only one of the apostles to deal very seriously with this doctrine in particular (Rom. 5:12ff.). Perhaps the other apostles passed over it because this doctrine was being handed down by tradition. Moses also touches on this doctrine in his prayer (Ps. 90:8): "Thou hast set our iniquities before Thee." There he shows clearly that in God's sight we are under wrath and that we suffer death because of God's wrath, which is aroused by the fact that our sins are known to God. The cause of these sins and of God's wrath is this, that in Paradise through Adam's fall this flesh became faulty so that it has a perverse fear and a perverse love toward God and toward itself. As I said, this doctrine was handed down by tradition, though Moses and David, and after them the apostle Paul, set it down in writing. Undoubtedly they drew this wisdom from the First Commandment and from the promises given to Abraham and to Adam. Since these promise a blessing, they make clear that this nature is under a curse and under the kingdom of the devil, in which there is darkness, hate of God, and mistrust.

This verse contains the reason why we all ought to confess that we are sinners, that all our efforts are damnable in the sight of God, and that God alone is righteous. This teaching is most necessary in the church; neither the pope nor the Turk believes it. I can testify from my own example that I did not yet know this teaching when I had been a doctor of theology for many years. They used to discuss original sin, but they said that it was removed in Baptism, and that even outside Baptism there was a light left in nature; if anyone followed this, grace would inevitably be given to him. They even taught that the natural powers of the demons had remained perfect and that they had only lost grace.[14] Who does not see the contradiction between the statement that the natural powers are perfect and the statement that nature is corrupted by sin? The will is indeed a natural thing. But they do not argue merely about willing, but about willing the good—and this they call natural. Here is the error. Will remains in the devil, it remains in the heretics; this, I admit, is natural. But that will is not good, nor does the intellect remain correct or enlightened. If we want to talk about natural powers on the basis of this psalm and on the basis of the Holy Spirit's manner of speaking, then we should call "natural" the fact that we are in sin and death and that we desire, understand, and long for things that are corrupt and evil. This agrees with the present psalm and can be proved from it.

Let this be enough about the confession of original or innate sin, which is hidden from the whole world and is not revealed by our powers, reasonings, or speculations, but is rather obscured, defended, and excused by them. We need the Word of God from heaven to reveal this uncleanness or fault of our nature. With faith in this Word let us confess that this is the way things are, even though all nature should object, as object it must. This is the most difficult teaching of this psalm, yes, of all Scripture or theology; without it, it is impossible to understand Scripture correctly, as the dreams of modern theologians prove.

Psalm 51:7

Thou wilt sprinkle me, Lord, with hyssop, and I shall be cleansed. Thou wilt wash me, and I shall be whiter than snow.

Thus far the prophet has condemned all righteousness, wisdom, and truth in general. He has exalted the single truth that is in secret, the

14 See above, p. 264 n. 6.

wisdom that is in a mystery, that confesses its sins and hopes for the mercy of the God who justifies sinners. The same thing is expressed in John 1:12–13: "To all who received Him, who believed in His name, He gave power to become children of God; who were born, not of blood nor of the will of the flesh nor of the will of man, but of God." There he universally condemns whatever reason and whatever "man," that is, whatever all men by their own nature and powers, can accomplish without the Holy Spirit. All he leaves is trust in the name of Jesus. To this general refutation he adds a special refutation of the righteousness of the Law or of Moses. He says that the sprinklings of Moses are nothing and that Moses does not truly sprinkle those whom he wants to sanctify, but that another and far more powerful sprinkling is necessary. . . .

Sprinkling with the blood of Christ

Let us seek the sprinkling of the Spirit and the inward washing which Peter (1 Pet. 1:2) calls "sprinkling with Christ's blood," by which all of us who hear and believe the Gospel of Christ are cleansed. The mouth of a man who teaches the Gospel is the hyssop and the sprinkler by which the teaching of the Gospel, colored and sealed with the blood of Christ, is sprinkled upon the church. Those who do not believe this Word are still sprinkled; the blood of Christ and the Word of Christ will judge them, but their unbelief will prevent them from being cleansed. The Sacraments, Baptism and the Lord's Supper, belong to this sprinkling, for in both we are sprinkled with the blood of Christ. In Baptism we are baptized into the death of Christ (Rom. 6:3), and in the Lord's Supper the body and blood of Christ are distributed to the church. In the ministry of the Word similarly we hear this sprinkling, that Christ has made satisfaction for the sins of the world. Here nothing remains but this: As we hear this in the Word and as it is offered and shown to us in the symbols of our faith, we should firmly believe, and we should strengthen our minds with trust in this sprinkling.

Here there is no difference between the present church of the faithful and the faithful in the Old Testament, except that they believed this sprinkling would come, while we believe that it has been manifested and completed. This is the summary of this verse: First, David rejects the cleansings of the Law as useless for righteousness; secondly, he asks to be sprinkled with the Word of faith in the coming Christ, who will sprinkle His church with His blood. He prays that he might hear and believe this Word, as the following shows more clearly. The saints in the Old Testament were saved by this faith, as we are also saved, although our condition is much better, because we see all this in a clear light. We do not merely hear it in the Word, but we also receive it wrapped in symbols, in Baptism and the Lord's Supper. Therefore Christ says (Luke 10:24): "Many kings and prophets desired to see what you see." Still it is the same faith by which both they and we are saved. If someone asks, therefore, how David could ask for this sprinkling with the blood of Christ though it had not yet been fulfilled, the answer is easy. The same sprinkling has always been in the world, by which believers were washed from their sins, namely, sprinkling with the blood of Christ. There has only been a difference of time, in that the sprinkling was future to them, while to us it is past and manifest. If anyone does not accept the sprinkling because of unbelief, this is the fault of his unbelief, not of the blood of Christ.

This teaching is easy, but it takes great effort to keep it and so to fortify your mind that you believe in the validity of no satisfaction, no work, no Law, no righteousness in the sight of God except this single sprinkling. Various thoughts tempt this faith. . . .

As long as we are outside temptation, it seems easy. But when the time of peace has gone away and we are in the midst of thoughts about the wrath of God, then we experience how much effort it takes to believe this firmly. Let everyone be warned not to presume anything. All this can be taught and heard and even believed, but to endure in temptation—this is a special gift of the Holy Spirit. It is so easy to fall into thoughts that are contrary to this teaching, thoughts about satisfactions and similar delusions of Satan. When you hear "satisfactions," therefore, declare that only that satisfaction is true which is called and is the satisfaction of faith, namely, that Christ Jesus bore your sins. If this satisfaction stands alone and pure, without any addition of your satisfactions, then you may chastise and mortify your flesh, then you may zealously exercise charity, serve your calling, and do everything that the Word of God permits you to undertake. This obedience is pleasing and acceptable to God because it is done with the right aim, namely, of obeying God and not setting up your own satisfaction. . . .

When we come to the doctrine of righteousness in the sight of God, we should simply reject all Law as useless for our justification and admit nothing but the law of the Spirit, the promise that Jesus Christ died on account of our sins. This is the Word of grace and promise, which does not demand anything of us as in the Law, but offers plenary satisfaction through the perfect victim, Christ, the victim who put an end to Moses and the whole Law. Therefore David so freely rejects the imperfect sprinkling of the Law and asks to be sprinkled not by the Levitical priest, but by God the Redeemer Himself so that his conscience might be cleansed with a cleanness that is whiter than snow. . . .

Whiter than snow

Here a theological question arises. How can we become "purer than snow" even though the remnants of sin always cling to us? I answer: I have always said that man is divided into spirit and flesh. Therefore as far as the total man is concerned, there remain remnants of sin or, as Paul calls them (2 Cor. 7:1), "defilements of body and spirit." Defilements of the spirit are doubt about grace, imperfect faith, murmurings against God, impatience, imperfect knowledge of the will of God, and the like. Defilements of the flesh are adultery, lusts, murder, brawls, and the like. The defilements of the spirit are increased in the world through heretics, the defilements of the flesh through other offenses, so that both spirit and body are polluted. Because of these defilements we are never as pure and holy as we really should be. Still we have obtained Baptism, which is most pure; we have obtained the Word, which is most pure; and in the Word and Baptism we have by faith obtained the blood of Christ, which is surely most pure. According to this purity, which in spirit and faith we have from Christ and from the Sacraments that He instituted, the Christian is rightly said to be purer than snow, purer than the sun and the stars, even though the defilements of spirit and flesh cling to him. These are concealed and covered by the cleanness and purity of Christ, which we obtain by hearing the Word and by faith.

We should note diligently that this purity is an alien purity, for Christ adorns and clothes us with His righteousness. So if you look at a Christian without the righteousness and purity of Christ, as he is in himself, even though he be most holy, you will find not only no cleanness, but what I might call diabolical blackness. Yet what does the pope do in his teaching but separate us from Christ, rob us of Baptism, the hearing of the Gospel, and the promises of God, and leave us by ourselves? This is to rob man of all purity and to leave nothing but sin. Therefore if they ask: "Sin always clings to man; how, then, can he be washed so as to make him whiter than snow?" you reply: "We should look at a man not as he is in himself, but as he is in Christ. There you will find that believers are washed and cleansed by the blood of Christ. Who is so profane as to deny that the blood of Christ is most pure? So why should a believer doubt his purity? Because he still feels the remnants of sin in himself? But all purity must be this alien purity of Christ and His blood. It must not be our own, which we put on ourselves." In a household, is not the son the heir of the father (Gal. 4:1–2)? Yet because of his immaturity he is carried, cared for, and ruled by a mere maid. If you look at the carrying here, is not the son, who is the heir, the servant of the maid, whom he is forced to obey? Yet he does not stop being the heir, for he is descended from the father and not from the maid. We should evaluate the Christian the same way and look at him as he was brought out of Baptism, not as he was born of his parents. Regeneration is stronger than the first birth, because it is not from man but from God and His promise, which our faith grasps, as the prophet now shows more fully.

Psalm 51:8

To my hearing Thou wilt give joy and gladness, and the humbled bones will rejoice.

There is good reason for my repeated statement that this psalm not only provides an example of justification in David but also presents the true teaching about the reason and manner of justification in all men. Thus this psalm is a sort of general rule how sinners become righteous. The last two verses have set forth a part of this rule, refuting all the other ways on which men rely for cleansing from their sins and reconciliation with God, either by the works of the Law or by other works they chose for themselves. He does not only require a hidden truth against hypocrisy, but he also requires another sprinkling than the one the Law had. To make this more clearly understood, he adds: "To my hearing Thou wilt give joy." It is as though he were to say: "Sprinkle me in such a way that Thou wilt give joy to my hearing, that is, that I might have peace of heart through the Word of grace." The emphasis falls on the noun "hearing," but the Hebrew reads a little differently: "Make me hear joy." The meaning is the same in either case. He simply wants the forgiveness of sins, which alone grants joy, to come only through the Word or only through hearing. For if you tortured yourself to death, if you shed your blood, if with ready heart you underwent and bore everything that is humanly possible—all this would not help you. Only hearing brings joy. This is the only way for the heart to find peace before God. Everything else that it can undertake leaves doubt in the mind. . . .

All this can be summarized as follows. When you become sad or feel divine wrath, do not look for any other medicine or accept any other solace than the Word, whether it is spoken by a brother who is present or comes from the spirit remembering a word you had heard earlier—like the passages: "I do not want the death of the sinner, but that he turn from his way and live" (Ezek. 33:11); "Life is in His will" (Ps. 30:5); "God is God of the living" (Matt. 22:32); "God so loved the world that He gave His only Son, that whoever believes in Him should not perish but have eternal life" (John 3:16). These and similar passages bring the hearing of gladness, whether they come from the mouth of another or from the inspiration of the Holy Spirit. This, too, is hidden truth and wisdom, which inexperienced men cannot grasp. Therefore the pope's teachers bring vastly different ways by which they want to heal troubled minds.

Hearing of gladness

In addition, this verse is an outstanding testimony to the adornment of the ministry of the Word or the spoken Word. Because he asks for the hearing of gladness, he clearly shows that the Word is necessary for consoling minds, whether it is brought by a brother or whether the Spirit suggests a word that once was heard. This verse battles, first, against those who hate or neglect the external Word and are captivated by their own vain and inane speculations. Secondly, it also battles against those who do not want to accept the Word in their anguish of mind, but either are unbelievers or flee from the Word to their works, as the others do to their speculations. Both are in error—the man of thought as well as the man of action. Only if you hear will you avoid error.

This is the doctrine for which we bear not only the name "heresy" but punishment, namely, that we attribute everything to hearing or to the Word or to faith in the Word—these are all the same—and not to our works. Yes, in the use of the Sacraments and in confession we teach men to look mainly at the Word, so that we call everything back from our works to the Word. The hearing of gladness is in Baptism, when it is said: "I baptize you in the name of the Father and of the Son and of the Holy Spirit" (Matt. 28:19); "He who believes and is baptized will be saved" (Mark 16:16). The hearing of gladness is in the Lord's Supper, when it is said, "This is My body, which is given for you" (Luke 22:19). The hearing of gladness is in confession, or, to call it by its more proper name, in Absolution and the use of the Keys: "Have faith. Your sins are forgiven you through the death of Christ." Although we urge the people to the Sacraments and to Absolution, still we do not teach anything about the worthiness of our work or that it avails by the mere performance of the work, as the Papists usually teach about the Lord's Supper, or rather about their sacrifice. We call men back to the Word so that the chief part of the whole action might be the voice of God itself and the hearing itself.

On the other hand, the pope omits the Word and argues about the form and power of the Sacraments or about contrition and attrition. In the schools I was so corrupted by this teaching that only with great labor, by the grace of God, was I able to turn myself solely to the hearing of gladness. If you wait until you are sufficiently contrite, you will never get to the hearing of gladness. I experienced this often enough in the monastery to my sorrow, for I was following this teaching about contrition. But the more contrite I was, the higher rose my sorrows and my conscience, and I could not accept the Absolution and the other consolations which those to whom I confessed brought me. This was the way I thought: "Who knows whether such consolations should be believed?" Later on, by chance I asked my preceptor, amid many tears, about these many temptations of mind, which I was suffering also because of my age. He said to me: "Son, what are you doing? Do you not know that the Lord Himself has commanded us to hope?" With this one word "commanded" I was so strengthened that I knew I should believe the Absolution which I had heard so often before. I had been so preoccupied with my foolish thoughts that I did not think I should believe the Word, but heard it as though it had nothing to do with me.

Therefore, being warned by my example and danger, teach the doctrine of justification which this verse manifests, namely, that righteousness comes only to him who believes the Word. Thus you may distinguish, as between heaven and earth, between the word of him who absolves you and your own intention or contrition. Even though it be the highest and most perfect, contrition is something very tiny in respect to righteousness. It is nothing at all by which to merit something or to make satisfaction. What sort of merit is there in acknowledging sin and sorrowing over it? So turn your eyes far away from your contrition, and with your whole heart pay attention to the voice of the brother absolving you. And do not doubt that this voice of the brother in the Sacrament or in absolution is divinely spoken by the Father, Son, and Holy Spirit Himself, so that you completely depend on what you hear, not on what you do or think.

Psalm 51:9

Turn away Thy face from my sins, and blot out all my iniquities.

Here, as you see, he again makes clear that he is not talking only about his sin of adultery, for he says: "Blot out all my iniquities." Here, too, he shows us the special experience that the saints have in this spiritual struggle. When the mind is fully occupied with the feeling of sin, then not even the righteous can have enough peace; but mixed with the hearing of gladness there remains a sorrow that will not let them get enough out of the hearing of gladness. They have the firstfruits and, as it were, the end of a finger to cool their minds (Luke 16:24). They do not have the "fullness of joy" (Ps. 16:11), but they hang by a thin strand when a thick rope would well be necessary to hold up the weight of their body. So the saints only begin to feel this hearing; they have not yet drawn enough from it to be drunk. Therefore in this verse David asks for an increase and perfection of this hearing, which will so fill his mind with this thought of mercy that nothing more will be left to trouble him.

Throughout our life we need this petition so that from day to day this knowledge and this trust in mercy might grow, as Paul (Col. 1:10) and Peter (1 Pet. 2:2) urge this growth of faith. You see the great danger that after we have read through one or another book, we persuade ourselves that we are doctors of theology. The examples of the sects are before our eyes. Although they have drawn hardly one drop of sound doctrine, still as the teachers of the world they have filled everything with false ideas of Baptism, the Lord's Supper, obedience to the Law of God, obedience to magistrates, and the like. Because they have never gone through these struggles of spirit nor grasped this teaching about trust in the mercy of God, it was easy for Satan to subvert them with false ideas. Therefore let us be warned by these horrible examples, pray with David for the growth of this faith, and say, "Lord, turn away Thy face from our sins, and blot out all our iniquities so that our peace and our joy may be full."

This same petition proves that the doctrine of justification is the kind of thing that can never be learned completely. Therefore it is true that those who have persuaded themselves that they know it fully have not even begun to learn it. Because every day new struggles arise from Satan or our flesh or the world or our conscience, prompting us to despair, wrath, lust, and other vices, how is it possible for this weakness of ours not to keep falling or breaking? Then, too, how many concerns arise in this life that gradually make us forget this gladness? Hence it is supremely necessary that we ask God to pour or sprinkle upon us this hearing of joy so that we are not covered again with the sadness that the feeling of sin brings on.

I understand this verse to be speaking of the increase of that peace and righteousness which conquers the feeling of God's wrath and of sin. Although the righteous truly have the forgiveness of sins, because they have trust in mercy and are in grace for Christ's sake, still the pangs of conscience and the remnants of sin that infest them do not stop. Hence it is a great power of the Holy Spirit to trust the grace of God and to hope that God is gracious and favorably disposed. Nor can this confidence be preserved without the most bitter struggles, aroused in our flesh by our daily occasions for trouble and sadness as well as by our inborn weakness and distrust. Even though today I may be of happy heart because of this hearing of joy, still something happens tomorrow to trouble me, when I remember that I did what I should have avoided or failed to do what I should have done. These storms and fluctuations never stop in the mind. Satan also keeps watch. When he notices that our hearts are not well fortified with the promises of God, he arouses other specters of wrath and trouble in us that melt our hearts like salt when it is thrown into the water. Therefore this prayer is necessary: "Turn away Thy face from my sins, and blot out all my iniquities." "All," he says, "whether past or present or future, for I sin daily. Blot out all of them, all, lest I fall into despair or forget Thy mercy." Here again you see that the forgiveness of sins is not in what I do but in the fact that by mercy God blots out, as Paul says about "the bond which is against us" (Col. 2:14).

We have finished the main part of this psalm, which deals with the principal doctrines of our religion, namely: What is repentance? What is sin? What is grace? What is justification? What are the causes of justification? The following section seems to me to pertain to the gifts of the Spirit that follow the forgiveness of sins. Paul maintains this distinction, that grace is one thing and the gift is another (Rom. 5:15). Grace means the favor by which God accepts us, forgiving sins and justifying freely through Christ.

Lectures on Genesis

1535–45

Martin Luther and his Wittenberg colleagues continued their theological negotiations with fellow Protestants and with the Church of Rome throughout the 1530s. Luther's lectures and writings during this period increasingly focused on the doctrine of the church and the unending struggle to maintain the Gospel. It was during this time that Luther undertook his final course of university lectures.

Luther began lecturing on the Book of Genesis at the beginning of June 1535. He never expected to finish the book before his death and often considered retirement. In the spring of 1538, Luther wrote that he was old and worn-out. Instead of continuing his lectures, he would rather enjoy the pleasures of an old man, spending time in the garden and marveling over God's creation of the trees, flowers, and birds.[1] *Although Luther frequently mentions that he is old and tired, he admitted that controversy made him feel young again.*[2] *He would not stop lecturing but would continue his attacks on the papacy and his defense of the Gospel!*

Luther's deteriorating health often interrupted the lectures on Genesis. He struggled with kidney stones, gout, incessant headaches, prolonged periods of weakness, fainting spells, and debilitating dizziness. He eventually needed a cane to move around. His eyes were failing. Despite these difficulties and the many other demands on Luther's time, he finished the lectures on Genesis in December 1545. His thirty-five-year career as university lecturer had come to an end. Luther closed his final lecture by saying he was weak and could do no more.[3] *One month later, in a letter to a friend, Luther more colorfully wrote that he was old, cold, one-eyed, and ready to die.*[4]

Despite Luther's infirmities, students and admirers marveled at the power of his lectures, his command of Scripture, and his interpretive insight. One such

1 Luther's letter to Justus Jonas, April 8, 1538, WA Br 8:209.12–14.

2 Luther's letter to Jacob Probst, September 15, 1538, WA Br 8:292.18–21.

3 LW 8:333.

4 Luther's letter to Jacob Probst, January 17, 1546, WA Br 11:263.3–4.

admirer wrote: "It was as if I were hearing an angel of the Lord."[5] *Luther's lectures on the first book of the Bible are another monument of his mature theology and confidence with the biblical text. Most commentators before Luther read Genesis allegorically. Whereas they "toiled exceedingly," Luther adhered to the historical and strict meaning, as he calls it.*[6] *This is especially true for the opening chapters of Genesis. Luther reads the beginning of Genesis and the account of God's creation literally. The heavens and earth were created by God in six days, and He rested on the seventh. Luther tabulated the history and determined that he was living 5,500 years after creation and in the last days.*[7]

The diverse events and themes of Genesis allow Luther to explore a number of topics in his lectures. The following excerpts fall into two parts. Part one focuses on creation, the fall, and the effects of sin on our world. Luther's historical reading of creation raises a number of perplexing exegetical and theological questions for him. How do we understand God resting from His work and yet continuing to govern and preserve His creation? How did God intend Adam and Eve to use the Sabbath before the fall? How were they to worship God? How long did Adam and Eve live in the garden before they sinned? The remaining excerpts in part one address the hope of salvation given to Adam and Eve following the fall, the effects of sin on the rest of creation and our natural endowments, God's use of created things to bestow His blessings and convey His grace, and, finally, a brief reflection on predestination.

Part two assembles Luther's comments on three major events from the life of the patriarch Jacob: the blessing by his father, Isaac (Genesis 27); his dream of a ladder extending to heaven (Genesis 28); and his wrestling with God (Genesis 32). Luther considers both the history and meaning of these events for Jacob and also for us. Jacob's life is one of blessing and trial; our life is the same. Luther dwells on Jacob's doubts and the torments of his heart and how faith in God's promises alone overcomes these trials.

Although Luther delights in the literal or plain sense of Genesis, he does not eschew allegory. There are times when Scripture records events that are meant to be read figuratively. For Luther, dreams or visions represent deeper truths in a way similar to Jesus' parables. Jacob's dream of a ladder extending to heaven with angels ascending and descending has a deeper significance for the discerning reader. For Luther, the ladder teaches the doctrine of Christ: that Christ is two natures, true God and man, in one person. This, Luther tells us, is the historical, simple, and literal sense of the passage.

---

5 Cyriakus Spangenberg (1528–1604), *Theander Lutherus* 70a–b, quoted in Robert Kolb, *Martin Luther and the Enduring Word of God* (Grand Rapids, MI: Baker Academic, 2016), 134.

6 LW 1:237.

7 *Supputatio annorum mundi* (1541), WA 53:1–184.

Jacob's wrestling with God is one of the most obscure passages in all of Scripture. Luther exhibits his profound interpretative gifts and pastoral insights in expounding Jacob's great struggle with God. We learn from Jacob that even the saints have doubts and often think they are abandoned by God. Luther insists, however, that when we suppose someone to be deserted by God, we should rather conclude that he is in fact in the arms of God and pressed upon His heart.

Lectures on Genesis[8]

Part One

Genesis 2:2

And on the seventh day God completed His work which He had made, and He rested on the seventh day from all His work that He had made.

God rested

Here a question arises. Moses says that the Lord rested on the seventh day from the work which He had done, that is, that He ceased to work on the seventh day. On the other hand, Christ says in John 5:17: "My Father works until now, and I work." Moreover, what Heb. 3:18 and 4:3 state concerning the rest pertains to this passage: "If they shall enter," not indeed into the Land of Promise but "into My rest."

We simply answer in this way: The solution is given by the text itself when it says: "The heaven and the earth were finished." The Sabbath, or the Sabbath rest, denotes that God ceased in such a way that He did not create another heaven and another earth. It does not denote that God gave up preserving and governing the heaven and the earth which had already been created. For in the preceding chapter Moses very plainly informs us about the manner of the creation when he says that God had created all things through the Word: "Let the sea bring forth fish; the earth, herbs, beasts," etc.; likewise: "Grow, fill the earth and the sea." These words are in force until today, and for this reason we see increase without end. Therefore if the world were in existence for an infinite number of years, the effectiveness of these words would not pass away; but there would be

8 The following excerpts are adapted from *Lectures on Genesis*, volumes 1–3, 5–6 of *Luther's Works: American Edition*, ed. Jaroslav Pelikan, Daniel E. Poellet, Walter A. Hansen, and Hilton C. Oswald, trans. George V. Schick and Paul D. Pahl (St. Louis: Concordia, 1958–70). Minor alterations have been made to the text for consistency in style, abbreviations, and capitalization. The annotations and subheadings are the work of the editor of this book.

continuous increase through the power of that Word or, to express myself so, of the original endowment.

Thus the solution is easy. God rested from His work, that is, He was satisfied with the heaven and earth which had then been created by the Word; He did not create a new heaven, a new earth, new stars, new trees. And yet God works till now—if indeed He has not abandoned the world which was once established but governs and preserves it through the effectiveness of His Word. He has, therefore, ceased to establish; but He has not ceased to govern. In Adam the human race had its beginning; in the earth the animal race, to use this expression, had its beginning through the Word; and in the sea that of the fish and of the birds had its beginning. But in Adam and in the first little beasts or animals they did not reach their end. Until today there abides the Word which was pronounced over the human race: "Grow and multiply"; there abides the Word: "Let the sea bring forth fish and birds of the heaven." Almighty, therefore, is the power and effectiveness of the Word which thus preserves and governs the entire creation.

Thus Moses has clearly established that the Word was in the beginning. But because all things grow, multiply, and are preserved and governed until now in the same manner as from the beginning of the world, it obviously follows that the Word still continues in force and is not dead. Therefore Moses' statement, "God rested from His work," is not to be understood of that course of events which involves their preservation and government but simply of the beginning, namely, that God had ceased creating classes, as they say in common speech, and new species or new creatures.

If you look at my person, I am something new, because sixty years ago I was nothing. Such is the judgment of the world. But God's judgment is different; for in God's sight I was begotten and multiplied immediately when the world began, because this Word, "and God said: 'Let Us make man,'" created me too. Whatever God wanted to create, that He created then when He spoke. Not everything has come into view at once. Similarly, an arrow or a ball which is shot from a cannon (for it has greater speed) is sent to its target in a single moment, as it were, and nevertheless it is shot through a definite space; so God, through His Word, extends His activity from the beginning of the world to its end. For with God there is nothing that is earlier or later, swifter or slower; but in His eyes all things are present things. For He is simply outside the scope of time.

Therefore these words, "God said: 'Let there be, grow, multiply,'" established the creatures as they are now and as they will be to the end of the world. But He ceased creating new ones. He did not create a new earth or a new heaven; but as He wanted the sun and the moon to course, so they still course. Just as at that time He filled the sea with fish, the heaven with flying things, and the earth with cattle, so these are complete, remain up to the present time, and are preserved. It is as Christ says (John 5:17): "My Father is working still, and I work." The Word which He spoke in the beginning is still in existence, as Ps. 33:9 says: "He spoke, and it came into being."

Does God continue to create?

But here another objection is voiced, namely: "How can it be true that God has created nothing new, when it is certain that the rainbow, or iris, was created at the time of Noah (Gen. 9:13)? Likewise, after Adam's fall the Lord threatens that the earth will produce thorns and thistles (Gen. 3:18), which it would not have produced if Adam had not sinned. Likewise, it is stated about the serpent that it would have to creep face down on the ground (Gen. 3:14), although without a doubt, in the state in which it was originally created, it walked upright, just as deer and peacocks do today. This is surely a new state of affairs, brought about by a new Word. Moreover, if Adam had not fallen into sin, wolves, lions, and bears would not have acquired their well-known savage disposition. Absolutely nothing in the entire creation would have been either troublesome or harmful for man. For the text states plainly: 'Everything that was created by God was good.' And yet, how troublesome they are! How many great afflictions of disease affect our body! I am passing over the fleas, the flies, and the spiders. And how great the dangers are from the other fierce and poisonous animals! But even if not one of these things is pertinent, surely this is something supremely new, that a virgin gives birth to the Son of God. Therefore God did not stop on the seventh day. He works not only by preserving His creation but also by changing and renewing His creation. Nor is it true, as was stated above, that God has refrained from creating new classes."

My answer is: Here Moses is speaking about the uncorrupted creation; if, therefore, man had maintained himself in the state of innocence in which he was created, no thorns or thistles or diseases would have come into existence, and beasts would not have become ferocious. This appears clearly enough from the fact that Eve speaks to a serpent with as little fear as we have when we speak to a charming little bird or a fawning puppy. Nor do I have any doubt that the serpent was a most beautiful creature, singularly endowed with a reputation for greater cleverness than the remaining beasts, just as little foxes, weasels, etc., have a reputation for cleverness.

Since Adam was still holy and innocent, all the living beings dwelt with him with the greatest delight, ready for every kind of service. If he had remained so, there would have been no fear of the flood; and, in consequence, iris, or the rainbow, would not have come into existence. But because of sin God changed many things. And on the Last Day there will be a far greater change and a renewal of the entire creature, which, as Paul says (Rom. 8:20), is now subjected to futility because of sin.

Therefore when Moses states that the Lord rested, he is speaking about the original state of the world. Because there was no sin, nothing new was created in it. There were neither thorns nor thistles, neither serpents nor toads; and if there were any, they were neither venomous nor vicious. Thus he is speaking about the creation of the world in its perfection. At that time the world was pure and innocent because man was pure and innocent. Now, when man is different on account of sin, the world, too, has begun to be different; that is, the fall of man was followed by the depravation and the curse of the creation. "Cursed is the earth," said God to Adam (Gen. 3:17–18), "on your account; thorns and thistles it will bring forth for you." On account of the sin of one single cursed Cain the earth is cursed so that even if it is tilled, it will not yield its best products. Later on there comes the flood because of the sin of the whole world, and the entire human race is destroyed. A few righteous people were preserved, however, lest the promise concerning Christ should not be fulfilled. But inasmuch as it appears that the earth was disfigured by sin, therefore I for one believe that the light of the sun also was more brilliant and beautiful when it was created, before man's sin.

In the theological schools the saying is current: "Distinguish the times, and you will bring the Scriptures into harmony."[9] Therefore what we say about the world after that wretched depravity which came in through sin must be far different from what we say about the original pure and unimpaired world. Let us consider an example that is before our eyes. Those who have seen the Promised Land in our time declare that it in no way resembles the favorable description which appears in Holy Scripture. Therefore when Count Stolberg had explored it with special care, he stated that he preferred his own lands in Germany.[10] On account of sin, on account of the wickedness and vileness of men, the land was

9 Augustine, *Sermon 32 on the New Testament* 10 (NPNF[1] 6:360).

10 Count Henry the Elder of Stolberg had been in the Holy Land in 1461 and in 1493 Count Henry the Younger also went on a pilgrimage there with Frederick the Wise. In his *Table Talk* Luther quotes the elder count as saying: "Is this the Promised Land? I would rather have the Golden Meadow!"—a section of Thuringia (no. 1223 [1530], WA TR 1:609.21).

made unfruitful, as Ps. 107:34 says. So Sodom, too, was a sort of paradise before it was destroyed by fire from heaven (Gen. 13:20).

Thus a curse generally follows sin, but the curse changes things so that the best becomes the worst. Therefore Moses is speaking about the perfection of the creatures as it was before sin. If man had not sinned, all the beasts would have remained obedient until finally God would have transferred man from Paradise, or from the earth; but after sin all things underwent a change for the worse.

In this way the solution proposed above stands: that in six days God finished His work, that is, that He ceased establishing classes; and whatever He wanted to make He made then. He did not say again: "Let there be a new earth, a new sea," etc. As to the fact that the Virgin Mary gave birth to the Son of God, it is clear that the reason also for this charitable act was the misfortune into which we fell through sin. God performed this marvelous and extraordinary work in such a way that He first revealed through His Word that He would do it in the future. Similarly, God indicated through His Word that other miracles would also take place in the future.

This, then, is the first disquisition concerning the statement that God finished the heaven and the earth and that He made nothing new. Now, that we may learn, this, too, should be explained: What is the Sabbath or the rest of God? Likewise, in what manner did God sanctify the Sabbath, as the text says?

Genesis 2:3

And God blessed the seventh day and sanctified it, because on it He had rested from all His work which God created, so that He made it.

In Matthew 12 Christ says that the Sabbath was made for man, not man for the Sabbath. But Moses says nothing here about man; he does not say in so many words that the Sabbath was commanded to man; he says that God blessed the Sabbath and that He sanctified it for Himself. Moreover, He did not do this to any other creature. He did not sanctify for Himself the heaven, the earth, or any other creature; but the seventh day He did sanctify for Himself. This has the special purpose of making us understand that the seventh day in particular should be devoted to divine worship. For "holy" is that which has been set aside for God and has been removed from all secular uses. Hence to sanctify means to set aside for sacred purposes, or for the worship of God. In this manner Moses rather frequently employs the expression, also of sacred vessels.

The worship of God

It follows, therefore, from this passage that if Adam had remained in the state of innocence, he nevertheless would have held the seventh day sacred. That is, on this day he would have given his descendants instructions about the will and worship of God; he would have praised God; he would have given thanks; he would have sacrificed; etc. On the other days he would have tilled his fields and tended his cattle. Indeed, even after the fall he kept this seventh day sacred; that is, on this day he instructed his family, of which the sacrifices of his sons Cain and Abel give the proof. Therefore from the beginning of the world the Sabbath was intended for the worship of God.

Unspoiled human nature would have proclaimed the glory and the kindnesses of God in this way: on the Sabbath Day men would have conversed about the immeasurable goodness of the Creator; they would have sacrificed; they would have prayed, etc. For this is the meaning of the verb "to sanctify."

Moreover, this also implies the immortality of the human race, as the Epistle to the Hebrews (8:11) learnedly expounds concerning God's rest on the basis of Ps. 95:11: "They shall not enter into My rest." For God's rest is eternal. Adam would have lived for a definite time in Paradise, according to God's pleasure; then he would have been carried off to that rest of God which God, through the sanctifying of the Sabbath, wished not only to symbolize for men but also to grant to them. Thus the physical life would have been blissful and holy, spiritual and eternal. Now we wretched men have lost that bliss of our physical life through sin, and while we live we are in the midst of death. And yet, because the Sabbath command remains for the church, it denotes that spiritual life is to be restored to us through Christ. And so the prophets have carefully searched those passages in which Moses intimates the resurrection of the flesh and life immortal.

Then it is also shown here that man was especially created for the knowledge and worship of God; for the Sabbath was not ordained for sheep and cows but for men, that in them the knowledge of God might be developed and might increase. Therefore although man lost his knowledge of God, nevertheless God wanted this command about sanctifying the Sabbath to remain in force. On the seventh day He wanted men to busy themselves both with His Word and with the other forms of worship established by Him, so that we might give first thought to the fact that this nature was created chiefly for acknowledging and glorifying God.

Moreover, this is also written that we might preserve in our minds a sure hope of the future and eternal life. All the things God wants done on the Sabbath are clear signs of another life after this life. Why is it necessary for God to speak with us through His Word if we are not to live in a future and eternal life? If we are not to hope for a future life, why do we not live like people with whom God does not speak and who do not know God? But because the divine Majesty speaks to man alone and man alone knows and apprehends God, it necessarily follows that there is another life after this life; to attain it we need the Word and the knowledge of God. For this temporal and present life is a physical life, such as all the beasts live that do not know God and the Word.

This is what the Sabbath, or the rest of God, means, on which God speaks with us through His Word and we, in turn, speak with Him through prayer and faith. The beasts, such as dogs, horses, sheep, and cows, indeed also learn to hear and understand the voice of man; they are also kept by man and fed. But our state is better. We hear God, know His will, and are called into a sure hope of immortality. This is the testimony of the clear promises concerning eternal life which God has revealed to us through His Word after giving those dark indications, like this one concerning the rest of God and the sanctifying of the Sabbath. And yet this one dealing with the Sabbath is rather clear. Suppose that there is no life after this life; does it not follow that we have no need of God or of His Word? What we need or do in this life we can have even without the Word. The beasts graze, live, and grow fat, although they do not have the Word of God or hear it. What need is there of the Word to get food and drink that has already been created?

Therefore that God gives His Word, that He commands us to occupy ourselves with the Word, that He issues orders for sanctifying the Sabbath and for His worship—all this clearly proves that there remains a life after this life and that man was created not for this physical life only, like the other animals, but for eternal life, just as God, who has ordered and ordained these practices, is eternal.

When did Adam fall?

But here another question arises, on which we touched above, namely, about the time of Adam's fall. When did he fall, on the seventh day or on another? Although nothing certain can be proposed, still I can readily imagine that he fell on the seventh day. On the sixth day he was created; Eve likewise was created toward evening or near the end of the sixth day, while Adam was sleeping. Early in the morning of the seventh day, which had been sanctified by the Lord, God speaks with Adam, gives him directions concerning His worship, and forbids him to eat the fruit of the tree of the knowledge of good and evil. This is the real purpose of the seventh day: that the Word of God be preached and heard. Henceforth both in the Scripture and in common usage the practice remained that the morning time was set aside for prayer and preaching, as Ps. 5:3 says: "In the morning I shall stand before Thee, and I shall see."

Thus early on the seventh day Adam appears to have heard the Lord charge him with the management of household and world affairs, and at the same time forbid him to eat the fruit. Satan was intolerant of this most magnificent creation and arrangement. He also envied man such great bliss, that an overflowing supply of everything was at hand for him on the earth and that after so blissful a physical life he had the sure hope of eternal life, which Satan himself had lost. And so, perhaps about noon, after God's conversation, he also converses with Eve. So it is wont to be to this day. Where the Word of God is, there Satan also makes it his business to spread falsehood and false teaching; for it grieves him that through the Word we, like Adam in Paradise, become citizens of heaven. And so he successfully incites Eve to sin. Moreover, the text states plainly that when the heat of the day had ended, the Lord came and condemned Adam, together with all his descendants, to death. I am easily convinced that all these events took place on the very Sabbath—and that one not complete!—on which Adam lived in Paradise and enjoyed its fruits.

And so through sin man lost this bliss. But Adam would not have spent his life in Paradise in idleness if he had remained in the state of innocence. On the Sabbath Day he would have taught his children; through public preaching he would have bestowed honor on God with the praises which He deserved; and through reflection on the works of God he would have incited himself and others to expressions of thanks. On the other days he would have worked, either tilling his field or hunting. But this would have been far different from the way it is done now. For to us work is something burdensome; but for Adam it would have been a supreme joy, more welcome than any leisure. Therefore just as the other misfortunes of this life remind us of sin and of the wrath of God, so work, too, and the well-known hardship of providing sustenance should remind us of sin and rouse us to repentance.

Genesis 2:8

And the Lord God planted a garden in Eden towards the east, in which He placed the man whom He had formed.

. . . At this point people discuss where Paradise is located. The interpreters torture themselves in amazing ways. Some favor the idea that it is located within the two tropics under the equinoctial point. Others think that a more temperate climate was necessary, since the place was so fertile. Why waste words? The opinions are numberless.

My answer is briefly this: It is an idle question about something no longer in existence. Moses is writing the history of the time before sin and the deluge, but we are compelled to speak of conditions as they are after sin and after the deluge. And so I believe that this place was called Eden either by Adam or at the time of Adam because of its fertility and the great charm which Adam beheld in it. And the name of the lost place persisted among his descendants, just as the names of Rome, Athens, and Carthage are still in existence today, although hardly any traces of those great states are apparent. For time and the curse which sins deserve destroy everything. Thus when the world was obliterated by the deluge, together with its people and cattle, this famous garden was also obliterated and became lost. Therefore it is vain for Origen and others to carry on senseless discussions.[11] Moreover, the text also states that it was guarded by an angel, lest anyone enter it. Therefore even if that garden had not perished as a result of the ensuing curse, the way to it is absolutely closed to human beings; that is, its location cannot be found. This is also a possible answer, although my first opinion, involving the deluge, seems more probable to me.

But what answer shall we give in regard to the passage in the New Testament (Luke 23:43): "Today you will be with Me in paradise"? Also regarding 2 Cor. 12:4: "I was snatched up into paradise"? Indeed, I myself, do not hesitate to assert that Christ and the thief did not enter any physical place. In Paul's case the matter is clear when he says that he did not know whether he was in the body or outside the body. Therefore I am of the opinion that in each of the two instances paradise designates the state in which Adam was in Paradise, abounding in peace, in freedom from fear, and in all gifts which exist where there is no sin. It is as if Christ said: "Today you will be with Me in paradise, free from sin and safe from death (except that the Last Day must be awaited, when all this will be laid open to view), just as Adam in Paradise was free from sin, death, and every curse, yet lived in the hope of a future and eternal spiritual life." Thus it is an allegorical paradise, as it were, just as Scripture also gives the name "Abraham's bosom" (Luke 16:22), not to Abraham's mantle but, in an allegorical sense, to that life which is in the souls who have departed in the faith. They have peace, and they are at rest; and in that quiet state they await the future life and glory.

11 Origen (ca. 185–ca. 254), one of the most prolific theologians of the early church, produced numerous commentaries on the Bible.

Genesis 2:9

For the Lord God had brought forth from the ground every tree that was beautiful to behold and delightful to eat. Also the tree of life was in the midst of Paradise, and the tree of the knowledge of good and evil.

Moses describes Paradise in such a way that he makes of God a gardener who, after planting his garden with great care according to his design, chooses one or more trees which he tends and loves more than the rest. One of these was the tree of life, created that man, by eating of it, might be preserved in full bodily vigor, free from diseases and free from weariness.

Here again man is set apart from the brutes, not only in regard to place but also in regard to the advantage of a longer life and one which always remains in the same condition. The bodies of the remaining living things increase in size and are stronger in their youth, but in their old age they become feeble and die. The situation of man would have been different. He would have eaten; he would have drunk; and the conversion of food in his body would have taken place, but not in such a disgusting manner as now. Moreover, this tree of life would have preserved perpetual youth. Man would never have experienced the inconveniences of old age; his forehead would never have developed wrinkles; and his feet, his hands, and any other part of his body would not have become weaker or more inactive. Thanks to this fruit, man's powers for procreation and for all tasks would have remained unimpaired until finally he would have been translated from the physical life to the spiritual. Therefore the remaining trees would have supplied delightful and most excellent food, but this one would have been like a medicine by which his life and his powers were forever maintained at their utmost vigor. . . .

And so when Adam had been created in such a way that he was, as it were, intoxicated with rejoicing toward God and was delighted also with all the other creatures, there is now created a new tree for the distinguishing of good and evil, so that Adam might have a definite way to express his worship and reverence toward God. After everything had been entrusted to him to make use of it according to his will, whether he wished to do so for necessity or for pleasure, God finally demands from Adam that at this tree of the knowledge of good and evil he demonstrate his reverence and obedience toward God and that he maintain this practice, as it were, of worshiping God by not eating anything from it.

Thus the statements which Moses has so far made deal with natural science or with economics or with politics or with jurisprudence or with medicine. But this is a matter of theology that here this statement about the tree is put before Adam in order that he may also have some outward physical way of indicating his worship of God and of demonstrating his obedience by an outward work. In a similar way the Sabbath, of which we spoke above, has to do chiefly with demonstrating inner and spiritual worship, with faith, love, prayer, etc.

But alas! Despite its fine purpose this method of showing outward obedience brought about a most wretched result. Similarly, we see even today that the holy and excellent Word is an offense to the wicked. Christ instituted Baptism to be a washing of regeneration (Titus 3:5). But haven't the sects stirred up a great offense on account of it? Has not the entire doctrine concerning Baptism been wretchedly corrupted? And yet what is more necessary to us than the institution of this very rite? In the same way it was necessary that man, as a physical being, also have a physical or external form of worship by means of which he might be trained according to his body in obedience to God.

Adam's church, altar, and pulpit

Thus this text truly pertains to the church or theology. After God has given man the administration of government and of the home, has set him up as king of the creatures, and has added the tree of life as a safeguard for preserving this physical life, He now builds him, as it were, a temple that he may worship Him and thank the God who has so kindly bestowed all these things on him. Today in our churches we have an altar for the administration of the Eucharist, and we have platforms or pulpits for teaching the people. These objects were built not only to meet a need but also to create a solemn atmosphere. But this tree of the knowledge of good and evil was Adam's church, altar, and pulpit. Here he was to yield to God the obedience he owed, give recognition to the Word and will of God, give thanks to God, and call upon God for aid against temptation.

Our reason indeed becomes provoked at the creation of this tree, since because of it we sinned and fell into the wrath of God and into death. But why does it not become provoked in the same way because the Law was given by God and later on the Gospel was revealed by the Son of God? Have not endless offenses of errors and heresies followed as a result of this? Therefore let us learn that some external form of worship and a definite work of obedience were necessary for man, who was created to have all the other living creatures under his control, to know his Creator, and to thank Him. If, therefore, Adam had not fallen, this tree would have been like a common temple and basilica to which people would have streamed. Similarly, later on, after our nature had become depraved, a definite place was set aside for divine worship: the temple at Jerusalem.

Now, after this tree has become the occasion of so awful a fall, it is correctly called by Moses the tree of the knowledge of good and evil on account of the unfortunate and wretched outcome.

Moreover, someone may ask here whether there was only one tree or several, and whether, in the fashion of Scripture, the singular is used for the plural, just as we speak collectively and say pear and apple when we have in mind the species and not the individual fruits. To me it does not appear at all preposterous that we understand the tree of life as a definite area in the midst of Paradise, a sort of grove in which there stood several trees of the species called arborvitae. It is also possible that the tree of the knowledge of good and evil is designated collectively as a wood or a grove, because it was somewhat like a chapel in which there were many trees of the same variety, namely, the trees of the knowledge of good and evil, from which the Lord forbade Adam to eat anything, or he would surely die. This tree was not deadly by nature; it was deadly because it was stated to be so by the Word of God. This Word assigns to all creatures their function and also preserves all creatures that they may not degenerate but that the distinct species may be preserved in endless propagation.

Thus it was brought about by the Word that the rock in the desert provided a most abundant supply of water (Num. 20:11) and that the bronze serpent healed those who looked at it (Num. 21:9). In this manner this one tree—or that particular kind of several trees in the midst of Paradise—killed Adam for not obeying the Word of God, not indeed because of its nature but because it had been so laid down by the Word of God. In this way we should also interpret the tree of life, from which God commanded Adam to eat as often as he desired to restore his powers; it was through the potency of the Word that the tree brought this about.

To our reason it appears very ludicrous for one fruit to be so injurious that the entire human race, in an almost infinite series, perished and died an eternal death. But the fruit did not have this power. Adam did indeed put his teeth into the fruit, but actually he put his teeth into a sting. This God had forbidden; this was disobedience to God. This is the true cause of the evil, namely, that Adam sins against God, disregards His order, and obeys Satan. The tree of the knowledge of good and evil was a good tree; it produced very fine fruit. But because the prohibition is added and man is disobedient, it becomes more injurious than any poison.

Similarly, because the Word of God inviolably declares (Exod. 20:15): "You shall not steal," anyone who appropriates the property of another is committing a sin. When the Jews in Egypt were commanded to seek to get money from their neighbors and to take it away with them (Exod. 3:22), this was not a sin; for they were exculpated by the command of God, to whom obedience is due in every situation. When a suitor loves a girl, desires her for his wife, and marries her, he does not commit adultery, even though the Law forbids desire; for matrimony was divinely instituted and commanded for those who cannot live a chaste life without it. The situation with respect to these trees is clearly the same. The tree of life makes alive through the potency of the Word of Him who gives the promise and ordains it so; the tree of the knowledge of good and evil kills through the potency of the Word of Him who issues the prohibition.

But it has its name "of the knowledge of good and evil," as Augustine says,[12] since after Adam had sinned because of it, he saw and felt not only what good he had lost but also into what great misery he had been hurled through his disobedience. So, then, the tree was good in itself; likewise, the command which had been added was good. Thus it was for Adam a tree of divine worship on which to show God his obedience by an outward work. But because of the sin which follows, it becomes a tree of curse. Now in a sort of digression Moses describes the garden at greater length.

Genesis 3:15

I shall put enmity between you and the woman and your seed and her Seed.

. . . This very clear promise is at the same time also very obscure, because God speaks in general of "the Seed of the woman."[13] Thus at the same time He makes all women suspect to Satan and worries him with endless concern and care. It is, therefore, an amazing instance of synecdoche.[14] "The woman's Seed," He says. This means all individuals in general; and yet He is speaking of only one individual, of the Seed of Mary, who is a mother without union with a male. Thus the first little expression, "I shall put enmity between you and the woman," seems to denote all women in general. God wanted to make all women suspect to Satan; on the other hand, He wanted to leave the godly with a very certain hope, so that they might expect this salvation from all who gave birth, until the real one came. In the same way this "her Seed" is spoken most individually, if I may use this expression, concerning the Seed which was born only to Mary of the tribe of Judah, who was espoused to Joseph.

This, therefore, is the text that made Adam and Eve alive and brought them back from death into the life which they had lost through sin. Nevertheless, the life is one hoped for rather than one already possessed.

---

12 Augustine, *The Literal Meaning of Genesis* 8.33–35 (WSA 1/13:365–67).

13 See below, pp. 459–62.

14 See above, p. 211 n. 4.

Similarly, Paul also often says (1 Cor. 15:31): "Daily we die." Although we do not wish to call the life we live here a death, nevertheless it surely is nothing else than a continuous journey toward death. Just as a person infected with a plague has already started to die when the infection has begun, so—because of sin, and death, the punishment for sin—this life can no longer properly be called life after it has been infected by sin. Right from our mother's womb we begin to die.

Through Baptism we are restored to a life of hope, or rather to a hope of life. This is the true life, which is lived before God. Before we come to it, we are in the midst of death. We die and decay in the earth, just as other dead bodies do, as though there were no other life anywhere. Yet we who believe in Christ have the hope that on the Last Day we shall be revived for eternal life. Thus Adam was also revived by this address of the Lord—not perfectly indeed, for the life which he lost he did not yet recover; but he got the hope of that life when he heard that Satan's tyranny was to be crushed.

Therefore this statement includes the redemption from the Law, from sin, and from death; and it points out the clear hope of a certain resurrection and of renewal in the other life after this life. If the serpent's head is to be crushed, death certainly must be done away with. If death is done away with, that, too, which deserved death is done away with, that is, sin. If sin is abolished, then also the Law. And not only this, but at the same time the obedience which was lost is renewed. Because all these benefits are promised through this Seed, it is very clear that after the fall our human nature could not, by its own strength, remove sin, escape the punishments of sin and death, or recover the lost obedience. These actions call for greater power and greater strength than human beings possess.

And so the Son of God had to become a sacrifice to achieve these things for us, to take away sin, to swallow up death, and to restore the lost obedience. These treasures we possess in Christ, but in hope. In this way Adam, Eve, and all who believe until the Last Day live and conquer by that hope. Death is indeed an awful and undefeated tyrant; but God's power makes nothing out of that which is everything, just as it makes all things out of that which is nothing. Look at Adam and Eve. They are full of sin and death. And yet, because they hear the promise concerning the Seed who will crush the serpent's head, they have the same hope we have, namely, that death will be taken away, that sin will be abolished, and that righteousness, life, peace, etc., will be restored. In this hope our first parents live and die, and because of this hope they are truly holy and righteous.

Thus we also live in the same hope. And, because of Christ, when we die, we keep this hope, which the Word sets before us by directing us to put our trust in the merits of Christ. It is vain to long for such perfection in this life that we become wholly righteous, that we love God perfectly, and that we love our neighbor as we love ourselves. We make some progress; but sin, which wars in our members (Rom. 7:23) and is present everywhere, either corrupts or altogether obstructs this obedience.

Therefore just as our very life can be called a death because of the death which lies ahead of us, so also our righteousness is completely buried by sins. By hope we hold fast to both life and righteousness, things which are hidden from our eyes and our understanding, but will be made manifest in due time. Meanwhile our life is a life in the midst of death. And yet, even in the midst of death, the hope of life is kept, since the Word so teaches, directs, and promises. Thus Ps. 68:20 offers the exceedingly beautiful comfort: "Our God is the God of salvation, the Lord of the issue of death." Let us give this title to God, not only because He grants aid in this temporal life—the devil also does this for those who worship him, as the examples of the heathen show—but because He is the Lord of the issue of death; that is, He frees those who are overwhelmed by death, and transports them into eternal life. This He does, as Moses teaches here, by crushing the head of the serpent.

Accordingly, we now find Adam and Eve restored, not indeed to the life which they had lost but to the hope of that life. Through this hope they escaped, not the firstfruits of death, but its tithes; that is, although their flesh must die for the time being, nevertheless, because of the promised Son of God, who would crush the head of the devil, they hope for the resurrection of the flesh and eternal life after the temporal death of the flesh, just as we do.

Genesis 3:17–19

But to Adam He said . . . the earth is cursed on your account. . . .

A broken creation

. . . Moreover, it appears here what a great misfortune followed sin, because the earth, which is innocent and committed no sin, is nevertheless compelled to endure a curse and, as St. Paul says Rom. 8:20, "has been subjected to vanity." But it will be freed from this on the Last Day, for which it is waiting. Pliny calls the earth a kind, gentle, and forbearing mother; likewise, the perpetual servant of the need of mortals.[15] But, as Paul points out, the earth itself feels its curse. In the first place, it does not

15 Pliny, *Natural History* 1.154–59.

bring forth the good things it would have produced if man had not fallen. In the second place, it produces many harmful plants, which it would not have produced, such as darnel, wild oats, weeds, nettles, thorns, thistles. Add to these the poisons, the injurious vermin, and whatever else there is of this kind. All these were brought in through sin.

I have no doubt that before sin the air was purer and more healthful, and the water more prolific; yes, even the sun's light was more beautiful and clearer. Now the entire creation in all its parts reminds us of the curse that was inflicted because of sin. Nevertheless, there have remained some remnants of the former blessing, namely, that the earth is, as it were, forced to work hard to yield those things that are necessary for our use, although they are marred by thorns and thistles, that is, by useless and even harmful trees, fruits, and herbs, which the wrath of God sows.

This curse was made more severe through the flood, by which the good trees were all ruined and destroyed, the sands were heaped up, and harmful herbs and animals were increased. Accordingly, where, before sin, Adam walked about among most fertile trees, in lovely meadows, and among flowers and roses, there now spring up nettles, thorns, and other troublesome sprouts in such abundance that the good plants are almost overwhelmed.

Consider a field that has been plowed and prepared for planting. The moment it has been sown, weeds and darnel come up more quickly than the crops that are useful for life. Unless they are destroyed with diligent care by the farmer every day, those pernicious plants gradually take possession of the field, and the good seed is choked. The earth indeed is innocent and would gladly produce the best products, but it is prevented by the curse which was placed upon man because of sin.

And so both the man and the woman bear the penalty of sin. The woman bears hers on her own body when she suffers distress in her function as childbearer, although the penalty is bearable; and the husband bears his penalty in the management of the household, when with difficulty and hard work he exercises authority in the home and supports his family. On his account the ground was cursed, although before sin no part of the earth was barren and inferior, but all of it was amazingly fertile and productive. Now the earth is not only barren in many places, but even the fertile areas are defaced by darnel, weeds, thorns, and thistles. This is a great misfortune, which might well lead Adam and all of us to self-destruction; but it is mitigated by the promise of the Seed, who will remove the penalty of eternal death, which is infinitely greater.

What is added—"in sorrow you will eat from it all the days of your life"—is readily understood. Who does not know what a hard life it is to be a farmer? It is not enough to ready the earth for planting, something which calls for work that is hard and varied. But also when the crop is developing, almost each individual day requires its definite tasks. I am saying nothing about the almost endless troubles from the sky, the harmful animals, and similar things, all of which increase this sorrow or hardship. Before sin there were not only no such troubles, but if Adam had not sinned, the earth would have produced all things, "unsown and uncultivated,"[16] more quickly than one could have hoped.

Furthermore, this misfortune which sin brought on was lighter and more bearable in many respects than that which followed the flood. Here mention is made only of thorns, thistles, and hard work. But now we learn from experience that countless others have been added. How many kinds of damage and how many diseases affect the crops, the plants and the trees, and finally everything that the earth produces! How much harm is done to the vegetables by harmful insects! Furthermore, frosts, lightning bolts, injurious dews, storms, overflowing rivers, settling of the ground, earthquakes—all do damage. Of all these things no mention is made in the words before us. Therefore I am fully of the opinion that because of the increase of sins the punishments were also increased and that these troubles were added to the curse of the earth.

But if it seems to someone that Moses includes all these when he says that the earth was cursed, I shall surely not argue with him. Yet no one will deny that as the sins increased, so also the troubles. Thus today we experience more frequent disasters to crops than in former times. The world is deteriorating from day to day.

There are clear indications that these misfortunes were brought upon Adam as a warning to the first world to maintain stricter order. But gradually, at the time of Noah, this maintenance of order weakened; people began to live more disorderly, until finally the earth was filled with violence, unrighteousness, and oppression. Then, just as more serious diseases in the body demand more powerful cures, so also other more severe or more frequent penalties had to be inflicted.

Accordingly, when the entire earth had been laid waste by the deluge, and every living thing on earth, with the exception of a few human beings, had been destroyed, the age which followed the time of Noah undoubtedly lived in the fear of God. But as the years advanced, they, too, were corrupted and depraved by Satan. Therefore a more stringent example was necessary, such as the destruction of Sodom and its surrounding cities. Similarly, Scripture says that the iniquities of the Amorites had to become full (Gen. 15:16). And finally the entire synagogue was destroyed

16 Homer, *Odyssey* 9.123.

when it had turned to paganism and manifest ungodliness. Rome also made great advances while the ancient maintenance of order was in effect; but when vices made their inroads, it also became necessary for punishments to draw closer.

The period when the Gospel first became known among us was rather respectable. Now there is almost no fear of God, our shortcomings grow daily, and false prophets are even making their appearance. What else can we hope for except that when our iniquities have become full, either everything will be destroyed, or Germany will pay the penalties for its sins in some other way? Thus it is a general truth that as sins increase, the penalties also increase.

Disease and misfortune

I spoke earlier about the damages suffered by the products of the earth. I am also convinced that the human body was healthier then than it is now. Proof of this lies in the length of life among people before the flood, which seems incredible to us. For the Lord does not threaten Adam with apoplexy, leprosy, epilepsy, and other pernicious evils.

When I was a boy, syphilis was unknown in Germany.[17] It first became known when I was about fifteen years old. Now even children in the cradle are stricken with this evil. In those days everyone was terrified by this disease, but now so little is thought of it that even friends who are bantering among themselves wish each other a case of syphilis.

Until my adult years the sweating sickness was an endemic disease, as the physicians call it.[18] Just as individual areas have their particular advantages, so, after they misuse them against God, they are also troubled and stricken with particular hardships. But this disease became common also in parts of inland Germany, far distant from the ocean. It is awful to hear that some have snakes in their bellies and worms in their brains. In my opinion these sicknesses were unknown to the ancient physicians, although they counted almost four hundred kinds of diseases.[19]

But if all these sicknesses had existed in the first world, how could Adam and others before Noah have attained such a great length of life? Therefore Moses is speaking only about the barrenness of the earth and the difficulty of providing food.

17 In his chronology of the world (*Supputatio annorum mundi*), Luther speaks of "a new disease, the French disease, otherwise known as the Spanish disease, which was brought to Europe, so it is said, from the newly discovered islands in the East. One of the great signs before the Last Day" (WA 53:169). This is one of Luther's few references to the discovery of the Americas.

18 The "sweating sickness" had broken out in Wittenberg in 1529.

19 Pliny, *Natural History* 20–27.

Anyone who desires to become wordy and wants to appear as an orator should count up all the evils of the human race. He will find such an abundant crop of misfortunes of every kind that he will have only one request to make of God: that He does not permit him to live a single hour among such great dangers.

Why are we speaking only about sicknesses? All creatures are against us, and they are all equipped for our destruction. How many people are there whom fire and water destroy? How great is the danger from wild or poisonous beasts? And they harm not only our bodies but also the foods which have been produced to support us. I am saying nothing about the fact that we ourselves are plunging into mutual slaughter as if there were no other plagues lying in wait for us.

And so if you look at human endeavors, what else is this life than daily conflict, treachery, robbery, and slaughter, in addition to the troubles which are brought upon us by foreigners? I do not think that before the flood all these were either as numerous or as severe as they are now. But because sins grew, the penalties were also increased.

Hence the misfortunes which were placed upon Adam were insignificant in comparison with ours. The more closely the world approaches its end, the more it is overwhelmed by penalties and catastrophes. But, to make it worse, the more the world is smitten, the more hardened and unconscious of its own evils it becomes. It is just as Prov. 23:35 says: "He drew me, but I felt it not; he beat me, but I felt no pain." This blindness is worse than all those misfortunes of the body.

Is it not an amazing and wretched thing? Our body bears the traces of God's wrath, which our sin has deserved. God's wrath also appears on the earth and in all the creatures. And yet we look at all these things with a smug and unconcerned attitude! And what of thorns, thistles, water, fire, caterpillars, flies, fleas, and bedbugs? Collectively and individually, are not all of them messengers who preach to us concerning sin and God's wrath, since they did not exist before sin or at least were not harmful and troublesome?

Despite what we know and see, therefore, we live in a darkness worse than that which covered Egypt (Exod. 10:21–23). Although everything on all sides warns us of God's wrath and all but forces it into our very eyes, we still ignore it and embrace this life as our only delight. Just as the sins increase, therefore, the smugness grows, too, and people become insensible and hardened toward their misfortunes.

Thus the evils are increased, not only in this life but also in the future life. I am speaking of the ungodly. For if a person in hell were to endure his punishments and tortures only with his feelings and did not realize that he had deserved the punishments he was enduring, his tortures would be more bearable. Similarly, we are unwilling to acknowledge our evils and, so to speak, "grieve them out." But this insensibility, which now prevents us from realizing our wretched state, will be removed in the future life. All our senses will be opened; not only will our body realize the punishment, but our very mind will realize the wrath of God and admit that we have deserved that wrath by our vileness. This will sharpen the tortures of the wicked and increase them in countless ways.

"Thorns and thistles it will bring forth for you." Here again we are reminded that the earth does not produce anything of this kind on its own, but because of Adam's sin, as He said above in so many words, "on your account." Therefore whenever we see thorns and thistles, weeds and other plants of that kind in a field and in the garden, we are reminded of sin and of the wrath of God as though by special signs. Not only in the churches, therefore, do we hear ourselves charged with sin. All the fields—yes, almost the entire creation—is full of such sermons, reminding us of our sin and of God's wrath, which has been aroused by our sin.

Therefore we should ask the Lord to take away this amazing insensibility from our eyes, our senses, and our hearts, so that, after being admonished so many times about our sin, we may rid ourselves of our smugness and walk in the fear of God.

Genesis 8:21

For the imagination of man's heart is evil from his youth.

Natural endowments corrupt

Careful note must be taken of this passage, since it clearly shows that the nature of man is corrupt. This knowledge of our corrupt nature is necessary above all else; without it the mercy and grace of God cannot be properly understood.

Accordingly, the sophists deserve our hate,[20] and we ought to indict the translator who gave rise to this error with his interpretation that the thinking of the human heart is not evil but is "inclined to evil."[21] This gives the sophists an opportunity to distort and get around the passages in which Paul declares that all are children of wrath (Eph. 2:3), that all commit sin (Rom. 5:12) and are under sin (Rom. 3:9). On the basis of

20 On Luther's use of "sophist," see above, p. 171 n. 14.

21 Luther laments the Latin Vulgate's poor translation of the Hebrew. It renders "the intention of man's heart is evil from his youth" as "the imagination and thought of man's heart are inclined to evil from his youth."

this passage they argue as follows: "Moses does not say that our nature is evil, but that it is inclined to evil. This tendency or inclination is under the control of the free will, and it does not impel man to evil"; or, to use their own words, it does not put man under compulsion.

Then they look for a reason for this opinion and declare that even after the fall man has a good will and a sound reason, inasmuch as the natural endowments have remained unimpaired, not only in man but also in the devil. Finally, they pervert Aristotle's axiom that reason is disposed toward what is best, and give it this meaning.[22]

... From this perverse opinion have originated many dangerous assertions, even some that are clearly false and ungodly, as, for instance, when they maintain: "When a man does that of which he is capable, God gives grace without fail."[23] With this trumpet signal, as it were, they have urged men on to prayers, fastings, bodily tortures, pilgrimages, and the like. Thus the world was convinced that if men did as much as they were able to do by nature, they were earning grace, if not by the merit of condignity, then by the merit of congruity.[24] The merit of congruity they have traced back to the idea that a work was not contrary to the Law of God but in accordance with the Law of God; for to an evil work punishment is due, not merit. The merit of condignity they ascribe not to the work itself but to the character of the work, if it was performed in a state of grace.

Of the same sort is the statement of Scotus that as a result of his natural endowments man is able to love God above all things, for the basis of this statement is the claim that the natural endowments are unimpaired. He reasons thus: A man loves a girl, who is a creature. But he loves her so desperately that he risks himself and his life for her. A merchant loves riches, and indeed so passionately that he undergoes a thousand perils provided he can make some profit. Therefore if there is such love for creatures, who rank far beneath God, how much more will man love God, who is the highest good? Hence God can be loved on the basis of the natural endowments alone.[25]

This is a fine conclusion, one worthy of a Franciscan monk! It shows that such a great theologian does not know what it means to love God. Our nature is so corrupt that it no longer knows God unless it is

22 Cf. Aristotle, *Nicomachean Ethics* 1102b15–16. Luther cites this phrase throughout his career. Cf. *Lectures on Romans* (1515–16), LW 25:345 (see above, p. 23).

23 See *Commentary on Psalm 51* (1532), LW 12:341–42 (see above, p. 290 and n. 12).

24 For a definition of these two types of meritorious acts, see the volume introduction above, p. ix; and above, p. 229 n. 10.

25 Cf. *Lectures on Romans* (1515–16), LW 25:261 (see above, p. 16); *Lectures on Galatians* (1531), LW 26:128 (see above, p. 232); *Commentary on Psalm 51* (1532), LW 12:345 (see above, p. 291).

enlightened by the Word and the Spirit of God. How, then, can it love God without the Holy Spirit? It is true that there is no desire for anything that is unknown. Hence our nature cannot love God, whom it does not know; but it loves an idol and the dream of its heart. Furthermore, it is so completely bound up in its love for the creatures that even after it has learned to know God from the Word, it still disregards Him and despises His Word, as the examples of our own people show.

Foolish and blasphemous statements of this kind are a sure proof that scholastic theology has clearly degenerated into a kind of philosophy that has no true knowledge of God. But because it does not know the Word, it also does not know God and is in darkness. Aristotle and Cicero, who are the most eminent men in this class, teach many things about the virtues and bestow superb praise on them because of their civil purpose; for they see that they are beneficial both in public and in private life. Concerning God, however, they teach nothing. They do not teach that His will and command are to be considered in preference to either public or private advantage; for men who do not have the Word lack the knowledge of this will of God.[26] Assuredly, the scholastic theologians have likewise been captivated by philosophical fancies and have failed to preserve the true knowledge either of God or of themselves. For this reason they have fallen into such fearful errors.

Genesis 19:14

So Lot went out and said to his sons-in-law . . . the Lord is about to destroy the city. . . .

. . . It is a general rule that whether something good is done through human beings or through angels, you must conclude that it has been done by the Lord and give Him the credit for it.

This rule is necessary, lest we make Moses a heretic and Lot an idolater who speaks of a creature as of the Creator. "The Lord," he says to his sons-in-law, "will destroy this place," although the angels had said that they would destroy this place. Therefore Lot does not consider the person of the angels; he considers God, who gives them the command.

Christ's statement in the Gospel (Matt. 19:4–5) is similar: "Have you not read that He who made them from the beginning made them male and female, and said: 'For this reason a man shall leave his father and mother'?" How shall we in this instance bring Moses into agreement with

26 For Luther, natural reason knows of God but not of God's will for us. Cf. *Lectures on Jonah* (1526), LW 19:53–55 (see above, pp. 130–31).

Christ? For Moses testifies in very clear words that this is Adam's statement, yet Christ asserts that God spoke in this manner.

My answer is: What Adam says, he says by divine authority. Therefore these words are not his own; they are God's. This, then, is the great glory with which the divine Majesty honors us: It works through us in such a manner that It says that our words are Its words and that our actions are Its actions, so that one can truthfully say that the mouth of a godly teacher is God's mouth and that the hand which you extend to alleviate the want of a brother is God's hand. Thus when Adam says to Cain (Gen. 4:6): "Why has your countenance fallen?" it is correct to say that these words are God's words, even though they were spoken by the mouth of Adam.

In this respect the heretics err greatly and associate things that have no connection when they argue about the spoken Word and the Sacrament and divest God altogether of the ministry; for he who does away with the Word and does not accept it as spoken by God does away with everything. Separate the Word from Baptism, from Absolution, and from the Lord's Supper, and they will be nothing.

Externals

Therefore it is not only a foolish but also an ungodly argument of the Sacramentarians[27] to maintain that externals are of no profit for salvation and then heap up examples and statements of Scripture such as (John 6:63): "The flesh is of no avail," etc. A distinction must be made among externals, and not all externals should thus be cast aside in general. Externals are rightly condemned as profiting nothing for salvation when they have been instituted by the will of man or, more correctly, rashly, without the Word of God. In other respects God wants to work through the service of His creatures. For this reason one must consider above all whether these externals are performed in accordance with the institution and will of God or not. If there is no Word or institution of God, then you are correct in saying that the externals profit nothing for salvation but even do harm. Thus Christ says (Matt. 15:9): "In vain do they worship Me with the precepts of men."

But if you see that the externals rest on the Word and were instituted by God's command, then worship those externals silently on bended knee, and say: "Not my pastor, not Peter, not Paul, commands this to be done; it is my Father in heaven who gives the command. Therefore I shall obey in humility, and I shall believe that this obedience will be profitable for salvation."

---

27 "Sacramentarians" rejected the real presence of Christ's body and blood in the Lord's Supper and like the "enthusiasts" embraced a spiritualizing view of Christianity. Cf. Luther, *Smalcald Articles* (1537) III VIII 3–13. See below, p. 414 n. 20.

This distinction is very necessary; for the heretics—either because they have no knowledge of it or disregard it—fall into ugly errors. The conclusion at which Schwenkfeld[28] arrives in the following manner is not universally and unqualifiedly true:

> Nothing external is profitable for salvation.
> Baptism, the preaching of the Gospel, and the Lord's Supper are externals;
> hence they are of no avail for salvation.

The major premise is clearly false, for one must make a distinction among externals. Some are wholly human and have been invented by human beings. Of these the major premise is true. But concerning those that have been instituted and commanded by God the major premise is not true; for they have been instituted for our salvation, as Christ says about Baptism (Mark 16:16): "He who believes and is baptized will be saved," and Paul (Rom. 10:10): "With the mouth confession is made unto salvation."

Thus the spoken Word is indeed the word of a human being, but it has been instituted by divine authority for salvation. For God wants to govern the world through angels and through human beings, His creatures, as through His servants, just as He gives light through the sun, the moon, and even through fire and candles. Here, too, you could say: "No external thing profits. The sun is an external thing. Hence it profits nothing; that is, it does not give light, it does not warm, etc." Who would put up with one who argues in such a silly way?

God's two powers

Therefore the rule of which I have also spoken above stands. It states that God no longer wants to act in accordance with His extraordinary or, as the scholastics express it, absolute power but wants to act through His creatures, whom He does not want to be idle.[29] Thus He gives food, not as He did to the Jews in the desert, when He gave manna from heaven, but through labor, when we diligently perform the work of our calling. Furthermore, He no longer wants to form human beings from a clod, as He formed Adam, but He makes use of the union of a male and a female, on whom He bestows His blessing. This they call God's "ordered" power, namely, when He makes use of the service either of angels or of human beings. Thus in the prophet Amos (3:7) there is the noteworthy statement that God does nothing that He does not first reveal to His prophets.

---

28 Caspar von Schwenkfeld (1489–1561) rejected Christ's real presence in the Lord's Supper and advanced an unorthodox Christology. Luther rejected his teachings and labeled him a heretic.

29 Scholastic theologians distinguished between God's absolute power (*de potentia absoluta*) and God's ordered power (*de potentia ordinata*).

But if at times some things happen without the service either of angels or of human beings, you would be right in saying: "What is beyond us does not concern us."[30] We must keep the ordered power in mind and form our opinion on the basis of it. God is able to save without Baptism, just as we believe that infants who, as sometimes happens through the neglect of their parents or through some other mishap, do not receive Baptism are not damned on this account. But in the church we must judge and teach, in accordance with God's ordered power, that without that outward Baptism no one is saved. Thus it is due to God's ordered power that water makes wet, that fire burns, etc. But in Babylon Daniel's companions continued to live unharmed in the midst of the fire (Dan. 3:25). This took place through God's absolute power, in accordance with which He acted at that time; but He does not command us to act in accordance with this absolute power, for He wants us to act in accordance with the ordered power.

In the schools they recite the statement of Dionysius that God works through His essence but that we work through a quality that has flowed down.[31] But who will understand this? He, however, who properly adheres to the canon we have set up can judge the pope and the world in all their wisdom, namely, that God regularly does everything through the ministry of human beings. Therefore nobody will obtain salvation through so-called spiritual speculations, without external things. Attention must be paid to the Word, and Baptism must be sought. The Eucharist must be received, and Absolution must be required. All these are indeed externals, but they are included in the Word. Hence the Holy Spirit works nothing without them.

The contemplative and active life

Formerly—before God revealed the light of the Gospel—much was written and said about the contemplative and the active life; and in the monasteries and convents monks and nuns who, on the whole, were very pious eagerly strove to have visions and revelations presented to them. Consequently, some even noted down all their dreams. Evidently they all waited for extraordinary illuminations without external means. What else is this than a desire to ascend into heaven without ladders? Consequently, these monks and nuns were very frequently deceived by delusions of the devil.

---

30 *Quae supra nos, nihil ad nos.* For this well-known proverb, attributed to Socrates, see Lactantius, *Divine Institutes* 3.20; Erasmus, *Adagia* 569.

31 Ps.-Dionysius the Areopagite, *On Divine Names* 5.3. Ps.-Dionysius, a fifth- or sixth-century Greek writer, attributed his writings to Dionysius, whom Paul had converted with his speech on the Areopagus (Acts 17:22–34). For this reason, Greek and Latin medieval theologians regarded his writings as apostolic and accorded him great authority.

Hence a certain father in the desert was correct in his judgment; for when he saw that his monks were given to such speculations, he warned them to refrain. He said: "If you think you are ascending into heaven and already setting one foot on the threshold of heaven, draw it back immediately, and do not follow with the other foot."[32] This man condemned speculations, or the contemplative life, which the unlearned and ignorant later on exalted with such great praises. Let him who wants to contemplate in the right way reflect on his Baptism; let him read his Bible, hear sermons, honor father and mother, and come to the aid of a brother in distress. But let him not shut himself up in a nook, as the sordid mob of monks and nuns is in the habit of doing, and there entertain himself with his devotions and thus suppose that he is sitting in God's bosom and has fellowship with God without Christ, without the Word, without the Sacraments, etc.

People of this kind speak most contemptuously of the active life, and I certainly had to pay a high price before I was freed from this error, for it pleases reason and seems to be a worship of angels, as Paul calls it (Col. 2:18). . . . For reason wants to move about among wonderful things that are beyond it. But beware of these snares of Satan, and set up a definition of the contemplative life different from the one they taught in the monasteries, namely, that it is the true contemplative life to hear and believe the spoken Word and to want to know nothing "except Christ and Him crucified" (1 Cor. 2:2). He alone, with His Word, is the profitable and salutary object of contemplation. Beware of forsaking Him; for those who have given up or disregarded the human nature or the flesh of Christ and speculate about God as the monks used to do and now Schwenkfeld and others are in the habit of doing are either driven to despair when they are overwhelmed by the clarity of the Majesty, or they foolishly exult and dream that they have been placed into heaven. . . . You should direct your attention to the ordered power of God and the ministrations of God; for we do not want to deal with the uncovered God, whose ways are inscrutable and whose judgments are unsearchable (Rom. 11:33).

We must reflect on God's ordered power, that is, on the incarnate Son, in whom are hidden all the treasures of the Godhead (Col. 2:3). Let us go to the Child lying in the lap of His mother, Mary, and to the sacrificial victim suspended on the cross; there we shall really behold God, and there we shall look into His very heart. We shall see that He is compassionate and does not desire the death of the sinner, but that the sinner should "turn from his way and live" (Ezek. 33:11). From such speculation

32 Elsewhere Luther attributes this story to Anthony the Great (ca. 251–356), the father of Egyptian monasticism. See *Sermons on John 14–16* (1533–34), LW 24:65.

or contemplation spring true peace and true joy of heart. Therefore Paul says (1 Cor. 2:2): "I determine to know nothing except Christ." We have leisure to speculate on this with profit.

Genesis 26:9

Isaac said to him: Because I thought, 'Lest I die because of her.'

Predestination

But it pleases me to take from this passage the opportunity to discuss doubt, God, and the will of God; for I hear that here and there among the nobles and persons of importance vicious statements are being spread abroad concerning predestination or God's foreknowledge. For this is what they say: "If I am predestined, I shall be saved, whether I do good or evil. If I am not predestined, I shall be condemned regardless of my works." I would be glad to debate in detail against these wicked statements if the uncertain state of my health made it possible for me to do so. For if the statements are true, as they, of course, think, then the incarnation of the Son of God, His suffering and resurrection, and all that He did for the salvation of the world are done away with completely. What will the prophets and all Holy Scripture help? What will the sacraments help? Therefore let us reject all this and tread it underfoot.

These are devilish and poisoned darts and original sin itself, with which the devil led our first parents astray when he said (Gen. 3:5): "You will be like God." They were not satisfied with the divinity that had been revealed and in the knowledge of which they were blessed, but they wanted to penetrate to the depth of the divinity. For they inferred that there was some secret reason why God had forbidden them to eat of the fruit of the tree which was in the middle of Paradise, and they wanted to know what this reason was, just as these people of our time say: "What God has determined beforehand must happen. Consequently, every concern about religion and about the salvation of souls is uncertain and useless." Yet it has not been given to you to render a verdict that is inscrutable. Why do you doubt or thrust aside the faith that God has enjoined on you? For what end did it serve to send His Son to suffer and to be crucified for us? Of what use was it to institute the sacraments if they are uncertain or completely useless for our salvation? For otherwise, if someone had been predestined, he would have been saved without the Son and without the sacraments or Holy Scripture. Consequently, God, according to the blasphemy of these people, was horribly foolish when He sent His Son, promulgated the Law and the Gospel, and sent the apostles if the only thing He wanted was that we should be uncertain and in doubt whether we are to be saved or really to be damned.

But these are delusions of the devil with which he tries to cause us to doubt and disbelieve, although Christ came into this world to make us completely certain. For eventually either despair must follow or contempt for God, for the Holy Bible, for Baptism, and for all the blessings of God through which He wanted us to be strengthened over against uncertainty and doubt. For they will say with the Epicureans: "Let us live, eat, and drink; tomorrow we shall die" (cf. 1 Cor. 15:32).[33] After the manner of the Turks they will rush rashly into the sword and fire, since the hour in which you either die or escape has been predetermined.

But to these thoughts one must oppose the true and firm knowledge of Christ, just as I often remind you that it is profitable and necessary above all that the knowledge of God be completely certain in us and that we cling to it with firm assent of the heart. Otherwise our faith is useless. For if God does not stand by His promises, then our salvation is lost, while, on the other hand, this is our comfort, that, although we change, we nevertheless flee for refuge to Him who is unchangeable. For in Mal. 3:6 He makes this assertion about Himself: "I the Lord do not change." And Rom. 11:29 states: "The gifts and the call of God are irrevocable." Accordingly, this is how I have taught in my book *On the Bondage of the Will* and elsewhere, namely, that a distinction must be made when one deals with the knowledge, or rather with the subject, of the divinity.[34] For one must debate either about the hidden God or about the revealed God. With regard to God, insofar as He has not been revealed, there is no faith, no knowledge, and no understanding. And here one must hold to the statement that what is above us is none of our concern.[35] For thoughts of this kind, which investigate something more sublime above or outside the revelation of God, are altogether devilish. With them nothing more is achieved than that we plunge ourselves into destruction; for they present an object that is inscrutable, namely, the unrevealed God. Why not rather let God keep His decisions and mysteries in secret? We have no reason to exert ourselves so much that these decisions and mysteries be revealed to us.

Moses, too, asked God to show him His face; but the Lord replies: "You shall see My back, but you will not be able to see My face" (cf. Exod. 33:23). For this inquisitiveness is original sin itself, by which we are impelled to strive for a way to God through natural speculation. But this is a great sin and a useless and futile attempt; for this is what

33 On the Epicureans, see above, p. 130 n. 3.

34 LW 33:138–47.

35 See above, p. 329 n. 30.

Christ says in John 6:65 (cf. John 14:6): "No one comes to the Father but by Me." Therefore when we approach the unrevealed God, then there is no faith, no Word, and no knowledge; for He is an invisible God, and you will not make Him visible.

Furthermore, God has most sternly forbidden this investigation of the divinity. Thus when the apostles ask in Acts 1:6, "Has it not been predestined that at this time the kingdom should be restored?" Christ says to them: "It is not for you to know the times" (Acts 1:7). "Let Me be hidden where I have not revealed Myself to you," says God, "or you will be the cause of your own destruction, just as Adam fell in a horrible manner; for he who investigates My majesty will be overwhelmed by My glory."

And it is true that God wanted to counteract this curiosity at the very beginning; for this is how He set forth His will and counsel: "I will reveal My foreknowledge and predestination to you in an extraordinary manner, but not by this way of reason and carnal wisdom, as you imagine. This is how I will do so: From an unrevealed God I will become a revealed God. Nevertheless, I will remain the same God. I will be made flesh, or send My Son. He shall die for your sins and shall rise again from the dead. And in this way I will fulfill your desire, in order that you may be able to know whether you are predestined or not. Behold, this is My Son; listen to Him (cf. Matt. 17:5). Look at Him as He lies in the manger and on the lap of His mother, as He hangs on the cross. Observe what He does and what He says. There you will surely take hold of Me." For "He who sees Me," says Christ, "also sees the Father Himself" (cf. John 14:9). If you listen to Him, are baptized in His name, and love His Word, then you are surely predestined and are certain of your salvation. But if you revile or despise the Word, then you are damned; for he who does not believe is condemned (Mark 16:16).

. . . Therefore we should detest and shun these vicious words which the Epicureans bandy about: "If this is how it must happen, let it happen." For God did not come down from heaven to make you uncertain about predestination, to teach you to despise the sacraments, absolution, and the rest of the divine ordinances. Indeed, He instituted them to make you completely certain and to remove the disease of doubt from your heart, in order that you might not only believe with the heart but also see with your physical eyes and touch with your hands. Why, then, do you reject these and complain that you do not know whether you have been predestined? You have the Gospel; you have been baptized; you have absolution; you are a Christian. Nevertheless, you doubt and say that you do not know whether you believe or not, whether you regard as true what is preached about Christ in the Word and the sacraments.

Lectures on Genesis
Part Two, Luther on Jacob

Isaac blesses Jacob (Genesis 27)

The blessing does not begin as yet, for the text goes on to state that Isaac asked: "Are you really my son Esau?" [v. 24]. But Moses means that when Isaac had touched and felt Jacob's hands, he was taken completely by surprise, dumbfounded, and out of his mind, and that with regard to this blessing he concluded and affirmed in his heart that it should be unalterable and permanent. It is as though he were saying: "The blessing has now been given and is definite." Thus later (v. 33) he will say to Esau: "And he shall be blessed." For it is the Holy Spirit who blesses through Isaac. Therefore one may not revoke or change anything. This was an extraordinary impulse and operation in the Holy Spirit. On this account he concluded within himself, after he had felt the hands and the neck, that he wanted to bless his son. Nor did he change his decision, even though many arguments were advanced against it.

Genesis 27:28–29

May God give you of the dew of heaven, and of the fatness of the earth, and plenty of grain and wine. Let peoples serve you, and nations bow down to you. Be lord over your brothers, and may your mother's sons bow down to you. Cursed be everyone who curses you, and blessed be everyone who blesses you!

This is the form of the blessing, and its first part pertains to the sustenance of the body; for without this we cannot live even in the kingdom of God so far as this life is concerned. For the body must be nourished if we must teach and govern the church. Accordingly, the first part pertains to the management of the household and to household supplies, in order that wife, children, and domestics may have the necessities of daily life. In the Lord's Prayer this is called "daily bread," that is, everything that is needed in the house for the sustenance of the body. "May God give you," says Isaac, "of the dew of heaven, and of the fatness of the earth, and plenty of grain and wine." These are temporal things. On earth we have need of the dew of heaven, that is, rain from heaven, and of the fatness of the earth, that is, fertility of the soil. For one sows in vain on rock, in water, or in a forest. One must sow in fertile and productive land. Then there is also need of rain. And he makes this part of the blessing rich and delightful enough; for he says that he would have plenty of grain and wine to live on, that he would live not only on water frugally and austerely, but would live in abundance and sumptuously. "You will have the wherewithal to take excellent care of your body," says Isaac. "Consequently, it will be nourished plentifully enough and amid an abundance of all things, not just barely." Thus Moses says in Deut. 32:15: "The loved one grew fat and frisky, became fat and gross and gorged."

Jacob's blessing

Accordingly, Jacob is sure of sustenance in the household for himself and his descendants. And that sustenance will not be meager. No, it will be sumptuous and luxurious. And one can surely see in the Books of the Kings how this promise was fulfilled. Therefore the godly should acknowledge that they have their earthly things because God gives and blesses. Nor should they dream, as the heathen and the unbelievers do, that either the good or the evil things in this life come about by chance. On the contrary, they should acknowledge that these great gifts come from God. Therefore they should be grateful to God for these benefits, as the apostles declare in Acts 14:17: "He did good and gave us from heaven rains and fruitful seasons, satisfying our hearts with food and gladness."

The monks and other unlearned people before these times taught contempt for temporal goods, vineyards, and fields. Yet they themselves regarded these with the greatest longing. They ate and drank what was finest and best. Contrary to these dreams of the monks, we should learn that physical benefits are also blessings of God.

The second part of the blessing has to do with the state and pertains to authority; for Jacob is appointed lord over peoples and nations. His descendants will be princes and kings, not only heads of households. For peoples will serve him when they will be subjected, not to heads of households but to princes and kings. Not only one people but many peoples and many tribes will be subject. This was also fulfilled at the time of the judges and the kings, when the children of Israel occupied the land of Canaan, when they not only subjected the Idumaeans but also exterminated all the peoples and kings of that land.

The third part of the blessing is spiritual and pertains to the priesthood. "The brothers born of the same father and the same mother will bow down to you. Perhaps they can enjoy the same authority in the state and in the household, but you alone will get the priestly authority." And this is the chief part of the blessing. Earlier he said: "Peoples will serve you, and the tribes of the earth will bow down to you." This bowing down is a civil matter. But this is something else and has reference to the brothers and sons of the same mother. Although it could be referred to the state, it is more properly understood of the third part of the blessing, since he had mentioned the state previously.

These, then, are the three hierarchies we often inculcate, namely, the household, the government, and the priesthood, or the home, the state, and the church. The home has the daily bread and is a daily realm, as it were. The government has things that are temporal and is more than a daily realm, because it endures throughout all time, excluding eternity. But the priesthood is above the household and the state; it pertains to the church and is heavenly and eternal. In this manner excellent provision has been made for Isaac's son; for he has been appointed the heir, so that he, together with his descendants, has his own household, realm, and church. And it is a rich and magnificent blessing by which he has been established with regard to the future inheritance, which he could hope and wait for with certainty and without any dispute.

The nature of the blessing

But this blessing is more than an empty sound of words or some verbal wish in which one person tells and wishes another person good things, as when I say: "May God grant you pious and obedient children." These words are nothing more than wishes with which I give nothing to the other person but only desire something eagerly for him, and it is a blessing that depends entirely on events and is uncertain. But this blessing of the patriarch Isaac states facts and is sure to be fulfilled. It is not a wish; it is the bestowal of a good thing—the bestowal with which he says: "Take these gifts which I am promising you verbally." For it is one thing when I say: "I would wish you to have a strong and healthy body, and to be gifted with fine talents," where the Word by which you get these things does not follow. It is another thing when I offer you a bag of money and say: "Take the thousand guldens[36] I am presenting to you," or when Christ says to the paralytic (Matt. 9:6): "Take up your bed and go home." According to an ordinary blessing, He would say: "Would that you were well and in full possession of your strength!" But the sickness would not be removed. Nor would a restoration of his strength ensue. Therefore it is only a verbal blessing.

In Holy Scripture, however, there are real blessings. They are more than mere wishes. They state facts and are effective. They actually bestow and bring what the words say. We also have blessings of this kind in the New Testament through Christ's priesthood, which is our blessing when I say: "Receive the absolution of your sins." If I said: "Would that your

36 On "gulden," see above, p. 112 n. 8.

sins were forgiven you; would that you were pious and in God's grace!" or "I wish you grace, mercy, the eternal kingdom, and deliverance from your sins," this could be called a blessing of love. But the blessing of a promise, of faith, and of a gift that is at hand is this: "I absolve you from your sins in the name of the Father and of the Son and of the Holy Spirit; that is, I reconcile your soul to God, remove from you God's wrath and displeasure, put you in His grace, and give you the inheritance of eternal life and the kingdom of heaven." All these things have the power to grant you forgiveness immediately and truly if you believe, for they are not our works; they are God's works through our ministry. Accordingly, they are not blessings that express wishes; they are blessings that have the power to bestow. When I baptize you in the name of the Father and of the Son and of the Holy Spirit, it is just as if I were saying: "I am snatching you from the hands of the devil and bringing you to God, and I am doing this truly and in fact."

In the same way the patriarchs had in their hands the power to bless, that is, to teach on the strength of a definite promise that their descendants would have sustenance, dominion, and the priesthood. This is no different from what it would be if Isaac were saying: "I am giving you grain; I am handing over to you dominion and the priesthood." The Jews treat these blessings too coldly; for they understand them only in a human way and as being expressed in the optative mood, not in a definite statement. But a blessing is the kind of statement that determines and settles something, a clinching statement or verdict. Such power is surely something great, for it really brings and grants physical goods for the household, temporal goods for the government, and spiritual goods for the priesthood. For this power they praised God, who had granted it to the men through whom He pronounced blessings and bestowed benefits of every kind.

Our blessing

But the fact that we see the very saintly patriarchs hand down and receive these goods with such sure faith, while we have such a cold and indifferent attitude toward our own blessing in the New Testament—this is great and deplorable wretchedness. I certainly am greatly ashamed of myself and chagrined whenever I compare myself with them. For look at this woman Rebecca, who lives in flesh and blood just as we do; and look at Isaac and Jacob. But with what a sure, living, and firm faith they are carried along to those future goods, so that they do not concern themselves about the presence of the flesh! Indeed, they seem to be sleeping and snoring in this physical life in view of the things that are promised to them for the future.

We have a richer gift, or surely one that is no smaller in measure and abundance. But we do not have the same faith; we snore, we are half dead, our eyes are dim-sighted, our ears are hard of hearing, our hearts falter and waver; they have, and they do not bother about what they have. For to pronounce Absolution, to administer the Sacraments of Baptism and the Lord's Supper, and to proclaim the forgiveness of sins from the Gospel is something far greater than if Isaac blesses Jacob. For it is just as if I were saying: "I give you the kingdom of heaven, power over the devil, and no matter how much you die, I keep you from perishing." Of course, we do not do this with our own strength; but we do it by virtue of the authority and command of God, who has given men the power to lead one another to eternal life through the priesthood of Christ.

Thus we indeed have far richer promises than they, but we also snore more and disregard this treasure of God's riches and goodness. For we are not grateful to God; we do not rejoice and exult wholeheartedly at this good fortune. We have it in great abundance; but we disregard and despise it, although everything is just as sure as those blessings of the patriarchs. Indeed, what is most horrible of all, the more abundantly we have, the more the world rages and persecutes.

Therefore the vigilance of the fathers, who accepted the promises and blessings with greater spirit and faith, should stir up our hearts and drive out this lethargy. Then we should make much of our gifts, which are equal to or greater than their gifts, even though they, too, are exceedingly great and excellent. We do not have the fathers speaking with us; but we have the Son of God Himself, as the author of the Epistle to the Hebrews says (1:2). We hear Him saying: "I absolve you, I give you the Keys of the kingdom of heaven, the power to baptize, to save, to tread demons and hell underfoot. I give you this divine power in order that you may do the same works that I do, and greater works than these" (cf. John 14:12).

But we, who are listless and sleepy, have thoughts like these: "Christ is true God and man. Consequently, it is not surprising that He bestows these gifts on men. But that men should give the gifts of this life and of the life to come to one another—this seems absurd, impossible, and unbelievable." But this was not the way the saintly fathers felt; they esteemed God's blessing very highly and gave thanks to God with rejoicing. Therefore we should blush when we compare ourselves with them, and we should censure and correct our sluggishness.

Jacob's trials

Now in the last part, the holy cross follows. Yet at the same time it is victory through and in the cross. For this is what Isaac says: "Cursed be everyone who curses you." This passage is taken from chapters 12 and 22, where the Lord says to Abraham: "You will be cursed, but I will turn the curse into a blessing." But the fact that Isaac pronounces this verdict shows that he has great power—power at which hell, together with its demons, and the whole world, with all its might, are compelled to tremble. For this is what he wants to say: "I know that these blessings will be odious to the devil, the world, and the flesh. I know that this is bound to happen, O Jacob. To be sure, I am heaping great gifts on you; I am exalting and glorifying you. For you will be a father without poverty, a king without hindrance, a priest and a saver of souls against the will of the gates of hell (cf. Matt. 16:18). But remember that all these things are a matter of promise, that they have not come to fulfillment in the complete victory which is still hoped for and in prospect. Therefore you will have these things in such a way that it will seem to you that you have nothing at all. For you will be assailed in the household, in the state, and in the church. The ungodly will envy you all these things, and you will be cursed by them in such a way that the curse has been made ready alongside the blessing. Although I am blessing you, the devil and the world will come, your brothers will come, and will curse you; they will persecute you and attempt to defeat and destroy your blessings."

And eventually the outcome was in accord with the prophecy. For how much Jacob suffered immediately after the beginning of the blessing! His brother, Esau, threatens him with death. Here the household cross is laid upon him. He is the father of descendants to come; but day and night he is in danger of his life, is exposed to murder at the hands of his brother, and with much concern and great difficulty he is spirited away by his parents in order that he may avoid this danger. He is compelled to be in exile in Syria for about twenty years. A fine blessing indeed! He surely could have thought: "Father, how does what you said about the dew of heaven and the fatness of the earth agree with such great troubles?" For he does not have even a crumb of bread when he goes to Syria. Poor and destitute, he serves for fourteen years, and in that servitude he suffers many indignities. For this reason his father warns him that he will feel the curse instead of the blessing.

But later, when the famine arises in the land of Canaan, he, together with his whole household, will be most seriously imperiled. In fact, he will be in extreme danger of his life. How cruelly and shamefully the children of Israel are eventually treated in Egypt! Where, then, is the blessing? I answer: "Man does not live by bread alone, but by every word that proceeds from the mouth of God" (Matt. 4:4). Man is buoyed up by the Word; he is sustained by the Word. Therefore even though for the present there is no bread in his household, yet he does not die. Nor is he forsaken. But faith in the Word of God feeds both his body and his soul in the midst of poverty and eventually also changes hunger into plenty and abundance. For "those who seek the Lord shall lack no good thing" (Ps. 34:9–10). On the other hand, it is stated about the rich: "The rich suffer want and hunger." And again (Ps. 37:2): "They will soon fade like the grass."

But this must be accepted and waited for with faith. Thus Jacob concluded in faith that nothing would ever be lacking in his household. And eventually the outcome was in very beautiful accord with this; when the blessing followed, he became richer than his father-in-law, Laban, but through trials. He was tried but not forsaken. For the blessing is assailed but not overcome. It is battered and jostled but not felled. Thus the psalm states (Ps. 118:13–14): "I was pushed hard, so that I was falling, but the Lord helped me. The Lord is my strength and my song; He has become my salvation." The Lord bestows a blessing mixed with patience and adorned with reminders of the holy cross, in order that we may be instructed in our trials and learn that our life depends not on bread alone but on every word of God. In the end, however, God surely and without fail supplies us with bread after we have been disturbed in faith about whether we are willing to believe God in His promises. For He makes a promise; but He tests us and withdraws His blessing, as though no blessing should be expected. But He really reflects on and is aware of the blessing when we feel the curse. Consequently, the blessing can be assailed and repressed; but, as is said about truth, it cannot be overwhelmed and subdued.

Our trials

And this was the curse or cross in the household that disturbed the patriarch harshly enough. But look also at the state among his descendants. Look at David, who was the first king according to the blessing, at how often, I ask you, his kingdom is shaken and in danger, as though it would collapse every moment, first at the time of Saul, then through his son Absalom and his wicked counselor Ahitophel. And at the time of Absalom his evil conscience was an additional factor. But despite this he buoyed himself up and sustained himself with God's promise, as is stated in Ps. 21:1: "In Thy strength the king rejoices, O Lord." Likewise (Ps. 63:11): "But the king shall rejoice in God; all who swear by Him shall glory." And in 2 Sam. 15:25–26 we read: "If I find favor in the eyes of the Lord, He will bring me back . . . but if He says: 'I have no pleasure in you,' behold, here I am, let Him do to me what seems good to Him." For the kingdom was promised to him and was established for him, but not without very great vexation and without trials on his part.

In the same way more of the curse than of the blessing is seen in the church. For this we, too, learn from experience—we who are in the same profession and to whom Baptism, the power of the Keys, and the Sacrament of the Altar have been given. But how many even very pious people there are whom Satan assails and infatuates to such an extent when he removes from their sight these heavenly blessings that they seem to retain nothing at all of these blessings! Indeed, they feel the curses and anguish of hell more than they feel the divine and heavenly blessings. Others rush into manifest acts of wickedness and manifest contempt, and cast the blessings aside. But those who retain these blessings and love them are so weak that they have need of many and frequent admonitions and repetitions to arouse them and to sharpen the Word of God in them, as Moses says (Deut. 6:7).

Meanwhile, however, nothing departs from the blessing. No, the blessing remains unalterable, firm, exceedingly rich, and greater than we understand. Paul has the same complaint when he says (2 Cor. 12:7) that a thorn was given him in the flesh and also (Acts 14:22) that we must enter the kingdom of heaven through many tribulations. Accordingly, curses will not be lacking. But go forth to face them more boldly, be strong, and cling steadfastly to the blessing, no matter how much everything seems to be full of a curse. For this is what we should conclude: It is sure that I have been baptized. I have heard the Word from the mouth of the minister. I have made use of the Sacrament of the Altar. This is the divine and unchangeable truth. Even though I am weak, it is sure and unalterable. They are exceedingly powerful and rich possessions, but the heart is slippery and vacillating when taking hold of them. But we should not deny them. This is the only thing against which we should be on our guard. And if we are unable to confess with a loud shout, let us at least make ourselves heard in a low murmur as best we can. If we cannot sing when we praise God, let us at least open our mouths, in order that we may continue steadfastly in the blessings into which the Son of God has placed us—the blessings which cannot be kept without a great struggle and trials of various kinds. For in this manner the fathers had sure and firm blessings, but not without a trial. And for this reason Christ so assiduously exhorts us to persevere. "By your endurance you will gain your lives" (Luke 21:19). You are children of the kingdom, your sins are forgiven, the devil has been overcome and laid low under your feet, sin and death will do you no harm; but you are blameless. Therefore bear the hostile curses with equanimity.

But after Isaac has mentioned the curses, that is, the cross and the trials which accompany those outstanding and rich blessings, he goes on to add: *"Blessed be everyone who blesses you!"* It is as though he were saying: "They will not all curse or assail you, but many will come who will bless you and share in your blessings. This will be the fruit of your trials if you continue steadfastly in the faith." Thus Christ says (John 12:24): "Truly, truly, I say to you, unless a grain of wheat falls into the earth and dies, it remains alone; but if it dies, it bears much fruit." One Christian who has been tried does more good than a hundred who have not been tried. For in trials the blessing grows, so that with its counsels it can teach, comfort, and help many in physical and spiritual matters. Thus in the world you are cursed, but at the same time you are filled with a heavenly blessing.

Genesis 28:10–11

Jacob left Beer-sheba, and went toward Haran. And he came to a certain place, and stayed there that night, because the sun had set. Taking one of the stones of the place, he put it under his head and lay down in that place to sleep.

Trusting in God's promises

The first point is altogether striking and is worthy of careful treatment. For it contains manifold and rich doctrine almost too grand for us to attain with our explanation. For Jacob goes into exile. He has been compelled to flee the rage of his brother and to leave to the fratricide the blessing owed to him. The latter, however, has been placated by the very fact that the possessor of the blessing flees and leaves him in full possession of it for so many years. These matters in the divine administration are undoubtedly foolish and absurd to our eyes, namely, that the heir who is destined to be the stone at the head of the corner is rejected by the builders (cf. Ps. 118:22; Matt. 21:42). He had been destined to be the ruler in the house, and the government of the house and the church was entrusted to him by divine authority. But to flee from and desert all this is not to have possession of the house or to govern the household and the church. Therefore reason concludes that in the divine promise there are meaningless and empty words, because the realization does not follow but tends in the opposite and contrary direction.

But these matters pertain to our doctrine; for theology is not philosophy, which looks at the things that are at hand, is inflated by prosperity, and is crushed when the same prosperity has been removed. Reason and all the Epicureans argue that God seems to be a liar, because He promises in a kindly manner and puts forth good words but gives things that are evil.[37] He gives Jacob a blessing and, on the other hand, allows it to be taken away. On the contrary, Esau, who has been cursed, remains in the house with his children, his wives, and his whole relationship, and governs everything just as previously he was head of the household and a priest of the church. Jacob goes into exile and abandons his blessing. This indeed is the administration of divine matters! The cornerstone must be rejected in order that we may learn to distinguish between divine and human government, and also that Jacob's blessing has not been lost, but that this is only a trial, to see whether he is willing to cling to it firmly in faith and to wait. For this way Abraham is also ordered to sacrifice his son, as though he were about to lose him (Gen. 22:2). Soon, however, he recovers him with greater glory and profit (Gen. 22:12). Thus David, after being anointed to be king (1 Sam. 16:13), lives in exile for ten years, is a servant of servants, and is king only in name and in accordance with the empty words which he heard from Samuel. Yet he holds out, and he perseveres in faith and expectation, until the outcome corresponds in richest abundance to the promise.

This is the constant course of the church at all times, namely, that promises are made and that then those who believe the promises are treated in such a way that they are compelled to wait for things that are invisible, to believe what they do not see, and to hope for what does not appear. He who does not do this is not a Christian. For Christ Himself entered into His glory only by first descending into hell. When He is about to reign, He is crucified. When He is to be glorified, He is spit on. For He must suffer first and then at length be glorified.

Moreover, God does this in order to test our hearts, whether we are willing to do without the promised blessings for a time. We shall not do without them forever. This is certain. And if God did not test us and postpone His promises, we would not be able to love Him wholeheartedly. For if He immediately gave everything He promises, we would not believe but would immerse ourselves in the blessings that are at hand and forget God. Accordingly, He allows the church to be afflicted and to suffer want in order that it may learn that it must live not only by bread but also by the Word (cf. Matt. 4:4), and in order that faith, hope, and the expectation of God's help may be increased in the godly. For the Word is our life and

37 According to Lactantius (ca. 250–ca. 325), an early Christian apologist, Epicurus formulated a riddle on the problem of evil and divine providence that perplexed many ancient philosophers. Epicurus argued that God is either willing to take away evil and unable, able and unwilling, unwilling and unable, or willing and able. The first three possibilities render God weak, hateful, or both and therefore cannot be true. And yet if God is willing and able, then why does He not take it away? See Lactantius, *On the Anger of God* 13.

salvation. If in this life the children of Adam can say and believe what is commonly stated, namely, that what is postponed is not taken away, why should we Christians not think and believe the same thing? . . .

Therefore is it not shameful that although we have such sure and firm promises about eternal life and the blessing, we still have doubts about God's will or at least are weak in faith? I have been baptized and have the hope of eternal life. Yet I cannot believe as firmly as would be the case if a prince promised me some estate and confirmed his promises by letter and seals. That strength and firmness of faith in this patriarch of ours is all the more praiseworthy. For when he is about to take up the government of the house which he has in accordance with the institution and blessing of God, he flees and leaves his adversary and enemy Esau in possession of the rule. Esau performs and enjoys everything that belonged to Jacob. Yet Jacob's faith is by no means shaken. It does not waver or fall away, even though it appears that the blessing is altogether vain and worthless. Yet I do not doubt—indeed, I gladly think—that those very saintly patriarchs were human beings, that they had flesh and blood just as we have. For if Peter, Paul, and the other apostles had flesh and blood, they were also afflicted with something that was human. For flesh and blood wrestle against the spirit.

Therefore there is no doubt that Jacob sometimes felt doubt and was tried. Was the blessing vain, or was it established? For his flesh was true flesh, and the devil was his foe. Accordingly, he felt not only an external trial, when he was forced to go into exile and was driven from his house and his own possession; but in addition there was an internal trial far more serious and on a far higher plane, when he thought: "What if your mother has deceived you? For you see that your brother remains in possession and acquires the blessing. What if God has changed His purpose? For Esau has the thing itself. I have nothing but meaningless words." And because of this twofold trial God will console him later with a new word.

Accordingly, one should learn patience from the examples of the patriarchs, who were tried in every way, yet not without sin, from which Christ alone was free (cf. Heb. 4:15). Surely Jacob was not tried without sin. He was not Christ Himself. Nor did he have a flesh free from sin. And he was tried as an example for us, in order that we might learn what faith is and what a Christian life is. For it is a life that has a definite promise which is not only postponed but brings the opposite to pass. Jacob should be king and priest by divine dispensation. But something happens that is far different from what has been promised. Then he thought: "Nothing will ever come of it; the outcome will not correspond to the promise." But faith wrestled against the flesh and said: "Flesh and Satan, you are lying;

for God has spoken and has made a promise. He will not lie, even if the opposite happens or I die in the meantime." Thus faith spoke and ordered the light to shine out of the darkness (cf. 2 Cor. 4:6). Therefore faith is not a laughable, cold quality that snores and is idle in the heart. No, it is agitated and harassed by horrible trials concerning the nothingness and the vanity of the divine promises. For I believe in Christ, whom I do not see. But I have His Baptism, the Sacrament of the Altar, and consolation through the Word and Absolution. Yet I see nothing of what He promises. Indeed, I feel the opposite in my flesh. Here, then, one must struggle and do battle against unbelief and doubt. . . .

Jacob's grief

But let us look at the words and the grammar. For these words are spoken with much feeling and indicate great sadness, namely, that after Jacob has been appointed ruler and heir, he leaves Beer-sheba and sets out for distant Haran. But everyone can make his own guess with what great grief the good and saintly patriarch was smitten. He undoubtedly traversed that long journey with many tears and with frequent sighs and sobs, for he fled in secret that he might hide himself from the fury of his brother, Esau, lest Esau pursue him, seize him on the journey, and do him some violence. Therefore he sets out alone, without a servant, without a guide or a companion. It certainly was great misery to go into exile and darkness in this way, to depart from father and mother, to leave that most pleasant association with his parents, and to allow his furious brother, together with his wives, to rule during his absence on that journey. Furthermore, Jacob was a human being subject to human feelings, just as we are. Indeed, the more spiritual he was, the more the wickedness of very evil men, likewise his own sins and troubles, affected and tormented his heart. For saintly men are very tender and are moved more deeply than those stocks and logs, the monks and the self-righteous. Therefore Jacob's departure was sad and troublesome enough without the danger which threatened from his brother. It was not a pleasant promenade; nor did he rest or proceed more slowly, as men do who feel secure and are safe from all snares. No, he hurried; he ran. Nor did his parents give him a companion in order that he might more easily conceal his departure from his brother, Esau. For Esau could have blocked his way and killed Jacob, as he had decided. But Moses uses the figure which they call hysteron proteron.[38] For Jacob fled before Esau discovered that he had fled.

Finally the fiery darts of the devil (cf. Eph. 6:16) were added to this great perturbation of his heart. In this way the devil incited him to think: "Behold, what have I done? I have seized the blessing of my brother,

38 A figure of speech that places the last in a series first.

have disturbed the house, and have enraged my brother and his whole household and relationship." Undoubtedly Jacob was not free from this trial; and although he overcame these trials, they nevertheless greatly tormented and distressed his heart. Accordingly, the saintly patriarch proceeded on his way in this great grief and unrest with worries and tears. For every circumstance was of such a nature that there was every reason for it to wring tears from him.

Genesis 28:12

And he dreamed that there was a ladder set up on the earth, and the top of it reached to heaven; and behold, the angels of God were ascending and descending on it!

Two kinds of saintliness

This is a very beautiful sermon and an extraordinary gem of this whole history, which should be accurately and carefully examined because, as we have often stated, in the legends and histories of the fathers and saints one should observe chiefly that God speaks with them. It is for this reason that they are saints and are called saintly. For there are two kinds of saintliness. The first is that by which we are sanctified through the Word. The second is that by which we are saintly on the basis of what we do and how we live. But these two kinds of saintliness must be most accurately distinguished. For the first and purest kind of saintliness is the Word, in which there is no fault, no spot, no sin; but it is so saintly that it needs no remission of sins, because it is God's truth, as we read in John 17:17: "Sanctify them in the truth; Thy Word is truth." In that saintliness we, who have been called through the Word, glory. It is outside us; it is not our work. It is not formal righteousness; but it is a heavenly saintliness communicated to us through the Word, and indeed through the spoken Word. Therefore we proclaim that righteousness and oppose it to all forms of righteousness and saintliness of the pope and all hypocrites, for it is unpolluted saintliness. I have the Word. I am saintly, righteous, and pure, without any fault and indictment, insofar as I have the Word. Thus Christ Himself says (John 15:3): "You are already made clean by the Word which I have spoken to you."

But the pope has no knowledge of this saintliness. All self-righteous people despise it and cling to the righteousness of the Law. They do not ascend to the heavenly saintliness by which we are acceptable before God because of His Word. Therefore the legends of the saintly patriarchs should be observed above all when God speaks with them. For from the Word you learn how great the saints are, even if they never performed a single miracle. Yet that is impossible. But before the flesh does anything, we are saintly through the Word. Therefore I conclude: "The Word is not my work. Consequently, when I glory in my work, I lose the Word. On the other hand, if I glory in the Word, my work perishes."

Of this no one can persuade the Papists, who constantly bark out that old saying, "Reason strives for what is best, etc." But let us remember that there are two kinds of saintliness. One is the Word, which is saintliness itself. But this saintliness is imputed to those who have the Word. And a person is simply accounted saintly, not because of us or because of our works but because of the Word. Thus the whole person becomes righteous. Therefore the church is called holy and we are called holy because we have irreprehensible holiness not from us but from heaven. And this saintliness should not be despised. Nor should we be ashamed to be called saintly. For if we do not glory in this saintliness, we do wrong to the true God, who sanctifies us with His Word. "But I am a sinner," you will say. "I know that you are a sinner, and if you were not, I would not want to sanctify you; you would have no need of the Word. But because you are a sinner, I sanctify you," says God.

The other saintliness is a saintliness of works. It is love, which does what is pleasing. Here not only God speaks, but I strive to follow God when He speaks. But because weakness clings to us, this righteousness is not pure. But the Lord's Prayer reigns, and it is necessary to pray: "Hallowed be Thy name" (Matt. 6:9). This pertains to our saintliness and the saintliness of works, which is formal and pertains to the saintliness of the Decalogue and the Lord's Prayer. But the first saintliness must be referred to the Symbol, to the Creed; for I do not take hold of the promise of the Word through the Ten Commandments. Nor do I do so through the Lord's Prayer. But with them I grasp my love and my works. Through faith, however, I take hold of the Word, that is, purity itself.

These things cannot be adequately stated and inculcated. Yet there is an easy distinction between the commandment and the promise. The Word, which justifies the believer without my love and my righteousness, is one thing. It is something else when I take hold of the commandments of God, so that I do not steal, do not commit adultery, etc. But the Papists are submerged in and overwhelmed by their own darkness to such an extent that when they hear this doctrine, they do not hear. Nor do we ourselves retain it firmly enough. Learn, therefore, from the reading of these histories what we have always been accustomed to do in our reading, namely, to linger at this passage, when God speaks with the patriarchs; for here the best and most precious things are to be read.

Jacob's dream

Now let us look at the sermon itself, and from it one surely sees in what great sadness and anguish of heart Jacob found himself. For he is in outer darkness, so to speak, driven from his home and fatherland, forsaken and solitary, uncertain where he can hide in safety. In addition, the devil has come—the devil, who is wont to torment afflicted hearts in a thousand strange ways, so that the truth of the common saying that no disaster is alone becomes apparent. For Satan "prowls around like a roaring lion" (1 Pet. 5:8) and seeks where he can most easily climb over the fence and with what stratagems he can overturn the leaning wagon. He climbs across where the fence is lowest; and if the wagon is unsteady, he turns it over completely. Thus temptation is added and piled up for those who are afflicted and tried, so that it hurls them headlong into despair, into blasphemy or impatience.

These are the works of the devil; these are his customary and constant snares. Therefore besides the physical cross and the exile, Jacob was undoubtedly assailed by the fiery darts of the devil (cf. Eph. 6:16). Perhaps he thought about how he had stolen the primogeniture and about how he had deceived his father. For in this way the devil is wont to make a great and enormous sin out of an excellent work. The fact that God speaks with him is a sign of this very grievous trial. For He is not wont to pour forth His discussions and words in vain. He does not speak unless an important and necessary reason impels Him to speak. Nor is He wont to address or to console those who laugh at Him, who exult and rage against Him in the pleasures or wisdom of the flesh, who live smugly, without fear of and reverence for God. "Wisdom is not found in the land of those who live pleasantly," says Job (cf. 28:13); it is found under the cross of those who are oppressed and are in conflict with spiritual trials. Then there is both a reason and a place for consolation; then God is present and consoles the afflicted, "lest the righteous put forth their hands to do wrong," as Ps. 125:3 says. And "He will speak peace to His servants" (cf. Ps. 122:8). For if He were absent too long, no one could endure and persevere in those trials and ragings. This, then, is a great consolation in his great and exceedingly sad perturbation, and it appears that this, rather than bodily exhaustion, lulled Jacob to sleep. For the devil came to terrify him within his heart while he was in flight and in exile.

But this is Jacob's dream: A ladder has been placed on the earth—a ladder which touches heaven with its top. On it the angels are ascending and descending. And the Lord Himself is reclining on the top of the ladder and is speaking that promise to this third patriarch. He is not speaking through a man. No, He Himself is speaking, a fact which, as we have stated, should be carefully observed in the histories of the fathers.

Allegory of the ladder

Moreover, the ladder is a picture or an image, as it were, that has to have a meaning. For the angels are spirits and fire, as we read in Ps. 104:4: "Who makest Thy angels spirits and Thy ministers a flaming fire." Therefore they have no need of a ladder on which to ascend or descend. Much less does God Himself have need of a ladder to recline on when He has to speak to Jacob, the heir of the promise. But the images and pictures suggested by this ladder have been explained in various ways, and it is not worthwhile to gather and recount them all.

Lyra says that the rungs refer to the patriarchs who are enumerated at the beginning of Matthew's Gospel in the genealogy of Christ.[39] For both sides indicate that Christ descends from sinners as well as from righteous men. The angels, he says, refer to the revelation of the incarnation of Christ—the revelation which took place through the fathers, the prophets, and the apostles. He interprets the ascent as the devotion of the saints when they pray. This thought is not irreverent. But it does not seem to be the principal explanation of allegory.

The *Glossa ordinaria* interprets the ascending angels as the blessed angels who minister to God in heaven.[40] Then it interprets the descending angels as those who do so to minister to men, as is written in Hebrews (1:14): "Are they not all ministering spirits sent forth to serve, for the sake of those who are to obtain salvation?" And in Dan. 7:10 we read: "A thousand thousands served Him; and ten thousand times ten thousand stood before Him."

Gregory calls the angels preachers who give thought to Christ when they ascend and later, when they descend to the church, serve the members of the church.[41] But who could enumerate all the speculations? Although they are godly, yet, like many things in the fathers, they have not been expressed at the right time or at the right place. It is true that a preacher must first ascend through prayer in order to receive the Word and doctrine from God. He should also study, learn, read, and meditate. Later he should descend and teach others. These are the twin duties of priests: to turn to God with prayer but to turn to the people with doctrine. But these matters should be left where they belong.

---

39 For Nicholas of Lyra, see below, p. 421 n. 9.

40 The *Glossa ordinaria* was the standard medieval commentary on the Bible. It assembled numerous comments from the fathers on the biblical text. Luther's reference to Pope Gregory the Great in the next paragraph is an example.

41 Gregory the Great, *The Book of Pastoral Rule* 2.5.

Jesus' interpretation

But because mention is made of this ladder in the first chapter of the Gospel of John, we should look rather at that text. For there the Lord Himself seems to interpret this picture. When Philip brings Nathanael to Christ, he says: "Behold, an Israelite indeed!" (John 1:47.) Here, as Augustine says, he reminds us of that ladder of Jacob, who is also called Israel.[42] This is what Christ says (John 1:50): "Because I said to you: 'I saw you under the fig tree,' do you believe? You shall see greater things than these." And He adds (v. 51): "Truly, truly, I say to you: 'You will see heaven opened, and the angels of God ascending and descending upon the Son of Man.'" We should believe and be content with this explanation of our Savior; for He has a better understanding than all other interpreters, even though they agree properly in this point, that this dream signified that infinite, inexpressible, and wondrous mystery of the incarnation of Christ, who was to descend from the patriarch Jacob, as God says: "In your seed, etc." Therefore He revealed to Jacob himself that he would be the father of Christ and that the Son of Man would be born from his seed. God did not speak this in vain. Indeed, He painted that picture of the ladder to comfort and console Jacob in faith in the future blessing, just as above (Gen. 22:18) He gave the same promise to Abraham and Isaac in order that they might teach and transmit it to their descendants as certain and infallible, and expect a Savior from their own flesh. In this way God strengthens Jacob, who, like the useless trunk of a tree, is wretched and afflicted in a foreign land; and by means of this new picture He transfers to him all the blessings, to assure him that he is this patriarch from whom the Seed promised to Adam will come.

Therefore we must understand the angels in their proper meaning, as Christ calls them in John 1:51, where He speaks of them as "the angels of God," that is, the blessed ones. They ascend and descend on Christ or upon Christ. The ladder signifies the ascent and the descent that are made by means of the ladder and by means of the rungs. If you remove the ladder, it signifies nothing else than the ascent and the descent. The angels, however, do not use a physical ladder or an imaginary one. Nevertheless, there is an ascent and a descent, that is, an angelic ladder, so to speak. This is the principal meaning, just as Christ Himself explains the descent and the ascent of the angels upon the Son of Man without a ladder.

Doctrine of Christ

But what is this ascent and descent? I reply that it is this very mystery that in one and the same person there is true God and man. Accordingly

42 Augustine, *Homilies on the Gospel of John* 7.23 (WSA 3/12:166–67).

the unity of the person fulfills this mystery. And we, who believe, fulfill the Word of Christ (John 1:51): "You will see . . . the angels . . . ascending and descending." For we believe in the one Lord, His only-begotten Son, born of the Virgin Mary, true God and man. This mystery is so great, so grand, so inexpressible, that the angels themselves cannot marvel at it enough, much less comprehend it. But, as is stated in 1 Pet. 1:12, these are "things into which angels long to look." For angels cannot rejoice and marvel enough at that inexpressible union and unity of the most diverse natures which they do not reach either by ascending or by descending. If they lift up their eyes, they see the incomprehensible majesty of God above them. If they look down, they see God and the divine Majesty subjected to demons and to every creature.

These are marvelous things: to see a man and the lowliest creature humbled below all, to see the same creature sitting at the right hand of the Father and raised above all the angels, and to see Him in the bosom of the Father and soon subjected to the devil, as is stated in Ps. 8:5: "Thou hast made Him a little lower than the angels." Likewise in Eph. 4:9: "He had descended into the lower parts of the earth." This is a wonderful ascent and descent of the angels, to see the highest and the lowest completely united in one and the same person, the highest God lying in the manger. Therefore the angels adore Him there, rejoice, and sing: "Glory to God in the highest" (Luke 2:14). On the other hand, when they consider the lowliness of the human nature, they descend and sing: "And on earth peace."

When we see the same thing in the life to come, we, too, shall feel and speak far differently from the way we feel and speak now. For now these are things such as the angels do not comprehend. Nor can they be satisfied. Indeed, they always desire to look into this inexpressible goodness, wisdom, kindness, and mercy poured out upon us when that person, who is the highest and is terrible in His majesty above all creatures, becomes the lowest and most despised. We shall see this wondrous spectacle in that life, and it will be the constant joy of the blessed, just as it is the one desire and joy of the angels to see the Lord of all, who is the same as nothing, that is, the lowest.

We carnal and ignorant human beings do not understand or value the magnitude of these things. We have barely tasted a drink of milk—not solid food—from that inexpressible union and association of the divine and the human nature, which is of such a kind that not only the humanity has been assumed, but that such humanity has been made liable and subject to death and hell yet in that humiliation has devoured the devil, hell, and all things in itself. This is the communion of properties. *God*, who created all things and is above all things, is the highest and the lowest, so that we must say: "That man, who was scourged, who is the lowest under death, under the wrath of God, under sin and every kind of evil, and finally under hell, is the highest God." Why? Because it is the same person. Although the nature is twofold, the person is not divided. Therefore both things are true: the highest divinity is the lowest creature, made the servant of all men, yes, subject to the devil himself. On the other hand, the lowest creature, the humanity or the man, sits at the right hand of the Father and has been made the highest; and He subjects the angels to Himself, not because of His human nature, but because of the wonderful conjunction and union established out of the two contrary and unjoinable natures in one person.

This, therefore, is the article by which the whole world, reason, and Satan are offended. For in the same person there are things that are to the highest degree contrary. He who is the highest, so that the angels do not grasp Him, is not only comprehended but has been comprehended in such a way, is so finite, that nothing is more finite and confined, and vice versa. But He is not comprehended except in that Word as in breasts in which milk has been set forth and poured. Faith takes hold of this Word, namely, "I believe in the Son of God, our Lord Jesus Christ, who was conceived by the Holy Spirit, born of the Virgin Mary (these are the breasts), suffered under Pontius Pilate, was crucified, dead, and buried; He descended into hell; the third day He rose from the dead; He ascended into heaven and sits at the right hand of God the Father Almighty, after subjecting all the angels to Himself." Here there is God and man, the highest and the lowest, infinite and finite in one person, emptying and filling all things.

This, then, is the ascent and descent of the angels of God and of the blessed, who look on this, pay attention to it, and proclaim it, as can be seen on the day of the nativity. They descend as though there were no God up in heaven. They come to Bethlehem and say: "Behold, I announce great joy to you, The Lord has been born for you" (cf. Luke 2:10–11). And in Heb. 1:6 we read: "When He brings the Firstborn into the world, He says: 'Let all God's angels worship Him.'" They adore Him as He now lies in the manger at His mother's breasts. Indeed, they adore Him on the cross, when He descends into hell, when He has been subjected to sin and hell, when He bears all the sins of the whole world. And they submit themselves forever to this lowest one. Thus, therefore, the angels ascend and see the Son of God, who is begotten from eternity. On the other hand, they descend when they see Him born in time of Mary. And whether ascending or descending, they adore Him.

This is how Christ explains this ladder. I regard this as the chief and proper explanation of this passage. And this is that great and indescribable dignity of mankind which no one can express, namely, that by this wonderful union God has joined the human nature to Himself. . . . Accordingly, the ladder is the wonderful union of the divinity with our flesh. On it the angels ascend and descend, and they can never wonder at this enough. This is the historical, simple, and literal sense.

Genesis 32:24

And Jacob was left alone. And a man wrestled with him until the breaking of the day.

This passage is regarded by all as among the most obscure passages of the whole Old Testament. Nor is this strange, because it deals with that sublime temptation in which the patriarch Jacob had to fight not with flesh and blood or with the devil but against God Himself. But that is a horrible battle when God Himself fights and in a hostile fashion opposes His opponent as though on the point of taking away life. He who wishes to stand and conquer in this struggle must certainly be a holy man and a true Christian. Accordingly, this story is obscure because of the magnitude of its subject matter, and because of its obscurity all other interpreters pass it by. It would also be permissible for us to pass it by. But we shall still say what we can.

Lyra has given some kind of explanation of this contest, but he could not explain all things correctly. Augustine resorts to allegory. But bare allegories should not be sought in the Holy Scriptures. For unless they have a story and a certain fact as a foundation, they are nothing else but fables like those of Aesop. Secondly, even if we have a story, it is not the business of all men to form allegories from it. Origen was not too successful, and Jerome had even less success with them, for they did not have a perfect knowledge of the narratives, without which no one can handle allegories successfully. So before all else the historical sense must be dug out. This teaches, consoles, and confirms. Afterward allegory embellishes and illustrates it as a witness.[43] But the narrative is the author, so to say, or the head and foundation of the matter.

We shall therefore make an attempt to see if we can dig out the true sense and doctrine of this passage. If we cannot attain it perfectly, we shall nevertheless not be very far from the mark. First of all, however,

43 See further below, "Luther on Allegory," pp. 466–86.

the hindrances of various opinions must be removed. Hosea adduces this passage when he says (Hosea 12:3–5): "In his manhood he strove with God. He strove with the angel and prevailed, he wept and sought his favor. He met God at Bethel, etc." From this all the interpreters infer that the man wrestling with Jacob was an angel, but we always observe this canon, that whenever Holy Scripture makes mention of apparitions, as above in Genesis 18, when three men meet Abraham, and the word "angel" is not expressly mentioned, there we do not interpret it as angels because it is clearly stated: "The Lord appeared to him," not an angel. But afterward, in chapter 19, when two angels go on to Sodom, we concede that they were angels.

So also in chapter 28:12–13, when Jacob sees the angels ascending and descending and the Lord stands on the ladder. Here we understand the Lord not as an angel, as those who ascend and descend are called angels by name, but as the Son of God, who was to become incarnate, our Lord Jesus Christ, who is true God and true man. By the communication of properties we say: "Man is on high above all creatures, and God is the lowliest one." This is the mystery "into which angels long to look" (cf. 1 Pet. 1:12), because on account of the unity of person they see God below but man above. So also we say: "Man sits at the right hand of God the Father." Likewise: "God descends into hell and ascends into heaven." This is the communication of properties concerning which we spoke more copiously above.

Wherever, therefore, the name of angel is not expressed, we do not understand it as angels. In this passage it is expressly stated: "You have prevailed with God," not only "you have striven with God" but "you have also conquered." Likewise, the statement follows later: "I have seen God face to face." . . .

Wrestling with God

But our opinion is this, that the wrestler is the Lord of glory, God Himself, or God's Son, who was to become incarnate and who appeared and spoke to the fathers. For God in His boundless goodness dealt very familiarly with His chosen patriarch Jacob and disciplined him as though playing with him in a kindly manner. But this playing means infinite grief and the greatest anguish of heart. In reality, however, it is a game, as the outcome shows when Jacob comes to Peniel. Then it will be manifest that they were pure signs of most familiar love. So God plays with him to discipline and strengthen his faith just as a godly parent takes from his son an apple with which the boy was delighted, not that he should flee from his father or turn away from him but that he should rather be incited to embrace his father all the more and beseech him, saying: "My father, give back what you have taken away!" Then the father is delighted with this test, and the son, when he recovers the apple, loves his father more ardently on seeing that such love and child's play gives pleasure to the father.

These games are very common on the domestic scene, but in the affairs and contests of the saints they are very serious and difficult. For Jacob has no idea who it is who is wrestling with him; he does not know that it is God, because he later asks what His name is. But after he receives the blessing, he says: "I have seen the Lord face to face." Then new joy and life arises from the sad temptation and death itself.

This, therefore, seems to be the teaching of this story, if only I could expound it according to its worth, that, according to the example of Jacob, God at times is accustomed to play with His saints, and, as far as He Himself is concerned, with quite childish playing. But to us whom He tempts in this way it appears far different. However, it is excellent and very salutary exercise and perfect instruction, and this is blessed with a very happy end, namely, that one learns "what is the good and acceptable and perfect will of God" (Rom. 12:2). To the flesh it cannot seem otherwise than an evil, troublesome, and gloomy will, but when we are weeping, God is smiling in a most kindly manner, and He takes pleasure in those who fear Him and hope in His mercy (cf. Ps. 147:11).

Moreover, the temptation to despair which usually accompanies this experience increases the grief and agitation of the flesh when the afflicted heart complains that it has been forsaken and cast off by God. This is the last and most serious temptation to unbelief and despair, by which the greatest of the saints are usually disciplined. He who is able to stand and endure in this temptation comes to the perfect knowledge of the will of God so that he is able to say with Jacob: "I have seen the Lord, etc. I did not think that the Lord meant so well with me." But before we reach this stage, life may be a trying experience. Therefore the teaching of this story concerning the temptations of the greatest saints is open and clear. With great delight they taste how kind the Lord is (cf. Ps. 34:8). But even though not all grasp or understand these contests, they are nevertheless not to be rejected for this reason. . . .

These matters must be dealt with carefully for the sake of those who will be future pastors of the churches. For there will always be some who will suffer these temptations. They should be cheered up and strengthened by the voice of the pastors in this manner: "In like manner, have confidence, my son; believe that you have been baptized, that you have been pastured and fed in the Lord's Supper and absolved by the laying on of hands, not mine, but God's, who has said to you: 'I forgive you your sins; I promise you eternal life.'" If they grasp this in firm faith, temptations and the spirit of blasphemy will vanish. For Abraham, too, undoubtedly felt great trepidation and consternation in his whole person when he was commanded to kill his son. In the meantime, however, he retained this faith by which he firmly determined that even if his son were reduced to ashes, he would nevertheless be the father of a posterity according to the promise. "What? Has God become a liar? Will the Lord tell lies? Or will He not keep His promises?" Such thoughts occurred to him. And yet he obeys the command, thinking: "Just as the Lord produced a son from my loins and from the womb of a worn-out and sterile mother, so also He will be able to revive him after he has been burned and reduced to ashes."

In this manner, Abraham also fought against *God*, which is one of the most serious and difficult of all struggles. But in this, God demonstrates His most perfect and excellent will. Although this struggle is not understood and cannot be endured except by the saints, nevertheless this teaching and consolation should be prominent to strengthen us so that we are not devoured by the devil, even though God is faithful, who will not let us be tempted beyond what we are able (cf. 1 Cor. 10:13). For that is what this example of Jacob teaches us. He was completely unequal to this great struggle and yet remained unconquered. But God conducts Himself in such a way toward him that he does not recognize that God is the wrestler. He thinks that it is an angel. But it is God who shows Himself as his adversary as though He wanted to kill him and deprive him of the promises and blessing and hand it over to his brother, Esau. Nor can anyone adequately express in words what his thoughts were on this occasion. But such thoughts as these undoubtedly occurred to him: "What sort of poor wretched being am I? Have I been created only to bear evils? I alone without respite am seized and afflicted by one evil after another. Of all men living, there is none more unfortunate than I am. I see my brother, Esau, reigning in triumph and growing and increasing with great glory, wealth, children, grandchildren, and revenues. What if God has changed His viewpoint, rejected me, and received my brother into favor?"

These were Jacob's thoughts, but they still remained thoughts. For nature and weak faith cannot, indeed, abstain from these, just as it cannot easily divest itself of other emotions such as impatience, wrath, and concupiscence. But they should remain only thoughts; they should not become axioms that are fixed and speak the final word or are established by our judgment and conscience. I cannot prevent my heart from being disturbed by strange vexations. Hence one should follow the advice of the hermit to whom a youth complained that he rather often experienced imaginations concerned with lusts and other sins and to whom the old man replied: "You cannot prevent the birds from flying over your head. But let them only fly, and do not let them build nests in the hair of your head. Let them be thoughts and remain such; but do not let them become conclusions." It is the mark of desperate men like Saul, Judas, and others to make conclusions out of thoughts, saying: "My punishment is greater than I can bear" (Gen. 4:13) and likewise: "I have betrayed innocent blood" (cf. Matt. 27:4). These men throw away the Word, faith, and prayer. That is making judicial sentences out of temptation. But Jacob does not throw away his faith, although he experienced a very serious temptation and had innumerable thoughts which those who are inexperienced in these matters do not understand.

The chief significance of this story, then, is the example of perfect saints and of temptations in high degree, not against flesh, blood, the devil, and a good angel but against God appearing in hostile form. For although Jacob does not know who this man is, he nevertheless feels that he has been forsaken by God or that God is opposed to him and angry with him. Therefore we retain the grammatical, or historical, sense; and when this is fixed, the allegories offer themselves spontaneously.

Genesis 32:26

Then He said: Let Me go, for the day is breaking.

If this wrestler is Christ, of what concern is the rising of the dawn to Him? My reply is that He assumed the character of a man and retained the same until He disclosed Himself. So the dawn also rises for Him in this character, and in the manner of all nations He had to return to His usual tasks. But Jacob said:

I will not let you go, unless you bless me

Why do you not let him go? Your thigh is hurt, and you are already lame; what will you do? "I feel no weakness," says Jacob. Who is strengthening you? "Faith, the promise, and, indeed, this weakness of faith." In this manner God is conquered when faith does not leave off, is not wearied, and does not cease but presses and urges on. So it makes its appearance in the Canaanite woman, with whom Jesus was wrestling when He said: "You are a dog; the bread of the sons does not belong to you" (cf. Matt. 15:26). The woman did not yield here but offered opposition, saying: "Even the dogs eat the crumbs that fall from their master's table." And so she was victorious and heard the excellent word of praise: "O woman, great is your faith!"

Such examples teach us that faith should not yield or cease urging or pressing on even when it is already feeling God's wrath and not only death and sin. This is the power and strength of the Spirit. Christ, while still wrestling with Jacob and with His omnipotence concealed, wants to be dismissed, but Jacob replies: "I will not let you go, unless you bless me." Why? "Because you said that I have been cursed, and for this reason my soul was confused. Therefore take back that sentence and bless me. You must provide me with a retraction, or I will not let you go. I have defeated you in strength of body. I will also overcome the words of your mouth, for my soul, which you said is lost and condemned, has toiled more vehemently than my body and arms. So I will not let you go unless you retract your judgment concerning me and give me the testimony that I have been blessed before God."

Genesis 32:27–28

And He said to him: What is your name? And he said: Jacob. Then He said: Your name shall no more be called Jacob, but Israel, for you have striven with God and with men, and have prevailed.

What is your name? Are you not Jacob? From whence, then, have you such great power and great strength? Now the temptation becomes somewhat milder, and Christ begins to lay aside His mask and to speak comforting and life-giving words. He now reveals Himself just as He did in the Gospel toward the Canaanite woman when He said (Matt. 15:28): "O woman, great is your faith." Her faith was very sharply attacked when He called her a dog. But she came back at Him, saying: "Seeing that You call me a dog, give me the crumbs which fall from the tables of the masters and which belong to the dogs." This was assuredly a beautiful and illustrious faith and an outstanding example which shows the method and skill of striving with God. For we should not immediately cast aside courage and all hope at the first blow but press on, pray, seek, and knock. Even though He is already thinking of leaving, do not cease but keep on following Him just as the Canaanite woman did, from whom Jesus could not conceal Himself but, as Mark says (7:25), she entered the house and fell at His feet.

Even if He hides Himself in a room in the house and does not want access to be given to anyone, do not draw back but follow. If He does not want to listen, knock at the door of the room; raise a shout! For this is the highest sacrifice, not to cease praying and seeking until we conquer Him. He has already surrendered Himself to us so that we may be certain of victory, for He has bound Himself to His promises and pledged His faithfulness with an oath, saying (John 16:23): "Truly, truly, I say to you, if you ask anything of the Father, He will give it to you in My name." Likewise (Mark 16:16): "He who believes and is baptized will be saved." These promises will never disappoint you, unless you refuse to follow and seek. In this case, through your fault, by snoring and sleeping, you lose the most certain promises and Christ Himself, because you refuse to enter this arena and take up the contest with God where the possession of these promises is seen and flourishes. This Man exercises Jacob until true strength and firmness of faith shows itself. For this reason, He changes his name. He says: "Your name shall no more be called Jacob. You were previously called a trampler because of your brother, but they have not yet imposed your true name on you. Your name will be *Israel*. For your fortitude and the invincible strength of heart by which you have conquered God and men have merited this." . . .

Yet He is not conquered in such a way that He is subjected to us, but His judgment, or His wrath and fury and whatever opposes us, is conquered by us by praying, seeking, and knocking, so that from an angry judge, as He seemed to be previously, He becomes a most loving Father and says (Matt. 15:28; Luke 7:50; cf. Matt. 8:13): "O woman, great is your faith. Your faith has saved you. As you have believed, so be it unto you. Oh, how you hurt Me with your cry!" It is the fullness of consolation that God exercises us in such a way and exhorts us to fight and shows that it is to Him a most pleasing sacrifice to be conquered by us.

But these matters must not be measured by the judgment of reason, which also tries to conquer God by its own strength and works. But God is conquered in this way as soon as He has surrendered Himself to us, so to say, and revealed Himself in His Word, promise, and Baptism. It remains that you should conquer those things which want to take this God away from you, namely, through the truth of the promises and faith. Or, if He pretends that He is unfriendly and angry with you inasmuch as He does not want to hear you and help you, then say: "Lord God, You have promised this in Your Word. Therefore You will not change Your promise. I have been baptized: I have been absolved." If you persistently urge and press on in this way, He will be conquered and say: "Let it be done unto you as you have petitioned, for you have the promise and the blessing. I have to give in to you. For a constant and persistent seeker and petitioner is the sweetest sacrifice."

Genesis 32:29–31

Then Jacob asked Him: Tell me, I pray, Your name. But He said: Why is it that you ask My name? And there He blessed him. So Jacob called the name of the place Peniel, saying: For I have seen God face to face, and yet my life is preserved. The sun arose upon him as he passed Peniel.

. . . But the wrestler conceals His identity and leaves him in uncertainty and doubt. The image of this Man is represented to Jacob in accordance with Jacob's feelings. Jacob does not understand, and so the Man does not reply to the question about the name, as though He meant to say: "I told you already previously that you have struggled and prevailed with God and men, and from this you should have gathered who I am." He does not want to tell him His name but proceeds to tempt, vex, and instruct him. But if Jacob had had a grip on himself and clouds were not obscuring the light of the sun, he would have understood more easily what was meant by being a conqueror of God and men. To be sure, he understands the words, but he does not comprehend the matter itself because he does not know that this is the Lord. He thinks: "Well, who are you, in whom I have conquered God and man?" But at length there follow the epiphanies of the Lord when He blesses him. Then, laying aside the mask, He manifests Himself, namely, that the wrestler is God and man, who would at length manifest Himself in our flesh and whom the Jews would crucify.

But what the blessing was Moses did not describe. Undoubtedly, it was that by which the fathers were blessed: "In your Seed all the nations will be blessed, etc. It is I, O Jacob, who have blessed you and will bless you." Therefore what Jacob could not see formerly when he was still a man but investigated and sought in doubt and uncertainty he understands and sees with great joy from the Word and blessing. "It is surely not You, my heavenly Father and Lord?" he thinks. "I thought that You were a specter or a man. Then You are the one who has blessed me, my father, Isaac, and my grandfather Abraham?"

This is the joyful climax of this contest. For now Jacob returns from hell to heaven, from death to life. It was certainly a very fierce and difficult contest which he had hitherto sustained. So he gives thanks to God and confesses his distress. Now he no longer wants this place to retain its former name but calls it Peniel, as though he meant to say: "It should not be called a struggle or vision of hell but a vision of God." Therefore he says: "*I have seen the Lord face to face.*" "And now I see clearly," he says, "that the wrestler who tested me was God Himself. Why was I so terrified? Why was I so alarmed? I did not know that this was the Lord my God."

Without any controversy we shall say that this man was not an angel but our Lord Jesus Christ, eternal God and future man, to be crucified by the Jews. He was very familiar to the holy fathers and often appeared to them and spoke with them. He exhibited Himself to the fathers in such a form that He might testify that He would at some time dwell with us in the form of human flesh.

This true explanation has not been discovered by us or taken over from others, but the man Himself manifests Himself by giving the name Israel to Jacob, and at this point Jacob says: "I have seen the Lord face to face." He Himself, our Lord Jesus Christ, tested Jacob not to destroy him but to confirm and strengthen him and that in this fight he might more correctly learn the might of the promise. Indeed, He added this strength and power to Jacob that he might conquer and joyfully praise the vision of the Lord.

In the grips of tribulation and the struggle itself he did not speak thus, just as others under the cross are never in the habit of uttering such happy and joyful words. But those who are godly and spiritual must nevertheless maintain the struggle and reach the point where they see the face of God, as was said previously concerning the woman of Canaan. She had seen and heard Christ, and when He withdrew into a house to conceal Himself, she followed Him there and pressed on until she succeeded in storming Christ's heart, which was too obstinate, it seemed, in repelling her. Having conquered in such a struggle, we can with the patriarch Jacob congratulate ourselves and boast that we have seen Peniel, that is, the face of the Lord. For in this way Jacob both attests the difficulty of the struggle which he had experienced and his joy; and he wants to say: "Good God, in what great troubles and difficulties I have been involved, and in what great consternation! But thanks be to God, for I have now withstood the struggle and am safe! My soul has been freed and rescued from these troubles, and now I give thanks to the Lord my God."

Genesis 32:31

And he limped because of his thigh.

. . . This is the story and simple meaning of this passage, which has been treated to the best of our ability, and I hope that it will also be plain to others. . . .

Jacob, therefore, has supplied the church of God with a very useful and beautiful example of faith struggling in infirmity, so that we should not think, as the monks imagined, that the fathers and prophets were senseless rocks and logs in whom there was no infirmity. Otherwise, we would have to despair, because we still experience the greatest infirmity in the flesh. For the flesh murmurs and does not want to suffer or to be trodden down. Therefore we complain and cry out that we are being treated unworthily. Let us, then, contemplate the holy patriarchs and comfort ourselves with their example since, indeed, they were not always firm and strong in faith.

Jacob was showered with the richest of consolations, not only with those he himself experienced but also with those that came upon his grandfather Abraham and his father, Isaac. Nevertheless, he wrestles with the greatest infirmity. So you should reflect: "I am not alone in being tempted concerning the wrath of God, predestination, and unbelief. I am not alone! All the saints, as many as have ever believed or now believe in *God's* Son, experience these struggles of temptation, by which either they themselves or the whole church are disciplined. For what is this whole assembly which is called the church? It is a tiny little flock of the most wretched, forlorn, and hopeless men in the sight of the world. What is this flock compared with the whole world, what is it compared with the kingdom of the Turks and France, indeed, compared even with our adversaries, the Papists?

So if you ask where the church is, it is nowhere in evidence. But you must not pay regard to external form but to the Word and to Baptism, and the church must be sought where the Sacraments are purely administered, where there are hearers, teachers, and confessors of the Word. If the church is still not in evidence, you should remember that our blessings are hidden and that their magnitude cannot be perceived in this life. Man is still wrestling, but he is not in any danger; indeed, this contest obtains a very joyful outcome.

Let us compose a proverb from this history: when you think that our Lord God has rejected a person, you should think that our Lord God has him in His arms and is pressing him to His heart. When we suppose that someone has been deserted and rejected by God, then we should conclude that he is in the embrace and the lap of God. So Jacob feels and thinks nothing else but that he will be destroyed. But when he takes stock of matters, he is held fast in the embrace of the Son of God. The example of Job in his humiliation and affliction teaches the same. For in this wonderful manner the Lord treats His saint (Ps. 4:3), namely, when we think that it is all over with us, He embraces and kisses us as His dearest sons. This is what Paul means when he says: "When I am weak, I am strong; when I die, I live" (cf. 2 Tim. 2:11; 2 Cor. 12:10).

Sermons on the Gospel of St. John

1537–39

The terms of the peace established between the Smalcald League and the Holy Roman emperor in 1532 called for a council of the Roman Church. In June 1536 the pope announced that a council would convene in Mantua, Italy, on May 23, 1537. The elector of Saxony, John Frederick, to whom Martin Luther dedicated his commentary on the Magnificat (see above, p. 38), requested a clear confession of faith from Luther on the critical issues of the Reformation. Luther composed a set of articles outlining his faith and the points of disagreement with Rome. When the elector read the articles, he declared them to be his faith. In the spring of 1537, the Smalcald League assembled to prepare for the council in Mantua. Although the league chose not to use Luther's articles, which are known as the Smalcald Articles, Luther arranged for their publication and regarded them as his final confession of faith. The council in Mantua never met. After repeated postponements by the pope, a council finally convened at Trent in December 1545.

Luther became very ill with kidney stones during the gathering of the Smalcald League. He thought he was going to die, and so did everyone around him. Although he was in no position to travel, Luther insisted on returning to Wittenberg. Along the way, he made his final confession of sins to Johann Bugenhagen. In this bleak hour, Luther made a sudden improvement. He began passing the stones, and his strength slowly returned. He considered his recovery a miracle. News quickly spread: "Luther lives!"

In the late spring of 1537, after recovering from his illness, Luther preached on Christ's sermon in John 14–16. Luther thought so highly of these sermons that he declared they were the best he had ever written. In July, Bugenhagen once again departed Wittenberg and went to Denmark to help organize the Reformation. Although he expected to be gone for only a few months, he did not return for two years. During his absence, Luther again assumed the preaching duties at St. Mary's, the city church. Before his departure, Bugenhagen had been preaching on the Gospel of John. When Luther took over, he claimed that neither he nor anyone else could remember where Bugenhagen had left off.

Therefore, he chose to start at the beginning of the Gospel. From July 1537 to September 1539 he preached on the first three chapters of St. John's Gospel. The excerpts below come from these two sets of sermons. In terms of chronology, the selections from John 14–16 were delivered before the selections from John 1–3.

The excerpts below focus on the Trinity and the doctrine of Christ. In the Smalcald Articles, Luther remarked that these two doctrines were not matters of dispute or contention with Rome. They misunderstood the work of Christ but rightly confessed His person. The challenge to these doctrines came from other Protestants. Luther's later writings and academic disputations attest to his growing concern that the faithful know how to speak correctly and accurately about the Father, Son, and Holy Spirit. In these sermons, Luther proclaims to the faithful in Wittenberg Scripture's teaching on the Trinity and the saving work of Christ, true God and true man.

Sermons on the Gospel of St. John[1]

I neither know nor can I ascertain from anyone where our pastor, Dr. Pomeranus, broke off in his sermons on the evangelist St. John, which he preached to us on Saturdays.[2] Therefore I make bold to go back to the beginning with my commentary on the evangelist. For the world—and particularly we in the church, who possess, preach, and confess God's Word—must remain conversant with this evangelist; to this end we must familiarize ourselves with his way of speaking. Therefore we propose to consider his Gospel in the name of the Lord, discuss it, and preach it as long as we are able, to the glory of our Lord Christ and to our own welfare, comfort, and salvation, without worrying whether the world shows much interest in it. Nonetheless, there will always be a few who will hear God's precious Word with delight; and for their sakes, too, we must preach it. For since God provides people whom He orders to preach, He will surely also supply and send listeners who will take this instruction to heart.

1 The following excerpts are adapted from *Sermons on the Gospel of St. John: Chapters 1–4*, volume 22, and *Sermons on the Gospel of St. John: Chapters 14–16*, volume 24 of *Luther's Works: American Edition*, ed. Jaroslav Pelikan and Daniel E. Poellot, trans. Martin H. Bertram (St. Louis: Concordia, 1957, 1961). Minor alterations have been made to the text for consistency in style, abbreviations, and capitalization. The annotations and subheadings are the work of the editor of this book.

2 Johann Bugenhagen was from Pomerania, thus Luther often refers to him by his nickname, Dr. Pomeranus. For more on Bugenhagen, see the introduction to *Sermon on the Mount* (1531), above, p. 147.

John 1:1–3

In the beginning was the Word, and the Word was with God, and God was the Word. He was in the beginning with God. All things were made through Him, and without Him was not anything made that was made.

From the very beginning the evangelist teaches and documents most convincingly the sublime article of our holy Christian faith according to which we believe and confess the one true, almighty, and eternal God. But he states expressly that three distinct persons dwell in that same single divine essence, namely, God the Father, God the Son, and God the Holy Spirit. The Father begets the Son from eternity, the Holy Spirit proceeds from the Father and the Son, etc. Therefore there are three distinct persons, equal in glory and majesty; yet there is only one divine essence.

The Second Person, the Son, and neither the Father nor the Holy Spirit, assumed human nature. He was born of the Virgin Mary when the day of redemption was to dawn. This Son of God, born of the Father in eternity, John first calls "the Word." He says: "In the beginning was the Word, and the Word was with God, and God was the Word." Later he speaks of His incarnation when he says (1:14): "And the Word became flesh." St. Paul speaks similarly in Galatians (4:4): "But when the time had fully come, God sent forth His Son, born of a woman."

I am wont to submit a rather plain and crude illustration in an effort to make this birth of the Son of God somewhat intelligible: As a human son derives his flesh, blood, and being from his father, so the Son of God, born of the Father, received His divine essence and nature from the Father from eternity. But this illustration, as well as any other, is far from adequate; it fails to portray fully the impartation of the divine majesty. The Father bestows His entire divine nature on the Son. But the human father cannot impart his entire nature to his son; he can give only a part of it. This is where the analogy breaks down.

Thus a painting of wine may possess the semblance and likeness of wine, but wine it is not. It does not quench the thirst and gladden the heart of man (Ps. 104:15). Likewise, a painting of water may have the appearance of water, but it is not real water which can be drunk or used for washing and cleansing; similarly, a human father imparts his nature to his son, but not his complete nature, only a fragment of it. In the Godhead, however, the entire divine nature and essence passes into the Son; yet the Son, who remains in the same Godhead with the Father, is one God together with Him. Likewise, the Holy Spirit partakes of the same divine majesty and nature with the Father and the Son.

This must be accepted by faith. No matter how clever, acute, and keen reason may be, it will never grasp and comprehend it. If it were susceptible to our wisdom, then God would not need to reveal it from heaven or proclaim it through Holy Scripture. So be governed by this fact and say: "I believe and confess that there is one eternal God and, at the same time, three distinct persons, even though I cannot fathom and comprehend this. For Holy Scripture, which is God's Word, says so; and I abide by what it states."

The first man to attack the doctrine of the divinity of Christ was the heretic Cerinthus, a contemporary of the apostles.[3] He presumed to fathom and comprehend this article with his reason. Therefore he declared that the Word was not God. And in order to support this view he cited the verse from Deuteronomy (6:4): "The Lord our God is one God"; and also (Deut. 5:7): "You shall have no other gods before Me." With this sham he worked great harm. He gained a powerful following. Many Jews attached themselves to him, even some of those who had believed in Christ. . . .

But now let us look at the text, for it is wonderful.

In the beginning was the Word, and the Word was with God, and God was the Word.

These introductory words to St. John's sermon about the eternal divinity of Christ, so wonderful and unprecedented, were also very strange and unusual to all wise and rational people. He affirmed clearly and distinctly that God is a Word and that this Word is with God, yes, is God Himself, as we shall hear later. John's expression on this subject is far more succinct and vivid than that of Moses, whose book begins with these words (Gen. 1:1–3): "In the beginning God created the heavens and the earth. . . . And God spoke a word, and there was light." St. John got the idea from Moses; but he is far more explicit in his statement that in the very beginning—antedating the creation of the universe, of the heavens, of the earth, or of any other creature—the Word existed, that this Word was with God, that God was this Word, and that this Word had existed from all eternity. This, I repeat, is a peculiar doctrine; it is foreign and strange to reason, and particularly to the worldly-wise. No man can accept it unless his heart has been touched and opened by the Holy Spirit.

3 Cf. Irenaeus (140–200), *Against the Heresies* 1.26, in *Ancient Christian Writers* (New York, NY: Newman Press, 1992), 90: "[Cerinthus] proposes Jesus, not as having been born of a Virgin—for this seemed impossible to him—but as having been born the son of Joseph and Mary like all other men, and that he excelled over every person in justice, prudence, and wisdom. After his baptism Christ descended on him in the shape of a dove from the Authority that is above all things. Then he preached the unknown Father and worked wonders. But at the end Christ again flew off from Jesus. Jesus indeed suffered and rose again from the dead, but Christ remained impassible, since he was spiritual."

It is as impossible of comprehension by reason as it is inaccessible to the touch of the hand.

Any attempt to fathom and comprehend such statements with human reason and understanding will avail nothing, for none of this has its source in reason: that there was a Word in God before the world's creation, and that this Word was God; that, as John says further on, this same Word, the only-begotten of the Father, full of grace and truth, rested in the Father's bosom or heart and became flesh; and that no one else had ever seen or known God, because the Word, who is God's only-begotten Son, rested in the bosom of the Father and revealed Him to us. Nothing but faith can comprehend this. Whoever refuses to accept it in faith, to believe it before he understands it, but insists on exploring it with his reason and his five senses, let him persist in this if he will. But our mind will never master this doctrine; it is far too lofty for our reason. Holy Writ assures us that faith alone can appropriate it. Let anyone who refuses to believe it let it alone. In the end only the Holy Spirit from heaven above can create listeners and pupils who accept this doctrine and believe that the Word is God, that God's Son is the Word, and that the Word became flesh, that He is also the Light who can illumine all men who come into the world, and that without this Light all is darkness. . . .

And now the evangelist begins to explain what this Word is in God. He says:

> *And God was the Word. . . . All things were made through Him, and without Him was not anything made that was made.*

Here you must take note of two words used by St. John: "existed" and "created." Whatever is created, did not exist before, as, for example, heaven, earth, sun, moon, stars, and all creatures, visible and invisible, did not exist before; they were created in the beginning. But whatever did not come into being, whatever was not begun, created, or made, and yet is and has its being—this must have existed previously. Thereby the evangelist powerfully attests to the fact that the Son of God, who is the image of the invisible God (Col. 1:15), was not created or made; for before the world, before all creatures, including the angels, were created, and before the beginning of things, the Speech or the Word was with God. And then we read that everything was created through this Speech or Word of God and that without Him nothing was made. This Word or Speech existed from the beginning of the creation of the world, approximately four thousand years before Christ's birth and incarnation; yes, He was in the Father's heart from all eternity. If that is true, it follows that this Word was greater and more sublime than anything created and made; that is, He must be God Himself. With the exception of God the Creator alone, everything was created—all creatures, angels, heaven, earth, man, and everything animate.

But now John declares that the Word already existed and had His being when God created all things in the beginning. He does not say: "God created the Word" or "The Word came into being" but "The Word was already in existence." We must deduce from this that the Word is not created or made, that He is no creature, but that all things were made by the Word, as the text which follows states. Therefore He must be God, if we accept the premise that the Word preceded all creatures.

To say that He, in His divine essence, is the Word of the eternal Father is a sublime way of introducing the discussion of the divine nature and majesty of our dear Lord and Savior Jesus Christ. Now every doubt has been removed, and it is easy for reason to draw the conclusion: If the Word existed from the beginning, before the inception of all things, then it must follow that this Word was God. Reason can readily make the distinction: anything that had its being before the creation of the world must be God, for there is nothing outside creation but the Creator. All that exists is either the Creator Himself or His creation, either God or creature. Now the Holy Spirit testifies through St. John: "In the beginning was the Word"; furthermore: "All things were made through Him." Therefore the Word cannot possibly be numbered among the creatures but has His eternal being in the Godhead. The incontrovertible and irrefutable deduction is that this Word is God. And this is also St. John's conclusion.

This is the text that establishes the divinity of Christ, given that we may know and believe that our Lord and Savior, born of the Virgin Mary, is also true and natural God, born of the Father in eternity. He is not to be counted among the angels; but He is the Lord and Creator of the angels and of all creatures, as Paul states in the first chapter of Colossians (1:16): "Through Him all things were created, in heaven and on earth, visible and invisible, both thrones and dominions."

If this conclusion is founded on Holy Scripture, which is the Word of God and abides forever (1 Pet. 1:25)—and the Scripture does testify clearly that the Word existed in the beginning, before the creation of any creature, and that all things were made by Him—then we Christians can come to no other opinion or conclusion than that the Word was not created or made but existed from eternity. This conclusion does not rest on reason.

And the Word was with God.

When God was creating the angels, heaven, earth, and all that is therein, and all things were coming into existence, the Word already existed. What was His condition? Where was He? To this St. John makes reply as well as the subject will permit: "He was with God, and He was God." That is to say: He was with God and by God; He was God in Himself; He was God's Word. The evangelist clearly differentiates between the Word and the person of the Father. He stresses the fact that the Word was a person distinct from the person of the Father, with whom He was. He was entirely separate from the Father. John wishes to say: "The Word, who was in the beginning, was not alone but was with God." Just as if I should say: "He was with me; he sits at my table; he is my companion." This would imply that I am speaking of another, that there are two of us; I alone do not constitute a companion. Thus we read here: "The Word was with God." According to reason, this would mean that the Word is something different from God. Therefore he continues and drives home his point: "And God was the Word." He does so, in order to forestall any attempt to separate the Word from God, that is, the Son from the Father, in view of the statement: "In the beginning was the Word, and the Word was with God." Now this gives the impression and sounds as if there were more than one. "You are right," he says, "inasmuch as you distinguish between the person of God and the person of the Word, since God is one person and the Word is another. Despite this, the Word, that is, the Son, is and remains eternal and true God together with the Father."

Our reason makes an entirely different deduction and says: "If you insist that the Word is with God, then are there two Gods?" Therefore St. John wants the three persons distinguished from one another within the one divine essence. And then he joins Them together again in order to avoid the impression that They are divided into three Gods, and in order to stress that there is only one God: God the Father, Son, and Holy Spirit, by whom all things were made. It is as if St. John were to say: "I wish to preach of a Word who became flesh but who was with God and beside God from the beginning. He could not be elsewhere than with God, since no creature existed as yet. It is true, I make mention of two, namely, God and the Word, that is, the Father and the Son. But this Word was with God, yet not as a separate, distinct God; no, He was the true, eternal God, of one essence with the Father, equal in might and glory. The distinction is that the Father is one person, and the Son is another person. Although the latter is a different person, He is nevertheless the same God as the Father. Although there are two of Them, yet the Son remains the one true God with the Father. The two persons are distinguished thus: It is the Father who speaks; the other person, the Son, is spoken."

There are two distinct persons; and still there is one single, eternal, natural God. The Holy Spirit is likewise a person, apart from the Father and the Son; and at the same time the Father, the Son, and the Holy Spirit are one divine essence and remain one God, three persons in the one divine essence. Therefore the Holy Trinity must be spoken of correctly and accurately: The Word, which is the Son, and God the Father are two persons but nevertheless one God; and the Holy Spirit is another person in the Godhead, as we shall see later.

He was in the beginning with God.

Again the evangelist reminds the reader that the Father and the Son are two distinct persons, equally eternal. But he does this in a manner which at the same time apprises him of the fact that the eternal Father sprang from no one, was not made, created, or born, while the Son, the image of the eternal Father, was born of the Father alone and was not made or created. Before Jesus Christ was Mary's Son and became flesh, He was with God and was true and eternal God of one divine essence with the Father, although a person distinct from the Father.

For want of a better term, we have had to use the word "person"; the fathers used it too. It conveys no other meaning than that of an *hypostasis*, an essence or substance which is in a class by itself, which is God. In this unique essence there are three persons but only one God, one single Godhead; there is only one God. Hence Jesus Christ is the Creator and Preserver of all things, together with God the Father, and—after His birth from the Virgin Mary—true God and also true man. . . .

Arius, the heretic, was the most artful and subtle of all the enemies [of the Trinity].[4] In order to support his blasphemous lie that Christ was not true and natural God, he invested it with a semblance of truth by alleging that in this text, "The Word was God," the term "God" did not refer to the true, natural God but to a titular deity. We might illustrate his viewpoint by saying that it is just as if a king were to call a distinguished and noble person a "prince" even though that person is not a real prince. Or I might say to someone before I depart on a journey: "Be the master of the house." In a similar manner, Arius declared, Christ was only called a god, since God had given Him the name and the commission: "Be a god on earth!" He was not really God by nature but was termed "God" in Holy Scripture because He was an unusual person who excelled all others.

And in order to dupe the people and deceive them with cunning speech, to blind them to his blasphemous lie, he declared that Christ was the best and the most glorious of all creatures, not only nobler and more precious than all visible creatures, than heaven, earth, sun, and moon, but also much more sublime and excellent than the angels, whom, together with all other creatures, God had created through Him.

4 On Arius, see above, p. 217 n. 6.

But he could not evade the words: "In the beginning was the Word, and the Word was with God"; he acknowledged that Father and Son were two distinct persons. But, as stated, he distinguished between them by making Christ a creature. However, the text, "In the beginning was the Word," staunchly refutes this position. For if He existed, then it is impossible that He should have been made or created; but together with the Father He was true and eternal God from all eternity, equal in power and majesty. And the blasphemous error of Arius was also mightily disproved and refuted by the words that follow:

All things were made through Him.

Augustine turns these words to good account against the Arians, who are given to pervert, to attenuate, to gloss and interpret so speciously all passages dealing with Christ's deity.[5] St. Augustine really presses them hard with this passage. And Arius found it impossible to surmount this obstacle, no matter how he perverted and glossed the words. They are indeed so clear that he could not circumvent them or twist them in any way.

Thus this text is a strong and valid attestation of the divinity of Christ. St. John includes every creature in his expression, for he says: "All things [for he who uses the word 'all' does not exclude anything] were made by the Word, who was in the beginning." Now Creator and creature are two distinct entities. He, the Word, already existed in the beginning when all things were made. From this fact the evangelist concludes that He not only antedated all creatures, but also that He was a co-worker and equal Creator of all things with the Father. In token and proof of this the work now shows and praises its Master. All that is made, is made through Him; He is the Creator of all creatures. Thus so far as Their divine nature is concerned, there is no difference between Him and the Father. We shall speak of the Holy Spirit later, when this subject is suggested by the text. According to His divine nature, He is the true God, who was in the beginning and was with God. This He actively demonstrated in the work of creation; for all creatures, angels, heaven, and earth were made by Him. In the fifth chapter of John, Christ declares (5:17): "My Father is working still, and I am working." And the text clearly asserts that He is coequal Creator: "All things were made through Him, and without Him was not anything made that was made." In the third chapter of Ephesians Paul says (3:9): "God created all things through Jesus Christ." And in Colossians (1:15–16): "He is the image of the invisible God, the firstborn of all creatures; for in Him all things were created, in heaven and on earth." And in

5 Augustine, *The Trinity* 1.9 (WSA 1/5:70–71).

Hebrews (1:2): "God has appointed the Son to be the heir of all things, and through Him He also created the world."

With these and kindred passages the article pertaining to the deity of Christ has been defended and maintained at all times in the church against all heretics. And it will assuredly also be preserved against the devil and his blasphemous followers until the end of the world. That we may not doubt but know and believe that our dear Lord and Savior, born of the Virgin Mary, is also the real, true, and natural God and Creator together with the Father and the Holy Spirit, we are assured here that the Father creates all things through the Son. . . .

True God and true man for our salvation

The devil is doing his worst against this article of the divinity and the humanity of Christ, which he finds intolerable. Christ must be true God, in accord with the powerful testimony of Scripture and particularly of St. Paul, who declares that in Him the whole fullness of the Deity dwells bodily (Col. 2:9); otherwise we are damned forever. But in His humanity He must also be a true and natural Son of the Virgin Mary, from whom He inherited flesh and blood as any other child does from its mother. He was conceived of the Holy Spirit, who came upon her and overshadowed her with the power of the Most High, according to Luke 1:35. However, Mary, the pure virgin, had to contribute of her seed and of the natural blood that coursed from her heart. From her He derived everything, except sin, that a child naturally and normally receives from its mother. This we must believe if we are not to be lost. If, as the Manichaeans allege, He is not a real and natural man, born of Mary, then He is not of our flesh and blood. Then He has nothing in common with us; then we can derive no comfort from Him.[6]

However, we do not let ourselves be troubled by the blasphemies which the devil, through the mouths of his lying servants, speaks against Christ the Lord—now against His divinity, now against His humanity—and by the attacks which he then makes against Christ's office and work. But we cling to the Scriptures of the prophets and apostles, who spoke as they were moved by the Holy Spirit (2 Pet. 1:21). Their testimony about Christ is clear. He is our Brother; we are members of His body, flesh and bone of His flesh and bone. According to His humanity, He, Christ, our

6 Manichaeans blended elements of Christianity with Eastern mysticism. They flourished in the early church and for a time could count among their numbers the young Augustine. Manichaeans, like the Gnostics and docetists before them, embraced a radical dualism between good and evil, light and darkness. The body was seen as evil and the spirit as good. Manichaeans were forced from the Roman Empire and traveled east. There is evidence of their existence as late as the seventeenth century in southern China.

Savior, was the real and natural fruit of Mary's virginal womb (of which Elizabeth, filled with the Holy Spirit, said to her in Luke 1:42: "Blessed is the fruit of your womb!"). This was without the cooperation of a man, and she remained a virgin after that.[7] Everything else that a mother imparts to a child was imparted by Mary, the mother of God's eternal Son. Even the milk He sucked had no other source than the breasts of this holy and pure mother.

To sum up, we must, first of all, have a Savior who can save us from the power of this world's god (2 Cor. 4:4) and prince (John 16:11), the devil, that is, from sin and death. This means that He must be the true, eternal God, through whom all believers in Him become righteous and are saved. For if He is not greater and more exalted than Moses, Elijah, Isaiah, or John the Baptist, He cannot be our Redeemer. But if, as God's Son, He sheds His blood to redeem us and cleanse us from sin, and if we believe this, rubbing it under the devil's nose whenever he tries to plague and terrify us with our sins, the devil will soon be beaten; he will be forced to withdraw and to stop molesting us. For the hook, which is the divinity of Christ, was concealed under the earthworm.[8] The devil swallowed it with his jaws when Christ died and was buried. But it ripped his belly so that he could not retain it but had to disgorge it. He ate death for himself. This affords us the greatest solace; for just as the devil could not hold Christ in death, so he cannot hold us who believe in Christ.

But, secondly, we must have a Savior who is also our Brother, who is of our flesh and blood, who became like us in all respects but sin. And in the children's Creed[9] we say, sing, and confess: "I believe in Jesus Christ, the only-begotten Son of God the Father Almighty, conceived by the Holy Spirit, not by Joseph, born of Mary, a true, natural man who suffered, was crucified, died, rose from the dead on the third day, ascended into heaven, and sits on the right hand of God, coequal with the Father in power and glory." With a cheerful heart I may declare: "I believe in Jesus Christ, God's only Son, who sits on His right hand as my Advocate. He

7 Luther, like all of the major reformers, confessed the perpetual virginity of Mary. In his sermon on John 2:12, he further explains: "But I am inclined to agree with those who declare that 'brothers' really means 'cousins' here, for Holy Writ and the Jews always call cousins brothers. Be that as it may, it matters little. It neither adds to nor detracts from faith. It is immaterial whether these men were Christ's cousins or His brothers begotten by Joseph" (*Sermons on the Gospel of St. John* [1537–39], LW 22:214–15).

8 Luther paraphrases Gregory of Nyssa's description of Christ's atonement. See Gregory of Nyssa, *Catechetical Oration* 24. The scriptural basis for this metaphor is Job 41:1. Luther also appeals to this metaphor in *Lectures on Galatians* (1531), LW 26:267.

9 *Kinderglaube* is Luther's designation for the Apostles' Creed.

is of my flesh and blood; yes, He is my Brother. For us men and for our salvation He came down from heaven, became incarnate, and died for our sins." And John, too, introduced his Gospel with the theme of the eternal deity of Christ when he said: "In the beginning was the Word"; "this Word," he added later, "became flesh." At the proper time we shall hear more about this. . . .

Thus this article that Christ is both very God and very man is the rock on which our eternal welfare and salvation are built. On this we are baptized; on this we live and die. St. John was preeminent among the apostles in his powerful portrayal of the deity of Christ the Lord, proclaiming as he did that the world, heaven, earth, and all creatures, visible and invisible, were created through the Word, that nothing was made except through this Word of the Father, and that for this reason He existed from eternity, preceding the creation of all creatures; for whatever existed before time, which is marked by a beginning and an end, must necessarily be eternal. . . .

All things were made through Him, and without Him was not anything made that was made.

Here St. John points out that Jesus is God and has been God from eternity, antedating the world and the beginning of all things, also that God created the world and all creatures through the Word, His only-begotten Son and divine wisdom. But he also says that through Him God still governs and preserves His creation and will govern and preserve it until the end of time. . . . God the Father initiated and executed the creation of all things through the Word; and now He continues to preserve His creation through the Word, and that forever and ever. He remains with His handiwork until He sees fit to terminate it. Therefore Christ says (John 5:17): "My Father is working still, and I am working." For just as we were created by Him without our own aid and agency, so we cannot maintain ourselves with our own might. Hence, as heaven, earth, sun, moon, stars, man, and all living things were created in the beginning through the Word, so they are wonderfully governed and preserved through that Word.

How long, do you suppose, would the sun, the moon, the entire firmament keep to the course maintained for so many thousands of years? Or how would the sun rise or set year after year at the same time in the same place if God, its Creator, did not continue to sustain it daily? If it were not for the divine power, it would be impossible for mankind to be fruitful and beget children; the beasts could not bring forth their young, each after its own kind, as they do every day; the earth would not be rejuvenated each year, producing a variety of fruit; the ocean would not supply fish—in short, none of the creatures, animals, or plants could propagate and perpetuate themselves, each after its own kind, as they do every year. If God were to withdraw His hand, this building and everything in it would collapse. The power and wisdom of all angels and men would not be able to preserve them for a single moment. The sun would not long retain its position and shine in the heavens; no child would be born; no kernel, no blade of grass, nothing at all would grow on the earth or reproduce itself if God did not work forever and ever.

Hence God does not merely create; but whatever He created He also preserves as it is—indeed, until the time He Himself has appointed for its termination. The day will come when the sun, the moon, and the stars will cease to be. But in the meantime He lets them shine. Year after year He produces grain anew, as we so clearly perceive. If it were not for His creative work, this grain would never grow. Thus when Christ the Lord declares (John 5:17): "My Father is working still, and I am working," He says in effect: "The Father is the sort of Creator who, after He has created all things, continues to occupy Himself forever and ever with the guidance and preservation of His creatures. So do I." Daily we can see the birth into this world of new human beings, young children who were nonexistent before; we behold new trees, new animals on the earth, new fish in the water, new birds in the air. And such creation and preservation will continue until the Last Day. God the Father, God the Son, and God the Holy Spirit do not rest from Their work, as craftsmen, shoemakers, and tailors do after they have completed their shoes and garments. No, They do not leave off working on Their creation until the end of time. Before one creature dies, They supplant it with another, to ensure the perpetuity of Their creation. . . .

Just as no creature was able to contribute toward its creation at the beginning, so it has not been able to work toward its preservation and the perpetuation of its kind. Thus as we human beings did not create ourselves, so we can do nothing at all to keep ourselves alive for a single moment by our own power. The fact that I grow and develop is God's work alone; without Him I would have died many years ago. If the Creator, who continues to work forever and ever, and His co-worker were to interrupt Their work, all would go to wrack and ruin in a twinkling. This truth prompts us to confess in the articles of our Christian Creed: "I believe in God the Father Almighty, Maker of heaven and earth." If He had not preserved us whom He created, we would have died and perished long ago, yes, even in the cradle or at birth. . . .

We must adhere to this view of creation. It is not true, as several heretics and other vulgar persons allege, that God created everything in the beginning, and then let nature take its own independent course, so that all things now spring into being of their own power; thereby they put God on a level with a shoemaker or a tailor. This not only contradicts Scripture, but it also runs counter to experience. In the doctrine of creation it is of primary importance that we know and believe that God has not withdrawn His sustaining hand from His handiwork. Therefore when St. John declares that everything made was made through the Word, one must also realize that all things created are also preserved by this Word. Otherwise they would not continue to exist very long.

John 1:14
And the Word became flesh.

The evangelist states: "The same Word of which I declared that it was in the beginning, through which all things were made, which was the Life and Light of man, became flesh." In scriptural parlance "flesh" denotes a complete human being, as in John 3:6, where we read: "That which is born of the flesh is flesh." It goes without saying that of a woman both body and soul are born, not an inanimate mass of flesh, a physical being of flesh and blood, designated by Scripture with that one word "flesh." Similarly, fleshly wisdom, glory, power, and strength are the equivalent of what we in the German tongue call human wisdom, glory, power, and whatever may be great and glorious in the world.

Thus the most precious treasure and the strongest consolation we Christians have is this: that the Word, the true and natural Son of God, became man, with flesh and blood like that of any other human; that He became incarnate for our sakes in order that we might enter into great glory, that our flesh and blood, skin and hair, hands and feet, stomach and back might reside in heaven as God does, and in order that we might boldly defy the devil and whatever else assails us. We are convinced that all our members belong in heaven as heirs of heaven's realm. . . .

We have beheld His glory.

What does this mean? The evangelist wants to say that Christ not only demonstrated His humanity with His actions, by dwelling among the people so that they could see Him, hear Him, speak with Him, and live near Him until His thirty-fourth year, by suffering cold, hunger, and thirst in this feeble and wretched human form and nature, but that He also displayed His glory and power in proof of His divinity. Of this He gave proof with His teaching, His preaching, His signs and wonders, convincing anyone of His Godhead who was not blinded and hardened by the devil, as the high priests and scribes were. By word and deed He proved that He was God by nature: He healed the sick and raised the dead; in short, He wrought more and greater miracles than any prophet before Him, in fact, than any other human being ever was able to do.

By way of illustration, as God brought forth heaven and earth through the Word, that is, through Him, even so He, too, performed all that He wished by uttering a word. For instance: "Little girl, I say to you, arise" (Mark 5:41); and: "Young man, I say to you, arise" (Luke 7:14); and: "Lazarus, come out!" (John 11:43); and to the paralytic: "Rise, take up your bed and go home; be delivered of your sickness" (Matt. 9:6); and to the lepers: "Be clean!" (Matt. 8:3; Luke 17:14). In a similar way He fed 5,000 men with five loaves of bread and two fish, prompting those who witnessed this miracle to say: "This is indeed the prophet who is to come into the world" (John 6:14). When a great storm arose on the sea and the Lord rebuked the winds and the sea, all those in His ship marveled, saying: "What sort of man is this, that even winds and sea obey Him?" (Matt. 8:27). With His words He also exorcised the evil spirits. All this He could accomplish with a single word.

As of the only-begotten of the Father.

This is the first time John calls the Word the only-begotten Son of the Father. In these words "as of the only-begotten of the Father," you have the evangelist's own explanation and the answer to your question regarding the meaning of his words: "In the beginning was the Word"; "All things were made through the Word"; "He was the Life and Light of men." Here you hear his own interpretation of them: "The Word, which was with the Father from eternity and is the Light of man, is called the Son, yes, the only-begotten Son of God. He alone is that, and no one else." Here we find the idea clearly stated which the evangelist wanted to convey earlier with the term "Word." Henceforth he intends to preach plainly of the kingdom of Christ. Hitherto he has done so with odd and obscure expressions which lack clarity in any language. But now he says: "This is God's only-begotten Son."

God has many sons and daughters besides; but He has only one only-begotten Son, of whom it is said that all was created through Him. The other sons are not the Word, through which all things were made; but they themselves were created through this only-begotten Son, who is coequal Creator of heaven and earth with the Father. All others became sons through the only-begotten Son, who is our God and Lord. There are many begotten sons; He alone is the only-begotten Son, begotten in the Godhead from eternity. Thus the Word, through which all things are made and preserved, was made flesh, that is, man, was born according to the flesh from the seed of Abraham and David, dwelt among us, and redeemed us from the curse and the power of the devil. By virtue of His incarnation and His eternal and glorious divinity we poor mortals who believe in His name become children of God, and God becomes our Father. We emphasize that Christ alone is, as St. Paul declares (Rom. 1:4), the only-begotten Son of God, through whom God creates, rules, and makes all things.

We must treasure this text and take comfort from it in hours of sadness and temptation. Whoever lays hold of it in faith is lifted out of his distress, for he is a child of eternal bliss. And to this honor he falls heir through the only-begotten Son, who is God from eternity. Now this Gospel begins to be lucid and clear. Until now the evangelist employed peculiar expressions, uncommon in any language, saying: "In the beginning was the Word"; "through the Word the world was made"; and "the Word became flesh." Who ever heard such speech before? But now all becomes plain and evident. Now the evangelist says: "The Word, of which I have spoken to you, is the only-begotten Son of God, true God and Creator with the Father, differing only in this, that He was born of the Father, and the Father not from Him." Thus we confess and pray: "And in Jesus Christ, His only-begotten Son." In Gen. 1:3 we find a similar expression: "God said." And, as already stated, John here adds the explanation.

That Jesus Christ is very God and very man, the only-begotten Son of the Father, begotten of Him in eternity, and born of the Virgin Mary in time, and that believers in Him are redeemed from sin and all evil—this is our Christian faith. This alone makes us Christians. It makes us adopted sons of God, but not His natural children; for Christ, our Head, alone is the natural, true, and only-begotten Son of God the Father. This Gospel should be highly prized and regarded by us, as the holy fathers also regarded it. For whoever has the Son is free from trouble, for then he is a child of God. Although he is not the only-begotten Son of God, he nonetheless becomes a son of God through Him, and as such he is His coheir and brother.

The evangelist also stated that "the Word became flesh and dwelt among us," as any human being dwells among men. We have learned that Christ was a natural man, and then we also beheld His glory as that of the only-begotten Son of the Father. This glory was demonstrated when He raised the dead and when He Himself arose from the dead by divine power. Thus He said in John 10:18: "I have power to lay My life down, and I have power to take it again." After His resurrection He showed Himself alive for forty days, imparting the Holy Spirit. Thus the same Word that became incarnate is "full of grace and truth." Accordingly, the evangelist differentiates between Christ and the patriarchs, Moses, and all the prophets; he exalts Him above all the others. It is as if he were saying: "In all ages there have been great men, though in some more than in others. For example, there were Adam, Noah, Abraham, Isaac, Jacob, Moses, Joshua, Samuel, David, Elijah, Elisha, all of whom proved by word and deed that they were friends and children of God. God worked many great miracles through them; they preached and taught, and their sermons and teachings were passed on to us as our inheritance through the records of Holy Writ. For this reason they were excellent and great men even in the eyes of the world. They believed in Christ as their Savior who was to come; and thus they were children of God, born of and from God, the same as we. They proved themselves by word and deed; and the glory we perceive in them is divine, not physical and earthly. The Old Testament Scriptures also bear witness to this. Nevertheless, they are in no respect comparable to the Word that became flesh." . . .

Full of grace and truth.

We Christians must learn to familiarize ourselves with this phraseology or diction of Holy Writ, indeed of the Holy Spirit, which is so strange to the heathen, to the worldly-wise, and to all unbelievers. This is the evangelist's meaning: "The Word, who became flesh and dwelt among us, whose sermons we heard and whose miracles we witnessed, lived and deported Himself in such a manner as to constrain us to say that He is the true and natural Son of God, full of grace and truth."

To bring about a better understanding of these words, we must contrast Adam and Christ. Through Adam's disobedience and fall original sin was passed on to us, so that we also fell victim to sin and death and incurred God's anger, His damnation, and eternal punishment. Thus we see nothing but God's wrath and disfavor in Adam. We find it reflected in our own wretched, burdensome, and brief life on earth, in all sorts of distress, in sickness, fear, want, misery, and grief, and, in the end, in death. This is why our harassed world laments and complains about this woeful life. Our daily experience also tells us that no one is sure of life even for a moment. One dies of the plague, another drowns, a third one is stabbed to death. And there is nothing more malodorous and filthier than the human carcass. For this reason we hurry to bury it, and in the grave it feeds the maggots. Although human misery is a daily spectacle, it usually affects few people until it strikes them directly. This world is a veritable vale of tears, an abode of sadness, a cheerless desert; for we behold Adam and all men full of God's disfavor, displeasure, wrath, curse, and condemnation. Adam is not full of grace.

By contrast, nothing but grace, love, peace, joy, and favor is evident in Christ. All of these are lavishly and profusely His, since He is the dear

Child of the heavenly Father. Therefore He is a far different man from Adam. The comparison between the two is like that of devil and angel. Whatever Christ says and does pleases God; His acts and words are none but the best. In Isa. 42:1 God says: "Behold My Chosen, in whom My soul delights." During Christ's Baptism in the Jordan and also on Mount Tabor the Father Himself called down from heaven in public testimony and said: "This is My beloved Son, with whom I am well pleased; listen to Him" (Matt. 3:17; 17:5).

Christ's words: "Your sins are forgiven" (Matt. 9:2) and those addressed to the deceased Lazarus: "Come out!" (John 11:43) are both well-spoken and also well-executed. And the Father adds His yea and amen to these words, so that everything Christ says and does is sheer grace, love, and joy; for He is the favorite, the only-begotten Son, who can do nothing amiss. Therefore we must never doubt the Word of Christ, our Lord. We must have our children baptized in accordance with His command and receive the blessed Sacrament; then God the Father will be well pleased for the sake of His beloved and only-begotten Son, through whom He made us acceptable and "chose us in Him before the foundation of the world" (Eph. 1:4). And, as John tells us later: "From His fullness have we all [he includes himself] received grace upon grace" (John 1:16).

John 1:18

No one has ever seen God; the only Son, who sits in the bosom of the Father, He has made Him known.

Holy Writ employs its own peculiar mode of expression, and we must familiarize ourselves with it. Here we have to ascertain the meaning of the phrase "to sit in the bosom of the Father." Ordinarily one does not speak of a father's "bosom" or of a man's "bosom" at all. Fathers take children into their "arms" or hold them against the "chest." It is customary, however, to speak of a mother's bosom, or to say that a maiden holds children to her bosom. The bosom is that which is encompassed by the two arms. We Germans use the terms "to embrace" or "to enfold in one's arms." The German translation does not fully capture the meaning of St. John's peculiar phrasing. He wants to say: We have received it from the only Son of God, who clings to the Father and rests snugly in His arms. John wishes to assure our hearts that the Word revealed by the Son must be absolutely trustworthy, since the Son rests in the bosom and in the arms of the Father, so intimately close to the Father that He is reliably informed about the decisions of His Father's heart.

St. John informed us earlier that the Law was given by Moses, and he also defined the truth which emanated from Christ. Our present statement follows on the heels of that one: "No one has ever seen God" except the only Son, who lies in the Father's arms. This text has caused much unnecessary distress in the higher schools. With concern the question has been raised: "Since no one has ever seen God, is it possible for one to know God or to arrive at a certainty of the existence of God with one's own innate powers?" The answer was yes, and St. Paul's words, recorded in Rom. 1:19f., were cited in corroboration: the existence of a God is evident to the Gentiles, perceived by them from the works of the creation, "so that they are without excuse." They are all acquainted with the law of nature. The Gentiles are all aware that murder, adultery, theft, cursing, lying, deceit, and blasphemy are wrong. They are not so stupid that they do not know very well that there is a God who punishes such vices. Furthermore, their reason tells them that the heavenly bodies cannot run their definite course without a ruler. Thus St. Paul says, Rom. 1:20f.: "The invisible nature of God, namely, His eternal power and deity, has been clearly perceived in the things that have been made, namely, in the creation of the world. . . . For although they knew God, they did not honor Him as God or give thanks to Him; but they became futile in their thinking, and their senseless minds were darkened. They were blinded and worshiped oxen, calves, hogs, storks, and snakes." Who can reconcile these statements? On the one hand, St. Paul says that man can know God; on the other hand, St. John clearly states that no one has seen God, be he ever so wise, clever, and smart, except the only Son of God, who revealed Him to us. Furthermore, Christ tells the Jews in John 8:54–55: "You claim to know God, but you do not know Him; you call Him your Father but do not know who He is." And let us note that here Christ is not rebuking the Epicureans,[10] those fat sows, or the smug scorners, or godless people, who are not interested in God, but the holy Pharisees, who were concerned about God and were seeking Him. It is they whom Christ informs: "If the Son, whom the Father embraces in His divinity, had not come to reveal God to us, no one would know Him." How can these statements be harmonized? The words "no one has ever seen God" exclude all those who seek God and try to find Him with their reason.

Two kinds of knowledge of God

Someday this question is going to cause trouble. But you must learn to answer it in the following way: There are two kinds of knowledge of God: the one is the knowledge of the Law; the other is the knowledge of the Gospel. For God issued the Law and the Gospel that He might be known through them. Reason is familiar with the knowledge of God which is based on the Law. It almost got hold of and sniffed God, for from

10 On "Epicureans," see above, p. 130 n. 3 and p. 343 n. 37.

the Law it saw the difference between right and wrong. The Law is also inscribed in our hearts, as St. Paul testifies to the Romans (Rom. 2:15). Although the same truth was stated still more clearly by Moses, it still remains true that all rational beings can of themselves determine that it is wrong to disobey father and mother and the government, to murder, commit adultery, steal, curse, and blaspheme. Therefore transgressors of the Law, whoremongers, murderers, and thieves were severely punished by the Romans and other pagan nations. Many books have been written about this subject. And these murderers, thieves, and similar rascals—if one collared them and did to them as they did to others—had to admit their wrongdoing in court; for their own conscience tells them that it is not right for one man to kill another. They have the content of the Law of God and the Ten Commandments written in their hearts by nature. They can recognize wrong both in themselves and in others; but while they censure others for infractions of the Law, they do not censure themselves. They, too, break the Law if they can do so in secret. St. Paul refers to this in Rom. 2:3, 20f. . . .

Reason can arrive at a "legal knowledge" of God. It is conversant with God's Commandments and can distinguish between right and wrong. The philosophers, too, had this knowledge of God. But the knowledge of God derived from the Law is not the true knowledge of Him, whether it be the Law of Moses or the Law instilled into our hearts. The people do not obey this Law, especially when they look about and observe that the greater the rogue, the greater his fortune. They infer that there is no God who punishes sin, and accordingly they follow the crowd bent on sin. Or those who would be the most pious argue: "I will honor father and mother, offend or murder no one, will not defraud anyone or rob him of his wife, child, property, and good name; if I conduct myself in this way, I shall be saved." Then from this knowledge of the Law come others, who want to do better but are not nearly as good as the aforementioned; in fact, they do not hold a candle to them.

To illustrate, let us take a monk. He depicts God to himself as enthroned in His heaven, tailoring cowls, shaving heads, and manufacturing ropes, coarse shirts, and wooden shoes. And then he imagines that whoever clothes himself in these not only merits heaven for himself but can also help others get to heaven. This is blindness beyond all blindness, as must be apparent to all. It is not one whit better than the blindness of the heathen, who worship oxen and calves and cannot be compared to those who seek to keep the Law of Moses or the dictates of the natural law. For what comparison is there between a friar's lousy, shabby jester's cap and cord, plus all his hocus-pocus, and the command to obey father, mother, and government? Even the heathen are superior to this group. They demonstrate a deeper knowledge of the Lord our God by their better comprehension of God's Commandments and demands. One might speak of this as sniffing the existence of God without tasting it. The heathen, the philosophers, and all wise people have progressed to a point where they recognize God through the Law. You have already heard, however, what is accomplished by this type of knowledge.

The other sort of knowledge of God emerges from the Gospel. There we learn that all the world is by nature an abomination before God, subject to God's wrath and the devil's power, and is eternally damned. From this the world could not extricate itself except through God's Son, who lies in the bosom of the Father. He became man, died, and rose again from the dead, extinguishing sin, death, and devil.

This is the true and thorough knowledge and way of thinking about God; it is called the knowledge of grace and truth, the "evangelical knowledge" of God. But this knowledge does not grow up in our garden, and nature knows nothing at all about it. Reason has only a left-handed and a partial knowledge of God, based on the law of nature and of Moses; for the Law is inscribed in our hearts. But the depth of divine wisdom and of the divine purpose, the profundity of God's grace and mercy, and what eternal life is like—of these matters reason is totally ignorant. This is hidden from reason's view. It speaks of these with the same authority with which a blind man discusses color. About this John says correctly: "No one has ever seen God; the only Son, who is in the bosom of the Father, He has made this known to the world."

The proper way to acquire a knowledge of God is the right-handed one, to know for sure what the thoughts and the will of God are. No human being can enlighten you on this. As a matter of fact, the human race stands in need of grace through the Son. Reason is confined to the first type of knowledge of God, which proceeds from the Law; and it speaks a vague language. All Turks, Jews, Papists, Tartars,[11] and heathen concede the existence of a God, the Creator of heaven and earth, who, as they say, makes life contingent on our observation of His commandments and prohibitions. The pope goes a step beyond this and also speaks about Christ, but what he says is merely historical. But the fact and the knowledge that all men are born in sin and are damned, that Christ, the Son of God, is the only source of grace, and that man is saved solely through Jesus Christ, who is the grace and truth—this is not Mosaic or legal knowledge but evangelical and Christian knowledge.

---

11 On the Tartars, see above, p. 183 n. 19.

Christian knowledge comes when I hear that the entire human race is so deeply steeped in sin that no one can or will keep God's Commandments, and that we would have had to condemn ourselves before the judgment seat of God if the Son of God had not come, assumed human nature, taken pity on us, and drowned our sins in His blood, thus saving those who believe in Him. No human reason has an inkling of this knowledge; there is not a trace of it in the books of the jurists and sages or even in the Law of Moses. Therefore the scholastics should not debate the question whether man, of himself, can discover that there is a God. They have always striven to know God from the Law, which is inscribed in every heart. But the question should not be "How can God be known from the Law?" but "How can He be known from grace and truth?" For the knowledge from the Law suggests itself automatically and very emphatically when one is terror-stricken or in the agony of death. But the knowledge of God in His grace was revealed from heaven and was otherwise entirely hidden to man. The first mode of knowing God is natural and universal and was reinforced by the Law of Moses. But the Law must not stand there in isolation; grace and truth must accompany it. And the knowledge of God in His grace is the skill and the wisdom which the Son alone has revealed to us. All the saints since the beginning of time either had to learn this, or they were lost. When Adam and Eve fell into sin, the knowledge of grace was at once divulged to them in the promise of Christ. They were told that the woman's Seed would crush the serpent's head (Gen. 3:15), which means that Adam should be saved through this grace which the promised Seed would bring to the world.

That is the spiritual and Christian knowledge of God. The other is carnal and earthly and issues from reason, for it is written in our hearts. But this knowledge must be proclaimed from above and take form in the heart; that is, one must learn that God confers grace through His beloved Son. Therefore behold how blind the world is in its way of knowing God. . . .

God seen properly only in Christ

To summarize, we have been so abominably corrupted by sin that we not only know nothing about our first and natural knowledge of God any longer, but we have also defected from the righteousness of the Law and fallen into lies. With our own fabricated works we presumed to reconcile God.

Thus reason recognizes God from the Law of Moses, as we find stated in Rom. 1:19, 32. But in the sense of the Gospel reason knows nothing of God. For this is a new revelation from heaven, which not only acquaints us with, and instructs us in, the Ten Commandments but also informs us that we mortals are all conceived in sin and are lost, and that no one keeps the Law, but that those who want to be saved will be saved solely through the grace and truth of Jesus Christ. Here is the depth of His nature; here is the will of God. May everyone be apprised, be he who he will—whether he has Moses on his side or whether he is totally submerged in his own righteousness—that there is no salvation or knowledge of God outside Christ. No one is approved by God unless he is marked with the grace and truth of the Son. This knowledge is concealed from reason. Even today the Papists and all the others are ignorant of it. I must come creeping to Christ and be found protected by the Son, attaining everything through His grace and truth. This is God's will and intent. This is knowing God aright. Thus after the fall Adam knew God through the Son, as did all the patriarchs and prophets. They hoped for the advent of the promised Messiah. Through Him they received grace from God. They did not linger with the Law, but through faith they looked to Christ. When they realized their inability to render perfect obedience to the Law, Christ appeared to their troubled and despondent hearts, proclaiming the Father's grace and will: He, the Son, would become incarnate of a virgin and would die for them. This is why we say that it is impossible to see God by means of the Law or by reason. No one can fathom Him, or climb to His heights. He is too lofty. He is seen only by those born of God, not by those born of the blood.

Whence comes the knowledge of the God of grace and truth? It is given by the only-begotten Son of God. The Son of God, who is in God and who Himself is God, is indispensable for this. For He comes from the Father, and He knows the truth. There is no other doctor, teacher, or preacher who resides in the Godhead and is in the bosom of the Father but the one Doctor, Christ. Humanly speaking, the Father enfolds Him in His arms and caresses Him. He who is in the divine essence descends from heaven to us and becomes man. Who else could have revealed God to us? Consult all the law books of the jurists, all the books of the philosophers and of all heathen. You will find that they do not exceed the knowledge of God contained in the Law of Moses, enjoining us not to steal, not to commit perjury, and to love government and parents. To know God from the Law with His back turned to us is a left-handed knowledge of Him. Therefore walk around God and behold His true countenance and His real plan. God is seen properly only in Christ. There we learn that all who wish to be saved must confess that they are damnable sinners and that they must rely on Him who is full of grace and truth. Thus they also attain grace and truth; this is the true mind of God. We must depend on Christ; this is the true knowledge of God.

Look at Holy Scripture. From the days of Adam, Christ has always revealed God to mankind. He never ceased proclaiming such a knowledge of God: that through Him we derive grace and truth, that is, life eternal. . . . When Moses desired to see God, saying: "Show me Thy face!" God said: "Indeed, if you would see Me, you would have to die; however, I will show you My back and My cloak, but to behold My face means death" (Exod. 33:18–20). Thus Moses viewed God's mercy from behind, as it is seen in the divine Word. As for the rest, Moses knew what he was to do; but he was not able to see God's plan and purpose.

Through the only-begotten Son and through the Gospel one learns to look directly into God's face. And when this happens, then everything in man dies; man must then confess that he is a blind and ignorant sinner who must forthwith appeal to Christ. When a monk clearly realizes in his heart that an alien righteousness, the righteousness accorded us by grace for Christ's sake, must save him, he will ask: "What am I to do now with my cowl, my monastic order, my rule?" Cowl and rule will be cast aside. All that he hitherto esteemed as sacred he now regards as dung, yes, as dead. His own righteousness and holiness, whatever has its origin in human power—all this must die, be committed to the grave, and interred. Man no longer wants any part in it. The knowledge of the Gospel is the face of God, the message that we have grace and truth through the death of Christ. Whoever does not have Christ, will not be saved—whether it be Moses, pope, cardinal, Mass, purgatory, vigils, and requiem—all this is nothing but death, death, yes, the devil himself. For God has placed His grace solely in the only Son. If we are without Him, we can fast ourselves to death, confess, observe vigils; but for all that we will never have a good and cheerful conscience. For this reason St. John here invites us never to lose sight of the mercy of God in Christ, for it all depends on Him. Let the Carthusians brag![12] All will be futile without the grace and truth of Christ. Life resides exclusively in the grace and truth of the dear Son of God, our Lord Jesus Christ. And only he who remains in Him knows God.

John 3:1

Now there was a man of the Pharisees, named Nicodemus, a ruler of the Jews.

To date we have discoursed on two chapters of St. John, and now we begin the third. But we could well afford to omit the beginning of this chapter, since it is customary to preach on it on Trinity Sunday; in

12 On the Carthusians, see above, p. 45 n. 6.

fact, almost the entire third chapter is considered at various times in the course of the church year. But, as the saying goes, "a good song bears repeating." And since the letters of kings and princes should be read two or three times or even oftener and one must listen attentively to them, much more ought we to meditate on God's Word night and day, as we are told in the first psalm (Ps. 1:2). It contains divine wisdom which can never be fathomed or fully comprehended, wisdom so infinite and inexhaustible that we can all find plenty in it to study.

This chapter stresses above all else that sublime topic: faith in Christ, which alone justifies us before God. You have often heard me say that the Christian life is made up of two parts, namely, first of faith and then of good works. A believer must be pious and must lead a good outward life. But the first part, faith, is the more essential. The second is never the equal of faith, although it is more highly prized by the world, which ranks good works above faith.

The pope fell from faith and lapsed into good works alone, many of which are of his own invention and choice. The Jews and the Turks did likewise; they steeped themselves in their good works. So it comes about that the second part, namely, good works, has always been esteemed more in the world than faith. Of course, it is true that we must perform good works, and these must be highly regarded. But beware, lest you emphasize these at the expense of Christ and of faith. For the greatest idolatry—yes, the very devil—ensues from too great an emphasis on works. This is what happened in the papacy and among the Turks. They overemphasize good works and entirely overlook faith in Christ. They do not laud and preach God's works but their own. But faith should be preached above all else, and then good works are to be taught. It is faith that takes us to heaven, without and before good works; for through faith we come to God.

This is the lesson which the Gospel of John imparts here through the story of Nicodemus. In his favor he has the second part, good works; he is praised because of these. He lived a holy and honorable life in the world and gave due attention to good works. But see how he fares! He comes to Christ under the cover of night for fear of the other Jews, the elders and the chief priests. Nicodemus was not one of the chief priests or one of the other priests; he was a pious and influential layman, an aristocrat or nobleman among the people, comparable to our counts and knights of today. John says that he was one of the aristocracy, a ruler in the civil government. For the burgomasters were the peers of the princes; therefore the Gospel speaks of them as "rulers" of the people. Joseph of Arimathea and others were such bigwigs. The other rulers probably sided with the priests, with Annas and Caiaphas, thinking it below their dignity to speak to Christ. But Nicodemus comes to Christ with an irreproachable character, with decency, honorableness, and obedience according to the Law of Moses. He is a respectable and honest councillor, a pattern for men in civil office. When he heard of the sermons and miracles of the Lord Christ, he felt impelled to come to Christ and confer with Him. He did not dare divulge his visit to anyone in the council, lest he have his head bashed in or be ejected from the council, exiled from the city, or stripped of all his property. The elders of the people all espoused the cause of the chief priests. In view of this, Nicodemus wants to call on Christ in secret and discuss a great and serious question with Him. He comes at night for fear of Caiaphas and the other chief priests and rulers of the people. He comes to Christ convinced of his own blamelessness and piety, and assumes that he will hear this opinion and statement from Christ's lips: "You are truly a pious man. Go, and continue on your course." But he now hears a strange sermon, one far different from what he had expected, enough to make him giddy and cause his head to reel.

Nicodemus realizes that Christ is a true prophet and teacher sent by God. He found proof for this in Christ's messages and miracles. And he says: "It is impossible that any other than one sent by God could perform such miracles." This is a strong testimony. Nicodemus speaks his mind frankly; he says that Jesus is a true prophet and teacher who bears this out not only with His words but also with His great miracles, which none but God can do. Thus he greets Christ with the words: "Rabbi, we know that You are a teacher come from God and that You teach the way of God correctly."

How does the Lord receive him? He surely lays him low at first, for his hope and good opinion of himself must be crushed and must vanish. Why? His confession that Christ is a teacher of the truth come from God and his praise of His miracles—these Christ accepts and lets stand. Then He replies: "My dear Nicodemus, I shall tell you the truth. Since you regard Me as a prophet of the truth, I shall also carry out this office and inform you of the truth. And this is the truth: Don't imagine that I am going to preach the Law and Moses to you, as is the custom in your schools and churches, where you pay much attention to the Ten Commandments and discuss Moses and the prophets aplenty, but without understanding them. I have come for the purpose of preaching to you a far different and far greater doctrine than has been preached to date in the schools and synagogues." Thus the Lord says in Matt. 23:2: "The scribes and the Pharisees sit on Moses' seat; so practice and observe whatever they tell you, but not what they do." The following words reflect the Lord's meaning:

John 3:3
Truly, truly, I say to you, unless one is born anew, he cannot see the kingdom of God.

These words greatly devaluate good works and the second part of the doctrine: the proclamation of good works. This does not imply that Christ rejects works utterly, for they are also commendable; but they must remain within their prescribed circle and sphere. Compared with the doctrine I am now discussing, namely, faith and regeneration, they are very insignificant. They cannot bring a man to heaven or advance him to that point where he feels a desire to behold heaven or to come into eternal life. No, one must be born again. Without this new birth there can be no membership in the church. These words of Christ are lucid and clear. Nicodemus is pious enough; he abounds in good works; and now he humbles himself and comes to the Lord Christ. Annas and Caiaphas would not have done this. Nicodemus confesses that Christ is a teacher of the truth. Still the Lord tells him: "Your humility and piety count for nothing, and you will not get to heaven unless you are born anew." . . .

Let me illustrate. A child which is to be born two years from now is still nonexistent. At present the maiden who is to carry and bear the child is still unmarried. The child which is to be born of her is nothing and can do nothing. Everyone must admit that one can do nothing until one has life. Therefore all works, however precious and fine they may be, are absolutely nothing if performed before regeneration; they are nothing but sin and death. Consequently, the Lord Christ judges that Nicodemus and all the Pharisees, yes, the entire Jewish nation, who do not accept Christ and believe in Him, are nothing at all; for they are not yet reborn.

. . . We teach in the very best way about good works and say that they can be performed by none but the regenerate, those who are born and created for good works; and we deny the claim of those who say that they perform good works even though they are not qualified—indeed, though they have not yet been born. Good works are necessary; but they are performed only by those who have been born as new persons, by those who can and must do them. If a carpenter is to build a house, it is necessary that the carpenter exist before he does the building. For what could he build if he has not yet been born? The same reasoning must be applied to all good works. What will the wearing of a cowl or a tonsure or many similar works benefit you? I ask you, does this cowl make you a newborn man? It surely does not. But this is true: a cowl covers many a rogue, but it makes no one pious. Of course, I may adorn myself with a cowl; but first ask yourself whether you are born anew, and then inquire about the good works you must do. However, people do not do this; they go right ahead to become monks and nuns on the assumption that they will be saved by means of such works. But make sure beforehand that you are born anew; if you are not, your works are worthless.

Therefore we teach that all the works of man are nothing and in vain apart from the new birth. And for this reason we call this the most important element in the instruction of the people, namely, that first of all they must be reborn. They must be told that they are all dead and that everything else, whatever there may be of conduct, orders, fasting, etc., avails nothing toward the attainment of the forgiveness of sin. First they must be born anew and become new persons.

But now we want to hear something about the nature of this birth. Its importance is stressed by the double oath with which Christ introduces His words. He says: "Truly, truly, I say to you, unless one is born anew." As if He were to say: "Do not imagine, Nicodemus, that you are saved by reason of your honesty and piety. Admittedly, one must live honestly, decently, and usefully in this world. If you do not, then Master Jack, the executioner, will appear on the scene with his sword and rope. He will make you act differently. He will say: 'What you do not want to do, you will be compelled to do!' But if you suppose that your good works are going to attain the kingdom of heaven for you, you will find them of no value. For these works and this piety give nothing but this temporal life to you. Thanks to them, you are not throttled or banished from house and home, wife and child, or hanged on the gallows. Thus if you are a citizen of Jerusalem, you can enjoy life, honor, and fame by reason of your respectability. But so far as the kingdom of heaven, the church, and the kingdom of Christ are concerned, you must remember to become a new man. You must think of yourself as an infant which as yet is not only incapable of a single work but, in fact, does not yet have life and existence." This is what Christians preach.

The Christian message informs us that, to begin with, we must become wholly different persons, that is, that we must be born anew. But how does this happen? By the Holy Spirit and by water (John 3:5). After I have been reborn and have become pious and God-fearing, then I go forth; and everything I do in that regenerate state is good.

John 3:4

How can a man be born when he is old? Can he enter a second time into his mother's womb and be born?

Nicodemus's reply betrays a bit of pique. He says: "I know well enough what it means to be born!" But he is thinking of an infant being born of its physical mother. Nicodemus wants to say: "You are a queer preacher with an odd message. You are a teacher come from God; but You have a low opinion of us, as though we were nonexistent and unborn. Have You no eyes? Don't You see me and the entire city of Jerusalem? Or do You want to say that this adult person, this body, must be crushed, squeezed flat, reduced to nothing, and return to its mother's womb?" If this were the meaning of Christ's words, then there would be no difference between birth and rebirth; then one birth would be like the other. Nicodemus believes that man cannot be born again except in a physical way, the only way he knows about.

Now the Lord replies more explicitly: "Reborn you must be, but not from your mother; for that birth would not be different from the first one. No, you must be born of the Spirit and of water; without this you cannot be saved." Now Christ explains His statement clearly and plainly enough, saying in effect: "I mean a spiritual birth." There are two types of birth. First, there is a physical birth from a woman. Thus we are all descended from Adam and Eve. Here Christ does not refer to this physical birth. He is speaking here of the spiritual birth, which comes from water and the Spirit. . . .

Christ discusses these matters at length with Nicodemus, but Nicodemus cannot understand them. For that matter, they cannot be understood unless one has experienced them and has been born spiritually. But let these words stand, and do not indulge in subtle arguments, even though they appear foolish and strange to reason. Take them in their simple sense, just as they read, not as some have interpreted them. . . . It is true that the word "water" does often symbolize temptation in Holy Writ, especially in the Psalms.[13] But here it cannot be interpreted that way; for here Christ is speaking of Baptism, of real and natural water such as a cow may drink, the Baptism about which you hear in the sermons on this subject. Therefore the word "water" does not designate affliction here; it means real, natural water, which is connected with God's Word and becomes a very spiritual bath through the Holy Spirit or through the entire Trinity. Here Christ also speaks of the Holy Spirit and teaches us to regard Baptism as a spiritual, yes, a Spirit-filled

13 Luther is thinking of passages such as Ps. 18:16 and Ps. 69:1–3.

water, in which the Holy Spirit is present and active; in fact, the entire Holy Trinity is there. And thus the person who has been baptized is said to be born anew. In Titus 3:5 St. Paul terms Baptism "a washing of regeneration and renewal in the Holy Spirit." In the last chapter of Mark we read that "he who believes and is baptized will be saved" (Mark 16:16). And in this passage Christ declares that whoever is not born anew of the water and the Holy Spirit cannot come into the kingdom of God. Therefore God's words dare not be tampered with. Of course, we are well aware that Baptism is natural water. But after the Holy Spirit is added to it, we have more than mere water. It becomes a veritable bath of rejuvenation, a living bath which washes and purges man of sin and death, which cleanses him of all sin.

Christ wants to say: "You are not yet born anew. But I have come to bring you a new way of being born again, namely, a rebirth by water and the Holy Spirit, and to proclaim to you the necessity of this rebirth. I bring you a washing of regeneration which gives you a new birth and transforms you into a new person." With this message the Lord gives Nicodemus and the entire Jewish nation a hard blow and a slap in the face; for they thought: "Lo, we are circumcised; we are the seed of Abraham and of Isaac; we have the Law or the Ten Commandments, the temple—all of which was arranged and commanded by God." Because of this they boasted that they alone would be saved. "No," says the Lord Christ, "I am ushering in a new order. Moses, the Law, the temple, and all Levitical service are now terminated. All those words are a thing of the past. Whatever is written concerning these things serves the purpose of pointing to Me that you may look for My coming and hear My message. My doctrine supplants that of Moses. And now I am not speaking of circumcision and of the temple but of a new washing." The entire Jewish nation was well aware that the Messiah would introduce a new doctrine. The Samaritan woman testified, according to John 4:25: "We know that when the Messiah comes, He will show us all things."

John 3:6

That which is born of the flesh is flesh, and that which is born of the Spirit is spirit.

Recently we heard the sermon in which the Lord told Nicodemus that unless a man is born anew of water and the Holy Spirit, he cannot come into the kingdom of God. Thereby He indicated that our salvation and blessedness does not depend on good works or the righteousness of the flesh but on our being born anew. This new birth must precede the good works. There is nothing hidden about it; it is to be known as a new birth from water and the Holy Spirit. That is how we must be born anew. It is not sufficient to be born of a woman, which is a birth of flesh and blood. This birth we experienced once. No, Christ says clearly and concisely that the birth referred to here must take place through water and the Holy Spirit. This new birth is Baptism. We are baptized in God's name, with God's Word, and with water. Thus our sin is forgiven, and we are saved from eternal death. The Holy Spirit is also bestowed on us; we receive a new nature, different from the one with which we were born. Through Adam we were involved in the realm of the devil, who is our master; death, sin, eternal damnation, and the devil's kingdom were born into us. But here we are reborn from death to life, from sin to righteousness; here we are transferred from the kingdom of the devil into the kingdom of God. You heard that the new birth is effected through the Holy Spirit and water, and that we are renewed through the power and the efficacy of Baptism. The new birth does not stem from our good works; but once we have been born anew, we begin to do good works, as we heard in the last sermon. Although this doctrine is assailed by the pope and the whole world, it is laid down here; and, I take it, so it will remain, regardless of who may adopt this doctrine. No one will ever strike a compromise between flesh and spirit. And begone with everyone who refuses to accept this doctrine!

That which is born of the flesh is flesh.

There is such a wide gulf between these two that it cannot be bridged. Flesh and spirit have nothing at all in common; man is either flesh, or he is spirit. Thus St. John declares: "That which is born of the flesh is flesh" or remains flesh. . . . Whether it be king, prince, or lord—all share the same kind of birth; and the people who have had only this physical birth are nothing but flesh. This implies a condemnation of all that is exalted and precious in the world, call it by whatever name you will: noble or ignoble, powerful, clever, judicious, rich, wise, rational, as well as all learned men. For whatever is born physically is a physical being. And if it does not have another birth, it will never be anything but a physical being which will perish. Truly, this cuts the ground from under our feet; yes, it really condemns us. . . .

Thus this verse passes an appalling sentence on the whole world, a sentence comparable to the one pronounced by St. Paul in the eleventh chapter of Romans, in which he says that "God has consigned all men to disobedience, that He may have mercy on all" (Rom. 11:32). Likewise in Rom. 3:23: "All have sinned and fall short of the glory of God." And in Eph. 2:8–9: "For by grace you have been saved through faith; and this is not your own doing, it is the gift of God—not because of works, lest any man should boast." If we really believed this, it would make us very humble. For is a man's birth of a woman, which is only a physical process and nothing spiritual, to be his greatest glory before God? After all, what would it amount to even though you were born a lord, or even if you were a king or the Turkish sultan, or possessed the most profound wisdom and intelligence on earth? My dear man, what would this really amount to? Nothing but flesh. In the eyes of the world all this may loom big and be greatly praised, but before God it means nothing. Why not? Christ answers this question here: "That which is born of the flesh is flesh"; a physical birth brings forth a physical object, and nothing more than a physical object. This is apparent from the bigwigs, whose might, honor, riches, glory, money, and goods all perish in the end.

Here Nicodemus is sharply lectured and taken to task. It will do him no good to have Moses and the entire Law on his side; despite all this he will remain flesh unless he is born anew. Christ wants to say: "Nicodemus, why do you persist in following Moses so long? You will still remain flesh." So what does the preaching of the Gospel profit the pope and the Turks? They hear and see it all. It is painted for them, written for them, sung and spoken for them. And still they refuse to be converted, for they remain the flesh they were when they were born. Nicodemus too. He and his Pharisees have the Law of Moses, the temple, and divine worship; and yet they remain flesh. We do not fare very differently today. To be sure, we hear the Gospel preached, sung, and read; but we do not become more pious or better as a result. For we are flesh and remain flesh. On the other hand:

That which is born of the Spirit is spirit.

As we have said, there is no way of reconciling the two: whatever is flesh remains flesh, and whatever is born of the Spirit is spiritual. But what is spiritual birth? It means that I am born again as a new being by Baptism and the Holy Spirit and that I believe in Christ. Then I do not expect riches, power, and glory from Him (as many a person looks exclusively for such things in the world) unless God has given me this before. And when the physical birth ends in death—whether this comes by fire or water, or whether I am interred in the earth—then I hope for and expect an eternal life, eternal joy and bliss. I shall be eternally saved even though I lose this life and lack the money and goods, the riches and power after which the world otherwise runs and races.

Thus we are reborn into a new life which is unlike the way of the world. Your natural mother cannot aid you toward this life with her body, her breasts, and the milk an infant drinks. An infant also has need of pap and cradle, clothes and shoes; it must be reared properly and decently.

All these elements of parental support and sustenance are part of physical birth. But when all this has had its day; when you lie in your grave and your good friend, your father, mother, government, and princes cannot accompany you but are powerless to help you; when strength and might forsake you, and you leave behind your popularity, honor, money and goods; when you are buried—then a new birth is required. Then it is necessary to look to another existence, an existence into which I am called by the Gospel and by Baptism, namely, when the Holy Spirit gives birth to me anew for eternal life, rearing, nourishing, and clothing me anew. This calls for other breasts and nipples, a different room and different garments, to nourish me and clothe me—to nourish and clothe me for eternal life and to make me fit for the kingdom of heaven.

Thus the spiritual birth is brought about by the Word of God, Baptism, and faith. Even now, while we sojourn on this earth, we are already in this birth if we believe. I stated earlier that the new birth or the spiritual life cannot be perceived by the five senses. It is invisible. Neither sword nor might, gold nor silver, neither crown, scepter, nor kingdom, can help to acquire this life; it is bestowed through the new birth. And this new life will endure when this physical life ends, when the physical birth vanishes and is reduced to dust. When the physical birth is no longer seen and felt, then the spiritual life will abide, and we shall be quickened and raised from the dead.

This birth is invisible and intangible; it is only believed. We believe that what issues from the spiritual existence is spiritual and that the chief treasure it dispenses is forgiveness of sin and eternal life. At the same time Christians must still participate in external existence too. While they are on earth, they let father and mother sustain them; they are still being governed, and they themselves govern; they eat, and they drink; they wear clothes and shoes, have house and home, money and goods. But all this they use as guests who journey across the countryside until they arrive in the city, which is their real destination.[14] Upon their arrival they do not care any longer for the inns which sheltered them en route. And while they are staying in the inn, they think to themselves: "Today I stay here as a guest, and tomorrow I journey forth again." Thus a Christian also reflects: "Today I am a guest here on earth. I eat and drink here; I live honestly and decently according to flesh and blood. But tomorrow I set out for eternal life in heaven, where I am a citizen and hold citizenship" (Phil. 3:20). Thus Christians pass through the years of their dependence on father and mother, through their time of eating and drinking, of

---

14 For a similar sentiment, see *Sermons on the First Epistle of St. Peter* (1522), LW 30:35 (see above, p. 105).

wearing clothes and shoes; and when they come to their end, they forsake all that is physical and enter into an infinite spiritual life, where they no longer have any use for their physical life and existence.

And now Christ says: "You must be one of the two, either a physical man or a spiritual man. Now choose which you want. There is no compromise: either physical or spiritual." He who chooses to be physical may be intent on good and easy days here on earth, on gorging and carousing, on indulging in all sensual pleasures; for after this life he gets nothing more. He will take along neither money nor goods, neither power nor riches, neither gold nor pearls—everything will remain behind. You may be a Turkish sultan, but this will not save you. But whoever would have eternal life must see to it that salvation is his after the conclusion of this life and that God is his Protector. He must be willing, if necessary, to abandon everything temporal for the sake of the Lord, in whom he is baptized and born anew. He will use all earthly things according to his necessity and pass through this temporal life into an eternal life which he neither sees nor understands nor comprehends but only believes. Whoever does not transcend physical birth will descend into the abyss of hell. Physical birth entails physical things, such as diapers and pap, father and mother; it concerns physical life and no more. But if you want salvation, you need different parents, who will bring you to heaven. This Christ does. By means of Baptism and the Word of God He places you and your Christianity into the lap of our dear mother, the Christian Church. This He accomplished through His suffering and death that by virtue of His death and blood we might live eternally.

John 3:13

No one has ascended into heaven but He who descended from heaven.

Doctrine of Christ

... According to reason, it does not ring true to say that Christ descended; but according to faith, it makes good sense. We also believe that Christ, our Savior, is the true Son of Mary and the only-begotten Son of God; and yet there are not two sons but only one Son of God the Father and of the Virgin Mary. We believe that He is eternal God and very man and that He has two natures, the divine and the human; nevertheless, there is only one Son, both God's and Mary's, and not two sons. In the fullness of time (Gal. 4:4) He assumed His humanity from the Virgin Mary, but His divinity He received from eternity from the Father. Thus this same Son of God, who was from eternity, is also the Son of the Virgin

Mary. There are two distinct natures but only one Son, Jesus Christ. This is our faith: that God has no other Son than the one born of the Virgin Mary, and that the Son, begotten by the Father before the beginning of the world, lies in the lap of Mother Mary.

We must hold to this faith in opposition to the heretics. The Turk contends that Mary was not the mother of the Son of God. The Nestorians said that Mary was not the mother of God but only of the man Jesus, who by nature was only her son.[15] They made two sons out of one. But there is only one Son; and yet there are two natures, which gave Mary the right to say: "This Son Jesus, whom I bore and suckled on my breasts, is the eternal God, born of the Father in eternity, and also my Son." And God says likewise: "Mary's Son is My only Son." Thus Mary is the mother of God.[16] And Christ, together with God the Father and the Holy Spirit, is very God from eternity who became man in time. So God the Father does not have a Son apart from Mary's, nor does Mary have a Son apart from God the Father's. This is the foundation on which our faith rests: that Jesus Christ has two natures even though He is one indivisible person. There are not two sons and two persons; there is one Son and one person.

But if we differentiate two sons in Christ, then it must follow that there are also two persons; this would nullify our redemption and the forgiveness of sin. No, the two natures must be the one Christ. Otherwise no satisfaction could have been rendered for our sins, and nothing would come of our salvation. If Christ were only man, His suffering would have been useless; for no man's suffering has ever been able to overcome my sin and yours, death and the power of the devil, God's wrath and eternal damnation. Therefore it was necessary for Him to be God and, in order to suffer, also true man. Furthermore, if there were two persons, He would not be able to sit at the right hand of God as merely a human being.

If reason wants to philosophize and rationalize here and say: "Tell me, how can the almighty God be born of a virgin and become man? How can God become man?" you reply: "I cannot understand it. But I must

15 Nestorius (ca. 381–451), bishop of Constantinople, rejected the title *Theotokos* for the Virgin Mary (see the next note) and was understood to teach a two-person Christology. This Christology was condemned at the Council of Ephesus in 431 and is commonly referred to as Nestorianism. Luther often has Ulrich Zwingli (1484–1531) and his Christology in mind when referring to Nestorius and Nestorianism. Cf. *On the Councils and the Church* (1539), LW 41:105.

16 *Theotokos*, a title used for the Virgin Mary, means "God-bearer." The term had been used in the church since the third century and became controversial during the fifth-century Christological debates. Cyril of Alexandria (ca. 376–444) defended the term, and Nestorius rejected it. The term affirmed the hypostatic union of Christ's two natures and was officially accepted at the Council of Ephesus (431) and the Council of Chalcedon (451).

believe that both, Mary and God, had one Son, born from the Father from eternity and from Mary in time, one person with two eternally inseparable natures." For Christ, God and man, refuses to be divided into two persons. If He were, we would be lost. Therefore this affords us the greatest comfort in every distress: that God and man are one and not two. Mary is to have no other Son than the one whom God, the heavenly Father, has. Nor is God, the heavenly Father, to have a different Son from the one Christ's mother has—with this distinction, however, that the Son assumed His human nature from the Virgin Mary and the divine nature from God, the heavenly Father. . . .

He who descended

Now we revert to our text, which is easily understood on the basis of what we have said: "No one has ascended into heaven but He who descended from heaven." Here Christ is really pointing to His two natures, which dwell in one person. He indicates that His Father is God and that His mother is human, that both have the one and the same Son, our dear Lord and Savior Jesus Christ, as our Creed also teaches. Inasmuch as Christ is God, He is in heaven above from eternity, together with the Father. When He was born of the Virgin Mary, however, He descended from heaven; but at the same time He remained in heaven. He also ascended into heaven, but He was also in heaven before His ascension.

The expression "descended" denotes that the Son, who was sent into the world by the Father but never left the company of the Father, became man, Mary's Son. Thus all the fathers, including St. Augustine, interpreted this word. That He descended means that God's Son assumed our poor flesh, became man, and was born of the Virgin Mary. He not only adopted our flesh but also descended into death and the grave, yes, into hell, as we confess in the Creed: "He descended into hell." And at the same time that He was the mighty God here on earth, He was and remained the mighty God in heaven. No place and no space can contain the Godhead, as it is written in the prophet (Isa. 66:1): "Heaven is My throne, and the earth is My footstool." He ascended again into heaven; yet He had been sitting continuously at the right hand of God, His heavenly Father. Yes, according to His deity, He was eternal. And yet He revealed Himself on earth, appearing personally and physically as man. He assumed a body and soul like ours. He was crucified. His thirst was quenched with vinegar. He died, was buried, and descended into hell. And all this involved no diminution of His Godhead. The only person who is called God and who existed from eternity is He who assumed humanity. Thus He is the Son of God and of Mary. When He was born of the Virgin, He became a human Son through her. . . .

Thus this text states that Christ descended from heaven; and after He had carried out His office here, He ascended again visibly into heaven, sits at the right hand of God, and rules there with might—not only according to His divine nature, as He did from eternity, but also according to His human nature. And everything—angels, principalities, and all creatures—everything is subject to the Son of Mary, very man; for divinity and humanity are now one essence and one person in Christ. In John 6:61–62 Christ says to His disciples: "Do you take offense at this? Then what if you were to see the Son of Man ascending where He was before?" In this chapter we also hear that He is above and that He is below, for He ascends as He is God's Son and He descends as He becomes man. According to His human nature, He dwelt on earth, died, and was buried; but according to His divine nature, He ascends into heaven again, where, in His divine nature, He had always remained. Thus Christ is the highest, the center, and the lowest; in short, He is the One and All. Thus St. Paul says to the Ephesians (4:8–10): "When He ascended on high, He led a host of captives, and He gave gifts to men. In saying, He ascended, what does it mean but that He also descended into the lower parts of the earth? He who descended is also He who ascended far above all the heavens, that He might fill all things." Therefore Christ is the highest and the lowest, and none can be found to compare with Him.

And so the Son of the Father is also Mary's Son, and Mary's Son remained true God. He retained His Godhead unaltered, when, according to His human nature, He came down to earth, became man, and descended into "the lower parts," namely, into hell, and then ascended again into heaven. And since there is only one Son, there cannot be two; but this one Son descended, ascended, and remained in heaven above. Therefore it is correct to say that God's Son descended, ascended, and remained in heaven above, although this one act, that of descending, was performed only according to His human nature. But since the two natures dwell in the one undivided person of Christ, one also ascribes to the divine nature what properly pertains to the human nature. For this reason it is not wrong to say: "The Son of God and of Mary descended into hell, suffered, and died" or "The Son of God and of Mary ascended into heaven and sits on the right hand of His heavenly Father." . . .

We are told here that Christ, true God and born as true man, descended according to His humanity, that God's Son died, descended into hell, and ascended again into heaven; that at the same time God remained in heaven, for the Godhead does not move about hither and thither but is omnipresent; and that according to His human nature, Christ ascended up above all. One may properly say that since there are two natures in one being and person, God's Son came down and entered the Virgin's womb and God's Son descended into hell. Although this really applied only to the human nature, by virtue of the personal union in Christ it is also ascribed to the other nature. That which applies to one nature applies to the entire person in the concrete.[17] We differentiate between the natures as we do between body and soul; however, there remains but one person. Thus Christ suffered for us not only with body and soul but also as the Son of God, as we confess in the articles of our Christian Creed: "I believe in Jesus Christ, God's only Son, our Lord, who was conceived by the Holy Spirit and born of the Virgin Mary." And this Son, born of Mary, is also God's Son, who later suffered, was crucified, ascended again into heaven, and seated Himself at the right hand of His Father. It is not two sons, but one Son. Up above He was born of the Father from eternity; here below He was born of Mary.

John 3:35

The Father loves the Son and has given all things into His hand.

Now the question arises again: How do we harmonize these two facts: that He is Lord over all and that at the same time He is a human being? If He is God, how could God give Him all? If He is God, He has always possessed everything. From the mere fact of His possessing all we deduce that He must be God; for God does not give everything in heaven and on earth to anyone unless he is God. Now if He is God and owns all, how can it be given to Him? This subject has often been discussed before in order to enable us to cope with the fanatics. You know about the

17 When discussing the doctrine of Christ, the "abstract" refers to His natures and the "concrete" to His person. Luther further explains this in his sermon on John 3:16 (*Sermons on the Gospel of St. John* [1537–40], LW 22:352): "Thus the words of this text indicate that God gave His Son for us and that the Son of Man died for us. There are not two Jesuses, the one coming from the Father and the other born of Mary. No, there is only one Jesus. Therefore the ancient fathers said that the attributes of both natures are ascribed and imputed to the whole person of Christ 'in the concrete,' creating a 'communication of properties,' a union in which the attributes of the one nature are imparted to the other. Each nature, of course, has its own peculiar character. For instance, it is peculiar to the human nature of Christ to be born of the Virgin Mary. The divine nature has different attributes. But since the person of Christ cannot be divided, there is a communion, which enables one to say: 'The infant Christ, who lies in the cradle and is suckled by the Virgin Mary, created heaven and earth.' Also: 'The Son of God who is with the Father from eternity nurses at His mother's breasts, is crucified, and dies.' 'For the communion of the natures also effects a communication of properties.' The ancient fathers diligently taught this and wrote about it."

communication of properties: two natures dwell in the Lord Christ, and yet He is but one person. These two natures retain their properties, and each also communicates its properties to the other.

Communication of properties

. . . The two natures, the human and the divine, are inseparable. They are so united in one person that the properties of the one nature are also attributed to the other. For instance, mortality is peculiar to human nature; now that the human nature is united in one person with the divine, death, exclusively the attribute of the human nature, is also ascribed to the divine. Now we can say: "God became man, God suffered, and God died." To attempt to separate humanity from divinity in any other way would be to lie; for God cannot die. However, if you say that the two natures dwell together in one person, you are expressing the truth. To be born and to be suckled are distinctive of human nature, for God does not drink milk. This would be inexplicable if man and God were not one person. But the two natures are so united in one person that it is correct to say: "The mother of God is a virgin; God is born." Since God and man are one person, the properties characteristic of humanity alone are attributed to the Deity; for the properties of the two natures are also united. Not to be born is also peculiar to the divine nature. In the Creed we pray and confess: "Who was conceived and who was born"—that is human; and "sits at the right hand"—that partakes of the divine, although it may also be human. Thus the Child who drinks His mother's milk is eternal; He existed before the world's beginning, and He created heaven and earth. Since the two natures are united in one person, the effect is that the properties are also united. Admittedly, the properties of the divine nature have nothing in common with human nature. I shall go beyond this and say that there is still less relation between God and man. Yet these two natures are so united that there is only one God and Lord, that Mary suckles God with her breasts, bathes God, rocks Him, and carries Him; furthermore, that Pilate and Herod crucified and killed God. The two natures are so joined that the true Deity and humanity are one. Now if the true God dwells in Christ, who was born of Mary, that is, the God who made and created all, we must say that the Deity and the humanity joined not only their natures but also their properties, except for sin.[18]

18 Cf. *Lectures on 1 John* (1527), LW 30:222: "We believe that Jesus Christ is one person, made up, to be sure, of two natures. Whatever is stated now about the person is stated about the whole person. But what the fanatics say, namely, that Christ suffered according to His humanity, is false. Scripture says that those two natures are in one person. Indeed, Scripture says—see Rom. 8:3—that the Jews crucified the Son of God, not His humanity. And in 1 Cor. 2:8 it is stated that if they had understood this, they would never have crucified the Lord of glory. Paul

Consequently, whenever Holy Scripture refers to Christ as a human being, we always confess His deity as well. In Ps. 110:1 we read: "Sit at My right hand." This is addressed exclusively to the human nature, but it is also to be applied to the divine nature; for Christ began to sit at the right hand after His ascension. His humanity had not occupied this place before this, but we cannot deduce from this that He had not previously sat there as God. Thus Christ, true man, is now called Lord over all; for He is true God. One dare not claim with Arius: "If He is ascending into heaven now, it must follow that He was not there before." No, He was in heaven before; but then He was not yet a man. Since His incarnation the two natures are united; and the divine nature confers its properties on the human, and, vice versa, the human on the divine. Throughout his entire Gospel, John speaks of Christ as a true and natural human being, and also as divine. Here he refers to Christ, who was born, was baptized, and has disciples, as a real human being; at the same time he declares that all that is God's alone was given into His hands. He employs the term "given to Him," which again applies to the human nature.

Thus the two natures are united in one person, and there are not two Christs. Therefore, when you hear it said that God gave all things into Christ's hands and that He raised Him from the dead, remember that this is spoken of Christ as man. Then again, when we hear the expression: "He is seated at the right hand of God the Father," bear in mind that the human nature is united with the divine. To be in heaven and to be on earth are one thing, just as to be crucified and to live are one thing. . . . If you are perplexed by the statement that Christ died and that He is alive, you might find it still stranger to hear that Christ is God and man in one person, that Christ died on the cross as a man, and that He nonetheless remains Christ in eternity.

You must learn to brush aside all such doubts and misgivings. We are also called Christians because we acknowledge Christ in His doctrine. How can anything be given to Him? According to His deity, He does not receive anything; but God gave all to Christ inasmuch as God and man are one person. Since the Son was man, God imparted to the man what was God's. And now, since it is given to the man, it is simultaneously given to God. Whoever apprehends and worships this man also

does not say that they would never have crucified His humanity. Thus in Luke 1:35 we read: 'The Child to be born of you will be called holy, the Son of God.' Because of the oneness of the person this passage does not say 'humanity.' Whatever is attributed to one, the same thing is also attributed to the rest. Indeed, it refers to the whole person. Christ Himself, the Son of God Himself, was delivered for us. For the granting of eternal life an eternal and inestimable price had to be given. 'He who gave His only Son for us,' we read in Rom. 8:32."

worships God; for He is God in essence. In the fourteenth chapter of John, Christ says to Philip: "He who beholds the Son also beholds the true God" (14:9). The person whom Thomas beholds declares: "I am the Way" (John 14:6). Thomas sees this person, but he does not know that He is the Way, the Truth, and the Life. Those are divine properties, for no man is a way to life. The fact that Christ is the way to life finds its explanation in this: that the person of Christ is not only human but is also God in essence. Therefore whoever hears and sees Him also hears God. Thus we read here: "The Father has given all things into His hands." Well, to have everything in one's hands is the equivalent of being God; for God "gives His glory to no other," as we read in Isaiah (42:8). Here He gives all to the Son, born of Mary, so that He may have all in His hands. How is that possible? Even before this He possessed everything. Previously He had not been man; but now, when He dies and rises again from the dead, the words apply that all things are given to the Son. Now you may say: "He who hangs suspended on the cross is Lord over all. Not until now does He receive the dominion effected by the union of the two natures. It was not like this before. Now He is glorified, and the news goes out to all that He is Lord over everything."

Thus the human nature in Christ shares in the glory of all the properties which otherwise pertain to God. Since the human nature, which did not possess these properties formerly, now receives them, the text properly states that all things are given to Him. Therefore it is true and proper to say that the Son of God and of Mary was from eternity; that Christ, the Son of God and of Mary, is still Lord over all; and that Christ, the Son of God, received all from the Father. Outside this man Christ, who was born of the Virgin Mary and who suffered, you must not seek God or any salvation and help; for He is God Himself.

John 14:16

If you love Me, you will keep My commandments. And I will pray the Father, and He will give you another Comforter, to be with you forever.

. . . But how can one reconcile the words "I will pray the Father" with the preceding statement, "Whatever you ask in My name, I will do" (v. 13)? There Christ shows that He is true God and that He Himself wants to give what they ask of Him; here He states that He will ask the Father to send them a Comforter. How can it be said of the true God that He will petition someone else? For it surely is not a quality of God to be subject to someone else and to be obliged to him for things received. No, He Himself is able to give and do all things.

Therefore when smart reason and clever minds hear such words of Christ, they exclaim at once: "Oh, those are not God's words; they are the words of a mere human being; for if He were God, He would have to say: '*I* will send you the Comforter.'" Thus they make bold to teach the Holy Spirit; they play wise with their grammar and logic, and tell us that the word "pray" is not applicable to God, and that for this reason Christ cannot be God. Then they emphasize and embellish this with their rhetoric, to make the Holy Spirit appear as a child, yes, as a fool, who does not know how to speak. No matter what the Holy Spirit does or says, it must be wrong. Thus they carp and give instruction. But they are not pious enough to bring the two verses together for comparison. They pick out one thing here and another thing there; and where they find a word or two, they pounce upon these and hoodwink people, to keep them from seeing what else Scripture has to say about this. Yes, if it were fair to take a word or two out of context and to ignore what precedes or follows, or what Scripture says elsewhere, then I, too, could interpret and twist all Holy Writ and any speech as I chose.

Christ speaks both as God and as man

But the rule is: You must look at the entire text, inclusive of the words that follow and those that precede. Then you will find that Christ speaks both as God and as man; then this will be powerful evidence, as we teach and believe, that Christ is both true man and true God. For how can one express in any words that He speaks as God and as man at the same time, since He has two distinct natures? If He were to speak as God at all times, one could not prove that He is also true man. And if He were to speak as true man at all times, one would never be aware that He is also true God.

Therefore Christ must alternate by sometimes using words that reflect His divine nature and at other times using those that are proper to the human nature. Yet it is the one person who speaks, sometimes as though He were only God and sometimes as though He were only man. For since Christ is both God and man in one person, why should He not also say both this and that of Himself without making a distinction? But here He employs both ways of speaking in rapid succession and in one sermon. For the same person who had said shortly before: "Whatever you ask, I will do it" also declares here: "I will pray the Father." This is done for the purpose of making this article certain and clear: that in this person there is neither purely Deity nor purely humanity, but that both the divine and the human nature are undivided in one person.

We have stated often enough that in the divine essence of Christ and the Father there are two distinct persons. Therefore when speaking of Christ here one must teach clearly that He is one person, but that there are two distinct natures, the divine and the human. Again, just as there the nature or the divine essence remains unmingled in the Father and in Christ, so also the person of Christ remains undivided here. Therefore the attributes of each nature, the human and the divine, are ascribed to the entire person, and we say of Christ: "The man Christ, born of the Virgin, is omnipotent and does all that we ask—not, however, according to the human but according to the divine nature, not by reason of His birth from His mother but because He is God's Son." And again, "Christ, God's Son, prays the Father, not according to His divine nature and essence, according to which He is coequal with the Father, but because He is true man and Mary's Son." Thus the words must be brought together and compared according to the unity of the person. The natures must always be differentiated, but the person must remain undivided.

And now since He is believed as one person, God and man, it is also proper for us to speak of Him as each nature requires. Some words reflect His human, others His divine nature. Therefore we should consider what Christ says according to His human nature and what He says according to His divine nature. For where this is not observed and properly distinguished, many types of heresy must result, as happened in times gone by, when some people asserted that Christ was not true God and others that He was not true man. They were unable to follow the principle of differentiating between the two types of discourse on the basis of the two natures.

Christ often spoke as the lowliest man on earth should hardly speak. For example, when He says: "I have not come to be served, but to serve" (Matt. 20:28). With these words He really makes Himself a servant among all men, although He is true God and Lord over all creatures, whom all must serve and worship. And in Ps. 41:4 He makes Himself a sinner and says that He is being punished because of sin. This, of course, is out of the question according to the divine nature. And again, He employs the speech of exalted majesty, such as no angel or creature should use, even though He was in the lowliest form and figure of His sojourn on earth. We read, for instance, in John 6:62: "Then what if you were to see the Son of Man ascending where He was before?"

Communication of properties

Yes, all that Scripture says of Christ covers the whole person, just as though both God and man were one essence. Often it uses expressions interchangeably and assigns the attributes of both to each nature. This is done for the sake of the personal union, which we call the "communication of properties." Thus we can say: "The man Christ is God's eternal Son, by whom all creatures were created, Lord of heaven and earth." And by the same token we say: "Christ, God's Son (that is, the person who is true God), was conceived and born of the Virgin Mary, suffered under Pontius Pilate, crucified and dead." Furthermore: "God's Son sits at meat with tax collectors and sinners, and washes the feet of the disciples." He does not do this, of course, according to the divine nature. But since this is done by one and the same person, it is correct to say that God's Son is doing it. Thus St. Paul declares in 1 Cor. 2:8: "If they had understood this, they would not have crucified the Lord of glory." And Christ Himself states in John 6:62: "What if you were to see the Son of Man ascending where He was before?" This is really spoken of the divine nature, which alone was with the Father from eternity; yet it is also said of the person who is true man.

In brief, whatever this person, Christ, says and does, is said and done by both, true God and true man, so that all His words and works must always be attributed to the whole person and are not divided, as though He were not true God or not true man. But this must be done in such a way as to identify and recognize each nature properly. If we want to speak correctly and distinctly of each, then we must say: "God's nature is different from man's. The human nature is not from eternity as the divine nature is; and the divine nature was not born temporally, nor did it die temporally, etc., like the human nature. And yet the two are united in one person. Therefore there is but one Christ, and we may say of Him: 'This man is God; this man created all things.' " Similarly, body and soul present two distinct entities in a natural and sound person; yet the two constitute but one person, and we ascribe the functions, activities, and offices of each to the whole person.

We say of every human being that he eats, drinks, digests, sleeps, wakes, walks, stands, works, etc., although the soul participates in none of these activities, but only the body. And yet this is said of the entire person, who has a body and a soul. For it is one person, by reason not only of the body but of both the body and the soul. Again, we say that man thinks, deliberates, and learns. According to his reason or soul, he can become a teacher or master, a judge, councillor, or ruler. Neither the body nor any one of its members gives him this competence. And yet we say: "He has a clever head; he is sensible, learned, eloquent, artistic." Thus it is said of a woman that a mother carries, bears, and suckles a child, although it is not her soul but only her body that makes her a mother. And still we ascribe this to the entire woman. Or if someone strikes a person on the head, we say: "He has struck Hans or Greta." Or if a member of the body is injured or wounded, we think of the whole person as being wounded.

I am using these simple illustrations to demonstrate how two distinct natures must be differentiated in the person of Christ and yet how this still leaves the person a whole and undivided entity. Whatever Christ says and does, both God and man say and do; yet each word and action is in accord with the one or the other nature. He who observes this distinction is safe and on the right path. He will not be led astray by the erroneous ideas of heretics, ideas which come into being solely because they do not properly join what belongs together and is united, or because they do not properly separate and distinguish what must be distinguished.

One and the same person

Therefore we must adhere to the speech and expressions of Holy Writ and retain and confess the doctrine that this Christ is true God, through whom all things are created and exist, and at the same time that this same Christ, God's Son, is born of the Virgin, dies on the cross, etc. Furthermore, Mary, the mother, does not carry, give birth to, suckle, and nourish only the man, only flesh and blood—for that would be dividing the person—but she carries and nourishes a son who is God's Son. Therefore she is rightly called not only the mother of the man but also the mother of God. This the old fathers taught in opposition to the Nestorians, who objected to calling Mary "mother of God" and refused to say that she had given birth to God's Son.[19]

Here we must again confess with our Creed: "I believe in Jesus Christ, God the Father's only Son, our Lord, born of the Virgin Mary, suffered, was crucified, died." It is always one and the same Son of God, our Lord. Therefore it is certain that Mary is the mother of the real and true God, and that the Jews crucified not only the Son of Man but also the true Son of God. For I do not want a Christ in whom I am to believe and to whom I am to pray as my Savior who is only man. Otherwise I would go to the devil. For mere flesh and blood could not erase sin, reconcile God, remove His anger, overcome and destroy death and hell, and bestow eternal life.

Furthermore, since the angels in heaven adore Him and call Him Lord as He lies in the manger, and say to the shepherds, according to Luke 2:11: "To you is born this day . . . a Savior, who is Christ the Lord," He must be true God. For the angels do not worship mere flesh or human nature. Therefore it follows that both God and man must dwell in this person. And when you speak of Christ, you speak of an undivided person, who is both God and man; and he who sees, hears, or finds Christ with the faith

19 See above, p. 397 n. 16.

of the heart surely encounters not only the man Christ but also the true God. Thus we do not let God sit idly in heaven among the angels; but we find Him here below, lying in the manger and on His mother's lap. We summarize and say: "Wherever we encounter this person, there we surely encounter the divine Majesty."

John 15:26–27

But when the Comforter comes, whom I shall send to you from the Father, even the Spirit of truth, who proceeds from the Father, He will bear witness to Me; and you also are witnesses, because you have been with Me from the beginning.

. . . In this text we again find the entire Holy Trinity recorded and named, all three persons of the divine Essence and Majesty: the Father, the Son, and the Holy Spirit. And here we must note first and particularly how Christ depicts the Holy Spirit as a Comforter against the evil spirit who rules in the world; He again calls Him (14:26) a Comforter and a Spirit of truth.

The devil has two weapons with which he assails the Christians respecting either their office or their own persons, in the hour of death or at other times. These weapons are sin and the penalty for sin. The stronger of these is the terror of sin; by means of this he renders the heart fearful and despondent by saying to it: "You have done this and that." He is a past master at this. He not only cites the sins which you yourself must confess, such as murder and adultery, and blows them up with his fiery breath to such proportions that your heart melts like salt in water; but he can also transform your good conduct and your best works into many kinds of sin and shame, so that you do not keep even a speck of them. Anyone who has engaged in real combat with him a few times is well aware of this.

Then the devil deals in the same way with the penalty for sin. He says: "With this or with that sin you have deserved to be broken on the wheel, to be put to the rack, to be killed a hundred times, and to be damned to eternal hell in addition." He makes things so hot and horrible that man considers heaven and earth too cramped and wants to hurl himself into fire from fright. Man lies there and tortures himself with thoughts such as these: "O Lord God, what have I done? If it is bad, it is not good; if it is good, it is far worse." If the devil takes hold of you there, and you do not know how to defend yourself, he has soon gained the victory.

Comforter

Therefore God has been gracious to us and has given us a Comforter to counteract this spirit of terror—a Comforter, who, as God Himself, is much stronger with His comfort than the devil is with his terror. And now when the devil also comes along with God's Law, advances against your works and your life, and shatters these so thoroughly that even your good works appear to be evil and condemned—an art in which he is a master and an excellent theologian—the Holy Spirit, on the other hand, will come and whisper consolingly to your heart: "Be of good cheer and unafraid. Go, preach, do what you have been commanded to do; and do not fear the terrors of sin, death, or the devil, even if these terrors present themselves in the name of God. God does not want to be angry with you, nor does He want to reject you; for Christ, God's Son, died for you. He paid for your sins; and if you believe in Him, these will not be imputed to you, no matter how great they are. Because of your faith your works are pleasing to God; they are adjudged good and well done even though weakness does creep in. Why do you let your sins be falsely magnified? Christ, your Righteousness, is greater than your sins and those of the whole world; His life and His consolation are stronger and mightier than your death and hell."

Thus He again makes the heart happy and bold, and inspires it with the courage and confidence to say: "Now I will believe in this Christ; I will preach Him and praise Him even if this should vex the world and all the devils. And although I am a sinner and have lived ever so wickedly, yet I will not on this account deny and reject this man; nor will I have such small regard for His suffering and death as you have, devil, when you try to make me believe that these are inadequate to cancel and extinguish all sin and your whole hell."

Behold, this leads to a confident and staunch heart that can scorn the devil with all his terror and torment, defy all his might, and say: "Sin, if you want to condemn me, you will first have to condemn Christ, my dear Savior, Priest, and Intercessor with the Father. Death, if you want to devour me, you must begin on top, with Christ, my Head. Devil and world, if you want to torment and frighten me, you must first pull Him down from His throne. In brief, I will fear nothing, even if lightning were to strike this moment and throw everything into confusion. For Christ is mine with His suffering, death, and life; the Holy Spirit, with His comfort; and the Father Himself, with all His grace. He sends the Holy Spirit to preach Christ into my heart and to fill it with His consolation. This is the main glory and prerogative of the Holy Spirit."

Spirit of truth

Secondly, He is also called a Spirit of truth who opposes all lies and false arguments. For the world, too, is always full of spirits, as the saying goes: "Wherever God erects a church, the devil builds his chapel or tavern next to it"; that is, wherever God's Word springs up in its purity, the devil ushers in sects, factions, and many false spirits, who also deck themselves with the glory and the name of Christ and His church. But it is all false to the core, without truth or certainty. Christ says: "I will give you the Spirit who makes you sure and convinced of the truth. Then you need no longer have any doubt regarding the truth of this or that article pertaining to your salvation, but you can be convinced of your stand and be judges competent to pass judgment on all other doctrines. Thus He will not only make you warriors and heroes, but He will also confer the doctorate on you and call you doctors and masters who can determine with certainty what is true or false doctrine in Christendom. The devil will not prove cunning enough, and no spirit will be smart enough, to falsify your doctrine or to lead you astray."

... Therefore Christ promises to give us a Spirit who will not only strengthen our hearts and increase our courage but will also make our faith sure, remove all doubt, and enable us to judge all other spirits. Such a promise is necessary, in order that we may successfully resist the devil's lies. For he can present these so attractively adorned and embellished "as to lead astray, if possible, even the elect," as Christ declares in Matt. 24:24. What would we have done if we had not had this sure conviction, given to us by the Spirit of truth? Who would have had the courage to chide and condemn such great and glorious semblance of truth as is found in the papacy? Or who would have such audacity today, since now they are beginning to bedeck themselves with holiness more than ever?

This Spirit of truth, however, steps forth boldly and pronounces the sentence: "This is the truth; that is fabrication, no matter how long it is adorned with the name of the church and of Christ, boasts of that name, and bears the semblance of the church." From its very inception Christendom has prevailed amid innumerable sects and lying spirits in the past. And it will prevail in the future. The church survives all this and retains its Baptism, Sacrament, Gospel, Christ, Ten Commandments, and prayer in all their purity. It judges and thus separates from itself all false doctrine and all opposition, even though the devil becomes an angel of light and appears in a form as beautiful and resplendent as God Himself, as he did to Christ according to Matt. 4:1ff. Inspired by this same Holy Spirit of truth, St. Paul calls himself a doctor or "a teacher of the Gentiles in faith and truth" (1 Tim. 2:7), that all the world may hear his message and that everyone who wants to remain undeceived and be saved may adhere to it and follow it.

Holy Spirit's sermon

In the third place, Christ says: "When you have been comforted and emboldened by the Holy Spirit, and your mind and understanding have been kept in the certain truth, He will also impel you to testify of Me. First He will bear witness internally in your hearts; then also externally by means of miraculous signs and by your confession and preaching. He will enable you who were with Me from the beginning to tell what you have heard and seen. Such testimony will exalt Me both against the angry lion and against the wily dragon, that is, the murderer and the spirit of lies." These words must be carefully noted; for with them Christ defined the work of the Holy Spirit or, rather, portrayed to us what His teaching and testimony would be and what it would not be. Christ says: "He will bear witness of none but Me. This will be known as the Holy Spirit's sermon. Therefore He will not be a Moses or a preacher of the Law such as you have had and still have; but I will put into His mouth another and more sublime sermon than the one Moses gave to you. Moses taught you nothing but the Law or the Ten Commandments, which he had received from God; he told you what to do and what not to do. But this One will make of you preachers and confessors who tell and testify, not of their own deeds and life but of Me."

This is the Holy Spirit's own specific office; by means of it one must discern all other doctrine. Consequently, the proponents of these doctrines will not have the glory and honor—although they want it and lay claim to it—that theirs is the Holy Spirit's doctrine or testimony. And herewith we can also defend and preserve ourselves against the devil's lies and false whisperings, with which he assails our heart and conscience and induces us to discuss our life and works on the basis of the Law before God's judgment seat. If I remain with him and associate with him, he strikes me down, and I am lost. Here he is too powerful, and no saint on earth can come off victorious against him; for before him he has God's Law, which no man on earth satisfies. But he can never go so far as to deny that Christ suffered and died for our sins, that He was buried, rose again, and now sits enthroned up in heaven for our sakes as our dear High Priest and our Mediator before God.

Admittedly the devil has the upper hand with the Law or the Ten Commandments. When he says, "You are a sinner!" I must say yes to this. But if he infers from this that I am to be damned and to become his own, I say no. For I still have a sermon or word, which is known as the Holy Spirit's testimony and the sermon about Christ: "You hold only Moses before my eyes; he proclaims God's command to me. But I must and will not remain in Moses' school. For I myself know and, unfortunately, know too well that I am a sinner. I will have no further discussion with you as to whether I have done something or nothing that is good. If my deeds are wrong, let them be wrong. But now I must and will hear and learn the Holy Spirit's message to me, namely, how Christ shed His blood for us, blotted out sin for me, overcame death, extinguished God's wrath and hell, and makes me an heir of eternal life solely through His suffering, death, and resurrection." This message the devil cannot abolish.

Therefore there is no other manner or way of comforting, strengthening, and instructing consciences and of protecting and defending ourselves than by this sermon and testimony of the Holy Spirit. With this doctrine I can condemn the devil and all his suggestions and arguments, and say: "You cite to me God's commandment and Law; I cannot object to this. But when I must stand before God's judgment seat, I must and will not discuss the things pertaining to my life; for I surely know in advance that these cannot pass muster there. You, however, you rogue, want to drown and submerge me in thoughts about how to fulfill the Law, about how to satisfy God through my own efforts and because of this to forget Christ, my Savior. In this way you tear me away from the testimony of the Holy Spirit."

Therefore he who has comprehended this revelation and testimony of the Holy Spirit can judge all such doctrine well and correctly and differentiate as follows: There are two types of life and work. The one is my life and work which must be carried out in accordance with the Ten Commandments; the other is that of Christ my Lord, which is recorded in my Creed. My salvation and happiness and all consolation for my conscience depend on the latter. With this differentiation I can meet the devil's attacks on me and say: "May God forgive me if my life does not conform perfectly to the Ten Commandments; but I cling to the life of this Man who died for me, whose Baptism and Sacrament I have received." This does not imply that one should not perform as many good works as possible. But now, when we are engaged in a battle with the devil and our own conscience, there must be no argument about this.

Here there must be a life and piety higher than the life and piety of all men; here there must be Christ our Lord, who died and rose again for me, and Baptism, which I have, not by virtue of my works but through Christ. This alone shall and must do what is required. Then I have certainty both with regard to doctrine and with regard to life; then I cannot fail. When the devil wants to make us pious, he emphasizes the importance of our life at the expense of faith; or when he has something special in mind and wants to make you clever and smart, he appeals to your reason in opposition to doctrine, just as he did in the case of the heretic Arius and to others. But if you cling to the Lord Christ's life and say: "I am not baptized on my or on any other man's life but solely on my Christ," he can gain nothing. Thus when the devil assails you by citing this sublime article of faith, refers you to your own intellect and wisdom, no longer discusses life but talks about how one should believe, and attacks the very foundation on which you build, then he will stress the subtle thoughts of reason and ask how this agrees. If at such a time you want to insure yourself against a fall, you must again say: "Listen to me. I do not believe my own reason and wisdom; my faith is expressed in the prayer of the children: 'I believe in God the Father, and in Jesus Christ, His only Son, and in the Holy Spirit.'" This is God's Word, which is proclaimed in the world through the Holy Spirit. The children know it, too, and the gates of hell will not overthrow it (Matt. 16:18).

The Holy Spirit proceeds from the Father

Finally, we must also speak about the essence of the Holy Spirit, since the text says that He is true God, as our Creed states: "I believe in the Holy Spirit." For no one but God alone is entitled to faith, and no one but Him—namely, God—who can give the faith that is necessary for eternal life should demand it. Consequently, since we believe in the Holy Spirit, we also believe in the true God.

This is sufficient to keep the simpleminded in their faith and to prevent them from listening any longer to the good-for-nothing wiseacres who want to be ingenious here and indulge in captious sophistries. For it is the business of scholars to fight against such persons in the schools and to expose and refute their false schemes. But this article of faith can be proved clearly and forcibly enough from our text, where it is stated: "The Holy Spirit, whom I shall send to you from the Father." Likewise "who proceeds from the Father."

These words testify and prove that the Holy Spirit is not a mere spirit—a creature, for example, or something apart from God and yet given to man by Him, or merely the work of God which He performs in our hearts—but that He is a Spirit who Himself is God in essence, who has His essence from the Father, and who was not created or made but proceeds from the Father and is sent by Christ. And Christ gives Him names which are personal names or indicate and name a distinct person. He calls Him the Comforter, for example. He also mentions personal works, as, for example, when He declares that He will bear witness of Christ. Then He says: "He will teach you all things" (14:26).

Here there is evidence enough that the Holy Spirit is a distinct person, a person separate from the Father and the Son. Christ says: "The Comforter, whom I shall send to you" and "who proceeds from the Father." And yet He is the same true and only God, since He is to perform works that God alone performs, such as illumining the hearts inwardly and bringing them to the true knowledge of God; kindling, creating, and strengthening faith in them; and comforting consciences and keeping them undismayed in the face of the terrors of devil and all creatures, etc. Apart from other passages, these words are strong and convincing enough to prove this article regarding the divine essence of the Holy Spirit. We shall hear more of this in the next chapter.

John 16:13

When the Spirit of truth comes, He will guide you into all the truth, for He will not speak on His own authority, but whatever He hears He will speak.

Here Christ makes the Holy Spirit a preacher. He does so to prevent one from gaping toward heaven in search of Him, as the fluttering spirits and enthusiasts do,[20] and from divorcing Him from the oral Word or the ministry. One should know and learn that He will be in and with the Word, that it will guide us into all truth, in order that we may believe it, use it as a weapon, be preserved by it against all the lies and deception of the devil, and prevail in all trials and temptations. For there is, after all, no other way and no other means of perceiving the Holy Spirit's consolation and power, as I have often demonstrated from Holy Writ and have often experienced myself. For I, too, am a half-baked theologian. This I say, lest I exalt myself over the great minds who have long ago ascended into the clouds beyond all Scripture and have nestled under the wings of the Holy Spirit. But experience has taught me all too often that whenever the devil catches me outside Scripture and sees that my thoughts are rambling and that I, too, am fluttering toward heaven, he brings me to the point of not knowing where God is or where I am. The Holy Spirit wants this truth which He is to impress into our hearts to be so firmly fixed that reason and all one's own thoughts and feelings are relegated to the background. He wants us to adhere solely to the Word and to regard it as the only truth. And through this Word alone He governs the Christian Church to the end.

20 Luther used the words "fanatics" and "enthusiasts" to refer to those who rejected the spiritual power of the external Word or Sacraments.

Here Christ defines the Holy Spirit's office and points out what and about what He is to teach. He constantly keeps in mind the false spirits and preachers who boastfully claim to have the Holy Spirit as well as others do and allege that what they say has emanated from the Holy Spirit. That is what the pope persuaded the entire world to believe. Thus the Holy Spirit establishes a wide difference among teachers and gives the right rule by which the spirits are to be tested. He wants to say that there are two kinds of teachers. There are some who speak on their own authority; that is, they evolve their message from their own reasoning or religious zeal and judgment. The Holy Spirit is not to be that kind of preacher; for He will not speak on His own authority, and His message will not be a human dream and thought like that of the preachers who speak on their own authority of things which they have neither seen nor experienced and, as St. Paul says in 1 Tim. 1:7, talk "without understanding either what they are saying or the things about which they make assertions." "No, His message will have substance; it will be the certain and absolute truth, for He will preach what He receives from the Father and from Me. And you will be able to recognize Him by the fact that He does not speak on His own authority—as the spirit of lies, the devil, and his mobs do—but will preach about what He will hear. Thus He will speak exclusively of Me and will glorify Me, so that the people will believe in Me." . . .

Speaker, Word, and Listener

This is the plain and simple meaning of this text concerning the office of the Holy Spirit. But here there is more to say about the person of the Holy Spirit, about how it is distinct from that of both the Father and the Son. For in the first place, when Christ refers to the Holy Spirit and says: "When the Comforter comes" (John 15:26), and "Whatever He hears He will speak" (John 16:13), and "He will glorify Me, for He will take what is Mine" (John 16:14), etc., He proves conclusively that the Holy Spirit is a true being in the Godhead, that He is Himself a distinct person who is neither the Father nor the Son. For all the following words indicate a special person: "the Comforter, who will come"; "whatever He hears He will speak." If He is to come or, as Christ said earlier, if He is to be sent or to proceed, also to hear and to speak, He must, of course, be something. Now He surely is not the Father, since the Father does not come and is not sent. Nor is He the Son, who has already come and now returns to the Father, and of whom the Holy Spirit will preach and whom He will glorify.

But Christ points in particular to the distinctive person of the Holy Spirit or His attribute, also to His divine essence together with the Father and the Son, when He says: "Whatever He hears He will speak." For here

Christ refers to a conversation carried on in the Godhead, a conversation in which no creatures participate. He sets up a pulpit both for the speaker and for the listener. He makes the Father the Preacher and the Holy Spirit the Listener. It is really beyond human intelligence to grasp how this takes place; but since we cannot explain it with human words or intelligence, we must believe it. Here faith must disregard all creatures and must not concentrate on physical preaching and listening; it must conceive of this as preaching, speaking, and listening inherent in the essence of the Godhead.

Here it is relevant to state that Scripture calls our Lord Christ—according to His divine nature—a "Word" (John 1:1) which the Father speaks with and in Himself. Thus this Word has a true, divine nature from the Father. It is not a word spoken by the Father, as a physical, natural word spoken by a human being is a voice or a breath that does not remain in him but comes out of him and remains outside him. No, this Word remains in the Father forever. Thus these are two distinct persons: He who speaks and the Word that is spoken, that is, the Father and the Son. Here, however, we find the Third Person following these two, namely, the one who hears both the Speaker and the spoken Word. For it stands to reason that there must also be a listener where a speaker and a word are found. But all this speaking, being spoken, and listening takes place within the divine nature and also remains there, where no creature is or can be. All three—Speaker, Word, and Listener—must be God Himself; all three must be coeternal and in a single undivided majesty. For there is no difference or inequality in the divine Essence, neither a beginning nor an end. Therefore one cannot say that the Listener is something outside God, or that there was a time when He began to be a Listener; but just as the Father is a Speaker from eternity, and just as the Son is spoken from eternity, so the Holy Spirit is the Listener from eternity.

Earlier we heard (John 14:26; 15:26) that the Holy Spirit is sent not only by the Father but that He is also sent by, and proceeds from, the Son. Therefore this Listener must be called the Listener of both the Father and the Son, not of the Father alone or of the Son alone. Christ has stated plainly: "The Comforter, whom I shall send to you from the Father." The expression "to send" has the very same connotation that the expression "to proceed from" has. For he who proceeds from someone is sent. Conversely, he who is sent proceeds from him who sends him. Consequently, the Holy Spirit has His divine essence not only from the Father but also from the Son, as the following words will illustrate further.

Thus these words confirm and teach exactly what we confess in our Creed, namely, that in one divine essence there are three distinct persons:

the Father, the Son, and the Holy Spirit. This is illustrated by means of a metaphor, or a picture of natural things, in order that we in our weakness may be able to know what is meant and to talk about it. But we cannot search it out or understand it. We must believe, and cling to, these words which we hear from Christ Himself, just as Christendom and especially the holy fathers and bishops did. They had disputations about this article, and they fought for and preserved it against the heretics and lying spirits who made bold to meditate on and to affect wisdom concerning these sublime, inscrutable matters beyond and apart from Scripture.

Treatise on the Last Words of David

1543

Martin Luther strongly believed the world would come to an end during his lifetime or soon thereafter. In his final years, as Luther's orneriness grew, so, too, did the number of his enemies. He continued to fight against Rome, the Sacramentarians, the fanatics, and the other Protestants who had abandoned Word and Sacrament. He also denounced with increased vigor and violent rhetoric the Jews and Turks. Although Luther's language belongs to his age and prejudices, there are historical factors that help us better understand why Luther opposed these groups, particularly the Jews, with such vehemence.

Luther lectured on the Book of Genesis from 1535 to 1545. A number of critical issues emerged for Luther. How does a Christian read and interpret the Old Testament? Luther had long explored this question in his writings and sermons. Although Luther had a place for allegory, responsible exegesis sought the plain sense of the text by focusing on the history and grammar of the book under consideration. Many other reformers in Luther's day agreed with him. They sought to establish the historical context of Moses or David when reading their books and argued that this stricter context determined the proper meaning of Scripture. These hermeneutical commitments led some to reject the doctrine of the Trinity.

The doctrine of the Trinity shaped and guided Christian confession and worship. The prayers, hymns, and liturgies of the Church were deeply trinitarian. And yet as early as the 1520s and increasingly throughout the 1530s and 1540s, a number of Protestants began rejecting the doctrine of the Trinity. Did Moses and David confess the Trinity? Was Jesus really the eternal Son of God, born of the Virgin Mary, true God and true man, or just a highly exalted but nonetheless created man? Was the Holy Spirit a distinct and eternal person or just a divine power or influence? These questions and more emerged from Protestant hermeneutics. Luther realized that he was not only partly responsible for this but also had embraced for a time this way of reading the Old

Testament. He labeled it a Jewish reading, an interpretation imitating the rabbis and practiced by the new Hebraists of his day.

For Luther, the attacks upon the Trinity were attacks upon the incarnation and upon the salvation won by Jesus Christ, the true Son of God, and delivered by the Holy Spirit through Word and Sacrament. Luther responded to these assaults upon the Gospel with all the talents he possessed. He preached on the Trinity by turning to the Gospel of John. He lectured on the Trinity at creation in his Genesis lectures. It was the Holy Spirit who blessed Jacob through Isaac. Jacob's ladder foretold the incarnation of the very One with whom he would later wrestle. Luther prepared future pastors and professors by leading academic disputations on the subtler points of Trinitarian theology, demonstrating the irreducible threeness and indivisible oneness of Father, Son, and Holy Spirit.[1] *At this time, Luther also composed and translated hymns on the certainty of God's Word, the Old Testament prophecies of Christ, the incarnation, and the Trinity.*[2] *Finally, Luther wrote formal theological works on the great creeds of the Church, among which he numbered the* Te Deum, *the early church's great hymn of praise.*[3] *All of these resources showed the importance of the church's theological grammar of faith for confessing the Trinity and the doctrine of Christ. This language was necessary for all believers, whether children or future pastors, whether his coarse Saxons or seasoned professors. This language belonged in sermons, hymns, and prayers as much as it belonged in academic disputations and theological treatises.*

The excerpt below comes from Luther's commentary on the last words of David. For Luther, David not only prophesied about the coming of the Messiah but also believed and confessed the Trinity. Luther divides his work into two parts. He begins with an exposition of David's last words from 2 Samuel 23 and then turns, in part two, to the rest of Scripture to show that Moses, Isaiah, and Daniel, among others, confessed the Father, the Son, and the Holy Spirit with the same conviction as John and Paul. The second part of the commentary also contains the clearest and most sustained discussion of the doctrine of the Trinity to be found in all of Luther's works.

1 Luther led academic disputations on John 1:14, on the humanity and divinity of Christ, on whether the divine essence generates, and on theological language. These are collected in WA 39/2.

2 See among other Luther hymns: "Lord, Keep Us Steadfast in Thy Word" (1541/1542), LW 53:305; "From Heaven the Angel Troop Came Near" (1543), LW 53:306–7; "Thou Who Art Three in Unity" (1543), LW 53:308–9.

3 *The Three Symbols* (1538), LW 34:197–229.

Treatise on the Last Words of David[4]

2 Samuel 23:1–7

St. Jerome reports that he was moved to translate the Bible anew from Hebrew into Latin by the sneering reproach of the enemies of Christ, the Jews, to the effect that Christians did not have the correct Bible in the version then in use throughout Christendom.[5] The reason given was that a number of words and letters were faulty and altogether different from the Hebrew. Prior to this, others had been induced to translate the Bible for the same reason, for instance, Aquila, Theodotion, Origen, and others, until at that time there were up to six translations, which they called *Hexapla*.[6] And in our day, too, so many are busying themselves with translating that history may repeat itself and there may be so many Bibles in the course of time and so many wiseacres who claim a mastery of the Hebrew tongue that there will be no end to it.

That will inevitably happen if we pay attention to what the Jews say and think of our Bible. After all, they are not in agreement among themselves, and they expound Scripture arbitrarily and quote out of context with their grammar. If we were to heed them, we could never acquire a uniform Bible, since every rabbi claims to be superior to the other. Furthermore, they all have to admit that the words in many a passage are incomprehensible to them. They are far from having one harmonious, perfect, and flawless Hebrew Bible, even from the point of view of grammar, to say nothing of theology, where they are so very incompetent.

Therefore such mockery of the Jews does not disturb me, and their opinion would not impel me to learn a single letter of the Hebrew language. The reason for that is this: We Christians have the meaning and import of the Bible because we have the New Testament, that is, Jesus

4 The following excerpt is adapted from *Treatise on the Last Words of David*, in volume 15 of *Luther's Works: American Edition*, ed. Jaroslav Pelikan and Hilton C. Oswald, trans. Martin H. Bertram (St. Louis: Concordia, 1972). Minor alterations have been made to the text for consistency in style, abbreviations, and capitalization. The annotations and subheadings are the work of the editor of this book.

5 Jerome produced a Latin translation of most of the books of the Bible from the original Hebrew and Greek. Many of Jerome's translations were incorporated into the Latin Vulgate. Prior to Jerome there were numerous Old Latin versions of the Bible which were translations of the Greek Old and New Testament.

6 The early church father Origen assembled the *Hexapla*, a six-columned edition of the Old Testament that reproduced the Hebrew text, a text transliterated into Greek, and the four available Greek translations of the Hebrew Old Testament. Luther mentions two of these Greek translations: the edition produced by Aquila (117–138) and the edition by Theodotion (second century). Origen also included the edition by Symmachus (second century) and the much older Septuagint.

Christ, who was promised in the Old Testament and who later appeared and brought with Him the light and the true meaning of Scripture. Thus He says in John 5:46: "If you believed Moses, you would believe Me, for he wrote of Me." Also Luke 24:44–45: "'Everything written about Me in the Law, the Prophets, and the Psalms must be fulfilled.' Then He opened their minds to understand the Scriptures."

For that is the all-important point on which everything depends. Whoever does not have or want to have this man properly and truly who is called Jesus Christ, God's Son, whom we Christians proclaim, must keep his hands off the Bible—that I advise. He will surely come to naught. The more he studies, the more blind and more stupid will he grow, be he Jew, Tartar,[7] Turk, Christian, or whatever he wants to call himself. Behold, what did the heretical Arians, Pelagians, Manichaeans, and innumerable others among us Christians lack?[8] What has the pope lacked? Did they not have the sure, clear, and powerful Word of the New Testament? What do the factions of our day lack? Do they not have the New Testament, clear and reliable enough? If the New Testament had to be translated in accord with each such stupid devil's mind, how many New Testaments, do you suppose, would we have to have? . . .

Just consider that excellent man Lyra.[9] He is a good Hebraist and a fine Christian. What good work he produces when he, in accord with the New Testament, opposes the Jewish concept. But whenever he follows his Rabbi Solomon,[10] how meaningless and unimpressive it sounds; it has neither hands nor feet, despite his good command of words and letters. Still he surpasses all the others, both the old and the new Hebraists, who follow the rabbis altogether too strictly. Indeed, in translating and expounding, one need not intentionally strain oneself to transmit the

7 See above, p. 183 n. 19.

8 On the Arian heresy, see above, p. 217 n. 6; on the Manichaean heresy, see above, p. 372 n. 6. Pelagius (ca. 354–ca. 418), a British monk, and his followers taught that people could make an initial movement toward salvation by their own efforts and apart from God's grace. Although condemned at the Council of Ephesus in 431, variations of Pelagianism continued to appear throughout the medieval period. When late medieval theologians argued that a person could merit first grace (*gratia gratis data*), they were met with the charge of Pelagianism. See further in the volume introduction, above, pp. viii–x.

9 Nicholas of Lyra (ca. 1270–1349) was the most accomplished and influential biblical scholar of the medieval church. Nicholas favored the plain sense of Scripture, knew Hebrew, and studied the interpretations of medieval rabbis. Luther often appeals to Nicholas of Lyra in his Old Testament commentaries.

10 Rabbi Solomon ben Isaac (1040–1105), more commonly known as Rashi, wrote influential commentaries on the Old Testament and the Talmud. A great deal of Lyra's rabbinical learning derived from Rashi.

concept of the rabbis and grammarians to us Christians. It is all too prone to stick to us of itself, automatically, just like pitch and glue, even if we deliberately guard against it. For the letters and the stories of the others blind the eyes and induce us occasionally to lose sight of the meaning of Christ where we should not, and thus the Jewish concept insinuates itself unawares, as every translator without exception has experienced. I, too, was not exempt from it.

In brief, if we do not apply all diligence to interpret the Hebrew Bible, wherever that is feasible, in the direction of the New Testament, in opposition to the interpretation of the rabbis, it would be better to keep the old translation (which, after all, retains, thanks to the New Testament, most of the good elements) than to have so many translations just because a few passages presumably have a different reading or are still not understood. This only confuses the memory of the reader, hinders his study, and leaves him in greater uncertainty than he was before.

To illustrate this, I have decided to discourse on the last words of David, not according to the German translation, in which I followed all the others to avoid the impression that I considered myself the only smart person. No, now I am going to be stubborn and follow none but my own spirit. He who dislikes this may ignore it. It is not the first time that I wrote something displeasing to others. I thank God that I am inured to that. I, on the other hand, do not approve of everything written by others either. Let everyone see how he may build on the foundation with gold or wood, silver or hay, gems or straw. The Lord's Day will bring this to light (cf. 1 Cor. 3:12–13).

2 Samuel 23:1

These are the last words of David.

The author means the words of David with which he is determined to die and depart this life. As one is wont to say: "This is my point of view; with it I will abide forever." For these are not the last words that David spoke during his lifetime, nor are they his last administrative speech, but they are his last will and testament. We Germans call this *Seelrecht*,[11] on which a person is willing to die and which is to be executed unaltered after his death. The jurists call it a "last will." A person may live a long time after this has been issued, and he may speak, do, and suffer much subsequently; it still remains intact as his testament, as his last will. In that sense these are also David's last words, that is, his soul's testament,

11 *Seelrecht* was the German word describing the provision one made for the salvation of his soul.

even though he spoke many a word, performed many deeds, and suffered much after this. . . .

The oracle of David, the son of Jesse.

How modestly David introduces his speech. He does not boast of his circumcision nor of his holiness nor of his kingdom, but he identifies himself simply as *the son of Jesse.* He is not ashamed of his lowly descent, that he was a shepherd. Yes, what is much more, he confesses his birth, in which he, like all men, came forth full of sin and guilty of death, for he wishes to speak of other matters, matters so sublime that no nobility of birth and holiness can be of advantage and no misery, whether sin nor death, can work harm.

The oracle of the man who is assured of the Messiah of the God of Jacob, the sweet psalmist of Israel.

Now David expresses himself clearly. He exalts himself extraordinarily and yet truthfully and without conceit. Here he no longer describes himself as the son of Jesse. This he did not inherit from his father nor learn from him nor acquire through his royal power or wisdom. This was conferred on him from above and without any merit on his part. In that he delights, that he exalts, and for that he is so very grateful. And what is it that he lauds so highly? He says: "In the first place it is that I am the man to whom God promised the Messiah of the God of Jacob, that the Messiah will descend from me, from my blood, from my tribe and family. I am sure and convinced of this not only because this has been promised me by God, whose words are certain and reliable and who will not lie to me, but also because I firmly believe this, because I hold to this unswervingly and immovably, knowing that I cannot be disappointed in this belief, and because I implicitly trust in God's Word with all confidence. Therefore I am cheerful and stand ready to live or to die when and how God wills. I know where I, or my soul, will abide, where I will leave it. I will not have it go astray or linger in doubt or depart wretchedly. I have God's definite assurance regarding His Messiah, and on that account I also have a firm and inflexible faith."

. . . For faith is and must be a confidence of the heart which does not waver, reel, tremble, fidget, or doubt but remains constant and is sure of itself. A similar idea is expressed in Isa. 40:8: "The Word of our God will stand forever." It "stands," that is, it is steadfast, it is certain, it does not give way, it does not quiver, it does not sink, it does not fall, it does not leave you in the lurch. And where this Word enters the heart in true faith, it fashions the heart like unto itself, it makes it firm, certain, and assured. It becomes buoyed up, rigid, and adamant over against all temptation, devil, death, and whatever its name may be, that it defiantly and haughtily despises and mocks everything that inclines toward doubt, despair, anger, and wrath; for it knows that God's Word cannot lie to it. . . .

Thus David . . . has the assurance of the promise, and also confidently believes, that the Messiah whom God has promised to the patriarch Jacob (Gen. 49:10: "The scepter shall not depart from Judah until Shiloh comes") would surely issue from his blood. And here the promise of the Messiah given to Jacob is seen anew and more clearly in David (as we shall see further) so that we can henceforth disregard the tribe of Judah and concentrate our attention on the house of David, from which, and from no other house in the tribe of Judah, the Messiah must most assuredly come. Yet even though these two, promise and faith, must go hand in hand—for where there is no promise, there can be no faith, and where there is no faith, there the promise comes to naught; but faith is not always uniformly firm but is assailed at times and becomes weak; the promise, on the other hand, as the eternal Word of God, remains equally firm and sure forever and ever—David is called . . . "affirmed," principally for this reason, that he has the firm promise, although he cannot apprehend and retain this without faith. Faith must also be present. So much about the first part.

Secondly, David boasts of being *the sweet psalmist of Israel*, that is, he did not keep this certain promise of the Messiah to himself nor for himself. For faith does not rest and declare a holiday; it bursts into action, speaks and preaches of this promise and grace of God, so that other people may also come up and partake of it. Yes, his great delight impels him to compose beautiful and sweet psalms and to sing lovely and joyous songs, both to praise and to thank God in his happiness and to serve his fellow men by stimulating and teaching them. Thus David glories in the fact here that he has indited many exquisite, sweet, and melodious psalms about the promised Messiah, which should be sung in Israel to the praise of God and, in fact, have been sung there, in which, simultaneously, both excellent prophecy and a lofty meaning have been preached and imparted to the people of Israel. And as David initiated the writing of psalms and made this a vogue, many others were inspired by his example and became prophets. These followed in David's footsteps and also contributed beautiful psalms, for example, the sons of Korah, Heman, Asaph, etc.

When David uses the word *sweet* he is not thinking only of the sweetness and the charm of the Psalms from a grammatical and musical point of view, of artistic and euphonious words, of melodious song and notes, of beautiful text and beautiful tune; but he is referring much more to the theology they contain, to the spiritual meaning. That renders the Psalms lovely and sweet, for they are a solace to all saddened and wretched consciences, ensnared in the fear of sin, in the torture and terror of death, and in all sorts of adversity and misery. To such hearts the Book of Psalms is a sweet and delightful song because it sings of and proclaims the Messiah even when a person does not sing the notes but merely recites and pronounces the words. And yet the music, or the notes, which are a wonderful creation and gift of God, help materially in this, especially when the people sing along and reverently participate. In 2 Kings 3:15 we read that the spirit of prophecy was aroused in the prophet Elisha by a psaltery, on which psalms were obviously played after the manner of David. David, too, often banished the evil spirit of Saul or restrained and subdued it with his lyre, as we read in 1 Sam. 16:23. For the evil spirit is ill at ease wherever God's Word is sung or preached in true faith. He is a spirit of gloom and cannot abide where he finds a spiritually happy heart, that is, where the heart rejoices in God and in His Word. St. Anthony also makes the comment that spiritual joy is painful to the devil.[12]

David calls his psalms the psalms of Israel. He does not want to ascribe them to himself alone and claim the sole glory for them. Israel is to confirm them and judge and acclaim them as its own. For it is essential that the congregation of God, or God's people, accept and ratify a word or a song; for the Spirit of God is to dwell in this people, and He wants to be honored and must be honored in His people. In that light we Christians speak of *our* psalmists. St. Ambrose composed many hymns of the church.[13] They are called church hymns because the church accepted them and sings them just as though the church had written them and as though they were the church's songs. Therefore it is not customary to say, "Thus sings Ambrose, Gregory, Prudentius, Sedulius," but "Thus sings the Christian church."[14] For these are now the songs of the church, which Ambrose, Sedulius, etc., sing with the church and the church with them. When they die, the church survives them and keeps on singing their songs. In that sense David wishes to call his psalms the psalms of Israel,

12 Anthony the Great, the father of Egyptian monasticism.

13 Ambrose of Milan was a gifted theologian, statesman, musician, and hymn writer. One of Ambrose's best-known hymns, "Veni, Redemptor gentium" ("Savior of the Nations, Come"), was used as evidence against Nestorius by Pope Celestine (r. 422–432) during the great Christological debates of the fifth century. This hymn was translated into German by Luther; see LW 53:235–36.

14 Pope Gregory the Great was credited with developing Gregorian chant or plainsong, the traditional music of the Latin liturgy. Prudentius (348–after 404/405) and Sedulius (fl. 430–450) were poets and hymn writers from the early church. See the hymns "Father, We Praise Thee," "Of the Father's Love Begotten," "From East to West," and "The Star Proclaims the King Is Here."

that is, the psalms of the church, which has the same Spirit who inspired them in David and which will continue to sing them also after David's death. He sensed in his spirit that his psalms would endure on and on, as long as Israel or God's people would endure, that is, until the end of time. And that is what has happened hitherto and will happen. Therefore they are to be called the psalms of Israel.

2 Samuel 23:2

The Spirit of the Lord has spoken by me, His Word is upon my tongue.

Here David begins to speak too strangely and too loftily for me. God grant that I may understand at least a bit of it despite that. For here he begins to talk about the exalted Holy Trinity, of the divine Essence. In the first place, he mentions the Holy Spirit. To Him he ascribes all that is foretold by the prophets. And to this and to similar verses St. Peter refers in 2 Pet. 1:21, where he says: "No prophecy ever came by the impulse of man; but moved by the Holy Spirit, holy men of God spoke." Therefore we sing in the article of the Creed concerning the Holy Spirit: "Who spake by the prophets." Thus we attribute to the Holy Spirit all of Holy Scripture and the external Word and the Sacraments, which touch and move our external ears and other senses. Our Lord Jesus Christ also ascribes His Word to the Holy Spirit, as He quotes Isa. 61:1 in Luke 4:18: "The Spirit of the Lord is upon Me, etc.," and as he quotes Isa. 42:1 in Matt. 12:18: "Behold, My Servant whom I have chosen. . . . I will put My Spirit upon Him." And in Luke 1:35 we read that the Holy Spirit will overshadow Mary, that He will touch her, take her blood and impregnate her, so that the Lord is described as "conceived by the Holy Spirit."

What a glorious and arrogant arrogance it is for anyone to dare to boast that the Spirit of the Lord speaks through him and that his tongue is voicing the Word of the Holy Spirit! He must obviously be sure of his ground. David, the son of Jesse, born in sin, is not such a man, but it is he who has been called to be a prophet by the promise of God. Should he who has such a Teacher to instruct him and to speak through him not be able to compose "sweet" psalms? "Let him who has ears to hear, hear! My speech is really not mine, but he who hears me hears God, and he who despises me despises God (cf. Luke 10:16). For I foresee that many of my descendants will not give ear to my word, and that will redound to their great detriment." Neither we nor anyone else who is not a prophet may lay claim to such honor. But we may do this as far as we are holy and possess the Holy Spirit, namely, in that we can boast of being catechumens and pupils of the apostles, in that we repeat and preach what we have heard and learned from the prophets and apostles and are convinced that the prophets taught this. In the Old Testament such people are called "sons of the prophets." They do not promulgate anything of their own or proclaim anything new, as the prophets do, but they teach what they have received from the prophets. They are, as David says, Israel, for whom he writes his psalms.

2 Samuel 23:3

The God of Israel has talked to me, the Rock of Israel has spoken; He who rules justly over men, He who rules in the fear of God.

Now we have three speakers. Above, David remarks that the Spirit of the Lord has spoken through his tongue. There the person of the Holy Spirit is clearly indicated to us Christians. Whatever Turks, Jews, and other ungodly persons believe we disregard. Thus we have heard that Scripture and our Creed ascribe to the Holy Spirit the external working, as He physically speaks to us, baptizes us, and reigns over us through the prophets, apostles, and ministers of the church. Therefore these words of David are also those of the Holy Spirit, which He speaks with David's tongue regarding two other Speakers. What does He say of these? First of all He speaks of the God of Israel and says that He has spoken to David, that is, has given him a promise. Which person of the Godhead this Speaker is we Christians know from the Gospel of John. It is the Father who said in the beginning (Gen. 1:3): "Let there be light." And His Word is the person of the Son, through which Word "all things were made" (John 1:3). The same Son the Spirit by the mouth of David here calls "*Rock*" *of Israel* and *just Ruler among mankind*. He, too, speaks, that is, the Holy Spirit introduces the Rock of Israel to let Him speak too. Thus all three persons speak, and yet there is but one Speaker, one Promiser, one Promise, just as there is but one God.

But as the outward working on man is ascribed to the Holy Spirit, so it is the attribute of the Son that He became incarnate and that He was appointed a Lord and Judge over all men and all creation. Ps. 8:4–6 sings: "What is man that Thou art mindful of Him, and the Son of Man that Thou dost care for Him? Yet Thou hast made Him little less than God and dost crown Him with glory and honor. Thou hast given Him dominion over the works of Thy hands; Thou hast put all things under His feet." Yet there is not a threefold dominion or three rulers, but there is one Lord and one dominion, which the Father has conferred on the Son, yes, on the man and the Son of Man, but undoubtedly not in this way, that He has eliminated Himself and the Holy Spirit from this dominion. Yet it is called the dominion of the man which God gives Him. Therefore the same man who is here called Ruler must be true

God, for He has possession of God's kingdom and is therefore equal to God in the one dominion.

For God gives His honor or His own kingdom to no one else. Thus He says in Exod. 20:3: "You shall have no other gods before Me," and in Isa. 42:8: "My glory I give to no other, nor My praise to graven images." But now since God bestows on this man and this Son of Man His honor and dominion—that is, subjects to Him all that has been created as it is subject to Him too—this man can be no other god or idol but must be the true and natural God together with the Father and the Holy Spirit. If we have the time and are endued with the grace, we shall later discourse on this subject on the basis of more similar passages, especially verses from the Psalms. But first let us dispose of these words of David in which he confesses the two sublimest doctrines of our faith so aptly, that there are three distinct persons in God, and that one of these, the Son, should become man and receive honor and dominion over all from the Father, that the Holy Spirit, who has previously proclaimed this through the mouth and lips of the prophets, should inscribe this into the heart of man by faith. And this is nothing but the work exclusively peculiar to the divine Majesty; for it is not the work of man or of angel first to promise this and then to create faith in the human heart. St. Paul declares (Eph. 2:8) that such faith "is the gift of God," effected and bestowed by the Holy Spirit.

Not everybody has the competency to note and to distinguish the three persons of the Godhead as distinct from one another as he reads Scripture and the Psalms. For if a carnal mind approaches these words here, he will read perfunctorily and cursorily: *The Spirit of the Lord has spoken by me, the God of Israel has talked to me, the Rock of Israel has spoken, the just Ruler among men, etc.* He will not think otherwise than that all these terms refer to God in one person with a superfluity of words. Or he falls into the Jewish blindness according to which they suppose that David is this just ruler, a ruler in the fear of God. They transform the promise into commands and laws, implying that he who aspires to rule over men must be just and God-fearing, although David enthusiastically and sincerely proclaims that these are words of promise of the Messiah of the God of Jacob and not precepts pertaining to worldly rulers.

Psalm 2

Such a person would fare the same way with Psalm 2, in which the three persons also speak separately, as three individual speakers. God the Father says (v. 6): "I have set My King on Zion, My holy hill." This King is certainly a person apart from Him who installs Him as King. And then the words follow immediately (v. 7) "I will tell of the decree." These words sound as if the Father were still speaking, and that is what reason would suggest, though, in fact, it is the King, the Son, as is apparent from what follows (v. 7): "The Lord said to Me, You are My Son, today I have begotten You." That this person is man is certain, for He is to preach and be the Messiah, as we hear in v. 2: "They rage against the Lord and His Messiah." But that He is God is proved by the words of the Father: "You are My Son, today I have begotten You," as we Christians well know. We find further proof of His Godhead in the fact that God makes "the ends of the earth His possession," together with the Gentiles and whatever the earth contains, which is the equivalent of God's own kingdom.

Furthermore, God orders man to kiss the Son (v. 11), or worship Him and serve Him with awe, concluding with the words: "Blessed are all who take refuge in Him." That can pertain only to God. The fact that not all obey Him in accord with the Gospel does not diminish His dominion over all creatures in the least. He who refuses to be under His grace must be subject to His wrath. He who will not rule with Him must, together with His enemies, be His footstool. He is Judge over the quick and the dead. Do you imagine that because Turk, pope, Jew, and the whole evil host of the world and the devil do not want His grace but rave against it they will on that account escape His might? They will surely be taught their lesson; for "He who sits in the heavens laughs. . . . Then He will speak to them in His wrath" (vv. 4–5). In brief, He is Lord and remains Lord, as God Himself is Lord; for God has given Him dominion over all. His power is certain and endures. Woe to him who does not accept this by grace. He will encounter this power coupled with wrath in all eternity.

Thus we again find two distinct persons here, the Father and the Son; and the Holy Spirit is present although not especially mentioned. It is He who composed and put into words this psalm, introducing the Father and the Son in Their own words. Thus the distinctive trinity of persons in one indivisible divine essence is professed here together with the fact that the Son is man and Messiah, just as this is professed in the last words of David. A carnal heart will pass over these words casually or suppose that David composed them in his capacity as a pious man about himself or about others. That is what the blind Jews do. But David does not let us attribute these words to him. "These are delightful and charming psalms of Israel," he says, "and I did not make them, but 'the Spirit of the Lord has spoken by me.'" After all, how could flesh and blood, reason and human wisdom, discourse on such sublime and incomprehensible matters? These are sheer foolishness and offense to them.

2 Samuel 7:11–16 and 1 Chronicles 17:10–14

Now to verify that this is really the opinion of David, that he, as just stated, believed this and died in that belief, we will discuss the words on which he based and by reason of which he indited such lovely psalms. We find them recorded in 2 Sam. 7:11–16 and in 1 Chron. 17:10–14. They read as follows:

> *Moreover the Lord declares to you that the Lord will build you a house. When your days are fulfilled to go to be with your fathers, I will raise up your Offspring after you, one of your own sons, and I will establish His kingdom. He shall build a house for Me, and I will establish His throne forever. I will be His Father, and He shall be My Son; I will not take My steadfast love from Him, as I took it from him who was before you, but I will confirm Him in My house and in My kingdom forever, and His throne shall be established forever.*

The first point made here is expressed in the words *The Lord declares to you that the Lord will build you a house.* This obviously refers to the house of David and signifies that his children are to possess the scepter of Judah until the advent of the Messiah. Enough has been said about this in that little booklet dealing with the Jews.[15] Here we again find the three persons of the Godhead: first the Holy Spirit, who speaks by the prophet Nathan. We heard before that Holy Scripture is spoken by the Holy Spirit in keeping with the words of David, *The Spirit of the Lord has spoken by me.* In like manner He speaks by all prophets. The Holy Spirit, furthermore, introduces the person of the Father when He says: "The Lord declares to you." And immediately after that He presents the person of the Son, saying *that the Lord will build you a house.* And yet it is but one God and Lord who speaks through Nathan, makes an announcement to David, and builds his house. All three are but one Speaker, one Announcer, one Builder. It is immaterial whether or not everybody's reason discerns these three persons in Scripture. I am well aware how the saucy prigs who make bold to instruct the Holy Spirit make annotations here and in similar passages.

Wherever in Scripture you find God speaking about God as if there were two persons, you may boldly assume that three persons of the Godhead are there indicated.[16] Thus in the passage under discussion we hear the Lord say that the Lord will build a house for David. Likewise we read in Gen. 19:24: "Then the Lord rained on Sodom and Gomorrah brimstone and fire from the Lord out of heaven." For the Holy Spirit is no fool or drunkard, who would speak one iota, much less a word, in vain. If the Lord, that is, the Son rains fire and brimstone from the Lord, that is, the Father, the Holy Spirit is simultaneously present. It is He who speaks

15 *On the Jews and Their Lies* (1543), LW 47:196–99.

16 Martin Chemnitz (1522–86) refers to this as Luther's rule. See Chemnitz, *Loci Theologici*, trans. J. A. O. Preus (St. Louis: Concordia, 2008), 1:90–91. Cf. Augustine, *The Trinity* 1.21 (WSA 1/5:81).

these words by Abraham, or whoever it might be, about the two Lords. And still these three are one Lord, one God, who rains fire and brimstone. Later we shall hear more examples illustrating that.

The second point is contained in the words *When your days are fulfilled to go to be with your fathers, I will raise up your Offspring after you, etc.* Here the text touching on the Messiah really begins. For these words cannot be spoken of Solomon, much less of any other son of David. They must refer to the true, unique Son of David, the Messiah, who was to come after the reign of Judah was ended. *He shall build a house for Me*, He says, *and I will establish His kingdom forever*. This house cannot be identical with the temple of Solomon, for immediately prior to this He says (1 Chron. 17:4–5): "You shall not build Me a house to dwell in. For I have not dwelt in a house since I led up Israel to this day." And in 1 Kings 8:27 Solomon himself declares: "But will God indeed dwell on the earth? Behold, heaven and the highest heaven cannot contain Thee; how much less this house which I have built!" And Isa. 66:1 expresses this thought still more forcefully: "Thus says the Lord: 'Heaven is My throne, and the earth is My footstool; what is the house which you would build for Me, and what is the place of My rest?' " . . .

Therefore this house, to be built by Messiah, the Son of David and of God, must necessarily be a different, a larger and more glorious, house. . . . Holy Scripture, in particular the New Testament, informs us about this house. It is the holy Christian Church, which extends to the ends of the earth. Furthermore, it is an everlasting house, a house that will endure and live forever, a house in which God remains and lives and keeps house forever. What a house and temple that will become!

Now let us consider the carpenter, or master builder, of this house. He is to be a man and a son of David, for the text speaks of *one of your own sons* (1 Chron. 17:11). Yet he is to build a house of God which is to be better and more glorious than heaven and earth and, in addition, is to stand forever. Whence will he derive the skill and the power for this? Neither man's nor angel's skill or might can come into question here, for angels cannot create heaven and earth, no, not even the least of the creatures. Much less is man able to do this. Therefore the builder of this house must be true God, who has the actual power of the divine nature to create heaven and earth and even much better things than that; that is, He must be omnipotent God, and yet He is not the person who says of Him *I will be His Father, and He shall be My Son, and He shall build a house for Me.* Here the persons are clearly and definitely distinguished as Father and Son, as Builder and Master of the house. Still they cannot be two Gods, nor can the Son be a separate or a different God. The First

Commandment precludes that possibility, saying (Exod. 20:3): "You shall have no other gods before Me." And (Deut. 6:4): "Hear, O Israel: The Lord our God is one Lord, or God."

We heard before that whenever Scripture speaks of the two persons of the Father and the Son, the Holy Spirit, the third person, is also present; for it is He who speaks those words through the prophets. Thus a believing heart finds powerful and well-grounded proof and testimony in this passage that God, the omnipotent Creator of heaven and earth, is the one true God, that there can be no other god beside Him, that there are, at the same time, three distinct persons, the Father, the Son, and the Holy Spirit yet in this way, that only the Son became man and David's Son. Undoubtedly the prohibition not to worship more than one God was impressed upon the people of Israel so strictly that they should not be offended when the Messiah should come and be proclaimed and believed to be God, as if He were minded, contrary to Moses, to teach more than one God, or a strange god, but that they should bridle their ears and hearts and be willing to learn how the First Commandment concerning one God is to be understood correctly and thoroughly. The text continues (1 Chron. 17:14):

I will confirm Him in My house and in My kingdom forever.

What does this mean? Let us give ear. As I have said above, the house is to be and to remain forever. Therefore the Master of the house must also be eternal and must be endowed with eternal and divine power. Here He continues His speech to David: "In the house which My Son and yours is to build for Me, He, as well as I, will be Master. He is to be My equal in this one house. I will install Him and decree that He is to own it just as I do." Now, we have heard that this house of God is larger and better and more glorious than heaven and earth. And if David's Son, the Messiah, is Master and Lord of this house, He is certainly also Master and Lord of heaven and earth and far superior to and better than these. For He who is Lord over this house, as God Himself is, must self-evidently be superior and be Lord over heaven and earth, as God Himself is. And that can be none other than the one God, Creator of heaven and earth. From this we deduce that Messiah, David's natural Son, must be true God and no strange god. For, as I have already said, God does not let a strange god be master of His own house. He must and will keep His honor and power for Himself and yield it to no one else. That should demonstrate clearly enough that Messiah, David's Son, is Lord and King in God's own kingdom, or that He is equal with God; for it is certain that God is here speaking of the Messiah. . . .

Now, he who would interpret the words *My house* and *My kingdom* in this passage as pertaining to the temple and to the people of Israel must also assume the further burden to adduce good and convincing proof that the temple in Jerusalem and the people of Israel in the land of Canaan have from the time of David until now remained intact continuously, for the text here clearly states that David's house shall remain forever and that the Messiah, David's Son, shall be eternally enthroned in God's house and kingdom. We Christians must concede that we are unable to prove this. We know that God's house, the temple in Jerusalem, has lain in ashes approximately 1,500 years, that David's house and kingdom and the people of Israel have also amounted to nothing for about 1,500 years, and that they have not had dominion or a kingdom in Canaan. We needs must adhere to our former interpretation and maintain that the words *My house* and *My kingdom* pertain to the eternal kingdom of God, in which He chooses to dwell and reign forever, which His Son and David's, the Messiah, was to build by His divine omnipotence and wisdom.

But let us lend ear to David himself and hear how he understood these words. In 1 Chron. 17:15–16 we read:

> *Nathan spoke all these words* (as given above) *to David. Then King David went in and sat before the Lord and said: "Who am I, O Lord God, and what is my house, that Thou hast brought me thus far?"*

Here David shows that he did indeed understand the words of God's promise spoken to him by Nathan (1 Chron. 17:13–14): *I will be His Father, and He shall be My Son . . . I will confirm Him in My house and in My kingdom forever.* Therefore he says *Who am I, and what is my house, that Thou hast brought me this far?* "Your promise that my house, that I, my Son, should reach such heights as to have Him occupy Your own eternal kingdom, be Lord and King, is too much glory and honor for me. O Lord God, where are You taking me?" He cannot find words to express himself in his great amazement. He speaks of *thus far.* "Whereto? Whereto? My dear God, am I, that is, my flesh and blood, to sit enthroned in Your eternal kingdom as Your equal? Then my flesh and blood, my Son and Your Son, must necessarily be true and very God, who sits enthroned as Your equal. O God, where are You taking me?" We read on (1 Chron. 17:17):

> *Thou hast regarded me as in the form of a man who is God the Lord on high.*

The translation of these words by almost all other Hebraists is far different. Several, however, and among these Bernhard Ziegler, bear witness to me that this passage may and must be translated grammatically as I did.[17] With these words David clearly states that his Son, the Messiah, will surely be true man, in form, manner, and size like any other man (Phil. 2:7), and yet up above and on high, where there is no manner of men, where only God is and governs, He is to be God the Lord. That is, I say, clearly the opinion of David tersely expressed. In view of this, he says above (v. 16): "Whither, whither are You, dear God, taking me?" And here: "Why do you regard me, unworthy human being that I am, that my Son should be King in Your eternal kingdom?" David knows full well that no other than the true God is entitled to be King in God's eternal kingdom. And since the Son of David is man and a person apart from the Father, who installs him in His kingdom, and since there cannot be two gods or more than one God, David here concludes that his Son, the Messiah, must be true and natural God, and yet none other God than the Father, but a separate person in the same one inseparable Godhead, and that the Holy Spirit, who as true God speaks these words through Nathan and David concerning the Father and the Son, is the third person in the same one Godhead.

That is the doctrine and the belief of the New Testament, namely, that Jesus of Nazareth, David's and the Virgin Mary's Son, is true man and God's natural, eternal Son, one God and three distinct persons together with the Father and the Holy Spirit. And since David's words in this passage amply reflect that meaning in accord with the general usage of the Hebrew tongue, we Christians must not seek or heed any other significance in them but regard this as the only correct one and look upon all other interpretations as worthless human imagination. The New Testament cannot err, nor can the Old Testament where it harmonizes and agrees with the New Testament.

You may feel tempted to ask here: "If the words of David and Nathan reveal the doctrine of Christ's deity so clearly, how do you explain that neither the holy fathers nor any other teacher discovered or ever mentioned this, and that you recent and young Hebraists just became aware of this now? Why do the Jewish rabbis not discern this?" We reply: After the days of the apostles the knowledge of the Hebrew language was scant and deficient. The dear fathers and teachers contented themselves with the New Testament, in which they found this doctrine and all others in great abundance. The prophets and apostles, however, did perceive the truth of this very well, as we shall hear later. It is perfectly natural that the rabbis did not see this; for he who is blind sees nothing. In Isa. 6:9 the

17 Ziegler (1496–1556) was professor of Hebrew at Leipzig and a frequent consultant to Luther and his colleagues on the translation and exposition of the Old Testament. Cf. *Table Talk* no. 5002 (1540), LW 54:375–76.

prophet says of them: "See and see, but do not perceive." And whoever must learn from them will surely also become blind. To be sure, we, too, would not be able to see it if we could not look the Old Testament straight into the eye because we are illumined by the New Testament. For the Old Testament is veiled without the New Testament (2 Cor. 4:3–4).

Consider our own times, in which we are preaching of the grace of Christ against our own presumptuous works and holiness. How few there are to see this or to accept it earnestly! Where does the fault lie? It is being preached and taught so lucidly; it is being read, written, sung, painted, and disseminated in every way, so that wood and stone could understand it if these were endowed with but a modicum of reason. And yet pope, kings, princes, bishops, scholars, lords, noblemen, burghers, and peasants do not see it but pass it by, blind with seeing eyes, deaf with hearing ears; for their heart does not concentrate on what lies close at hand but roves about elsewhere. Thus the prophets also foretold clearly enough in their day that Christ was to be God and Lord over all, as David does here. However, only a few paid this any heed and believed it; the others were blind and deaf to it and followed the voice of their heart and their own fancy. This is termed a mystery, and a mystery it remains. Let him who understands this and is sincere in his belief thank God and pay no attention to the great multitude of scorners.

Isaiah

Do you not suppose that Isaiah read this text intently? For he says in chapter 9:6–7: "For to us a Child is born, to us a Son is given; and the government will be upon His shoulder, and His name will be called 'Wonderful, Counselor, Mighty God, Everlasting Father, Prince of Peace.' Of the increase of His government and of peace there will be no end, upon the throne of David, and over His kingdom, to establish it and to uphold it with justice and with righteousness from this time forth and forevermore." Here Isaiah takes the words out of Nathan's mouth, as he prophesies that the Messiah will be an eternal King and Father in God's kingdom. And he also calls Him God, for the word literally, to be sure, means "power"; but when it is a proper name, as here, its meaning throughout Scripture is God, who alone has power. Both Jews and Hebraists have to admit that. Thus Isaiah concurs with David and the New Testament, affirming that Christ is an eternal King and the true God. And it follows that His kingdom must be divine and everlasting, established on the throne of David, etc.

In particular has he studied the concept "everlasting kingdom" in the passage where God says to David by Nathan (1 Chron. 17:14): *I will confirm thy Son in My kingdom forever*, and he feels instinctively that this is spoken, as David says, of a man who must be God, up above. For to possess the eternal kingdom of God and to be King there cannot belong to a mere man, nor can this refer to a transitory, temporal, and earthly kingdom which will terminate and the king of which must die and his children after him. No, here the Son of David is to be an eternal King in the everlasting kingdom of God. And as Isaiah agrees, "of the peace there will be no end," and He, the Son of David, the Child, born and given to us, shall be an "Everlasting Father and a Prince of Peace . . . from this time forth and forevermore." Consequently, He must be God, who is able to bestow and preserve such eternal peace by His divine power.

Isaiah witnesses to the eternity of the Messiah's kingdom in a number of passages; for instance, in chapter 51:4–5: "Listen to Me, My people, and give ear to Me, My nation; for a law will go forth from Me, and My justice for a light to the peoples. My righteousness draws near speedily, My salvation has gone forth." And a little while later he says (v. 6): "My Salvation will be forever, and My Righteousness will never be ended." This is the eternal Righteousness of which Dan. 9:24 says: "Seventy weeks of years are decreed . . . to bring in everlasting Righteousness." This refers to the Messiah; thus all old Hebraists have interpreted it. Mere man or angel cannot be called "eternal Righteousness and Salvation"; no, these terms signify God Himself. And yet He is also David's Son, natural man, and a person distinct from the one who speaks about Him and calls Him "My Salvation, My Righteousness." The Holy Spirit is the third person present; it is He who says this about the other two. In 1 Cor. 1:30 the New Testament speaks of "Christ Jesus, whom God made our Wisdom, our Righteousness and Sanctification and Redemption." That is in accord with Isaiah, and Isaiah is in accord with Paul.

In Isa. 60:19–20 we read in like manner: "The sun shall be no more your light by day, nor for brightness shall the moon give light to you by night; but the Lord will be your everlasting Light, and your God will be your Glory. Your sun shall no more go down, nor your moon withdraw itself; for the Lord will be your everlasting Light, and your days of mourning shall be ended." Here it is clearly stated that the Lord and our God Himself will be our everlasting Light. Here the one Lord speaks about the other. Indeed, in the entire chapter it is not Isaiah who is speaking but the Lord. It is He who says: "The Lord will be your everlasting Light." Who is the Lord who speaks these words? Without a doubt, God the Father. Who is the Lord of whom He says: "The Lord will be your everlasting Light"? Without a doubt, God the Son, Jesus Christ. For here we find the great name of God, Jehovah, which our Bibles print with capital letters, LORD, in contradistinction to the other names. Who is it who speaks these words by the tongue of Isaiah? Without a doubt, God the Holy Spirit, who speaks by the prophets, introducing the person of the Father, who, in turn, speaks of the eternal Light, that is, of His Son, Jesus of Nazareth, the Son of David and of Mary.

Such an eternal Light, yes, such a Lord, cannot be a mere angel, nor a man either. Isaiah's prophecy agrees with the New Testament, in which Jesus often calls Himself a light. In John 1:4–5 we read: "The life was the light of men. The light shines in the darkness, but the darkness has not grasped it." Since this is in agreement with the New Testament, Isaiah's prophecy should cheerfully be interpreted as referring to none other than Jesus Christ, who has not prepared a transitory kingdom under this sun and this moon for us; no, He Himself wants to be our eternal Light, Sun and Moon, Life and Salvation. Thus He says in Isa. 51:6 above: "Lift up your eyes to the heavens and look at the earth beneath; for the heavens will vanish like smoke, the earth will wear out like a garment; and they who dwell in it will die like gnats; but My Salvation will be forever, and My Righteousness will never be ended." . . .

Daniel

Let us also consult Daniel, who declares in chapter 7:13–14: "I saw in the night visions, and behold, with the clouds of heaven there came one like a Son of Man, and He came to the Ancient of Days and was presented before Him. And to Him was given dominion and glory and kingdom, that all peoples, nations, and languages should serve Him; His dominion is an everlasting dominion, which shall not pass away; and His kingdom one that shall not be destroyed." Christians understand this verse well. However, now we want to observe how this agrees with the New Testament. He beholds a Son of Man in the clouds, which undoubtedly signifies that His kingdom is not to be of this world, that it is not to be transitory and temporal, but that it is to be heavenly and eternal. He says that "the Ancient of Days," that is, God the Father, gave Him dominion over all, that His power is to endure forever and is not to pass away. This eternity, or this everlasting kingdom, cannot be conferred on any mere creature, neither angel nor man, for it is a divine dominion, God's own dominion. If God were to divest Himself of His eternal dominion and His eternal kingdom, what would He have or have left? He would keep nothing at all, He would destroy Himself since there would then be another in possession of the eternal dominion. Obviously there can be nothing beyond and outside of this eternal dominion. Eternal dominion embraces everything and will not tolerate anything superior to it or anything outside of it. This must be God Himself and nothing else.

This passage from Daniel also powerfully presents the doctrine of the Godhead in three persons and of the humanity of the Son; for the person who gives must be distinct from the person who receives. Thus the Father bestows the eternal dominion on the Son, and the Son receives it from the Father, and this is from eternity; otherwise this could not be an eternal dominion. And the Holy Spirit is present, inasmuch as He speaks these words through Daniel. For such sublime and mysterious things no one could know if the Holy Spirit would not reveal them through the prophets. It has been stated often enough above that Holy Scripture is given through the Holy Spirit. In addition, the Son is nevertheless also a Son of Man, that is, a true human being and David's Son, to whom such eternal dominion is given. Thus we note that the prophets did indeed respect and understand the word "eternal," which God used when He addressed David through Nathan and said (1 Chron. 17:14): "I will install My Son and yours in My eternal kingdom."

Here is where Mr. Smart Aleck, reason, takes offense, presuming to be ten times wiser than God Himself, asking: "How can God take His eternal dominion and bestow it on someone else?" What would He be retaining for Himself? Did we not say above that God says in Isa. 42:8: "My glory I give to no other, nor My praise to graven images"? And it is particularly impossible for God to bestow this on a human being, who has not existed from eternity, as God has, but who had a beginning in time, who was born and who is mortal, as we Christians confess and preach of Jesus Christ, David's and Mary's Son. The Jews, Mohammed, the Turks, and the Tartars also belong to this category of superintelligent people. With their spoonful or nutshellful of brain they can comprehend the incomprehensible essence of God and say that since God has no wife, He can also have no son. Fie, fie, fie upon you, devil, together with Jews and Mohammed and all who are the disciples of blind, deaf, and wretched reason in these exalted matters, which none but God alone can fathom, which we grasp only in the measure in which the Holy Spirit has revealed them to us through the prophets.

Christ's two natures

We Christians, illumined by the New Testament, can answer these objections clearly and definitely and say: Christ, our Lord, has two births, or two natures, in one indivisible person; for He is one Christ and not, as the stupid mind of Nestorius madly maintains, two Christs.[18] According to the first birth, He received, not in time but from all eternity, the everlasting dominion, or the Godhead, from the Father. The Father gave this to Him in its entirety and in its perfection, as He Himself possesses

18 See above, p. 397 n. 15.

it from eternity. He did not transfer this to Him in the sense that He Himself divested and deprived Himself of it; but He gave the Son the selfsame dominion and none other which He Himself had fully and completely from eternity and which He retains in all eternity. For there are not two Godheads, but both persons are one Godhead. The words of Isa. 42:8 ever remain true: "My glory I give to no other, nor My praise to graven images." For the Son is no separate god or idol, but together with the Father He is the one true and eternal God.

Christ Himself speaks about this when He says in John 16:15: "All that the Father has is Mine." He does not say: "The Father no longer has anything; I alone have everything now," or: "The Father has everything alone; I have nothing." But He says: "The Father has it all, but, this 'all' that He has is Mine." That is patently saying that the Father and the Son compose one single Godhead. And of this "all" of the Father which belongs to the Son the Holy Spirit also partakes, as Christ says in the same passage: "He will take what is Mine." Which "Mine"? Without a doubt, from the "Mine" which the Father has. Thus the Holy Spirit takes from both, from the Father and the Son, the same complete Godhead from eternity. Christ also says in John 5:26: "As the Father has life in Himself, so He has granted the Son also to have life in Himself," and in vv. 21 and 23: "As the Father raises the dead and gives them life, so also the Son gives life to whom He will . . . that all may honor the Son, even as they honor the Father." All of this is said of the first, eternal, divine birth.

According to the second, the temporal, human birth Christ was also given the eternal dominion of God, yet temporally and not from eternity. For the human nature of Christ was not from eternity as His divine nature was. It is computed that Jesus, Mary's Son, is 1,543 years old this year. But from the moment when Deity and humanity were united in one person, the man, Mary's Son, is and is called almighty, eternal God, who has eternal dominion, who has created all things and preserves them "through the communication of attributes" (*per communicationem idiomatum*), because He is one person with the Godhead and is also very God. Christ refers to this in Matt. 11:27: "All things have been delivered to Me by My Father," and in Matt. 28:18: "All authority in heaven and on earth has been given to Me." To which "Me"? "To Me, Jesus of Nazareth, Mary's incarnate Son. I had this from My Father from eternity, before I became man, but when I became man, it was imparted to Me in time according to My human nature, and I kept it concealed until My resurrection and ascent into heaven, when it was to be manifested and glorified." Thus St. Paul declares in Rom. 1:4, He was glorified, or "designated Son of God in power." John speaks of this as being "glorified" in chapter 7:39: "As yet the Spirit had not been given, because Jesus was not yet glorified."

Now note that Daniel speaks about the Son of Man, who receives eternal dominion from God, in almost the same way as Isaiah does and as also Nathan and David do, saying that God would install David's Son as King in His eternal kingdom; and, as David states, this is spoken of a man "who is God the Lord on high." Oh, that we Christians would recognize this ineffable grace which both the Old and the New Testament contain in such rich measure! Alas, that we do not rejoice and show forth our gratitude as we should! It would not be surprising if a Christian heart that thoroughly pondered and grasped the import of this would die for joy and again be quickened by joy. How amazing it is that God is man and converses with us humans, that He lives and especially that He dies for us! David grows mute and numb with ecstatic joy; he can utter no more than (1 Chron. 17:16): *What am I, O Lord God, and what is my house, that Thou hast brought me thus far?*

All of this revolves about the words recorded in 1 Chronicles 17, on which, as already stated, the last words of David are based, which assert that Christ must be very God and very man. And whatever further thoughts might well forth from that text we shall consider later with God's help. The prophets that followed David, as well as David himself, derived much proof of Christ's deity and of His humanity from this. Take, for example, Ps. 110:1: "The Lord says to My Lord, Sit at My right hand, until I make Your enemies Your footstool." What else can be the significance of the phrase "to sit at My right hand" than to sit enthroned equal with God, that is, to be seated in the eternal kingdom of God? For Christ does not sit at God's head or at His feet, neither above Him nor below Him, but at His right, as His peer, so that the heaven is also His throne and the earth His footstool. Thus Christ says in Matt. 28:18: "All authority in heaven and on earth has been given to Me," and in Mark 16:19 we read: "He was taken up into heaven and sat down at the right hand of God." And when Christ asks the Pharisees in Matt. 22:43–44: "If Christ is David's Son, how is it then that David, inspired by the Spirit"—that is, the Spirit speaks by him—"calls Him Lord, saying, 'The Lord said to My Lord, Sit at My right hand'?" they were unable to make reply. . . .

Now the Father is not Christ or David's Son, and Christ is not the Father; and yet He is to sit at the right hand of the Father as His equal and partake of one kingdom, dominion, honor, and everything with Him. But God tolerates no peer to share equal honor and dominion with Him. Therefore Christ, David's Son, must be true God and one God with the Father and of equal throne with Him. For there can be no more than one

God in accord with the First Commandment, which reads: "Thou shalt have no other gods besides Me." And the Holy Spirit is also present as the one true God. It is He who speaks to us men through David and through all the prophets and reveals and teaches us every truth of the Godhead. Thus David declares (2 Sam. 23:2): *The Spirit of the Lord has spoken by me.* And Christ Himself states in Matt. 22:45: "If David thus calls Him Lord, how is He his Son?" To be sure, without the Spirit he would neither call Him that nor know in what way Christ is his Son and his Lord. The Holy Spirit, however, is not Christ the Son nor the Father. He cannot be another God. It follows cogently that there is but one God and yet three separate persons, Father, Son, and Holy Spirit, from eternity to eternity.

Christ often called David

It may perplex some to hear David say: *Who am I? What is my house?* Also: *Thou hast regarded me as a man who is God the Lord on high* (1 Chron. 17:16–17). After all, God did not say to David: "You shall be My son; I will establish you in My eternal kingdom." No, God says to David: "Your Son shall be My Son; Him will I place in My eternal kingdom" (cf. 1 Chron. 17:13–14). Why does David alter the words of God and refer them to himself, as though he were the man *who is God the Lord on high?* Well, as you hear, David is the father of this Son; the latter is to issue from his family and his blood. Now it is natural that a father glories in the honor that comes to his son as much and more than the son does himself. He wishes every honor and every good thing for his son more than he does for himself. And again, any contumely and dishonor the son experiences saddens the father more than if this were heaped on him himself. Therefore, when he says: *What is my house?* not only David but his whole house exults here over the glory that a Son should issue from their flesh and blood who would sit at the right hand of God.

. . . Therefore it is not unfitting for a father to praise and thank God for his son's honor in words like these: "O dear God, who am I and what do You make of me that You honor me so highly and elevate the issue of my flesh and blood to such a lordship? It is I on whom this honor and this joy are bestowed; for, after all, it is my flesh and blood which at present is still in me and with me, but which is to be born some time in the future."

In the prophets our Lord Jesus is therefore often called by the name of His father David. In Hosea 3:5 we read: "Afterward the children of Israel shall return and seek the Lord their God, and David their King; and they shall come in fear to the Lord and to His goodness in the latter days." Here David means our Lord Christ, and He is given equal honor with God and is called the Lord, whom they will seek and honor. They will seek and honor God and their King in the same way, just as we honor the

Father and the Son with the same faith. We do not honor the Father with one faith and the Son with a different one. The third person, the Holy Spirit, is also present here. It is He who utters these words through Hosea and who teaches us to believe.

Likewise, we read in Ezek. 34:23–24: "And I will set up over them one Shepherd, My Servant David, and He shall feed them: He shall feed them and be their Shepherd. And I, the Lord, will be their God, and My Servant David shall be Prince among them." Here Christ is called "David" and "God's Servant." He is called "God's Servant" also in Isa. 52:13 and in many other places. And St. Paul, who again and again proclaims Christ as very God, makes Him a servant in Phil. 2:5–7: "Have this mind among yourselves, which you have in Christ Jesus, who, though He was in the form of God, did not count equality with God a thing to be grasped, but emptied Himself, taking the form of a servant, etc." Let us ask the apostle how he can talk so absurdly. If Christ is equal with God, how can He be a servant and assume the form of a servant? If He is a servant, how can He be God and in the form of God? We Christians, of course, know and understand this very well, but the Jews confidently harden themselves with this passage from Ezekiel. They stubbornly insist on their opinion—I am tempted to say, on their madness. Let them go their way.

Similarly, in Jer. 30:8–9 we read: "And it shall come to pass in that day, says the Lord of hosts, that I will break the yoke from off their neck, and I will burst their bonds, and strangers shall no more make servants of them. But they shall serve the Lord their God and David their King, whom I will raise up for them." Here Christ is again called "David." The Jews, both the young and the old, have to interpret this verse as referring to the Messiah. However, they misunderstand the words "the yoke" and "the bonds." They assume that these allude to the Babylonian captivity. But all three chapters in a row speak distinctly of the redemption which the Messiah is to work, that is, the redemption from sin and death, which the Law sets at us and of which the Jews and reason are ignorant. This is how Christians and whatever has been Christian since the beginning of the world conceive of these words, etc.

Jeremiah in this verse at the same time makes his King David true God. He identifies God with this David and unites Him in one and the same honor which the children of Israel are to render Him. For if this David were not true God, God would not place Him beside Himself and say: "They shall serve the Lord their God and David their King," for it is written: "Thou shalt serve no other God but the Lord your God. Him alone you must fear and serve" (cf. Deut. 6:13–14; 10:20). Thus the words of Jeremiah harmonize with 1 Chron. 17:14–17: "I will confirm your Son in My eternal kingdom, who is man and who, simultaneously, is God the Lord on high, who is honored and served equally with the Father." And the Holy Spirit, who speaks these words through Jeremiah and teaches us to believe and understand them, must be the third person present here. And this is one God, beside whom we honor and serve no other.

Moses and John agree

This should be sufficient about the text of 1 Chronicles 17, on which David's last words are based to show that Christ is God and that He is man, descended from David. Now we may again revert to David's last words and bring them to a close, in which he professes that Christ is his Son and in which he praises Him as his God, in accord with the verse (1 Chron. 17:17): "Thou hast regarded me as a man, who high above, or up above, or on high is God the Lord" . . . However, since this is such fine subject matter and we, unfortunately, are such a small number together with the apostles and prophets, who concern themselves with Christ, the crucified David and eternal God, we want to discourse further on David's last words before we conclude them and take leave of them. This we do for the strengthening of our faith and in defiance of all devils, Jews, Mohammedans, Papists, and all other enemies of this Son of David.

In the first place we want to give Moses, the fountainhead, the source, the father, and teacher of all prophets, a hearing. We want to test him to see whether we find him to be a Christian, whether he supports our position, since Christ Himself mentions him by name and says in John 5:46: "Moses wrote of Me." And if he wrote of Christ, he must, of course, have prophesied and proclaimed Him and enjoined all prophets who followed him to write and to preach of Christ. This they have done diligently, so that all Jews, young and old, know that a Messiah was to come. But Moses lies buried and is hidden from them, and no one knows where he is interred. Therefore we shall authorize and commission two faithful and reliable legates or ambassadors to look for him, find him, rouse him, and fetch him hither. These two are the evangelist John and the apostle Paul. I wager that these two will hit the mark and not miss. However, I do not want you to forget what I said earlier, namely, that I would like to discuss here the proposition: Wherever the Hebrew text readily yields to and harmonizes with the New Testament, this is and must be the only right interpretation of Scripture. All else, whatever Jews, Hebraists, and anybody else may babble against this to make it agree with their stippled, tormented, and coerced grammar, we must certainly consider sheer lies.

All right! John begins his Gospel with the words: "In the beginning was the Word, and the Word was with God, and the Word was God. He was in the beginning with God; all things were made through Him, and without Him was not anything made that was made." This is the speech of St. John, or, rather, of the Holy Spirit, who quickens all things. Now let us see whether John is able to find Moses with these words and to raise him from the dead. Moses has a very acute sense of hearing. He steps forth immediately and says: "Here I am; for just as you, John, speak about the Word, I, too, have spoken and still speak about the Word. You are taking the words out of my mouth. In the beginning of my book I, too, said of creation: 'And God said, "Let there be light"; and there was light. . . . And God said, "Let there be a firmament in the midst of the waters." . . . And God said, "Let the waters under the heavens be gathered together into one place, and let the dry land appear." . . . And God said, "Let the earth put forth vegetation, plants yielding seed." . . . And God said, "Let there be lights in the firmament of the heavens to separate the day from the night," ' etc." (cf. Gen. 1:3, 6, 9, 11, 14).

Here Moses is in accord with John, saying that there was a Word in the beginning of creation, through whom God said, that is, created and made, everything. Moses is not muttering or stammering here. These are not ambiguous and obscure words. The grammar is definite, too, on this point, that where there is a speaker, there is also a *logos*, a word, or speech. We care not if the Jews, heretics, and Mohammed dream up their own interpretation here in opposition to the Christian belief. We have Moses' text and grammar on our side. This states plainly and clearly that God spoke in the beginning before the advent of any creature and that there is a Word through whom God says everything. This is affirmed in John 1. The dear fathers, Hilary, Augustine, Cyril, and others dealt with this Gospel amply and forcefully, rendering any further discourse on our part superfluous. Their books are still extant.[19] For the present it suffices that we see and hear for ourselves how spontaneously and naturally and manifestly and exactly Moses agrees with John. Even blind reason cannot deny this but, in accord with definitive grammar, must concede that they speak one and the same language about the Word, through whom God created and made everything in the beginning.

Both of them, Moses and John, wish to indicate by which means, with which tool, or from what God made such a great work, the whole universe. There was no material at hand, no wood or stone; there was absolutely nothing available with which the world was created. It was solely the Word through whom it was made. The Word, however, was not made, but was with God from the beginning when He made all things,

19 See Hilary (ca. 315–367), *On the Trinity* 2.10–23; Augustine, *Homilies on the Gospel of John*; and Cyril of Alexandria, *Commentary on John*.

as Moses here says: "God said, 'Let there be'" this and that, etc. By the Word, he says, all things came into being. But there can be nothing with God outside of creation which is not God itself. It follows that the Word must be God Himself, as great and as mighty as God Himself, since all things were made by Him. And yet this cannot be the person who speaks the Word. The speaker and the Word must be two separate beings. And again, these cannot be two gods because there is only one true God. There is of necessity only one Creator of heaven and earth, not two or three creators, or gods. Thus Moses and John concur in their testimony that God and the Word are surely two distinct persons and that these two are, nonetheless, but one Creator and God, indivisible in the one divine essence.

David and Psalm 33

This is how David read and understood Moses when he wrote in Ps. 33:6: "By the Word of the Lord the heavens were made, and all their host by the Breath of His mouth." He says that the heavens and all that is in and on it are "made." My dear man, made out of what? Out of nothing. By what? By God's Word and the Breath of His mouth. Does not David's speech here coincide with that of Moses? Does he not wish to say with practically the same words that God said, "Let there be the heaven," and the heaven came into being? But if the heaven with all that is therein came into being and was made by God's Speech, or Word, then the earth with all that is therein indubitably also came into being and was made by the same Word. Now, the Word is not the heaven nor the earth, nor anything that is in them, nor anything that is made together with these by the Word. Therefore it must be God Himself, and, at the same time, a person apart from the Speaker, who makes all things through the Word, united in one indivisible essence of divine power, might, and effect. But if we have the Word, it is easy to discover the third person in David's speech: "All their host by the Breath of His mouth."

The author uses the word "made" only once, saying: "By the Word of the Lord the heavens were made, and all their host by the Breath of His mouth." He mentions three distinct persons, namely, the Lord, His Word, and His Breath; and yet he does not set up more than one Creator, without any differentiation. All things are made. By whom? By one Creator, who is Lord, Word, and Breath. The Lord does not do His own work separately, the Word does not do His own work separately, and the Breath does not do His own work separately. All three distinct persons are but one Creator of the work of each. And each one's work is that of all three persons as that of one Creator and Master. For as the Lord creates the heavens, the Word creates the same and no different heavens, and the

Breath creates the same and no different heavens. It is one essence that creates, and it is one creation that all three persons create. And again, just as the Lord creates the host of the heavens by His Spirit (as the text says: "And all their host by the Breath of His mouth"), thus the Breath creates the same and no other host of the heavens, and the Word creates the same and no other host of the heavens.

External works of the Trinity

Therefore a Christian must here take careful note not to mingle the persons into one person nor to divide and separate the one divine essence into three persons, as Athanasius sings in his Creed.[20] For if I ascribe to each person a distinct external work in creation and exclude the other two persons from this, then I have divided the one Godhead and have fashioned three gods or creators. And that is wrong. Again, if I do not ascribe to each person within the Godhead, or outside and beyond creation, a special distinction not appropriate to the other two, then I have mingled the persons into one person. And that is also wrong. Here the rule of St. Augustine is pertinent: "The works of the Trinity toward the outside are not divisible."[21] The works performed by God outside the Godhead must not be divided, that is, one must not separate the persons with regard to the works and ascribe to each its distinct external work; but one must distinguish the person within the Godhead and yet ascribe, externally, each work to all three without distinction.

Let me illustrate this with an example. The Father is my God and Creator and yours, who created you and me. This same work, your creation and mine, was also performed by the Son, who is also my God and Creator and yours, just as the Father is. Likewise, the Holy Spirit created the selfsame work, that is, you and me, and He is my God and Creator and yours as well as the Father and the Son. This notwithstanding, there are not three gods and creators, but one God and Creator of us both. With this creed I guard against the heresy of Arius and his ilk, to keep me from dividing the one divine essence into three gods or creators and to help me retain in the true Christian faith no more than the one God and Creator of all creatures.

---

20 Although attributed to Athanasius (ca. 296–373), the Athanasian Creed, also known as the *Quicunque vult*, is a Western creed written in Latin during the fifth or sixth century. The Creed rehearses the theological grammar used by the church to confess the Trinity and the person of Christ.

21 Luther writes this in Latin: *opera trinitatis ad extra indivisa sunt*. Cf. Augustine, *The Trinity* 1.7 (WSA 1/5:70).

Distinguishing marks of the persons

On the other hand, when I go beyond and outside of creation or the creature and move into the internal, incomprehensible essence of divine nature, I find that Holy Scripture teaches me—for reason counts for nought in this sphere—that the Father is a different and distinct nature from the Son in the one indivisible and eternal Godhead. The difference is that He is the Father and does not derive His Godhead from the Son or anyone else. The Son is a person distinct from the Father in the same, one paternal Godhead. The difference is that He is the Son and that He does not have the Godhead from Himself, nor from anyone else but the Father, since He was born of the Father from eternity. The Holy Spirit is a person distinct from the Father and the Son in the same, one Godhead. The difference is that He is the Holy Spirit, who eternally proceeds both from the Father and from the Son, and who does not have the Godhead from Himself nor from anyone else but from both the Father and the Son, and all of this from eternity to eternity. With this belief I guard against the heresy of Sabellius and his ilk,[22] of Jews, Mohammed, and all others who presume to be smarter than God Himself. Thus I refrain from jumbling the persons together into one person, but I retain, according to the true Christian belief, three distinct persons in the one divine and eternal essence, all three of which are, over against us and all creatures, one God, Creator and Worker of all things.

Perhaps all of this is too abstruse or subtle for us Germans and should, more reasonably, be confined to the universities. But since the devil whips his tail about in these last days and would fain stir up all sorts of heresy again; and since the world, even aside from this, hankers and longs to hear something novel and is weary of the salutary doctrine, as St. Paul prophesied (2 Tim. 4:3); and since the door has thereby been left open for the devil to bring in what he will: it is useful and necessary that at least a few, both laymen and scholars, especially pastors, preachers, and schoolteachers, also learn to reflect on such vital doctrines of our faith and to express them in German. But may he for whom this is too complicated stay with the children and confine himself to the catechism and pray against the devil and his heresy, against the Jews and against Mohammed, lest he succumb to temptation. But since we have entered upon this subject, we will cite more illustrations of this doctrine for those who are interested, and demonstrate that the one Godhead is not to be

22 Sabellius was a third-century figure who thought of the Son as a different mode of the Father's existence rather than as an eternally distinct person in His own right. Sabellius's views were embraced and enlarged upon by others. These diverse views were collectively rejected as Sabellianism in the early church.

divided nor the persons intermingled. This we do to strengthen and to profess our faith.

Baptism of Christ

When St. John baptized our Lord in the Jordan, heaven opened and the Holy Spirit descended physically in the form of a dove, and the Father's voice was heard to say: "This is My beloved Son; with whom I am well pleased" (cf. Luke 3:22; 2 Pet. 1:17). Here we find a dove, a creature which not only the Holy Spirit but also the Father and the Son had created. As I was saying: "The works of the Trinity to the outside are not divisible," whatever is creature has been created by God the Father, the Son, and the Holy Spirit as one God. Still, the dove is called only Holy Spirit, or, as Luke says, it was only the Holy Spirit, who descended in the form of a dove. And the Christian Creed would by no means tolerate that you say of the dove: That is God the Father, or That is God the Son. No, you must say: That is God the Holy Spirit, although God the Father, the Son, and the Holy Spirit are but one God. You may say very correctly of the dove: That is God, and there is no God beyond that one. And yet it would be incorrect for you to say: That is God the Father; that is God the Son. You must say: That is God the Holy Spirit.

In like manner, the voice that says "This is My beloved Son, etc.," is a creature created not only by the Father but also by the Son and the Holy Spirit. As I was saying: "The works of the Trinity, etc." Outside the Godhead all creatures are created equally by all three persons as by one God, and over against the creature all three persons are one God. And again, with regard to the three persons the creature is but one work and not three works. And yet this voice is called, and is, none but the Father's. As a Christian you cannot say of the voice: That is God the Holy Spirit or that is God the Son. No, you must say: That is God the Father, although God the Holy Spirit and God the Son and God the Father are but one God. You may say very correctly of this voice: That is God, and there is no God beyond that. But it would be incorrect to say: That is God the Son or God the Holy Spirit. No, you must say: That is God the Father.

Of Christ's humanity we say similarly: It is a real creature created by the Father, the Son, and the Holy Spirit. We would not permit the Creed to state that the Father alone or the Son alone or the Holy Spirit alone created this creature, or humanity; this is "an indivisible work of the Trinity," a work which all three persons created as one God and Creator of one and the same work. Thus the angel Gabriel says to the Virgin Mary in Luke 1:35: "The Holy Spirit will come upon you, and the power of the Most High will overshadow you." "Not only the Holy Spirit," says he, "will come upon you but also the Most High, that is, the Father will overshadow you with His power, that is, with His Son, or Word. And 'the Child to be born of you' will be called the Son of the Most High." Thus the entire Trinity is present here as one Creator and has created and made the one work, the humanity. And yet it was only the person of the Son that united with the human nature and became incarnate, not the Father nor the Holy Spirit.

Of this man you cannot say: That is God the Father or that is God the Holy Spirit; but you must say: That is God the Son, although God the Father, the Son, and the Holy Spirit are one God, and although you can say very correctly of the man: That is God, and there is no other god beside Him. And yet it would be incorrect to say: That is God the Father or God the Holy Spirit. No, you must say: That is God the Son, as St. Paul declares in Col. 2:9: "For in Him the whole fullness of Deity dwells bodily." And yet the Father and the Holy Spirit are not thereby deprived of their Godhead but are one God together with the Son and man Christ. Here you observe how the three persons are to be believed as distinct within the Godhead and are not to be jumbled together into one person and that, for all of that, the divine essence is not to be divided to make three gods. Viewed from without, from the point of view of the creature, there is but one Creator, so completely one that even the creature forms which the three persons individually take are the single work of all three persons of the one God.

. . . We must understand here that all three persons, as one God, created the one humanity, clothed the Son in this, and united it with His person, so that only the Son became man, and not the Father or the Holy Spirit. In the same way we should think also of the dove which the person of the Holy Spirit adopted and of the voice which the person of the Father adopted; also the fiery tongues on the Day of Pentecost, in which the person of the Holy Spirit was revealed; also the wind and whatever else is preached in Christendom or in Holy Scripture about the operation of the Holy Spirit.

Doctrine of appropriation

Here one might reasonably ask: Why, then, do we say, or, rather, why does Holy Scripture teach us to say: "I believe in God the Father, Creator of heaven and earth," and not to mention also the Son as Creator? Also, why do we say: "I believe in Jesus Christ, who was conceived by the Holy Spirit?" Also, why do we say that the Holy Spirit quickens us and that He spoke by the prophets? Here the peculiar and distinctive works are being assigned externally to each person by way of differentiation. This is perhaps too subtle, too, for simple Christians who want to adhere to their plain faith that God the Father, the Son, and the Holy Spirit are one God, etc. However, it is necessary to discourse on this subject in Christendom and to learn to understand it in order to withstand the devil and his heretics. In the first place, it is certain that God wants to be known by us, here on earth by faith, yonder by sight, that He is one God and yet three persons. And according to John 17:3, this is our everlasting life. To this end He gave us His Word and Holy Scripture, attested with great miracles and signs. We must learn from it. To attain that knowledge of God, it is surely necessary that He Himself instruct us, that He reveal Himself and appear to us. By ourselves we could not ascend into heaven and discover what God is or how His divine essence is constituted. Well, for this purpose He employs visible elements in His creation, as Scripture teaches us, so that we may comprehend this; for invisible creatures do not make an impression on our senses.

Accordingly, you must view the creature in two different ways; in the first place, as a creature, or work, per se, absolutely, created or made in this or that way by God. In that sense all creatures are God's work, that is, the single work of all three persons without distinction. This we have already heard. For in that respect they manifest no distinctive revelation of the three persons, since they are all the same single work of the three persons as of the one God. Secondly, you must view the creature not per se, absolutely, but relatively, according to each one's function, as God uses them toward us. Here God takes His creature, which all three persons as one God have created, and uses it as an image, or form, or figure in which He reveals Himself and in which He appears. Here distinctive images, forms, and revelations of the three separate persons come into being. Thus God employs the dove to become an image, or revelation, of the Holy Spirit. This is a distinctive image, which does not portray the Father or the Son but only the Holy Spirit. The Father, the Son, and the Holy Spirit want the dove to depict and reveal distinctively only the person of the Holy Spirit, to assure us that God's one essence is definitely three separate persons from eternity. That is why Luke 3:22 states: "The Holy Spirit descended upon Him in bodily form, as a dove."

In the same way, we say of the Son that He is revealed to us in His humanity, or, as St. Paul says in Phil. 2:7, "taking the form of a servant, being born in the likeness of men." And this form, or humanity, is not the image, or revelation, of the Father or of the Holy Spirit, although it is the same single creation of all three, Father, Son, and Holy Spirit, but it is the peculiar and special form and revelation of the Son alone. For thus it has pleased God, that is, Father, Son, and Holy Spirit, that the Son should be revealed to and recognized by humankind in this form, or figure, of humanity as a person apart from the Father and the Holy Spirit in one eternal essence of divine nature. In like manner we should profess that the Father was revealed to us in the voice. This form, or figure, is not a revelation of the Son or of the Holy Spirit but only of the Father, who in that distinctive form wants to manifest Himself to us as a person distinct from the Son and the Holy Spirit in one, indivisible divine essence.

You may also choose a crude example illustrating this from grammar. When the priest baptizes or absolves, he uses the words: "In the name of the Father and of the Son and of the Holy Spirit." All of these words in our mouth are the creation and work of God (as we and all that we have are), and not one word is distinctively only that of the Father or of the Son or of the Holy Spirit, but it is the work of all three persons, the single creation of the one God. However, in accordance with this interpretation, or revelation, you must not say that the words "of the Father" signify all three persons, but specifically only the Father, and the words "of the Son" specifically only the Son, and the words "of the Holy Spirit" specifically only the Holy Spirit—all in one Godhead. Thus these words, or their interpretation, reveal to us that there are three distinct persons in the one Godhead. For the priest does not say: "In the names," as of many, or as though each person had a special name and essence. No, he says: "In the name," as in the name of one being and yet three distinct persons.

Accordingly, you observe that the creature must be considered in a twofold manner, as a reality and as a symbol, that it is something per se, created by God, and that it is also used to signify or teach something else, something which it is not of itself. Smoke is a reality, a thing per se and at the same time a sign of something else, something which it is not but which it indicates and reveals, namely, fire. St. Augustine comments at length on this in *On Christian Doctrine*.[23] But here in this sublime subject it means more. For the humanity of Christ is not a mere sign or a mere figure, as the dove and the voice also are not empty figures or images. No, the humanity in which God's Son is distinctively revealed is complete, it is united with God in one person, which will sit eternally at the right hand of God, as was promised to David in 1 Chron. 17:12 above. The dove is a figure assumed for a time by the Holy Spirit to reveal Himself, but it was not united with Him forever. No, He again shed this form, as angels, too, adopt human form, appear in it, and later again abandon it. The same is true of the voice of God the Father. There is no promise involved that it should be so forever, but it is a temporary revelation.

23 Augustine, *Teaching Christianity* 2.1 (WSA 1/11:129).

Trinitarian language of faith

When we confess in the children's Creed: "I believe in God the Father Almighty, Creator of heaven and earth," we do not mean to imply that only the person of the Father is the almighty Creator and Father. No, the Son is likewise almighty, Creator, and Father. And the Holy Spirit is likewise almighty, Creator, and Father. And yet there are not three almighty creators and fathers but only one almighty Creator and Father of heaven and earth and of us all. Similarly, the Father is our Savior and Redeemer, the Son is our Savior and Redeemer, and the Holy Spirit is our Savior and Redeemer, and yet there are not three saviors and redeemers, but only one Savior and Redeemer. Likewise, the Father is our God, the Son is our God, and the Holy Spirit is our God, and yet there are not three gods, but only one God. Likewise, the Holy Spirit sanctifies Christendom, so does the Father, so does the Son, and still there are not three sanctifiers, but only one Sanctifier, etc. "The works of the Trinity to the outside are not divisible."

All of this has been said so that we may recognize and believe in three distinct persons in the one Godhead and not jumble the persons together nor divide the essence. The distinction of the Father, as we have heard, is this, that He derived His deity from no one, but gave it from eternity, through the eternal birth, to the Son. Therefore the Son is God and Creator, just like the Father. But the Son derived all of this from the Father, and not, in turn, the Father from the Son. The Father does not owe the fact that He is God and Creator to the Son, but the Son owes the fact that He is God and Creator to the Father. And the fact that Father and Son are God and Creator they do not owe to the Holy Spirit; but the Holy Spirit owes the fact that He is God and Creator to the Father and to the Son. Thus the words "God Almighty, Creator" are found as attributes of the Father and not of the Son and of the Holy Spirit to mark the distinction of the Father from the Son and the Holy Spirit in the Godhead, again, the distinction of the Son from the Father and the Holy Spirit, and the distinction of the Holy Spirit from the Father and the Son; namely, that the Father is the source, or the fountainhead (if we may use that term as the fathers do) of the Godhead, that the Son derives it from Him and that the Holy Spirit derives it from Him and the Son, and not vice versa.[24]

Beyond this internal distinction of the persons, there is also the external difference, in which the Son and the Holy Spirit are revealed. The Son is revealed in humanity, for the Son alone became man, He alone was conceived by the Holy Spirit, was born of the Virgin Mary, suffered and died for us, as our Creed informs us. However, it is also correct to say that

---

24 Cf. Augustine, *The Trinity* 4.29, 4.32 (WSA 1/5:174, 177); John of Damascus, *On the Orthodox Faith*, 1.8.

God died for us, for the Son is God, and there is no other God but only more persons in the same Godhead. Only the Holy Spirit was diversely revealed in the fiery tongues, in the gifts, in the variety of languages and miraculous signs, etc., although the humanity was created by all three persons, and the fiery tongues and the gifts of the Holy Spirit are the creation and work of all three persons, as we have heard sufficiently for the present. We have precious books on this subject by St. Augustine, Hilary, and Cyril at our disposal. And this article of faith remained pure in the papacy and among the scholastic theologians, and we have no quarrel with them on that score.

Some people worry and wonder whether they are addressing the person of the Father or the divine Essence when they pray the Lord's Prayer. It is not at all surprising that strange thoughts come to a person in this extremely mysterious and incomprehensible article of faith and that occasionally one of these goes away and a word miscarries. But wherever the basis of faith remains intact, such splinters, chips, or straws will not harm us. But the foundation of faith, as we have heard, is this, that you believe that there are three persons in the one Godhead and that each person is the same, one, perfect God, in other words, that the persons are not intermingled and the Essence is not divided but the distinction of persons and the unity of the Essence is preserved. For it is this mystery, of which, as we read in 1 Pet. 1:12, the angels cannot behold and wonder their fill in all eternity and about which they are in bliss through all eternity. And if they were able to satisfy their longing, their happiness would end too. We, too, shall behold this, and it will make us eternally blissful, as the Lord says in John 17:3: "And this is eternal life, that they know Thee the only true God, and Jesus Christ, whom Thou hast sent." In the meantime, faith must cling to the Word, for reason cannot do otherwise than assert that it is impossible and contradictory that there should be three persons, each one perfect God, and yet not more than one God; that only the Son is man; that he who has the Father and the Son will surely learn to know the Holy Spirit from the Father and the Son.

You have heard earlier that the Father is the God and Father of us all, that the Son is the God and Father of us all, that the Holy Spirit is the God and Father of us all, and that, for all of that, not more than one God is our Father. For the essence is undivided, therefore no matter which person you may mention, you have named the one true God in three persons, since each person is the same, one, perfect God. In this you cannot err or go wrong. For Jesus Christ is no other God or Father or Creator than the Father or the Holy Spirit, even though He is a different person. The same is true of the Father and of the Holy Spirit. Hence it would not only be incorrect but also impossible and futile for you to restrict the name "Father" to the person of God the Father and to the exclusion of the Son and the Holy Spirit; for that would be dividing the divine Essence and eliminating the Son and the Holy Spirit. That is out of the question. For according to such a manner of personal paternity, the Father has no more than one Son, and the Son has no more than one Father. He is not such a Father to you, and you are not such a Son to Him. No, this is the only-begotten Son of the Father from eternity, as Ps. 2:7 says: "The Lord said to Me, 'You are My Son, today I have begotten You.'" But you are a temporal son of all three persons, of one God, and may be 30, 40, or 50 years of age, depending upon the time of your birth and Baptism.

As the works of the Trinity to the outside are indivisible, so the worship of the Trinity from the outside is indivisible. Whatever God does to the creature is done by all three persons without distinction. For there is one divine Essence of all three persons, and what we or the creature do to each person of the Godhead we do to the one God and to all three persons without distinction. In relation to us He is one God; within Himself He is distinctive in three persons. Thus Christ Himself says in John 14:9–10: "Philip, he who has seen Me has seen the Father; how can you say, 'Show us the Father'? Do you not believe that I am in the Father and the Father in Me?" And in John 5:23 we read: "All may honor the Son, even as they honor the Father." And in John 10:30: "I and the Father are one." We mean to say: "One entity, one essence, one God, one Lord." At this point "the Jews took up stones again to stone Him" (John 10:31). In John 5:17–18 we read: "'My Father is working still, and I am working.' This was why the Jews sought all the more to kill Him, because He not only broke the Sabbath but also called God His Father, making Himself equal with God, etc."

I am going to discontinue this subject now. It had been my intention to write an essay, but I have fallen into preaching. Read the Gospel of St. John; it teaches this all in rich measure. We have established that Moses agrees with St. John in the assertion that the Word was in the beginning, that by Him all things were made; that this Word cannot be a creature or anything created and yet is something distinct from God, or a person different from God, whose this Word is. For since He was not made but all things were made by Him, He must be God, Creator of all things, for it is certain that outside of creation, which is made, there can be naught but God, who makes it. And yet the Word, the God and Creator by whom all things are made, is distinct from the Speaker, or from Him who speaks the Word. Thus Moses is now our witness; he has become a Christian and is teaching the same doctrine that we Christians teach, namely, that God had a Word in the beginning, by whom all things were made, just as John writes.

Moses and Paul agree

Now let us briefly lend an ear also to the other legate, St. Paul, how he salutes Moses and appeals to him. In Col. 1:15–17 he has this to say of our Lord Jesus Christ: "He is the image of the invisible God, the firstborn of all creation; for in Him all things were created, in heaven and on earth, visible and invisible, whether thrones or dominions or principalities or authorities—all things were created through Him and for Him. He is before all things, and in Him all things hold together." To be sure, these words cannot be spoken of Christ according to the human nature; for He was not man "before all things." At present it is only 1,543 years ago that He became man. This is indeed a mighty and powerful verse in proof that Christ is eternal God, Creator of heaven and earth, and that to the present day and forevermore everything exists and is preserved and is made by Him, also all that is exalted in heaven and on earth, angels and spirits, the visible and the invisible. On this point Paul is in perfect agreement with John, who says (1:3): "All things were made through Him, and without Him was not anything made that was made." If Moses hears and approves the words of John, he surely also gives ear to and agrees with these words of Paul and says: "Yes, my dear Paul, in Genesis 1 I recorded the same truth which you and John voiced, namely, that all things are created by the Word."

In 1 Cor. 10:4 Paul says furthermore: "They drank from the spiritual Rock which followed them, and the Rock was Christ." If Christ was contemporaneous with the children of Israel and accompanied them, if it was He from whom they drank spiritually and on whom they were baptized spiritually, that is, if the children of Israel believed in the future Christ as we do in the Christ who appeared, then Christ must be true and eternal God. For you cannot believe in angels—that is an honor to which God alone is entitled. Nor can the angels be our spiritual food; God Himself must be that. Likewise, in 1 Cor. 10:9 Paul writes: "We must not put Christ to the test, as some of them did and were destroyed by serpents." What do we make of that? Does not Moses write again and again that it was the Lord Jehovah, the one true God, whom the children of Israel put to the test? In Exod. 17:2 he says: "Why do you put the Lord to the proof?" And in Num. 14:22 the Lord declares: "They have put Me to the proof these ten times." If this is the Lord of whom Moses writes, how can it be Christ, of whom St. Paul writes? But they must both be correct; for the Holy Spirit does not contradict Himself.

It follows cogently and incontrovertibly that the God who led the children of Israel from Egypt and through the Red Sea, who guided them in the wilderness by means of the pillar of cloud and the pillar of fire, who nourished them with bread from heaven, who performed all the miracles recorded by Moses in his books, again, who brought them into the land of Canaan and there gave them kings and priests and everything, is the very same God, and none other than Jesus of Nazareth, the Son of the Virgin Mary, whom we Christians call our Lord and God, whom the Jews crucified, and whom they still blaspheme and curse today, as Isa. 8:21 declares: "They will be enraged and will curse their King and their God." Likewise, it is He who gave Moses the Ten Commandments on Mount Sinai, saying (Exod. 20:2–3): "I am the Lord your God, who brought you out of the land of Egypt . . . . You shall have no other gods before Me." Yes, Jesus of Nazareth, who died for us on the cross, is the God who says in the First Commandment: "I am the Lord your God." How the Jews and Mohammed would rant if they heard that! Nevertheless, it is true and will eternally remain true. And he who disbelieves this will tremble before this truth and burn forever.

Here is Moses, who states so lucidly that all things were created by the Speech, or the Word, of God. And in Ps. 33:6 David declares: "By the Word of the Lord the heavens were made." If the heavens are made by the Word, then every other creature is also made by Him; for he who makes one creature makes them all, and he who does not make them all is unable to make any. Thus Moses and David agree with John and Paul, and both join them in saying: "All things were made and created by the Word, or by Christ." Now, if all things were made by Him and if nothing was made without Him, as the text of all four declares—Moses, David, John, and Paul—then what they call "all things" must include and not exclude the exodus from Egypt and whatever else happened in the midst of the people of Israel, yes, all that everywhere has taken place since creation and still takes place and will take place. These are powerful and important words which declare that all is made by Him and, as Moses puts it, "God said, and there was." Even if Moses does not use the name "the Son" or "Christ" grammatically, he nonetheless names and professes the Speech, the Word, by whom all things are made. Thereby he indicates that in God there is one who speaks and another who is the Word, and yet there is but one Creator of all creatures. Something had to be reserved for the New Testament, too, so that in it the Father, the Son, and the Holy Spirit might clearly be named, whom the Old Testament calls the Speaker, the Word, and the Spirit of the Lord.

Father, Son, and Holy Spirit

Therefore it is of no avail to Jews, Turks, and heretics to feign great religious zeal and to boast against us Christians of their belief in the one God, the Creator of heaven and earth, and that they devoutly call Him Father. These are nothing but inane and empty words with which they take the name of God in vain and misuse it contrary to the Second Commandment. Thus Christ says to the Jews in John 8:54–55: "It is My Father who glorifies Me, of whom you say that He is your God. But you have not known Him." It is indeed extremely inconsistent to call God "Father" and not to know who He is. For if you were to ask such a very saintly Jew, Turk, or heretic whether he believes that this one God, Creator of heaven and earth (whose name they exalt so piously and whom they call Father—although all this falsely), really is a Father and has a Son in the Godhead outside of creation, he would be horrified in his great holiness and would regard this as frightful blasphemy. And if you would ask further whether the same, one God, Creator, Father (as they call Him with their lying mouths) is also a Son, who has a Father in the Godhead, he would stuff up his ears in his great zeal, gnash his teeth, and worry that the earth might swallow you and him. And if you continue to ask whether the same, one God, Creator, and Father (as they boastfully call Him) is also a Holy Spirit, who has the Father and the Son, from whom He derives His divine essence, this superholy man would run away from you as though you were the vilest devil just come from hell.

Here you can note that they do not know what God is. When they speak of God, Creator, and Father, they do not know what they are saying. For if God is not to be the God (as Holy Scripture teaches us) who is a natural Father, who has a natural Son, and both have a natural Holy Spirit, all in one divine essence, God is nothing; He is no God at all. Consequently they have no God, except that they sinfully and shamefully misuse the name of God and fabricate their own god and creator, who is to be their father and they his children. They rob God of His natural fatherhood, of His one natural Son, and of the natural Holy Spirit, that is, of the entire true Godhead. Instead, they impute to God their vain dream and their lies of God, Creator, and Father. Yes, they confer on their fabrication, that is, on the devil, this holy name of God. The devil is their god and father, the father of all lies. At the same time, they presume to be the dearest little children and the holiest saints.

It is a settled matter, and thus God Himself revealed Himself to us, that He is one God, Creator, and Father of heaven and earth; that this same, one God, Creator and Father of all the world, is a natural Father of one Son in the Godhead; that this same, one God, Creator and Father of all the world, is one natural Son of the Father in the Godhead; that the same, one God, Creator and Father of all the world, is a Holy Spirit, proceeding from the Father and the Son in the Godhead. For the three distinct persons are one God, Creator and Father of all the world. And each person is the same complete, one God, Creator and Father of all the world. And when you call upon Jesus Christ, saying: "My dear Lord God, my Creator and Father, Jesus Christ, one, eternal God!" you need have no concern that the Father and the Holy Spirit are resentful on that account, but you may know that you immediately call upon all three persons and the one God, no matter which person you may address. You cannot call upon one person without including the others, since there is one indivisible divine essence in all and in each person. On the other hand, you cannot deny any one person without denying all three and without denying God entirely, as we read in 1 John 2:23: "No one who denies the Son has the Father."

I say it is not wrong but laudable if you invoke Jesus Christ thus. The church sings similarly of the Holy Spirit: "Come, O Father of the wretched."[25] However, it is better to observe and not disregard the order of the persons, as the apostles do and as the church, emulating them, does when they mention the name of the Father in supplication or prayer, for example, in the Lord's Prayer, etc. For He is the fountainhead or the wellspring (so to say) of the Godhead in the Son and the Holy Spirit, and when the Father is mentioned, the Son cannot be divorced from Him but must simultaneously be named and meant. Likewise the Holy Spirit is named and meant together with the Father and the Son, because none of the persons can be a separate God apart from the others. Thus say St. Paul (2 Cor. 1:3) and St. Peter (1 Pet. 1:3): "Blessed be the God and Father of our Lord Jesus Christ, the Father of mercies." Christ Himself always gives precedence to the Father in the Gospel and ascribes everything to Him, and yet He says (John 5:23): "That all may honor the Son as they honor the Father," and (John 16:15): "All that the Father has is Mine." The only difference is this, that the Father is the first person, from whom the Son derives everything, and not vice versa. However, the fact that a sin may be committed distinctively against the Father or against the Son or against the Holy Spirit is related to the revelation of the persons and not to the division of the essence. We have dealt a little with this subject above, and elsewhere it has been treated more in detail.

25 These are the opening words of the second stanza of the hymn "Veni, Sancte Spiritus" of Stephen Langton, who died in 1228.

Moses and the incarnation

But what is to be our attitude over against St. John's further statement about the Word: "The Word became flesh"? That, I suppose, cannot be harmonized with the Word about which Moses writes: "God said, Let there be light!" or David says: "By the Word of the Lord the heavens were made." Moses, or (as we believe) the Word Himself, commands on Mount Sinai (Exod. 20:4; Deut. 5:8): "You shall not make yourself a graven image or likeness of anything that is in heaven above or that is in the earth beneath." John does not make an image but a creature and a man, saying (John 1:18): "The Word became flesh." Paul does the same when he declares (Rom. 1:3; Gal. 4:4) that He was David's Son, or Seed, born of a woman. Therefore Moses must be speaking of another Word, a Word by whom all things were made. Nothing can be created by man, who himself is a creature. Paul and John are contradicting themselves when they make Him a man and yet say that all was created by Him.

Let us see whether we can find a similar statement in Moses. In Gen. 3:15 he writes that God said to the serpent: "I will put enmity between you and the woman, and between your seed and her Seed; He shall bruise your head, and you shall bruise His heel." It is obvious that God is not speaking of an ordinary serpent here, which slithers through the grass or the water and devours young frogs, but of a serpent which at that time was a beautiful and very intelligent animal. It was not merely able to speak but also to discuss profound divine questions and commands, just as though it had learned it in heaven. This gift was imparted to no other creature except to angels and men. And by means of this gift, the serpent wrought such harm as to lure man into sin and eternal death with the glittering pretense of God's name. This was not a common and silly little snake, such as eat little frogs, but a snake that devours the entire world. It was the cursed devil who dwelt in the snake, who brought death into the world through sin. Of this murderer, teacher of sin, and world-devourer God is here speaking and saying that his head will be crushed, that is, that his power, death and sin, will be destroyed and life and righteousness be restored.

And that is to be effected by the Seed of the woman. As the devil worked man's fall through a woman who issued from man without the participation of a woman, thus the Seed which will issue from a woman without the participation of a man will bring about the devil's downfall. This Seed of the woman will have to be a man, or a son, for in Scripture the seed of man obviously means the offspring, the son of a man. The unusual feature in this passage is that this child, or man, is called "Seed of a woman." Otherwise the word "seed" regularly refers to the seed of a man, or a father. We read, for example, of Abraham's seed, of David's seed, etc. Throughout Moses and the prophets the word "seed" means the man's seed. Thus Moses here agrees with Luke and Matthew, stating that this woman is to be a virgin who will become a mother solely through her own seed and without the cooperation of a man. And since this is in accord with the New Testament, we Christians, following the previously acknowledged rule, concede no other interpretation either to the Jew or to the devil.

In brief, it is certain that this Seed of a woman is to be a man. But, in addition, He must also be God, lest Moses be accounted an idolatrous prophet of the devil; for he imputes to this Seed the power which is proper to no creature but to God alone, namely, to abolish death and the murderer, sin and God's wrath, and to restore righteousness and life. My dear friend, no angel individually or all angels collectively will be able to do that. This calls for a mightier and more exalted man than all angels and creatures. I repeat, Moses must be a damned and idolatrous prophet if he attributes to the seed of a woman works such as strangling and overcoming death and sin, raising from the dead, and justifying, when this seed of a woman is a mere creature and not the one God Himself, who alone can quicken, as John 1:4 says of the Word: "In Him was life."

Reason itself must, of course, admit that he who is competent to crush death underfoot is also able to restore life, that he who can destroy sin can restore righteousness; for the removal of death is nothing else than restitution of life, and the remission of sin is nothing else than restitution of righteousness, of which the serpent, that is, the devil in the serpent, basely defrauded Adam and Eve together with all their descendants and all the children of men. It was he who through his lies brought sin and death down upon them. The text in Gen. 2:17 reads clearly enough: "Of the tree . . . you shall not eat, for . . . you shall die." Against this the liar and murderer replied: "You may indeed eat of it without suffering death. In fact, you will become like God and know everything." As I said before, all of this speaks about the sin and death which the serpent caused and ushered into the world. Therefore the crushing of the serpent can mean nothing else than the demolition of his work and power, as St. Paul says in 2 Tim. 1:10: "Christ abolished death and brought life and immortality to light." We pay the commentaries no heed which Jews, Mohammed, and others scribble and scrawl. It suffices us that Moses is in agreement here with the New Testament.

This interpretation, that the Seed of a woman must be God, who should crush the devil's head, was held also by Adam and Eve. For according to Gen. 4:1, when Eve had given birth to Cain, she perhaps supposed that because he was the first man born on earth he would be the foremost, and she assumed that he was to be the Seed of the woman and that she was to be that woman, or mother. This prompted her to exclaim: "I have the man, the Lord!" as though she were to say: "This is undoubtedly the man, the Lord, the Seed of woman, of whom God spoke, etc." She calls the child man and Lord, or God; for here we find the great and proper name of God, Jehovah, which indicates nothing else than God alone in His nature or essence. And "man," when used alone and without the accompanying word for woman, does not simply designate a male such as all men are, but an ideal and outstanding man, as we Germans, too, say: *Das ist ein Mann! Das will ein Mann werden!* ("He is every inch a man!") Similarly, Eve means to say here: "I have borne a son, who will develop into a real man, yes, he is *the* man, God Himself, who will do it, crush the serpent, as God assured us." How is this possible? How could the idea come to her which induced her to say of this child: "I have the man, the Lord," if she had not understood God's statement to mean that the woman's Seed would have to be God, who would carry out what God had told them?

Without a doubt Eve was not the only one to interpret these words thus. Very likely Adam discussed this with her long before this, and they cherished this verse and drew comfort from it against sin and death, which were to be abolished by this Seed and replaced by the forfeited innocence and life. In the absence of that comfort they would have despaired. And it is not God's will or way that His eternal Word, such as this is, should be spoken in vain and understood by no one. In Isa. 55:11 He says: "My Word shall not return to Me empty, but it shall accomplish . . . that for which I sent it." Now, there were only two people here who could understand it. Therefore they must have understood it profitably, blissfully, and correctly, entirely as we Christians do and before us all prophets did.

But our poor, unhappy Mother Eve was mistaken in her assumption that she was that woman simply because there was no other woman on earth besides her. In her great desire and longing, she hoped that her son was to be the Seed, the man Jehovah. She was too impatient and hasty; but no one can reprove her for her desire to be rid of sin and death, that is, of the devil, so soon. However, God had not said to her: "Your seed is to do it." Nor had He said to Adam: "Your wife's seed is to be the one." No, He reads their proper text to both of them, one that all children of men will still feel to the end of time. But to the serpent God turned and said: "As for you, on the other hand, I will provide Him who shall crush your head. He will be the Seed of a woman. I will fell you haughty, powerful, evil spirit by the Son of Man, so that all men in turn will run you down and tread you underfoot as you have now done to Adam and Eve." This our dear Lord Jesus Christ did, does, and ever will do, who together with God the Father is one Jehovah. Amen.

Someone may interpose here: How do you account for it that no Christian or Jew has seen such a meaning in this passage? All other translators do it differently. The Latin reads: "I have gotten a man through God." Other Hebraists say: "I have gotten the man from the Lord." That does not interest me now. Above, I repeatedly reserved the right to decline having a teacher here and to present my own views in the translation. If it pleases no one else, it is sufficient that it pleases me.[26] . . .

Seed of Abraham

The words of Moses in Gen. 22:18, containing God's promise to Abraham and confirmed with an oath, are also pertinent here: "By your Seed shall all Gentiles of the earth be blessed." . . . Thus the divine blessing, promised to Abraham's seed, is also an active, real, and live blessing, which provides what the blessing promises. It is promised and issued against the curse under which the serpent brought us through Adam's disobedience and sin. Here the promise of the Seed of the woman is renewed, and henceforth it is to be known as Abraham's Seed. Later it was called David's Seed, and finally the Virgin's Seed. Therefore the blessing in the Seed of Abraham here means the same as earlier (Gen. 3:15): The Seed of the woman shall crush the serpent's head, that is, He shall remove sin and death and restore innocence and life. For sin and death are the curse under which we would have to languish eternally if we were not again blessed by this Seed, that is, if we were not again made alive and righteous, holy and blessed. Yes, thus we are blessed in this Seed of Abraham. Indeed, on account of this blessing we glory in being Gentiles, we accept it by faith, we are very haughty, proud, and arrogant over against the devil and his power, over against death and sin and whatever else there may be. We sing and say: In the Seed of Abraham, of David, of the woman Mary we have remission of sin, ablution of sin, redemption from sin, liberation from death and every other evil; for it is He "whom God made our Wisdom, our Righteousness and Sanctification and Redemption" (1 Cor. 1:30), our Blessing, our Consolation, our Life, and our Joy in eternity. May God be praised for this forever. Amen.

And if this Seed of Abraham produces and works such a powerful and effective blessing among the Gentiles, He cannot be a mere man,

26 Luther had uttered a similar sentiment in 1517 about the first publication of his own work, *The Seven Penitential Psalms*. See Luther's letter to John Lang, March 1, 1517, LW 48:39–40.

able to wish a person a good morning and no more—something all men are able to do—but He must be the one true and natural God, who is able to administer this blessing mightily. For to abolish sin and death, to bestow righteousness and life, is not the work of a human being or of an angel, but to do this is the exclusive domain of the one eternal and divine Majesty, the Creator of heaven and earth. And again, if He is to be Abraham's Seed, that is, his child and son, He cannot only be God, but He must also be a true and natural man, proceeding from the flesh and blood of Abraham; that is, He must be both God and man in one person. Furthermore, since He is not the person who says to Abraham of this Seed and person: "In your Seed shall all the Gentiles be blessed," He must be a different and distinguishable person, for He who says to Abraham: "In your Seed, etc.", is not Abraham's Seed, but He is referring to another who is to be Abraham's Seed. We naturally conclude that these are two different persons. And yet there remains but the one undivided God in His one divine essence. The Third Person is also at hand. It is He who expresses these words about the two persons orally through Moses or the angel. As we said before, the utterance of the oral word is the special function and the distinctive revelation of the Holy Spirit; just as Christ's humanity is His particular and special revelation.

Christology

... Thus all of Scripture, as already said, is pure Christ, God's and Mary's Son. Everything is focused on this Son, so that we might know Him distinctively and in that way see the Father and the Holy Spirit eternally as one God. To him who has the Son, Scripture is an open book; and the stronger his faith in Christ becomes, the more brightly will the light of Scripture shine for him.

Now, if you believe and understand that Christ is very God and very man, as Scripture teaches us, then see to it that you do not separate the person of Christ nor intermingle the two natures or the divine and the human essence into one essence, but that you differentiate between the natures and preserve the one person. For many wiseacres have come to grief on this point, that they have insisted either on uniting Deity and humanity into one nature or on dividing them into two persons, as Nestorius and Eutyches and their like did.[27] The Jews and Turks presume to be extraordinarily smart, supersmart, and look down upon

27 On Nestorius, see above, p. 397 n. 15. Eutyches (ca. 378–ca. 454), a monk from Constantinople, taught that Christ had one nature and one person after the union of the divine and human natures in Mary's womb. Nestorius's Christology was condemned by the Council of Ephesus in 431 and Eutyches's Christology was condemned by the Council of Chalcedon in 451.

us Christians as great dolts. If Christ is God, they say, how can He die like a man, for God is immortal? If He is man, how can He be God's Son, for God has no wife? . . .

All right, let these miserable fools go their way and think themselves smart until they are surfeited with it. But you cling firmly to the Christian faith, taught us by Scripture, that Jesus Christ is true God and God's Son, and also true man, David's and Mary's Son, and yet not two Sons, two men, two persons, but one Son, one person, of and in two distinct natures, Deity and humanity. For just as you, as we heard earlier in the doctrine of the Godhead, must guard against jumbling the three persons into one person or separating the essence, or nature, into three Gods, but must retain the three distinct persons in one divine Essence; so you must here beware, lest you separate, or divide, the one person into two persons or mingle the two natures into one nature, but you must preserve the two distinct natures in one person. And just as the two natures unite in one person, thus also the names of the two natures unite in the name of the one person. In Latin this is known as "communication of idioms or properties." By way of illustration: He who is called man and who was born of the Virgin Mary and was crucified by the Jews must also be called the Son of God. And we must say that God was born of Mary and was crucified by the Jews; for God and man are one person. There are not two Sons, the one of God, the other of Mary, but He is just one Son, God's and Mary's.

If you were to concur with Nestorius and say that God, or Jesus, God's Son, was not born of Mary nor crucified by the Jews but that this was experienced only by the man, Mary's Son, then you would create two persons, you would split the one person into two, so that there would be one person who is born and crucified and another person who is not born and crucified. Each nature would thus become a person in itself, and there would be two distinct Sons. This is tantamount to saying that God did not become man but that He remains God, a person in Himself, apart from the man, and the man a person in himself, a person apart from God. That will not do; it will not hold its ground against Scripture, for it says in John 1:14: "And the Word became flesh," and in Luke 1:35: "The child to be born will be called holy, the Son of God." And the catechism states: "I believe in Jesus Christ, God's Son, conceived by the Holy Spirit, born of the Virgin Mary," etc. It does not say that God's Son is a different person but the same one who was born of Mary and became her Son.

On the other hand, if you were to say with Eutyches that the man Jesus, Mary's Son, is not Creator of heaven and earth, or that He is not God's Son, who is to be worshiped, you would again divide the person and split it into two persons. Just recently a silly bloke opened his big mouth and exclaimed that we Christians lived so precariously, worshiping a creature as God. That stupid fool does not read Scripture nor any books but dreams of such sublime matters in his own ignorant head. He is a conceited smart aleck. Nestorius separates the persons, tearing the humanity away from the Deity and making each nature an independent person. In consequence, only the man Christ was crucified. Eutyches, however, tears the humanity away from the Deity, also making each nature an individual person. The result is that God must be worshiped divorced from and apart from the human nature. But Scripture and the Creed speak thus: When we worship the man born of Mary, we do not worship a detached person, a person apart from and outside of God, a separate, independent person. No, we worship the one true God, who is one God with the Father and the Holy Spirit, and who is one person with His humanity. . . .

Thanks and praise be to God in all eternity that we Christians know that Messiah is God's one eternal Son, whom He sent into the world to take our sins upon Himself, to die for us, and to vanquish death for us. Thus Isa. 53:6, 10 says very clearly: "All we like sheep have gone astray . . . and the Lord has laid on Him the iniquity of us all. . . . He made Himself an offering for sin, etc." Therefore we exult and rejoice that God's Son, the one true God together with the Father and the Holy Spirit, became man, a servant, a sinner, a worm for us; that God died, and bore our sins on the cross in His own body; that God redeemed us through His own blood. For God and man are one person. Whatever the man does, suffers, and speaks, that God does, suffers, and speaks; and, conversely, what God does and speaks, that the man does and speaks. He is both God's and Mary's Son in one undivided person and in two distinct natures. . . .

Conclusion

Let this be my translation and exposition of David's last words according to my own views. May God grant that our theologians boldly apply themselves to the study of Hebrew and retrieve the Bible for us from those rascally thieves. And may they improve on my work. They must not become captive to the rabbis and their tortured grammar and false interpretation. Then we will again find and recognize our dear Lord and Savior clearly and distinctly in Scripture. To Him, together with the Father and the Holy Spirit, be glory and honor in eternity. Amen.

Luther on Allegory

Martin Luther often criticizes the allegories of the church fathers in his lectures and sermons. He does not, however, reject the allegorical reading of Scripture. He dismisses allegory when it undermines or ignores the historical character of Scripture. For Luther, the historical sense alone supplies true and sound doctrine. Allegories adorn or embellish the historical account.

Luther further distinguishes between good and bad allegories based on their subject matter. He argues that early church commentators such as Origen and Jerome offer merely moral and philosophical allegories. Although these may advance good thoughts, allegories should clarify doctrine and comfort consciences. These theological allegories, as Luther calls them, always proceed from the rule of faith. As long as the insight of the interpreter conforms to the rule of faith and seeks to enhance our understanding of that faith, it may be accepted, even if the allegory itself is unconvincing.

The excerpts below provide a small window into Luther's understanding and use of allegory.

Lectures on Deuteronomy (1525)[1]

I have added brief allegories, almost for every chapter. This is not because I attach great importance to them, but I want to forestall the silly attempts at allegorical interpretation that some make. We see that Jerome, Origen, and other ancient writers did not employ a sufficiently felicitous and helpful method of devising allegories, since they direct everything to manners and works, whereas everything should rather be applied to the Word and to faith.[2] Indeed, they exercised themselves in pure allegories, namely, in the talk of crazy persons. Lest readers be deceived by a false idea in allegories, I reckoned it worth the effort to show them that it is a proper allegory when, so far as possible, they discover in every allegory

1 The following excerpt is adapted from *Lectures on Deuteronomy*, in volume 9 of *Luther's Works: American Edition*, ed. Jaroslav Pelikan and Daniel E. Poellot, trans. Richard R. Caemmerer (St. Louis: Concordia, 1960). Minor alterations have been made to the text for consistency in style, abbreviations, and capitalization. The annotations and subheadings are the work of the editor of this book.

2 On Jerome, see above, p. 86 n. 3. On Origen, see above, p. 313 n. 11.

the ministry of the Word or the progress of the Gospel and of faith. For this is the purpose of whatever figures or meanings there are in the Law and the people of Moses. . . .

This admonition I have often given elsewhere I repeat here and shall give again: that the Christian reader should make it his first task to seek out the literal sense, as they call it. For it alone is the whole substance of faith and Christian theology; it alone holds its ground in trouble and trial, conquers the gates of hell (Matt. 16:18) together with sin and death, and triumphs for the praise and glory of God. Allegory, however, is too often uncertain, and is unreliable and by no means safe for supporting faith. Too frequently it depends on human guesswork and opinion, and if one leans on it, one will lean on a staff of Egyptian reed (Ezek. 29:6). Therefore we should beware of Jerome, Origen, and similar fathers or read them with independent judgment. Yes, we should beware of that whole Alexandrian school, which the Jew Philo extols, according to the testimony of Eusebius and Jerome, for having once excelled in the pursuit of such allegorical interpretation.[3] For later writers unhappily imitated their example; which was adopted with excessive praise. They constructed and taught arbitrarily from Scripture according to their liking, until some shaped the words of God into the most absurd monstrosities; and, as Jerome also complains about his own time, they drag Scripture into contradiction with itself by citing proofs that do not apply, a crime of which he himself was also guilty.

Such are those who nowadays expound almost the whole Bible, wherever they find a word in the feminine gender, concerning the Blessed Virgin. Likewise those who build monasteries from the dwelling place of Martha and make our schoolmasters out of the mighty in Israel, and numberless similar wonders. . . . Hence the rule of Paul should be observed here, that allegories should be kept in second place and be applied for the strengthening, adorning, and enriching of the doctrine of faith, or, as he says in 1 Cor. 3:11ff., they should not be the foundation but be built on the foundation, not as hay, wood, and stubble but as silver, gold, and gems. This is done when, according to the injunction of Rom. 12:6, prophecy is according to the analogy of faith, namely, that you first take up a definite statement set down somewhere in the Scriptures, explain it according to the literal sense, and then at the end connect to this an allegorical meaning which says the same thing. Not as though the

3 Philo of Alexandria (ca. 20 BC–ca. AD 50) was a Jewish writer thoroughly conversant in the Platonism of his day. He interpreted the Books of Moses allegorically and philosophically and exercised a considerable influence on later Christian interpreters.

allegorical meaning proved or supported the statement of doctrine; but it is proved or supported by the statement, just as a house does not hold up the foundation but is held up by the foundation.

In order that we may safely allegorize here, Paul, in 2 Cor. 8:7ff., leads the way by treating the entire story of Moses in a most ample allegory, comparing the glory of his face with the glory of the face of Christ. According to this example, you can rightly weave an allegory, making of Moses the ministry of the Law, sin, and death, likewise of Christ the ministry of the Gospel, grace, and life, just as he beautifully sets this forth to the Romans in the fourth and eighth chapters and elsewhere. Furthermore, Paul makes the point that the one face of Moses was seen in two ways, veiled and unveiled. The veiled one he relates to those who by the ministry of the Law are moved only to works and hypocrisy; they never understand the power of the Law, but their heart remains blinded when they read the Old Testament, so that they neither recognize nor yearn for the glory of Christ. The unveiled he relates to those who do not work through the Law but recognize sin and are slain, so that they yearn for grace.

Deuteronomy 15: The sabbatical year

The year of the release of debt is the whole time of grace, because the kingdom of Christ is nothing but the constant forgiveness of debts, so that they are forgiven. But that a debt is not forgiven to a stranger denotes that outside the church of God there is no remission of sins. For forgiveness cannot be granted to those who do not want it, who justify themselves and despise the church. Therefore repayment is to be demanded from them until they pay; that is, one must not yield to them but must always demand in order that they may think and act differently, until they repent. But to the repenting brother everything is to be forgiven. For where faith remains, there are no sins that are not forgivable and not to be remitted; but where unbelief remains, there are no sins that are not to be condemned and that should go unpunished. To lend on interest to no one, and to be lent to on interest by all, means to live so righteously that a man owes no one, but all owe him; for he harms no one, but is harmed by all. That there should be no poor, and if there are, that they should be helped, is to bear with those who are weak in faith and morals, to teach and exhort, and to pray for them without deceit, from perfect singleness of heart; and such there will always be among us (v. 11). To send away a Hebrew slave brother with something for the journey is not only to forgive his guilt but also to help with an additional gift of love.

Although this slave, by actual allegory, is the people of the Law and serves a hard bondage, yet when the year of release comes, the freeman is not only set free from the Law by the Gospel but is honored through the Word of the Gospel, by which he lives. For he served in a double bondage, inasmuch as he did the works of the Law and thereby earned nothing except that his master, the Law, flourished more. For the more we labor under the Law, the more it demands, the more powerful it becomes, and the less it is fulfilled, while hatred of the Law steadily increases. Yet in the meantime he also neglects his own interests; that is, he does not achieve a trusting conscience but loses what he could have gained outside the Law through the Gospel. The fact that his ear is pierced with an awl and he remains a slave forever means that the man now free in spirit nevertheless subjects his flesh the more strongly to the Law and by means of the iron and rigid Law forces it to obedience, as Paul says (1 Cor. 9:27): "I pommel my body and subdue it." Thus he remains a slave and a freeman at the same time.

Not to plow with a firstborn ox and not to shear the firstborn sheep signifies that the righteousness of faith is not to be abused for our own convenience or glory but in an upright manner to bring offerings to God to His glory and honor. For it is not of our doing or under our power to control it; but it is God's alone, who makes and gives it. Thus Paul does not want to rule over the faith of the Corinthians (2 Cor. 1:24). This allegory, therefore, pertains especially to ministers of the Word; they should not subject the people by faith to their laws and to the works ordained by them but should offer them up subject to God alone, to be ruled by faith. Just so Paul boasts in Rom. 15:16 that he so hallows the Gospel that the offering of the Gentiles becomes acceptable; that is, through the Gospel he offers up the Gentiles to God that they may be subject not to him, Paul, but to God. And what do the ministers of the Word do when they subject us to their works except that they shear us and seek their own advantage and glory, namely, our wool and produce?

That it should not have a blemish denotes that one's conscience should be sound by faith and not want to be justified and please God by works and by faith simultaneously. Therefore He vigorously attacks this fault also in Mal. 1:7ff., because His faith and doctrine are no joking matter.

Lectures on Isaiah (1527–28)[4]

The Call of Isaiah (Isaiah 6:1–8 ESV)

In the year that King Uzziah died I saw the Lord sitting upon a throne, high and lifted up; and the train of His robe filled the temple. Above Him

4 The following is adapted from *Lectures on Isaiah: Chapters 1–39*, in volume 16 of *Luther's Works: American Edition*, ed. Jaroslav Pelikan and Hilton C. Oswald,

stood the seraphim. Each had six wings: with two he covered his face, and with two he covered his feet, and with two he flew. And one called to another and said: "Holy, holy, holy is the LORD of hosts; the whole earth is full of His glory!" And the foundations of the thresholds shook at the voice of him who called, and the house was filled with smoke. And I said: "Woe is me! For I am lost; for I am a man of unclean lips, and I dwell in the midst of a people of unclean lips; for my eyes have seen the King, the LORD of hosts!" Then one of the seraphim flew to me, having in his hand a burning coal that he had taken with tongs from the altar. And he touched my mouth and said: "Behold, this has touched your lips; your guilt is taken away, and your sin atoned for." And I heard the voice of the Lord saying, "Whom shall I send, and who will go for Us?" Then I said, "Here I am! Send me."

Allegory

The Lord sitting in glory is Christ at the right hand of the Father. The temple is His church or heaven. The fact that He appears in visible form indicates that He is man, for everywhere the appearance of God denotes the humanity of Christ. Now He rules in the church through His humanity, but finally as the glorious God. The seraphim are the apostles and preachers of the Word. Winged angels everywhere signify the ministry of the Word. The two wings are the two Testaments, or the testimonies of the Law and the Prophets. The flying denotes the course of the ministry. "The Lord gives the command; great is the host of those who bore the tidings" (Ps. 68:11). There are many indeed, but all of them with one accord preach the same Christ. Veiling the face and feet means that the life of the godly is hidden in Christ. The feet signify conduct. Faith is not seen and its conduct is not grasped by the ungodly; in fact, it may seem strange and stupid to them. John 3:8 says: "You hear the sound of it, but you do not know whence it comes or whither it goes." Christians certainly live without glory in the world.

The seraphim stood ready to serve the Lord. Their cry is a declaration of preaching. "Holy, holy, holy." "No one has ascended into heaven but He who descended from heaven, etc." (John 3:13). And chapter 16: "He will convince the world of sin and of righteousness and of judgment" (John 16:8). Those who boast of their own holiness do not cry, "Holy is the Lord God," but as desecrators of God's name they make their boast in man. The "Sanctus" in the Mass is a song for the boys. But the preacher is the public singer of it. As long as we live, there is never enough singing.

---

trans. Herbert J. Bouman (St. Louis: Concordia, 1969). Minor alterations have been made to the text for consistency in style, abbreviations, and capitalization. The annotations and subheadings are the work of the editor of this book.

When Peter sang this song in Acts 2:37, "they were cut to the heart and said to Peter and the rest of the apostles, 'Brethren, what shall we do?' "

There will never be a lack of fruit and faith for the true preaching of Christ and for His purified holiness. Just as here, too, the lintels of the temple, that is, the house itself, were shaken by their voice, so also those who are in the church are moved by the Gospel and do not belong to the number of the blinded. Paul says the Gospel "is bearing fruit and growing" "in the whole world" (Col. 1:6). It makes an impression because it is high and exalted. The conscience is terrified when it hears that everything is condemned and Christ alone is holy, and He alone enlightens every man coming into this world (John 1:9).

The house was filled with smoke. In other places, such as Exod. 40:34 and 1 Kings 8:10, Scripture says that clouds filled the house and calls the cloud the glory of the Lord. And it denotes a "smoking" faith, one that knows that all our own things are defiled. Here Christ dwells, a light rising and justifying after the old man has been put to death. Confession then follows this hovering smoke, and the confession is: "Holy, holy, holy is the Lord of hosts." Then the severe judgment of God is felt, which forcibly elicits the confession. This is the first part of penitence, namely contrition, which shakes the thresholds and raises the smoke, namely, a feeling of the divine Word condemning the entire human righteousness. Then comes the seraph, that is, the preacher of the Gospel, which is the fiery coal, and promises the forgiveness of sins for Christ's sake and lifts one up to righteousness. Therefore "through the Law comes knowledge of sin" (Rom. 3:20), through the Gospel comes the knowledge and reception of grace and righteousness. The glowing coal is the Word kindled by the Holy Spirit in love, whereby those who have been put to death are revived by the cry of the seraphim. To touch the mouth is to strike the heart with the Gospel, which is sweet to the bitter heart. Then the heart is a fit vessel for honor, because it will go for the Lord, that is, it will be His instrument for teaching others, hearing and breaking through, even though with danger, the last comfort. A remnant will be saved, even though not all hear the Word and many spit it out.

Isaiah 13: History and allegory

Let us forewarn here concerning allegory that it may be handled wisely in the Spirit. For playing games with the Sacred Scriptures has the most injurious consequences if the text and its grammar are neglected. From history we must learn well and much, but little from allegory. You use allegory as an embellishment by which the discourse is illustrated but not established. Let history remain honest. It teaches, which allegory does not do. But this is what it means to teach: to instruct the conscience about what and how it should know, to nourish faith and the fear of God. In history you have the fulfillment of either promises or threats. Allegory does not pertain to doctrine, but to doctrine already established it can be added as color. The painter's color does not build the house. The human body does not consist of a garland or a beautiful garment. Even so faith is not established by means of allegories.

Here you have the threats against Babylon that it would be destroyed, although this seemed impossible to the whole world. You also have the promise that Israel would be liberated, which likewise seemed impossible. Console yourself with this in every trouble. Do not lose hope, consider that God is truthful and that He can accomplish what He has promised, even though there were a hundred Babylons to be destroyed. Israel was held in physical captivity, you in a spiritual one. If you have faith, God will deliver you in the same way and will not forsake you. In this way the histories must be treated, and allegories will be profitable. Then make the application to the pope and the bishops. Formerly there was no hope whatever that the realm of the pope would be laid waste. Rome is the true Babylon, and these things are said of Rome at least in a general way, if not in specific detail. For in general all the ungodly will perish. The defenders of the pope are struck with fear; they do not know how to interpret Scripture. They howl and hiss for the pope; they have become hairy satyrs, ostriches, owls, dragons, etc. They have divested themselves of all humanity and godliness.

Furthermore, another allegory can be derived from this passage and from all wars against human and carnal righteousness, which though strong as long as the body is healthy, are nevertheless put in jeopardy in the death struggle. Babylon is carnal righteousness and a conscience priding itself on its reliance on works. The Persians and Medes are the Law of God that touches the heart. All of these, namely, those showy and lofty works, the Law flattens out; it judges them unclean and condemns them. Then follow fear, torments, griefs. The sun is darkened, etc. There is no help. Would that many would successfully get away, because those who are captured are put to death. Here neither gold nor wisdom nor power is of any avail. The Law does not leave any part of the hypocritical righteousness but removes it all like Sodom. This becomes an allegory through the Law and the Gospel.

Lectures on Genesis (1535–45)[5]

Genesis 1–3: Creation

According to our ability, we have treated all these facts in their historical meaning, which is their real and true one. In the interpretation of Holy Scripture the main task must be to derive from it some sure and plain meaning, especially because there is such a variety of interpreters—Latin, Greek, and Hebrew too. Almost all of these not only do not concern themselves with the story but bury it and confuse it with their nonsensical allegories.

The ridiculous procedure which Origen and Jerome follow in these chapters is well-known. Everywhere they depart from the historical account, which they call "the letter that kills" and "the flesh"; and they bestow lofty praise on the "spiritual meaning," of which they have no actual knowledge. In fact, Jerome followed Origen as his teacher. The same thing happens in our time; those who are influential, either through their native ability or through their eloquence, strive with all their power to persuade their hearers that the historical accounts are dead matter and useless for building the churches. Thus it came about that with common zeal we rashly strove for allegories. When I was a young man, my own attempts at allegory met with fair success. It was even permissible to come up with foolish ideas, since these great teachers of the churches, such as Jerome and Origen, had at times given wide range to their imagination. And so anyone who was somewhat more skilled in contriving allegories was also regarded as a rather learned theologian. Augustine, too, was led astray by this conviction; and, especially in the instance of the Psalms, he disregards the historical sense and has recourse to allegories. They were all convinced that, especially in the historical accounts of the Old Testament, the allegories represented the spiritual meaning; but the historical account itself, or the literal sense, represented the carnal meaning.

But, I ask you, is this not a desecration of the sacred writings? Origen makes heaven out of Paradise and angels out of the trees. If this is correct, what will be left of the doctrine of creation? Particularly for beginning students of the Sacred Scriptures it is, therefore, necessary that when they approach the reading of the ancient teachers, they read them with discretion, or rather with the definite intention to disapprove of those

5 The following is adapted from *Lectures on Genesis: Chapters 1–5* and *Lectures on Genesis: Chapters 6–14*, volumes 1–2 of *Luther's Works: American Edition*, ed. Jaroslav Pelikan and Daniel E. Poellot, trans. George V. Schick (St. Louis: Concordia, 1958, 1960). Minor alterations have been made to the text for consistency in style, abbreviations, and capitalization. The annotations and subheadings are the work of the editor of this book.

statements for which there is less support. Otherwise they will be led astray by the authority of the name of the fathers and teachers of the church, just as I was led astray and as all the schools of the theologians were. Ever since I began to adhere to the historical meaning, I myself have always had a strong dislike for allegories and did not make use of them unless the text itself indicated them or the interpretations could be drawn from the New Testament.

But it was very difficult for me to break away from my habitual zeal for allegory; and yet I was aware that allegories were empty speculations and the froth, as it were, of the Holy Scriptures. It is the historical sense alone which supplies the true and sound doctrine. After this has been treated and correctly understood, then one may also employ allegories as an adornment and flowers to embellish or illuminate the account. The bare allegories, which stand in no relation to the account and do not illuminate it, should simply be disapproved as empty dreams. This is the kind which Origen and those who followed him employ. Where can it be proved from Scripture that Paradise denotes heaven and that the trees of Paradise refer to the angels? These ideas have been thought up as something most absurd and altogether useless.

Therefore let those who want to make use of allegories base them on the historical account itself. The historical account is like logic in that it teaches what is certainly true; the allegory, on the other hand, is like rhetoric in that it ought to illustrate the historical account but has no value at all for giving proof. In these circumstances an allegory has value, as when we say that heaven denotes the church, but that earth denotes the governments and the political order. Christ Himself calls the church the kingdom of heaven and the kingdom of God; but the earth is called the land of the living, where kings and princes rule.

Similar is the allegory which Paul employs: that Adam and Eve, or marriage itself, is a type of Christ and the Church (Eph. 5:32). This allegory is ingenious and full of comfort, for what more delightful statement can be made than that the Church is the bride and Christ the Bridegroom? It expresses that most happy association and bestowal of all the gifts which the Bridegroom possesses, as well as the obliteration of the sins and all the misfortunes with which the poor bride is burdened. Therefore it is a most delightful saying when St. Paul states (2 Cor. 11:2): "I have espoused you to one husband that I may present you to Christ as a chaste virgin."

Likewise, in Rom. 5:14 he states: "Adam was the first figure of Him that was to come." How? "For just as through Adam many have died, much more has the grace of God and the gift by grace, which is of one man, Jesus Christ, abounded unto many." See how well this allegory ties in with the historical account as its basis.

Similarly, in Gal. 4:24 Paul makes two testaments out of Sarah and Hagar. Let those who want to devise allegories follow this lead and look for their basis in the historical account itself.

Earlier we heard the statements about the Seed of the woman and that of the serpent. On this historical account Christ bases His parable about the enemy who sows evil seed, that is, wicked doctrine and evil ideas (Matt. 13:24–30). Who does not realize that these allegories are more appropriate, more enlightening, more profitable, and better than those which Augustine, Lyra, and others devised about the relationship of the higher and the lower mind?[6]

Dealt with in this manner, what else can the closed Paradise and the cherubim with their swords, stationed to guard Paradise, signify than that without faith in Christ man can endure neither the Law nor the Gospel? Paul speaks this way when he says that the Jews were unable to look at Moses' shining face and that Moses was compelled to place a veil before his face (2 Cor. 3:7).

The tree of death is the Law, and the tree of life is the Gospel, or Christ. Those who do not believe in Christ cannot draw near to these trees. They are prevented by the sword of the angel, who cannot put up with hypocrisy and corrupt righteousness. But for him who acknowledges his sin and believes in Christ, Paradise remains open. He brings with him not his own righteousness but Christ's, which the Gospel announces to all so that we all may place our reliance on it and be saved.

There is no need at all for dwelling at greater length on this matter of allegory. Let this reminder suffice: that those who wish to make use of allegories, make use of those which the apostles point out and which have a sure basis in the words themselves or in the historical account. Otherwise it will happen that we build chaff and stubble on the foundation, and not gold (1 Cor. 3:12).

Genesis 6–9: The flood

At last we have finished the story of the flood, which was related by Moses at considerable length as an awful example of the vast and almost boundless wrath of God, which no words can adequately express. It remains for us to say something about the allegorical meaning, although I have often asserted that I take no great delight in allegories. Nevertheless, I was so enchanted by them in my youth that under the influence of the examples of Origen and Jerome, whom I admired as the greatest

6 For Augustine's discussion of the higher and lower mind, see *The Trinity* 12 and especially 12.10 (WSA 1/5:327–28) for the allegory referred to by Luther.

theologians, I thought that everything had to be turned into allegories. Augustine, too, makes frequent use of allegories.

But while I was following their examples, I finally realized that to my own great harm I had followed an empty shadow and had left unconsidered the heart and core of the Scriptures. Later on, therefore, I began to have a dislike for allegories. They do indeed give pleasure, particularly when they have some delightful allusions. Therefore I usually compare them to pretty pictures. But to the same extent that the natural color of bodies surpasses the picture—even though, as the poet puts it, the pictures are adorned with the colors of an Apelles,[7] which closely approximate nature—the historical narrative itself surpasses the allegory.

In our own age the unlearned mob of the Anabaptists, no less than the monks, are in the clutches of an excessive zeal for allegories. Because of this they have a great affection also for the more obscure books, such as the Revelation of John and the worthless fabrication going by the name of Ezra, which appears in translation in the last two books.[8] There one is free to fabricate anything whatever. We recall that Münzer, that rebellious spirit, turned everything into allegories.[9] But truly, he who either fabricates allegories without discrimination or follows such as are fabricated by others is not only deceived but also most seriously harmed, as these examples show.

Hence allegories either must be avoided entirely or must be attempted with the utmost discrimination and brought into harmony with the rule in use by the apostles, of which I shall say something a little later. Let us not fall into these abominable and ruinous absurdities because of the example not only of the theologists but also of the canonists, or rather the "asinists"—something to which the decretals and decrees of His Most Execrable Lordship, the pope, bear witness.[10]

Yet these remarks must not be understood to mean that we condemn all allegories indiscriminately, for we observe that both Christ and the apostles occasionally employed them. But they are such as are conformable to

7 Apelles (fl. fourth century BC) was a highly esteemed painter in the ancient world.

8 The Vulgate numbered four books of Esdras. The final book, Esdras 4, which Luther refers to here, is an apocalyptic writing belonging to the Apocrypha. English Bibles identify Esdras 1 and 2 as the canonical books of Ezra and Nehemiah and, somewhat confusingly, number the two apocryphal books as Esdras 1 and 2. See *The Apocrypha: The Lutheran Edition with Notes*, ed. Edward A. Engelbrecht (St. Louis: Concordia, 2012), 282–307.

9 Thomas Müntzer or Münzer (ca. 1489–1525), an early friend and supporter of Luther, served as pastor in Zwickau and Allstedt. Müntzer embraced a mystical and spiritualist theology, subordinating the external Word to the internal working of the Holy Spirit. He was executed in 1525 for his role in the Peasants' War.

10 On the decretals, see above, p. 28 n. 28.

the faith, in accordance with the rule of Paul, who enjoins in Rom. 12:6 that prophecy or doctrine should be conformable to the faith.

When we condemn allegories, we are speaking of those that are fabricated by one's own intellect and ingenuity, without the authority of Scripture. The others, which are made to agree with the analogy of the faith, not only embellish doctrine but also give comfort to consciences.

Thus Peter turns this very story of the flood into a beautiful allegory when he says in 1 Pet. 3:21–22: "Baptism, which corresponds to this, now saves us, not as a removal of dirt from the body, but as an appeal to God for a clear conscience, through the resurrection of Christ from the dead," who is at the right hand of God, swallowing up death in order that we may be made heirs of eternal life, and "who has gone into heaven, with angels, authorities, and powers subject to Him." This is truly a theological allegory, that is, one in agreement with the faith and full of comfort.

Of the same nature is Christ's allegory in John 3:14 about the serpent that was raised up in the desert and those who looked up at it and were healed from its bite. Likewise Paul's (1 Cor. 10:4): "Our fathers all drank from the supernatural rock."

These allegories are such that they not only agree nicely with the subject matter but also instruct hearts about faith and are profitable to the conscience.

Consider, on the other hand, the majority of the allegories of Jerome, Origen, and Augustine. These men do not concern themselves with the faith when they devise allegories; they look for philosophical ideas, which are profitable neither for morals nor for the faith, not to mention that they are even rather silly and absurd.

We have previously heard Augustine's allegory about the creation of the man and the woman. He applies it to the upper and the lower part of the human being, that is, to reason and the emotions. But, I ask you, what is the value of this fabrication?

The pope deserves praise for piety and learning in the matter of allegories when he thunders thus from his exalted position: "God made two large luminaries, the sun and the moon. The sun is the papal office, from which the imperial majesty derives its light, just as the moon does from the sun."[11] Oh, such audacious insolence and such villainous desire for power!

Similarly, in this historical account they compare the ark to their own church, in which the pope is with his cardinals, bishops, and prelates. The laity, however, is swimming in the sea; that is, it is involved in secular

11 See Pope Innocent III (r. 1198–1216), *Sicut universitatis conditor*, promulgated November 3, 1198.

affairs and would not be saved unless those helmsmen of the ark, or the church, held out to the swimmers either planks or ropes to draw them into the ark. The monks everywhere have used such a picture to depict the church.

Origen has better sense than the popes, for he usually devotes his allegories to matters of morality. Nevertheless, he should have observed Paul's rule, who enjoins that the analogy of the faith must be preserved in prophecy; for this edifies and is truly applicable to the church. Concerning morals the philosophers of the heathen, too, are capable of giving instruction, although they are completely without a knowledge of faith.

Flood and Baptism

In his letter to the Corinthians (1 Cor. 10:2) Paul declares that the Israelites were baptized under Moses in the cloud and in the sea. If in this passage you look merely at conduct and words, then Pharaoh, too, was baptized, but in such a way that he perished with his men, while Israel passed through safe and unharmed. Similarly, Noah and his sons are preserved in the baptism of the flood, while the entire remaining world outside the ark perishes because of this baptism of the flood.

These are fitting and learned statements, for Baptism and death are interchangeable terms in the Scripture. Therefore Paul says in Rom. 6:3: "As many of us as have been baptized, have been baptized into the death of Christ." Likewise, Christ says in Luke 12:50: "I have a Baptism to be baptized with, and how I am constrained until it is accomplished!" And to His disciples He said (Mark 10:39): "You will be baptized with the Baptism with which I am baptized."

In accordance with this meaning, the Red Sea is truly a baptism, that is, death and the wrath of God, as is manifest in the case of Pharaoh. Nevertheless, Israel, which is baptized with such a baptism, passes through unharmed. Similarly, the flood is truly death and the wrath of God; nevertheless, the believers are saved in the midst of the flood. Thus death engulfs and swallows up the entire human race; for without distinction the wrath of God goes over the good and the evil, over the godly and the ungodly. The flood that Noah experienced was not different from the one that the world experienced. The Red Sea, which both Pharaoh and Israel entered, was not different. Later on, however, the difference becomes apparent in this: those who believe are preserved in the very death to which they are subjected together with the ungodly, but the ungodly perish. Noah, accordingly, is preserved because he has the ark, that is, God's promise and Word, in which he is living; but the ungodly, who do not believe the Word, are left to their fate.

This difference the Holy Spirit wanted to point out in order that the godly might be instructed by this example to believe and hope for salvation through the mercy of God, even in the midst of death. For they have Baptism joined with the promise of life, just as Noah had the ark. Hence even though the death of the wise man and of the fool is the same (Eccl. 2:16)—for Peter and Paul die no differently from the way Nero and other ungodly men die later on—they nevertheless believe that in death they will be preserved for eternal life. Nor is this an idle hope; for they have Christ to receive their spirits. On the Last Day He will revive also the bodies of believers for eternal life.

This allegory is of great value and serves to comfort our hearts, for it points out how differently things will turn out in the end. If you heed the eyes of the flesh, Solomon's statement is true (Eccl. 2:16) that the wise man and the fool die alike and that the righteous man dies as though he were not beloved of God. But here the eyes of the spirit must be applied and the difference noted: Israel enters the Red Sea and is saved, but when Pharaoh follows on the heels of Israel, he is submerged by the waters and perishes. Therefore the death by which the godly and the ungodly perish is the same; indeed, the death of the godly is almost always ignominious, while that of the ungodly is grand and magnificent. But in the eyes of God the death of sinners is the worst, while the death of the saints is precious (Ps. 116:15); for it has been sanctified by Christ, through whom it becomes the beginning of eternal life.

Just as the deluge and the Red Sea are helpers, as it were, to deliver Noah and Israel from death and to preserve their life, so our own death, if we abide in the faith, is clearly the opportunity for life. When the children of Israel were in extreme peril, the sea suddenly opened and stood to the right and to the left like an iron wall, so that Israel passed through without danger. Why did this happen? Manifestly in order that in this manner death might serve life. For this is the divine power by which the assaults of Satan are overcome, as was the case in Paradise. There, too, he was endeavoring to kill the entire human race with his poison. But what happens? Through what was truly a "happy guilt," as the church sings, it was brought about that the Son of God came down into our flesh and delivered us from such great evils.[12]

Accordingly, this allegory teaches, comforts, and encourages us in an excellent manner. As a result, we fear neither death nor sin but disdain all dangers while we give thanks to God for calling us and dealing with us in

12 Luther refers to the *Exsultet* sung at the Easter Vigil and the line: "O happy fault that merited such and so great a Redeemer" [*O felix culpa, quae talem ac tantum meruit habere redemptorem*].

such a way. Death itself, by which the entire world perishes, is compelled to serve life, just as the flood, in which the rest of the world perished, was the occasion to preserve Noah; and the Red Sea, by which Pharaoh was destroyed, served the welfare of the children of Israel.

This must be applied also to other trials. We must learn to disdain dangers and to have hope even when no hope appears to be left, so that when death or any other danger befalls us, we may encourage ourselves and say: "Behold, here is your Red Sea, your flood, your baptism, and your death. Here your life—as a philosopher used to say about those who were going to sea—is barely a handbreadth away from death. But do not be afraid. This danger is like a handful of water, whereas through the Word you have a flood of grace. Therefore death will not destroy you but will be a thrust and aid toward life." Far from being able to destroy the Christian, death is the most immediate escape from death. For the death of the body immediately precedes the liberation of the spirit as well as the resurrection of the flesh. Similarly, in the flood it is neither the earth nor the trees nor the mountains that carry Noah; it is the flood itself, even though it kills the rest of the human race.

Therefore the prophets have reason for their frequent praise of the wonderful deeds of God, such as the passage through the Red Sea, the exodus from Egypt, and the like. For there the sea, which by nature cannot do otherwise than overwhelm and destroy man, is compelled to stand still and protect him, lest he be covered by its waves. Hence that which by its nature is nothing but wrath becomes grace for those who believe; that which is nothing but death becomes life. Thus whatever misfortunes there are, of which this life surely has countless numbers and by which our bodies and goods are beset—all this will be turned into salvation and joy if you are in the ark, that is, if you believe and lay hold of the promises made in Christ; for death, which carries you away, must be turned into life, and hell, which engulfs you, into a way to heaven.

It is for this reason that in 1 Pet. 3:21 Peter declares that we, too, are saved through water in Baptism, which is symbolized by the flood, because pouring water over us or immersing us is death. And yet from that death or immersion there arises life because of the ark in which we are preserved, that is, because of the Word of promise to which we hold fast. The canonical Scriptures put forward this allegory, and it is something not only trustworthy but also worthwhile in every way. We should consider it carefully, for it provides glorious comfort even in extreme perils.

Ark

To this allegory the fathers added another, one derived from the geometrical shape and proportion of the ark. From the crown of the head to the sole of the foot the human body is six times longer than it is wide. Now the ark was fifty cubits wide; but its height was six times greater, namely, 300 cubits. Hence they declare that the ark signifies the man Christ, to whom all promises apply. Therefore those who believe in Him are saved; and in the flood, that is, in death itself, they remain alive.

This thought is not unscholarly. Nor is it unattractive. I am most pleased that it is conformable to the faith. Therefore even if there were an error in the application, the basis nevertheless is sure and solid. There is no doubt that the Holy Spirit used various ways to depict the promises that were to be realized through Christ and the wonderful way in which the human race was to be saved through faith in Christ. If one devises allegories in this manner, therefore, they are nevertheless not ungodly or offensive, even though they may be somewhat inappropriate.

Thus if someone should state that Christ is the sun and the church the moon, illuminated by the grace of Christ, he might be in error; nevertheless, his error is such that it rests not on an incorrect basis, but on a solid one. But when the pope declares that the sun is the papal office and the moon is the emperor, then not only is the application silly and foolish, but even the basis is evil and wicked. Such allegories are thought out and devised not by the Holy Spirit, but by the devil, the spirit of lies.

In order to comfort and strengthen our hearts, allegories must be directed toward the promises and toward the teaching of the faith, as the example of Peter teaches us. Because he sees that Noah is delivered in the midst of death and that the ark is the means of life, the ark is properly made to signify Christ. For it takes a divine power to save in the midst of death and to carry across to life. Thus in Ps. 68:20 Scripture calls God the one who delivers from death and makes death an occasion or even an aid to life. . . .

Raven

Now that we have presented this picture of the ark and the meaning of the flood on the basis of the canonical Scriptures, something must also be said about the remaining portions of the historical account: about the raven which did not return; and about the doves, the first of which returned when she did not find a place where she could set her foot, the second returned and brought back an olive branch, and the third did not return, because the earth had now been cleared of water.

In our discussion of the historical account we stated that these events took place for the comfort of Noah and his sons, to give them the assurance that the wrath of God had come to an end and that He was now reconciled. It was not through her own effort that the dove brought back the olive branch; this was a divine power and miracle, just as the serpent in Paradise did not speak by its own effort but through the influence of the devil, by whom it was possessed. Just as in that instance the serpent spoke under the influence of Satan and seduced mankind into sin, so in this instance the dove did not bring back the olive branch through her own effort and instinct but under God's influence, in order that Noah might derive sure comfort from this most delightful sight. For the fruit of the olive tree is not the food of a dove, which likes wheat, barley, or peas.

It is certain, therefore that this miraculous action had some particular meaning, especially since the prophets also frequently mention doves in their prophecies about the kingdom of Christ, such as Ps. 68:13 and Isa. 60:8. In the Song of Songs, Solomon also seems to take special delight in the name of the dove. Therefore the picture that this allegory presents should not be regarded with complete indifference; it should be treated with fitting skill.

The allegory that the scholars fabricated about the raven is familiar. They were of the opinion that because ravens are fond of carrion, they represent carnal people like the Epicureans, who delight and indulge in carnal pleasures.[13] The thought is indeed good, but it is not fully satisfactory; for this allegory is merely moral and philosophical, the sort that Erasmus has been accustomed to fabricate, somewhat after the pattern of Origen.

We for our part should look for a theological allegory. Those moralists fail to note, in the first place, that Scripture praises the raven for not leaving the ark of its own accord; it is sent out by Noah as his messenger, to investigate whether the waters have ceased and the wrath of God has come to an end. But the raven does not return, nor is it the bearer of a favorable omen. It remains outside the ark; and although it goes and comes, it does not let itself be caught by Noah but remains outside the ark.

All this agrees most beautifully with the ministry of the Law. The black color characteristic of the raven is a symbol of sadness, and the sound of its voice is unpleasant. All the teachers of the Law who teach a righteousness of works are of the same kind: they are ministers of death and of sin. Thus Paul calls the ministry of the Law the ministry of death: "The Law kills" (2 Cor. 3:6); "the Law brings wrath" (Rom. 4:15); "the Law causes sin to increase" (Rom. 5:20).

And yet Moses is sent by God with this doctrine, just as Noah sends out the raven. God wants people to be instructed about morals and a holy life, and He wants His wrath and sure punishments announced to the transgressors of the Law. Nevertheless, such teachers are nothing else

---

13 See above, p. 130 n. 3.

than ravens; they fly back and forth around the ark and bring no sure pronouncement of a reconciled God.

It is characteristic of the Law that its teaching cannot make fearful consciences sure, strengthen and comfort them. Rather it frightens them, because it does nothing else than teach what God demands from us, what He wants us to do. Moreover, it bears witness against us through our conscience, because not only have we not done the will of God revealed in the Law, but we have even done the opposite.

Hence it is correctly stated about the teachers of the Law in Ps. 5:9: "There is nothing sure in their mouth." (Our translation has: "In their mouth is no truth.") For when they present their doctrine in their most perfect manner, they say: "If you do this and if you do that, you will be saved." Therefore when the scribe gives a superb formulation of the teaching of the Law, Christ answers him ironically (Luke 10:28): "Do this, and you will live." He shows him that the teaching is holy and good, but that since we are imperfect, the guilt lies on us, who neither keep nor can keep it.

We, therefore, declare correctly that by the works of the Law—not those dealing with ceremonies but those chief ones dealing with the love of God and one's neighbor—we are not justified. The reason is that we cannot perform them.

What is more, we have the right to censure the effrontery of our opponents, who shout that when we deny the righteousness of works, we are forbidding good works and condemning the Law of God. We would be doing this if we did not acknowledge that the raven had been sent out from the ark by Noah. We do assert that the raven was sent out from the ark; but this we deny, either that there was no raven or that it was a dove. Yet all the shouts, calumnies, and abuses of our adversaries aim to force us into the lie of making a dove out of the raven.

. . . So far as moral precepts are concerned, one cannot find fault with the industry and earnestness of the heathen. Nevertheless, they are all inferior to Moses, who gives instruction not only in morals but also in the worship of God. Yet it is true that he who stops with Moses has nothing but the raven flying back and forth outside the ark; of the dove and of the olive branch he has nothing. . . .

Dove

What Moses relates about the dove is really a delightful likeness of the Gospel, especially if you carefully trace the characteristics of the dove, which are ten in number: (1) it is devoid of malice; (2) it does no harm with its mouth; (3) it inflicts no damage with its claw; (4) it picks up clean grain; (5) it feeds other young birds; (6) instead of singing, it moans; (7) it stays near water; (8) it flies in flocks; (9) it nests in a safe place; (10) it flies swiftly. . . .

The New Testament relates that the Holy Spirit appeared in the form of a dove. Therefore we rightly apply the allegory to the ministry of grace.

Moses relates that the dove did not fly to and fro about the ark, like the raven; but she was sent out, and when she did not find a place to light, she returned to the ark and was caught by Noah.

This dove is a figure of the holy prophets, who were indeed sent to teach the people; but the flood, that is, the era of the Law, had not yet come to an end. Thus although David, Elijah, and Isaiah did not live to see the era of grace or of the New Testament, they were nevertheless sent to be messengers of the end of the flood, even though it had not yet ended. After they had performed their mission, they returned to the ark, that is, they were justified and saved without the Law through faith in the blessed Seed, in whom they believed and for whom they were waiting.

After this dove another is sent out; it finds the earth dry and not only the mountains but also the trees free of water. This one alights on an olive tree and brings to Noah a branch she plucked.

Scripture suggests this allegory also, since in several passages it compares olive oil to grace or mercy or the forgiveness of sins. This the dove brings in its mouth, to represent the outward ministry or the spoken Word. For the Holy Spirit does not—as the enthusiasts and the Anabaptists, truly fanatical teachers, dream—give His instruction through new revelations outside the ministry of the Word.[14] God wanted the branch of a green olive tree brought to Noah by mouth, to make us realize that in the New Testament, when the flood or the era of wrath comes to an end, God wants to reveal His mercy to the world through the spoken Word.

The messengers of this Word are doves, that is, devout men and without malice, full of the Holy Spirit. Isaiah (60:8) likewise compares the ministers of the Gospel, or of grace, to doves that are flying to familiar windows. Even though Christ commands His disciples in Matt. 10:16 to imitate doves in their simplicity, that is, to be sincere and without venom, He nevertheless urges them to be wise as serpents; that is, they should be on their guard against insincere and treacherous people, and they should be cautious, the way a serpent in a fight is said to protect its head with extraordinary skill.

That the olive tree is green, this agrees with the Word of the Gospel, which endures forever and is never without fruit. The psalm (1:3) also compares people who apply themselves to the Word to a tree whose leaves do not fall. We heard nothing like this when we spoke about the

---

14 On the Anabaptists, see above, p. 148 n. 4.

raven flying to and fro near the ark. Hence this dove, the second one to be sent out, is a type of the New Testament, where forgiveness of sin and grace are plainly promised through the sacrifice of Christ. That is why in the New Testament the Holy Spirit wanted to appear in the form of a dove.

The third dove did not return. When the promise of the Gospel, announced to the world through the mouth of a dove, has been fulfilled, there is nothing left to do, and no new doctrine is expected. All we still expect is the revelation of the things we have believed. Hence this also serves to give us a sure testimony that this doctrine will endure until the end of the world.

The text also expressly mentions the time. It states that after Noah had sent out a dove for the first time, he waited seven days. These seven days are the time of the Law, which had to precede the time of the New Testament.

Similarly, it is said of the second dove that it returned to the ark toward evening and was carrying an olive branch. The last age of the world is set aside for the Gospel. Nor should any other kind of doctrine be expected. For this reason Christ compares the Gospel to a supper (Matt. 22:2; Luke 14:16).

The doctrine of the Gospel has been in the world ever since our first parents fell, and by various signs God confirmed this promise to the fathers. The earlier times knew nothing of the rainbow, circumcision, and other things that were ordained later on. But all ages had the knowledge of the blessed Seed. Since this has been revealed, there is nothing left except the revelation of what we believe and our flight with the third dove into another life, never to return to this wretched and distressful life.

Conclusion

These are my thoughts about this allegory. I wanted to present them briefly. Allegories do not deserve as much time as do the historical accounts and the articles of faith.

Origen, Jerome, Augustine, and Bernard allegorize a great deal. The trouble is that since they spend too much time on allegories, they call hearts away and make them flee from the historical account and from faith, whereas allegories should be so treated and designed that faith, to which the historical accounts point in every instance, may be aroused, increased, enlightened, and strengthened. As for those who do not pay attention to the historical accounts, it is no wonder that they look for the shade of allegories as pleasant bypaths on which to ramble.

We see that in the papacy the music of the chants is very pleasing, although the words are commonly not only inappropriate but even wicked and contrary to Scripture. Thus with their foolish allegories the scholars have often corrupted the good sense of a historical account, the sense that was profitable for faith.

I have often stated what kind of theology there was when I began to engage in this sort of study. It was continually stated that the letter kills (2 Cor. 3:6). Therefore I disliked Lyra above all other exegetes, because he tried to ascertain the literal meaning with such care. But now, just because of this commendable quality, I prefer him to almost all other interpreters of Scripture.[15]

I urge you with all possible earnestness to be careful to pay attention to the historical accounts. But wherever you want to make use of allegories, do this: follow closely the analogy of the faith, that is, adapt them to Christ, the church, faith, and the ministry of the Word. In this way it will come to pass that even though the allegories may not be altogether fitting, they nevertheless do not depart from the faith. Let this foundation stand firm, but let the stubble perish (1 Cor. 3:12–15).

---

15 On Lyra, see above, p. 421 n. 9.

Subject Index

Scripture Index

Old Testament